Studies in Diversity Linguistics

Chief Editor: Martin Haspelmath
Consulting Editors: Fernando Zúñiga, Peter Arkadiev, Ruth Singer, Pilar Valenzuela

In this series:

1. Handschuh, Corinna. A typology of marked-S languages.

2. Rießler, Michael. Adjective attribution.

3. Klamer, Marian (ed.). The Alor-Pantar languages: History and typology.

4. Berghäll, Liisa. A grammar of Mauwake (Papua New Guinea).

5. Wilbur, Joshua. A grammar of Pite Saami.

6. Dahl, Östen. Grammaticalization in the North: Noun phrase morphosyntax in Scandinavian vernaculars.

7. Schackow, Diana. A grammar of Yakkha.

8. Liljegren, Henrik. A grammar of Palula.

9. Shimelman, Aviva. A grammar of Yauyos Quechua.

10. Rudin, Catherine & Bryan James Gordon (eds.). Advances in the study of Siouan languages and linguistics.

11. Kluge, Angela. A grammar of Papuan Malay.

12. Kieviet, Paulus. A grammar of Rapa Nui.

13. Michaud, Alexis. Tone in Yongning Na: Lexical tones and morphotonology.

ISSN: 2363-5568

Tone in Yongning Na
Lexical tones and morphotonology

Alexis Michaud

language
science
press

Alexis Michaud. 2017. *Tone in Yongning Na: Lexical tones and morphotonology* (Studies in Diversity Linguistics 13). Berlin: Language Science Press.

This title can be downloaded at:
http://langsci-press.org/catalog/book/109
© 2017, Alexis Michaud
Published under the Creative Commons Attribution 4.0 Licence (CC BY 4.0):
http://creativecommons.org/licenses/by/4.0/
ISBN: 978-3-946234-86-9 (Digital)
      978-3-946234-87-6 (Hardcover)
      978-3-946234-68-5 (Softcover)
ISSN: 2363-5568
DOI:10.5281/zenodo.439004

Cover and concept of design: Ulrike Harbort
Typesetting: Luise Dorenbusch, Benjamin Galliot, Guillaume Jacques, Alexis Michaud, Sebastian Nordhoff, Thomas Pellard
Proofreading: Eran Asoulin, Rosey Billington, Mykel Brinkerhoff, Henriëtte Daudey, Aude Gao (Gao Yang 高扬), Andreas Hölzl, Lachlan Mackenzie, Maria Isabel Maldonado, Claudia Marzi, Jean Nitzke, Sebastian Nordhoff, Ikmi Nur Oktavianti, Ahmet Bilal Özdemir, Ludger Paschen, Brett Reynolds, Alec Shaw
Fonts: Linux Libertine, Arimo, DejaVu Sans Mono, Charis SIL, AR PL UMing
Typesetting software: XƎLATEX

Language Science Press
Unter den Linden 6
10099 Berlin, Germany
langsci-press.org

Storage and cataloguing done by FU Berlin

Language Science Press has no responsibility for the persistence or accuracy of URLs for external or third-party Internet websites referred to in this publication, and does not guarantee that any content on such websites is, or will remain, accurate or appropriate.

À mon père

Contents

Acknowledgments   xiii

Abbreviations and conventions   xvii

For quick reference: Lexical tones and main tone rules   xxv

1   Introduction   1
    1.1   The Na language   2
        1.1.1   Endonym and exonyms   2
        1.1.2   Dialect classification and issues of phylogeny   9
        1.1.3   A review of Na language studies   14
    1.2   Project and method   22
        1.2.1   The aim: Detailed description of a level-tone system . .   22
        1.2.2   Theoretical backdrop   23
        1.2.3   Field trips and collaboration with consultants   27
        1.2.4   Elicitation methods   35
        1.2.5   Online materials   38
    1.3   A grammatical sketch of Yongning Na   45
        1.3.1   Word order   47
        1.3.2   Tense, aspect and modality   48
        1.3.3   Question formation   48
        1.3.4   Existential sentences   48
        1.3.5   Sentence-final particles   50
        1.3.6   Noun and noun phrase   50
        1.3.7   Verb and verb phrase   51

2   The lexical tones of nouns   53
    2.1   A static inventory of tone patterns   53
    2.2   A dynamic view, bringing out the tonal categories   57
        2.2.1   Monosyllabic nouns: Six tonal categories   57
        2.2.2   Disyllabic nouns: Eleven tonal categories   58

	2.3		Phonological analysis	59
		2.3.1	A floating H tone	60
		2.3.2	Word-final H tone and the 'flea' H tone category	69
		2.3.3	A postlexical rule for all-L tone groups	72
		2.3.4	Tonal contours as sequences of level tones	72
		2.3.5	An alternative analysis of //LM// and //LH//	73
		2.3.6	Cases of neutralization of //LM// and //LH//	76
		2.3.7	On the anchoring of tones to word boundaries	77
	2.4		General observations about the system	78
		2.4.1	Usefulness of an autosegmental approach	78
		2.4.2	Recapitulation of the lexical tone categories	79
		2.4.3	M as a default tone	87
		2.4.4	The notation of tonal categories in lexical entries	88
		2.4.5	Attested and unattested lexical tones	90
		2.4.6	Phonological regularities and morphotonological oddities	91
3	**Compound nouns**			**93**
	3.1		Determinative compound nouns. Part I: The main facts	94
		3.1.1	The role of the number of syllables	95
		3.1.2	How the tone patterns were collected	97
		3.1.3	Surface phonological tone patterns	98
		3.1.4	Analysis into underlying tone patterns	105
	3.2		Determinative compound nouns. Part II: Discussion	113
		3.2.1	LM-tone determiners	118
		3.2.2	M-tone determiners	119
		3.2.3	L-tone determiners	120
		3.2.4	H-tone determiners: #H, H# and H$	121
		3.2.5	MH-tone determiners	122
		3.2.6	Determiners carrying LM+MH# tone or LM+#H tone	122
		3.2.7	Cases of neutralization of tonal oppositions on the head	123
		3.2.8	A tendency to avoid long-distance movement of tones	125
		3.2.9	Brief remarks about slips of the tongue	126
		3.2.10	Perspectives for comparison across speakers	127
		3.2.11	Exceptional items	129
	3.3		Coordinative compounds	133
		3.3.1	The main facts	133
		3.3.2	Discussion: Tonal variability and lexical diversity	141
		3.3.3	Compound given names and terms of address	144

	3.4	Compound nouns containing adjectives	148
		3.4.1 A productive construction: N+Adj+relativizer	148
		3.4.2 Lexicalized compounds of N+Adj structure	151
		3.4.3 N+Adj combinations in the process of lexicalization	158
		3.4.4 A lexicalized compound of Adj+N structure	160
		3.4.5 A lexicalized compound of V+Adj structure	160
	3.5	Concluding note	161
4	**Classifiers**		**163**
	4.1	Numeral-plus-classifier phrases	164
		4.1.1 Elicitation procedures	164
		4.1.2 Results: Nine tonal categories for monosyllabic classifiers	167
		4.1.3 The tones of classifiers and of corresponding free forms	177
		4.1.4 Indirect confirmation for the H, MH, M and L categories	179
		4.1.5 Degree of tonal complexity and amount of mistakes	180
		4.1.6 About variants of tone patterns	181
		4.1.7 Disyllabic classifiers	183
		4.1.8 Two numerals plus a classifier	183
		4.1.9 Conclusions	185
	4.2	Demonstrative-plus-classifier phrases	187
	4.3	Tonal interactions with a preceding noun	189
	4.4	Concluding note	192
5	**Combinations of nouns with grammatical elements**		**195**
	5.1	Derivational affixes: Gender suffixes and kinship prefix	195
		5.1.1 Introduction to gender suffixes	195
		5.1.2 The facts	197
		5.1.3 Discussion	205
		5.1.4 Other suffixes for 'male'	211
		5.1.5 The kinship prefix /ə˧-/	213
	5.2	Reduplication	216
		5.2.1 Reduplication of numeral-plus-classifier phrases	217
		5.2.2 A reduplicated nominal suffix	217
	5.3	Possessive constructions containing pronouns	219
		5.3.1 The 1st, 2nd and 3rd person pronouns	220
		5.3.2 The pronoun 'oneself'	224
	5.4	Monosyllabic enclitics, suffixes, and postpositions	227
		5.4.1 L-tone morphemes	227
		5.4.2 M-tone morphemes	231

		5.4.3	MH-tone morphemes	236
		5.4.4	A H-tone morpheme	236
	5.5	Disyllabic postpositions		238
	5.6	Adverbs		240
		5.6.1	The homophonous adverbs /la˦/ 'only' and 'too, and' . .	241
		5.6.2	The adverb /pɤ˦to˩/ 'even'	242
	5.7	Concluding note		242
6	Verbs and their combinatory properties			245
	6.1	The lexical tones of verbs		245
		6.1.1	Overview	245
		6.1.2	About subsets of M-tone verbs	249
		6.1.3	Adjectives as distinct from verbs	251
	6.2	Reduplication		252
	6.3	Prefixes		258
		6.3.1	M-tone prefixes	258
		6.3.2	L-tone prefixes	261
		6.3.3	The marking of spatial orientation on verbs	263
	6.4	Monosyllabic postverbal morphemes		275
		6.4.1	L tone	276
		6.4.2	M tone	278
		6.4.3	H tone	283
		6.4.4	MH tone	285
	6.5	Disyllabic postverbal morphemes		288
		6.5.1	M.H tone	288
		6.5.2	M.L tone	291
	6.6	Combinations of postverbal morphemes		293
		6.6.1	Postverbal morphemes preceded by the negation prefix .	293
		6.6.2	Postverbal morphemes preceded by the interrogative . .	297
	6.7	Morphemes surrounding adjectives		298
		6.7.1	Addition of reduplicated suffixes to adjectives	298
		6.7.2	Demonstrative and intensive constructions	298
	6.8	Object followed by non-prefixed verb		300
		6.8.1	The facts	301
		6.8.2	Evidence of the opposition between //LM// and //LH// .	304
		6.8.3	About tonal variants	304
		6.8.4	Exceptional combinations	306
		6.8.5	Noun plus copula behaves tonally like O+V	307

		6.8.6	Interrogative pronoun and verb	307
	6.9		Object and prefixed verb	308
		6.9.1	The facts	309
		6.9.2	Data analysis	310
	6.10		Subject and verb	315
		6.10.1	The facts	316
		6.10.2	Variants resulting from a division into two tone groups	317
		6.10.3	Noun plus existential verb behaves tonally like S+V	320
7	Tone assignment rules and the division of utterances into tone groups			321
	7.1		A summary of tone-to-syllable association rules	323
		7.1.1	The phonological tone rules	323
		7.1.2	About the ordering of rules	327
		7.1.3	A discussion of alternative formulations	328
		7.1.4	Implications for the tones of sentence-final particles	329
	7.2		The division of utterances into tone groups	331
		7.2.1	Morphemes that constitute a tone group on their own	332
		7.2.2	Topicalized constituents always end a tone group	334
		7.2.3	Options left to the speaker	335
		7.2.4	Some general tendencies	337
		7.2.5	Extreme cases of tonal integration	341
		7.2.6	Two cases of resistance to tonal integration	345
		7.2.7	Illustration: Sample derivations	345
	7.3		Cases of breach of tonal grouping and their consequences	347
		7.3.1	Non-final contours as a stylistic option	347
		7.3.2	The emergence of extrametrical syllables	351
		7.3.3	Further examples of extrametrical elements	354
		7.3.4	Deviant tone patterns and Mandarin loanwords	354
	7.4		Concluding note	356
8	From surface phonological tone to phonetic realization			357
	8.1		Introduction	357
		8.1.1	Definition of terms	360
		8.1.2	About tools for intonational transcription	363
		8.1.3	Intonation in level-tone languages: A review	365
	8.2		Syntactic intonation: Phrasing and junctures	369
	8.3		Pragmatic intonation	371
		8.3.1	Emphatic stress and its toned-down avatars	372
		8.3.2	Focalization by intonational means	375

	8.4	Intonational modifications as a path towards the loss of lexical tone	382
	8.5	Key factors in the phonetic implementation of tone	386
		8.5.1 Intonational background of function words	386
		8.5.2 The absence of oppositions between /L.M/ and /L.H/, or between /H.M/ and /H.L/	387
		8.5.3 Anticipatory dissimilation in M.L and M.H sequences	388
		8.5.4 Resetting of reference values at junctures between tone groups	391
		8.5.5 The realization of rising contours	391
	8.6	By way of recapitulation: Examples of mistaken tonal identification	392
		8.6.1 Anticipatory dissimilation before a L tone	392
		8.6.2 Interplay between morphosyntax and phonology	393
		8.6.3 Resetting at junctures between tone groups	393
		8.6.4 The effects of pragmatic intonation	394

9 Yongning Na tones in dynamic-synchronic perspective 397

- 9.1 Gap-filling in tonal paradigms . . . 398
- 9.2 Disyllabification . . . 403
  - 9.2.1 A dynamic analysis of compound nouns . . . 403
  - 9.2.2 Possible origins for disyllables in view of their tone . . . 406
  - 9.2.3 Recovering the tones of nouns on the basis of compounds 407
- 9.3 Analogy . . . 408
  - 9.3.1 General principles . . . 408
  - 9.3.2 Analogy in Yongning Na morphotonology . . . 409
- 9.4 The influence of bilingualism with Mandarin . . . 409
  - 9.4.1 Loss of tone categories that do not surface in isolation . 411
  - 9.4.2 Simplification of morphosyntactic tone rules . . . 412
  - 9.4.3 Straightening out irregular tone patterns . . . 414
  - 9.4.4 Cases where MH tone fails to unfold: Towards a syllable-tone system? . . . 414
  - 9.4.5 A topic for future research: Influence of language contact on intonation . . . 416

10 Typological perspectives 419

- 10.1 Tonal typology . . . 419
  - 10.1.1 Level tones and phonetically complex tones . . . 420
  - 10.1.2 Typological profile of Na prosody . . . 423
- 10.2 Assessing the complexity of the Na tone system . . . 425
  - 10.2.1 Partly regular morphotonology . . . 425

		10.2.2	Nouns and verbs: A comparable degree of complexity? .	425
		10.2.3	More progressive spreading than regressive spreading: A typologically common pattern	426
		10.2.4	The dual status of the M tone is not a typological rarity .	427
	10.3	Tonal vs. non-tonal intonation		427
		10.3.1	Instances of intonational tones in the world's languages	427
		10.3.2	Doubtful cases of intonational tone: Crossing the fine line between intonation and tone?	428
		10.3.3	Conditioning factors for the development of intonational tones	433

11 Yongning Na in its areal context — 437
- 11.1 Naxi and Laze: Close relatives, but not part of a convergence area — 437
- 11.2 Comparison with Pumi . . . . — 438
  - 11.2.1 The tone group and its ties with information structure — 438
  - 11.2.2 Other similarities . . . . — 440
- 11.3 Comparison with Yi . . . . — 440
- 11.4 Contact between two-level and three-level tone systems . . . . — 441

12 Conclusion — 443

Appendix A: Vowels and consonants — 447
- A.1 Consonant and vowel charts . . . . — 448
- A.2 Syllable nuclei: Vowels and syllabic consonants . . . . — 452
  - A.2.1 Consonantal nuclei . . . . — 452
  - A.2.2 Close vowels . . . . — 457
  - A.2.3 A neutral vowel: /ə/ . . . . — 459
  - A.2.4 Nasal rhymes . . . . — 461
  - A.2.5 The open vowels /ɑ/ and /æ/, and the vowel /ɤ/ . . . . . — 465
  - A.2.6 A note on phonetic diphthongization . . . . — 466
  - A.2.7 A note on vowel harmony . . . . — 466
- A.3 Initial consonants . . . . — 468
  - A.3.1 On-glides . . . . — 468
  - A.3.2 Initial glottal stop . . . . — 470
  - A.3.3 Initial /ʁ/ as a phonemicized empty-onset filler . . . . . — 470
  - A.3.4 Velar and uvular stops . . . . — 471
  - A.3.5 Retroflex stops and affricates . . . . — 472
  - A.3.6 Laterals /l/ and /ɬ/, and retroflexes /ɭ/ and /ɻ/ . . . . . . — 473
  - A.3.7 The glottal fricative /h/ and the sound [f] . . . . — 474

A.4		Comments about the inventory of syllables	475
	A.4.1	Combinations of a dental stop and /æ/ vowel seem recent	477
	A.4.2	A marginal combination: Dental stop plus /ɤ/	477
	A.4.3	After alveolopalatals, is the rhyme /o/ or /jo/?	478
	A.4.4	Phonemic status of the retroflex nasal	479
	A.4.5	The palatal nasal	479
	A.4.6	Syllables introduced by Mandarin borrowings	480
A.5		Articulatory reduction: Reduced forms and their lexicalization	481
A.6		Expressive coinages and phonostylistic observations	483
	A.6.1	Onomatopoeia and ideophones	483
	A.6.2	Phonostylistic observations	484
	A.6.3	Expressive uses of reduplication	485

Appendix B: Historical and ethnological perspectives — 487

B.1		The history of Yongning in outline	487
	B.1.1	Prehistory	487
	B.1.2	Empires and indigenous chieftains	492
	B.1.3	The People's Republic of China	495
B.2		Ethnic classification: Naxi, Mongolian, Mosuo, or Na	496
B.3		Anthropological research: The fascination of the Na family structure	501
	B.3.1	Surveys conducted in the 1960s	502
	B.3.2	Marxist interpretation of the Na family structure	505
	B.3.3	Cai Hua's *A society without fathers or husbands*	505
	B.3.4	Studies of Na society in comparative perspective	509
	B.3.5	Present-day sociological studies	514

References — 517

Index — 561

Name index . . . 561
Language index . . . 568
Subject index . . . 570

Acknowledgments

> [Writing a grammar] takes an individual who loves language in general, the target language in particular, and is trained and happy to spend time doing this work.
>
> (Nurse 2011: xxiv)

I am grateful to my teachers for long years of patient and inspiring training. Laurent Danon-Boileau, my first linguistics tutor, advised students to study lesser-documented languages. I realized at once that this was what I wanted to do: to apply myself to the documentation of a lesser-known language. In 1994, reading Michel Launey's newly published description of Classical Nahuatl as "an omnipredicative grammar" (Launey 1994), my imagination was fired by the mention (p. 16) of the professional and personal coincidences that had led him to study a language remote in time and space, which yielded groundbreaking insights into human language. I dreamt of making a scientific contribution by exploring a distant language and culture. I finally experienced this wonderful blend of discovery, excitement and fulfilment in my fieldwork in Southwest China.

Many thanks to Jacqueline Vaissière for undertaking to raise a novice steeped in the cloudiest romanticism to the status of Doctor in phonetics, and for her continued guidance over the years.

My work on Yongning Na began in 2006, at the same time as I joined the *Langues et Civilisations à Tradition Orale* (LACITO) research centre within *Centre National de la Recherche Scientifique* (CNRS). With its tradition of immersion fieldwork and in-depth research on endangered languages, LACITO proved a stimulating and congenial work environment. I am grateful for the opportunity allowed me by CNRS of staying in China in 2011–2012 for fieldwork, through a temporary affiliation with the *Centre d'Etudes Français sur la Chine contemporaine* (CEFC). I would also like to thank the Institute of Linguistics, Academia Sinica for hosting me for three months (January to March 2011). From November 2012 to June 2016, I was based at the International Research Institute MICA

(Hanoi, Vietnam), in a stimulating environment allowing for close collaboration with colleagues from Asia and elsewhere. Special thanks to the heads of the institute, Phạm Thị Ngọc Yến (succeeded in 2015 by Nguyễn Việt Sơn) and Eric Castelli, for their support and encouragement.

I am grateful to the Dongba Culture Research Institute (丽江市东巴文化研究院) in Lijiang and the Horse-Tea Road Culture Research Centre (云南大学茶马古道文化研究所) in Kunming for facilitating administrative and practical matters; special thanks to Li Dejing 李德静 and Mu Jihong 木霁弘. At Yunnan University, many thanks are due to Duan Bingchang 段炳昌, Wang Weidong 王卫东, Zhao Yanzhen 赵燕珍 and Yang Liquan 杨立权 for their sensitive management of fieldwork-related administrative matters.

Many thanks to Picus Ding for putting me in touch with the Mosuo scholar Latami Dashi 拉他咪·达石 (lɑ˧tʰɑ˧mi˧ tæ˧ʂɯ˧), and to Latami Dashi for supporting and encouraging my work with his mother Mrs. Latami Dashilame 拉他咪·达石拉么 (lɑ˧tʰɑ˧mi˧ tæ˧ʂɯ˧-lɑ˩mv̩˩) over the years. I am grateful to the Yongning Na language consultants (in particular my main consultant, Mrs. Latami Dashilame) for their patience and support.

Many thanks to connoisseurs of the Na culture and language for our exchanges, and for their useful comments on draft versions: Lamu Gatusa 拉木·嘎吐萨 (Chinese pen-name: Shi Gaofeng 石高峰), Liberty Lidz, Christine Mathieu, Pascale-Marie Milan and Ho Sana 何撒娜. Special thanks to Roselle Dobbs for extensive discussions and vigorous text editing over the years. Many thanks to the three anonymous reviewers for wonderfully thorough and helpful reviews, and to Chen Yen-ling 陳彥伶, Katia Chirkova, Denis Creissels, Stéphane Gros, Nathan Hill, Guillaume Jacques, Martine Mazaudon, Boyd Michailovsky, Frédéric Pain, Phạm Thị Thu Hà, Annie Rialland, Martine Toda and Meng Yang for their useful comments on draft chapters.

Many thanks are also due to Séverine Guillaume, the engineer in charge of the Pangloss Collection (an online archive of recordings of rare languages), for her help in the archiving of the annotated audio recordings that constitute the empirical foundations of the present volume. Many thanks to Luise Dorenbusch for conversion of the original draft to LaTeX. Many thanks to Guillaume Jacques, Thomas Pellard and Sebastian Nordhoff for their help with LaTeX. Many thanks to Jérôme Picard for drawing the map. Many thanks to the series editor, Martin Haspelmath, to the Language Science Press coordinator, Sebastian Nordhoff, and to the wonderful team of volunteers who proofread the volume. Remaining errors and shortcomings are mine alone.

Many thanks to my wife and my daughter for their patience and support.

So many people have supported this project that I must apologize for those names that should be here but were inadvertently left off the list.

Fieldwork on Yongning Na was funded through two grants from the *Agence Nationale de la Recherche* (ANR, France): PASQi (ANR-07-JCJC-0063) and Himalco (ANR-12-CORP-0006). The present book is a contribution to the Labex project "Empirical Foundations of Linguistics" (ANR-10-LABX-0083).

Abbreviations and conventions

Interlinear glosses

Glosses follow the Leipzig Glossing Rules, with some additions.

A	agent marking (adposition)
ABILITIVE	abilitive (suffix)
ABL	ablative (adposition)
ADJ	adjective
ADVB	adverbializer (suffix)
AFFIRM	affirmative (particle)
ALL	allative
ASSOCIATIVE	associative plural
AUG	augmentative
CAUS	causative
CERTITUDE	a use of the copula described by Lidz (2010:497) as "an epistemic strategy that marks a high degree of certitude"
CLF	classifier
CNTR	contrastive
COM	comitative
COMPLETION	completion (suffix)
COP	copula
DAT	dative
DEM	demonstrative
DESIDERATIVE	desiderative (suffix)
DIM	diminutive
DISC.PTCL	discourse particle
DIST	distal
DU	dual
DUR	durative
EXCL	exclusive
EXIST	existential (verb)

FUT	future
IMM.FUT	immediate future
IMMINENCE	imminence (prefix): the event is imminent
INCL	inclusive
INTERROG	interrogative (particle or pronoun)
INTJ	interjection
INTS	intensifier
N	noun
NEG	negation
NMLZ	nominalizer
NUM	numeral
O	object
OBLIGATIVE	obligative (suffix)
PERMISSIVE	permissive
PFV	perfective
PL	plural
POSS	possessive
PROG	progressive
PROH	prohibitive
PROX	proximal
PST	past
RECP	reciprocal
REDUPL	reduplication
REL	relativizer
REP	reported-speech particle
S	subject
SG	singular
TOP	topic marker (suffix)
V	verb
1	first person
2	second person
3	third person

Verbs are glossed in the infinitive, as 'to fly', 'to say', 'to lead', 'to go', and so on, in order to clarify that the intended English gloss is the verb, not the noun.

Other abbreviations and symbols

cs	centisecond: a unit of time equal to 0.01 seconds
F	focalization of the word that precedes (through local intonational modification of tone: see §8.3.2)
F_0	fundamental frequency (a standard abbreviation in phonetics)
F1, F2…	Female language consultant number 1, 2… (this is a standard convention in phonetics; the numbering is chronological, referring to the set of Naish recordings that have been collected since 2002)
H	High tone
L	Low tone
M	Mid tone
M1, M2…	Male language consultant number 1, 2…
p.c.	personal communication
=	clitic boundary
-	affix boundary
.	syllable boundary
σ	syllable (a standard convention in phonology)
|	tone group boundary (see Chapter 7)
~	reduplication (example: /wɤ˩~wɤ˩/)
≈	free variation: variation that is not conditioned by phonological or morphosyntactic parameters (example: [tɕɥe] ≈ [tɕɥi]). In this volume, the tilde ~, commonly used in linguistics as a symbol for free variation, is reserved for reduplication.
↑	emphatic stress on syllable that follows (see §8.3.1)
#	word boundary (see Chapter 2); by extension: the boundary of the entire expression to which a tone pattern is associated (see Chapters 3-6)
$	a symbol used in H$, one of the lexical categories of H tones

–	morpheme break, used in the representation of the tone pattern of an expression made up of two (or more) morphemes. Thus, for a dimorphemic compound noun, –L refers to a L tone that attaches after the morpheme break (i.e. on the second noun: the head noun), and LM–L indicates that the first noun gets LM tone and the second gets L. (In earlier publications on Yongning Na, the symbol used was a superscript circle °, but this use of the symbol conflicted headlong with Africanist usage, in which L° refers to a *level* L tone: a tone that contrasts with L through the absence of a phonetic falling contour.)
//ʐwæ˥//	underlying phonological form (a vertical bar is more usual, but in this volume the vertical bar is used for tone group boundaries)
/ʐwæ˧/	surface-phonological form
[ʐwæ˧]	phonetic realization
*ʐwæ˧	a reconstructed form
†ʐwæ˧	a form that is predicted on the basis of regular rules, but unattested
‡ʐwæ˧	incorrect (ungrammatical) form; note that the asterisk is not used, to preclude confusion with reconstructed forms
::	phonological correspondence between two languages or dialects (a standard convention in historical linguistics)

References to online annotated recordings of Yongning Na

One-click links from the electronic version of this book to the examples cited are not yet available, unfortunately. Interested readers need to locate the document in the list of Yongning Na recordings in the archive, open it, and navigate down to the cited sentence. Examples from the online texts are referred to in the following format: text identifier followed by a dot followed by the sentence number. For instance, Sister.27 refers to sentence 27 in the narrative referred to for short as 'Sister'. For some of the stories, several versions were recorded. In these cases, the version number is indicated after the text identifier, without a separator: thus, Dog2.35 refers to sentence 35 in the second version of the narrative 'Dog'.

Here is a list of texts, providing the correspondences between identifiers and full titles.

Agriculture	Agriculture: agricultural activities over the course of the year
BuriedAlive	Buried alive: how a young woman ran into great trouble because of her greed
Caravans	Caravans: about the trade which flourished in the area in the second quarter of the twentieth century
ComingOfAge	Coming of age: the ritual performed at age thirteen
Dog	Dog: how dog and man exchanged their lifespans
Elders	Elders: elders and ancestors
FoodShortage	Food shortage: how parents set out to sell children, and then changed their mind
Funeral	Funeral: how funeral rites used to be conducted
Healing	Healing: how diseases used to be treated through rituals
Housebuilding	Housebuilding: the process of building a house
Lake	Lake: how the Lake was created
Mountains	Mountains: some beliefs associated to the mountains around Yongning
Mushrooms	Mushrooms: which ones are collected for cooking and for medicine
Renaming	Renaming: how one used to change a child's name to give it a happier start in life
Reward	Reward: how the heavens rewarded an honest man
Seeds	Seeds: how mankind obtained seeds and learnt to grow crops
Sister	Sister: the sister's wedding
Tiger	Tiger: how the tiger attacked a woman and her daughter
TraderAndHisSon	Trader and his son: how a trader taught his son how to handle the ups and downs of commerce

For elicited phonological and morphotonological data, the correspondences between identifiers and full titles are as follows.

AccompPfv	Verbs illustrating the various tone categories, in the frame ACCOMPLISHED+VERB+PERFECTIVE
CoordCompounds	Coordinative compounds, 1
CoordCompounds2	Coordinative compounds, 2: pairs of numerals in association with 'year', 'month' or 'day'
DemClf	Demonstrative-plus-classifier phrases, 1
DemClf2	Demonstrative-plus-classifier phrases, 2
DemClf3	Demonstrative-plus-classifier phrases, 3
DetermCompounds1to4	The tones of compound nouns: body parts of animals, documents 1 to 4
DetermCompounds5	The tones of compound nouns: body parts of animals, document 5 (verifications)
DetermCompounds6	The tones of compound nouns: body parts of animals, document 6 (verifications)
DetermCompounds7	The tones of compound nouns: body parts of animals, document 7 (extensive set)
DetermCompounds8to10	The tones of compound nouns: body parts of animals, documents 8 to 10 (complements)
DetermCompounds11	The tones of compound nouns: body parts of animals, document 11 (a few verifications)
DetermCompounds12	The tones of compound nouns: body parts of animals, document 12
DetermCompounds13	The tones of compound nouns: body parts of animals, document 13 (compounds with the noun 'sheep')
DetermCompounds14	The tones of compound nouns: body parts of animals, document 14
DetermCompounds15	The tones of compound nouns: body parts of animals, document 15 (a few compounds with the noun 'cat')

DetermCompounds16	The tones of compound nouns: cultural objects and peoples
LocativePostp	Nouns followed by locative (spatial) postpositions: 'beside', 'behind', 'to the left', 'to the right'
NounsEven	Nouns followed by 'even'
NounsInFrame	Disyllabic nouns placed in a carrier sentence: 'This is (a/the) N', in order to bring out their tone patterns
NumClf (41 documents)	The titles of all 41 documents follow the same format: "Numeral-plus-classifier phrases. Tone: T. Classifier: C. Range: 1 to n", where T is the lexical tone, C the class of objects to which this classifier applies, and n the end value of the range of numerals: either 30 or 100.
ObjectVerb	Data illustrating the tone patterns of object-plus-verb combinations, 1
ObjectVerb2	Data illustrating the tone patterns of object-plus-verb combinations, 2
ObjectVerb3	Data illustrating the tone patterns of object-plus-verb combinations, 3
OnlyAnd	Nouns followed by the morpheme 'only' (homophone: 'and')
PalatalizedApicalized	Words illustrating the opposition between two apicalized high front vowels following alveolo-palatal initials
PossessPro	Possessive constructions with pronouns, without an intervening particle
SpatialOrientation	Spatial orientation: combinations among verbs and prefixes (or adverbials) indicating spatial orientation
SubjectVerb	Data illustrating the tone patterns of subject-plus-verb combinations

VerbDurative	Verbs illustrating the various tone categories, in the frame DURATIVE+V+PROGRESSIVE
VerbProhib	Verbs of all tone categories preceded by the PROHIBITIVE, 1
VerbProhib2	Verbs of all tone categories preceded by the PROHIBITIVE, 2
VerbReduplObj	Reduplicated verbs (tones: M, H, L and MH) preceded by an object
VerbReduplObj2	Reduplicated verbs of all tone categories preceded by an object

Photographs and figures

Photographs and figures are my own.

Translation of citations

Unless a reference to a translated version is provided, English translations of citations are my own.

For quick reference: Lexical tones and main tone rules

This volume is organized in analytical order: setting out facts, and gradually advancing towards an analysis. This mode of exposition replicates the progression of analysis during fieldwork, working up from the surface facts. The aim is to allow the reader to evaluate the analysis step by step, and to reflect on possible alternatives, rather than proposing a complete analysis from a top-down perspective. A drawback of this choice is that the main facts about the tone system are not grouped in one place, and can be difficult to look up. The present reference section is the place to go to re-check (i) the inventory of tones for nouns and verbs, (ii) the meaning of the custom notations used for the tone categories of Yongning Na (H#, #H and the like), (iii) the list of phonological tone rules, and (iv) three sets of tables presenting combination rules: those that hold in determinative compound nouns, subject-plus-verb combinations, and object-plus-verb combinations, respectively.

The tones of nouns and verbs

The copula and the possessive are used as tests to determine the lexical tone of a noun, because their surface tone changes according to the tone category of the target word. The use of different contexts of elicitation can be likened to the use of chemicals in the processing of photographic films: in the same way as a blend of chemicals is required to convert the latent image to a visible image, several contexts need to be used to reveal underlying tone. Together, the copula and the possessive suffice to bring out all the categories of nouns. For nominal classifiers (Table 2), nine tonal categories were brought out by examining tonal patterns in association with numerals. For verbs (Table 3), the seven categories are arrived at by piecing together evidence from four contexts: in isolation; with a preceding NEGATION prefix, /mɤ˩-/ or accomplished prefix, /le˧-/; and in association with the object 'a bit', /ɖɯ˧-kʰwɤ˩$/.

Table 1a: The lexical tone categories of monosyllabic nouns. From §2.4.2.

analysis	in isolation	+COP	+POSS	//example//	meaning
// LM //	LH	L+H	L+H	bo˧˥	pig
// LH //	LH	L+H	L+H	ʐæ˧˥	leopard
// M //	M	M+L	M+M	lɑ˧	tiger
// L //	M	L+LH	L+M	jo˩	sheep
// #H //	M	M+H	M+M	ʐwæ˥	horse
// MH# //	MH	M+H	M+H	tsʰæ˧˥	deer

Table 1b: The lexical tone categories of disyllabic nouns. From §2.4.2.

analysis	in isolation	+COP	+POSS	//example//	meaning
// M //	M.M	M.M+L	M.M+M	po˧lo˧	ram
// #H //	M.M	M.M+H	M.M+M	ʐwæ˧zo#˥	colt
// MH# //	M.MH	M.M+H	M.M+H	hwɤ˧li˧˥	cat
// H$ //	M.H	M.M+H	M.M+M	kɤ˧ʂe˥$	flea
// H# //	M.H	M.H+L	M.H+L	hwæ˧tsæ˥	squirrel
// L //	L.LH	L.L+H	L.L+H	kʰɤ˩mi˩	dog
// L# //	M.L	M.L+L	M.L+L	dɑ˧ji˩	mule
//LM+MH#//	L.MH	L.M+H	L.M+H	õ˩dv˧˥	wolf
//LM+#H//	L.M	L.M+H	L.M+M	nɑ˩hĩ#˥	Naxi
// LM //	L.M	L.M+L	L.M+M	bo˩mi˧	sow
// LH //	L.M	L.M+L	L.M+L	bo˩ɬɑ˥	boar

Table 2: One example of each of the nine tonal categories of monosyllabic classifiers. From §4.1.2.

classifier	tone	description: classifier for...
ɖwæ˦	H$_a$	steps (of stairs)
ɲi˦	H$_b$	days
hɑ̃˧˦	MH$_a$	nights
kv˧˦	MH$_b$	people, persons
nɑ˧	M$_a$	tools
dzi˧	M$_b$	pairs of non-separable objects, e.g. shoes
dze˩	L$_a$	pairs of separable objects, e.g. pots, bottles
dzi˩	L$_b$	trees, bamboo
ʐv̩˩	L$_c$	lines, patterns (in weaving or drawing)

Table 3: The seven tonal categories of monosyllabic verbs: analysis into H, M, L and LH tones. From §6.1.1.

tone	example	in isolation	NEG	ACCOMP	V+'a bit'
H	dzɯ˦ 'to eat'	M	M.H	M.H	M.M.M
M$_a$	hwæ˧$_a$ 'to buy'		M.M	M.M	M.H.L
M$_b$	tɕʰi˧$_b$ 'to sell'				M.M.M
M$_c$	bi˧$_c$ 'to go'			M.L	n.a.
L$_a$	dze˩$_a$ 'to cut'	LH	M.L		M.M.H
L$_b$	tʰɯ˩$_b$ 'to drink'				M.M.MH
MH	lɑ˧˦ 'to strike'	MH	M.MH	M.MH	M.H.L

Notational conventions for tones

L	Low tone
M	Mid tone
H	High tone
#	word boundary; by extension: the boundary of the entire expression to which a tone pattern is associated (e.g. a compound noun or a numeral-plus-determiner phrase)
H#	final High tone: this H gets anchored on the last syllable of the expression to which it is associated
#H	floating High tone: this H gets anchored *after* the word boundary, i.e. on a following morpheme, if one is available and can serve as a host. In some contexts, the floating H tone does not surface (for want of syllabic association) but lowers following tones to L.
MH#	final Mid-to-High tone, realized either as a rising contour on the last syllable of the expression, or, where the morphotonological context allows, as M tone on the last syllable of the expression and H tone on (the first syllable of) the morpheme that follows
H$	a type of H tone (analyzed in §2.3.2) exemplified by the noun 'flea', and nicknamed the 'flea' tone or 'gliding' tone. When a word carrying this tone is pronounced in isolation, the H tone associates to its last syllable: /kɤ˧ʂe˥/ 'flea' has a M.H tone sequence at the surface phonological level. When the copula is added, the result is /kɤ˧ʂe˧ ɲi˥/ 'is (a/the) flea', with H tone on the copula. When the noun is followed by the possessive, no H tone reaches the phonological surface: the observed form is /kɤ˧ʂe˧=bɤ˧/ 'of (a/the) flea', with M tone on both syllables of the noun and also on the possessive.
–	In the representation of the tones of expressions containing two (or more) morphemes, such as compound nouns, the symbol – refers to the morpheme break. Thus, –L refers to a L tone that attaches after the morpheme break, i.e., in the case of a compound noun, on the head noun. LM–L indicates that the morpheme before the morpheme break (i.e., in a compound, the determiner) gets LM tone and the noun after the break gets L tone.

The seven phonological tone rules (from §7.1.1)

Rule 1: L tone spreads progressively ("left-to-right") onto syllables that are unspecified for tone.

Rule 2: Syllables that remain unspecified for tone after the application of Rule 1 receive M tone.

Rule 3: In tone-group-initial position, H and M are neutralized to M.

Rule 4: The syllable following a H-tone syllable receives L tone.

Rule 5: All syllables following a H.L or M.L sequence receive L tone.

Rule 6: In tone-group-final position, H and M are neutralized to H if they follow a L tone.

Rule 7: If a tone group only contains L tones, a post-lexical H tone is added to its last syllable.

Combination rules in determinative compounds, S+V combinations, and O+V combinations

Table 4a: The underlying tonal categories of σ+σ compound nouns. Leftmost column: tone of determiner; top row: tone of head. From §3.1.4.

tone	LM; LH	M	L	H	MH
LM; LH	LH	LM	LH	LM+#H	LM+MH#
M	−L	#H	−L	#H	MH#
L	L				
H	#H−	#H			−L
MH	H#			H$	

Table 4b: The underlying tonal categories of σσ+σ compound nouns. Leftmost column: tone of determiner; top row: tone of head. From §3.1.4.

tone	LH; LM	M	L	H	MH
M	−L	#H	−L	#H	−L
#H	H#	#H			
MH#		MH#			H#
H$	#H−	#H	H$	#H	H#−
L	L+H#	L			L+H#
L#	L#−				
LM ı MH#	LM+MH#−	LM+MH#	LM+H$		
LM+#H		LM+#H	LM+H#	LM+#H	LM+H#
LM	LM−L	LM	LM−L		LM+MH#
LH	LH				
H#	H#−				

Table 4c: The underlying tonal categories of σ+σσ compound nouns. Leftmost column: tone of determiner; top row: tone of head. From §3.1.4.

tone	M	#H	LM	MH#	LM+#H	H$	L	L#	LM+MH#; LM+#H; LM; LH	H#
LM; LH	M	#H		LM+#H	LM+MH# / L+#H−	LM+H$	L+#H−	L+#H− / L+H#	L+#H−	LM+H# / L+H#
M	M	#H	LM+#H	MH#		H$	−L	−L#	−L	H#
L	L				L+H#	L+H#	L	L+H#	L+#H−	L+H#
#H	H#	#H	#H	#H−		−L / H#	#H−	H#	#H−	H#
MH				MH#	#H−					#H

Table 4d: The underlying tonal categories of σσ+σσ compound nouns. Leftmost column: tone of determiner; top row: tone of head. From §3.1.4.

tone	M	#H	MH#	H$	L	L#	LM+MH#; LM+#H; LM; LH	H#
M	M	#H	MH#	H$ / #H–	–L	–L#	LM+MH#; LM+#H; LM; LH	H#
#H	H#	#H–	#H–	H$ / #H– / H#	#H–	H#	MH#–	
MH#	MH#	MH#		#H– / H#–			MH#–	
H$	#H	#H		#H– / H#–			#H–	
L	L+H#	L	L+H#	L+H#	L+#H–	L+H#	L+#H–	L+H#
L#	L#–							
LM+MH#	LM+H#	LM+#H	LM+MH#–	LM+MH#– / H#	LM+MH#–	LM+MH#–	LM+MH#–	LM+H#
LM+#H				LM–H$	LM+#H–			
LM	LM–		LM+MH#		LM–L	LM–L#	LM–L	
LH	LH							
H#	H#–							

Table 5: The tone patterns of subject-plus-verb combinations, in surface phonological transcription. From §6.10.1.

tone of noun	tone of verb					
	H	M_a	M_b	L_a	L_b	MH
LM, LH	L.H	L.M+M	L.M+M	L.H	L.H	L.MH
M	M.M+L	M.M+M	M.M+M	M.L	M.L	M.MH
L	M.M+L	L.L	M.M+M	L.L	L.L / M.L	L.L
H	M.M+L	M.M+L	M.M+L	M.MH	M.MH	M.L
MH	M.H	M.H	M.H	M.MH	M.MH	M.H
M	M.M.M+L	M.M.M+M	M.M.M+M	M.M.L	M.M.L	M.M.MH
#H	M.M.M+L	M.M.M+L	M.M.M+L	M.M.MH	M.M.MH	M.M.L
MH#	M.M.MH	M.M.MH	M.M.MH	M.M.MH	M.M.MH	M.M.H
H$	M.M.M+L	M.M.M+L	M.M.M+L / M.M.M+H	M.M.MH	M.M.MH	M.H.L
L	L.L.L	L.L.L	L.L.L	L.L.L	L.L.L	L.L.H
L#	M.L.L	M.L.L	M.L.L	M.L.L	M.L.L	M.L.L
LM+MH#	L.M.M+L	L.M.M+L	L.M.M+L	L.M.MH	L.M.MH	L.M.H
LM+#H	L.M.M+L	L.M.M+M	L.M.M+M	L.M.L	L.M.MH	L.M.MH
LM	L.M.M+L	L.M.M+M	L.M.M+M	L.M.L	L.M.L	L.M.MH
LH	L.H.L	L.H.L	L.H.L	L.H.L	L.H.L	L.H.L
H#	M.H.L	M.H.L	M.H.L	M.H.L	M.H.L	M.H.L

Table 6: The tone patterns of object-plus-verb combinations. From §6.8.1.

tone of noun	tone of verb					
	H	M_a	M_b	L_a	L_b	MH
LM	L.M+L̄	L.M+M	L.M+M	L.M+L	L.M+L	L.MH
LH	L.L / L.H	L.H	L.L / L.H	L.H	L.H / L.L	L.MH
M	M.M+L	M.M+M	M.M+M	M.L	M.L	M.MH
L	L.L	M.M+M	M.M+M / L.L	L.L	L.L / M.L	L.L
H	M.M+L	M.L	M.M+L	M.H	M.MH	M.L
MH	M.H	M.H	M.H	M.H	M.MH	M.H
M	M.M.M+L	M.M.M+M	M.M.M+M	M.M.L	M.M.L	M.M.MH
#H	M.M.M+L	M.M.L	M.M.M+L	M.M.H	M.M.MH	M.M.L
MH#	M.M.MH	M.M.H+L	M.M.MH	M.M.H	M.M.MH	M.M.H
H$	M.M.M+L	M.H.L	M.M.M+L	M.M.H	M.M.MH	M.H.L
L	L.L.L	L.L.H	L.L.L	L.L.H	L.L.L	L.L.H
L#	M.L.L	M.L.L	M.L.L	M.L.L	M.L.L	M.L.L
LM+MH#	L.M.M+L	L.M.H	L.M.M+L	L.M.H	L.M.MH	L.M.H
LM+#H	L.M.M+L	L.M.L	L.M.M+L	L.M.H	L.M.L / L.M.MH	L.M.L
LM	L.M.M+L	L.M.M+M	L.M.M+M	L.M.L	L.M.L	L.M.MH
LH	L.H.L	L.H.L	L.H.L	L.H.L	L.H.L	L.H.L
H#	M.H.L	M.H.L	M.H.L	M.H.L	M.H.L	M.H.L

xxxiv

1 Introduction

The aim of this book is to provide a description and analysis of the tone system of Yongning Na (also known as Mosuo), a Sino-Tibetan language spoken in Southwest China.

The richness of this system is immediately apparent when one examines a sentence. Example (1a) is the first one that I transcribed: I had just arrived at my future teacher's house; my luggage had been left at someone's house along the main road, some fifty meters from the house. I asked my teacher's son, who can speak fluent Mandarin, to translate an explanation for me: "I have brought a lot of stuff; I have to go back [to the main road] and pick it up now". This yielded (1a). Later I elicited (1b) as a simpler form.

(1)   a.   njɤ˦   ʐi˩   bi˩   -zo˩   -ho˧.
           1SG   to_take   to_go   OBLIGATIVE   DESIDERATIVE
           'I have to go and take [my luggage] now.' (Field notes, 2006)

       b.   njɤ˦   bi˦   -zo˦   -ho˩.
           1SG   to_go   OBLIGATIVE   DESIDERATIVE
           'I have to go. / I'm afraid I have to leave.' (Field notes, 2006)

The difference in the lexical tone on the main verb (in 1a: /ʐi˩/ 'to take'; in 1b: /bi˦/ 'to go') is reflected in the tones of the following syllables, all the way to the end of the sentence.

This book proposes an analysis of the underlying system: lexical tone categories, phonological rules that apply inside tone groups, and combination rules that apply in various types of phrases (i.e. *morphotonological* rules). As a preview of the results concerning lexical tones, (1a–1b) are provided below (as 2a–2b) with morpheme-level transcriptions indicating lexical tone by means of tone symbols supplemented by subscript letters $_{a\ b\ c}$ to distinguish subcategories of lexical tones. The following chapters provide full details on this system, and describe how the tones of entire sentences obtain from the lexical tones.

(2) a. njɤ˧ ʐi˩ bi˩-zo˧-ho˩.
    njɤ˩ ʐi˩ₐ   bi˧_c   -zo˧ₐ   -ho˩
    1SG   to_take to_go   OBLIGATIVE DESIDERATIVE
    'I have to go and take [my luggage] now.'

b. njɤ˧ bi˧-zo˧-ho˩.
    njɤ˩ bi˧_c   -zo˧ₐ   -ho˩
    1SG   to_go   OBLIGATIVE DESIDERATIVE
    'I have to go. / I'm afraid I have to leave.'

To set the stage for these analyses, §1.1 presents the Na language and provides a review of Na language studies. (Historical and ethnological perspectives are presented in Appendix B.) §1.2 sets out the research programme behind the present study, and presents the language consultants, the data elicitation methods, and the online documentation available on this language. A quick grammatical sketch is provided in §1.3, presenting general properties of the language such as basic word order and the structure of noun and verb phrases, which serve as the backdrop to the discussion of morphotonology in the following chapters.

1.1 The Na language

1.1.1 Endonym and exonyms

Yongning Na is a Sino-Tibetan language spoken in Southwest China, astride the border between the provinces of Yunnan and Sichuan, at a latitude of 27°50' N and a longitude of 100°41' E. Speakers of the language refer to it as /na˩ʐwɤ˩/: 'Na language'. The structure of this compound, made up of a noun and a verb, is shown in (3).

(3) na˩ʐwɤ˩
    na˩   ʐwɤ˩_b
    endonym: Na to_speak
    'the language of the Na', i.e. 'the Na language'

The name 'Yongning Na' was coined by Liberty Lidz (2006) by associating the people's endonym with the name of the place where the language is spoken: the plain of Yongning 永宁, a basin located close to Lake Lugu 泸沽湖, a lake of about fifty square kilometres (see Map 1.1). The lake creates a microclimate that is suitable for farming despite the high altitude (about 2,800 meters above sea level).

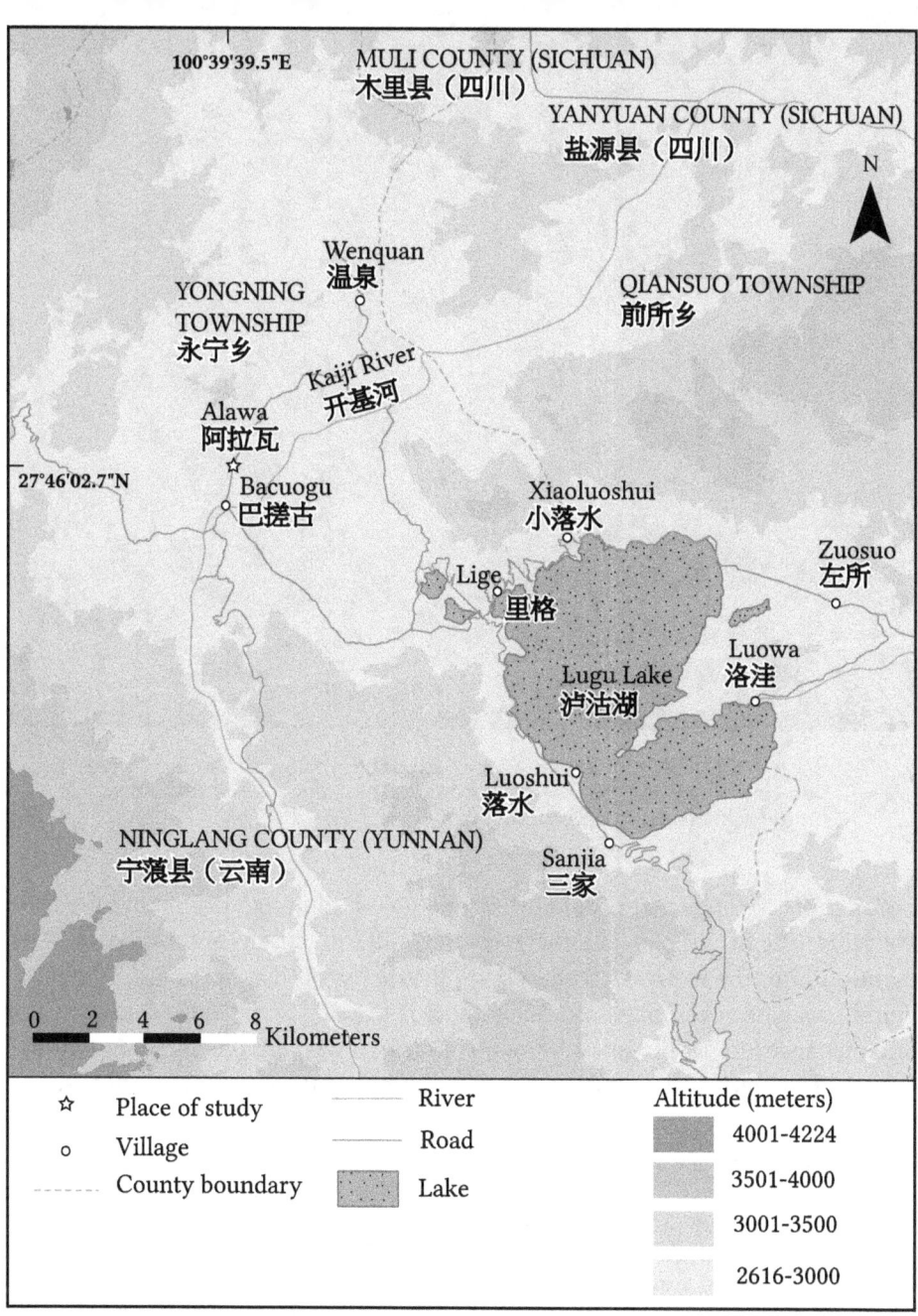

Map 1.1: A sketch map of the Yongning area. *Designed by Jérôme Picard. Sources: Geofabrik, ASTER GDEM (a product of METI and NASA) and OpenStreetMap.*

Photo 1.1: The plain of Yongning seen from the West, with Gemu Mountain (in Na: **kɤ˩mv˧**) in the background. The Lake is behind the pass on the right-hand side. Autumn 2006.

Yongning Na appears in the Glottolog database (glottolog.org) under the code *yong1270*. The Ethnologue language code is NRU, an acronym for 'Narua', a romanization of the expression shown in (3): /nɑ˩ʑwɤ˩/ 'Na language'. The number of speakers is estimated at 47,000 in the Ethnologue database, based on the Summer Institute of Linguistics' own sources (Lewis, Simons & Fennig 2016).[1] Ethnonymy reflects the high degree of ethnic, cultural and linguistic intricacy of

---

[1] The figure of 47,000 speakers includes people who do not use the name /nɑ˩ʑwɤ˩/ to refer to their native language. This is a drawback of the name 'Narua', proposed in a report to the Summer Institute of Linguistics asking for a language code distinct from Naxi. By contrast, the Glottolog inventory of languages adopts the name 'Yongning Na', based on principles such as that (i) "language names (like city names) are loanwords, not code-switches" (Haspelmath 2017), a principle which leads to favour 'Na language' over its equivalent in Na: /nɑ˩ʑwɤ˩/ 'Na language', romanized as 'Narua', and (ii) "language names may have a modifier-head structure", so that the name 'Yongning Na' is interpreted with the intended meaning of 'Yongning variety of the Na language'.

the Sino-Tibetan borderlands (Gros 2014a). Table 1.1 presents (i) two endonyms, (ii) the name by which the Naxi 纳西 (a closely related ethnic group) refer to the Na, and (iii) a Chinese exonym found in various sources, under various avatars, for close to two thousand years, and which currently enjoys renewed favour for reasons discussed in Appendix B (§B.2).

The most likely interpretation of the endonym /naɬ/ is that it means 'black'. Use of ethnonyms meaning 'black' or 'white' is widespread in the area; in Yongning, the Na coexist with the Pumi 普米, who call themselves /tʰóŋmə/ 'white people'.

> The designation **tʰóŋ** 'white' sets the Pumi apart from some surrounding ethnic groups whom they designate as **nʲæ̌** 'black': the **goŋnʲæ̌** 'Nuòsū (Yí) 彝' ('black skin') and the **nʲæmɜ̌** 'Na (Mósuō) 摩梭' ('black person'). (Daudey 2014: 2)

Among the Yi 彝 (formerly known as 'Lolo'), there is a distinction between 'black' and 'white' castes. "The Nasoid groups are also known as Black Lolo, and the assimilated groups connected with them – either Nasoid groups who have become Sinicized, or others who have become assimilated to the Nasoid groups, often by capture or conquest – are called 'white' to denote the fact that they do not 'fit' in the Nasoid clan structure" (Bradley 1979: 53).

> In northeastern Yunnan and western Guizhou, the designation *Nasu* (the black ones) refers to a group of Yi who were the overlords of a series of feudal kingdoms between the 9th and the 20th centuries; they were often contrasted to other, subordinate groups who referred to themselves as white. In the Liangshan region of southwestern Sichuan, on the other hand, Black bones (*Nuoho*, called Black Yi in Chinese), and White bones (*Quho*, called White Yi in Chinese), refer to the aristocratic and commoner castes into which the society is divided – the term *nuo*, or 'Black' also means 'heavy', 'important', or 'serious'. At the same time, the aristocratic caste is also associated with darker colored clothing (...). In this case, it appears that historically the color of the clothing is derived from the color name given to the people, rather than the other way around. What is most important here is to realize that the association of people and colors in this region has little or nothing to do with the imagined color of the people themselves, but rather is part of a complex symbolic system that both reflects and is reflected in the styles and colors of people's clothing. (Harrell 2009: 102)

Table 1.1: The names of the Na: endonyms and exonyms.

transcription	language	romanized equivalents	Chinese equivalents	meaning
nɑ˩	Na	Na (Cai 1997; Lidz 2010)	Nà 纳 (Yáng Fúquán 2006)	'black'
ɬi˩-hĩ˩	Na	Hli-khin (Rock 1963), Hli-hing (Shih 1993)	Lǐxīn 里辛 (Shih 2008: 15)	'People of the Centre'
ly˩-ɕi˩	Naxi	Lü-khi (Rock 1963)	Lǚxi 吕西 (Guō Dàliè & Hé Zhìwǔ 1994: 8)	as above: 'People of the Centre'
origin not established yet	Chinese	Moso (Cordier 1908; Nishida 1985; Shih 1993; McKhann 1998; Luo 2008), Mo-So, Mosuo (Knödel 1995)	Móshā 摩沙, Móxiē 磨些, Móxiē 麼些, Móxiē 摩些, Mósuō 摩娑, Móxiē 末些, Móhuò 磨荍, Mósuān 莫俊, Mósuō 摩梭	*not established yet*

6

The name of Yongning in Na is /ɬi˧di˩/, interpreted by Shih (2010: 23) as 'the peaceful land', relating it to the verb /ɬi˩/ 'to rest, to relax'. This folk etymology fits nicely with the author's celebration of Na society's ideals of harmony (the title of the volume is *Quest for harmony: The Moso traditions of sexual union and family life*). But phonetic correspondences with Naxi do not support this analysis, and demonstrate instead that the Na name of Yongning, /ɬi˧di˩/, means 'the central land, the heartland'. The linguistic argument is as follows.

Yongning is called /ly˧dy˩/ in Naxi (Hé Jírén, Zhào Qìnglián & Hé Jiézhēn 2011: 201). This cannot be a recent borrowing from Na, because Na does not have a rounded close front vowel /y/. If the present form of the Na word were borrowed into Naxi, /ɬi˧di˩/ would be interpreted as /li˧di˩/ by Naxi ears, with a straightforward correspondence for /d/ and /i/ (which are present in both languages) and a reinterpretation of Na /ɬ/ as Naxi /l/ in the absence of an unvoiced lateral in Naxi. The presence of the vowel /y/ in Naxi /ly˧dy˩/ strongly suggests that the word is cognate with Na. It could be a calque (a root-for-root translation from Na to Naxi, by a bilingual speaker who was able to interpret the Na word), but it is not a phonetic loanword.

The noun's second syllable is easily analyzed: it means 'earth, place, land' (Na: /di˩/, Naxi: /dy˩/), a root found in many place names in both languages: it is used as a locative nominalizer (Lidz 2010: 559). As for the first syllable, in view of Na data alone it could have a number of different interpretations. It could indeed be related to the verb 'to rest', /ɬi˩/, as in the folk etymology of Yongning as 'the land of rest, the peaceful land' adopted by Shih Chuan-kang.[2] But it could equally be related to 'moon', /ɬi˧/ (as in the disyllable /ɬi˧mi˧/ 'moon'); to 'ear', /ɬi˧/ (as in /ɬi˧pi˩/ 'ear'); to 'middle', /ɬi˧/ (as in /ɬi˧gv˧/[3] 'middle part'); or to 'Bai' (an ethnic group), through truncation of the disyllable /ɬi˧bv˧/ 'Bai'. Any of these roots combined with /di˩/ 'earth, place' would yield the form /ɬi˧di˩/ by application of regular tone rules.

Moreover, the search needs to be extended further in view of the existence of some words that are irregular in terms of their tone patterns: the tones of some disyllabic words do not correspond to the tones of their two monosyllabic roots as expected in view of synchronically productive rules (as explained e.g. in §3.2.11 and §5.1.3.5). This suggests that one needs to relax tonal constraints when searching for the origin of the first syllable of the name /ɬi˧di˩/. Widening the

---

[2] The main language consultant reports this folk etymology in the document FolkEtymology, available online.

[3] For the sake of simplicity, this noun is provided here in surface phonological transcription. Its underlying form is //ɬi˧gv#˩//, with a floating High tone. This tonal category is analyzed in §2.3.1.

search to /ɬi/ roots of all tone categories yields the following additions to the list of possible origins for the first syllable in the name /ɬi˧di˩/ 'Yongning': the nouns 'roebuck' (/ɬi˩/), 'turnip' (in the disyllable /ɬi˩bi˩/), 'trousers' (in /ɬi˩qʰwɤ˩/), and 'wrath, anger' (in /ɬi˩ʁɑ˩/), as well as the verbs /ɬi˩/ 'to measure' and /ɬi˧/ 'to dry in the sun'. Language-internal evidence thus allows for a broad range of hypotheses: is /ɬi˧di˩/ 'the peaceful land, the land of rest', 'the land of the moon', 'the land of ears', 'the land of the middle', 'the land of the Bai people', 'the land of the roebuck', 'the land of turnips', 'the land of trousers', 'the land of wrath', 'the land of measurements' or 'the land of sun-drying'? It would be unwise to exclude some of these possibilities on grounds of semantic implausibility: a study of place names in various languages of China (Yáng Lìquán & Zhāng Qīnghuá 2011) confirms the great extent of toponymic creativity.

The decisive evidence comes from comparison with Naxi. Of all the above possibilities, only one is supported by the existence of a cognate in Naxi. The root /ly˧/ means 'centre' in Naxi, as does /ɬi˧/ in Na. This leads to an interpretation of the name /ɬi˧di˩/ (and of Naxi /ly˧dy˩/) as 'the central land, the heartland'. This interpretation can then be passed on to historians and anthropologists; it makes excellent sense in view of Yongning's geographic position, and of the role of the Yongning area in the history of Naish peoples (about which see Appendix B), but the crucial evidence is linguistic, relying on the historical-comparative method. In Na, /ɬi˧di˩/ can have more than ten different interpretations; likewise, in Naxi, /ly˧dy˩/ could be given various etymologies, such as 'land of grain', 'land of Asian crabapple, *Malus asiatica*', 'central land', 'land of watchfulness', or 'quaking land, trembling land'. It is through looking for matches between the Na and Naxi words (technically known as *cognate words*), and examining their phonetic correspondences, that the final result can be arrived at.

'The Centre, the Central land', /ɬi˧di˩/, is an apt designation from the point of view of linguistic richness, as most of the diversity of the Naish language group (the lower-level subgrouping to which Na belongs: see §1.1.2) is found in and around the plain of Yongning, within a radius of less than a hundred kilometres. The name 'People of the Centre', /ɬi˧-hĩ˧/,[4] refers to the inhabitants of the plain of Yongning. Ironically, this name is not in common use in the dialect under study here, which is located squarely inside the Yongning plain, whereas it is still used by a community of speakers who moved from Yongning to the peripheral region of Shuiluo 水落 (in the neighbouring county of Muli 木里) several centuries ago.

---

[4] For the sake of simplicity, this noun is provided here (and also in Table 1.1) in surface phonological transcription. Its underlying form is //ɬi˧-hĩ#˧//, with a floating High tone. This tonal category is analyzed in §2.3.1.

1.1.2 Dialect classification and issues of phylogeny

1.1.2.1 Dialect classification: The heritage of mid-20th century surveys

The language spoken in Yongning was investigated in 1979 by the linguists He Jiren 和即仁 and Jiang Zhuyi 姜竹仪, who classified it among Eastern Naxi dialects (Hé Jírén & Jiāng Zhúyí 1985: 4, 104–116). The division of Naxi into Eastern and Western dialects was initially advanced cautiously, as a working hypothesis based on relatively short stays in the field in 1956 and 1957 as part of the national survey of the languages spoken within the borders of the People's Republic of China.

> From our analysis and comparison of the available linguistic and cultural materials, we propose a preliminary division between two dialects, Western and Eastern. But due to the very short amount of time [that could be devoted to this research] and the shortcomings of our experience, it is difficult to tell whether this division tallies with the actual language situation… (Hé Jírén & Hé Zhìwǔ 1988: 120)[5]

The Western dialect area thus proposed by and large corresponds to the area ruled by the Naxi chieftains of Lijiang from the 14th to the 18th century (see Appendix B, §B.1.2). The Eastern dialect area is located to its east and north-east, across the Yangtze river, in the present-day counties of Ninglang 宁蒗, Yanyuan 盐源, Muli 木里, and Yanbian 盐边. Within the Eastern dialect area, three sub-dialects were distinguished by He Jiren & He Zhiwu: Yongning 永宁, Guabie 瓜别 and Beiquba 北蕖坝.

This classification came to be used as the standard in Chinese scholarship. It was also taken up in the inventory of languages maintained by the Summer Institute of Linguistics: *Ethnologue: Languages of the World* (Gordon 2005). Naxi used to appear in Ethnologue under the language code NBF, which covered all the dialects, i.e. giving the name "Naxi" the same extension as in Chinese scholarship. As from 2010, "Eastern" dialects of Naxi were granted an entry of their own in this inventory, under the romanized name "Narua" (code: NRU). The former language code NBF is now split into (i) Naxi proper (new code: NXQ), corresponding to "Western Naxi" in Chinese terminology, and (ii) "Narua" (code: NRU), corresponding to "Eastern Naxi" in Chinese terminology. In detail, however, the division into dialects proposed for "Narua" is identical with that proposed by He

---

[5] *Original text*: 我们从现有的语言和人文材料来加以分析和比较，将纳西语初步分划为西部和东部两个方言。不过时间短促，经验不足，这样分划不知是否符合客观现实情况……

& Jiang for "Eastern Naxi". The total number of speakers was estimated at about 40,000 on the basis of early surveys (Hé Jírén & Jiāng Zhúyí 1985: 107); the same figure is taken up by Yang (2009). As mentioned at the outset of this chapter, the Ethnologue entry indicates a figure of 47,000 as of 2012.

No large-scale dialectal comparison was conducted in the half-century that followed the first dialect survey. The list of "subfamilies" (zhīxì 支系) of the "Naxi nationality" (Nàxīzú 纳西族) provided by Guō Dàliè & Hé Zhìwǔ (1994: 5–9) could serve as a useful reference for such a survey, keeping in mind that this list was essentially based on ethnological criteria, rather than on linguistic data. Reliable descriptions of the language varieties that these authors grouped under the label "Naxi" are required for fine-grained dialectological and comparative research. The present volume aims to contribute to this long-term endeavour by offering a synchronic description of the tone system of one specific language variety.

1.1.2.2 Issues of phylogeny: The position of Na and Naxi within Sino-Tibetan

The position of Naxi and Na within Sino-Tibetan is a topical issue in Sino-Tibetan historical linguistics. Naxi was classified as a member of the "Lolo branch" (Yi) by Shafer (1955); however, Shafer clarified that this language, to which he referred as "Mosso", was among those for which there was "[t]oo little data or too irregularly recorded" (p. 103, note 37). His classificatory proposal for Naxi, as for the other languages placed in the "Unclassified" set within the "Lolo branch", was thus tentative. Bradley (1975b) took up the issue on the basis of advances in the comparative study of Lolo (Yi) languages. He noted that "[w]hile a large proportion of Nahsi vocabulary is plausibly cognate to Proto-Burmese-Lolo (*BL) and Proto-Loloish (*L) forms reconstructed in Bradley 1975a, there is only limited systematic regularity of correspondence. Moreover, the tonal and other developments postulated for *BL and *L by Matisoff are not reflected in Nahsi". The lack of regular correspondences, and the absence in Naxi of shared innovations deemed characteristic of Loloish and Burmese-Lolo, led Bradley to conclude that Naxi is "certainly not a Loloish language, and probably not a Burmish language either" (p. 6).

Some scholars, especially in mainland China, nonetheless maintain the classification of Naxi as a member of the Yi/Lolo group. Gài Xìngzhī & Jiāng Zhúyí (1990) base this renewed claim on the high percentage of phonetically similar words between Naxi and Yi/Lolo, though without verifying the regularity of sound correspondences. Lama (2012) includes Naxi among the set of thirty-seven Lolo-Burmese languages among which he proposes subgroupings by two methods,

(i) searching for candidates for the status of shared innovations, and (ii) conducting automated computation. The latter approach consists of performing Bayesian inference of phylogeny using MrBayes, and computing phylogenetic networks by means of SplitsTree. These two software are applied to a 300-word list from the thirty-seven languages. No judgments of cognacy are passed on the 300 word sets fed as input to the computational procedure, which apparently assumes cognacy in all cases as a default hypothesis. By definition, these methods lead to proposals for subgrouping without questioning the premise that the languages at issue all belong to the same branch.

In light of the conclusion reached by Bradley (1975b), if one looks outside Lolo-Burmese for languages most closely related to Naxi and Na, suggestive evidence comes from comparison with the neighbouring languages Shixing 史兴语 (also known as Xumi; see Huáng Bùfán & Rénzēng Wàngmǔ 1991 and Chirkova, Chen & Antolík 2013) and Namuyi 纳木依语 (Lāmǎ 1994; see also Sūn Hóngkāi 2001, Yáng Fúquán 2006, and Lakhi, Bum & Stuart 2010), but full-fledged comparison has not been carried out yet, and the state of phonological erosion of these languages is a major impediment to comparative studies.

Sun Hongkai, who included Shixing (Xumi) and Namuyi within a "Qiangic" language group which he defined on the basis of typological similarities, proposed that Naxi (understood as encompassing Naxi and Na) is an "intermediate language" ("*línjiè yǔyán* 临界语言") between Loloish and Qiangic (Sūn Hóngkāi 1984).[6] This compromise view amounts to projecting the presence of Yi-like and Qiangic-like typological features into the indefinite past of Naxi. By a similar reasoning, the presence of words of Sinitic (Chinese), Tai-Kadai and Mon-Khmer origin in Vietnamese could lead to its classification as an intermediate language straddling the divide between these three language families. Historical linguists, however, favour an approach in which borrowings and other changes in the language are gradually identified, one layer after another, eventually resulting in a detailed account of the language's evolution that includes the influences to which the language was subjected through the ages. Thus Maspero, in his study on Vietnamese, identified Chinese elements as belonging to a later layer than Tai-Kadai and Mon-Khmer elements:

---

[6] The original statement is the following: "纳西语经常被认为是彝语支的语言，大家知道，纳西语在彝语支中是不太合套的一种语言 [David Bradley, Proto-Loloish, 1978: 14]，纳西语动词的互动范畴和彝语支完全一致。此外纳西语方言中还有一些语音、词汇和语法现象，与羌语文语言相一致。纳西语是彝语支和羌语支之间的"临界"语言。即在语言谱系分类上兼有两种语言集团的不同的特征。也就是说，纳西语同时兼有彝语支和羌语支所特有的某些特征，而动词互动范畴，则是纳西语兼有羌语支的一种重要的语法特征。" (Sūn Hóngkāi 1984: 14)

> Pre-Annamite was born out of the fusion of a Mon-Khmer dialect with a Tai dialect; the fusion may even have involved a third language, which remains unidentified. At a later period, the Annamite language borrowed a huge number of Chinese words. (Maspero 1912: 118)[7]

Four decades later, Haudricourt further attempted to tease apart the Tai-Kadai and Mon-Khmer components, emphasizing that the notion of "language fusion" can be misleading.

> If we admit that there is no such thing as "fusion" between languages, and that genealogical relatedness must be assessed on the basis of core vocabulary and grammatical structure, we are led to consider that the modern form of a language is not determined by its genealogical origin, but by the influences to which it is subjected in the course of its history. (Haudricourt 1953: 121–122)[8]

Haudricourt identified a greater proportion of Mon-Khmer words in basic vocabulary as opposed to words of Tai stock, and came to the conclusion that Vietnamese is a Mon-Khmer language. Importantly, this proposed phylogenetic affiliation by no means constitutes a denial of the considerable influence of language contact in the course of history – a point emphasized e.g. by Dimmendaal (2011: 268-271), citing Manessy (1990).

> It is important to realise that there is no principled way in which one can argue that language x has become "mixed", i.e. embedded with foreign language material, to an extent where it should be classified as non-genetic, or multi-genetic. There are scales or degrees of borrowing, and it is precisely for this reason that it is *not* a useful taxonomic principle to talk about non-genetic or multi-genetic developments. (Dimmendaal 2011: 271)

There is no hard-and-fast dividing line between cases of contact that are considered to result in language replacement – where the vocabulary inherited from

---

[7] *Original text*: Le préannamite est né de la fusion d'un dialecte mon-khmer, d'un dialecte thai et peut-être même d'une troisième langue encore inconnue, et postérieurement, l'annamite a emprunté une masse énorme de mots chinois.

[8] *Original text*: Si l'on admet qu'il n'y a pas de « fusion » de langues, et que l'apparentement généalogique doit être fondé sur le vocabulaire de base et la structure grammaticale, on sera conduit à penser que ce qui donne sa forme moderne à une langue n'est pas son origine généalogique, mais les influences qui s'exercent sur elle au cours de son histoire.

an earlier language is considered as a substratum: piecemeal vestiges of a language that has been replaced by another, e.g. Basque or Celtic elements in Romance languages – and cases where the earlier component still appears substantial enough to motivate classification of the modern language as belonging to that earlier component's language family, e.g. the Mon-Khmer component in Vietnamese.

Returning to Yongning Na, the traditional tools of comparative-historical phonology appear as the most reliable to unravel this language's history and clarify its relationship to other languages within the Sino-Tibetan family. There is widespread agreement about the method: "it is only by searching for lexical and morphological parallels on all sides and by establishing the phonetic equations for such parallels that we can finally decide the genetic relationship of a doubtful group" (Shafer 1955: 98). To what extent this endeavour is successful depends, as Shafer was keenly aware, on the empirical basis: the abundance and reliability of available data.

A tentative family tree was proposed in a preliminary comparative study (Jacques & Michaud 2011) based on Yongning Na, Lijiang Naxi, and Laze – a language spoken in Muli County. The use of a tree representation does not amount to downplaying the importance of areal diffusion. In the Sino-Tibetan family, waves of mutual influence are so strong that concerns about the applicability of the tree model have been voiced for decades (Benedict 1972; Matisoff 1978). Still, the tree model is useful, as one of the tools in the historical linguist's toolbox: it serves to set out one's working hypotheses about degrees of phylogenetic closeness between languages – hypotheses which serve as the basis for attempting comparisons and proposing reconstructions at various historical depths. In a context of continuing debates about models and methods (see e.g. François 2014; Jacques & List submitted), it appears necessary to emphasize that the researcher's aim when proposing a tree model is not to float new proposals about classification for classification's sake, but to clarify assumptions made in historical comparison. The real aim is to document the evolution from the hypothesized common ancestor of a language group to the attested language varieties.

The proposal that Yongning Na, Lijiang Naxi, and Laze join into a Naish lower-level subgroup is supported by shared innovations, in particular structural similarities in the tones of numeral-plus-classifier phrases that cannot have been acquired through contact (the argument will not be repeated here: readers are referred to Michaud 2011). It is further proposed that the Naish subgroup joins with Shixing (Xumi) and Namuyi into a Naic subgroup. At a third, more speculative level, Naic joins with Ersuish (called Ersuic in the historical study of Yu 2012; see also the reference grammar of Ersu by Zhang 2013) and Qiangic, to form a Na-Qiangic node. Na-Qiangic further joins with Lolo-Burmese, to form a Burmo-Qiangic higher-level grouping, provisionally placed on a par with Bodic, Sinitic, and other primary branches. This is represented visually as Figure 1.1. This working hypothesis encourages the search for cognates between Naic languages, Ersuish, and Qiangic. Needless to say, in this research programme, comparison with Lolo-Burmese languages is also essential to progress in the historical study of Naish languages: all the languages listed in Figure 1.1 are uncontroversially related, as members of the Sino-Tibetan family, so that comparative analysis of data from all these languages makes sense.

Systematic comparison between Naic and Lolo-Burmese (conducted e.g. by Lǐ Zǐhè 2015) holds potential for clarifying to what extent their typological similarities are due to (i) inheritance, (ii) parallel changes (unrelated developments, from a typologically similar starting-point: e.g. the development of retroflex consonants from initial consonant clusters), and (iii) language contact. There remains considerable room for progress in the reconstruction of the various lower-level subgroups within Sino-Tibetan, including Naish; in turn, progress in documentation and lower-level reconstruction holds potential for a refined understanding of the broader picture of Sino-Tibetan historical linguistics.

1.1.3 A review of Na language studies

Historical sources in Chinese offer fascinating glimpses into the language spoken in Yongning centuries ago. The *Yuan Yi Tongzhi*《元一统志》, a book dated 1286, provides Chinese phonetic equivalents for present-day Lijiang and Yongning as 样渠头 and 楼头 (present-day Mandarin: *yàngqútóu* and *lóutóu*), respectively. In the variety of Chinese recorded in the 14th-century rhyme table *Zhongyuan Yinyun*《中原音韵》, the initial of 头 is unvoiced; however, using the reconstruction of 'Phags-pa by Coblin (2007), it is interpreted as *dəw, i.e. with the same voicing features as present-day Na and Naxi. The name 楼头 reconstructs as *ləw dəw (Jacques & Michaud 2011: 487), which is clearly cognate with the present-day name of Yongning in Na (/ɬi˧di˩/) and Naxi (/ly˧dy˩/), discussed in Appendix B (§B.3.4). This word by itself is sufficient to establish that this place name dates back at least eight centuries; it also provides evidence on a disputed point of Chinese historical phonology, suggesting that the standard dialect of Yuan dynasty Chinese (Northern Mandarin) retained voiced obstruents (Jacques & Michaud 2011: 487). On the topic of tone, on the other hand, we have not been able to extract evidence from these early notations: examples are few, and too little is currently known about tone in both Yuan dynasty Chinese and Yuan dynasty Naish languages – not to mention the possibility that tone was simply ignored

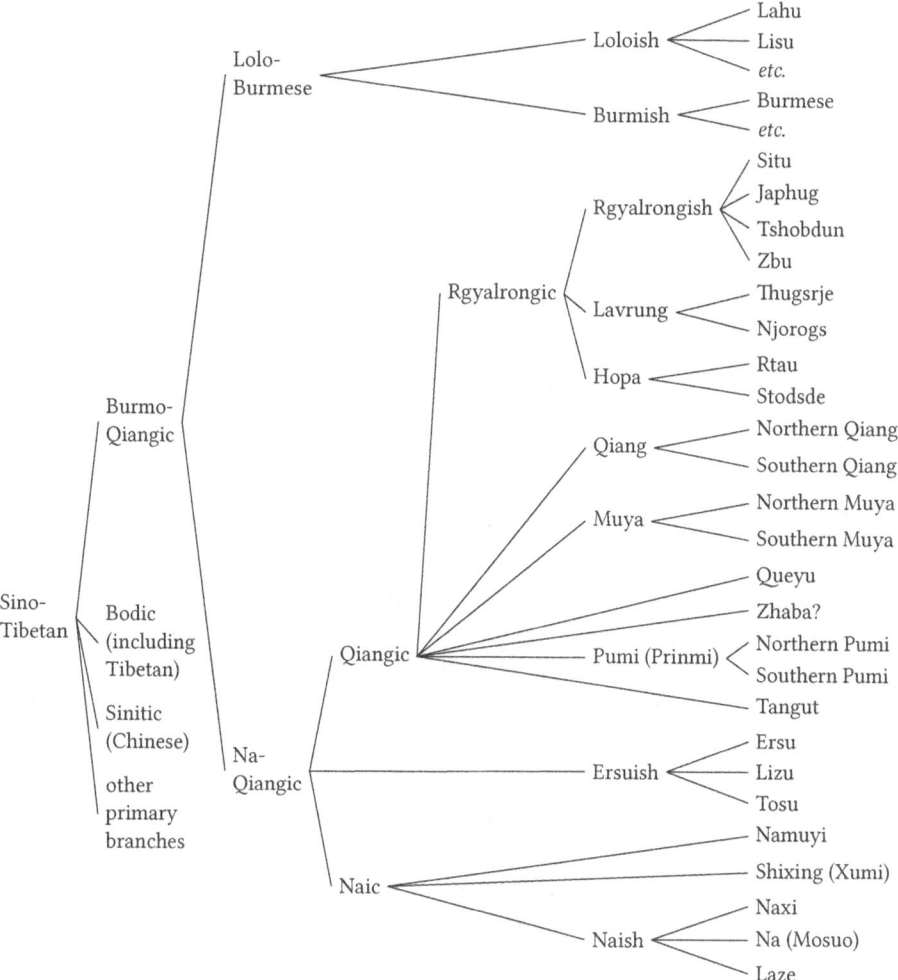

Figure 1.1: A tentative family tree showing the position of Yongning Na within Sino-Tibetan.

in the process of selecting a Chinese equivalent for local terms. The notes of explorers of the turn of the 20th century likewise provide little information about the language and less about tone, and will therefore not be discussed here; readers are referred to Michaud & Jacques (2010) and references therein. The present review of Na language studies focuses on contemporary linguistic research.

1.1.3.1 Information about Na in the *Brief description of the Naxi language*

He Jiren & Jiang Zhuyi's 1985 *Brief description of the Naxi language* mainly focuses on the dialects spoken in the Lijiang plain, but the volume includes a word list of Yongning Na, as well as some observations on phonology, syntax, and dialectal diversity (pp. 107–116; see also Jiāng Zhúyí 1993).

The transcription is not phonemicized, and may not be fully consistent. Only four tones are transcribed over monosyllables: LM (˧˩), M (˧), ML (˩˧), and H (˥), whereas the analysis presented in this volume brings out six categories (LM, LH, M, L, H and MH: see Chapter 2). He & Jiang based their linguistic research on an analogy with Naxi, a language which both of them could speak: He Jiren as a native speaker, Jiang Zhuyi as a second-language learner. Naxi has a four-way tonal opposition over monosyllables: High, Mid, Low (realized phonetically as low-falling), and Rising. When listening to Yongning Na, He & Jiang failed to distinguish the low-rising and mid-rising tones. Moreover, they report a difference between M and H tones in word-initial position, which in fact does not exist. Of course, it may also be that the dialect they investigated differs considerably from that spoken by the consultants who collaborated with me, but this is considered less likely in view of the great phonetic proximity between their word list and the data reported here. It is not uncommon for phonemic and tonal analyses based on data collected during short field trips to differ greatly across authors, due to incomplete phonemicization of the data (as pointed out by Matisoff 2004: 329).

Returning to tones M and H in Yongning Na, in the language variety described here (Alawa dialect) these two tones are neutralized to M in isolation (see §2.3.1.2). Phonetic realizations of this tone (which, under a Praguian approach, can be referred to as an architoneme) vary freely in the upper half of the speaker's tonal space, so that an investigator who starts out from the hypothesis that there are H-tone monosyllables and M-tone monosyllables would be able to hear differences in pitch that seem to support the hypothesis. The same process of pre-existing assumptions affecting linguistic observation happened to me in the early stages of fieldwork: in my initial transcriptions, there were H-tone words and M-tone words. I later discovered that there was no such opposition in isolation. In Alawa, the phonological M and H tones can only be brought out by placing the words in context, e.g. adding the copula (as explained in Chapter 2). The distinction between H and M tones made by He and Jiang on the basis of citation forms (words said in isolation) is thus spurious (unless, as mentioned above, there is a considerable gap between the tone systems of the dialects at issue). 'Field', glossed as 'earth' (dì 地), is transcribed with a High tone: /lɣ˥/, when in fact it carries Mid tone: //lɣ˧// (the double slashes are used in this volume to distinguish lexical forms from surface phonological ones). 'Man' is transcribed as /xĩ˧/, with M tone; this is indeed the tone that the word carries in isolation, but its behaviour in context reveals that its lexical tone is H (my transcription: //hĩ˥//).

The distribution of Low(-falling) and Low-rising tones in He & Jiang's data is a puzzle to me, since no monosyllables are pronounced with Low tone in isolation in the language variety that I investigated. Examples include 'plain, flatlands', 'water' and 'goose', transcribed as /dɣ˩/, /dʑi˩/ and /o˩/; these three items have different tones in my data: LH tone for 'plain', L tone for 'water', and LM for 'goose'. My best guess is that, in the speech of He & Jiang's consultants, L was a (relatively infrequent) free variant of LH in citation form. It is also possible that their word list combines data from several speakers, and is not dialectally homogeneous. The Naxi data in the same volume is a case in point: the authors present the data as coming from the dialect of the township of Qinglong 青龙 (present-day Changshui 长水), the home of Jiang Zhuyi's teacher He Zhiwu 和志武, but some data was contributed by He Jiren on the basis of his native dialect, Yangxi 漾西. In the absence of indications about the origin of each piece of data, it is extremely difficult to determine which data comes from which dialect.

There are also some issues with He & Jiang's transcription of vowels and consonants, as is to be expected of initial field notes. Nasality is transcribed only in two syllables, /xĩ/ (as in 'man', transcribed /xĩ˧/; my data: //hĩ˥//) and /ɣ̃r/ (the only example is 'bone', transcribed /ʂa˧ɣ̃r˧/; my transcription: //ʂæ˧ɭ̝̃˩//), whereas the investigation reported in the present volume brings out eight nasal rhymes. Another point of difference is that He & Jiang do not transcribe the uvular consonants reported in Chapter A of this volume. Such discrepancies may be due to the fact that the variety described by He & Jiang had fewer phonemes than that described here; but it is not implausible that they failed to distinguish some sounds that were in fact contrastive.

Conversely, some vowel differences transcribed by He & Jiang may be spurious. The word list contains examples of /li/ (as in /li˧/ 'to look') and /lie/ (as in /lie˩/ 'tea'). In my data 'tea' and 'to look' have the same initial and rhyme. The vowel /i/ is slightly diphthongized towards [e], and thus close to [lie], which explains why it could be sometimes heard as [i] and sometimes as [ie] before the investigator's ear attunes to the vowel system of Yongning Na. Once again, it is also theoretically possible that these two words did not have the same phonemes in the dialect investigated by He & Jiang.

1.1.3.2 A study of kinship terms, with phonetic observations: Fù Màojì (1980)

The linguist Fu Maoji 傅懋勣 visited Yongning in May and June 1979 with He Jiren and Jiang Zhuyi. He collected data in the village of /dʐɤ˩bɤ˧-ʁwɤ˩/ (Jiabowa 甲波瓦) for a study about kinship terms, presented at the 12th International Conference on Sino-Tibetan Languages and Linguistics (Paris, 1979), then published in Chinese and in French translation (Fù Màojì 1980; 1983). The paper is a testimony to the appeal of Na family structure beyond the circle of professional anthropologists (see Appendix B, §B.3). The article has an appendix containing notes about phonetic transcription. It is interesting to examine these notes in light of a full-fledged phonemic analysis, picking up in retrospect some groundbreaking observations, such as the recognition of uvular /q/, /qʰ/ and /ʁ/. Fu Maoji also recorded the approximant /ɹ/, noting that it can appear in front of a vowel (i.e. as an initial consonant) or constitute a syllable on its own; this is no different from the analysis proposed in this volume (see Chapter A), where the notation chosen is as a retroflex, /ɻ/.

However, Fu Maoji's felicitous insights come together with more puzzling proposals. For instance, his set of uvular consonants includes the fricative /χ/, which closer analysis of the target dialect would probably show never to contrast with velar realizations, as in all the Naxi and Na dialects recorded to date. Supposing that, during their joint field trip, He Jiren and Jiang Zhuyi examined Fu Maoji's notations, they could rightly be skeptical of inclusion of /χ/ in the inventory, and their doubts could then extend to Fu Maoji's (correct) proposal of uvular /q/ and /qʰ/ as distinct phonemes. There are further possible reasons for disbelief on their part: the uvular sounds [q] and [qʰ] are also found in Naxi, where the scope of allophonic variation of velar stops extends well into the uvular region. This can lead speakers of Naxi to the assumption that uvulars in other Naish varieties are also allophones of velars. Moreover, the phonological environments in which /k/ and /kʰ/ contrast with /q/ and /qʰ/ in Yongning Na are restricted (for details, see Appendix A, §A.3.4).

Other problematic aspects of Fu Maoji's notation include (i) a distinction between plain and laryngeally constricted /u/, /v/ and /z̩/ rhymes, (ii) a proposed set of three rhotic vowels in addition to the approximant rhyme [ɹ], and (iii) an analysis whereby /i/ contrasts with /e/ but /i/ is realized as [e] after apical and apical-dental consonants. There is still some way to go from these notes to a working phonemic notation. As for tone, Fu Maoji's classification into three categories, mid-rising, high-flat, and mid-falling, demonstrates that he commendably chose to start fresh and establish the language's tonal categories on their own terms instead of interpreting them in terms of the Naxi tone system; but again, he did not quite reach the stage at which the relevant categories would have emerged. The piecemeal nature of the report goes some way towards explaining why He Jiren and Jiang Zhuyi did not avail themselves of Fu Maoji's data in their 1985 book. It should however be remembered that conducting fieldwork in Yongning in 1979 was an achievement in itself.

1.1.3.3 An outline of Yongning Na by Yang Zhenhong (2009)

An outline of Yongning Na was published by Yang Zhenhong 杨振洪, a speaker of this language from /ə˩by˩-ʁwɤ˩/ village (Abuwa 阿布瓦村), close to the current location of the Yongning high school (original publication in Chinese: Yáng 2006; English translation by Liberty Lidz, with improvements made after consulting with the author, published as Yang 2009). This outline by and large follows the structure of He & Jiang's description of Naxi. Some parts of the discussion of phonetics and phonology may require further analysis: among consonants, uvular and retroflex stops are not granted phonemic status; concerning tone, the analysis is based on the four tones attested in Naxi, which entails some limitations. Informal exchanges with the author (in 2011) suggest that there are in fact more tone categories in the dialect at issue. Like various other researchers, Yang Zhenhong uses descriptive tools developed for syllable-tone systems such as those of Sinitic languages, which do not constitute a fully adequate means to describe tone in Na. (A similar problem was encountered in studies of Pumi – also known as Prinmi – where advances were finally realized by researchers with a knowledge of other types of tone systems, such as those of Japanese dialects: see Ding 2001; 2006; Jacques 2011a.)

1.1.3.4 Lexical materials

An anthology of everyday words and expressions in the Mosuo language (Zhíbā Ěrchē & Xǔ Ruìjuān 2013) presents vocabulary and expressions arranged by semantic field. The authors are a native speaker from the Lake Lugu area and a doctor in linguistics from Yunnan University. Their fieldwork is described as covering the Yongning plain and the Lake area, but with the Yongning plain as the main research area (p. 2).

Approximations in phonetic notation are so numerous that they make the volume unreliable as a work of reference. Voicing contrasts were challenging for the linguist in the team, whose training was mainly focused on the theory and practice of teaching Chinese as a foreign language. Thus, the name of the mountain /kɤ˧mv̩˩/ is transcribed as /gə⁵⁵mu⁵⁵/, with a voiced initial (p. 17 and elsewhere). The mountain's name in Chinese, *Gemu* 格姆山, may have exerted an influence here. Conversely, the adjective /dʐɤ˩˥/ 'good' is transcribed as /tɕa¹³/, with an unvoiced initial. Some phonemes, such as uvulars, are absent from the notations.

1.1.3.5 Collections of oral literature: Na ritual texts

In the Yongning plain, Tibetan Buddhism (of the Gelugpa school) co-exists with a local tradition of ritual practitioners, called /dɑ˧pɤ˥/. Unlike those of the Naxi, the rituals are not written – although some written characters are used by the Na for computing days in divination: see Yáng Xuézhèng (1985) and Lǐ Dázhū (2015: 163-189). The absence of a written form explains in part why these rituals have attracted less attention than those of the Naxi. The much smaller size and socio-political weight of Yongning as compared with Lijiang, and the difficulty of access to the area until the late 20th century, also go a long way towards explaining why there were few efforts for documenting this aspect of the Na oral tradition.

A bilingual collection published by a native speaker of the language (Āzémíng Cìdázhū 2013) contains (i) a phonetic approximation of each syllable by means of a Chinese character, (ii) a transcription of each syllable in the International Phonetic Alphabet, (iii) a Chinese gloss for each syllable, and (iv) a translation into Chinese for each line. (Most lines contain five, seven, or eight syllables.) This volume is best reserved for readers already familiar with the language, who will be able to identify part of the glosses by making allowance for transcription habits influenced by the *Pinyin* system for the romanization of Chinese. For instance, /p/, /t/ and /k/ are apparently used to transcribe aspirated /pʰ/, /tʰ/ and /kʰ/, respectively, like *p, t, k* in *Pinyin*: 'white', transcribed as /puə/ in this book (p. 4), has an aspirated initial in Na. Tone is not indicated.

During the 2010s, Latami Dashi started a documentation programme aiming at the publication of an extensive collection of translated and annotated rituals with accompanying video. This work was in progress at the time of publication of the present volume.

In-depth study of Na rituals, and comparison with Naxi rituals, holds great promise for an improved understanding of Na cultural dynamics (see Mathieu 2015 and references therein). This study would require a good command of Tibetan philology, an in-depth knowledge of Tibetan Buddhism, and other skills far beyond my field of expertise. A piecemeal observation can be offered to suggest the type of issues of cultural contact related to Na religion: twentieth-century reports suggest that monks and /dɑ˧pʏ˧/ coexisted peacefully, with an established division of labour. One would call the /dɑ˧pʏ˧/ to perform a ritual when killing pigs; the monks on prescribed days of the calendar; and both monks and /dɑ˧pʏ˧/ for the most important events, such as funerals. This peaceful coexistence, and the occasions for contact offered by the rites where both participated, apparently resulted in a measure of convergence. The Na /dɑ˧pʏ˧/ show signs of influence from the highly ritualized behaviour of Buddhist monks. They prepare their rituals with an attention to detail that approaches that of Buddhist monks, asking for all the necessary paraphernalia in advance, such as butter, candles, water, and different types of flour. By contrast, the Yi ritual specialists (called 'Bimo' 毕摩 in Chinese) have a habit of requesting objects and accessories suddenly at any point during a ritual, as if acting on their inspiration (Latami Dashi, p.c. 2008). The gestures of the /dɑ˧pʏ˧/ have also come to resemble those of monks. Conversely, some monks are reported to study the Na horoscope – one of the fields of competence of the /dɑ˧pʏ˧/.

1.1.3.6 Liberty Lidz (2010), *A descriptive grammar of Yongning Na (Mosuo)*

By far the most thorough description and analysis of Yongning Na to date is Liberty Lidz's Ph.D. dissertation (Lidz 2010), *A descriptive grammar of Yongning Na (Mosuo)*. It concerns the variety of Yongning Na spoken in the village of Luoshui 落水, on the shore of Lake Lugu. The dissertation, based on in-depth fieldwork, provides a description of the morphosyntax of the language, and contains 150 pages of transcribed and annotated narratives.

Concerning tone, it has been noted that "[t]he tonal system of Luoshui Narua calls for further analysis. Surface phonological tones are transcribed employing three tonal levels, but a reanalysis in terms of two levels would seem possible in many cases. Mention is made of prolific tone sandhi processes, but tantalisingly, these processes are not elaborated on" (Dobbs & La 2016). It is not unusual for reference grammars to leave open some issues of prosody, such as the status of tone, or of stress (Zeitoun 2007: 26); in the case of Yongning Na, a division of labour has been tacitly established between Liberty Lidz and myself, whereby I would take up the task of conducting detailed investigations into tone. Such is the aim of the present volume.

1.2 Project and method

1.2.1 The aim: Detailed description of a level-tone system of East Asia

Tonal changes permeate numerous aspects of the morphosyntax of Yongning Na. Importantly, they are not the product of a small set of phonological rules, but of a host of rules that are restricted to specific morphosyntactic contexts. Guillaume Jacques (p.c. 2009) notes that irregular morphology in Yongning Na, as also in other Naish languages (and in Pumi), mostly consists of irregular morphotonology. The richness of this aspect of the language calls for a book-length description, applying "the old philological virtue of exactitude" (Scherer 1885: 152) to this system, in order to arrive at a reasonably comprehensive account.

A search for full-fledged, book-length descriptions of similar systems in other languages suggests that such reference works remain relatively scarce, even concerning the extensive Bantu branch of the Niger-Congo family of languages, famous for the richness of its morphotonology.

> Theoretical linguistics is primarily concerned with advancing the theoretical enterprise, and tends to produce short pieces – chapters, articles, squibs. It does not have the writing of grammars as a priority, and few of the theoretical grammars of African languages written during the heyday of transformational theory during the 1960s and 1970s have stood the test of time. (…) Are there enough grammars of sub-Saharan African, especially Bantu, languages? The answer is no. (…) The overwhelming impression is that of the small number of real grammars, and the number is not increasing. (Nurse 2011: xxiii–xxiv)

In addition to quantitative scarcity, there is also an issue of breadth and depth of coverage for those languages that have been the object of book-length descriptions. Linguistic fieldwork consists in "going into a community where a language is spoken, collecting data from fluent native speakers, analysing the data, and providing a comprehensive description, consisting of grammar, texts and dictionary" (Dixon 2007: 12). This all-out endeavour entails decisive advantages for understanding the language as a whole, as it functions in its social setting. But breadth of scope can occasionally conflict with depth of investigation of individual topics, such as tone. "No variety of Bambara has heretofore been the object of a systematic tonological description aiming at full coverage"[9] (Creissels 1992: 199; see also

---

[9] *Original text*: aucun parler bambara (…) n'a jusqu'ici fait l'objet de ce qui mériterait d'être considéré comme une description tonologique systématique visant à l'exhaustivité.

Clements 2000; Hyman 2005). "Even the 'well described' languages often suffer from a lack of examples, by which to test the descriptive or theoretical claims" (Nurse 2011: xxiii). Similar observations recur in literature concerning tone systems from various areas of the world. In the field of Mesoamerican languages, the following plea for better documentation of tonal morphology emphasizes the urgency of the work.

> We need full paradigms in grammars of tonal languages, not just rules, abstract representations or examples of how a given form is used in a natural context. This is a cordial invitation to descriptive linguists to enrich the field with new data on inflection. It matters. It matters in a time when most languages with complex morphology are dying. By doing so, we will be paying tribute both to the languages and to the field of linguistics, because in a hundred years from now, when all of us are gone, it will only be our data that shall remain for future linguists to continue increasing our understanding of our human languages. (Palancar 2016: 134)

In the field of Sino-Tibetan studies, occasional misrepresentation of the (often complex) tone systems is not unheard of, as noted e.g. by Sun (2003b) for Tibetan and Post (2015: 188) for Tani and languages of Northeast India in general. Fortunately, languages with level-tone systems and rich morphotonological systems are the object of active research. Two grammars of Pumi, a language that uses two tonal levels, are now available (Daudey 2014; Ding 2014). The present account of Yongning Na tone is intended as a contribution to this development in Sino-Tibetan studies.

At the present stage, the aim is to arrive at a precise description, which constitutes the necessary basis for further work. Consequently, this volume contains many tables setting out the paradigms in full. There is room for some progress in terms of economy of description: for instance, identifying a set of morphotonological combination patterns as default for a certain category of morphemes, and rewriting the data for other categories as *identical to the standard pattern, except for...*, instead of setting out all the data in tabular form. Modelling the morphotonology of Yongning Na, with computer implementation (finite-state modelling), is among the author's long-term projects, mentioned in the conclusion (Chapter 12).

1.2.2 Theoretical backdrop

This study is theory-informed, not theory-driven: the aim is not to bring selected data to bear on topical issues in phonological or morphological debates, but to attempt an in-depth description of a language as it functions. This goal is common to all linguists, and matters more than theoretical differences. An overarching guiding principle is to exercise the greatest vigilance to steer clear of Procrustean models. The theoretical backdrop to the present research is intended to be as unobtrusive as possible, as befits language description and analysis. Linguistic models will be mentioned as the necessity arises.

In a nutshell, the method used here essentially rests on the basic principles of classical structural-functional phonology, as set out in handbooks of phonological description (for instance Martinet 1956: 15, 34–47). It is difficult to select a quote that would neatly summarize the main tenets of this approach. Martinet devoted an entire volume to setting out *A functional view of language* (Martinet 1962). The excerpt below is from another English-language volume, entitled *The internal conditioning of phonological systems*.

> A dynamic conception of language presupposes that we do not deal with it as we would with a dead body in the morgue, but try to look at it as a means of satisfying some of the human needs, and essentially that of communication. In other terms, it derives from a functional view of language (…). [E]xperience has shown that even if language is often used for the satisfaction of other needs as, for instance, that of communion, it is, in the last analysis, mutual understanding that determines the choices of the speakers. (…) At every point in time, with every speaker, what is said and how it is said will show a balance between the desire to communicate, and inertia, be it individual, i.e. reduction of energy, or social, i.e. preservation of traditional forms at the expense of personal comfort and communicative efficiency. (Martinet 1996: 2–3)

A major source of change is the constant competition between the tendency towards phonological integration on the one hand and the tendency towards phonetic economy on the other. Phonological integration tends to fill structural gaps in phonological systems, while phonetic economy tends to create phonological gaps. A simple example can be drawn from tones: having five level tones (Top, High, Mid, Low, Bottom) could be seen as phonologically economical, since in such a system tone alone allows for numerous lexical distinctions, and the combinations of the five levels open up immense possibilities for tonal morphology and morphotonology. But having five level tones is phonetically uneconomical, because the distinction between a large number of level tones is perceptually difficult, e.g. distinguishing sequences such as Top+High, Top+Mid, and High +Mid.

In synchronic description, attention to the conflicting factors that are constantly at play in speech communication leads to adopt the method advocated by Martinet under the name of "dynamic synchrony" (Martinet 1990). The focus is on synchronic description, but flatly synchronic description is enriched by observations about current tensions within the system, assessing which of the competing variants are innovative and which are conservative. Thus synchrony and diachrony gradually combine. Not much is known at present about the diachrony of level-tone systems in Sino-Tibetan. Case studies in dynamic synchrony can yield convergent evidence on diachronic tonal changes and their conditioning. Ultimately, what is needed is an approach that attempts to formulate generalizations about sound change that are independent of any particular language or language group. The aim is to build an inventory of types of sound change and arrive at an improved understanding of the conditions under which they occur. Haudricourt labels such an approach *panchronic* (Haudricourt 1940; 1973; see also Hagège & Haudricourt 1978). Panchronic laws are obtained by induction from a typological survey of precise diachronic events whose analysis brings out their common conditions of appearance. In turn, panchronic laws can be used to shed light on individual historical situations. The idea is that, out of the pool of potential changes, the direction of evolution observed in a given language depends in part on the state of its phonological system: which phonemic oppositions are found in the language, which phonotactic constraints they are subject to, which role they play in the morphophonology, and so on. (For an example, see Jacques 2011a.)

A challenging mid- to long-term goal for historical research will consist in modelling the origin and evolution of level-tone systems with the same degree of precision attained in studies of classical tonogenetic processes in Sinitic, Austroasiatic and Tai-Kadai, which constitute a success story of panchronic phonology. Diachronic comparison shows that a voicing opposition can turn into a phonation-type opposition, a tonal opposition, or a vowel quality opposition (Haudricourt 1965; Ferlus 1979). In the Mon language, for instance, the voicing opposition on initial consonants transphonologized to two contrastive phonation types; in Vietnamese, it resulted in an increase in the number of lexical tones; and in Khmer, it resulted in an increase of the number of vowels. Phonation-type oppositions are now known to be the first stage in the transphonologization. This stage is characterized by the relaxation of the larynx for syllables with formerly voiced initials. At that stage, the phonetic cues to this opposition include, in addition to phonation type proper, some differences in pitch, as well as differences in vowel articulation. This was already noted for a conservative variety of Khmer by Henderson (1952), and is confirmed by experimental studies of Mon (Abramson, Tiede & Luangthongkum 2015 and references therein). At a later stage, one or the other of the cues becomes dominant: this is where the evolution branches into the Khmer type (where vowel quality stabilizes as the new distinctive property) and the Vietnamese type (where the distinctions become tonal). A major structural parameter in this branching is whether the language already has tones at the time when the transphonologization takes place. If the language already has tones, the transphonologization of voicing oppositions creates a split in the tone system; otherwise it becomes a vowel quality opposition, creating a two-way split in the vowel system. Examination of numerous East and Southeast Asian languages confirms this model, simultaneously offering opportunities for further refinements to the model through the study of tonogenetic processes in progress, e.g. Brunelle (2012) on Cham; Kirby (2014) on Khmer; Yang, Stanford & Yang (2015) on Lalo; and Pittayaporn & Kirby (2017) on Cao Bằng Tai.

Panchronic phonology is close (at least in my view) to *evolutionary phonology*, a theory of phonology that aims to combine insights from historical phonology and experimental phonetics, to provide "a general link between neogrammarian discoveries, advances in modern phonetics, and phonological theory" (Blevins 2004: xiii). The emphasis on phonetic bases of change, building on Ohala (1989), encourages a continuous and mutually profitable dialogue between experimental phonetics and historical phonology. Evolutionary phonology, like panchronic phonology, thus constitutes a long-term research programme that holds promise of an increasing degree of precision and explicitness in modelling historical change. While it is possible to pinpoint some differences in the stated principles and methods (see Labov 1994: 601, Andersen 2006, Iverson & Salmons 2006, Mazaudon & Michailovsky 2007 and Smith & Salmons 2008), I believe that the common aim – to explain synchronic states in terms of the processes that lead up to them, and to arrive at general laws of sound change – is more important than theoretical differences, and that practitioners of panchronic phonology, evolutionary phonology or other approaches to the typology of sound systems and sound change share the same essential goals.

This may seem far too much diachronic background for a synchronic monograph, but I believe that it is useful for synchronic descriptions such as the present volume to have a long-term diachronic agenda. In historical linguistics, as in phonetics/phonology, "the devil is in the detail" (Nolan 2003), and the patient sifting of fine points of tonal description helps develop a feel for the diachronic evolution of tone systems. (Chapter 9 is devoted to issues of synchronic variation and diachronic change.)

1.2.3 Field trips and collaboration with consultants

The present results are based on data collected since 2006. Four field trips to the village of Alawa were conducted from 2006 to 2009. Excluding the time spent on travel and on organizational tasks, the duration of these stays was 50 days in 2006, 35 days in 2007, 58 days in 2008 and 40 days in 2009. From July 2011 to October 2012, I had the wonderful opportunity of staying in China for long-term fieldwork. As my main consultant had by that time moved to the town of Lijiang to take care of a granddaughter, I was based in this town too, working with her for an average of two hours a day. In 2013, 2014, 2015 and 2016, I made short field trips to Lijiang and Yongning, still working mainly with the same consultant.

Currently standard procedures for data collection, as reflected in the 'Method' section of papers in phonetics journals, tend to avoid any mention of personal contacts between the investigator and the subjects. Such mentions would be worse than irrelevant, they would be suspicious, since exchanges with consultants beyond providing instructions are viewed as a contaminagen: a threat to the objectivity of the experiment. "The subjects were unaware of the purpose of the experiment" is considered a commendable state of affairs. However, to linguists who have experience of working in collaboration with consultants, whether in a language lab or in the field, it is clear how deeply the relationship established with the consultant influences research. A close look at data collection in language laboratories suggests that important dimensions in the selection of language consultants and the formulation of instructions tend to be overlooked. Worries are seldom voiced about the bias introduced by the use of professional linguists, or multilingual students, as subjects, despite the existence of well-documented differences across speakers: clearly, different people have different abilities (see e.g. Audibert, Aubergé & Rilliard 2008).

Of course, different research purposes call for different data collection methods, and it would be thoroughly unreasonable to expect all investigators to develop personal familiarity with subjects who participate in their research. Nevertheless, it is clear that, in the process of describing a language, mutual understanding between the investigator and consultants is of the essence. In this light, the personal details presented here are not simply fieldwork anecdotes: in my view they represent relevant information on data collection.

1.2.3.1 First steps in the search for consultants

On the first field trip, Mr. Latami Dashi, a native speaker of Na and a researcher in ethnology based in the Ninglang county seat to whom I had been introduced by Picus Ding, accompanied me to his family's house, where I was invited to reside during all my stays in Yongning. He volunteered to work as a consultant. (His code in the database of Naish speakers is M18.) Mr. Latami has near-native command of both Southwestern Mandarin and Standard (Beijing) Mandarin. It was immediately obvious to both of us, when we began an elicitation session, that long years of daily practice of Mandarin had taken their toll on his proficiency in Yongning Na. He offered to help find a speaker who had a relatively homogeneous linguistic experience, having lived continuously in Yongning since childhood. For my part, I wanted to work with a male speaker, for a technical reason: spectrogram reading and electroglottographic analysis, two techniques that I planned to use, are easier to perform on data from male speakers. Also, we agreed to look for a speaker whose age ranged between 35 and 65. Younger speakers have limited command of the language; as for the oldest speakers, they are often the most proficient in Na, but at a certain age speech becomes less audible and communication with strangers more difficult.

Mr. Latami therefore set out to look for a suitable consultant in the neighbourhood. The procedure as he narrated it to me was the following. He invited a candidate over to his place after dinner, treated him to liquor and sunflower seeds, and launched a conversation about how the language was being lost by the younger generation. Then he explained that there was currently a foreigner staying in the house, who wanted to study and record everyday language; and he asked if the person would agree to work as language consultant.

Several acquaintances were thus invited, said they would consider the proposal, and eventually declined. There may have been a number of reasons for this. Mr. Latami's point of view is that, for want of knowing the ins and outs of linguistic fieldwork, they were suspicious of potential misuse of the information that they would provide, and wary of the blows that their reputation would suffer if their name became associated with debatable materials about Na language and Na culture. There are enough examples of ludicrously simplified depictions of Na culture produced to cater for the tourist industry (as reviewed in Appendix B, §B.3.5) to justify their cautious stand.

On the other hand, these people have known Mr. Latami since he was a child, and they would have reason to trust that he would not collaborate in a research project that may harm the image of the community. In his own research on Na culture, Mr. Latami takes care to gather viewpoints from a number of relatives and acquaintances. After he has finalized a draft of one of his books, he circulates copies to Na people who are literate in Chinese and asks for their comments. Only after he has received their criticisms, corrections and comments, and worked them into the final version, does the book go to press. This offers no absolute guarantee against resentment on the part of community members concerning the contents of the book in its final form, but it could go some way towards allaying suspicions.

The negative response of these Na speakers on being invited to participate in data collection can be considered as providing an insight into traditional Na society as a highly conservative agricultural society where deviant behaviour meets with sharp reproach. This is not without consequences for language: "the strong networks typical of rural life" (Milroy & Milroy 1985: 379) favour not only archaism, but also the development of innovations that tend to complexify morphology – a process opposite to what happens in cases of creolization. For instance, reflecting on the case of the development of person agreement marking on complementizers in Bavarian German (reported by Bayer 1984), Peter Trudgill speculates that this only happens in tightly-knit rural communities. The example given is (4), where *ob* 'whether' receives second-person agreement *-st* (Trudgill 2011: 82, 112–113).

(4) ... obst   du   noch   Minga   kummst
        whether   you-SG   to   Munich   come

   'whether you are coming to Munich'

To return to Yongning Na, the development of the rich morphotonology described in the present volume may have been favoured by the same social factors that initially led potential consultants to decline sharing their knowledge of Na with me.[10]

Mr. Latami Dashi's mother seconded her son's efforts to convince potential consultants that they should not be intimidated by the tasks proposed to them, explaining that the purpose was not to collect folklore, but to study the everyday language, and that the initial stage of the work was as simple as saying the words for 'head', 'hand', and so on. While she did not succeed in convincing others, she eventually convinced herself, and volunteered as a consultant.

1.2.3.2 Main language consultant

My Na language teacher is Mrs. Latami Dashilame /lɑ˧tʰɑ˧mi˩ tæ˧ʂɯ˧-lɑ˩mv˩/. (Her code in the database of speakers of Naish languages is F4.) She was born in 1950 into a family of commoners – the majority group among the Na, distinct on

---

[10] I am aware that this link is hypothetical and looks a lot like a "just-so story": an *ad hoc* and unverifiable speculation. Some observations on the dynamics of Yongning Na morphotonology are set out in Chapter 9.

the one hand from the chieftain's family, which constituted the nobility, and on the other hand from the serfs. Her birthplace is the hamlet called /ə˧lɑ˧-ʁwɤ˧/,[11] close to the monastery of Yongning, called *dgra med dgon pa* in Tibetan, a name rendered in Chinese as *Zhāměisì* 扎美寺. The full address is: Yúnnán province, Lìjiāng municipality, Nínglàng Yí autonomous county, Yǒngníng district, Ālāwǎ village (云南省丽江市宁蒗彝族自治县永宁乡阿拉瓦村). This place is referred to in this volume as 'Alawa'. The founding of this hamlet is recounted in the narrative Elders3 (about the narratives and other online resources, see §1.2.5.1). My teacher later established a home of her own in a neighbouring hamlet, slightly closer to the road leading to the Yongning marketplace.

My teacher is attached to traditions, closely associated with the teachings of her grandmother, whom she remembers as an outstanding character who tactfully managed a large household. In narratives, she refers to her grandmother as /ə˧si˧/, 'great-grandmother, ancestor of the third generation', the term of address used by her own children – a way to point her out to the next generation as a model. My teacher is considered locally as a connoisseur of Na customs: in the last two decades or so, villagers experiencing doubts about how a certain ceremony should be performed would come to ask her for instructions.

On the other hand, she is well aware of how deeply Na society has been transformed since her childhood, and she does not cling to a bygone past. She is an open-minded character, gaily deriding in retrospect the prejudices that used to prevail in Na villages. For instance, in an account of the introduction of vegetables such as courgettes and eggplants in Yongning, she reports that distrustful and indignant villagers would warn, "Don't eat those: they are grown in shit!" but that these new crops were eventually adopted, along with traditional Chinese methods for fertilizing soil (narrative: Housebuilding2). In her childhood, my teacher was one of the actors in a film about the Na and their unusual family structure "without fathers or husbands" (discussed in Appendix B, §B.3): *'A-zhu' marriage among the Naxi of Yongning.*[12] Later, one of her sons became an an-

---

[11] For the sake of simplicity, this noun is provided here in surface phonological transcription. Its underlying form is //ə˧lɑ˧-ʁwɤ#˧//, with a floating High tone. This tonal category is analyzed in §2.3.1.

[12] I was not able to access this film. Chinese title: 《永宁纳西族的阿注婚姻》. Black and white. Duration: about 60 minutes (6 film portions of 10 minutes each). Production date: about 1966. Advisor: Qiū Pǔ 秋浦. Scenario: Zhān Chéngxù 詹承绪 and Yáng Guānghǎi 杨光海. Director: Yáng Guānghǎi 杨光海. Photography: Yuán Yáozhù 袁尧柱. Sound recording: Zhào Déwàng 赵德旺. Animations: Zhèng Chéngyáng 郑成杨. Narration: Zhōu Qìngyú 周庆瑜. Summary: "Before Liberation, the Naxi of the people's commune of Yongning, in Ninglang Yi Autonomous County, lived in a feudal society, but they preserved distinctive characteristics of primeval matriarchal societies. They had matriarchal households in which the maternal side constituted

Photo 1.2: The main language consultant, Mrs. Latami Dashilame (lɑ˧tʰɑ˧mi˩ tæ˩ʂɯ˧-lɑ˩mv˩), shopping at the Yongning marketplace. Spring 2008.

thropologist, specializing in Na society, and she met a number of his colleagues. She witnessed how the Na of Yongning became an object of curiosity and fantasy, and how Na culture became folklorized for the promotion of the tourist industry.[13] Her experiences and reflections shook some of the beliefs that had been passed on to her by her grandmother, such as Buddhist faith. While conscientiously going through the prescribed rituals on a day-to-day basis, her belief in Buddhist teachings such as reincarnation was faltering, although without affecting her commitment to the ideals of benevolence and respect of others. The narratives recorded show her awareness of the cultural relativity of the waning customs and traditions of the Na, to which she nonetheless remains attached.

---

the core of the family. They retained a style of marriage ('A-zhu' marriage) in which men did not take wives into their family, and women did not marry into another family. This documentary film records this form of matrimony according to the facts." *Original text*: "在云南省宁蒗彝族自治县永宁公社的纳西族，解放前处于封建领主社会，但长期以来还保存着原始母系社会特征，保存着以母系为核心的母系家庭，保存着男不娶，女不嫁的"阿注婚姻"。男阿注到女阿注家过夜，晚上来白天走的"半同居"婚姻生活。本片对这种婚姻形式、特点和母系家庭作了如实的记录。" The film is part of a series about "ethnic minorities" initiated in 1957: 少数民族社会历史科学纪录片.

[13] One example among many is a report done for the French tabloid *Paris Match*. The magazine's special issue "China is changing" ("La Chine change", May 2001) contained no fewer than ten pages dedicated to the "Mosuo" (pp. 52–61), including an interview with Latami Dashi and his mother Latami Dashilame (p. 60).

Unlike more traditional parents in whose view the monastery was the most prestigious prospect for boys, she encouraged her children – girls as well as boys – to study in the Chinese school system, which she felt was a better gateway to an existence free from daily toil in the fields. Her four children have all found employment outside Yongning, one of them in the county town of Ninglang, two in Lijiang, and one in faraway Shenzhen (Guangdong). Although she lived continuously in the village from the time of her birth, and hardly ever left the plain of Yongning (and, indeed, seldom left her village) until she came over to the city of Lijiang to look after a newborn granddaughter in 2010, she was always well aware of the wider world.

Her experience that, beneath the differences in local customs, the human heart is the same everywhere, surfaces in places in the narratives that she agreed to record during the course of our collaboration. She likes to point out similarities between the situations described in her narratives and present-day situations. For instance, mentioning apprentice monks' hopes of finding a good master, she brought out the analogy with my study of Na, for which I likewise needed attentive teachers, as did her grandson at a university in Kunming. Following her instruction, I have always called her 'mother' (/ə˧mɑ˧/), and have been the grateful object of her affectionate care throughout my stays. She is a model of tact, masterfully fine-tuning relations within the family and beyond. She has been a patient and encouraging teacher, despite her declining health and her heavy workload as a mother and a grandmother. While conceivably proud of raising four children under harsh circumstances, she has a strong sense of humour and was never inclined to pose as guardian angel, muse, or Madonna (to cite Baudelaire's impassioned wording: "l'Ange gardien, la Muse et la Madone").

She was a stutterer during her adolescence, but later overcame this difficulty. I may not have noticed had I not been informed, but I now interpret the rare cases of stuttering that occur in recorded audio documents as remnants of this earlier difficulty. Also, she is known in the community as a person who talks fast. Finally, although she has never suffered from any major otorhinolaryngological ailments, she has noticed changes in her voice over the years, and is no longer able to sing the high-pitched songs of the Na. The reason is partly social: according to local habits, singing is an activity for young people. The voices of singers over the age of forty (fifty at a push) are considered unattractive, and it is unusual for a women past fifty to sing songs. On the occasion when my teacher agreed to sing a song (understanding that this may be a useful part of documenting the language, and that most members of the younger generation do not get to learn traditional songs anymore), it appeared that lack of practice over the years had made her unable to perform songs.

She never travelled to Na villages outside the Yongning plain, such as Labai or the Na villages in Muli county. She can speak a little Southwestern Mandarin Chinese, and borrows common Chinese words when speaking Na, but her proficiency was very limited until she moved to Lijiang in 2010 and found herself in a predominantly Chinese-speaking environment. Apart from initial vocabulary elicitation, which was done in Chinese, fieldwork was conducted in Yongning Na, the consultant providing explanations in her own language, without translation into Chinese. This certainly made the elicitation process slower than it would have been with a bilingual consultant, but monolingual fieldwork also has its advantages, allowing the investigator to develop a better command of the language.

In addition to phonological materials, the set of texts by consultant F4 grew from one traditional story to a set of over one hundred monologues (addressed to the investigator) about topics that she selected. The consultant does not view herself as a skilled performer of oral literature: she was not tutored to become the depositor of a heritage of oral traditions, a role reserved to men in the local tradition of ritual practitioners (called **dɑ˧pɤ˧**, and related to the Naxi **to˧mbɑ˩**: see Fāng Guóyú & Hé Zhìwǔ 1995; Lǐ Dázhū 2015). She gave in to the wishes of the investigator, a linguist who was greedy for narratives and audio recordings in general. Knowing that I have a side interest in history, ethnicity and sociology, she talked about life in Yongning in "the old times", a conveniently vague epoch which includes her childhood and youth. The result is a set of monologues that belong to ordinary, casual speech as opposed to codified performance of oral texts (to use a distinction set out in Dournes 1990). On the other hand, she is aware of how much is at stake when narrating oral history, and how narratives about the past can be used. (About the didactic and mobilizational power of personal stories in "an oral history regime", see Bulag 2010: 100-105.) She therefore exerts caution to steer clear of topics that she feels to be sensitive. This results in a degree of evenness and uniformity of style that entails strong limitations in terms of speaking styles (the recordings are monologues, and are predictably less lively than dialogues) as well as in terms of contents. No claims are made of having achieved a balanced corpus in any sense. From the point of view of morphotonology, the main concern was to have sufficiently abundant materials to be able to confirm some (if not all) of the elicited tonal combinations by matching them with data which, in the phonetician's admittedly crude categories, belong to "spontaneous speech" as opposed to phonological elicitation sessions.

1.2.3.3 Other language consultants

During the first field trip (2006), as work with consultant F4 began, I reflected on possibilities to extend the work to other speakers. I had in mind the textbook arguments for working with several speakers.

> Data from varied sources can guard against distortions resulting from dressage, the observer's paradox, faulty questioning, or prescriptive influences of one individual's idiolect. Working with several speakers will provide the researcher with points of comparison so that he or she can learn to distinguish between reliable and unreliable data. (Chelliah & Reuse 2011: 180–181)

In the family where I stayed, two members were living in Yongning all the year round: F4, and a daughter-in-law: the wife of her second son. Her daughter-in-law (speaker code: F5), born in 1973, accepted to act as language consultant for basic elicitation, while declining to record any continuous texts such as narratives or dialogues, explaining that she did not feel up to the task. Unlike F4, who after a couple of days eliciting vocabulary agreed to record a narrative, F5 maintained her initial decision not to record anything other than short responses to my questions, except for a few short songs recorded in 2007.

Both F4 and F5 had relatively little spare time, so I would work with one or the other depending on who was available at the time. One day in December 2007 when both were busy, F5 asked a niece to "replace" her for a work session. This offered an opportunity to get insights into the speech of the younger generation. This speaker, F6, was born in 1987. As a high school student in the Ninglang county seat, she only came back home for holidays. Vocabulary elicitation showed that she knew few words, and that her Na phonological system was highly simplified. These observations are reported in a joint book chapter with Latami Dashi: "A description of endangered phonemic oppositions in Mosuo (Yongning Na)" (Michaud & Latami 2011; Chinese translation: Michaud & Lātāmī 2010).

In 2008, two more speakers were recorded. The first was Mr. /ho˧dʑɯ˧tsʰe˩/ (Chinese: He Jiaze 何甲泽), hereafter M21, born in 1942. He was a retired cadre (*gànbù* 干部), and had lived two years in Kunming and three in Yongsheng. But elicitation tasks proved challenging for him, due to some hearing difficulties: he reported full deafness in one ear and highly reduced sensitivity in the other. His experience of various dialect areas also made him more changeable in linguistic behaviour than the investigator would have wished. Specifically, it did not prove feasible to elicit consistent tone patterns for compound nouns from M21, as some patterns that had been elicited in one session were dismissed in another, only to be reasserted with full confidence at a later point. Later, M21's youngest son, /ɖɯ˩dʐɯ˧/ (Chinese: He Duzhi 何独知), born in 1974, kindly agreed to participate in the linguistic investigation. His command of Na appears comparable to that of F5. Like F5, M21 and M23 declined to record anything except vocabulary, phrases and sentences.

1.2.4 Elicitation methods

1.2.4.1 Examination of transcribed texts and direct elicitation

"Texts are the lifeblood of linguistic fieldwork. The only way to understand the grammatical structure of a language is to analyse recorded texts in that language" (Dixon 2007: 22). Following classical methods in linguistic fieldwork, observations from continuous speech (in the case of the present study, mostly narratives) are verified and further investigated through elicitation. A fair amount of transcribed narrative has been collected: more than four hours in total. But a considerably greater amount would be necessary to be able to study the language's tonal grammar on the basis of these texts alone. Not all possible tonal combinations in compound nouns are found in these texts, and no amount of continuous speech would be enough to obtain all the combinations of numerals from 1 to 100 with the various tonal categories of classifiers, as required for the study of numeral-plus-classifier phrases (Chapter 4). Systematic elicitation was therefore used to investigate one area after another of the tonal grammar of Yongning Na.

Larry Hyman, reflecting on his study of the tones of another Sino-Tibetan language (Thlangtlang Lai), makes the following observation:

> Clearly the speaker had never heard or conceptualized noun phrases such as "pig's friend's grave's price", "chief's beetle's kidney basket" (…). It would not impress any psychologist, and it would definitely horrify an anthropologist. (…) However, when I need to get 3×3×3×3=81 tonal combinations to test my rules, the available data may be limited, or the language may make it difficult to find certain tone combinations. I am personally thankful that speakers of Kuki-Chin languages are willing to entertain such imaginary notions. It is most significant that the novel utterances are produced with the appropriate application of tone rules. (Hyman 2007a: 34)

Using this method, L. Hyman completed elicitation of data on Thlangtlang Lai tone within six hours (Hyman 2007a: 9). Such swift progress is possible when the linguist is fortunate to work with consultants possessing high metalinguistic abilities, who enter into the linguistic reasoning, and collaborate with the linguist as colleagues. Famous cases include François Mandeville, a speaker of Chipewyan (Athabaskan family) who "possessed the extraordinary ability to dictate texts and to explain forms with lucidity and patience" (Li 1964: 132).

In the case of Yongning Na, the relationship with the consultants was somewhat different. In the course of our collaboration, they developed an understanding of a linguist's interests and aims. In particular, dozens of hours working together made the main consultant familiar with the investigator's body language, so she would understand a repetition-beseeching glance upward from the laptop screen, or volunteer an explanation when a lengthy pause suggested that the investigator was experiencing a doubt. On the other hand, the main consultant did not develop metalinguistic intuitions beyond the notion of full homophony between two words. She did not reach the stage where she would indicate that the tone of a word is like the tone of another word, much less name a category by letter or number. The main consultant did not become a collaborator in the sense of studying tools for transcribing her language and discussing the inventory and analysis of phonemes and tonemes, i.e. gaining training in linguistics. So she did not provide feedback on analytical choices or on the transcriptions. This clarification appears useful, in light of the recommendation that "linguists should make it a practice to explicitly indicate whether the tonal categories have been recognised by native speaker consultants and whether words cited have been confirmed in those categories by native speakers, or whether those categories are the result of the linguist's own analysis" (Morey 2014: 638). I would be delighted to work with native speakers as fellow linguists, and hope that there will be opportunities for this in future.[14]

1.2.4.2 The issue of cross-speaker differences

One of the findings from the systematic study of compound nouns (reported in Chapter 3) was the high degree of cross-speaker difference.

It is a general observation that tone is highly susceptible to dialectal variation, and in view of existing reports it appears that the greater Yongning area is the

---

[14] I was fortunate to co-supervise the M.A. thesis of a native speaker who conducted a comparative study (Ā Huì 2016) on the tone systems of her own dialect – that of the village of Shèkuǎ 舍垮 – and of Ālāwǎ 阿拉瓦, studied in the present volume. This was of the highest interest for me, of course. But A Hui's work did not include verification of the analyses that I propose for Ālāwǎ: A Hui worked out the tone categories of her own dialect, and she did a comparison with transcribed recordings that I provided, without questioning my notations. The two systems are fairly different: that of Shèkuǎ is based on two levels only (High and Low), as against High, Mid and Low in Ālāwǎ.

part of the Naish-speaking area that has the richest tone systems and the greatest dialectal diversity. In this light, differences observed within the same village, and even within the same family, did not come as a huge surprise.

Another factor of diversity is the gap between age groups created by ongoing language shift to Chinese. F4's four children are more proficient in Chinese than in Yongning Na. All four left Yongning to work. Two married Han Chinese spouses without any command of Na; one married a Na spouse from a different dialect area (**lo˧gv˩**; in Chinese: Běiqúbà 北渠坝) and difficulties of mutual comprehension led the wedded pair to communicate in Chinese instead; one married a Na spouse from Yongning (F5) but works in Shenzhen (Guangdong) and seldom returns home. The generation of her four grandsons and granddaughters has even less command of Na, even though it was F4 who took charge of them in their early years. But there are also notable differences in tonal terms between the speech of F4 and that of her daughter-in-law F5, despite their living under the same roof. Documenting the tone system of several speakers is not simply a matter of verifying data: the description is to be conducted separately for each speaker, only comparing the results as a second step. Another difficulty was that transcribed texts are necessary in order to confirm at least part of the patterns obtained through systematic elicitation, but speakers F5, M21 and M23 declined to record narratives. Had they agreed, arriving at a sizeable collection of texts for each of the four speakers would have represented a formidable amount of work – not to mention the difficulty for the investigator of keeping the four systems distinct.

1.2.4.3 A dilemma: tonological depth vs. sociolinguistic breadth

Clearly, it did not appear feasible to explore all areas of the tone system with the same degree of detail for four speakers. This led to the following dilemma: either limiting the extent of investigation (for instance, focusing on compound nouns, or on numeral-plus-classifier phrases) but eliciting data from a broad sample of speakers, to arrive at adequate sociolinguistic coverage; or extending the investigation to more parts of the linguistic system, working towards a complete picture of the tonal grammar of one speaker, with occasional extension of the investigation to other speakers.

The second option was preferred: attempting as complete a description as possible of the entire linguistic system. Work with consultant F4 appeared more promising because of her much stronger proficiency in Na than the two younger consultants (F5 and M23) and of her relatively homogeneous linguistic lifecourse, as opposed to M21's long years of practice of various dialects of Na and of Chinese. Basing the work primarily on data carefully verified with F4 appeared to be a reliable starting-point for later comparative work, including cross-speaker and cross-dialect studies.

The ultimate research goal, viewed as a collective endeavour, is to document in great detail the synchronic tone systems of a number of research locations in the Na-speaking area, and, on this solid empirical basis, to conduct comparisons and gradually reconstruct the history of the evolution of tone systems. Ideally, this would lead to a complete account of the origin and development of tone systems in Naish, shedding light on all the stages that led from a non-tonal stage to each of the present-day varieties. This is clearly a long-term endeavour; the first task to be addressed is to attempt a description of the tonal system of one dialect in its full synchronic complexity.

The analyses of Yongning Na tone reported in the present volume are therefore based on data from consultant F4, unless otherwise mentioned.

1.2.5 Online materials

1.2.5.1 Transcribed and translated narratives and phonological materials

A guiding principle in the present research is that a close association between documentation and research is highly profitable to both. If it is true, as Whalen (2004) puts it, that "the study of endangered languages has the potential to revolutionize linguistics", and that "the vanguard of the revolution will be those who study endangered languages", then it is all the more unfortunate that "enormous amounts of data – often the only information we have on disappearing languages – remain inaccessible both to the language community itself, and to ongoing linguistic research" (Thieberger & Nordlinger 2006; see also Woodbury 2003; 2011). "[L]anguage documentation as a paradigm in linguistic research" has been described as having benefits such as the following:

(i) making analyses accountable to the primary material on which they are based;

(ii) providing future researchers with a body of linguistic material to analyse in ways not foreseen by the original collector of the data; and, equally importantly,

(iii) acknowledging the responsibility of the linguist to create records that can be accessed by the speakers of the language and by their descendants. (Thieberger et al. 2016: 1)

The necessity of making primary data available was emphasized with specific reference to the analysis of tone at a symposium on "Cross-linguistic studies of tonal phenomena":

> The point to be made is extremely simple: declare the status of the primary data for what it is, and allow an evaluation of the data and its subsequent interpretation to take place in view of the declared status of the data. (…) I in no way imply that the wealth of impressionistic data which we have on tonal phenomena are inherently wrong or that they misrepresent the situation in any particular language. (…) What I do, however, argue for is an unashamed scientific approach to the handling of tonal data, abiding with generally accepted criteria of scientific practice. This will not only raise the credibility of analyses, but may even lead to objective empirical testing of particular theories. (Roux 2001: 366)

Accordingly, the recordings conducted in Yongning have been made freely available online, document after document, since 2011. The recordings are mostly narratives and lexical or phonological elicitation sessions. They are accompanied by metadata (information about the recordings), and, to the greatest extent possible, by full transcriptions and translations. A list of documents is provided in the Abbreviations section.

The data is hosted by the Pangloss Collection[15] (Michailovsky et al. 2014), a language archive developed at the research centre *Oral Tradition: Languages and Civilizations* (LACITO) of the French National Centre for Scientific Research (CNRS) since 1994. The goal of this archive is to preserve and disseminate oral literature and other linguistic materials in (mainly) endangered or poorly documented languages, giving simultaneous access to sound recordings and text annotation.

For some of the Yongning Na recordings, an electroglottographic signal was collected simultaneously with the audio. The electroglottographic signal allows for high-precision measurement of the voice's fundamental frequency, as well as of other glottal parameters.[16] Documents that comprise an electroglottographic signal are accompanied by a special icon in the list of resources (Figure 1.2).

The list of resources is generated automatically from the archive's catalogue. As of 2017, it was arranged by date of deposit. This does not make it easy to locate

---

[15] Address of the interface as of 2017: http://lacito.vjf.cnrs.fr/pangloss/index_en.html

[16] About electroglottography, see the initial report of the invention: Fabre (1957); a synthesis: Baken (1992); some caveats: Orlikoff (1998); discussions about parameters that can be measured: Henrich et al. (2004), Michaud (2004a); and applications to the study of specific linguistic issues, e.g. Brunelle, Nguyễn & Nguyễn (2010) and Kuang & Keating (2014).

Figure 1.2: Screen shot of the beginning of the list of Yongning Na resources in the Pangloss Collection.

a document in this list, or to get a feel for the state of the corpus. A description of the corpus is therefore provided as a static HTML document. It is available by clicking on the language name ('Na') at top of page. This description is arranged by dialect and by type of contents. Explanations about data collection are also provided. A passage from this presentation (which is maintained and gradually improved over the years) is shown in Figure 1.3. For instance, the recordings of numeral-plus-classifier phrases which appear as a list towards the bottom of Figure 1.2 are arranged in table form on the presentation shown in Figure 1.3, making it much easier to see at a glance which recordings are available. Figure 1.4 shows a passage from one of the documents as displayed on the web interface: transcription, translation, and time-aligned audio. The original files can also be downloaded (no login is required).

The Na documents are archived with provisions for long-term conservation, and will continue to be accessible despite future changes that may take place in the Uniform Resource Locator of the Pangloss Collection's web interface. Stable internet links to directly access a specific location within a text are currently under development at the archive; the aim is "to offer readers the means to interact instantly with digital versions of the primary data, indexed by transcripts" (Thieberger 2009). Seamless navigation between grammars and data is clearly the way to go, providing one-click links to the texts where cited examples are taken from. It is hoped that, by the time the next edition of this volume is released, tools for resolving a multimedia document's identifier will be all set up and working, allowing for links from the digital book that will direct the user straight to the relevant passage in the online data. In the meantime, it did not appear advisable to provide hyperlinks to the archive's current interface, because URLs are likely to change in future.

Embedding audio excerpts of the cited examples in the PDF file of this volume would have been a technical possibility, but this would not have reached the goal of connecting the analyses to the data: allowing the reader to navigate between the book and the online documentation where the examples can be examined in context. At present, it remains necessary for users to go to the Pangloss Collection's online interface, and to locate the document at issue either on the internet page presenting the Na documents or in the automatically generated list of documents.

The availability of these audio and electroglottographic data with synchronized transcriptions makes it possible for interested persons to get a feel for the data; it also allows for further research into a broad range of phonetic topics. Given the amount of time that is necessary to produce a state-of-the-art experi-

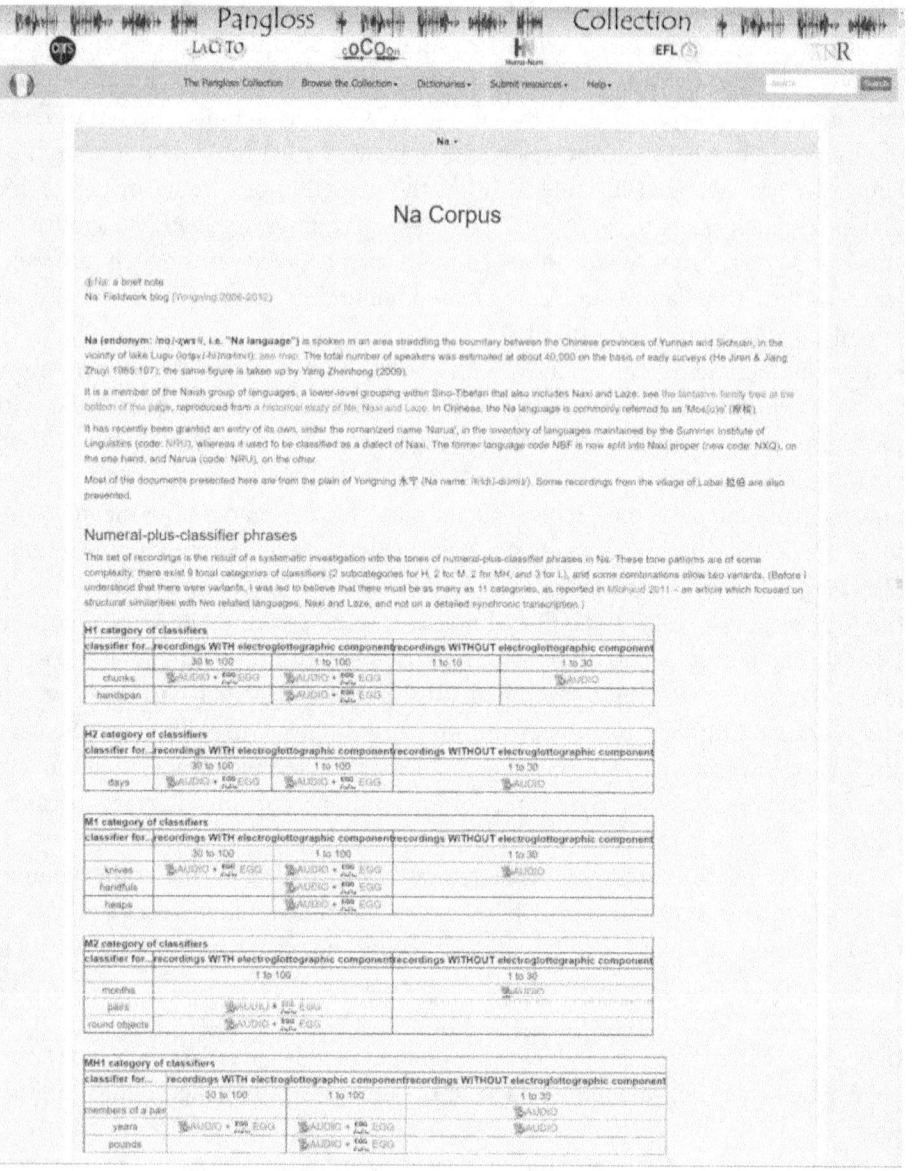

Figure 1.3: Static HTML page presenting the Na resources.

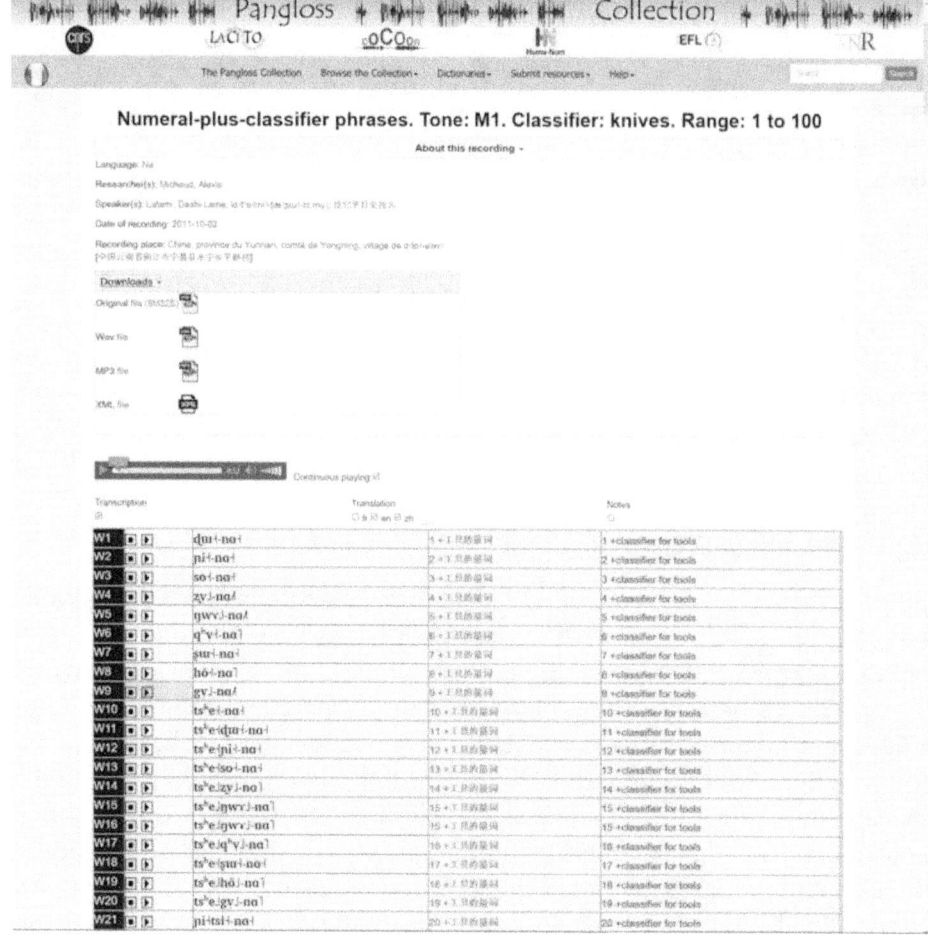

Figure 1.4: A passage from one of the documents as displayed on the web interface: transcription, translation, and time-aligned audio.

mental phonetic investigation, it is simply impossible for linguists who are working at the description of an entire language (or of several languages) to launch into a phonetic study to substantiate and refine each of their observations; on the other hand, it appears feasible to collect a sufficient amount of data for interested colleagues to conduct such a study. To take the example of recorded data about numeral-plus-classifier phrases (analyzed in Chapter 4), here are two examples of phonetic phenomena that could be studied in the future on the basis of the recorded Yongning Na data.

43

(i) The implementation of tone

The electroglottographic signal has not been exploited so far, except for its occasional use in auditory verification (the pitch can be clearer when listening to the electroglottographic signal than when listening to the audio). This signal could serve in future for a phonetic study of the implementation of tone in Yongning Na. There is a large gap between phonological representations in terms of sequences of level tones, on the one hand, and observed fundamental frequency curves, on the other: from a phonetic point of view, "both F_0 height and F_0 velocity are relevant parameters (…) even for the simplest level tone languages" (Yu 2010: 1). A study of the implementation of tone sequences in Yongning Na would be a useful addition to the existing literature on contextual tonal variation and segmental effects on tone, as studied by Abramson (1979), Gsell (1985) and Gandour & Potisuk (1992) for Thai, and Xu (1997; 1998) for Mandarin.

(ii) The weakened (hypo-articulated) realization of repeated words

When a consultant pronounces a sequence of numeral-plus-classifier phrases, such as /ɖɯ˧-kʰwɤ˥ | ɲi˧-kʰwɤ˥ | so˩-kʰwɤ˩ | zʲ˧-kʰwɤ˧/ ('one piece, two pieces, three pieces, four pieces…'), the tone of the classifier changes (e.g. High in /ɖɯ˧-kʰwɤ˥/ and /ɲi˧-kʰwɤ˥/, Low-to-High in /so˩-kʰwɤ˩/, and Mid in /zʲ˧-kʰwɤ˧/) but its consonants and vowels do not. As a result, the speaker's attention focuses on the realization of the new information (essentially: the correct tone sequence for the phrase); in terms of the continuum from hyper-articulation to hypo-articulation (Lindblom 1990), the classifier is hypo-articulated. Specifically, the unvoiced lateral /ɬ/ in classifiers such as /ɬi˧/ 'month' and /ɬi˩/ 'armspan' is occasionally realized as voiced, despite the existence of a voicing opposition between /ɬ/ and /l/ in Na. Pursuing such observations would shed light on the field of allophonic dispersion of Na phonemes. Due to the nature of the corpus, numerous tokens of each numeral and classifier are available, offering a good basis for statistical treatments.

Importantly, the documents are also open to entirely different uses, including aesthetic enjoyment of a voice captured through the wonder of high-fidelity recording, and preserved unchanged through the magic of digital technology. I for one am not insensitive to the luxury of listening to the Yongning Na recordings at leisure. After a recording session is over, the qualms and concerns of fieldwork recede, leaving room for "the fecund miracle of communication within solitude", to cite Proust's eulogy of reading.[17]

---

[17] *Original text:* la lecture, dans son essence originale, dans ce miracle fécond d'une communication au sein de la solitude (…) (*Journées de lecture*, in *Pastiches et mélanges*, Paris: Gallimard, 1919, p. 257).

1.2.5.2 Dictionary

A dictionary of Yongning Na (Michaud 2015a) is available online (i) as an online dictionary in HTML format, (ii) as a PDF document, and (iii) in database format. Entries and examples have translations into English, Chinese and French. There are two supplementary files in the version deposited in the HAL archive.

(i) The file NaDictionary.xml contains the entire database in XML format following the ISO standard LMF (Francopoulo 2013).

(ii) The file NaDictionary.txt contains the entire database in SIL's Toolbox format (MDF). This is the source file on which the editing is done.

This dictionary is conceived of as a work in progress: successive versions will be released, probably every two years or so. Hosting in the HAL preprint archive guarantees long-term preservation.

1.2.5.3 Bibliography

An online bibliography of Naish studies (studies about Naxi, Na, Laze and related languages) was started in 2015, as a Zotero group (Duong 2010) called 'Naish languages'. The emphasis is on linguistics, but the team of contributors would also like to include ethnological/anthropological, historical, and sociological work. Any visitor can consult this bibliography; people interested in contributing to its enrichment and maintenance are welcome to get in touch.

1.3 A grammatical sketch of Yongning Na

This last introductory section is a quick grammatical sketch of Yongning Na, presenting general properties of the language such as basic word order and the structure of noun and verb phrases, which serve as the backdrop to the discussion of morphotonology in the following chapters. A more substantial sketch is found in Lidz (2016).

There is no inflectional morphology in Na. Suppletion is only observed for 'to go': nonpast /**bi˧**_c_/, as in (5), past /**hɯ˧**/, as in (6), past perfective /**hɤ˩**_a_/, as in (7), and imperative /**hõ˧**/, as in (8). Note that the nonpast form in (5) is translated as a preterite, a tense commonly used for narratives in written English.

(5) ɖɯ˧-ɣ˧ lɑ˧ **bi˩** | pi˧-dʑo˩ | ʐv˩-kv˩ tɕɯ˩-kv˩ mæ˩!
ɖɯ˧-ɣ˧   lɑ˧   **bi˩**ᶜ   pi˩   -dʑo˩   ʐv˩-kv˩
one-CLF.individual   only   **to_go.NONPAST**   to_say   TOP   four-CLF
tɕɯ˩   -kv˩   mæ˩
to_lead   ABILITIVE   OBVIOUSNESS

'If only one [man] went, he could lead four [horses]! / If a man went alone, he would lead up to four horses!' (Caravans.119)

(6) ɨ˩tʂʰe˧-ɖɯ˩mɑ˩ | tsʰi˧ɲi˧ | ə˧tse˧ **hɯ˧-ɨ˩**?
ɨ˩tʂʰe˧-ɖɯ˩mɑ˩   tsʰi˧ni#˩   ə˧tse$˩   **hɯ˧**ᶜ   -ɨ˩
given_name   today   INTERROG:why   **to_go.PST**   INCEPTIVE

'Why has Erchei Ddeema gone away today? / How come Erchei Ddeema has left the house?' (BuriedAlive2.14)

(7) "næ˧=ɨ˩-se˩ | ə˧mv˩ le˩-ji˩~ji˩-ze˩! | se˧kʰɯ˩-ʁo˩ni˩ le˩-po˩ ji˩~ji˩-ze˩!"
| pi˧-kv˩ mæ˩, | ho˧di˧ **hɤ˧-dʑo˩**!
næ˧=ɨ˩   -se˧   ə˧mv˩   le˧-   ji˧ᶜ   ~   -ze˧
2PL   TOP   elder_brother   ACCOMP   to_come   RED   PFV
se˧kʰɯ˩-ʁo˩ni˩   le˧-   po˩   ji˧ᶜ   ~   -ze˧   pi˩
satin_headdress   ACCOMP   to_bring   to_come   RED   PFV   to_say
-kv˩   mæ˩   ho˧di˧   **hɤ˩**ₐ   -dʑo˧
ABILITIVE   OBVIOUSNESS   Sichuan   **to_go.PST.PFV**   PROG

'When [one's brothers] had gone away [on a caravan] to Sichuan, [people in the village] would say: "You, your brother is going to come back! [He] will bring back a satin headdress [for you]!" ' (Caravans.35)

(8) no˧ | wɤ˩ | tsʰo˧qʰwɤ˩ **hõ˩**!
no˩   wɤ˩   tsʰo˧qʰwɤ˩   **hõ˧**
2SG   again   tonight   **to_go.IMPERATIVE**

'Go again tonight!' (Reward.63)

Reduplication of verbs and adjectives is widely used to convey reflexivity and intensification (see §6.2).

In the lexicon, a major driving force towards the creation of disyllables is the pressure of homophony, caused by the dramatic phonological erosion of the Naish languages as compared with proto-Sino-Tibetan. For instance, [ji˧] can mean 'jar', 'ox', 'to do', 'to draw' and 'to inform'. 'Jar' is generally disyllabic: [**ji˧mi˧**], adding the syllable for 'mother', which has grammaticalized uses as a female suffix and an augmentative suffix (see §5.1). In that instance, the disyllabic form simply replaces the monosyllable.

1.3.1 Word order

Word order is S+O+V, or, to be more accurate: "[i]n unmarked, non-idiomatic, pragmatically neutral constructions, subject-object-verb word order is most common" (Lidz 2007: 48). Adverbials can appear at various places. Agent marking is not obligatory: "agents are unmarked more frequently than they are marked, both in conversation and narrative" (Lidz 2011: 51). Like the agent adposition /ɳɯ˧/, the dative suffix /**-ki˧**/ is optional. These morphemes allow for a deviation from standard word order; they also serve purposes of disambiguation, as in (9), where the presence of a noun phrase marked as dative clarifies that the verb /**so˧**/ is to be understood in its meaning of 'to teach', and not in its meaning of 'to study; to imitate', since the latter's object cannot take a dative particle. The context of (9) is the following: the speaker saw me sitting ready for an elicitation session, silently hoping that someone could give me some of their time. There was a real uncertainty as to who that would be, as I was working with two consultants within the household at the time. No subject is indicated in the first part of the sentence ('After feeding the pigs'), as it is obvious from the situation that the feeding is done by the person who speaks. On the other hand, the explicit mention of both semantic roles in the second part of the sentence thoroughly answers the concerns of its addressee.

(9) bo˩-hɑ˧ | le˧-ki˧ le˧-se˩-ze˩, | njɤ˧ ɳɯ˧ | no˧-ki˧ | nɑ˩ʑwɤ˧ so˩-bi˩!
bo˩ hɑ˧ le˧- ki˧ₐ le˧- se˩ₐ -ze˧ njɤ˩ ɳɯ˧
pig food ACCOMP to_give ACCOMP to_finish PFV 1SG A
no˩ -ki˧ nɑ˩ʑwɤ˩ so˩ₐ -bi˧
2SG DAT Na_language to_teach/to_study IMM.FUT

'After feeding the pigs, I will teach you Na (myself) / I shall come over for a language lesson!' (Sentence transcribed on the fly in 2008)

As is well-attested across the Himalayas, nominals, including pronouns, need not appear if they can be understood from the discourse context. This applies to any definite argument of the verb, the head of a relative clause, or the head of a complex noun phrase. Another areal characteristic is that topic markers are the morphemes with the highest frequency of occurrence.

1.3.2 Tense, aspect and modality

Tense, aspect and modality are expressed through a host of post-verbal particles and some pre-verbal particles, such as durative /tʰi˧-/, accomplished /le˧-/, perfective /-ze˧/ and experiential /-dʑɯ˧/. 'To go', /bi˩ₑ/, is grammaticalized to express immediate future, and /se˩ₐ/ 'to complete' as a completion marker (both are placed post-verbally). Na stands at a great typological distance from a language such as Wolof, where one predicative marker associated to the verb encodes the greater part of the grammatical content (Creissels & Robert 1998; Guérin 2015). In Na, as in Loloish (Yi) languages such as Lahu (Matisoff 1973) or Lalo (Björverud 1998), particles have rich combinatory potential. Combinations among particles create a wealth of highly dialect-specific nuances; these nuances are best appreciated by examining examples in context.

1.3.3 Question formation

In yes/no questions, the verb is preceded by an interrogative particle /-ə˩/, as illustrated in (10). In *wh*-questions, exemplified by (11), the interrogative pronoun occupies the same slot as the noun phrase would in a statement.

(10)   njɤ˧ my˩ | ə˩-ɲi˩?
       njɤ˩   my˩   ə˩-   ɲi˩
       1SG   daughter   INTERROG   COP

   'Is this my daughter? / Are you my daughter?' (BuriedAlive3.107)

(11)   ɲi˩ ɳɯ˧ | ə˧ma˧-qa˧ tɕʰo˧ bi˩?
       ɲi˩   ɳɯ˧   ə˧ma˧   -qa˧   tɕʰo˩   bi˩ₑ
       INTERROG.who   A   mother   COMITATIVE   together   to_go

   'Who is going to go together with mama? / Who is going to accompany mama?' (FoodShortage2.17)

1.3.4 Existential sentences

There exist several existential verbs in Na, as in many other Sino Tibetan languages. One is preferred for animates, as illustrated in (12). One is "used with things that stand, protrude, or are perpendicular to a plane" (Lidz 2010: 358), as in (13), and another is "used with objects within a container" (Lidz 2010: 361) – including abstract containers such as narratives: see (14). In contrast to the above three, there is an existential for entities that are diffuse, as it were: those that can neither be counted nor held within a container (which would allow for making them quantifiable): an example is shown in (15). Finally, there is a generic existential, illustrated in (16).[18]

(12) hĩ˧ a˥ʁo˧ dʐo˧
     hĩ˥   a˩ʁo˧   dʐo˩ᵦ
     person home EXIST.ANIMATE

'there are people at home' (Reward.11)

(13) tɕʰi˧ tʰi˧-di˩-ɲi˩ mæ˩!
     tɕʰi˥   tʰi˧-   di˩ₐ   -ɲi˩   mæ˧
     thorn   DUR   EXIST CERTITUDE OBVIOUSNESS

'There are some thorns [on barley], not? / [barley] has beard, hasn't it!' (FoodShortage.43)

(14) dɑ˧pɤ˧ qʰwæ˧-qo˩ | qv˧ɬɨ˧ | tʰi˧-ʐi˩-kv˩ mæ˩!
     dɑ˧pɤ˧   qʰwæ˧   -qo˧   qv˧ɬɨ#˥
     priest_of_local_religion message inside name_of_a_mountain
     tʰi˧-   ʐi˥   -kv˥   mæ˧
     DUR   EXIST ABILITIVE OBVIOUSNESS

'Mount qv˧ɬɨ#˥ is mentioned in the tales of the Daba priests!' *Literally:* 'Mount qv˧ɬɨ#˥ exists in the tales of the Daba priests' (Mountains.120)

(15) ə˧tso˧-mɤ˧-ɲi˩ | le˧-ʂe˧, | le˧-ji˥!
     ə˧tso˧-mɤ˧-ɲi˩   le˧-   ʂe˧ₐ   le˧-   ji˥
     all_sorts_of_things ACCOMP to_get ACCOMP EXIST

'We get all sorts of things (all the necessary paraphernalia for a ritual, a feast…) [so that] we have it (at hand for when we need it) / We get all sorts of things ready (for the ritual / the feast)!' (Source: field notes.)

(16) dzɯ˧-di˧ mɤ˧-dʐo˥
     dzɯ˥   -di˩   mɤ˧-   dʐo˧ᵦ
     to_eat NMLZ NEG EXIST

'there was nothing to eat / there was no food left' (FoodShortage2.4)

---

[18] Lidz (2010: 359) reports an additional existential verb in the Luoshui dialect, "used for the passing of time": "/ku33/ EXIST.T [Existential: Used with past existence of time] seems to have something of a connotation of 'pass,' and may be a fairly recent grammaticalization from a lexical verb". In the Alawa dialect (studied in the present volume), this verb, /gv˧ₑ/, retains the lexical meaning 'to flow, to go by, to elapse (time); to take place, to occur (event)'.

1.3.5 Sentence-final particles

Among sentence-final particles, several are epistemics or evidentials: /tsɯ˦/ for hearsay, /mv˧/ for affirmation, /le˩/ for exclamation, and /mæ˧/ to convey obviousness. Combinations between sentence-final particles allow for a considerable range of nuances. Their meaning in context obtains through an interplay with intonational cues: the three-level tone system does not considerably constrain a sentence's intonation; it leaves ample room for the expression of nuances of doubt, surprise and other attitudes and emotions by intonational means, such as overall raising of the pitch register, pitch range expansion, lengthening, and changes in phonation type. (This topic is taken up in Chapter 8.)

1.3.6 Noun and noun phrase

The classifier, preceded by a numeral or a demonstrative, follows the head noun, as in the phrase 'a dumb person' in (17). A numeral and a classifier also constitute a well-formed phrase, which can receive a suffix, as in the phrase 'a family' in the same example (17). The counting system is decimal.

(17) ɖɯ˧-ʑi˩=i˩-dʑo˩ | zo˧bæ˩ | ɖɯ˧-v˧ dʑo˩ tsɯ˩ | mv˩!
      ɖɯ˧ ʑi˩ᵦ   =i˩   -dʑo˩   zo˧bæ˩   ɖɯ˧
      one CLF.households ASSOCIATIVE TOP   dumb_man   one
      v˧   dʑo˩ᵦ   tsɯ˩   mv˩
      CLF.individual EXIST REP   AFFIRM

'It is said that, in a household, there was a dumb man.' (Lake3.3)

Classifiers are numerous; many still correspond transparently to a noun. Some 'self-classifiers' are used without a head noun, e.g. /ɖɯ˧-kʰv˧/ 'one year' (not ‡ kʰv˧ ɖɯ˧-kʰv˧ 'year one-year'). Classifiers are discussed in Chapter 4.

The order in compounds is *determiner+determined*, but a few lexicalized items made of adjective plus noun have the reverse order, e.g. 'dry field' /pv˧lv˧/ ('dry' +'field'). Compounds are discussed in Chapter 3.

There is no gender or agreement.

There are proximal and distal demonstratives. The proximal demonstrative, /tʂʰɯ˩/, is homophonous with the third person singular pronoun. There are inclusive and exclusive second-person pronouns, and collective forms referring to 'me and my kin', 'you and your kin', etc. Pronouns in Na behave syntactically like nouns (as in languages such as Chinese, Japanese, Bambara and Zarma: Creissels 1995: 29) and not as pronominal indices.

The clause relativizer is /-hĩ˧/, illustrated in (18).

(18)   go˧mi˧ | tʰi˧-ki˧-hĩ˧ | tʂʰɯ˧-ʐi˧...
       go˧mi˧   tʰi˧-   ki˧ₐ   -hĩ˧   tʂʰɯ˧   ʐi˩ᵦ
       younger_sister   DUR   to_give   REL   DEM.PROX CLF.households
       'the family to which the younger sister pledged herself... / the household which the woman entered upon marriage...' (Sister3.18)

1.3.7 Verb and verb phrase

Directionality is expressed before the verb, by /gɤ˩-/ 'upward', /mv˩-/ 'downward', or disyllabic expressions (§6.3.3). Verb serialization is used for many constructions including resultatives, equivalents of Chinese 'de 得' constructions, and the expression of movement (Lidz 2010: 397-405). Imperatives are simply conveyed by intonational means: the syntactic structure is the same as for statements, except for the verb 'to go', which has a distinct imperative form, as explained at the outset of this section (§1.3).

Adjectives can be considered as stative verbs: they "can take aspect marking, be negated, and can be modified by the intensifier" (Lidz 2010: 362). The intensifiers are /ɖwæ˩/, which appears before the adjective ('very ADJ') or verb ('V a lot') and /ʐwæ˩/ (which means 'extremely', and only appears with adjectives). The copula is not used with adjectives. It can be added after any verb to convey certainty (Lidz 2010: 354).

In addition to the discussion of the lexical tones of nouns (Chapter 2) and verbs (§6.1), the following chapters return to various syntactic phrase types in which tone changes occur: compound nouns (Chapter 3), phrases containing nominal classifiers (Chapter 4), combinations of content words with grammatical elements (nouns in Chapter 5 and verbs and adjectives in §6.2-6.7), object and verb (§6.8-6.9), and subject and verb (§6.10).

2 The lexical tones of nouns

This chapter focuses on the lexical tones of nouns; it is customary in tonal studies to proceed "from the tones of nouns to the general organization of the system" (Rialland & Sangaré 1989; see also Hyman 2014: 526-527). In Yongning Na, tonal oppositions are partly neutralized when words are spoken in isolation. This casts a subtle veil on the tone categories, hiding some of them from the casual observer. Because of these cases of neutralization, issues concerning the behaviour of nouns in context will also be broached in this chapter, which thus serves as an introduction to the Yongning Na tone system as a whole.

The chapter is organized in analytical order. It starts out from a static inventory of tone patterns over domains of different lengths, and gradually progresses towards an analysis. This mode of exposition replicates (as far as possible) the progression of analysis during fieldwork, working up from the surface facts. The aim is to allow the reader to evaluate the analysis step by step, and to reflect on possible alternatives, instead of proposing a complete analysis from a top-down perspective.

2.1 A static inventory of tone patterns

Words spoken in isolation (often referred to as *citation forms*) are what one starts out from in the earliest stages of fieldwork. Table 2.1 presents an overview of the tone patterns over monosyllabic nouns spoken in isolation. It was not possible to find a minimal set (words distinguished solely by tone) due to the relatively low number of monosyllabic nouns in the language.

At this initial stage, the essential information is that provided in the leftmost column in Table 2.1, describing the three patterns as follows: a non-rising, non-low pattern; a low-rising pattern; and a mid-rising pattern. The second column of Table 2.1 proposes preliminary labels for the three patterns using level tones: L(ow), M(id), H(igh), and their combinations. All that this second column does at the moment is to suggest how the three categories might be viewed in terms of L, M and H phonological levels. Justification for the use of a level-tone analysis comes from morphophonological alternations in which the tones partake;

Table 2.1: Tone patterns attested over monosyllabic nouns spoken in isolation.

phonetic realization	preliminary label	example
non-rising, non-low	M ? H ? HM ?	/z̺wæ/ 'horse'
low-rising	LM ? LH ?	/bo/ 'pig'
mid-rising	MH ?	/tsʰæ/ 'deer'

evidence of this will be provided later on in the course of the analysis. The question-mark in the column 'preliminary label' is intended to emphasize that these labels were given in a first pass; some were modified later on in the course of the analysis, as will be explained below.

The three surface patterns are the same for monosyllables that belong to other word classes, such as verbs. The restrictions on the tones of monosyllables spoken in isolation are the following.

(i) There are no examples of contrastive falling contours.

(ii) There is no opposition between a high tone and a mid tone: only one type of non-low, non-rising tone is observed. Its realizations occupy the entire upper part of the tonal space, varying from mid to high, with a flat or falling contour. The choice of the label M (rather than H) for this pattern will be explained further below, at the stage of phonological analysis.

(iii) There is only one contour that starts on a low pitch. Using level-tone labels, this observation can be stated as follows: there is no opposition between LM and LH.

(iv) There are no examples of low, non-rising tones.

Over disyllabic nouns, seven patterns are observed, as shown in Table 2.2. Since lexical roots are monosyllabic, disyllables result from various processes, such as addition of the female gender suffix /-miɭ/, found in 'dog' and 'sow' (this suffix will be studied in detail in §5.1.2). At the present point in the exposition, the aim is to propose a static inventory including all attested tonal categories of disyllabic nouns, irrespective of their internal structure.

Table 2.2 includes two unattested combinations, marked with a double dagger (‡) in the *preliminary label* column. If the tone of the first syllable is non-low, there are four observed tonal patterns on the second syllable: low, mid, high, and

Table 2.2: Tone patterns attested over disyllabic nouns spoken in isolation.

1st syllable	2nd syllable	preliminary label	example
non-low	low	M.L ?	/dɑ.ji/ 'mule'
non-low	low-rising	‡ M.LM	–
non-low	mid-rising	M.MH ?	/hwɤ.li/ 'cat'
non-low	mid	M.M ?	/po.lo/ 'ram'
non-low	high	M.H ?	/hwæ.tʂæ/ 'squirrel'
low	low	‡ L.L	–
low	low-rising	L.LM ? L.LH ?	/kʰɤ.mi/ 'dog'
low	mid-rising	L.MH ?	/õ.dʋ/ 'wolf'
low	mid (or high)	L.M ? L.H ?	/bo.mi/ 'sow'

mid-rising. If the tone of the first syllable is low, there are three attested patterns on the second syllable: low-rising, mid, and mid-rising.

The restrictions on the distribution of tones on disyllables can be described in static terms as follows.

(i) Only two tones contrast on the first syllable: low and non-low. There can be no contour on the first syllable.

(ii) A non-low tone cannot be followed by a low-rising tone.

(iii) A disyllable cannot be low throughout.

(iv) There is no contrast between a low+mid pattern and a low+high pattern.

There are also strong limitations on tone patterns over three syllables: only twelve patterns are attested. The data in Table 2.3 is from trisyllabic nouns whose degrees of lexical integration differ even more from one another than those of the disyllables in Table 2.2. The trisyllabic nouns in Table 2.3 range from transparent compounds, such as 'Year of the Dragon' and 'Year of the Snake', to fully indecomposable words, such as 'lips'. (A hyphen is placed between the two parts of decomposable compounds.) In the same way as for disyllables, the focus here is on the static inventory; the rules relating the tones of compounds to those of their components will be analyzed later (in Chapter 3).

Since there is a three-way opposition in tonal levels on the second syllable, these three levels are labelled as 'low', 'mid' and 'high', whereas for the first

Table 2.3: Tone patterns attested over trisyllabic nouns spoken in isolation.

1st σ	2nd σ	3rd σ	preliminary label	example	meaning
non-low	mid	mid	M.M.M ?	dzɣ.qʰwʀ.tṣe	awl
non-low	mid	low	M.M.L ?	mʋ.gʋ-kʰʋ	Year of the Dragon
non-low	mid	high	M.M.H ?	njo.bi.li	lips
non-low	mid	mid-rising	M.M.MH ?	bʋ.zʋ-kʰʋ	Year of the Snake
non-low	low	low	M.L.L ?	mo.jo.mi	owl
non-low	high	low	M.H.L ?	æ.tse.pʰæ	kneebone
low	low	mid	L.L.M ?	tʰo.kʰʋ.mi	male dog
low	low	low-rising	L.L.LM ?	dʐɯ.nɑ.mi	wilderness
low	mid	mid	L.M.M ?	tʰɑ.ʐwæ.mi	donkey
low	mid	high	L.M.H ?	æ.li.pʰæ	mirror
low	mid	mid-rising	L.M.MH ?	bi.pʰʋ-dʐɯ	flood
low	mid	low	L.M.L ?	bæ.bʋ-bʋ	ladybird

syllable, where there is no opposition between mid and high, the two levels are simply labelled 'low' and 'non-low'.

In view of the information in Tables 2.1-2.3, the following generalizations can be proposed:

(i) A non-low tone can be followed by one of four tones: low, mid, high, or mid-rising.

(ii) A low tone can be followed by low, low-rising, mid, or mid-rising.

(iii) A high tone can only be followed by a low tone.

(iv) Non-final syllables never carry a contour.

(v) An entire word cannot carry low tone on all of its syllables. L.L.L is not permitted in trisyllabic nouns, any more than L.L in disyllabic nouns and L in monosyllabic nouns, even though L.L is found in syllable 1 and 2 positions in some trisyllabic nouns, and also in syllable 2 and 3 positions in some other trisyllabic nouns.

(vi) There can never be a trough: a tone surrounded by higher tones (non-low followed by low followed by mid, for instance).

From the above data alone, it is not yet possible to know whether these generalizations concern the level of the word, the phrase, or entire sentences, since "words produced in isolation are minimal utterances showing both lexical and utterance-level (post-lexical) features" (Himmelmann 2006: 164). To preview the results of later analysis, the relevant domain is a unit between the word and the utterance, which could be called a phonological phrase. The term adopted here is *tone group* because the defining characteristic of this phonological unit is that it serves as the domain of tonal processes. Tone groups are discussed in detail in Chapter 7.

A dynamic approach to the tone categories of nouns sheds light on the above generalizations about static inventories.

2.2 A dynamic view, bringing out the tonal categories

A dynamic view brings out six tonal categories for monosyllabic nouns, and eleven categories for disyllabic nouns. While reading through this section, the reader may want to make an occasional leap forward to Table 2.7, which presents a synthetic overview of the full picture of the tone system for nouns as it finally emerges from the analysis. This table is also reproduced in the 'Quick reference' section at the beginning of this volume.

2.2.1 Monosyllabic nouns: Six tonal categories

It was mentioned above that there are three patterns for monosyllables spoken in isolation: low-rising; non-low; and mid-rising. The set of nouns realized as non-low in isolation is not homogeneous, however. Take, for example, the behaviour of /jo/ 'sheep', /ʐwæ/ 'horse' and /lɑ/ 'tiger', all of which are realized with a non-low tone in isolation. In association with the copula, these yield: /jo˩ ɲi˧˥/ 'is (a/the) sheep', with low tone on the noun and rising tone on the copula; /ʐwæ˧ ɲi˥/ 'is (a/the) horse', with mid tone on the noun and high tone on the copula; and /lɑ˧ ɲi˩/ 'is (a/the) tiger', with mid tone on the noun and low tone on the copula. Since the morphosyntactic context is the same,[1] these three words must be considered to be representatives of three different lexical tone categories.

---

[1] To preview the results of analyses set out further below, in §6.1, the copula carries a lexical L tone. In isolation, it surfaces with a rising tone, analyzed as LH.

These three tone categories all neutralize to non-low when the noun is spoken in isolation.

The set of nouns realized as low-rising in isolation, such as /z̻æ/ 'leopard' and /bo/ 'pig', is not homogeneous either. Although differences do not surface in combination with the copula, as they do for non-low nouns, in other contexts, such as object-plus-verb combinations, /z̻æ/ 'leopard' and /bo/ 'pig' have different behaviours. For example, 'has bought leopards' is /z̻æ˩ hwæ˦-ze˩/, with a L tone on the perfective suffix /-ze/, whereas 'has bought pigs' is /bo˩ hwæ˦-ze˦/, with M tone on the suffix.

Out of the three surface patterns on monosyllables in isolation, only one (MH) corresponds to a single phonological set: all the words realized with MH tone in isolation have the same tone pattern in a given morphosyntactic context. The two others constitute the neutralization of two or more lexical categories: the low-rising contour corresponds to two lexical categories, and the non-low tonal realization corresponds to three categories (see Table 2.7a). To sum up, a dynamic view brings out six tonal categories of monosyllables.

2.2.2 Disyllabic nouns: Eleven tonal categories

The same procedure as above was also applied to disyllabic nouns, i.e. looking at the behaviour of nouns in different morphosyntactic contexts, in order to find out how many tone categories need to be distinguished.

It was discovered that the nouns realized with a M.M pattern in isolation belong to two distinct categories: one after which the copula carries L tone, and one after which the copula carries H tone. One set is illustrated by /po˦lo˦/ 'ram', /po˦lo˦ ɲi˩/ 'is (a/the) ram'. The other is illustrated by /z̻wæ˦zo˦/ 'colt', /z̻wæ˦zo˦ ɲi˥/ 'is (a/the) colt'.

Likewise, the nouns realized with a M.H pattern in isolation make up two distinct sets, the one illustrated by /kv˦ʂe˥/ 'flea', /kv˦ʂe˦ ɲi˥/ 'is (a/the) flea', the other by /**hwæ˦tʂæ˥**/ 'squirrel', /**hwæ˦tʂæ˥** ɲi˩/ 'is (a/the) squirrel'.

Finally, the nouns realized with a L.M pattern in isolation (which could also be transcribed as L.H: there is no opposition between a L.M pattern and a L.H pattern, as mentioned above) fall into no fewer than three categories. These three categories are brought out by intersecting evidence from two contexts: with a following copula, and with a following possessive, as shown in Table 2.4. Addition of the copula sets apart a category exemplified by the Na word for 'Naxi', after which the copula receives H tone. Addition of the possessive sets apart a category exemplified by 'boar', which depresses the tone of the possessive to L, as opposed to its realization as M for the other words. While the evidence used

Table 2.4: Examples illustrating the existence of three tone categories of nouns neutralized to L.M in isolation.

in isolation	meaning	with copula	with possessive
/naJhĩ˧/	Naxi	naJhĩ˧ ɲi˥	naJhĩ˧ = by˧
/boJmi˧/	sow	boJmi˧ ɲiJ	boJmi˧ = by˧
/boJɬa˧/	boar	boJɬa˧ ɲiJ	boJɬa˧ = byJ

to bring out the tone categories is morphotonological (looking at the behaviour of nouns in context), the tone categories are lexical, since the difference in the surface phonological tone strings shown in Table 2.4 must be ascribed to a difference between the lexical items at issue, and hence, to a difference in lexical tone category.

In total, this yields eleven tonal categories of disyllables.

2.3 Phonological analysis of the tone categories of nouns

As reported in the preceding paragraphs, a number of tonal categories were brought out on the basis of their different behaviour in various morphosyntactic contexts. The phonological analysis of these categories is up against an issue of circularity, since the tone categories of the simplest units – monosyllabic nouns – can only come to light through examination of their combinations with various other morphemes whose tone categories, at this stage, have not been analyzed either. In practice, however, bootstrapping is often required when analyzing a new language variety: groping for a correct analysis by trial and error.

A step forward in the analysis of the tones of nouns was made possible by progress in the analysis of the tones of other morphemes. Through an analytic process set out further below, it was realized that the copula carried lexical L tone, and that the possessive carried lexical M tone. On this basis, it became possible to propose a phonological analysis for each of the tone categories of nouns.

The two tonal categories of nouns illustrated by /la˧ ɲiJ/ 'is (a/the) tiger' and /ʐwæ˧ ɲi˥/ 'is (a/the) horse' were analyzed as follows. In the first case, the copula surfaces with its own lexical tone. 'Tiger' represents the simplest case, analyzed as having lexical M tone, a phonological tone identical with the surface tone in this context. (The same analysis is proposed for the category of disyllables illustrated by /po˧lo˧/ 'ram'.) In the second case, 'horse', the copula surfaces with a H tone which must be supposed to be projected onto it by the noun. 'Horse', therefore, exemplifies a tone category characterized by a H tone which can only surface on a following syllable: a floating H tone. This phenomenon warrants a separate subsection to explain the motivation for using this label.

2.3.1 A floating H tone

2.3.1.1 Theoretical backdrop: a quick introduction to floating tones

Floating tones, sometimes called vowelless tones (Goldsmith 2002: 84), are entities postulated to explain categorical modifications of the tonal string. Floating tones do not surface directly, but affect the tones of neighbouring morphemes. For instance, the definite article in Bamana (Mande subgroup of Niger-Congo) has a floating L tone as its signifier, illustrated in (1-2). The examples are reproduced as (1a) and (2a) with tone indicated by means of accents; equivalents using tone letters are provided as (1b) and (2b).

(1) a. Mùsò té yàn
      woman NEG.be here
      'There is no woman/there are no women here.'

   b. Mu˩so˩ tɛ˥ yan˩
      woman NEG.be here
      'There is no woman/there are no women here.'

(2) a. Mùsó-ˋ té yàn
      woman-ART NEG.be here
      'The woman is not here.'

   b. Mu˩so˥- ˩ tɛ˥ yan˩
      woman-ART NEG.be here
      'The woman is not here.'

In (2), there is ample evidence of the presence of a floating L tone: it is manifested through two phonological phenomena. First, contact between the L tone of the noun 'woman' and the floating L tone of the definite article results in the addition of a H tone at the end of the noun, due to a general rule inserting a buffer high tone between two low tones, hence /mùsó/ (L.H) instead of /mùsò/ (L.L). Second, the floating L tone triggers downstep[2] because the following morpheme,

---

[2] Downstep is a distinctive lowering of tone; about the history of this notion, see Rialland (1997). Downstep is not indicated in the example transcript, because it is a phonological consequence of the presence of a floating L tone. Alternatively, one could transcribe the downstep (the usual convention is as an exclamation mark) instead of the floating L: /Mùsó !té yàn/.

the negation marker /té/, carries H tone.[3]

Comparative evidence typically reveals that floating tones originate in the reduction (complete segmental ellipsis) of a syllable. The Bamana article is considered to originate in *-ò; the full form (a vowel and a tone) "is still attested in numerous varieties spoken on the geographic periphery of the Manding area: Mandinka, Xasonka, Worodugukan, Marka-Dafin, some Kagoro dialects" (Vydrin 2016).

A purely tonal morpheme occurs when a morpheme that was segmentally expressed, as a syllable carrying a tone, is reduced to a mere tone, and is only manifested through its association with another morpheme. This is not the only scenario, however: a morpheme can acquire a floating tone through the loss (complete segmental ellipsis) of one of its syllables. For instance, disyllabic verbs are postulated for earlier states of the Igbo language; later "the syllabicity of the final syllables is lost, leaving floating tones, which (...) shift to the left and knock the first tones off in front of the verb morpheme" (Hyman & Shuh 1974: 94).

Concerning the choice of terms, Voorhoeve (1967: 424) used the labels "presegmental tonemes" and "postsegmental tonemes". He was still looking for an adequate cover term for both sets, and seems to have been aware of the awkwardness of the pleonastic label "nonsegmental tonemes", which he grazed (but avoided) by using "nonsegmental H and L". He put forward the notion of *floating tones* in 1971. In the early 1970s, tonologists still felt that it was necessary to enclose this recently coined term in quotation marks at first occurrence, as in the following commentary about Fe'Fe' (Bantu, Niger-Congo):

> [In the word 'pot' /càg ´/] an earlier high tone suffix was present. Historically, there was an accompanying vowel, but synchronically, a mere "floating" high tone is posited. (...) [T]his high tone causes the preceding L tone to raise to a raised-low tone via the process of low-raising. (Hyman & Shuh 1974: 86)

The term gradually caught on, and is currently standard in Bantu studies (see e.g. Franich, O'Connor & Barnes 2012: 33).

---

[3] An alternative analysis of the Bamana facts, following Dumestre (1987: 24-25), is that the tone change is from L.H.H to L.L.H, rather than from L.L.L to L.H.L. Assuming that the category of nouns exemplified by /mùsó/ 'woman' has a lexical LH pattern simplifies the analysis of trisyllables. So the underlying and surface tones of 'woman' in (2) would be the same (LH), whereas a change from the underlying form to the surface form would be hypothesized to occur in (1). However, this has no bearing on the analysis of floating tones: all authors agree that the floating tone does trigger downstep of the following H in (2).

Carry-over of the notion of floating tone to one of the lexical H tone categories of Yongning Na is motivated by the fact that the Na tone at issue is never realized over the word to which it is lexically attached: this H tone can only be anchored to a following morpheme. "Floating tone" is used in the present volume as a synchronic concept, "the concept of *floating* having here the meaning of non-realised tones in an isolated context" (Somé 2000: 61).

An important caveat is that the use of this concept borrowed from the field of Bantu tone studies does not imply the same diachronic analysis as proposed for floating tones in Bantu, where all floating tones are assumed to originate in the segmental ellipsis of a syllable. Floating tones in Bantu result from the loss of segmental materials that were formerly present; by contrast, in Yongning Na, comparative evidence (set out in §2.3.1.3) suggests that the evolutionary mechanism at play was different.

2.3.1.2 The synchronic facts about the floating tone in Yongning Na

An example illustrating the floating H tone category of the Alawa dialect of Yongning Na is the monosyllable for 'horse', realized in isolation as /ʐwæ˧/. The word for 'colt', realized in isolation as /ʐwæ˧zo˧/, offers a neat opportunity to extend the analysis to disyllables: the H tone that appears in /ʐwæ˧zo˧ ɲi˥/ 'is (a/the) colt' is interpreted as reflecting the floating H tone lexically attached to the noun 'colt', in a way that is exactly parallel to /ʐwæ˧ ɲi˥/ 'is (a/the) horse'.[4]

Since this floating H tone is the only type of H tone that may be lexically attached to a monosyllable, it is convenient to transcribe it as a simple H tone on monosyllabic nouns in the dictionary and in examples within this volume: e.g. 'horse' is transcribed as //ʐwæ˥//. (The double slashes are used in this volume to distinguish underlying phonological forms from surface phonological ones.) For disyllables, however, there is an opposition between this floating H tone and a word-final H tone (as in /hwæ˧tsæ˥/ 'squirrel'). This complexity of syllabic anchoring makes it necessary to use a nonstandard symbol: a symbol not used in the International Phonetic Alphabet. Desperate tones call for desperate measures. The pound symbol # was chosen to stand for the end of a lexical word, adopting a notation of the word as /ʐwæ˧zo#˥/, and of the tonal category as #H.

To repeat this important point with another example, the #H-tone word 'little brother' and the M-tone word 'little sister' have the same tonal pattern in iso-

---

[4] Noun-plus-copula combinations behave tonally like object-verb combinations, of which a detailed account is presented in Chapter 6. The rules yielding the surface phonological tone pattern are syntactically conditioned: not all combinations of a #H tone and a L tone yield a /M...M.H/ sequence.

lation (M on both syllables: /gi˧zɯ˧/ 'little brother', /go˧mi˧/ 'little sister'), but the former yields /gi˧zɯ˧ ɲi˥/ 'is little brother' (tone sequence: M.M+H), the latter /go˧mi˧ ɲi˩/ 'is little sister' (tone sequence: M.M+L). The analysis proposed is that 'little brother' has a final H tone which remains unassociated unless it can associate to a following syllable: a H tone that is floating at the end of the word. The association of this floating H tone requires specific morphosyntactic conditions. For instance, the H tone does not surface when the noun is followed by the possessive clitic /=bv̩˧/: thus, **gi˧zɯ˧=bv̩˧** 'of (a/the) little brother' is tonally identical to /**go˧mi˧=bv̩˧**/ 'of (a/the) little sister'.[5]

2.3.1.3 The floating H tone of Alawa corresponds to an overt H tone in two neighbouring dialects

Observations on a neighbouring dialect, that of the village of /pʰɤ˧dʐo#˥/ (in Chinese: Labai 拉伯村), offers indirect supporting evidence for the H tone postulated for the tonal category of the Alawa dialect illustrated by 'horse'. My only contact with the Labai dialect so far has been through two work sessions with Mr. Lamu Gatusa 拉木·嘎吐萨, a researcher at the Academy of Social Sciences in Kunming. The monosyllables of Alawa analyzed as having a (floating) H tone correspond to monosyllables with H tone in Labai. Examples are presented in Table 2.5a. When one of the #H-tone words in Table 2.5a is spoken in isolation, its H tone does not surface (//M// and //#H// are neutralized to /M/), whereas H-tone items are realized as such in Labai. The #H::H correspondence among monosyllables is the tonal correspondence that has the most examples. The only exception is (in the order Alawa::Labai) **hæ̃˩::hæ̃˥** for 'gold' (shown at bottom of Table 2.5a), for which no explanation can be offered at present. For the sake of completeness, Table 2.5b shows the correspondences for syllables carrying M tone in Labai. (A recording of some of the words is available online from the Pangloss Collection; the title of the resource is: M28_Vocabulary.) Importantly, all the monosyllables that belong to the M tone category in Alawa correspond to M-tone monosyllables in Labai.

On disyllables, the floating H tones of Alawa also correspond to H tones in Labai: disyllables that have #H tone in Alawa have a H tone on their second syllable in Labai. Disyllables that have M tone in Alawa likewise carry M tone on both of their syllables in Labai. Some examples are provided in Table 2.6.

---

[5] Whether the floating H tone surfaces or not in a given context is not simply an issue of syntactic class of the added morpheme. To preview data set out in §5.4.1, another clitic, the COLLECTIVE, can host a floating tone. Such complexities explain why tone in Yongning Na requires a book-length description and analysis.

Table 2.5a: Tone correspondences between Alawa and Labai for monosyllabic nouns carrying H tone in Labai.

gloss	Alawa /in isolation/	//lexical form//	Labai	correspondence
earth	tʂe˧	tʂe#˥	tɕi˥	#H::H
hail	dzo˧	dzo#˥	dzo˥	#H::H
sky	mv˧	mv#˥	mv˥	#H::H
fire	mv˧	mv#˥	mi˥	#H::H
star	kɯ˧	kɯ#˥	kɯ˥	#H::H
snow	bi˧	bi#˥	mbi˥	#H::H
pond	ɖwæ˧	ɖwæ#˥	ɳɖwæ˥	#H::H
canal	qʰæ˧	qʰæ#˥	qʰæ˥	#H::H
urine	dʐɯ˧	dʐɯ#˥	ɳɖʐɯ˥	#H::H
gall	kɯ˧	kɯ#˥	kɯ˥	#H::H
blood	sʁ˧	sʁ#˥	sʁ˥	#H::H
head	ʁo˧	ʁo#˥	ʁo˥	#H::H
Pumi	bʁ˧	bʁ#˥	bʁ˥	#H::H
man	zo˧	zo#˥	zo˥	#H::H
bronze	æ̃˧	æ̃#˥	æ˥	#H::H
salt	tsʰe˧	tsʰe#˥	tsʰe˥	#H::H
gold	hæ̃˧	hæ̃˩	hæ̃˥	L::H

Another neighbouring dialect, that of the village of Wujiao 屋脚, just across the border with the county of Muli in Sichuan (四川凉山州木里县屋脚乡), yields similar correspondences: lexical field notes kindly provided in 2012 by Xu Duoduo 许多多, then a graduate student at Tsinghua University, reveal that words that belong in the #H tone category in Alawa (neutralized with M in isolation) have an overt H tone in Wujiao. This H tone is phonetically transcribed by Xu Duoduo as ⁵³ (high-to-mid) on the basis of commonly observed realizations in isolation, but in the absence of a ⁵⁵ (high level) tone in her notes this can confidently be interpreted as a H tone. Examples include [kʰv⁵³] 'dog' (homophone: 'to steal'), [kv⁵³] 'garlic' and [hṽ⁵³] 'hair'. The corresponding words in Alawa are phonologically identical, except that the H tone is floating: //kʰv#˥// 'dog', //kʰv#˥// 'to steal', //kv#˥// 'garlic' and //hṽ#˥// 'hair'. No counterexample has been found.

Table 2.5b: Tone correspondences between Alawa and Labai for monosyllabic nouns carrying M tone in Labai.

gloss	Alawa	Labai	tone correspondence
small dike	bo˧	mbu˧	M::M
intestine	bʏ˧	bʏ˧	M::M
dew	dʐʏ˧	ndʐɯ˧	M::M
wind	hæ̃˧	hæ̃˧	M::M
tobacco	jɤ˧	jɤ˧	M::M
field	lʏ˧	lʏ˧	M::M
wound	mi˧	mi˧	M::M
hole	qʰʏ˧	qʰɚ˧	M::M
serf	wɤ˧	wɤ˧	M::M
liquor/spirits	ʐɯ˧	ʐɯ˧	M::M
water	dʐɯ˩	dʐɯ˧	L::M
lake	hi˩	hɯ˧	L::M
thread	kʰɯ˩	kʰɯ˧	L::M
silver	ŋv˩	ŋv˧	L::M
bridge	dzo˩	ndzo˧	L::M
iron	ʂe˩	ɕi˧	L::M
bone	ɻ̃˥	ɚ̃˧	H::M
pond	ɖwæ˥	ɳɖwæ˧	H::M
rib	ɬo˥	hõ˧	H::M
earth	di˧˥	di˧	LH::M
rain	hi˧˥	hɯ˧	LH::M

The above comparisons provide neat confirmation for the H tone category independently postulated for the Alawa dialect. Needless to say, the tonal correspondences between Alawa, Labai and Wujiao call for a systematic investigation, based on much more extensive data than has been collected so far for Labai and Wujiao. The tone system of Labai warrants an in-depth study in its own right, and a detailed comparison with Alawa, Lataddi (Dobbs & La 2016) and other dialects. The tone system of Wujiao appears at first blush to be more similar to that of Alawa, but nonetheless with enough differences to necessitate a detailed description.

Table 2.6: Examples illustrating the M::M and #H::MH tone correspondences for disyllabic nouns between Alawa and Labai.

correspondence	meaning	Alawa	Labai
M::M	little sister	go˧mi˧	go˧mi˧
	ancestor	ə˧pʰʏ˧	ə˧pʰə˧
	Bai	ɬi˧bʏ˧	li˧bʏ˧
	mother	ə˧mi˧	ə˧mi˧
	body	gʏ˧mi˧	gʏ˧mʏ˧
	heel	mʏ˧tʰɯ˧	mi˧tʰɯ˧
	thigh	do˧bæ˧	do˧bæ˧
	buttock	do˧bʏ˧	do˧bʏ˧
	nostril	ɲi˧qʰʏ˧	ɲi˧qʰə˧
	back	gʏ˧dʏ˧	gʏ˧dʏ˧
	breast	ʁa˧pʏ˧	ŋga˧pʏ˧
	belly	bi˧mi˧	bi˧mi˧
	plait	hæ̃˧pʀ˧	hæ̃˧pʀ˧
	sun	ɲi˧mi˧	ɲi˧mi˧
	moon	ɬi˧mi˧	li˧mi˧
	stone	lʏ˧mi˧	lʏ˧mi˧
	powder	tsa˧bʀ˧	tsa˧mba˧
	hot spring	ɻ̩˧qʰʏ˧	ə˧qʰə˧
	paddy field	ɕi˧lʏ˧	ʂɯ˧lʏ˧
#H::MH	little brother	gi˧zɯ#˥	gɯ˧zɯ˥
	grandson	zʏ˧ʏ#˥	zʏ˧ʏ˥
	granddaughter	zʏ˧mi#˥	zʏ˧mi˥
	sole	mi˧bʀ#˥	mi˧bʀ˥
	nose	ɲi˧gʀ#˥	ɲi˧ŋgʀ˥
	craftsman	po˧dʐɯ#˥	po˧dʐʏ˥
	forehead	to˧kʀ#˥	to˧kʀ˥
	host	da˧pʏ#˥	nda˧pʏ˥

2.3.1.4 The creation of floating H tones: a consequence of phonotactic constraints?

The correspondence between floating H tones in Alawa and overt H tones in Labai raises the issue of whether an earlier overt H tone became floating in Alawa, or conversely, an earlier floating H tone became an overt H tone in Labai. Cross-linguistically, the more common scenario is that of overt tones being set afloat by changes in metrical structure. For instance, in Manding languages (Mande branch of Niger-Congo), it has been hypothesized that, at one stage of language history, there were heavy syllable rhymes, VV or VN, which could carry up to two tonal levels, and that, at a later stage exemplified by Bambara, the distinction between heavy rhymes and light rhymes was lost, and the second tone on former heavy rhymes became floating (on Bambara: Creissels & Grégoire 1993; see also Konoshenko 2008 on interesting developments in Liberian Kpelle related to the delinking of H in an earlier LH category).

It seems reasonable to hypothesize that in Naish languages too the diachronic change was from overt tones to floating tones. A specificity of Alawa, as compared with Labai, is the prohibition of tone-group-initial H tone. A consequence of this exceptionless rule is that, at the surface phonological level, it is impossible to have H tone on a monosyllable said in isolation. Supposing that there used to be a *H tone on monosyllables, the opposition between tone categories M and H for monosyllables was threatened when the number of possible contrasts over a group-initial syllable collapsed from three (H, M, L) to two (M, L). Delinking the H tone could be seen as a response to this threat, preserving the lexical distinctions.[6]

As for disyllables, supposing that there used to exist nouns carrying a *H.M pattern, their initial H tone was also affected when the prohibition against tone-group-initial H tone set in. In the abstract, one could imagine that this initial H tone would be set afloat as a response, like the H tone of monosyllabic nouns. But this scenario does not take into account the state of the tone system as a whole. The representation shown in Figure 2.1 brings out the implausibility of a change whereby initial H tone on disyllabic nouns is set afloat whereas the tonal cate-

---

[6] The argument that H tones are set afloat *in order to preserve lexical distinctions* is to be wielded with great care, since any merger is possible: some phonological oppositions are irreversibly lost in the course of language history. "The linguistic system, with its myriad phonetic and semantic pressures effecting changes simultaneously and at times antagonistically, always emerges functionally unscathed, its semantic clarity intact" (Silverman 2015: 697). For now, I am content to record the fact that the tonal oppositions were maintained; finding out *why* it was so is much more arduous.

gory of nouns characterized by a final H tone remained unchanged. It does not appear likely that the *HM category could stride over the *MH category, as it were, to yield a floating tone (scenario 1). Instead, the change affecting word-initial H tones probably created a push chain, represented as scenario 2 in Figure 2.1: initial H moves to final position, and *final* H is set afloat.[7] Scenario 2 is supported by the observed correspondences between Alawa and Labai shown in Table 2.6: disyllables with a floating H tone in Alawa correspond to disyllables with final H tone in Labai.

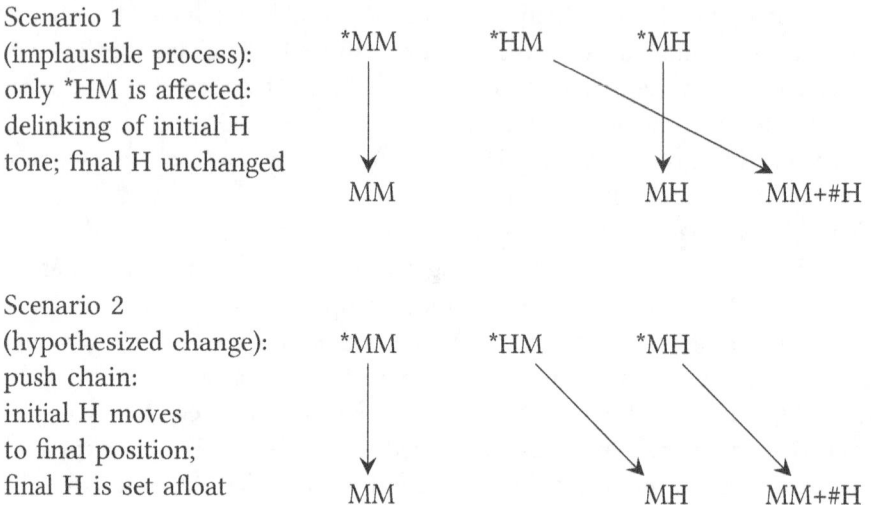

Figure 2.1: Two scenarios of evolution for *MM, *HM and *MH tone patterns over disyllabic nouns.

To conclude this brief foray into diachronic territory, a caveat is in order. The scenarios set out in Figure 2.1 presuppose that, at the time of the change, the rest of the system was as it is now: that the present-day M and H# categories have not changed their nature since then. They also presuppose that the state of affairs found in Labai is more conservative than that found in Alawa: the tone patterns found in Labai are simply copied into Figure 2.1 with the addition of an asterisk, as if they were proto-forms. These assumptions are not unreasonable in view of the close proximity between the two dialects. Still, the history of these dialects is not without complexities, witness the diversity of tonal correspondences for monosyllables shown in Table 2.5a. The logical next step in diachronic analysis

---

[7] I am grateful to Henriëtte Daudey and Denis Creissels for closely-argued discussion of this topic.

would be to conduct a full-fledged comparison of the tone systems of Alawa and Labai. As pointed out in the introduction (§1.2.4.3), the ultimate research goal, viewed as a collective endeavour, is to document in detail the synchronic tone systems of a number of research locations in the Na-speaking area, and gradually reconstruct the history of the evolution from a non-tonal stage to each of the present-day varieties. For the present argument, let us simply conclude that there is solid comparative evidence for a process of delinking of H tones that resulted in the present-day floating H tones of the Alawa dialect.

2.3.2 Word-final H tone and the 'flea' H tone category

It was mentioned above that the words 'squirrel' and 'flea', realized with a M.H pattern in isolation (as /**hwæ˧tsæ˥**/ and /**kv˧ʂe˥**/, respectively), have different lexical tones.

The former has a simple tonal behaviour: its H tone attaches to the last syllable of the lexical word. This is where it appears in all contexts. Under the present analysis, the first syllable of the word receives a M tone by default, yielding a surface phonological M.H pattern.[8]

The latter, on the other hand, is much more elusive. 'Flea' is a fitting example word for the tone category to which it belongs, serving as mnemonic of its propensity to hop around with less predictability than its host could hope for. When a word carrying this tone is pronounced in isolation, the H tone associates to its last syllable: /**kv˧ʂe˥**/ 'flea' has a M.H tone sequence at the surface phonological level. When the copula is added, the result is /**kv˧ʂe˧ ɲi˥**/ 'is (a/the) flea', with H tone on the copula; this is the same surface phonological pattern that is observed with the floating H tone, as exemplified by /**gi˧zɯ˧**/ 'little brother', /**gi˧zɯ˧ ɲi˥**/ 'is (a/the) little brother' (tone pattern in isolation: M.M, as opposed to M.H for 'flea'). When the noun is followed by the possessive, no H tone reaches the phonological surface: the observed form is /**kv˧ʂe˧ = bv˧**/ 'of (a/the) flea', with M tone on both syllables of the noun and also on the possessive. Again, this pattern is the same as that observed with the floating H tone: /**gi˧zɯ˧ = bv˧**/ 'of (a/the) little brother'. This raises the issue of the mode of association of the 'flea' H tone. It does not sit on the lexical word's last syllable, and it does not float in

---

[8] This pattern might also be analyzed as consisting of a MH contour associated to the first syllable, and projecting its H part onto the second syllable. This word-initial MH tone would contrast with the tone category MH#, in which the MH contour is associated to the word's last syllable (for example: /**hwɤ˧li˧**/ 'cat'). There is however no evidence that the tone at issue consists of a MH contour. The analysis adopted here is therefore as a lexical-word-final H tone, transcribed as H#.

the same sense as the 'little brother' (#H) tone, which is never realized on the word to which it is lexically associated.

One possibility that was entertained at earlier stages of reflection about this type of H tone is that its association could be specified relative to a unit higher than the word. In Na, the syllable is the smallest relevant unit for tonal association and the tone-bearing unit at the surface phonological level, and the tone group is the highest relevant unit: successive tone groups are entirely independent from the point of view of their phonological tones. In-between these two levels, one may propose to distinguish additional levels:

- the lexical word, to which tone categories are lexically associated
- the tonal word: a combination of lexical words, such as noun plus verb in S+V or O+V combinations, and noun plus noun in compounds
- the tonal phrase: a tonal word plus any added clitics and affixes

I proposed in an article written in 2013 and published in 2015 that the 'flea' H tone attached to the right edge of the tonal phrase (Michaud 2015b). While lexically associated to a word, this type of H tone would hop all the way to the right of this higher prosodic domain. In cases where the last syllable in the tonal phrase is a suitable host, the H tone attaches to it; otherwise, such as in the case of the possessive suffix, the H tone remains unassociated, and does not make it to the surface phonological level.

Upon further reflection, the search for a defining characteristic of the 'flea' H tone category with respect to a given level in the prosodic hierarchy does not appear as a promising strand of analysis. This tone has a propensity to be realized later than the word to which it is lexically associated, but it shares this behaviour with the floating H tone. For instance, the main consultant's family name has the 'flea' H tone; when spoken in isolation, it is realized as /laɨtʰaɨmi˥/; when the associative clitic /=ɟɨ˩/ is added to it, it yields /laɨtʰaɨmiɨ=ɟɨ˥/ 'the Latami family; the Latamis'; and addition of the agent adposition /ŋɯɨ/ yields /laɨtʰaɨmiɨ=ɟɨ-ŋɯ˥/ 'by the Latami family'. Impressionistically, this may seem to be typical of the behaviour of the 'flea' tone: hopping, or gliding, all the way to the right edge of the tonal phrase, as the morphotonological opportunity for it arises. But this behaviour is not a defining characteristic of the 'flea' H tone category: the floating H tone yields the same results in association with these added syllables. The behaviour of the various lexical tones in combination with other morphemes, as set out in tabular form in Chapters 2 to 6, provides ample evidence that metaphorical descriptions of the tones (as semi-personified entities) will not take us very far. It would be misleading to build a narrative account of the process whereby the noun's H tone would 'hop' or 'glide' onto the verb. The synchronic reason that the copula receives H tone when following the 'flea' H tone is because there is a morphotonological rule to that effect.

Thus, it does not appear feasible to pinpoint the exact phonological nature of the 'flea' H tone category by proposing one defining characteristic. Instead, it is more appropriate to view it first and foremost as one of the tones within the system, defined by the set of oppositions in which it enters in the full range of morphotonological contexts. The special feel of a tone can warrant giving it a nickname, as a convenient label, referring to the 'little brother' tone (#H) as a *floating* H tone, and to the 'flea' H tone as a *gliding* H tone, for instance; but this label should not be mistaken for a definition. The symbol chosen for transcribing the 'flea' H tone is H$, where the dollar sign '$' is added to distinguish this tone from the other two lexical H tones: H# (lexical-word-final H tone) and #H (floating H tone). The choice of an arbitrary symbol (the dollar sign) is intended to reflect the abstract nature of this tone category, as one of the distinctive tones within the tone system of Alawa.

This category is small, with only forty-five example words in the dictionary (Michaud 2015a) as against 180 examples for the word-final H tone category, H#, and 345 examples for the floating H tone category, #H. But it is firmly attested, and there are productive rules of compounding, prefixation and suffixation that feed into this category (as will be set out in later chapters).

To sum up, disyllabic (and polysyllabic) nouns with H tone must be divided into three categories, labelled H#, H$ and #H. A H tone on the last syllable of a disyllabic or polysyllabic noun may have different origins. It may be the realization of a High tone that is anchored to the last syllable of the lexical word: H#. Or it may be the realization of H$ tone. It is impossible to distinguish these in isolation. The third of these categories – #H – denotes a noun that carries a floating H tone. In order to find out the lexical tones of words, they have to be heard in various contexts. For nouns, these are: tone-group-final position (as when they are spoken in isolation); tone-group-internal position; and when followed by a clitic such as the possessive. (On the notion of tone group: see Chapter 7.) The lexical tone can be identified with certainty by matching up the behaviour of the word in these various contexts.

2.3.3 An added complexity concerning L tone: A postlexical rule for all-L tone groups

'Sheep', realized in association with the copula as /joꜜ ɲiʌ/ (i.e. with a low-rising contour on the verb), is a case where the noun's phonological tone is hypothesized to surface as such: a L tone. A slight complexity is that the copula which follows it surfaces with a low-rising tone. This makes sense in view of the exceptionless observation that an utterance cannot carry low tone on all of its syllables. The sequences L+L (monosyllabic noun+copula) and L.L+L (disyllabic noun +copula) cannot surface as such, due to a general prohibition against all-L tone groups in the Alawa dialect of Yongning Na. The contour observed at the end of a sequence of L tones is interpreted as resulting from the post-lexical addition of an extra tone. (This phonological rule is formulated in §7.1.1 as Rule 7: "If a tone group only contains L tones, a post-lexical H tone is added to its last syllable".) The same applies to the tonal category of disyllables exemplified by /kʰvꜜmiʌ/ 'dog'.

Concerning the transcription of low-rising contours, the choice between notation as LM or LH could appear as a nonissue, insofar as there is no contrast (at the surface phonological level) between LM and LH contours. But in the case of /joꜜ ɲiʌ/ 'is (a/the) sheep' or /kʰvꜜmiʌ/ (realization of 'dog' in isolation), there is a language-internal argument for analyzing the endpoint of the contour (a postlexical tone) as H rather than M. As will be set out in §2.4.3, the M tone in Na is a phonologically inert tone; if the postlexical tone added to all-L sequences were M, this would be the only instance of rule leading to the addition of a M tone to a syllable that already hosts another tone. The postlexical tone added at the end of a sequence of L tones is therefore analyzed as H, and the rising contour found in the nouns 'dog' and 'wilderness', and in the phrase 'is a sheep', will hereafter be written as LH, hence /kʰvꜜmiʌ/, /dʐɯꜜnɑꜜmiʌ/ and /joꜜ ɲiʌ/, respectively.

The issue of why monosyllabic L-tone nouns in isolation surface with M tone and not with a LH contour (consisting of their lexical L tone plus a postlexical H tone) is addressed in §2.4.6.

2.3.4 Tonal contours as sequences of level tones

As mentioned in the static overview presented earlier, there are no phonological falling contours in Alawa: no syllables carry phonological tones HL, HM, or ML. Also, tone-group-initial H is never observed.

Rising contours, on the other hand, do exist. They are restricted to the last syllable of a tone group: a rising contour is not found on a non-group-final syllable, except in some special cases discussed in §7.3. The two observed contours are M-to-H and L-to-H (the latter constituting the neutralization of underlying LM and LH). Unlike the low-rising contour, the phonological behaviour of the mid-rising contour, MH, is straightforward. When the word is tone-group-final, the contour is realized as such: a rising tone with a non-low starting-point, e.g. in /tsʰæ˧˥/ 'deer' and /hwɤ˧li˧˥/ 'cat'. (Note that when a word is pronounced in isolation, it constitutes a tone group on its own: the beginning of the word is also the beginning of the tone group, and the end of the word is also the end of the tone group.) When there is a following syllable within the tone group, the MH contour unfolds, projecting its H part onto that syllable. Unlike the floating High tone (#H), which cannot attach to a following clitic, the MH contour can unfold over any syllable. With the copula, this yields /tsʰæ˧ ɲi˥/ 'is (a/the) deer' and /hwɤ˧li˧ ɲi˥/ 'is (a/the) cat'. With the possessive, it yields /tsʰæ˧=bv̩˥/ 'of (a/the) deer' and /hwɤ˧li˧=bv̩˥/ 'of (a/the) cat'. This constitutes strong evidence in favour of analyzing the contour tones of Yongning Na as sequences of level tones.

To preview the result of analysis, low-rising contours also lend themselves to decomposition into levels. But they raise some subtle issues for description and analysis, which are addressed in the paragraphs that follow.

2.3.5 An alternative analysis of the //LM// and //LH// categories: Could the two terms of the opposition be //LM// and //LML//?

Concerning the two categories of tones neutralized to a low-rising tone in isolation, illustrated by /zæ˩˧/ 'leopard' and /bo˩˧/ 'pig', at least two analytical options are open. Assuming (for reasons which will be explained below) that the perfective suffix carries a M tone unless affected by what precedes, the L tone on the suffix in (3), contrasting with the M tone in (4), could be put down to a floating L tone, parallel to the floating H tone found in the tone categories illustrated by 'horse'. This tone would remain unassociated when 'to buy leopards' is spoken without a suffix, and associate to the suffix when one is available.

(3) zæ˩ hwæ˧-ze˩
    zæ˩˧   hwæ˧   -ze˧
    leopard to_buy PFV
    'has bought leopards'

73

(4) boJ hwæ˦-ze˦
    bo˩   hwæ˦   -ze˦
    leopard to_buy PFV
    'has bought pigs'

The underlying tone pattern of 'to buy leopards' would then be //LML//, as against a simpler underlying //LM// pattern for 'to buy pigs'. (Remember that double slashes are used for underlying phonological tone, as opposed to simple slashes for surface phonological tone.) In turn, the difference between these two object-plus-verb phrases would be put down to a //LML// vs. //LM// tone contrast on the noun. The //LML// sequence could also be transcribed as //LM+#L//: //LM// followed by a floating L tone.

But another analytical option is suggested by the static observation that a H tone is always followed by L tones within a speech unit which is referred to here as a *tone group* (about which see full details in Chapter 7). In this light, the lowering of the tone of the perfective suffix in (3) could be ascribed to the presence of a preceding H tone, which depresses the tones of all the syllables that follow it: the phonological form would be //z̠æJ hwæ˥-zeJ//.[9] In turn, the H tone carried by the verb 'to buy' in this construction would originate in a lexical LH tone on the noun 'leopard'.

Of these two options, the second is currently favoured because floating L tones are not required anywhere else in the description of the language. There are strong reasons to use the concept of floating H tone in the description of this dialect's morphotonology (including pieces of comparative-diachronic evidence set out in §2.3.1.4), whereas positing a floating L tone would be an *ad hoc* theoretical move. Still, there is no overwhelming evidence for rejecting the analysis of the tone of the 'leopard' category as a sequence of three levels: LM, plus a floating L tone (LM+#L). Such cases of analytical indeterminacy are important to understanding the evolutionary potential of the system – a topic which will be taken up in Chapter 9.

Under the present analysis, the tone categories //LM// and //LH// contrast not only on monosyllables but also on disyllables. These two tones surface in the same way except when the word is followed by a clitic. For instance, //**boJmi˦**// 'sow, female pig' and //**boJɬa˥**// 'boar, male pig' are realized with the same surface phonological tone pattern, not only in isolation but also when followed by

---

[9] The L tone on the perfective suffix is not a phrase-level phenomenon: there are contexts where a clause-final (and utterance-final) suffix carries a tone other than L, e.g. in (4) and in /æJ **hwæ˦-ze˦**/ 'bought chicken'.

the copula. In Alawa, L.M.L and L.H.L never contrast with each other at the surface phonological level, nor do L.M and L.H in final position in a tone group; it is therefore possible to transcribe the surface forms as /bo˩mi˧/ or /bo˩mi˥/ for 'sow' and /bo˩mi˧ ɲi˩/ or /bo˩mi˥ ɲi˩/ for 'is (a/the) sow'; and as /bo˩ɬɑ˧/ or /bo˩ɬɑ˥/ for 'boar' and /bo˩ɬɑ˧ ɲi˩/ or /bo˩ɬɑ˥ ɲi˩/ for 'is (a/the) boar'. The contexts that allow for telling apart these two lexical tone categories are exemplified by /bo˩mi˧=bv̩˧/ 'of (a/the) sow' vs. /bo˩ɬɑ˧=bv̩˩/ (which could also be transcribed /bo˩ɬɑ˥=bv̩˩/) 'of (a/the) boar': in the latter expression, the possessive clitic //=bv̩˧// receives L tone.

For the first category, 'sow', the analysis of the tone pattern as LH is ruled out: if one were to transcribe this as /bo˩mi˥/, then one would have to transcribe the form with the possessive as /‡ bo˩mi˥=bv̩˥/ 'of (a/the) sow', since the possessive surfaces with the same tonal level as the noun's second syllable; but the tone sequence H+H is never observed elsewhere in the Alawa dialect of Yongning Na. By an exceptionless rule, a syllable following a H-tone syllable receives L tone; this will be referred to in §7.1.1 as "Rule 4". (The full set of rules is also given in the 'Quick reference' section at the outset of this volume.) In view of the above argument, 'of (a/the) sow' is transcribed as /bo˩mi˧=bv̩˧/, and the category illustrated by 'sow' is analyzed as //LM//, hence //bo˩mi˧//.

As for 'boar', a phonological analysis as //bo˩ɬɑ˥// makes good phonological sense, insofar as all the tones that follow are lowered to L, as expected following a H tone. When a word of this tonal category is followed by the possessive //=bv̩˧//, the latter carries L tone; this is the same as after a disyllable with H# tone, as shown in (5a-5b), where the notation as LH for 'boar' is adopted.

(5) a. hwæ˧tsæ˥=bv̩˩
hwæ˧tsæ˥ =bv̩˩
rat POSS
'of (a/the) rat'

b. bo˩ɬɑ˥=bv̩˩
bo˩ɬɑ˥ =bv̩˩
boar POSS
'of (a/the) boar'

In addition, all compounds involving the tone category of 'boar' ('boar's head', 'boar's blood', and so on) have the same pattern, which can be described as L followed by H followed by a sequence of L tones (L.H.L...). This is again parallel to the //H#// category, where the tone pattern of all compounds is M followed by H followed by a sequence of L tones (M.H.L...).

Under the present analysis, disyllables and monosyllables both undergo a neutralization of the underlying //LM// and //LH// categories when they are realized in isolation.

For disyllables of the 'sow' and 'boar' types, as for monosyllables of the 'pig' and 'leopard' types discussed at the outset of the present section (§2.3.5), an alternative to the //LM//-vs.-//LH// analysis would be an analysis as //LM// vs. //LML//. The tone pattern of 'sow' would be analyzed as //LM//, and that of 'boar' as //LML//. This analysis equally captures the fact that the tones of syllables following nouns of the 'boar' type are lowered to L: by Rule 5 ("All syllables following a H.L or M.L sequence receive L tone"), L.M.L can only be followed by more L tones. This is the analysis that I chose at first, including in the Yongning Na glossary deposited in 2011 in the Sino-Tibetan Etymological Dictionary and Thesaurus (STEDT). Describing this tone category as a sequence of three levels did not seem exceedingly complex at the time, in view of the complexity of other categories, such as //L+MH// and //LM+#H//. However, those two lexical tone categories are composed of two parts, one associating to the beginning of the word, the other to its end; //LML// would be the only pattern specifying three levels in a row. Moreover, it would be the only category for which a //ML// contour would be posited. Notation as //LH// is therefore adopted here. One may nonetheless keep in mind that an analysis as //LML// would also be possible. Such cases of analytical uncertainty do not merely constitute recondite topics for the phonologist to ponder, they also provide insights into the system's potential for change, since language learners also face these competing analytical options when constructing their own phonological systems.

2.3.6 Cases of neutralization of the opposition between //LM// and //LH//: Is the product /LM/ or /LH/?

Monosyllables of //LM// and //LH// tone categories, such as //**bo**˩// 'pig' and //**zæ**˩// 'leopard', are realized in isolation with the same tone: a low-rising contour. Phonetically, a low-to-mid realization and a low-to-high realization are both acceptable. My consultants sometimes corrected my productions of this tone category because the starting-point was not low enough, which entails risks of confusion with //MH//. On the other hand, they never corrected me for a mistaken endpoint (too high or too low).

In an attempt to find out to what extent there is a preference for a phonetically [Mid] or phonetically [High] endpoint for the low-rising contour, I tried fishing for corrections from consultant F4 on several occasions, producing two variants of words such as 'pig' and 'leopard', both with a low starting-point, one with what I intended as a moderate rise (approximately up to F₀ mid-range), and one which I intended as a strong, rapid rise towards a [High] final target. I asked the consultant to choose which of the two productions sounded better. The answer was always 'both are correct' (/ɲi˧-bæ˧ | ho˩/: *two-CLF correct*).

The choice made here is to transcribe the product of the neutralization of //LM// and //LH// as /LH/ at the surface phonological level; but there is no decisive phonetic argument for this notation. The product of tone neutralization tends to be phonetically less definite than the product of consonantal neutralization. For instance, the opposition between coronal and retroflex stops in Yongning Na is neutralized in front of /ɯ/, and the product of neutralization is clearly a retroflex: [ʈʰɯ] is a well-formed syllable in Yongning Na, and [tʰɯ] is not. On the other hand, the product of the neutralization of //H// and //M// in isolation occupies the entire portion of the phonetic tone space corresponding to these two tones: it is a non-low tone, and it may not prove appropriate to assign it a more precise phonetic label, such as either 'high' or 'mid'. (Issues of phonetic implementation of tone sequences are taken up in Chapter 8.)

2.3.7 On the anchoring of tones to word boundaries

The M and L tone categories of the Alawa dialect of Yongning Na are hypothesized to associate to the *first* syllable of a lexical item, and to spread from there onto the entire word; as for H tone (or rather, the three categories of H tones), its association is specified respective to the *last* syllable of the lexical item. There are thus tone categories that are anchored to the beginning of the word, and others to its end. Two of the tone categories have both anchorages: they are made up of two parts, the first of which is anchored at the beginning of the lexical word, and the second at its end. These two categories are //LM+#H// and //LM+MH#//, exemplified in Table 2.7b by //na˩hĩ#˥// 'Naxi' and //õ˩dy˥// 'wolf', respectively. The '+' sign in //LM+#H// and //LM+MH#// denotes the juncture between these tones' first and second part. Thus the H tone in the phrase /na˩hĩ˧ ɲi˥/ 'is (a/the) Naxi' is interpreted as the manifestation of a floating H tone, and the lexical tone of this category analyzed as //LM+#H//: a //LM// contour plus by a floating H tone, //#H//. Likewise, //LM+MH#//, exemplified by //õ˩dy˥// 'wolf', is analyzed as a tonal category consisting of two parts: a //LM// tone, plus a final //MH// contour. In both cases, the pound symbol indicates the syllabic anchoring of the second part of these two-part tone categories: after the end of the lexical word for //LM+#H//, and at the end of the lexical word (i.e. on its last syllable) for //LM+MH#//.

These two tone categories may seem awfully complex, being composed of two parts each of which associates at a different end of the same word. The complexity is real, and probably goes a long way towards explaining why there are only two such tone categories in Alawa, and not the full range of combinations that would be theoretically possible: there is no //LM+H$// tone, for instance. On the other hand, seen from inside the Na tone system, the behaviour of these two tone categories, //LM+#H// and //LM+MH#//, is not all that complicated, as it results straightforwardly from that of the constituent elements. The tones only need to be specified as consisting of two parts, each of which takes care of its own mode of association, like when they appear on their own. The mode of association of the first part of the tone (the //LM// part) in //LM+#H// and //LM+MH#// is straightforward; likewise for the second part (//#H// and //MH#//, respectively). As suggested by the '+' symbol in //LM+#H// and //LM+MH#//, the complexities in these two-part tone categories add up; they do not multiply.

2.4 General observations about the system

Some generalizations emerge from the observations made above. There are three tonal levels in Yongning Na, H(igh), M(id) and L(ow). The tone-bearing unit is the syllable, more specifically the syllable rhyme. There is no distinction in terms of syllable weight, and thus no need for a decomposition into moras: any syllable rhyme, including syllabic consonants, can function as a tone-bearing unit for one or two tonal levels. Out of six theoretically possible contours (HM, HL, MH, ML, LH, and LM), only the three rising contours (MH, LH and LM) are attested as lexical categories, illustrated on monosyllables by //tsʰæ˩// 'deer', //ʐæ˧// 'leopard' and //bo˥// 'pig'. Moreover, at the surface phonological level, (i) contours are restricted to tone-group-final position, and (ii) LM and LH are neutralized to LH. Stated differently, each syllable within a tone group carries one of three levels: H, M or L, and the last syllable can carry one of the following: H, M, L, MH, or LH. There are no phonological falling contours (HL, HM or ML) on a single syllable, only rising contours.

The following paragraphs propose an overview of the system of lexical tones for nouns, and some reflections on its structure.

2.4.1 Usefulness of an autosegmental approach

A first general observation that can safely be made in view of the data presented so far is that tone in Yongning Na is best analyzed in terms of autosegmental models: models in which the tones are *auto*nomous from the *segments* (i.e. vowels and consonants). These models were originally developed for Subsaharan tone systems, but have been convincingly applied to certain languages of the Tibeto-Burman area (see, in particular, Hyman & VanBik 2002). The choice of these descriptive concepts is motivated by language-internal evidence; it is by no means dictated by *a priori* theoretical commitments. I am fortunate to be familiar with two strikingly different tone systems of Asia: that of Yongning Na, which has phonetically simple and morphophonologically complex tones, and that of Northern Vietnamese, which has phonetically complex and morphophonologically inert tones. To me, it is clear that Yongning Na is to be described as having a level-tone system, unlike Vietnamese in which "there are no objective reasons to decompose (…) tone contours into level tones or to reify phonetic properties like high and low pitch into phonological units such as H and L" (Brunelle 2009c; see also Brunelle, Nguyễn & Nguyễn 2010; Kirby 2010; 2011). This issue is discussed further in §10.1.1.

2.4.2 Recapitulation of the lexical tone categories

Tables 2.7a and 2.7b set out the analysis of the six tone categories of monosyllabic nouns and the eleven categories of disyllabic nouns. To date, no single morphosyntactic context bringing out all the tonal contrasts of nouns has been found: each context brings out only some of the oppositions, whereas others are neutralized. For instance, addition of the copula brings out the opposition between //M// and //#H// tones, which is neutralized in isolation. On the other hand, addition of the copula neutralizes the tonal contrasts that appear in isolation among //#H//, //MH#// and //H$// on disyllables: all three yield /M.M+H/ with the copula, whereas they are realized as /M.M/, /M.MH/ and /M.H/ respectively in isolation. So it is necessary to elicit a word in several contexts to determine its lexical tone. Tables 2.7a and 2.7b provide information on the tone categories (i) in isolation, (ii) when followed by the copula //ɲi꜒//, in frame (6), and (iii) when followed by the possessive clitic //=bv̩˧//.

(6) tsʰuɥ ˍˍˍˍˍˍ ɲi
    DEM.PROX *target item* COP
    'This is (a/the) ˍˍˍˍˍ.'

A recording of disyllabic nouns in frame (6) is available online; its identifier is: NounsInFrame.

This set of three contexts is sufficient to bring out all oppositions, except that between //LM// and //LH// on monosyllables, which only surfaces in a very re-

Table 2.7a: The lexical tone categories of monosyllabic nouns.

analysis	in isolation	+COP	+POSS	//example//	meaning
// LM //	LH	L+H	L+H	bo˩	pig
// LH //	LH	L+H	L+H	ʐæ˩	leopard
// M //	M	M+L	M+M	lɑ˧	tiger
// L //	M	L+LH	L+M	jo˩	sheep
// #H //	M	M+H	M+M	ʐwæ˥	horse
// MH# //	MH	M+H	M+H	tsʰæ˥	deer

stricted number of contexts. (As was mentioned above, §2.2.2, one such context is in association with the verb 'to buy': for instance, the //LM//-tone word 'pig' yields /bo˩ hwæ˧-ze˧/ 'bought pigs', whereas the //LH//-tone word 'leopard' yields /ʐæ˩ hwæ˧-ze˩/ 'bought leopards'.)

The proximal demonstrative //tsʰɯ˥// always carries the same surface tone in (6), regardless of the tonal category of the following item; as a consequence, only the tonal pattern of the rest of the sentence is indicated in Table 2.7a–b. On the other hand, no tone is indicated for the copula in frame (6), because its surface tone changes according to the tone category of the target word.

Dots indicate boundaries between syllables within the lexical word, and the '+' sign indicates the junctures between the noun and a following morpheme. For instance, the information provided in Table 2.7b for disyllabic L-tone nouns is: L.LH in isolation, and L.L+H with copula and with possessive clitic. As an example, the word 'dog' is /kʰv̩˩mi˩/ in isolation, yielding /kʰv̩˩mi˩ ɲi˥/ 'is (a/the) dog' and /kʰv̩˩mi˩=bv̩˥/ 'of (a/the) dog'.

The leftmost column ("analysis") presents the lexical tone categories. The three following columns contain surface phonological transcriptions. Examples in the column before last are transcribed according to the phonological tone categories, following conventions set out in §2.4.4.

In view of this picture of the tone system of nouns, the distributional observations made above can be flipped around. For instance, instead of stating that "a monosyllabic noun that carries a M tone in isolation may belong in one of three distinct underlying categories", it can now be said that the three non-contour lexical tones, //M//, //L// and //#H//, all neutralize to /M/ when a monosyllable is said in isolation. Among disyllables, //M// and //#H// neutralize to /M.M/; //H$// and //H#// neutralize to /M.H/; and //LM//, //LH// and //LM+#H// neutralize to /L.M/.

Table 2.7b: The lexical tone categories of disyllabic nouns.

analysis	in isolation	+COP	+POSS	//example//	meaning
// M //	M.M	M.M+L	M.M+M	po˧lo˧	ram
// #H //	M.M	M.M+H	M.M+M	ʐwæ˧zo#˥	colt
// MH# //	M.MH	M.M+H	M.M+H	hwɤ˧li˥	cat
// H$ //	M.H	M.M+H	M.M+M	kv˧ʂe˥$	flea
// H# //	M.H	M.H+L	M.H+L	hwæ˧tsæ˥	squirrel
// L //	L.LH	L.L+H	L.L+H	kʰv˩mi˩	dog
// L# //	M.L	M.L+L	M.L+L	dɑ˧ji˩	mule
//LM+MH#//	L.MH	L.M+H	L.M+H	õ˩dv˥	wolf
//LM+#H//	L.M	L.M+H	L.M+M	nɑ˩hĩ#˥	Naxi
// LM //	L.M	L.M+L	L.M+M	bo˩mi˧	sow
// LH //	L.M	L.M+L	L.M+L	bo˩ɬɑ˥	boar

When the possessive clitic //=bv˧// is added after a monosyllabic noun, yielding, for example, /tsʰæ˧=bv˥/ 'of the deer', contours unfold over the two syllables of the resulting combination: //LH// yields /L+H/ (as does //LM//, following neutralization with //LH//), and //MH// yields /M+H/.

This last point offers evidence for the distinction between contours (//LM//, //LH// and //MH#//) on the one hand and the floating H tone (//#H//) on the other. The second part of a contour is realized on the possessive; the floating H tone is not.[10]

A schematic representation in successive stages is presented in Figure 2.2, taking as an example a disyllabic noun that belongs in the //MH#// tone category.

---

[10] How come the possessive clitic gets a H level when the noun has a MH contour, but not when the noun has a floating H tone? One way to think of it (which admittedly amounts to no more than an *ad hoc* conjecture, based on the investigator's non-native introspection) is that providing anchorage for a //#H// tone is quite a different matter from hosting a H tone level that is part of a //MH#// tone anchored to a preceding syllable. The //MH#// tone has a stable anchorage on the noun's last syllable, which allows it to express itself in the usual way, unfolding over two successive syllables: the noun's last syllable, which gets the M part of the contour, and the clitic, which gets its H part. The H level is jutting out from the noun, as it were: it is part of a MH sequence which is firmly moored at one of its ends (the M part), though not at the other. This can be thought of as a case of "tonal protrusion": the contour holds firm, its M part sitting on the noun's last syllable, and its H part jutting out over the clitic. By contrast, the //#H// tone does not get to express itself because the stage of anchorage is not reached in the first place. In derivational terms, a distinction is to be made between *tonal anchoring* and the later stage of *contour unfolding*.

Stage 1 is the input: the noun has //MH#// tone, and the copula has //L// tone.[11] Stage 2 shows the anchoring of the MH tone pattern onto the last syllable of the lexical word. This is part of this lexical tone's specification, as indicated by the symbol # in the label MH#. Stage 3 represents one-to-one mapping of levels to available syllables. The MH contour associates to syllables one by one, starting from its point of anchorage, namely the noun's last syllable, which receives M. The H level associates to the following syllable: the copula. This leaves no syllable available for the copula's lexical L tone, which remains unassociated, and does not surface at all. The first syllable of the noun, which has not been assigned a tone in the above process of association of the lexical tone, remains toneless. Stage 4 represents the hypothesized process whereby it receives a M level, by default. Stage 5 is the surface phonological result.

For this tonal category of nouns, the process of association for the possessive clitic //=bɤ˧// is the same, as shown in Figure 2.3.

By contrast with MH#, the floating H tone (#H) does not anchor to any of the syllables of the word to which it is lexically attached, and the possessive clitic is unable to provide such anchorage. Since this H tone receives syllabic anchorage neither onto the word to which it is lexically attached, nor on the possessive clitic that follows it, it remains unassociated, and does not surface at all in this context. This is represented as Figure 2.4. The figure for the 'flea' tone, H$, would be identical with Figure 2.4: the possessive clitic is not a suitable host, so that the H$ remains unassociated, and does not surface at all in this context.

The behaviour of the word-final H tone (H#) is shown in Figure 2.5: in this case, the L tone on the clitic results from an exceptionless phonological rule whereby all tones following H are lowered to L (see §7.1.1).

These step-by-step representations go into more detail than tonologists with an experience of level tones may find necessary. It does not appear indispensible to draw similar figures for the other lexical categories of Yongning Na, though this could be offered as an exercise for an introductory phonology class.

---

[11] About the copula's tone, see the argument set out in §6.1.

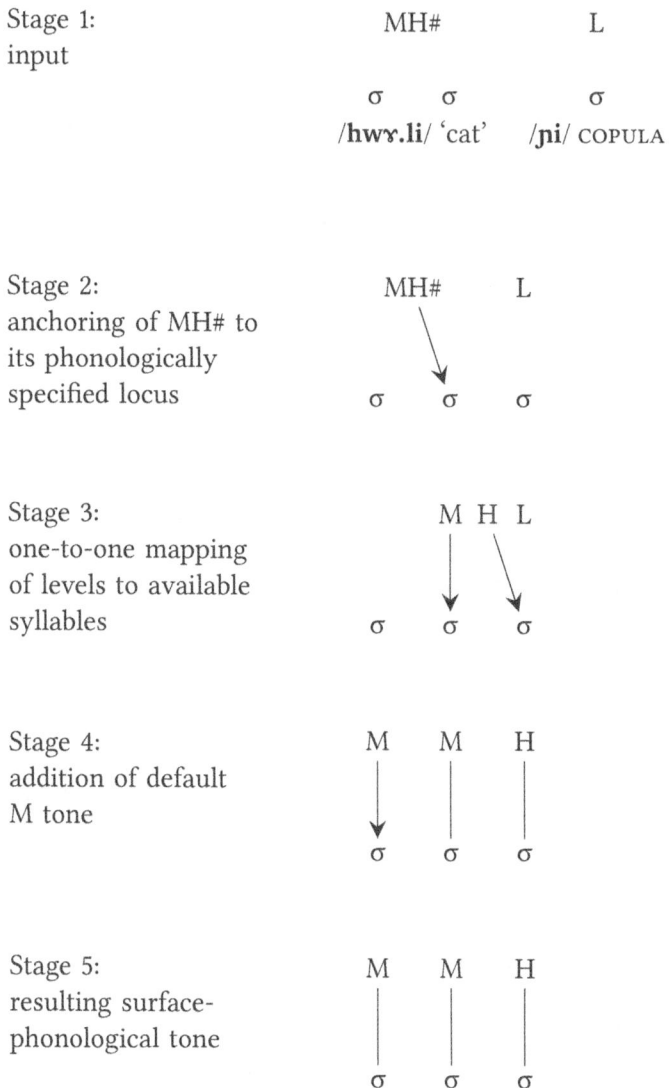

Figure 2.2: A detailed representation of tone-to-syllable association for /hwɤ˧li˧ ɲi˧˩/ 'is (a/the) cat'.

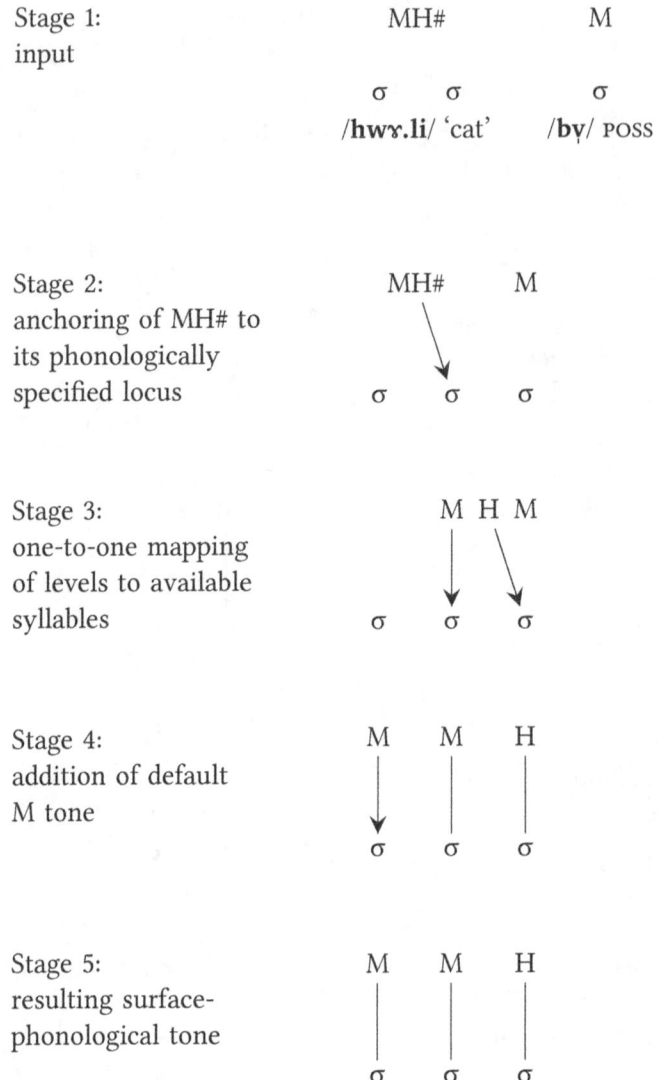

Figure 2.3: A detailed representation of tone-to-syllable association for /hwɤ˧li˧=bʏ˩/ 'of (a/the) cat'.

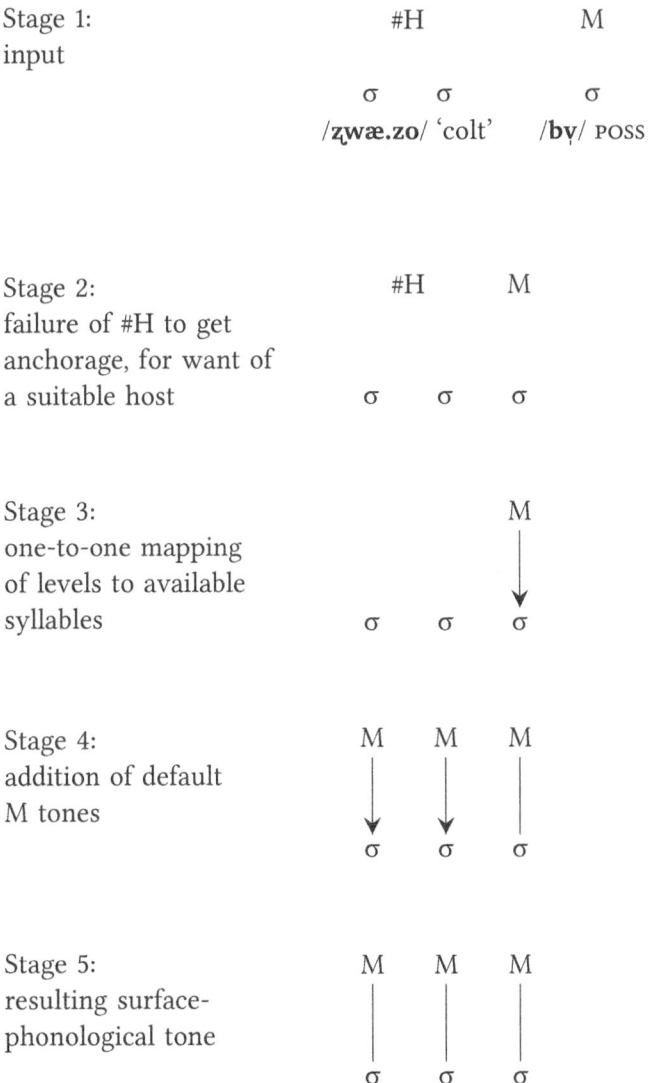

Figure 2.4: A detailed representation of tone-to-syllable association for /ʐwæ˦zo˦=bɣ˦/ 'of (a/the) colt'.

Stage 1:
input

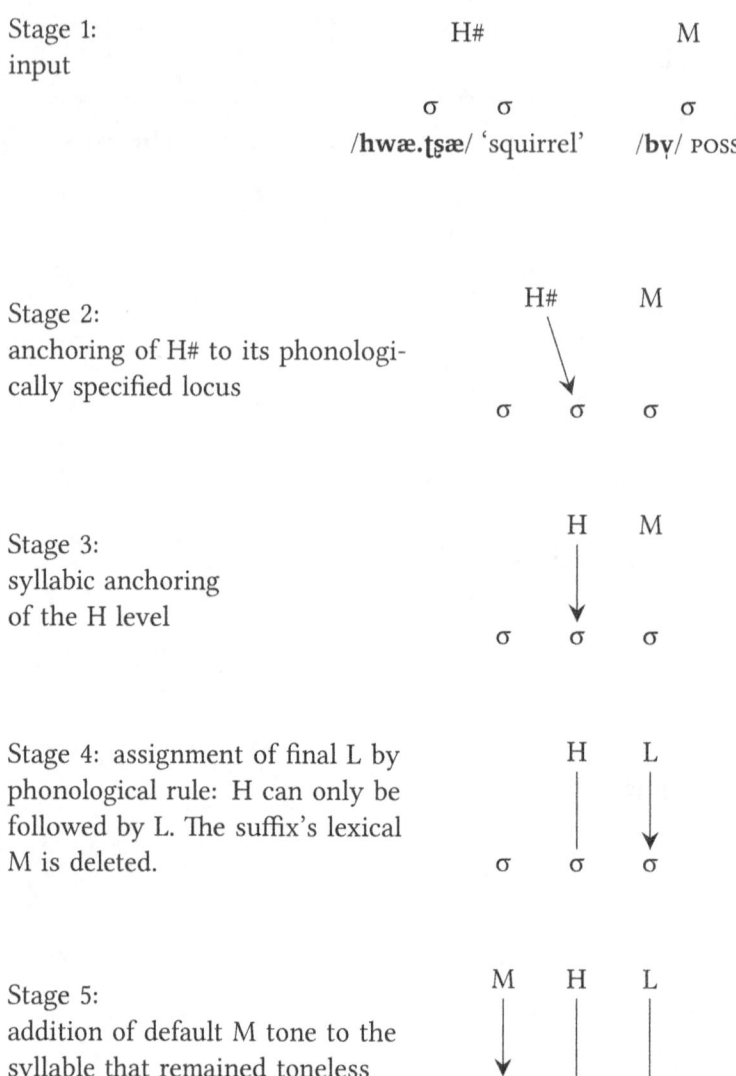

Stage 2:
anchoring of H# to its phonologically specified locus

Stage 3:
syllabic anchoring of the H level

Stage 4: assignment of final L by phonological rule: H can only be followed by L. The suffix's lexical M is deleted.

Stage 5:
addition of default M tone to the syllable that remained toneless

Figure 2.5: A detailed representation of tone-to-syllable association for /hwæ˧tʂæl=byˌ/ 'of (a/the) squirrel'.

2.4.3 M as a default tone

The analysis set out above assumes that M serves as a default tone: syllables that are not specified for tone receive M. For instance, a //#H// tone carried by a disyllabic noun can only manifest itself on a following word: the H tone, though lexically attached to the noun, never appears on the noun itself. Both syllables of the noun receive /M/ tone in the surface phonological form. Under the present analysis, this is understood as default tone assignment. Likewise, /M.L/ is observed as a surface pattern on disyllabic and polysyllabic words, such as /dɑ˧ji˩/ 'mule', but this pattern is analyzed as the manifestation of a lexical-word-final L tone (notation: //L#//), the /M/ tone on the first syllable being a default tone, not a lexically specified tone. Evidence for this analysis will be presented in the course of the discussion, adducing evidence from the combinatorial properties of tones, such as the tone rules that apply in compounding.

One may be tempted to push this analysis further and try avoiding specifying the M tone anywhere in the inventory of lexical tones. As stated above, disyllables such as /dɑ˧ji˩/ 'mule', with a surface phonological M.L pattern, are analyzed as having a final L (notation: //L#//), the M tone on the first syllable being a default tone, whereas disyllables such as /bo˩mi˧/, with surface L.M, are analyzed as having a phonological //LM// tone, i.e. specifying phonologically the M tone of their second syllable. The reason for this analysis is that L tone spreads progressively ("left-to-right") onto syllables that are unspecified for tone (this is referred to as Rule 1; see §7.1 for further detail). In Table 2.7b, disyllables that carry L tone on both of their syllables are accordingly analyzed as possessing a simple lexical L tone. In transcriptions, L tone is indicated on both syllables by convention (e.g. the word for 'dog' is written //kʰv˩mi˩//), so as to stay close to surface forms, but at a lexical level, these words are analyzed as carrying a simple //L// tone. Disyllabic nouns that have a /L.M/ pattern (L on first syllable, M on second syllable) are analyzed as having a phonological /M/ on the second syllable, blocking L-tone spreading.

Under an approach dispensing with M at the lexical level, the syllabic anchoring of all L tones would need to be specified. This would to some extent be parallel to H tones, which fall into three categories that have different modes of association to the syllabic string: H#, H# and H$. However, if the L.M pattern were reanalyzed as a word-initial L tone, it would be necessary to specify that it does not spread, unlike other L tones. Reanalyzing the //LM// category as a non-spreading L, contrasting with a spreading L, is a theoretical possibility, but one which (at present) appears to me as less consistent with the rest of the description than positing a combination of two levels as the underlying lexical tone.

Yet another alternative would be to analyze the /L.H/, /M.L/ and /L.L/ surface patterns as the realization of initial //L//, final //L//, and //L.L// (with L tone specified on both syllables), respectively, avoiding any reference to L-tone spreading. However, L-tone spreading is such a commonly attested process in the Alawa dialect of Yongning Na that this does not appear as a promising strand of analysis.

Moreover, any description avoiding M tones at the lexical level would require another device to describe MH contour tones, since they cannot be described simply as H tones. It would be necessary to posit a separate type of H tones: a contour-creating H tone, in addition to the three types recognized so far.

For these various reasons, it seems reasonable to adopt a model using M in the lexical specification of some of the categories.

2.4.4 The notation of tonal categories in lexical entries

This section explains the choices made for the notation of tonal categories in lexical entries (as head words in dictionary entries, and in interlinear glossing of texts), as exemplified for nouns in Table 2.7a–b.

One typographical option would be to indicate the phonological category in superscript at the beginning or end of the word, e.g. //ʐwæ$^{\#H}$// for 'horse', and //õ.dv$^{LM+MH\#}$// for 'wolf'. This notation, which separates tone from vowels and consonants, makes good sense in view of the analysis proposed here: that tone in Na is lexically associated to entire lexemes, not to individual syllables. On the other hand, working out the tone-to-syllable mapping requires complete familiarity with the mapping rules of Yongning Na. So it appeared better to offer a transcription that looks more similar to the surface phonology, indicating a tone at the end of each syllable. Following standard usage, International Phonetic Alphabet tone letters (Chao 1930) were chosen: ˥ for High, ˧ for Mid, ˩ for Low, ˩˧ for Low-to-Mid, ˩˥ for Low-to-High, and ˧˥ for Mid-to-High.

This is strictly equivalent to Africanist notation by means of accents: for instance, //bo˩˧// 'pig' could be written as //bǒ// in Africanist notation, and //ʐæ˩˥// 'leopard' as //ʐæ̌//. Tone letters are favoured over accents for want of a satisfactory solution to the typographic issue of combinations of diacritics, e.g. how to indicate a rising contour on a syllable such as /ĩ̯/.

Instead of tone letters, numbers are favoured in Chinese-language publications. The strict equivalents would be the following: ˥ corresponds to ^{5}, ˧ to ^{3}, ˩ to ^{1}, ˩˧ to ^{13}, ˩˥ to ^{15}, and ˧˥ to ^{35}. There are further complexities here, however. Chinese authors use at least two numbers for each tone: one for its beginning and one for its endpoint. To reflect the insight that there is no phonologically relevant change in pitch in the course of the H, M and L tones, these three level tones could be transcribed by doubling the number indicating their relative pitch level, transcribing the H tone as ⁵⁵, the M tone as ³³, and the L tone as ¹¹. But this notation would differ from Chinese linguists' conventions, because the systematic use of at least two numbers leads them to pay attention to any differences in pitch between a tone's beginning and endpoint (differences which are crucial in the description of systems where tones do not simply consist of sequences of levels: see §10.1.1). For instance, since the L tone in Yongning Na is often realized phonetically as a fall in pitch, rather than as a flat, sustained low pitch, it will be transcribed by Chinese linguists as ²¹ or ³¹ (e.g. the L tone of Naxi is transcribed as ³¹ by Hé Jírén & Jiāng Zhúyí 1985). Notation as ¹¹ would not be an accurate representation of the Low tone's phonetic realization, and would thus be counterintuitive to users accustomed to this system. Notation as ³¹ would obscure the phonological nature of the L tone, however, wrongly suggesting that tones "31" (i.e. L tone in the present description) and "13" (i.e. LM tone) are each other's mirror image.¹² For tonologists accustomed to Chinese-style tone numbers, I therefore strongly recommend using the following set of equivalences, which may initially seem counterintuitive, but which are less likely to lead to phonological misinterpretations: ⁵⁵ for ˥, ³³ for ˧, ¹¹ for ˩, ¹³ for ˩˧, ¹⁵ for ˩˥, and ³⁵ for ˧˥.

In the process of mapping tonal categories to syllables written in the International Phonetic Alphabet, some cases are simple: for instance, the tone category LM can be represented by associating both levels to a monosyllable, for instance //bo˩˧// 'pig', and distributing them over the two syllables of a disyllable, for instance //bo˩mi˧// 'sow'. But not all cases are that straightforward, making it necessary to provide detailed explanations about the notational choices made here.

The first choice consists in writing the floating H tone of monosyllabic nouns as a simple H tone, without indicating in the notation that this tone is floating. Thus, 'horse' is transcribed simply as //ʐwæ˥//, rather than //ʐwæ#˥//. The reason for this choice is that, on monosyllables, there is only one type of H tone, namely this floating H, that can only surface after the syllable to which it is lexically attached. In the absence of a distinction among types of H tones, it appeared economical to dispense with the added pound symbol '#', which indicates the tone's mode of syllabic association (namely: after the word's last syllable).

For nouns of two syllables or more, on the other hand, there are three types of H tones, namely H#, #H and H$, so an indication about syllabic anchorage

---
¹² Reflections about notational choices for level tones and their influence on the phonological analysis of tone in Naish languages are set out in Michaud (2013b).

cannot be dispensed with when transcribing the lexical form of nouns. At least two diacritics need to be used to make the three-way distinction among H#, #H and H$. The first of these three is indicated by a simple H-tone mark ˦ on the last syllable, as its mode of anchoring appears as phonologically simplest: sitting inert on the last syllable, and never moving from there. Hence //**hwæ˧tʂæ˦**//, not //**hwæ˧tʂæ˦#**//, for 'squirrel'. The motivation for indicating a Mid tone ˧ on the first syllable of this word is to keep the notation of lexical forms close to the surface phonological forms: when a disyllable with lexical H#, #H or H$ tone is realized in isolation, its first syllable carries M tone, interpreted here as a default tone (added to a syllable that is lexically unspecified for tone: see §2.4.3). When writing the lexical (deep-phonological) form of words, it appeared better to indicate a tone for each syllable. The same reasoning leads to notation as //**ʐwæ˧zo#˦**//, not //**ʐwæ.zo#˦**//, for 'colt' ; //**kv̩˧ʂe˦$**//, not //**kv.ʂe˦$**//, for 'flea'; and //**hwɤ˧li˦**//, not //**hwɤ.li˦**//, for 'cat'.

In the case of the L tone, the choice to indicate a tone for each syllable introduces some redundancy. For instance, 'dog' is transcribed as //**kʰv̩˩mi˩**//, not //**kʰv̩˩mi**//: the L tone is indicated on both syllables.

Conversely, the tone pattern analyzed as LM+#H is, by convention, represented in the lexical form of disyllables simply as L on the first syllable and #H on the second, because indicating the M tone as a tone letter would wrongly suggest the presence of a contour on the syllable to which it would be associated. Hence, the notation chosen is //**nɑ˩hĩ#˦**// for 'Naxi (person)'.

2.4.5 Attested and unattested lexical tones

The static regularities that came to light in §2.1 can be reformulated in dynamic terms, as resulting from a set of phonological tone rules. These tone rules are set out in §7.1.1, and discussed throughout Chapter 7, which also presents the phonological unit within which the rules apply: the tone group. Here is a preview of the full set of rules; the reader will need to make frequent reference to it when reading the following chapters.

- Rule 1: L tone spreads progressively ("left-to-right") onto syllables that are unspecified for tone.
- Rule 2: Syllables that remain unspecified for tone after the application of Rule 1 receive M tone.
- Rule 3: In tone-group-initial position, H and M are neutralized to M.
- Rule 4: The syllable following a H-tone syllable receives L tone.

Rule 5: All syllables following a H.L or M.L sequence receive L tone.

Rule 6: In tone-group-final position, H and M are neutralized to H if they follow a L tone.

Rule 7: If a tone group only contains L tones, a post-lexical H tone is added to its last syllable.

The key facts for the present discussion are the following: (i) L tone spreads progressively ("left-to-right"), (ii) all tones following H are lowered to L, and (iii) H and M are neutralized to M in tone-group-initial position. These generalizations, together with the observation that there are no falling contours on a single syllable, rule out all of the unattested lexical tone patterns for monosyllables, and most of the unattested patterns for disyllables, such as ‡ H.L, ‡ H.M, ‡ M.LM, and ‡ ML.M. On the other hand, there is a combination that is compatible with the language's phonotactics and yet unattested: there is no //LM+H$// lexical tone category of disyllables, whereas there are //LM+MH#// and //LM+#H// categories. (As for //LM+H#//, it is undistinguishable from //LH//, since for a disyllable both formulae result in the same tonal assignment: L on the first syllable, and H on the second.) This gap can be interpreted as evidence that //H$// is relatively marginal in the system.

2.4.6 Phonological regularities and morphotonological oddities

Looking back at the data in Table 2.7a–b, it is tempting to look for phonological regularities that would capture all the observed patterns. However, such a search would come up against facts that resist phonological generalizations. For instance, there is no obvious reason why L should surface as M in isolation. This may have to do with the prohibition of all-L tone groups (about which see §2.3.3), and *a fortiori* all-L utterances; but for verbs this is repaired by adding a post-lexical final H tone, so that verbs with lexical //L// tone surface with a /LH/ contour when they are spoken in isolation (see Table 6.2). If the tone system were based on a set of phonological rules (rules applying uniformly in all morphosyntactic contexts), lexical //L// on a noun would be expected to surface as /LH/, not as /M/. A similarly puzzling case is that of the //L// tone on disyllabic nouns. A word such as //kʰv̩˩mi˩// 'dog' yields /kʰv̩˩mi˧/ in isolation, as expected, but when followed by the copula it yields /kʰv̩˩mi˩ ɲi˥/ 'is (a/the) dog': the copula loses its lexical //L// tone. There is no obvious reason why this should be so: one could have expected a /L.L.L/ sequence, //†kʰv̩˩mi˩ ɲi˩//, realized as /†kʰv̩˩mi˩ ɲi˧/ following the addition of a post-lexical H tone to avoid an all-L tone group.

This asymmetry in the tonal treatment of the copula after a //L//-tone noun, depending on the number of syllables in the noun, points to a crucial aspect of Yongning Na tone: many tone rules have narrowly restricted fields of application; they apply in highly specific morphosyntactic contexts, and are sensitive to the number of syllables (and internal makeup) of the morphemes at issue.

These reflections about the overall outlook of the Yongning Na tone system will be taken up in §10.2, in light of the account of Na morphotonology to which we now proceed (Chapters 3-6).

3 Compound nouns

Tonal processes applying within the noun phrase constitute a major part of the Yongning Na tone system. They also shed light on evolutionary processes. In Na, as in other Sino-Tibetan languages that have undergone considerable phonological erosion (such as Tujia 土家语, Bai 白语, Namuyi 纳木依语, or Shixing 史兴语), many roots that used to be phonologically distinct have become homophonous. As a consequence, there exists a strong tendency towards disyllabification. The study of synchronic tonal processes reveals which processes – such as compounding and affixation – feed into which categories of disyllabic nouns. It also brings out, by contrast, those disyllabic nouns whose tones are different from what one would expect in view of currently productive rules. In turn, this draws attention to these outlier nouns, raising the issue of where they got their tone from – whether they date back to a time when different tone rules applied, for instance.

Tonal phenomena taking place within the noun phrase in Na will be presented in the following order: compounds (this chapter); numeral-plus-classifier phrases (Chapter 4); and combinations between nouns and grammatical morphemes (Chapter 5).

Compounding is a highly productive word formation process in Na. "Compounding is the prevalent morphological process" (Lidz 2010: 344). This is also true of many other languages of East and Southeast Asia (on Sinitic: Arcodia 2012: passim). Determinative compounds (the *tatpuruṣa* compounds of Sanskrit grammar) are more common than coordinative compounds (Sanskrit *dvandva*). In Yongning Na, determinative compounds, such as 'tiger's skin', and coordinative compounds, such as 'mother and daughter', do not follow the same tone rules. For instance, the determinative compound 'nanny goat's back', /**tsʰɯ˧mi˧-gʏ˩dʏ˩**/, carries H# tone (a final H tone), whereas the coordinative compound 'father and mother', /ə˧dɑ˧-ə˧mi#˥/, carries tone #H (a floating H tone), even though the input tones are the same: both 'nanny goat' and 'father' have H$ tone, and both 'mother' and 'back' have M tone. Determinative compounds and coordinative compounds are therefore presented separately.

3.1 Determinative compound nouns. Part I: The main facts

In Yongning Na, the order of constituents in determinative compounds is determiner plus head, as is generally the case in Sino-Tibetan (Michailovsky 2011).

In some tonal languages, possessive constructions (genitival syntagms) and compounds (complex lexemes) are distinguished by their tone patterns. In Kita Malinke (Mande branch of Niger-Congo), for instance, 'the meat of the cow' is /mìsí sùbû/, and 'beef, cow meat' is /mìsì-súbú/ (Creissels & Grégoire 1993). The latter is characterized by tonal compactness (*compacité tonale*): the tone pattern of the compound is determined by that of its first component, which is the determiner. Similarly, in Yongning Na, no tonal change takes place in possessive constructions, whereas tonal changes take place in compounds – although the tone changes are more complex than in Malinke, as will be explained further down. In Na, the two constructions are conspicuously different: in possessive constructions, the possessive /=bv˧/ is added after the determiner, before the head, e.g. /hwɤ˧li˧/ 'cat', /ɭv˧/ 'brains', /hwɤ˧li˧=bv˧ | ɭv˧/ 'brains of the cat'. The first noun – the determiner – and the possessive particle form a single tone group. As for the second noun (the head), its tone pattern remains the same as in isolation. By contrast, the tones of compounds are not simply the concatenation of those of their constituents. The present analysis progresses in increasing order of abstraction, from the surface phonological patterns of compounds to the underlying system.

Determinative compounds are sometimes divided into "free" and "fixed" combinations. The former consist of two nouns that are not habitually associated, e.g. /gi˧nɑ˧mi˧-njɤ˩lɯ˩/ 'bear's eye': the two nouns are combined into a noun phrase in the context of a given utterance. The latter constitute lexicalized combinations, e.g. /ʐi˩hỹ#˩/ 'body hair (of humans)', literally 'monkey's hair'. There is a cross-linguistic tendency for compounds to stray away from regular morphophonological patterns and from the semantics that one would expect on the basis of their constituting elements. But the meaning may be specialized whereas the phonological form remains undistinguishable from that of a newly coined compound; conversely, the phonological form may be irregular whereas the meaning is as expected on a flatly synchronic basis.

> Thus in Zarma, *háw bíi* /ox/black/ is a syntagm with a perfectly regular form, which would be expected to mean 'black ox', but which refers to the buffalo – an animal that resembles the ox, and whose colour is black. In *cùrò bíi*, one easily recognizes *cúrò* 'bird' and *bíi* 'black', but the meaning is 'guinea fowl'; in this case, semantic specialization is accompanied by

a tonal irregularity: a syntagm meaning 'black bird' would be expected to have the form *cúrò bîi*. (Creissels 1991: 121)¹

The lack of straightforward match between semantic regularity and morphophonological similarity needs to be taken into account when exploring a tone system. Semantics cannot be used as the sole criterion to tease apart morphophonologically irregular compounds. The distinction made in this chapter is therefore not between "fixed" and "free" combinations, but between regular and irregular combinations. From a morphotonological point of view, the relevant parameter is whether the tone pattern of a compound follows productive rules or not.

3.1.1 The role of the number of syllables

Tonal changes in compounding are only observed when the second term – the head – has fewer than three syllables, i.e. in combinations of the form σ+σ, σ +σσ, σσ+σ, σσ+σσ, σσσ+σ, or σσσ+σσ. Otherwise no tone change takes place (for instance in σ+σσσ, σσ+σσσ, or σσσ+σσσ). What matters is thus not the total number of syllables of the resulting compound, but the number of syllables of the head. An illustration is provided by examples (1a–1c).

(1)   a.   lo˧ʂv˩ | -hi˩na˧mi#˥
           lo˧ʂv˩   hi˩na˧mi#˥
           Luoshui (village name)   lake

           'Lake Lugu' (*literally:* 'the lake of Luoshui')

    b.   ɬi˧di˩-di˩mi˩
           ɬi˧di˩   di˧mi˧
           Yongning (place name) large_plain

           'Yongning plain'

    c.   gi˧na˧mi˧-njɤ˥lɯ˩
           gi˧na˧mi#˥   njɤ˩lɯ˧
           bear   eye

           'bear's eye'

---

¹ *Original text*: Ainsi en zarma, *háw bîi* /bœuf/noir/ est un syntagme de formation parfaitement régulière dont on attendrait qu'il signifie « bœuf noir », mais qui désigne le buffle (animal semblable au bœuf et de couleur noire). Dans *cùrò bîi*, nous reconnaissons facilement *cùrò* « oiseau » et *bîi* « noir », mais la signification est « pintade » ; dans ce cas, le figement sémantique s'accompagne d'une irrégularité tonale : le syntagme signifiant « oiseau noir » serait *cúrò bîi*.

The place names in (1a) and (1b) have the same syntactic structure: /lo˧ʂv˩/ (Chinese: Luòshuǐ 落水) is the name of a village on the shore of Lake Lugu, and /ɬi˧di˩/ is the name of Yongning. The relationship in both cases is between determiner and head: 'the lake of /lo˧ʂv˩/', 'the plain of /ɬi˧di˩/'. In (1a), both parts of the compound retain their lexical tones: /lo˧ʂv˩/ 'Luoshui' and /hi˩nɑ˧mi#˩/ 'lake'. The compound 'Lake Lugu', /lo˧ʂv˩ | -hi˩nɑ˧mi#˩/, is to be analyzed as consisting of two tone groups (this is reflected by the symbol '|', which indicates a tone group boundary); if it constituted one tone group, its tone pattern would be ‡ **lo˧ʂv˩-hi˩nɑ˩mi˩**, by application of Rule 5: "All syllables following a H.L or M.L sequence receive L tone". (For a list of the tone rules, see §7.1.1.) In (1b), the expected tone change takes place, by application of Rule 5: the lexical tone of 'plain' is M (/di˧mi˧/), but in the context of this compound it is lowered to L. Example (1c), from /**gi˧nɑ˧mi#˩**/ 'bear' and /**njɤ˩ɭɯ˧**/ 'eye', illustrates the fact that tonal change takes place in compounds with a three-syllable determiner, provided that the head comprises no more than two syllables.

It is clear from the data set out below (Table 3.4 and following tables) that heads undergo more tonal changes than determiners in compounding. In particular, there are numerous cases where a H tone that originates lexically on the determiner associates to the last syllable of the head. If this happens in a σσ+σ compound, the distance between the syllabic position to which the tone is lexically attached and the syllabic position of the tone in the surface phonology is no greater than one syllable. In a σσ+σσ compound, this distance increases to two syllables. The same process applying to a σσ+σσσ compound would become rather unwieldy, as it would result in a H tone moving three syllables away from its original position in the lexical representation. This is by no means a cognitive impossibility: staggeringly complex tonal phenomena are firmly attested in the world's languages, and by some estimates the Alawa dialect of Yongning Na would rate as a complex system. Still, it seems clear that in this instance the observed pattern (dividing the compound into two parts) is a strategy to bypass tonal computation, thereby avoiding a source of complexity. The asymmetrical state of affairs whereby σσσ+σσ compounds undergo tonal change, but σσ+σσσ compounds do not, makes intuitive sense in light of the amount of tonal computation that the latter require.

There is thus a preference (in this particular language and dialect) for tonal processes that do not result in tonal movements of more than two syllables at a time. Long-distance movement of tones is avoided. This observation will be taken up in §3.2.8.

3.1.2 How the tone patterns were collected

Some lexicalized compounds can be found in narratives, e.g. /ə˧mi˧-ʁæ˧ʈv̩˩/ 'mother's neck' in Tiger2.86. Others were encountered during lexical elicitation sessions, and are consigned in my dictionary of Yongning Na (Michaud 2015a). In order to obtain all possible tonal combinations of determiner and head, systematic elicitation was also used. The main language consultant, F4, was reluctant to accept semantically implausible combinations. She gradually understood that the unusual combinations that I put forward were designed to obtain a particular sequence of tones; she nonetheless retained a strong commitment to a common-sense use of language. In the consultant's view, compounds such as 'flea's back' and 'flea's liver' did not stretch plausibility too far, and I gratefully recorded them. But she would definitely not have accepted combinations such as 'chief's beetle's kidney basket' (to cite an example used by Hyman 2007a, taken up in Evans 2010: 225). Compounds that did not make sufficiently good sense, such as 'woman's blood', were produced either as possessive constructions – an English equivalent would be 'blood of a/the woman', as opposed to the desired 'woman's blood' – or as an ungrammatical expression consisting in the mere juxtaposition of the citation forms of the two words.

It was nonetheless possible to obtain all combinations in the end, by searching through the word list to arrive at the least implausible combinations, and discussing possible contexts with the consultant. In the case of 'woman's blood', her argument was that there is nothing specific about the blood of women, and thus no need to distinguish it from that of men: women's blood is no more and no less than human blood. To get round this issue, the imagined context was that a man-eating demon feels an urge to drink *woman's blood*. Each combination was then checked multiple times by using different example words for the same tonal combination, and eliciting tokens several times during different elicitation sessions. This made the elicitation process slower than it would have been with a consultant who readily agreed to create any combination. A consultant's conservative behaviour may have some advantages, however: one might have suspicions that a consultant whose imagination runs free from the trammels of common sense could occasionally take similar liberties with the language's ordinary rules.

Transcribed recordings of over 1,500 compounds are available online from the Pangloss Collection (references: DetermCompounds1 through DetermCompounds16), providing, for each compound, the input tones and the lexical forms of the determiner and the head, as shown in Figure 3.1. In all cases where examples are also found in texts, the tone patterns are identical with those obtained through elicitation. Table 3.1 provides an example word for each tonal category of noun used to build compounds referring to body parts.

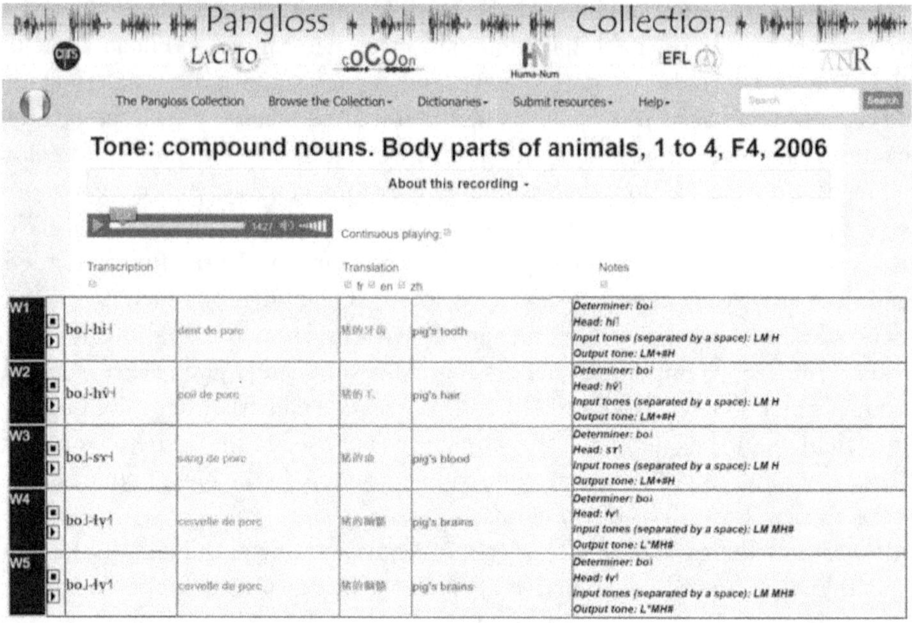

Figure 3.1: First lines of the document DetermCompounds1 as displayed in the online interface.

3.1.3 The facts: Surface phonological tone patterns

The tone patterns of compound nouns in Alawa are set out in Tables 3.2a–e as a function of the tones of their constituting elements. The tone of the determiner is indicated in the leftmost column, and the tone of the head in the top row. For instance, 'tiger' /lɑ˧/ carries lexical M and 'skin' /ɣɯ˩/ carries lexical LM; the tone of the compound 'tiger's skin' can be found at the intersection of row M and column LM in Table 3.2a. The information 'M.L' provided in the cell at the intersection of row M and column LM indicates that the surface phonological tone of the compound at issue is M.L: /lɑ˧-ɣɯ˩/ 'tiger's skin'. Tables 3.2a and 3.2b present monosyllabic heads, and Tables 3.2c and 3.2d disyllabic heads.

Like simple nouns, compounds need to be elicited in at least two contexts to bring out their lexical tone categories, because the opposition between tone

Table 3.1: Example words used to elicit body-part compound nouns.

tone	determiners	meaning	heads	meaning
LM	boʌ	pig	ɣɯʌ	skin
M	la˧	tiger	bv˧	intestine
L	joɬ	sheep	mʁɬ	fat
#H	ʐwæ˥	horse	sʁ˥	blood
MH#	tsʰæ˧˥	deer	ɬy˧˥	brains
M	po˧lo˧	ram	gv˧dv˧	back
#H	ʐwæ˧zo#˥	colt	ɲi˧gʁ#˥	nose, snout
MH#	hwʁ˧li˧˥	cat	qv˧tsæ˧˥	throat
H$	hwʁ˧mi˥$	she-cat	hu˧mi˥$	stomach
L	kʰvɬmiɬ	dog	nvɬmiɬ	heart
L#	da˧jiɬ	mule	ɬi˧piɬ	ear
LM+MH#	õɬdv˧˥	wolf	ji˩tsæ˧˥	waist
LM+#H	naɬhĩ#˥	Naxi person	ɲæɬqʰæ#˥	eye sand, rheum
LM	æɬmi˧	hen	ɲʁɬɯ˧	eye
LH	boɬɬa˥	boar	hi˩zæ˥	uvula
H#	hwæ˧tsɯ˥	rat	ʁæ˧ty˥	neck

categories such as //M// and //#H// is neutralized in isolation. Compound nouns, like simple nouns, were elicited (i) in isolation and (ii) in frame (2).[2]

(2) tsʰɯ˧ | _____ ɲi.
    tsʰɯ˥   _____   ɲiɬ
    DEM.PROX   *target item*   COP
    'This is (a/the) _____.'

---

[2] Frame (2) is reproduced from example (6) of Chapter 2. In (2), the lexical tones of the demonstrative and of the copula are indicated in the interlinear glosses, building on the findings reported in the course of Chapter 2. The tone-group boundary separating the demonstrative from what follows is also indicated, by means of the vertical bar symbol '|'. No tone is indicated for the copula in the surface phonological representation (the first line of the example) because its surface tone changes according to the tone category of the target noun.

In cases where the copula surfaces with its lexical L tone, only one tone pattern is indicated in the corresponding cell in the table. For instance, 'tiger's skin' is /lɑ˧-ɣɯ˩/ (tone: /M.L/), and the copula surfaces with L tone after this compound: /lɑ˧-ɣɯ˩ ɲi˩/ 'is tiger's skin'. The information provided in Table 3.2a in the cell at the intersection of row M and column LM is therefore simply 'M.L': the fact that only one pattern is provided means that this pattern is unchanged when a copula is added. On the other hand, in cases where the copula bears a tone other than its lexical L tone, the tonal string that is obtained when adding the copula is indicated after a comma. For instance, the information 'M.M, M.M.H' provided at the intersection of row M and column M in Table 3.2a indicates that the tonal string of the compound at issue is M.M when said in isolation, e.g. /lɑ˧-bv̩˧/ 'tiger's intestine', and that addition of a copula yields a M.M.H pattern: /lɑ˧-bv̩˧ ɲi˥/ 'is tiger's intestine'.[3]

When there are tonal variants, alternatives are separated by slashes. For instance, the indication 'M.L.L/M.M.H' in row #H, column H$ of Table 3.2c means that these compounds can have either of two patterns: M.L.L or M.M.H, e.g. /ʐwæ˧-hu˩mi˩/ or /ʐwæ˧-hu˧mi˥/ for 'horse's stomach'. For the sake of typographical economy, sequences of four M tones (M.M.M.M) have been abbreviated to 'M...M'. Adjacent cells with identical contents have been grouped by using boxes in dashed lines. For instance, the tone pattern of any disyllabic compound with a L-tone determiner is /L.LH/, hence all the cells in the 'L' row in Table 3.2a are grouped into one box delimited by dashed lines, containing the indication 'L.LH'. This process has not been pushed to an extreme, however. The purpose of Table 3.2a is to set out the facts in a legible and unambiguous way; this is only one step towards the long-term goal of arriving at a full-fledged linguistic model, with new ways of modelling regularities and irregularities within paradigms (Sagot & Walther 2013).

In view of the rarity of three-syllable nouns, only one three-syllable determiner was used: /gi˧nɑ˧mi#˥/ 'bear' (tone: #H). The data is set out in Table 3.2e.

---

[3] In 3.2a, there are no examples of simple M.M: all disyllabic M.M compounds plus copula yield M.M.H, so that the 'M.M.H' part in 'M.M, M.M.H' may seem redundant. But this piece of information is not superfluous, because the surface tone pattern M.M on a disyllable always needs disambiguation in Yongning Na: /M.M/ constitutes the neutralization of underlying //M// and //#H// tones, illustrated in Chapter 2 by the nouns //po˧lo˧// 'ram' and //ʐwæ˧zo#˥// 'colt', respectively.

Table 3.2a: Surface phonological representation of the tones of compound nouns. Monosyllabic determiner and monosyllabic head. Leftmost column: tone of determiner; top row: tone of head.

tone	LH; LM	M	L	H	MH
LM	L.M			L.M, L.M.H	L.MH
LH	L.H	L.L	L.H		
M	M.L	M.M, M.M.H	M.L	M.M, M.M.H	M.MH
L	L.LH				
H	M.H	M.M, M.M.H			M.L
MH	M.H			M.H, M.M.H	

Table 3.2b: Surface phonological representation of the tones of compound nouns. Disyllabic determiner and monosyllabic head. Leftmost column: tone of determiner; top row: tone of head.

tone	LH; LM	M	L	H	MH
M	M.M.L	M.M.M, M.M.M.H	M.M.L	M.M.M, M.M.M.H	M.M.L
#H	M.M.H	M.M.M, M.M.M.H			M.M.L
MH#	M.M.H	M.M.MH			M.M.H
H$	M.M.H	M.M.M, M.M.M.H	M.M.H, M.M.M.H	M.M.M, M.M.M.H	M.H.L
L	L.L.H	L.L.LH			L.L.H
L#	M.L.L				
LM+MH#	L.M.H	L.M.MH	L.M.H, L.M.M.H		
LM+#H	L.M.H	L.M.M, L.M.M.H	L.M.H	L.M.M, L.M.M.H	L.M.H
LM	L.M.L	L.M.M	L.M.L	L.M.M, L.M.M.H	L.M.MH
LH	L.H.L				
H#	M.H.L				

101

Table 3.2c: Surface phonological representation of the tones of compound nouns. Monosyllabic determiner and disyllabic head. Leftmost column: tone of determiner; top row: tone of head.

tone	M	#H	MH#	H$	L	L#	LM+MH#; LM+#H; LM; LH	H#
LM; LH	L.M.M	L.M.M, L.M.M.H	L.M.MH / L.H.L	L.M.H, L.M.M.H	L.M.L	L.M.L / L.L.H	L.H.L (=L.M.L)	L.M.H / L.L.H
M	M.M.M	M.M.M, M.M.M.H	M.M.MH	M.M.H, M.M.M.H	M.L.L	M.M.L	M.L.L	M.M.H
L	L.L.L.H			L.L.H	L.L.L.H	L.L.H	L.H.L	L.L.H
#H	M.M.H	M.M.M, M.M.M.H	M.H.L	M.L.L / M.M.H	M.H.L	M.M.H	M.H.L	M.M.H
MH#	M.M.H	M.M.M, M.M.M.H	M.M.MH	M.H.L	M.H.L	M.M.H	M.H.L	M.M.H

102

Table 3.2d: Surface phonological tones of compound nouns. Disyllabic determiner and disyllabic head. Leftmost column: tone of determiner; top row: tone of head.

tone	M	#H	MH#	H$	L	L#	LM+MH#; LM+#H; LM; LH	H#
M	M..M	M..M, M..M.H	M..MH	M.M.M.H, M..M.H / M.M.H.L	M.M.L.L	M.M.M.L	M.M.L.L	M.M.M.H
#H	M.M.M.H	M..M, M..M.H	M.M.H.L	M.M.M.H, M..M.H / M.M.H.L / M.M.M.H	M.M.H.L	M.M.M.H	M.M.H.L	M.M.M.H
MH#		M..MH	M.M.H.L	M.M.H.L / M.M.M.H	M.M.H.L	M.M.M.H	M.M.H.L	M.M.M.H
H$		M..M, M..MH	M.M.H.L / M.H.L.L		M.M.H.L	M.M.M.H	M.M.H.L	M.M.M.H
L	L.L.L.H	L.L.L.H	L.L.H.L	L.L.L.H	L.L.H.L	L.L.L.H	L.L.H.L	L.L.L.H
L#	M.L.L.L	M.L.L.L				L.M.M.H	L.M.H.L	L.M.M.H
L+MH#	L.M.M.H	L.M.M.M, L.M.M.M.H	L.M.H.L		L.M.H.L	L.M.M.H	L.M.H.L	L.M.M.H
LM+#H			L.M.H.L	L.M.M.H,	L.M.H.L			
LM	L.M.M.M		L.M.M.M.H	L.M.M.M.H	L.M.L.L	L.M.M.L	L.M.L.L	
LH	L.H.L.L							
H#	M.H.L.L							

Table 3.2e: Surface phonological representation of the tones of compound nouns. Compounds with a trisyllabic #H-tone determiner: 'bear'+body part.

head		compound	
form	tone	surface form	surface tone
ɣɯ˧ 'skin'	LM	gi˧nɑ˧mi˧-ɣɯ˥	M.M.M.H, M.M.M.H.L
bʏ˧ 'intestine'	M	gi˧nɑ˧mi˧-bʏ˧	M.M.M.M, M...M.H
mʁ˩ 'grease'	L	gi˧nɑ˧mi˧-mʁ˥	M.M.M.MH
sʁ˥ 'blood'	H	gi˧nɑ˧mi˧-sʁ˧	M.M.M.M, M...M.H
ɬv˥ 'brains'	MH	gi˧nɑ˧mi˧-ɬv˩	M.M.M.L
gv˧dv˧ 'back'	M	gi˧nɑ˧mi˧-gv˧dv˧	M.M.M.M.M, M...M.H
ɲi˧gʁ˧ 'nose'	#H	gi˧nɑ˧mi˧-ɲi˧gʁ˧	M.M.M.M.M, M...M.H
qv˧tsæ˥ 'throat'	MH#	gi˧nɑ˧mi˧-qv˥tsæ˩	M.M.M.H.L
hu˧mi˥$ 'stomach'	H$	gi˧nɑ˧mi˧-hu˧mi˥	M.M.M.M.H, M...M.H
nv˩mi˩ 'heart'	L	gi˧nɑ˧mi˧-nv˥mi˩	M.M.M.H.L
ɬi˧pi˩ 'ear'	L#	gi˧nɑ˧mi˧-ɬi˧pi˥	M.M.M.M.H
ji˩tsæ˥ 'waist'	LM+MH#	gi˧nɑ˧mi˧-ji˥tsæ˩	M.M.M.H.L
njʁ˩lɯ˧ 'eye'	LM	gi˧nɑ˧mi˧-njʁ˥lɯ˩	M.M.M.H.L
ʁæ˧tv˥ 'neck'	H#	gi˧nɑ˧mi˧-ʁæ˧tv˥	M.M.M.M.H

3.1.4 Analysis into underlying tone patterns

The surface tonal strings found on compounds, as reported in Tables 3.2a–e, can in most cases be reduced to simple tone categories, such as //L//, //LM// or //LH//, by examining them in light of the phonological tone rules set out in §7.1.1. Here are two examples.

- The sequence /L.LH/ can be interpreted as the realization of a simple //L// tone: it spreads over the two syllables of the compound, yielding //L.L//, and this sequence is further supplemented by a post-lexical H tone due to Rule 7 ("If a tone group only contains L tones, a post-lexical H tone is added to its last syllable").

- The sequence /M.M/ in /lɑ˧-bv˧/ 'tiger's intestine' could be the realization of underlying //M// or //#H// (recall that //#H// is a H tone that is floating, and can only be realized after the lexical item at issue). The fact that the copula receives a H tone when it follows this compound (/lɑ˧-bv˧ ɲi˥/ 'is tiger's intestine') reveals that the underlying tone pattern is #H.

The result of analysis is presented in Tables 3.3a–e, which contain all the information required to generate the surface phonological patterns of compounds, following the standard tone-to-syllable association rules.

In the description of these patterns, reference needs to be made to a juncture that is internal to the tone group: one that separates the determiner from the head. This juncture is indicated by the symbol '–'; the same symbol will be used in the description of numeral-plus-classifier phrases in Chapter 4. Thus, –L refers to a L tone attaching to the second part of an expression. For example, the output –L indicated in Table 3.3d for a disyllabic determiner carrying M tone (first row) and a disyllabic head carrying L tone (sixth column) means that the determinative compound carries L tone on its second part, i.e. after the juncture between the two nouns. For instance, the combination of /po˧lo˧/ 'ram' and /nv̩˩mi˩/ 'heart' yields a compound with L tone on its second part, hence /po.lo.nv̩˩mi/ (L tone associates to the first syllable after the juncture between the two nouns). Association of tones to the other three syllables then follows from the regular phonological tone rules of Yongning Na: the L tone spreads onto the following syllable (by Rule 1), hence /po.lo.nv̩˩mi˩/; and the first two syllables receive M tone (by Rule 2), yielding /po˧lo˧-nv̩˩mi˩/. A step-by-step representation of this simple example is provided in Figure 3.2. A similar representation is provided in Figure 3.3 for #H– (a floating H tone attaching to the first part of the expression):

the #H tone is inserted before the juncture between the two nouns, i.e. it associates to the second syllable of the compound. From there, the H tone attaches to the following syllable (this is the defining property of the #H tone category, which associates *after* the syllable to which it is lexically attached), i.e. on the third syllable. Finally, the first and second syllables receive M tone by Rule 2, and the fourth syllable receives L tone by Rule 4.

Four tonal categories of head nouns always behave the same way in compounds: the opposition among LM, LH, LM+#H and LM+MH# is neutralized. These tone categories for heads are therefore pooled together in Tables 3.3a–e. Among determiners, the opposition between LH and LM on monosyllables is neutralized; accordingly, these two tones are also pooled together in the tables.

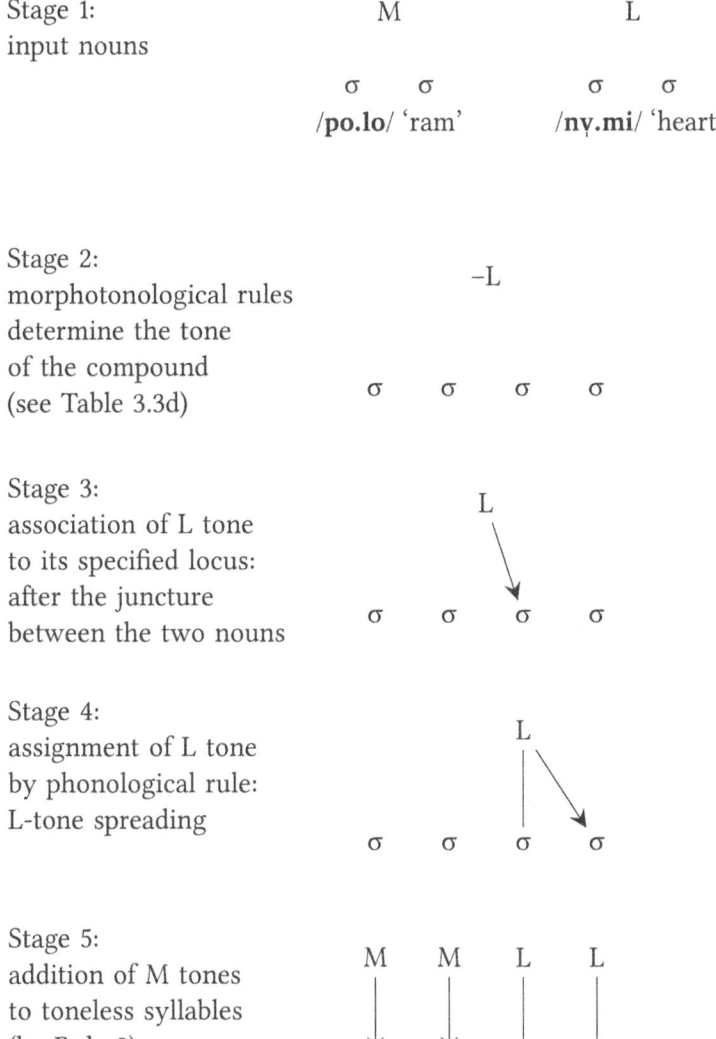

Figure 3.2: First illustration of the anchoring of tones relative to a morpheme break inside a complex expression (notation: '−'): step-by-step representation of tonal association of the −L tone of the compound /po˧lo˧-ɲv̩˩mi˩/ 'rat's stomach'.

107

Stage 1:
input nouns

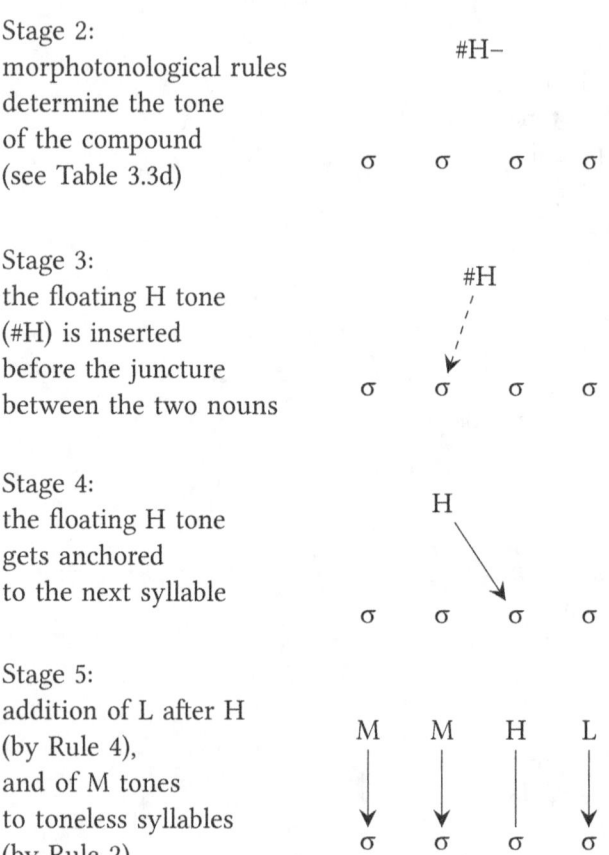

Stage 2:
morphotonological rules
determine the tone
of the compound
(see Table 3.3d)

Stage 3:
the floating H tone
(#H) is inserted
before the juncture
between the two nouns

Stage 4:
the floating H tone
gets anchored
to the next syllable

Stage 5:
addition of L after H
(by Rule 4),
and of M tones
to toneless syllables
(by Rule 2)

Figure 3.3: Second illustration of the anchoring of tones relative to a morpheme break inside a complex expression (notation: '–'): step-by-step representation of tonal association of the #H– tone of the compound /hwɤ˧li˧-qʌ˥tsæ˩/ 'cat's sound / cat sounds'.

108

Table 3.3a: The underlying tonal categories of compound nouns. Monosyllabic determiner and monosyllabic head. The tone of the determiner is indicated in the leftmost column, and the tone of the head in the top row.

tone	LM; LH	M	L	H	MH
LM; LH	LH	LM	LH	LM+#H	LM+MH#
M	−L	#H	−L	#H	MH#
L	L				
H	#H−	#H			−L
MH	H#			H$	

Table 3.3b: The underlying tonal categories of compound nouns. Disyllabic determiner and monosyllabic head. The tone of the determiner is indicated in the leftmost column, and the tone of the head in the top row.

tone	LH; LM	M	L	H	MH
M	−L	#H	−L	#H	−L
#H	H#	#H			
MH#		MH#			H#
H$	#H−	#H	H$	#H	H#−
L	L+H#	L			L+H#
L#	L#−				
LM+MH#	LM+MH#−	LM+MH#	LM+H$		
LM+#H		LM+#H	LM+H#	LM+#H	LM+H#
LM	LM−L	LM	LM−L		LM+MH#
LH	LH				
H#	H#−				

Table 3.3c: The underlying tonal categories of compound nouns. Mono-syllabic determiner and disyllabic head. The tone of the determiner is indicated in the leftmost column, and the tone of the head in the top row.

tone	M -	#H	MH#	LM+#H	LM+MH# / L+#H-	H$	L	L#	LM+MH#; LM+#H; LM; LH	H#
LM; LH	LM		LM+#H	LM+MH# / L+#H-	LM+H$		L+#H-	L+#H- / L+H#	L+#H-	LM+H# / L+H#
M	M	#H	MH#		MH#	H$	-L	-L#	-L	H#
L	L				L+H#	L+H#	L	L+H#	L+#H-	L+H#
#H	H#	#H	#H	#H-		-L / H#	#H-	H#	#H-	H#
MH			MH#		MH#	#H-				#H

Table 3.3d: The underlying tonal categories of compound nouns. Disyllabic determiner and disyllabic head. The tone of the determiner is indicated in the leftmost column, and the tone of the head in the top row.

tꞇɔne	M	#H	MH#	H$	L	L#	LM+MH#; LM+#H; LM; LH	H#
M	M	#H	MH#	H$ / #H–	–L	–L#	–L	H#
#H	H#	MH#	#H–	H$ / #H– / H#	#H–	H#	#H–	
MH#		MH#	#H– / H#–	#H– / H#			MH#–	
H$		#H					#H–	
L	L+H#	L	L+H#	L+H#	L+#H–	L+H#	L+#H–	L+H#
L#	L#–							
LM+MH#	LM+H#	LM+#H	LM+MH#–	LM+MH#– / H#	LM+MH#–	LM+H#	LM+MH#–	LM+H#
LM+#H				LM–H$	LM+#H–			
LM	LM–		LM+MH#		LM–L	LM–L#	LM–L	
LH	LH							
H#	H#–							

Table 3.3e: Examples and underlying tonal categories of compound nouns with a trisyllabic, #H-tone determiner: 'bear'+body part.

head		compound	
form	tone	underlying form	underlying tone
ɣɯ˩˧ 'skin'	LM	gi˧na˧mi˧-ɣɯ˥	H#
bv˧ 'intestine'	M	gi˧na˧mi˧-bv#˥	#H
mʁ˩ 'grease'	L	gi˧na˧mi˧-mʁ˧˥	MH#
sʁ˥ 'blood'	H	gi˧na˧mi˧-sʁ#˥	#H
ɬy˧˥ 'brains'	MH	gi˧na˧mi˧-ɬy˩	L#
gv˧dv˧ 'back'	M	gi˧na˧mi˧-gv˧dv#˥	#H
ɲi˧gʁ˧ 'nose'	#H	gi˧na˧mi˧-ɲi˧gʁ#˥	#H
qv˧tsæ˧˥ 'throat'	MH#	gi˧na˧mi˧-qv˥tsæ˩	#H–
hu˧mi˥$ 'stomach'	H$	gi˧na˧mi˧-hu˧mi˥$	H$
nv˩mi˩ 'heart'	L	gi˧na˧mi˧-nv˥mi˩	#H–
ɬi˧pi˩ 'ear'	L#	gi˧na˧mi˧-ɬi˧pi˥	H#
ji˩tsæ˧˥ 'waist'	LM+MH#	gi˧na˧mi˧-ji˥tsæ˩	#H–
njʁ˩ɭɯ˧ 'eye'	LM	gi˧na˧mi˧-njʁ˥ɭɯ˩	#H–
ʁæ˧tv˥ 'neck'	H#	gi˧na˧mi˧-ʁæ˧tv˥	H#

3.2 Determinative compound nouns. Part II: Discussion

Let us now proceed to an analysis of the patterns presented above. At this point, it may be useful to speculate about possible ways in which the tones of the determiner and head could combine. Some languages, such as Mandarin, have no tone change at all in compounds, showing that tone change is not necessary to compounding. A first theoretical possibility would thus be the simple concatenation of the input tones. Under such a configuration, given the *determiner-head* order of Yongning Na compounds, the tone of the determiner would express itself first, and given the limitations on tone sequences within a tone group (summarized as Rules 1–7), this would leave little room for the tone of the head to express itself. Since a H tone precludes the expression of any other tone on following syllables (by phonological rules 4 and 5), determiners carrying a lexical tone containing a H level (i.e. one of #H, H$, MH#, LM+MH#, LM+#H and H#) would neutralize all tonal oppositions on head nouns. Likewise, the L level in the lexical categories L and L# would spread rightward all the way to the end of the compound noun. The tone of the head could only express itself when the determiner has M tone: M plus L would yield –L, M plus #H would yield #H, and so on.

A second possibility would be the complete neutralization of tonal oppositions on the determiner, or on the head. Neutralization of oppositions on the determiner would seem odd, because the linear order is determiner-first, and processes of tone spreading and tone reassociation in Yongning Na are mostly perseverative (towards following syllables, not preceding syllables), so that the loss of tonal oppositions among determiners would drastically reduce the number of tone patterns on compounds at the surface phonological level. Neutralization of tonal oppositions on the head is attested in the neighbouring language Shixing (also known as Xumi), where only the tone of the determiner expresses itself, i.e. all tonal oppositions on the head are neutralized, and the 3×3 tonal combinations among nouns boil down to three patterns on compounds (Chirkova & Michaud 2009).

A third possibility would be the assignment of a replacive tone in compounds. This is reported to be widespread in the Mande subgroup of the Niger-Congo family, e.g. in Dan-Gwɛɛtaa (Vydrin 2016) and Kpelle (Welmers 1969; 1973: 132; Konoshenko 2014b: 239). In Naish (the lower-level subgroup within Sino-Tibetan to which Yongning Na belongs), on the other hand, no case of replacive tone has been observed to date.

The state of affairs found in Yongning Na bears some similarities to the first and second theoretical possibilities: there is a tendency for output tone patterns to consist of the concatenation of input tones, and there is a measure of neutralization of tonal oppositions (output tone patterns are fewer than input combinations). On the one hand, about half the patterns can be straightforwardly explained in terms of successive association of the two input tones, followed by application of the general rules governing the adjustment of successive tones within a tone group. On the other hand, it was not found possible to capture the other half of the patterns by means of a set of rules.

The tone patterns of determinative compounds thus present a composite picture (play on words intended). Since not all the tone patterns of compounds follow either of the three theoretical possibilities mentioned above, it must be acknowledged that compounds have tone rules of their own, which differ subtly from successive association of the two input tones.

This conclusion may come as a slight disappointment to the linguist, whose job is to account for all observations through a model that is as simple and elegant as possible. Here, as in many other domains of the Yongning Na tone system, it is clear that the gap between the lexical tones of words and their tonal realizations in context is not simply a matter of sandhi rules operating on a phonological level. (Some clarifications about the terms 'tone sandhi', 'morphotonology' and 'tonal morphology' are set out in §8.1.1.) The behaviour of the three-syllable noun 'bear', /gi˧nɑ˧mi#˥/, as a determiner is a case in point: it patterns almost like disyllabic #H-tone nouns, such as 'colt', /ʐwæ˧zo#˥/, but not quite. When the head is a L-tone monosyllable, the output tone is MH#, instead of #H when the determiner is disyllabic.

In view of these observations, the present discussion of the combinations in Tables 3.3a–e is arranged by increasing degree of complexity.

The simpler cases can be described as follows: the tone of the determiner expresses itself first, and after that the tone of the head expresses itself to the extent allowed by the tones already assigned. The tone patterns of compounds in which the tone of the determiner is H#, LH or L# are so simple as to appear trivial: in these three cases, only the tone of the determiner expresses itself. When the determiner has H# tone (a H tone associated to its last syllable), tonal oppositions on the head are neutralized, irrespective of the number of syllables: see the last rows of Tables 3.3a–e. The compound carries H#–, i.e. a H tone on the last syllable of the determiner. This can be interpreted as the result of the straightforward association of the H# tone to the determiner: H on its last syllable, and M on its first syllable, by default. The lowering of all the following tones to L results from Rules 4 and 5: "A syllable following a H-tone syllable receives L tone" and "All syllables following a H.L or M.L sequence receive L tone". This is shown in Figure 3.4, using 'rat's stomach' (/**hwæ˧tsɯ˥-hu˩mi˩**/) as an example. In this compound, no trace is left of the H$ tone (the 'flea' tone) carried by the head.

The same analysis can be extended to the two other tone categories of disyllables after which all tonal oppositions are neutralized: LH and L#. Application of one of these tone patterns to the first part of the compound (the determiner) precludes any tone other than L on the following syllables, by Rules 4 and 5. The L# tone pattern of the latter results in association of a L tone to the second syllable of the determiner, whose first syllable receives M by default; this M.L sequence precludes, again, any tones other than L on the next syllables, by Rule 5.

In the other cases, which constitute a majority, the tonal oppositions on the head are not entirely neutralized: the tone of the compound cannot be arrived at without knowledge of the tone of the head noun. This observation casts doubt on the adequacy of the representation proposed in Figure 3.4, which assumes determiner-driven tonal association. If the process were one of step-by-step association of the tones of the determiner, then of the head, one would expect neutralization of all tonal oppositions on the head when the determiner carries MH# tone. On the analogy of Figure 3.4, one would expect the behaviour shown in Figure 3.5, i.e. that the tone pattern for 'cat's ear' would be ‡ **hwɤ˧li˧-ɬi˥pi˩**. But the observed tone is H#: /**hwɤ˧li˧-ɬi˧pi˥**/.

Note that the double daggers ‡ added to the labels 'Stage 2', 'Stage 3' and 'Stage 4' in Figure 3.5 aim to emphasize that this representation is only proposed to bring out the *ad hoc* nature of the representation in Figure 3.4: tone association in compounds is not always determiner-driven. The representation in Figure 3.4 nonetheless appears to correspond to a reality, but one that is specific to H# tone. This tone is anchored onto a word's final syllable; in compounding, when the first element of the compound (the determiner) carries H# tone, this tone remains moored onto the final syllable of the first element in the compound.

A few of the combinations in Tables 3.3a–e appear counter-intuitive in terms of the input tones. For instance, a M-tone determiner plus a M-tone monosyllabic head combine to a compound with a floating H tone, #H. This result could go so far as to cast doubt on the correctness of the analysis of the tone category of the two components of the compound as M, since this tone is expected to be inactive (see §2.4.3). However, while a disyllabic determiner with M tone and a monosyllabic head with M tone likewise yield a compound with #H tone, a compound made of a M-tone determiner and a disyllabic M-tone head carries a simple M tone. The analysis of the lexical category as M does not appear mistaken: the unexpected #H output is not the result of a general phonological rule of Na whereby any combination of two M tones would produce a floating H;

Stage 1:
input

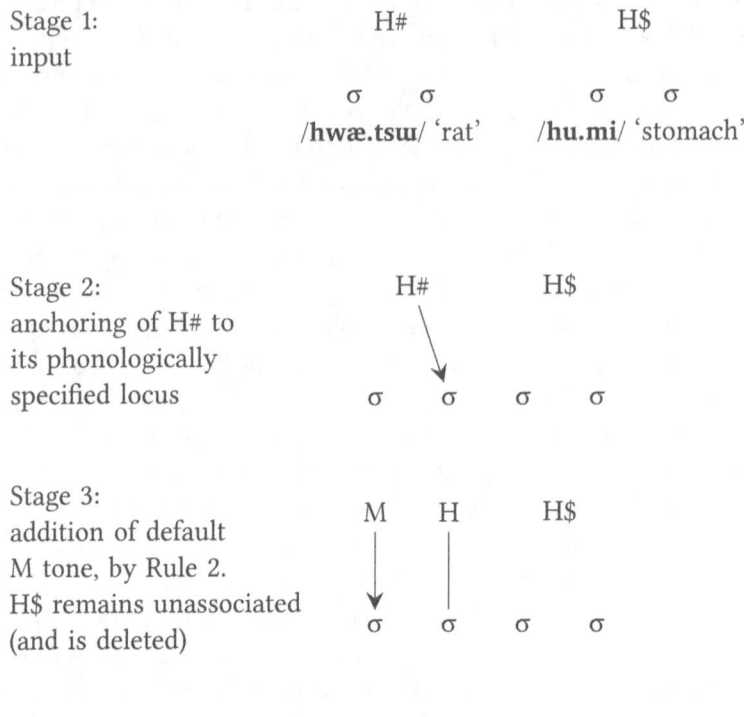

Stage 2:
anchoring of H# to
its phonologically
specified locus

Stage 3:
addition of default
M tone, by Rule 2.
H$ remains unassociated
(and is deleted)

Stage 4:
assignment of L tone
by Rules 4 and 5.

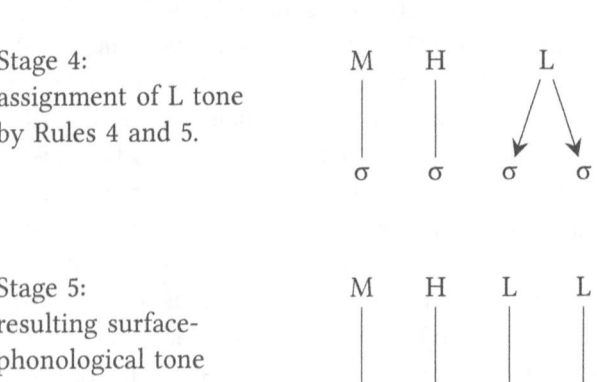

Stage 5:
resulting surface-
phonological tone

Figure 3.4: A hypothesis about how H# tone on the determiner associates to the entire compound. Example: /hwæ˧tsɯ˧-hu˩mi˩/ 'rat's stomach'.

116

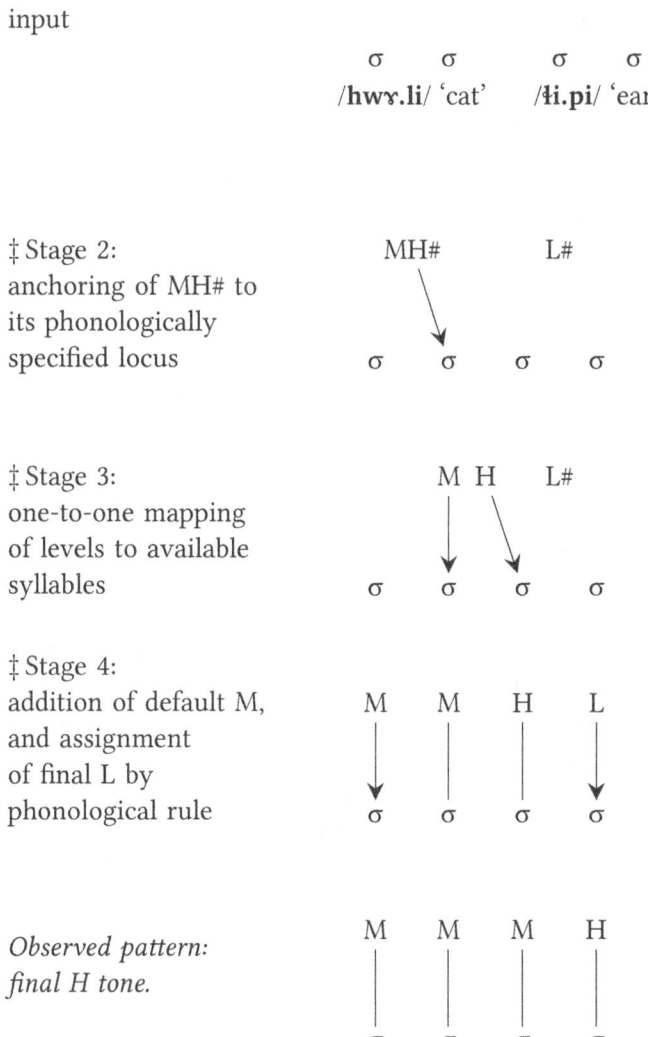

Figure 3.5: Tone-to-syllable association expected for 'cat's ear' under the mistaken hypothesis of determiner-driven tone association: ‡ **hwʁ˦li˦-ɬi˥pi˩**, as contrasted with the observed pattern: /**hwʁ˦li˦-ɬi˦pi˥**/.

117

it results from the *morpho*phonological rules that apply in this specific syntactic construction, and which need to be specified for each combination of input tones (hence their presentation in table form, as Tables 3.3a–e).

The following discussion of the more complex tone patterns is arranged by tone of the determiner.

3.2.1 LM-tone determiners

A LM tone on the determiner results in the assignment of L on the first syllable of the compound, and M on its second syllable, in all cases. A relatively high number of tone sequences are allowed after /L.M/; accordingly, some of the tone categories of the head manifest themselves in full. Over three syllables, one may observe /L.M.L/, /L.M.M/, and /L.M.H/. Over four syllables, ‡ L.M.L.M and ‡ L.M.L.H are ruled out because the sequence /M.L/ can only be followed by /L/, by virtue of Rule 5 ("All syllables following a H.L or M.L sequence receive L tone"). The tones that are compatible with the realization of an initial LM pattern are observed to manifest themselves: LM plus #H, LM plus MH#, LM plus H$ and LM plus H# are realized as such – a concatenation of the two input tones. As expected, a M tone on the head has no effect on the final tone pattern, which is simply LM. Likewise, the combinations LM plus #L and LM plus H# for quadrisyllabic compounds surface as such.

Some of the surface patterns are analytically indeterminate. For instance, the result of the combination of a monosyllabic LM determiner and a monosyllabic MH# head is L.MH (e.g. /boɈ-ɬɣ˦/ 'pig's brains'). This could be analyzed as L–MH#: L on first part, and MH# on second part. Or it could be analyzed as LM+MH#: the LM portion of the pattern yields L on the first syllable and M on the second, and the MH# portion of the pattern expresses itself by the assignment of a MH contour to the last syllable, in this case also the second syllable. Both analyses are equivalent insofar as they generate the same output, but it appears simpler to describe this tone pattern as the concatenation of the two input tones, analyzing it as //LM+MH#//. Under this analysis, the pattern is the same for trisyllabic compounds and quadrisyllabic compounds (σσ+σ and σσ+σσ); the different surface patterns (L.M.MH for σσ+σ, and L.M.M.H for σσ+σσ) result straightforwardly from the general rules of tone-to-syllable mapping summarized in §7.1.

In the case of a disyllabic compound with a LM-tone determiner, a L or LM tone on the head cannot express itself, since the determiner's LM contour has already projected its endpoint (M) on the second syllable. While the M tone can in some respects be considered as default (see §2.4.3), as the endpoint of a LM contour it counts as a fully specified tone. Such cases are not typologically infrequent;

this point will be returned to in the discussion in Chapter 10. In derivational terms, this interpretation of the Yongning Na facts could be phrased as follows: at the point when the tone of the head could come into play, both syllables of the compound are already specified for tone, resulting in the neutralization of LM, M and L as the second components of σ+σ compounds with a LM determiner.

On the other hand, if the compound has three or four syllables, a L or LM tone on the head can express its L tone, resulting in L.M.L on three-syllable compounds, and in L.M.L.L on four-syllable compounds (by virtue of Rule 5: "All syllables following a H.L or M.L sequence receive L tone").

To sum up, the tones of all compounds with a LM determiner obtain through the concatenation of that of their two components, modified by subsequent application of the phonological rules that apply to tone groups (as recapitulated in Chapter 7).

3.2.2 M-tone determiners

After M-tone determiners, the L and LM tones on heads are neutralized due to Rule 5 ("All syllables following a H.L or M.L sequence receive L tone"). Apart from these two, one would expect the tone of the second component of the compound to express itself fully, because M behaves in some respects as a default tone (see §2.4.3) and is expected to be phonologically neutral (inert). This prediction is not entirely realized, however. As mentioned at the outset of this chapter, the tone pattern #H (a floating H tone) that results from the combination of a M-tone determiner with a monosyllabic M-tone head does not conform to the regularities observed for the other combinations. The #H– variant for disyllabic M-tone determiner plus H$-tone head is likewise unexplained. A third unexpected pattern is the –L output of the combination of disyllabic M with monosyllabic MH#, which one would expect to surface as MH#, as is the case in each of the other combinations, i.e. σσ+σσ, σ+σσ, and σ+σ. These three cases confirm an observation made above: some combinations are not simply the product of a set of rules applying throughout the tone system. As a child, F4 (the main consultant for the present study) apparently learnt a great number of tone patterns individually, acquiring morphotonology in a comparable way to children learning the morphology of Rgyalrongic or Kiranti languages, to cite two subgroups of Sino-Tibetan that have flamboyant morphology (Michailovsky 1975; Van Driem 1990; Sun 2000; Jacques 2004). But it may be too late to investigate children's acquisition of Yongning Na morphotonology in the form documented in this volume: in the mid-2010s, school-age children in the Alawa village were exposed to a great deal of Mandarin, and the chances that much morphotonology would be passed down to them seemed small. (The influence of bilingualism with Mandarin constitutes the topic of §9.4.)

3.2.3 L-tone determiners and what they reveal for the analysis of the head noun

The first of the seven phonological tone rules of Yongning Na is that L tone spreads progressively ("left-to-right") onto syllables that are unspecified for tone. The tone patterns of compounds with L-tone determiners provide an interesting testing-ground for determining whether or not the lexical tones which have an initial M tone in their surface form are specified for tone on their first syllable: if they were, that initial M tone would be expected to block L-tone spreading; on the other hand, if that syllable is unspecified for tone, it should receive a L tone through spreading.

The observed patterns lend support to the analysis of the disyllables with High tone (#H, H$, and H#) as unspecified for tone on the first syllable: if the head has one of these tones, a L tone on the determiner spreads onto the first syllable of the head.

The same analysis can be extended to the L# tone, a type of L tone that associates in word-final position. L plus L# yields H#, e.g. /kʰv̩˧mi˩/ 'dog' and /ɬi˧pi˩/ 'ear' yield /kʰv̩˧mi˩-ɬi˩pi˥/ 'dog's ear', where the L tone on the first syllable of the head is analyzed as resulting from L-tone spreading. (More below about the H part in this compound's tone pattern.)

The weight of this argument is admittedly decreased by the fact that the tone patterns after a L-tone determiner cannot be generated through the application of a set of general rules. It is not entirely clear to what extent the processes involving L tone in this particular morphosyntactic context (determinative compounds) relate to the general rule of L-tone spreading. If the determiner is monosyllabic and combines with another monosyllable, all oppositions are neutralized; the compound carries L tone. In the other three length combinations (σσ+σσ, σσ+σ, σ+σσ), the picture is more complex. A floating H tone (#H) on the head is always disregarded, and the result is L. In combination with a M-tone head, the result is L except for σσ+σσ which yields L+H#: a sequence of L tones and a final H (surface phonological tone sequence: L.L.L.H). The presence of a final H is not due to a general rule preventing the L tone from spreading more than one syllable to its right: for instance, the compound //jo˩-gv̩˩dv̩˩// 'sheep's back' (input tones: L and #H) carries a simple L tone, which spreads over the two syllables of the head. (It surfaces as /jo˩-gv̩˩dv̩˥/, with a final rise, due to post-lexical H-tone addition: Rule 7.) A combination of L and L on disyllables also yields a result that is unexpected under the hypothesis that the tones of the determiner and head are simply concatenated: L+#H− (surface form: L.L.H.L).

The behaviour of L-tone determiners in compounds resists phonological generalizations, just like that of M-tone determiners (studied in the previous section: §3.2.2). For instance, in some cases it could seem as if dissimilation were at play. In the example /kʰy˩mi˩-ny˥mi˩/ 'dog's heart', from a L plus L input, there is a H tone on the first syllable of the head. This looks like a case of dissimilation whereby the L tone on the head dissimilates to an initial H tone. But a L plus L input yields a simple L output for words of other lengths (σσ+σ, σ+σ and σ+σσ), clarifying that there is no general (phonological) mechanism of dissimilation between successive L tones. Here again, it appears that the tone combination rules are learnt individually.

3.2.4 H-tone determiners: #H, H# and H$

For the H tones (#H, H# and H$) as for the L tone, there are differences in the tone of the compound depending on the number of syllables of the head noun. Attempts at generating the tones of these compounds from the input tones on the basis of a set of rules were unsuccessful. A general observation can be made nonetheless:

> A floating H (#H) and a tone-group-final H (H$) are never observed to reassociate more than one syllable to their right.

This regularity is specific to determinative compounds. It does not hold in other parts of the morphotonology, witness example (3), where H$ tone moves two syllables away from the word to which it is lexically attached (the family name /la˧tʰa˧mi˥$/ 'Latami').

(3) la˧tʰa˧mi˧=ɻ̍˧ ŋɯ˥
    la˧tʰa˧mi˥$ =ɻ̍   ŋɯ˧
    Latami (family name)   ASSOCIATIVE   A
    'by the Latamis' (Source: field notes.)

In combinations with a monosyllabic head, the #H tone is preserved in six cases out of ten. As this tone attaches at the end of the word that carries it, this amounts to a one-syllable shift to the right from its original position. In combinations with a disyllabic head, the #H tone is never present in the output, as if it could not move more than one syllable away from its original position without changing its nature. Eight of the sixteen combinations have a fixed, word-final H tone instead (H#).

In this light, the H# tone that occurs on H#-plus-H# combinations (with a disyllabic head) is to be interpreted as originating in the H# tone of the head, not of the determiner.

The above generalization also captures the fact that the H$ tone never surfaces on compounds with a disyllabic head. On the other hand, no hypothesis can be proposed as to why it surfaces when the head is a L-tone monosyllable but does not surface in association with any other monosyllabic head. Interestingly, the seven combinations that have two or three variants all involve a H$-tone head noun, pointing to the relatively greater instability of this tone category as compared with the other types of H tones.

Compounds with a #H-tone determiner have the same output tone whether the determiner is monosyllabic or disyllabic. This is taken as a confirmation of the initial hypothesis that the tone category of monosyllables illustrated by /ʐwæ#˥/ 'horse' and the category of disyllables illustrated by /gi˧zɯ#˥/ 'little brother' are phonologically identical. For the sake of typographical simplicity, and in the absence of an opposition among different types of H tones on monosyllabic nouns, 'horse' is transcribed as /ʐwæ˥/ rather than /ʐwæ#˥/, omitting the information on the segmental anchoring of its H tone.

3.2.5 MH-tone determiners

In determinative compounds, MH tone, like other tones containing a H level, is not observed to move more than one syllable to the right. In σσ+σ (that is, when the head is monosyllabic and the determiner disyllabic), a MH tone on the determiner moves onto the last syllable of the compound. In σ+σ, on the other hand, the MH tone does not move as a whole: it appears to remain associated to the determiner, and to project its H level onto the head – except when the head has a #H or MH tone. Again, those are simply piecemeal observations: no set of rules can be proposed to generate the tones of these compounds from the input tones.

3.2.6 Determiners carrying LM+MH# tone or LM+#H tone

The behaviour of LM+MH# and LM+#H when they appear on determiners provides evidence for their phonological analysis. These two lexical categories unfold as L.M over the first two syllables of polysyllabic compounds. This offers support for the analysis of these tones proposed in the previous chapter (§2.4.2):

both contain a LM pattern. If LM+MH# were analyzed as L+MH#, dispensing with the first M in the expression 'LM+MH#', its initial L level would be expected to spread, creating a sequence of Ls, followed by a final MH contour. Likewise, reanalysis of LM+#H as L+#H would not at all be promising, despite the apparent gain in descriptive economy: if this tone's first part were a simple L tone, its behaviour in compounds would be incomprehensible.

Apart from this observation, the interpretation of individual combinations is not straightforward. The cases that seem to make good sense in terms of the input tones do not greatly outnumber those that seem opaque. For instance, LM+MH# followed by a monosyllable with #H or MH yields a pattern comprising a tone-group-final H tone (H$), exactly like a combination of monosyllables with MH on the determiner and #H or MH on the head. But the parallel ends here: if the head is a L-tone monosyllable, a MH-tone determiner yields a final H tone (H#), whereas a LM+MH# determiner yields a tone-group-final H (H$).

3.2.7 About cases of neutralization of tonal oppositions on the head

Four tonal categories of disyllabic head nouns always behave in the same way: the oppositions among LM, LH, LM+#H and LM+MH# are neutralized. This neutralization is not a direct result of the application of the seven phonological tone rules set out in §7.1.1 and listed at several places in this volume (including the 'Quick reference' section). In principle, one could imagine a morphotonological rule whereby L tone on the determiner and LM+MH# on the head would yield L–LM+MH# on the compound, through the simple concatenation of the two tones. Thus, 'sheep's waist' (input tones: L and LM+MH#) would not be /jo˩-ji˥tsæ˩/, but ‡ **jo˩-ji˩tsæ˥**. Such a compound would not violate conditions on well-formedness. What may be the reasons why it is not attested?

As observed at the outset of §3.2, in the simpler cases the tone of the determiner expresses itself first, and after that the tone of the head expresses itself to the extent allowed by the tones already assigned. The four categories LM, LH, LM+#H and LM+MH# all have an initial L tone; in almost all cases, expression of this L tone on the head results in the creation of a /H.L/ or /M.L/ sequence at the juncture between the determiner and the head. Taking the simple example of a M-tone determiner, such as /po˧lo˧/ 'ram', and a LM+MH#-tone head, such as /ji˩**tsæ**˥/ 'waist', tone assignment can be hypothesized to take place as follows:

(i) the M tone of the determiner associates first; this yields M tone on the first two syllables of the compound /po.lo-ji.tsæ/ 'ram's waist', hence /po˧lo˧-**ji.tsæ**/;

(ii) since the tone of the determiner is M, a tone that does not spread, the tone of the head can express itself, by "left-to-right" association of its tone pattern; its first syllable receives L, through association of the first tone level in the LM+MH# pattern, yielding /po˧lo˧-ji˩tsæ/;

(iii) the last syllable receives L tone through application of one of the phonological rules that govern tone association in the Alawa dialect of Yongning Na, namely Rule 5: "All syllables following a H.L or M.L sequence receive L tone". This yields /po˧lo˧-ji˩tsæ˩/.[4]

The situation illustrated by /po˧lo˧-ji˩tsæ˩/ 'ram's waist' is widespread: cases where the tone pattern of the compound can be analyzed as the result of the successive association of the tones of the determiner and the head (with any adjustments required by the phonological tone rules). How come the combination of input tones L and LM+MH# does not follow this general pattern?

Let us hypothesize that, at an earlier historical stage, input L and LM+MH# for a σ+σσ string yielded L.L.MH (phonologically: L+MH#) by successive association of the two input tones. At that stage, supposing that the rest of the system was as it is now, the output L+MH# must have been an outlier. Among the tone patterns of compound nouns with a L-tone determiner, it was the only one that contained anything other than L and H tones, because it was the only combination in which a tone pattern beginning in L could express itself fully on the head without contravening phonological rules. Apart from this one combination, the opposition between LM, LH, LM+#H and LM+MH# tones was always neutralized on compounds' head nouns by application of Rule 5: "All syllables following a H.L or M.L sequence receive L tone". Thus, this combination was the only counterexample to a local pattern of neutralization. It appears possible that speakers modified this unique output (*L+MH#) by analogy with the more common pattern.

In other words, the scenario is at follows. First, an almost complete pattern of neutralization resulted from a phonological rule. The exception was *L+MH#,

---

[4] Another way of thinking of it would be to consider that the lexical tone pattern of the head gets associated in full, yielding ‡ po˧lo˧-ji˩tsæ˧, and that this expression, which does not constitute a well-formed tone sequence due to the presence of a trough in the middle (the L in the M.M.L.MH sequence), is repaired by deletion of the final MH sequence and its replacement by L. Rule 5 could then be rephrased as Rule 5': "All syllables following a H.L or M.L sequence are lowered to L". Rule 5' would apply after association of the entire LM+MH# tone pattern, whereas under the present account, Rule 5 applies as soon as the M.L sequence is created, i.e. as soon as a L tone associates to the syllable /...-ji˩.../. Since both views have the same practical implications, the choice of one or the other can be made freely in view of one's theoretical preferences.

from input L and LM+MH#. Later, neutralization was made exceptionless (in this corner of Yongning Na morphotonology) by a process of analogy: the one and only exception was regularized. This change created greater uniformity in the inventory of tone patterns of compounds, as it resulted in the current pattern of full neutralization of LM, LH, LM+#H and LM+MH# tones on compounds' head nouns. On the other hand, it detracted from the regularity of the correspondences between input tones and output tones, by adding an exception to the pattern of successive association of the tones of the determiner and the head. (The simplicity of the successive-association pattern makes it pleasing to the phonologist, but apparently less so to the speakers of the language: the simplicity of rules is one thing; the simplicity of output forms is another matter.) The new output for the combination of input L and LM+MH# was more similar to the tones of other compounds, but it had to be learnt individually.

This is admittedly a purely speculative scenario. But formulating this kind of hypotheses can be useful in order to see the tone combination rules as a coherent whole, rather than a mere collection of pieces of information. Successive association of the two input tones in compounds may never have been an exceptionless rule at any diachronic stage: on the contrary, cases where the output tone obtains by successive association of the input tones may conceivably have been *fewer* in number at some point in the past than they are now. But it is nonetheless useful to reason in terms of one prototype (in this case: successive association), listing and analyzing the combinations that do not obey this simple pattern, and looking for structural factors that may shed light on these cases. Further progress in this strand of research will require broader dialectal coverage than is available at present. The general topic of the diachronic dynamics of the Yongning Na tone system is taken up in Chapter 9.

3.2.8 A tendency to avoid long-distance movement of tones

It was noted at the outset of this chapter, when discussing compounds of five syllables and more, that there was in Yongning Na a tendency to avoid processes that would result in long-distance movement of tone, namely reassociation of a H tone more than two syllables away from the word to which it is lexically attached. This tendency is confirmed by observations about the tone patterns that result from compounding. A floating H tone (#H) on the determiner plus a M tone on the head yields a final H tone (H#) on the compound, not a floating H tone (#H). A consequence is that the H tone does not move further away, as a floating tone would do. To propose an impressionistic description of the process: the H tone only floats once; at the outcome of the compounding process, its mode of association does not retain any potential for further movement. It appears highly significant that the only σσ+σσ compounds that carry a floating H tone result from an input where the head had this tone in the first place, i.e. cases where the floating H tone does not move in the process of compounding. It seems as if a floating H tone loses its ability to float when it becomes modified by compounding.

Likewise, when the determiner carries H$ or MH#, the H level in the lexical tone tends to remain close to the determiner's last syllable, even though the nature of this H level's anchoring is sometimes modified in compounding (as set out in §3.2.4).

The association of L tone to long stretches of syllables does not constitute a counterexample to the tendency to avoid long-distance movement of tones. This is tone spreading, neutralizing all tonal oppositions on a portion of the tone group; it is not an instance of tonal movement (reassociation of a tone away from the word to which it is lexically attached).

3.2.9 Brief remarks about slips of the tongue

Hesitations, variants, and tonal slips of the tongue can offer insights into the tone system. A full-fledged study of this captivating topic would require more fine-grained tools than have been employed so far. The boundary between an acceptable variant and a commonly occurring mistake is not altogether clear, and the main consultant's judgments sometimes wavered between one and the other. While the greatest care was exercised to verify the data, the initial dichotomy between mistakes and acceptable variants would need to be followed up by specific experiments to ascertain the degree of acceptability of variants along a precise scale. (On the notion of gradient acceptability, see Kirby & Yu 2007; Coetzee & Pater 2008; Goldrick 2011.) An attempt at quantifying and analyzing mistakes is proposed in the discussion of numeral-plus-classifier phrases (§4.1.5); for compounds, only some preliminary remarks can be offered here.

To explore slips of the tongue, it is useful to take into account, for each of the surface phonological tone patterns, (i) the rules from whose application it can result, and (ii) the morphosyntactic constructions in which it is attested. For instance, the L tone category is not attested in any σσ+σ determinative compound (see Table 3.3b), so that cases where a σσ+σ compound is realized erroneously with a L tone cannot be put down to analogy with other σσ+σ compounds. (Examples include the realization of 'dog's brains' as ‡ kʰɣ˩mi˩-ɬɣ˩ instead of /kʰɣ˩mi˩-ɬɣ˥/ in the recording DetermCompounds12.) It may be relevant here that σ+σσ compounds with the same tonal input yield a L tone (see Table 3.3c):

the slip of the tongue may be an example of interference between the tone rules that apply on compounds with different syllabic patterns. But the erroneous pattern could also result from the mistaken application of a phonological rule of tone spreading, Rule 1: "L tone spreads progressively onto syllables that are unspecified for tone" (see §7.1.1). In that case, the mistake would consist in pairing the words together with a solely phonological adjustment instead of a morphophonological one.

Tonal slips of the tongue ("slips of the larynx"?) in the recorded Na data could also be adduced to argue that there is a special closeness between certain pairs (or subsets) of tonal categories. The M tone category seems more liable to confusions with #H than with other tones. For instance, errors involving /la˧/ 'tiger' consist in the substitution of the tone pattern expected for a #H-tone word: ‡ la˧-ɬv˩ 'tiger's brains', instead of /la˧-ɬv˧/, and ‡ la˧-hu˩mi˩ 'tiger's stomach', instead of /la˧-hu˧mi˩$/. (There are two instances of both of these mistakes; the recordings are: DetermCompounds6 and DetermCompounds7.) There are also instances of substitutions among H$, MH# and H#, e.g. ‡ hwɤ˧li˧-sʁ˩ instead of /hwɤ˧li˧-sʁ˧/ for 'cat's blood', and ‡ hwɤ˧li˧-ɬv˧ instead of /hwɤ˧li˧-ɬv˩/ for 'cat's brains'. Finally, the speaker sometimes gets confused between the LM+H# and LM+MH# tones.

3.2.10 Perspectives for comparison across speakers

The entire data set discussed here was provided by the consultant of reference, F4. Data was also elicited from three other speakers: F5, who is F4's daughter-in-law; M21, a relative of F4, belonging to the same generation; and M23, who is M21's son. All three are less proficient speakers than F4, due to long stays away from Yongning in the case of M21, and to a generation gap in the case of F5 and M23, both proficient speakers of Southwestern Mandarin.

Unsurprisingly, some cross-speaker differences are observed. Analysis of this data is crucial to understanding the dynamics of the tone system. Some of the differences reflect the fact that the nouns at issue belong in different categories in the speech of the other consultants. For instance, 'flea' is /kv˧ʂe˩$/ in F4's speech (LH tone), whereas in M21's speech it is /kv˧ʂe#˧/ (#H tone). Likewise, 'boar' is /bo˩ɬa˧/ in F4's speech (LH tone), whereas in M21's speech it fluctuates between /bo˩ɬa˧/ and /bo˩ɬa˧/ (LM+MH# tone). The difference in tones for 'boar's nose' between the two speakers – /bo˩ɬa˧-ɲi˩gɤ˩/ for F4 (tone: LH), and /bo˩ɬa˧ɲi˧gɤ#˧/ (tone: LM+#H) for M21 – is interpreted not to have originated in a difference in the rules that determine the tonal output for compounds, but in a difference in input tones. Both compounds follow the regularities summarized in Tables 3.3a–e, but the input combination is different.

This situation requires a full checkup of each consultant's tone system and lexicon as a preliminary to the selection of compound nouns for elicitation. On this basis, cross-speaker differences in the tone rules can be brought out.

To begin with a comparison within close age groups, Table 3.4 presents two differences between F4 and M21.

Table 3.4: Differences between speakers F4 and M21 in the tones of compounds.

input tones	output tones, with example compounds		
	F4	M21	meaning
M+M (σ+σ)	#H	L#	
	la˧-bv̩#˥	la˧-bv̩˩	tiger's intestine
#H+H$ (σσ+σσ)	H#, H$, or #H–	–L	
	ʐwæ˧zo˧-hu˧mi˥	ʐwæ˧zo˧-hu˩mi˩	colt's stomach

The output that is obtained when combining two M tones over monosyllables is different for the two speakers, and this output is odd in both cases: why not use a simple concatenation of the input tones, yielding M tone for the compound, as happens for the other M+M compounds (σσ+σσ, σσ+σ and σ+σσ)? For both F4 and M21, the output differs from what would be expected as default. The combination of input #H and H$ over disyllables (σσ+σσ) is also different for the two speakers, who both refused the other's variant when I tried it on them.

An interesting characteristic of these different patterns is that they nonetheless have a family resemblance: M21's patterns are not that different from F4's. M21 has –L tone on the phrase 'colt's stomach' (σσ+σσ); this same –L tone is found in F4's data, when monosyllabic input nouns with these tones are combined into a compound (σ+σ). Such observations suggest that subtle processes may be at play, whereby individuals bound by social ties tend towards a degree of convergence. One could speculate that, in cases where speakers wish to promote a feeling of community, for instance in relaxed discussions with a relative, they tend to accommodate to their interlocutor's tone patterns, occasionally adopting new patterns so as to emphasize linguistic common ground over differences. Since one and the same surface tone pattern is open to several phonological interpretations (e.g. /M.M/ may be the realization of underlying //M// or //#H//), this process of accommodation can result in a proliferation of divergent variant forms from one speaker to another. Speakers' adoption of tone patterns from their customary interlocutors could thus explain the extent of the observed pool of morphotonological variation. By a related process, speakers may tend to select from within this pool of variation those patterns that they feel will be most accessible to their addressee: avoiding, among possible variants, those that are felt to be most sharply at variance with the addressee's linguistic habits. Conversely, self-assertive speakers who want to distance themselves from the addressee could favour linguistic patterns that they feel are most different from those used by the addressee: this would be a possible path whereby a variant acquires prominence and eventually comes to be generalized by that speaker.

To test these hypotheses, one could examine dialogues, for instance comparing F4's tone patterns in conversations with different family members – whose tone patterns will need to be described with the greatest possible precision. This is a perspective for future research; it holds promise of bringing out mechanisms that play a key role in the evolution of the tone system, thereby shedding light on the system's synchronic outlook.

3.2.11 Exceptional items

Some compounds possess lexical tones that differ from those that would be expected on the basis of their constituting elements. The irregularity can be due to the determiner, as in the first four lines of Table 3.5, or to the head, as in its last line. These examples are discussed one by one below.

3.2.11.1 The noun 'Naxi'

The noun 'Naxi' (/naˍhĩ#˦/, tone: LM+#H) yields irregular results in two quadrisyllabic compounds (see the recording DetermCompounds16):

(i) with MH# tone: /naˍhĩ˧-kʰɯ˧dʑi˩/ 'Naxi leggings'. The regular tone pattern would be †naˍhĩ˧-kʰɯ˧dʑi˦ (underlying tone: LM+MH#–); however, this pattern is not acceptable. The observed tone is LM+#H–. An example of the regular tone pattern is /naˍhĩ˧-ŋwɤ˧pʰæ˦/ 'Naxi tile'.

(ii) with L tone: /naˍhĩ˧-ba˧la˦/ 'Naxi clothes'. The regular tone pattern would be †naˍhĩ˧-ba˦la˩ (underlying tone: LM+#H–, which can also be described as LM+MH#–), but it is not acceptable. The observed tone is LM+H#. An example of the regular tone pattern is /naˍhĩ˧-ʂɯ˧tʰi˩/ 'Naxi knife'.

'Naxi' has a special status in Yongning Na. On the one hand, it refers to an ethnic group perceived as distinct from the Na: the Naxi of the Lijiang plain, some

Table 3.5: Compounds whose tones differ from those that would result from the application of the synchronic tone rules.

observed compounds	tone pattern	expected pattern	irregular word	meaning	tone
nɑɭhĩ˩-kʰɯ˧dʑi˩ 'Naxi leggings'; **nɑɭhĩ˩-bɑ˧lɑ˥** 'Naxi clothes'	LM+#H−; LM+H#−	LM+MH#−; LM+#H−	**nɑɭhĩ#˥**	Naxi	LM+#H
ɲi˧gʶ˩-dʑɯ˥ 'mucus'	MH#	#H	ɲi˧gʶ#˥	nose	#H
mv˧-ʁo˥ 'sky'	H#	#H	mv˥	sky	#H
ji˧bv˥ 'cows' stable'	MH#	#H	ji˥	ox	#H
lv˧imi˧-tsɑ˩bʶ˧ 'fine sand'; qʰɑ˧dze˧-tsɑ˩bʶ˧ 'sweetcorn flour'; dze˧ɭɯ˧-tsɑ˩bʶ˧ 'wheat flour'	−L	M	**tsɑ˩bʶ˧**	powder	M

130

of whom settled in Yongning since the early 20th century but still retain their distinct costumes and language (on the cultural divide between the Naxi and Na, see Appendix B, in particular the end of §B.3.4). On the other hand, it is made up of the endonym of the Na, compounded with the word for 'person, human being', so that its independence from 'Na' is problematic. The exceptional treatment of this noun may have to do with the perceived necessity of handling the term in such a way as to attempt to avoid its perception as a compound meaning 'Na person'.

3.2.11.2 The nouns 'nose' and 'hair'

'Nasal mucus' is /ɲi˧gʌ˧-dʐɯ˩/ (tone: MH#); on the basis of the input nouns, /ɲi˧gʌ#˩/ 'nose' and /dʐɯ˩/ 'water', the expected tone would be #H (/†ɲi˧gʌ-dʐɯ#˩/). 'Hair (on the head)', /ʁo˧hỹ˩/, has the same tone (MH#); for this word, too, the expected tone would be #H: /†ʁo˧hỹ#˩/ (the input nouns both have H tone: /ʁo˩/ 'head; top' and /hỹ˩/ 'hair').

The etymology of these two words is self-evident. On the other hand, mucus is not just a kind of water ('nose-water'). The difference between hair on the head and on the body may seem smaller, but many languages have different roots for the two, e.g. French and Lao (Enfield 2006: 187-188). In Na, the compounds referring to 'hair (on the head)' and 'body hair' are lexicalized compounds ('body hair' is /ʐi˧hṽ#˩/, literally 'ape hair'). The irregular tone patterns of these two words may reflect an early lexicalization. The discrepancy between the tones of these items and the output of the currently productive tone rules for compounds may be due to different tone rules that applied at the time when these compounds were created. Or they may result from an evolution of the compounds away from the regular tone pattern, triggered by the perception of their status as lexical units rather than compounds. This second possibility might sound less plausible than the first, but item-by-item tone change accompanying lexicalization is a salient characteristic of the tone system of Laze, a language closely related to Na,[5] so this possibility should not be lightly dismissed.

---

[5] There are four lexical tones for Laze monosyllables (for predicates: H, M, L and MH; for nouns: H, M, L and a floating H tone); in theory, this could yield as many as sixteen tone patterns over disyllables, but only seven are observed. Tone changes occur as lexicalization takes place. Numerous combinations of two input tones other than H yield H+H. For instance, 'dog' is /kʰɯ˧/, and 'to beat' is /dɯ˩/. Their combination should yield M.L, but it comes out as H.H. This is a key process in the lexical integration of disyllables in Laze (Michaud 2008a; 2009; Michaud & Jacques 2012).

3.2.11.3 The noun 'flour, powder'

The word for 'powder, flour' is /tsa˧bɤ˧/, with M tone. According to the synchronically productive rules, the combination of this word with /lv̩˧mi˧/ 'stone', /qʰa˧dze˧/ 'sweetcorn' and /dze˧ɭɯ˧/ 'wheat' should yield a simple M-tone output, e.g. †lv̩˧mi˧-tsa˧bɤ˧ for 'fine sand'. But the observed forms, shown in Table 3.6, all carry a M.M.L.L tone pattern, corresponding to underlying −L (a L tone on the second part of the compound).

Table 3.6: Irregular compounds with /tsa˧bɤ˧/ 'flour, powder'.

determiner	compound with /tsa˧bɤ˧/ 'flour, powder' as head noun		
	expected tone: M	attested tone: −L	meaning
/lv̩˧mi˧/ 'stone'	†lv̩˧mi˧-tsa˧bɤ˧	lv̩˧mi˧-tsa˩bɤ˩	fine sand
/qʰa˧dze˧/ 'sweetcorn'	†qʰa˧dze˧-tsa˧bɤ˧	qʰa˧dze˧-tsa˩bɤ˩	sweetcorn flour
/dze˧ɭɯ˧/ 'wheat'	†dze˧ɭɯ˧-tsa˧bɤ˧	dze˧ɭɯ˧-tsa˩bɤ˩	wheat flour

The principle applied in the present study is that two lexical items of like phonological structure whose tones differ in at least one morphosyntactic context need to be recognized as belonging to different lexical tone categories. Mechanical application of this principle would lead to recognition of /tsa˧bɤ˧/ 'flour, powder' as the sole example of an umpteenth (twelfth) tonal category of disyllabic nouns. But it makes much more sense to try to explain the irregular behaviour of the compounds in Table 3.6 by other factors.

The word /tsa˧bɤ˧/ is a Tibetan loanword (from *rtsam pa* 'roasted flour'). The lowering of the tones on the latter part of the compounds in Table 3.6 echoes observations about a larger set of words of Tibetan origin: given names. These compounds will be referred to for short as 'Tibetan compounds'; this topic will be taken up in the analysis of proper names in §3.3.3.

3.2.11.4 The noun 'sky'

The disyllabic form of the noun 'sky' is /mv̩˧ʁo˩$/. The monosyllabic root for 'sky' is /mv̩˩/; if the second syllable were /ʁo˩/ 'head; top', one would expect the compound to have #H tone (on the basis of the regularities set out in Tables 3.2a–e). But the second syllable could also be the postposition 'on' – itself likely to be grammaticalized from 'head'. This postposition is not in common use anymore (the common form is //**bi˩**// 'on; at': see §5.4.1); this is an obstacle to establishing its lexical tone and studying its combinatory properties.

3.3 Coordinative compounds

3.3.1 The main facts

In the closely related language Naxi, the tones of coordinative compounds are simply the concatenation of those of their constituents, e.g. /ɲi˧ny˩-jæ˧kæ˩zɯ˧/ 'wife and husband' from /ɲi˧ny˩/ 'wife' and /jæ˧kæ˩zɯ˧/ 'husband'.[6] In Yongning Na, on the other hand, coordinative compounds are tonally active, to an extent comparable with determinative compounds.

Coordinative compounds are less common than determinative compounds, however, and less easy to elicit systematically. Syntactically, coordinative constructions can be applied to any pair of nouns. This is exemplified by the names of public houses in English. Combinations like "Fox and Hounds" or "Dog and Duck" refer to hunting traditions; others, such as "Bear and Ragged Staff", refer to heraldry. Once the pattern is established, new coordinative combinations can be created at will, such as the humorous "Snail and Salad", where the relationship between the two terms – and their relationship to the food served in the pub – is offered to the customer's fancy. In Yongning Na, any two nouns can be coordinated by means of the conjunction /lɑ˧/ 'and', but coordinative compound nouns are not as easy to coin: the two nouns must refer to entities that are commonly paired together.

Three sources were found: pairs of animal names of the two sexes, and their offspring, such as 'ewe and ram', 'ram and ewe', 'ewe and lamb', and 'ram and lamb'; pairs of kinship terms, such as 'uncle and nephew' and 'mother and daughter'; and successive numerals followed by the same classifier, such as 'two or three years', 'five or six months' or 'four or five days'. A broad sample of the first two sets can be found in the online recording CoordCompounds; the third set is found in CoordCompounds2. The consultant (F4) preferred to remain within the bounds of common sense, and non-matching pairs such as 'mother and nephew'

---

[6] This tonally inert compound is of little phonological interest; on the other hand, it has some ethnolinguistic interest. As the Naxi of Lijiang like to point out, this compound places the wife in front of the husband, in contradiction of Confucian principles.

or 'grandmother and brother' were avoided. The data is set out in Tables 3.7a-3.7i. As elsewhere, a slash separates variants. Some tone patterns that were proposed by the investigator and refused by the consultant are indicated, with a double dagger ‡, in the output column: for instance, in view of the existence of two variants for the combination /zv̩˩ɬi˩-ŋwʁ˩ɬi/ ≈ /zv̩˩ɬi˩-ŋwʁ˥ɬi˩/ 'four or five months', whose input nouns both have L tone, it was attempted to apply the L tone pattern of the variant /zv̩˩ɬi˩-ŋwʁ˩ɬi/ to other combinations of two L-tone nouns, such as 'nephews and nieces', /ze˩v̩˩-ze˩mi˩/. The fact that the L variant is not possible for these expressions (‡ ze˩v̩˩-ze˩mi/) is indicated through the mention '(‡ L)' in the output column.

Three suffixes appear repeatedly in the table: the female/augmentative suffix /-mi˩/, the male suffix /-pʰv̩˥/, and the child/male/diminutive suffixe /-zo˥/. These suffixes are discussed in more detail in §5.1.

Most examples are quadrisyllabic, from two input disyllables (σσ+σσ). The two disyllabic examples (σ+σ) at the top of Table 3.7a are written without a hyphen, on the basis of the intuition that they are more strongly integrated than the others. Trisyllabic examples are of the structure *disyllable plus monosyllable* (σσ +σ), showing a preference for coordinative compounds where the first term has at least as many syllables as the second. Hexasyllabic compounds can be created, e.g. /ŋwʁ˩-ɬi˩mi˩-qʰv̩˥-ɬi˩mi˩/ (Dog2.64) 'the fifth and sixth months'.

Table 3.7a: Coordinative compounds of fewer than four syllables, arranged by input tones.

compound	meaning	input	output
mv̩˧di˥	universe ('sky'+'earth')	H and LM	MH#
zo˧mv̩˥	child ('son'+'daughter')	H and LH	H#
ə˧mi˧-mv̩˩	mother and daughter	M and LH	−L
ə˧mi˧-zo#˥	mother and son	M and H	#H
ə˧dɑ˧-mv̩˥	father and daughter	H$ and LH	H#
ə˧dɑ˧-zo#˥	father and son	H$ and H	#H

Table 3.7b: Quadrisyllabic compounds with M as the first input tone.

compound	meaning	input	output
ə˧pʰv̩˧-zv̩˧v̩#˥	great-uncle and great-nephews	M and M	#H
ə˧pʰv̩˧-zv̩˧mi#˥	great-uncle and great-nieces		
ə˧si˧-ə˧pʰv̩#˥	3ʳᵈ-generation ancestors		
ə˧si˧-zv̩˧mi#˥	(great-)grandmother and granddaughters		
ə˧si˧-zv̩˧v̩#˥	great-grandmother and grandsons		
gv̩˧dv̩˧-gv̩˧mi˧	(human) body	M and M	M
jo˧mi˧-po˧ɬo˧	ewe and ram		
dʐwæ˧mi˧-dʐwæ˧pʰv̩˧	male and female sparrow		
ɖɯ˧ɬi˧-ɲi˧ɬi˧	one or two months		
ɲi˧ɬi˧-so˧ɬi˩	two or three months	M and M	−L
bæ˧mi˧-bæ˧pʰv̩#˥	female and male duck	M and #H	#H
bæ˧mi˧-bæ˧zo#˥	female duck and duckling		
bv̩˧mi˧-bv̩˧zo#˥	female yak and yak calf		
ʂɯ˧ɬi˧-hõ˧ɬi#˥	seven or eight months	M and H$	#H
ə˧mi˧-ze˩mi˩	aunt and niece	M and L	−L
ə˧mi˧-ze˩v̩˩	aunt and nephew		
bv̩˧mi˧-bv̩˩ʂwæ˩	female and male yak		
dzo˧mi˧-dzo˩pʰv̩˩	female and male lizard		
so˧ɬi˧-zv̩˩ɬi˩	three or four months		

Table 3.7c: Quadrisyllabic compounds with #H as the first input tone.

compound	meaning	input	output
gi˧zɯ˧-go˧mi#˥ bæ˧zo˧-bæ˧mi#˥ bæ˧pʰv˧-bæ˧mi#˥	little brothers and sisters duckling and female duck male duck and female duck	#H and M	#H
tsʰɯ˧zo˧-to˧qa˥	kids and little nanny goats	#H and M	H#
ʐv˧v˥-ʐv˩mi˩	grandchildren	#H and #H	H#–
hwɤ˧pʰv˧- hwɤ˧zo#˥ / hwɤ˧pʰv˧-hwɤ˥zo˩	tom-cat and kitten	#H and #H	#H / #H–
ho˧mi˧-ho˧pʰv#˥ / ho˧mi˧-ho˥pʰv˩	female and male pheasant		
dʑi˧mi˧-dʑi˧zo#˥ / dʑi˧mi˧-dʑi˥zo˩	female and baby buffalo		
dʑi˧zo˧-dʑi˧mi#˥ / dʑi˧zo˧-dʑi˥mi˩	baby and female buffalo		
lɑ˧mi˧-lɑ˧pʰv#˥ / lɑ˧mi˧-lɑ˥pʰv˩	female and male tiger		
lɑ˧mi˧-lɑ˧zo#˥ / lɑ˧mi˧-lɑ˥zo˩	female and baby tiger		
ʐv˧ɲi˧-ŋwɤ˧ɲi#˥ / ʐv˧ɲi˧-ŋwɤ˥ɲi˩	four or five days		
ʁv˧pʰv˧-ʁv˧mi#˥	male and female crane	#H and MH	#H
hwɤ˧pʰv˧-hwɤ˧mi˥ hwɤ˧zo˧-hwɤ˧mi˥	tom-cat and she-cat cats: kitten and parents	#H and H$	H#
ŋwɤ˧ɲi˧-qʰv˩ɲi˩ ʂɯ˧ɲi˧-hõ˩ɲi˩	five or six days seven or eight days	#H and H$	–L
ʐwæ˧zo˧-ʐwæ˥mi˩ / ʐwæ˧zo˧-ʐwæ˧mi˥	colt and mare	#H and L	#H– / H#
pʰɤ˧pʰv˧-pʰɤ˥mi˩ / pʰɤ˧pʰv˧-pʰɤ˧mi˥	male and female hyena		
gv˧ɲi˧-tsʰe˩ɲi˩ / gv˩ɲi˩-tsʰe˩ɲi˥	nine or ten days	#H and L	–L / L+H#
kʰv˧zo˥-kʰv˩mv˩ / kʰv˧zo˧-kʰv˧mv˥	male and female puppies	#H and H#	H#– / H#

136

Table 3.7d: Quadrisyllabic compounds with MH# as the first input tone.

compound	meaning	input	output
ə˧zi˧-ə˧pʰy˥	elders, grandparents	MH# and M	MH#
æ˧my˧-go˧mi˥	sisters, female siblings	MH# and M	H#
ə˧zi˧-zv̩˥ly˩	grandmother and grandsons	MH# and #H	#H–
ə˧zi˧-zv̩˥mi˩	grandmother and granddaughter		
æ˧my˧-gi˥zɯ˩	brethren, brothers		
ɖɯ˧kʰv̩˧-ɲi˥kʰv̩˩	one or two years	MH# and MH#	MH#–
ə˧v˧-ze˥v˩	uncle and nephew	MH# and L	MH#–
ə˧v˧-ze˥mi˩	uncle and niece		
zo˧hỹ˧-my˥zo˩	descendants		
ɲi˧kʰv̩˧-so˧kʰv̩˥ (‡ ɲi˧kʰv̩˧-so˥kʰv̩˩)	two or three years	MH# and L	H#
ʂɯ˧kʰv̩˧-hõ˥kʰv̩˩ / ʂɯ˧kʰv̩˧-hõ˧kʰv̩˥	seven or eight years	MH# and H#	MH#– / H#

Table 3.7e: Quadrisyllabic compounds with H$ as the first input tone.

compound	meaning	input	output
tsʰɯ˧mi˧-po˧lo˥	nanny goat and billy goat	H$ and M	H#
ə˧dɑ˧-ə˧mi#˥	father and mother, parents	H$ and M	#H
qʰʏ˧ɬi˥-ʂɯ˩ɬi˩	six or seven months	H$ and M	H#–
ə˧ɲi˧tsʰi˧ɲi#˥ ə˧ji˧-tsʰi˧ji#˥ tsʰæ˧mi˧-tsʰæ˧zo#˥	these days these years doe and stag	H$ and #H	#H
hwɤ˧mi˧-hwɤ˧zo#˥ / hwɤ˧mi˧-hwɤ˧zo˥$	she-cat and kitten	H$ and #H	#H / H$
hwɤ˧mi˧-hwɤ˥pʰʏ˩ / hwɤ˧mi˧- hwɤ˧pʰʏ#˥ / hwɤ˧mi˧-hwɤ˧pʰʏ˥$	she-cat and tom-cat	H$ and #H	#H– / #H / H$
qʰʏ˧ɲi˥-ʂɯ˩ɲi˩ / qʰʏ˧ɲi˧-ʂɯ˥ɲi˩ / qʰʏ˧ɲi˧-ʂɯ˧ɲi#˥ (‡ qʰʏ˧ɲi˧-ʂɯ˧ɲi˥$) hõ˧ɲi˥-gʏ˩ɲi˩ / hõ˧ɲi˧-gʏ˥ɲi˩ / hõ˧ɲi˧-gʏ˧ɲi#˥ (‡ hõ˧ɲi˧-gʏ˧ɲi˥$)	six or seven days eight or nine days	H$ and #H	H#– / #H– / #H
ɲi˧ɲi˧-so˧ɲi˥ (‡ ɲi˧ɲi˥-so˩ɲi˩)	two or three days	H$ and MH#	H#
dɯ˧ɲi˧-dɯ˥hɑ̃˩ (‡ dɯ˧ɲi˧-dɯ˧hɑ̃˥)	one day and one night		#H–
tsʰæ˧mi˧-tsʰæ˧zo#˥ dɯ˧ɲi˧-ɲi˧ɲi#˥	doe and fawn one or two days	H$ and H$	#H
hõ˧ɬi˥-gʏ˩ɬi˩ ɲi˧ɲi˥	-so˩ɲi˩	eight or nine months two or three days	H$ and L	H#–
ə˧ji˧-ʂɯ˥ji˩	in the past	H$ and LM+#H	#H–

138

Table 3.7f: Quadrisyllabic compounds with L as the first input tone.

compound	meaning	input	output
bv̩˩ʂwæ˩-bv̩˥mi˩ / bv̩˩ʂwæ˩-bv̩˩mi˩	male yak and female yak	L and M	L / L+#H−
kʁ˩pʰv̩˩-kʁ˩mi˥ / kʁ˩pʰv̩˩-kʁ˥mi˩	male and female falcon		
dzo˩pʰv̩˩-dzo˩mi˩ / dzo˩pʰv̩˩-dzo˥mi˩	male and female lizards		
mv̩˩zo˩-ə˥mi˩ / mv̩˩zo˩-ə˩mi˥	young woman and (her) mother	L and M	L+#H− / L+H#
gv̩˩ɬi˩-tsʰe˥ɬi˩ / gv̩˩ɬi˩-tsʰe˩ɬi˥	nine or ten months		
mv̩˩zɯ˩-ni˥mi˩	brothers and sisters	L and #H	L+#H−
ʐwæ˩mi˩-ʐwæ˩zo˩	mare and colt	L and #H	L
so˩ɲi˩-ʐv̩˩ɲi˩	three or four days		
ŋwʁ˩ɬi˩-qʰv̩˥ɬi˩	five or six months	L and H$	#H−
ji˩mi˩-ʐʁ˥qo˩	cow and calf	L and L	L+#H− (‡ L)
ze˩v̩˩-ze˥mi˩	nephews and nieces		
ji˩bv̩˩-ji˥mi˩	bull and cow		
pʁ˩mi˩-pʁ˥pʰv̩˩	female and male frog		
pʰʁ˩mi˩-pʰʁ˥zo˩	female hyena and hyena pup		
ʐv̩˩ɬi˩-ŋwʁ˩ɬi/ / ʐv̩˩ɬi˩-ŋwʁ˥ɬi˩	four or five months	L and L	L / L+#H−
so˩kʰv̩˩-ʐv̩˩kʰv̩˥	three or four years	L and L#	L+H#

Table 3.7g: Quadrisyllabic compounds with L# as the first input tone.

compound	meaning	input	output
ʐwæ˧sɯ˩-ʐwæ˩zo˩	stallion and colt	L# and #H	L#–
ʐwæ˧sɯ˩-ʐwæ˩mi˩	stallion and mare	L# and L	L#–
gv˧kʰv˩-tsʰe˩kʰv˩	nine or ten years		
ʐv˧kʰv˩-ŋwɤ˩kʰv˩	four or five years	L# and L#	L#–
ŋwɤ˧kʰv˩-qʰv˩kʰv˩	five or six years	L# and H#	L#–

Table 3.7h: Quadrisyllabic compounds with LM as the first input tone.

compound	meaning	input	output
a˩ʁo˧-ʑi˧dv˧	the household	LM and M	LM–
pv˩tsɯ˧-pv˧mi˩	small and large combs	LM+MH# and L	LM+MH#–
pɤ˩tɕi˧-pɤ˧mi˩	tadpole		
æ˩mi˧-æ˧ʂwæ˥	hen and cock	LM and H#	LM+H#
æ˩mi˧-æ˧tsɯ˥	hen and chicks		
bo˩mi˧-bæ˧bv˥	sow and piglets		
ʐæ˩pʰv˧-ʐæ˩mi˩	male and female leopard	LM and LM+#H	LM–L
dv˩mi˧-dv˥pʰv˩	female and male weasels	LM+#H and LM	LM+#H–
a˩mi˧-a˥pʰv˩	female and male goose	LM+#H and LM	LM+#H–
ɖɯ˩zo˧-ɖɯ˥mi˩	female and male mule	+#H	

Table 3.7i: Compounds of four to six syllables with H# as the first input tone.

compound	meaning	input	output
qʰv˧kʰv˥-ʂɯ˩kʰv˩	six or seven years	H# and MH#	H#–
hõ˧kʰv˥-gv˩kʰv˩	eight or nine years	H# and L#	H#–
æ˧ʂwæ˥-æ˩mi˩	cock and hen	H# and LM	H#–
ŋwɤ˧ɬi˩mi˩-qʰv˩ɬi˩mi˩	the fifth and sixth months		

140

3.3.2 Discussion: Tonal variability and lexical diversity

The existence of variants was already observed for some determinative compounds (see Tables 3.3a–e), but the overall proportion of combinations that have variants is low: 7 combinations out of 257, all of which have H$ tone on the head noun. For coordinative compounds, on the other hand, less regularity is observed. There are not only tonal variants, but compounds with identical input tones and different outputs. Among quadrisyllabic compounds, two different outputs (on different examples) are found for no fewer than six tonal combinations: those with input tones M and M, #H and M, MH# and M, H$ and M, H$ and #H, and L and #H. A seventh combination, #H and #H, even has three different outputs. For quadrisyllabic compounds, the proportion of tone combinations with two or three different outputs is about one out of four.

The general picture is thus one of great tonal diversity. But coordinative compounds are not simply characterized by a general looseness of their tone patterns, whereby two or three tonal variants would be acceptable for any combination of input tones. In cases where the same tonal input yields different tones in different coordinative compounds, it was attempted to substitute one for the other. For instance, input H$ and M nouns yield a compound with #H tone in the case of 'little brothers and little sisters', //gi˧zuɯ˧-go˧mi#˥//, but a compound with H# tone in the case of 'kids and little nanny goats', //tsʰuɯ˧zo˧-to˧qa˥//; it was therefore attempted to substitute tones #H and H# for each other on coordinative compounds. These attempted variants were rejected by the consultant, as shown in Table 3.8. Clearly, each coordinative compound comes to carry a habitual tone pattern to the exclusion of others. Cross-speaker comparison (within the family, then extending the comparison to other micro-dialects) will be necessary to explore the paths of development of idiosyncratic preferences.

Table 3.8: Attempted tonal variants for coordinative compounds.

meaning	input tones	attested form		attempted variant	
little brothers and little sisters	H$ and M	gi˧zuɯ˧-go˧mi#˥	#H	‡ gi˧zuɯ˧-go˧mi˥	H#
father and mother	H$ and M	ə˧da˧-ə˧mi#˥	#H	‡ ə˧da˧-ə˧mi˥	H#
kids and little nanny goats	H$ and M	tsʰuɯ˧zo˧-to˧qa˥	H#	‡ tsʰuɯ˧zo˧-to˧qa#˥	#H
nanny goat and billy goat	H$ and M	tsʰuɯ˧mi˧-po˧lo˥	H#	‡ tsʰuɯ˧mi˧-po˧lo#˥	#H
ancestors	MH# and M	ə˧zi˧-ə˧pʰy˦	MH#	‡ ə˧zi˧-ə˧pʰy˥	H#
sisters	MH# and M	æ˧my˧-go˧mi˥	H#	‡ æ˧my˧-go˧mi˦	MH#

The diversity of tone patterns relates in subtle ways to the semantic diversity of coordinative compounds. Importantly, it is not always possible to arrive at the meaning of coordinative compounds simply on the basis of their two constituents. For instance, /hwɤ˧zo˧-hwɤ˧mi˩/, made up of 'kitten' and 'she-cat', does not mean 'kitten and she-cat' (the child and the mother), but refers to cats in general, as a species. The terms for male and female puppies, /kʰv˧zo#˩/ and /kʰv˧mv#˩/ respectively, have come to be used as names for human newborns: an unlovely name is purposely chosen to repel demons who may be lurking around to take their lives.[7] The real name is only given after a couple of months, or sometimes as late as one full year after birth. The two terms /kʰv˧zo#˩/ and /kʰv˧mv#˩/, and their compound /kʰv˧zo˧-kʰv˩mv˩/, have become culturally specialized and have ceased to be used to refer to real puppies. There is thus a broad range of situations, from elicited combinations which the consultant may never have conceptualized before (such as 'male and female jackal') to highly lexicalized expressions. This sheds indirect light on the observed tonal diversity. However, the overall number of examples is too small to determine with confidence which outputs are currently productive. The logical next step to investigate this issue would be to test the degree of lexicalization of the various compounds.

The tone patterns observed to date are summarized in Tables 3.9a and 3.9b. When two different (and mutually exclusive) patterns are observed over different compounds, these patterns are separated by a semi-colon. In cases of free variation (over the same compound), the patterns are separated by a slash. In order to save space, tone categories for which there are no examples are simply omitted from the table.

Table 3.9a: The tones of coordinative compounds with monosyllabic second noun. A question mark indicates that no example was found.

type of 1st noun	tone of 1st noun	tone of 2nd noun		
		LM	L	#H
monosyllables	#H	MH#	H#	?
disyllables	M	?	-L	#H
	H$	?	H#	#H

Sixty percent of the combinations are identical with those found on determinative compounds. There is a considerable proportion of combinations for which

---

[7] This is known in Chinese as "milk name" (乳名 rǔmíng), and constitutes one of the types of "names intended to avoid attracting the unwanted attention of gods, sparing the name-bearers the misfortunes wrought by the god's wrath or jealousy" (Chen 2016: 118).

Table 3.9b: The tones of coordinative compounds consisting of two disyllables. A question mark indicates that no example was found.

tone of 1st noun	2nd noun							
	M	#H	MH#	H$	L	LM+#H	LM	H#
M	M; #H	#H	?	?	−L	?	?	?
#H	H#; #H	H#−; H#/#H−	#H	H#	#H− / H#	?	?	H# / H#−
MH#	MH#; H#	MH#−	?	?	MH#−	?	?	?
H$	H#; #H	#H; #H− / H#	#H−	#H	?	#H−	?	?
L	L+H# / L+#H−	L; L+#H−	?	?	L+#H−	?	?	?
L#	?	L#−	?	?	L#−	?	?	?
LM+MH#	?	?	?	?	LM+MH#−	?	?	?
LM+#H	?	?	?	?	?	LM+MH#−	LM+MH#−	?
LM	LM−	?	?	?	?	LM−L	?	LM+H#
LH	?	?	?	?	?	?	?	?
H#	?	?	?	?	?	?	H#−	?

143

no example was found; to the cells containing a question mark in the table must be added the empty columns, which are omitted from the table. Only 35 combinations were observed, out of a theoretically possible 223 (6×6 for σ+σ compounds, 11×6 for σσ+σ compounds, and 11×11 for σσ+σσ compounds). Since there is nothing to restrict input combinations, the gaps in Tables 3.9a and 3.9b must be considered accidental. This is due in part to the limitations of available materials, but the scarcity of examples, and the diversity of their tone patterns, also provides food for morphotonological thought: coordinative compounds are much less common than determinative compounds. It may be that there is no such thing as a full-fledged set of productive tone combination rules governing their tone patterns, and that newly minted coordinative compounds are based on analogy with the best example at hand: a lexicalized compound perceived (on grounds that may fluctuate) as liable to the same tone rules. A touch of expressivity may also be involved in the process: greater weight placed on one of the two elements in the compound, on semantic-stylistic grounds, could contribute to the selection of one tone pattern rather than another. This would constitute a clue to the observed diversity.

3.3.3 Compound given names and terms of address

Compound given names and terms of address constitute two specific areas in the morphotonology of Yongning Na: they do not follow the regularities brought out above for other coordinative compounds.

In Yongning, given names are of Tibetan origin. They consist of a combination of two disyllabic names. For instance, /ji˧tɕi˧-ɖɯ˧ma˩/ is made up of /ji˧tɕi˧/ and /ɖɯ˧ma#˥/; /ɖɯ˧dʐɯ˧-tsʰɯ˩-i˩/ is a combination of /ɖɯ˧dʐɯ˧/ and /tsʰɯ˧i#˥/. Table 3.10 provides a list: disyllabic names, and attested combinations. The corresponding forms in Written Tibetan were proposed by Nathan Hill and Tsering Samdrup (p.c. 2016), and remain to be confirmed by eliciting the written forms from a monk in Yongning. Question marks indicate uncertain identifications. A dash '–' indicates that no forms are found in the set of recorded texts (and additional data will be necessary).

The tones of the second name are lowered to L in all cases, even when they could in theory be expressed without contravening any phonological rule. For instance, /ɖɯ˧dʐɯ˧/ and /tsʰɯ˧i#˥/ could combine as ‡ ɖɯ˧dʐɯ˧-tsʰɯ˧i#˥, by successive association of the tones of the two nouns. The expression ‡ ɖɯ˧dʐɯ˧-tsʰɯ˧i#˥ would not violate phonological conditions of well-formedness: there exist some four-syllable expressions that carry just this tone pattern, such as /na˩ba˧-ʁa˧lɯ#˥/ (the name of a mountain). The lowering to L of the second part

Table 3.10: Yongning Na given names and identifications with Tibetan names proposed by Nathan Hill and Tsering Samdrup.

name	Tibetan	attested combinations
ɖɯ˧dʑɯ˧	Rdo rje	ɖɯ˧dʑɯ˧-tsʰɯ˩ɻ̍˩, ɖɯ˧dʑɯ˧-ɬɑ˩-tsʰo˩
ɖɯ˧ma#˥	Sgrol ma	ɖɯ˩ma˧-ɬɑ˧tsʰo˩, ɖɯ˩ma˧-pv˩tʰɯ˩
dʐʁ˩tsʰi#˥	Bde skyid?	dʐʁ˩tsʰi˥-ɖɯ˩ma˩, dʐʁ˩tsʰi˥-pv˩tʰɯ˩
gʌ˧ma˧	?	gʌ˧ma˧-tsʰɯ˩ɻ̍˩
ji˧ʂɯ˥	Ye shes	ji˧ʂɯ˥-ti˩ɖo˩
ji˧tɕi˧	Yid ches?	ji˧tɕi˧-ɖɯ˩ma˩, ji˧tɕi˧-ɬɑ˩mʌ˩
kʁ˧zo#˥	Skal bzang?	kʁ˧zo˧-tsʰɯ˩ɻ̍˩
ki˧zo#˥	?	ki˧zo˧-ɖɯ˩ma˩, ki˧zo˧-ɬɑ˩mʌ˩
lɑ˩ma˩	Bla ma	–
ɬɑ˧mʌ˥$	Lha mo	–
ɬɑ˧tsʰo#˥	Lha mtsho	–
nɑ˧dʑi#˥	Rnam rgyal	–
ɲi˩ma#˥	Nyi ma	–
no˩bv˧	Nor bu	no˩bv˧-tsʰɯ˩ɻ̍˩
no˧no˧	?	no˧no˧-ɖɯ˩ma˩
pæ˩pʰæ˧	Spen pa?	–
pi˧ma˧	Padma	pi˧ma˧-ɬɑ˩mʌ˩, pi˧ma˧-ɬɑ˩tsʰo˩
pʰi˧tsʰo#˥	Phun tshogs	pʰi˧tsʰo˧-ɖɯ˩dʑɯ˩
pv˩tʰɯ˧	Bu phrug? Bu khrid?	–
ɻ̍˩tsʰe#˥	Rin chen	ɻ̍˩tsʰe˧-ɖɯ˩ma˩, ɻ̍˩tsʰe˧-tsʰɯ˩ɻ̍˩
tɑ˩dʐʁ#˥	Dar rgyes?	–
tæ˧ʂɯ˧	Bkra shis	tæ˧ʂɯ˧-ɖɯ˩ma˩, tæ˧ʂɯ˧-ɬɑ˩mʌ˩, tæ˧ʂɯ˧-pæ˩pʰæ˩, tæ˧ʂɯ˧-tæ˩tʌ˩, tæ˧ʂɯ˧-tsʰi˩ti˩
tæ˩tʌ#˥	Dgra 'dul?	–
tɕʰi˧dʌ#˥	Spyi 'dul?	–
ti˧ɖo˥	?	–
tsʰi˧ti#˥	?	–
tsʰɯ˧ɻ̍#˥	Tshe ring	tsʰɯ˧ɻ̍˧-lɑ˩mʌ˩, tsʰɯ˧ɻ̍˧-ɖɯ˩ma˩, tsʰɯ˧ɻ̍˧-ɬɑ˩mʌ˩, tsʰɯ˧ɻ̍˧-pʰi˩tsʰo˩

of compound names only applies to given names, not to compound names made up of a term of address and a two-syllable given name. For instance, a woman named /ki˧zo#˩/ may be addressed as /ə˧mi˧-ki˧zo#˩/ ("Mother **ki˧zo#˩**, Aunt **ki˧zo#˩**") by her nephews and nieces. This term of address is not realized as ‡ ə˧mi˧-ki˩zo˩, as would be the case if it were treated in the same way as compound given names. So the lowering of the last two syllables in given names, such as /ɖɯ˩dʐɯ˧-tsʰɯ˩-i̥˩/ and all the other examples in Table 3.10, is puzzling: it cannot be put down to the application of tone rules that apply throughout the Yongning Na tone system. Nor can it be explained as the result of a process of lexicalization that would have taken place at an earlier stage in the language's history: the lowering process clearly has the status of an exceptionless synchronic rule, applying to all compound given names. Speakers retain a clear awareness of the two parts of the compound names as distinct components, each of which has a lexical tone of its own. One of the two parts of the given name serves as the usual term of address; it may be the first or (less commonly) the second. For instance, the name that was bestowed on me by a priest of the Yongning monastery is /ʝi˧ʂɯ˩-ti˩ɖo˩/; F4 chose to call me by the second part of that compound given name: /ti˧ɖo˩/, which she pronounced with its own lexical tone, not as a stump retrieved from the compound (in which case she would have said it with L tone).[8] This is one of many pieces of evidence demonstrating that compounds such as /ʝi˧ʂɯ˩-ti˩ɖo˩/ are readily decomposable.

---

[8] F4's son (M18) argued that the shortened name should be /ʝi˧ʂɯ˩/, but F4 maintained her initial choice, providing no further explanation than that she preferred /ti˧ɖo˩/. The choice depends in part on considerations of homonymy within the extended family: there are so few names that homonymy is a real issue, and concerns about inappropriate use of proper names runs deep in Asian cultures. This is evidenced by the taboo on using the names of important characters (emperors, but also one's elders) in China and neighbouring countries, a practice known as *bìhuì* 避讳 (studied in detail by Adamek 2012). In Yongning Na, the concern is not limited to elders, as illustrated by the following anecdote. In the course of telling the story BuriedAlive2, consultant F4 realized that the name of the woman protagonist, /ɨ˩tsʰe˧-ɖɯ˩ma˩/, happened to be that of a member of her household. The consultant immediately substituted another name, /no˩bv̩˧-tsʰɯ˩i̥˩/, exempt from association with family members. The character in the story has a less than glorious role; the coincidence of names threatened to build an unwanted association between the family member and the character's shameful behaviour. The concern was such that F4 would have preferred me to delete the recording of this version of the story altogether, so as to leave no trace of this unfortunate coincidence of names. But we had already spent much time working on the transcription, so I was not overjoyed at the prospect of outright deletion of the files. Fortunately, the consultant found comfort in the explicit disclaimer which is present on the recording, to the effect that the character's name was /no˩bv̩˧-tsʰɯ˩i̥˩/ and *not* /ɨ˩tsʰe˧-ɖɯ˩ma˩/, and she agreed that we should complete the transcription and allow access to this linguistic document.

Should the tonal lowering of the latter part of compoun given names be considered as another instance of a tone rule applying in a highly specific morphosyntactic context: a tone combination rule that holds in given names, and nowhere else – not even in other sets of proper names, such as place names?

Interestingly, a similar process of lowering is found in compounds involving the word for 'powder, flour': /tsɑ˧bɤ˧/ (as reported in §3.2.11.3). According to the synchronically productive rules, the combination of this word with /lv˧mi˧/ 'stone', /qʰɑ˧dze˧/ 'sweetcorn' and /dze˧lɯ˧/ 'wheat' should yield a simple M-tone output, e.g. †lv˧mi˧-tsɑ˧bɤ˧ for 'fine sand'. But the observed forms, shown in Table 3.6, all carry a M.M.L.L tone pattern, corresponding to underlying –L (a L tone on the second part of the compound), just like the compound given names in Table 3.10. The label 'Tibetan compounds' is proposed for these compounds. From a synchronic point of view, this label may seem invalid, since none of the consultants has any knowledge of Tibetan (either spoken or written) and hence any awareness of Tibetan loanwords as such. The hypothesis here is that at some earlier point in time – one to four centuries ago? – speakers of Yongning Na who had some knowledge of Tibetan (a smattering would have been enough) applied a specific tonal treatment to compounds containing Tibetan words, by imitation of what they perceived as the Tibetan pattern. Tibetan was a prestige language in Yongning at least since the fourteenth century, and up until the mid-twentieth century (see Appendix B, §B.1), so it is not unlikely that processes of imitation of prosodic patterns took place. This may have happened at the time when the Tibetan words were borrowed, or at a later stage, when speakers of Yongning Na who were aware of the status of these words as Tibetan in origin made efforts to copy (what they felt to be) Tibetan prosodic patterns. Cases of contact with a prestigious language can result in a range of unusual changes by imitation, including hypercorrections: see Meillet (1936: 99-103) on a possible case concerning Germanic and Romance, and Ferlus (2001) on cases in the Vietic subgroup of Austroasiatic; a highly speculative application to Tibetan has also been proposed (Ferlus 2003).

Supposing that imitation of Tibetan was at play in these compounds, it remains to be explained why lowering tone to L on the latter part of compounds had a Tibetan ring to Na ears, and at which point in history the adoption of this prosodic pattern took place. For want of a command of Tibetan, I am not in a position to investigate topics of historical contact with this language - one of many topics that remain for future investigations.

3.4 Compound nouns containing adjectives

The tonal categories of adjectives will be brought out in §6.1.3. As a background to the discussion in the present section, here is a preview of the results: the four tonal categories of adjectives are L, M, H, and MH, with a subdivision among L-tone items, distinguishing L_a and L_b.

Compounds containing adjectives are a difficult topic in Yongning Na, not least because they are the product of lexicalization, and cannot be elicited systematically by asking consultants to coin compounds on the fly to bring out a full set of synchronic rules, as can be done for *noun plus noun* compounds. As a preliminary to the study of lexicalized compounds, it is useful to present adjectival phrases.

3.4.1 A productive construction: N+ADJ+relativizer

In Yongning Na, the association of adjectives to nouns is realized by the construction N+ADJ+relativizer/nominalizer /-hĩ˧/. For instance, //ɖɯ˩a// 'big'[9] yields //ɖɯ˩-hĩ˩// '(which is) big', and //ʂɯ˧// 'new' yields //ʂɯ˧-hĩ˧$// '(which is) new'. These are added after the noun as a separate tone group, as in (4)-(7).

(4) ɲi˧zo˧ | ɖɯ˩-hĩ˩
     ɲi˧zo˧   ɖɯ˩ₐ   -hĩ˩
     fish   large   NMLZ
     'big fish'

(5) pʰi˧ | ʂɯ˧-hĩ˧
     pʰi˧   ʂɯ˧   -hĩ˧
     linen_cloth   new   NMLZ
     'brand new linen cloth'

(6) tɕʰo˩ | ʂɯ˧-hĩ˧
     tɕʰo˩   ʂɯ˧   -hĩ˧
     ladle   new   NMLZ
     'new ladle'

---

[9] As explained on the first page of the introduction, morpheme-level transcriptions indicate lexical tone by means of tone symbols supplemented by subscript letters ₐ ᵦ ᵪ to distinguish subcategories of lexical tones. The subcategories for verbs and adjectives are set out in Table 6.2 of §6.1.1. The pound symbol # is also part of the apparatus to transcribe the different categories of lexical tones, as was explained in §2.3.1.

(7) qʰwɤ˧ | ʂɯ˧-hĩ˧
     qʰwɤ˧ ʂɯ˧ -hĩ˧
     bowl   new NMLZ
     'new bowl'

No tonal interaction takes place between the noun and adjective. If an intensifier is substituted for the relativizer, the construction becomes a statement, as in (8). The construction (9) likewise means 'the fish is big'.

(8) ɲi˧zo˧ | ɖɯ˧ | ʐwæ˩.
     ɲi˧zo˧ ɖɯ˩ₐ ʐwæ˩
     fish   large INTS
     'The fish is very big.'

(9) ɲi˧zo˧ | ɖɯ˧.
     ɲi˧zo˧ ɖɯ˩ₐ
     fish   large
     'The fish is big.'

In example (10), the numeral-plus-classifier phrase has the effect of nominalizing a construction that would otherwise mean 'the fish is/was really big', rather than 'a very big fish'.

(10) ni³³ zɔ³³   ɖɯ⁵⁵ ʐwæ¹³ ɖɯ³³ mi³¹
     fish   big   INTS   one   CLS
     鱼   大   很   一   量词
     'a very big fish' (example 187 from Lidz 2010: 215; her glosses and tone marking. CLS: classifier; ⁵⁵: High tone; ³³: Mid tone; ³¹: Low-falling tone; ¹³: Low-rising tone.)

The word order Noun+Adjective in a noun phrase always signals a lexicalized item: to use a textbook example from English, a phrasal, nonlexicalized 'black bird' as distinct from 'blackbird' requires a relativizer (examples are provided a few lines below). For instance, //ʐɯ˧na˩//, from //ʐɯ˧// 'liquor/spirits' and //na˩ᵦ// 'black', does not mean 'black liquor, liquor of a black colour', but refers to a specific type of strong, high-quality spirits. This is a disyllabic noun, requiring an entry of its own in the dictionary; it is not a phrasal construction (a description associating a quality to the entity that the noun refers to). The nouns //ə˧mi˧-ɖʐɯ˩// and //ə˧mi˧-tɕi˩//, referring to the mother's older sisters and younger sisters respectively, are lexical units, even though they can still be transparently analyzed as made up of //ə˧mi˧// 'mother' plus the adjectives //ɖʐɯ˩ₐ// 'large' and //tɕi˩ₐ// 'small'.

There also exist compounds with the adjectives 'big' and 'small' for maternal uncles, //ə˧v˧//: //ə˧v˧-tɕi˩// for 'mother's younger brother', and //ə˧v˧-ɖʐɯ˧// for 'mother's elder brother'. However, constructions with the relativizer //-hĩ˩// are more common: to clarify whether one is referring to the mother's elder brother or younger brother, the former is called /ə˧v˧ | ɖʐɯ˩-hĩ˧/, and the latter /ə˧v˧ | tɕi˩-hĩ˧/, as shown in (11a–11b).

(11)   a. ə˧v˧ | ɖʐɯ˩-hĩ˧
          ə˧v˧   ɖʐɯ˩ₐ   -hĩ˩
          uncle big   NMLZ

        'mother's elder brother, elder maternal uncle'

   b. ə˧v˧ | tɕi˩-hĩ˧
          ə˧v˧   tɕi˩ₐ   -hĩ˩
          uncle small NMLZ

        'mother's younger brother, younger maternal uncle' (Caravans.75, 76, 78, 79, 177–179, 196, 259, Elders3.23, 31, 32)

The study of successive occurrences within the same text confirms that the construction with the relativizer/nominalizer //-hĩ˩//, although it may seem cumbersome, is the standard construction to associate an adjective to a noun. This construction is not followed by a synthetic, compact N+ADJ construction at later occurrences. For instance, example (13) follows example (12) at a distance of a few sentences inside the same narrative, and both contain the same construction with nominalizer.

(12) mv˩zo˧ | ɖʐɯ˩-hĩ˧, | zo˧my˩ | ɖʐɯ˩-hĩ˧ | ɖɯ˧-ɭɯ˧ dʑo˩ tsɯ˩.
       mv˩zo˩   ɖʐɯ˩ₐ -hĩ˩   zo˧my˩ ɖʐɯ˩ₐ -hĩ˩ ɖɯ˧-ɭɯ˧ dʑo˩ᵦ
       young_lady large   NMLZ child   large   NMLZ one-CLF   EXIST
       tsɯ˩
       REP

'It is said that [this couple] had a big girl, a big child (=a child who thought very seriously for her age).' (Reward.59)

(13) mv˧zo˧˥ | ɖɯ˩-hĩ˩-ki˩ (…)
      mv˧zo˧˥   ɖɯ˩ₐ   -hĩ˩   -ki˧
      young_lady   large   NMLZ   DAT

'to his elder daughter, [the father said…]' (Reward.65)

This is a notable difference from Naxi. For instance, 'important person, great personage; adult' in Naxi is /hi˧-ɖɯ˩/ 'person'+'big'. In Yongning Na, the same concept is: /ɖɯ˩-hĩ˥/, 'big' plus relativizer, with 'person' as the implicit referent (e.g. Sister.13, 14, 34, Sister3.31, 36, 38, 41, and BuriedAlive3.5).

3.4.2 Lexicalized compounds of N+ADJ structure

The adjectives that appear in lexicalized combinations with nouns in the examples provided above are //nɑ˩ᵦ// 'black, dark', //ɖɯ˩ₐ// 'large' and //tɕi˩ₐ// 'small'. Is it a coincidence that 'black' is also the adjective used in the textbook example of English *black bird* and *blackbird*? The compound noun *blackbird* refers to *Turdus merula*, a species of thrush, while the combination of noun and adjective *black bird* refers to any bird of a black colour. The former, *blackbird*, carries stress on the first element of the compound (for short: "first-element stress"), whereas the latter, *black bird*, carries last-element stress: primary stress on *bird*. The meaning of *black bird* can be deduced from the meaning of its elements and the meaning of the construction, whereas the meaning of *blackbird* cannot be arrived at on the basis of the meaning of the elements. First-element stress is generally interpreted as a marker of degree of lexicalization. It has been observed, in a study of English, that "the number of adjectives that work in the way that *black* does in our *exemple-type* seems to be very restricted" (Bauer 2004: 9). Examples are shown in Table 3.11. But at the end of a quest using corpus-query tools to explore hypotheses about the relevance of factors such as the frequency of the particular collocations and contrasting patterns of premodification, the author concludes that the gaps in English adjective-plus-noun compounds are likely to be accidental. In Na, as in English, adjectives that appear in compound nouns do not constitute a closed set.

In English, there is variation across speakers (and even for one and the same speaker) in judgments about stress patterns, and in stress assignment in actual speech. In Yongning Na, on the other hand, noun-plus-adjective compounds are conspicuously different from attributive constructions, since the latter comprise

Table 3.11: Types of adjectives that appear in compound nouns in English (from Bauer 2004: 9).

type of adjectives	examples	example compounds
some colour adjectives	*black, blue, brown, green, grey, red, white*	*blackboard, blue-tit, brownstone, greenfly, greyhound, redfish, whiteboard*
grand in words of family relationships	*grand*	*grandfather*
a miscellaneous set of monosyllabic gradable adjectives	*broad, dry, free, hard, hot, mad, small, sweet* (among others)	*broadcloth, dry-cell, freepost, hardboard, hotbed, madman, small-arm, sweetcorn*
a small set of non-gradable monosyllabic adjectives	*blind, dumb, first, quick* (= 'alive'), *square, whole*	*blindside, dumbcluck, first-day, quicksand, squaresail, wholestitch*
a very small number of disyllabic adjectives	*bitter, narrow, silly*	*bitter-cress, narrow-boat, sillyseason*

a relativizer. This makes it easy to identify these compounds in Yongning Na. Their tonal analysis, however, is not straightforward. Examples are shown in tabular form, arranged by the tone of the adjective: L_a in Table 3.12, L_b in Table 3.13, M in Table 3.14, and H in Table 3.15.[10] (No compounds with MH-tone adjectives have yet been observed.) All these items are lexicalized: for instance, the phrase /tsʰæ˧nɑ˥/ refers to a legendary stag, which only spirits are able to hunt down; it is thus different from an attributive construction ('black-coloured deer').

---

[10] The subscript letters $_a$ $_b$ $_c$ added to the tones serve to distinguish subcategories of lexical tones. The subcategories for verbs and adjectives are set out in Table 6.2 (§6.1.1).

Table 3.12: Examples of compounds containing the L_a-tone adjectives /mo˩ₐ/ 'old', /ɖɯ˩ₐ/ 'large', /tɕi˩ₐ/ 'small', and /pʰv˩ₐ/ 'white'. Note that no monosyllabic form is attested synchronically for 'stone' and 'ard'.

head noun			compound		
form	tone	meaning	form	tone	meaning
hĩ˥	H	person	hĩ˧mo˥	H#	elderly person
ʐwæ˥	H	horse	ʐwæ˧mo˥	H#	old horse
si˥	H	wood	si˧mo˥	H#	old wood, old tree
lv˧mi˧	?	stone	lv˧mo˥	H#	old stones
tsʰo˩	L	human being	tsʰo˩mo˩	L	old man
æ˩gv˩	?	ard[a]	æ˩mo˥	LH	used ard (out of use)
ʁo˥	H	head	ʁo˧ɖɯ˦	MH#	tadpole
zo˥	H	son	zo˧ɖɯ˧	M	eldest son
mv˦	LH	daughter	mv˩ɖɯ˩	L#	eldest daughter
ə˧mi˧	M	mother	ə˧mi˧-ɖɯ˩	L#	mother's elder sister
ə˧v˦	MH#	maternal uncle	ə˧v˧-ɖɯ˦	MH#	mother's elder brother
ə˧bo˥$	H$	paternal uncle	ə˧bo˧-ɖɯ˦	MH#	father's elder brother
mv˦	LH	daughter	mv˩tɕi˥	LH	youngest daughter
zo˥	H	son	zo˧tɕi˥	H#	youngest son
ə˧mi˧	M	mother	ə˧mi˧-tɕi˩	L#	mother's younger sister
ə˧v˦	MH#	maternal uncle	ə˧v˧-tɕi˥	H#	mother's younger brother
ə˧bo˥$	H$	paternal uncle	ə˧bo˧-tɕi˥	H#	father's younger brother
tɕɯ˧	M	cloud	tɕɯ˧pʰv˩	L#	white cloud

[a] The ard, also known as scratch plough, is the type of ploughing implement used in Yongning. Unlike the plough, the ard has a symmetrical share that traces a shallow furrow but does not invert the soil (Haudricourt & Jean-Brunhes Delamare 1955).

Table 3.13: Examples of compounds containing the L_b-tone adjective /na˩ˌb/ 'black'.

head noun			compound		
form	tone	meaning	form	tone	meaning
hỹ˥	H	hair	hỹ˧na˩	L#	wild animal
ʂe˥	H	meat	ʂe˧na˩	L#	lean meat
si˥	H	wood	si˧na˥	H#	deep forest
kʰv˥	H	dog	kʰv˧na˥	H#	dog (in formal speech)
tɕʰi˥	H	thorn	tɕʰi˧na˥	H#	prinsepia
ʐɯ˧	M	liquor/spirits	ʐɯ˧na˩	L#	high-quality spirits
njɤ˧˥	LH	eye	njɤ˧na˩	L#	eyeball
ʂʰæ˧˥	MH	deer	ʂʰæ˧na˥	H#	legendary black stag

Table 3.14: Examples of compounds containing the M-tone adjectives /pɤ˧/ 'dry', /bæ˧/ 'stupid', /tʰi˧/ 'clever', /tsʰi˧/ 'hot' and /ʂæ˧/ 'long'.

head noun			compound		
form	tone	meaning	form	tone	meaning
hɑ˥	H	food	hɑ˧pɤ˩	L#	dry cooked rice (as opposed to gruel)
zo˥	H	son	zo˧bæ˩	L#	idiot
mv˧˥	LH	daughter	mv˩tʰi˩	L	clever woman
dʑɯ˩	L	water	dʑɯ˩tsʰi˩	L	hot water
zɯ˧	M	life	zɯ˧ʂæ˧	M	long life

Table 3.15: Examples of compounds containing the H-tone adjectives /qʰæ˥/ 'cold' and /ɖæ˥/ 'short'.

head noun			compound		
form	tone	meaning	form	tone	meaning
dʑɯ˩	L	water	dʑɯ˩qʰæ˩	L	cold water
zɯ˧	M	life	zɯ˧ɖæ#˥	#H	short life

In terms of tone, the compounds exhibit some diversity. Of the five compounds that relate to monosyllabic roots with H tone, three have L# tone, and two have H# tone. This is not related to any obvious structural property of the compounds: the compound /hỹ˧na˩/, literally 'black hair', does not refer to a type of hair, but to 'wild animal', referring by synecdoche to the *possessor* of dark hair;[11] on the other hand, the compound /ʂe˧na˩/, literally 'dark meat', refers to a sort of meat (lean meat). (In the Indian linguistic tradition, /hỹ˧na˩/ 'black hair' for 'wild animal' would be referred to as a *bahuvrīhi* compound: a compound that denotes a referent by a certain characteristic.) Semantically, there is no salient difference either. In the L#-tone compounds for 'dark hair' and 'lean meat' the adjective /na˩ᵦ/ can be argued to have a literal interpretation as 'black, dark': traditionally, pigs and cattle were only slaughtered once a year, so that fresh meat was the exception; the norm for lean meat was the preserved sort, with a dark brown colour. By contrast, prinsepia (/tɕʰi˧na˦/) is not black or dark-coloured, and /kʰv˧na˦/ for 'dog' carries no hint of hair colour, so it may be argued that one of the two tone patterns corresponds to a semantically bleached use of the adjective. But this is less clear in the case of /si˧na˦/, 'wood'+'dark', for 'deep forest': here the semantic indication of darkness seems present. Analysis of this issue is made more difficult by the rarity of lexical items sharing the same tone as 'black', //na˩ᵦ//: the only other example observed to date is //dʑɤ˩ᵦ// 'good' (see §6.1.3).

A similar lack of one-to-one correspondence between input tones and output tone is also found for compounds containing the adjective /ɖɯ˩ₐ/ 'large, big'. The compound nouns /zo˧ɖɯ#˦/ 'eldest son' and /ʁo˧ɖɯ˦/ 'tadpole' (literally 'big head') have different tones (#H and MH#, respectively), although both are made up of a noun root that has H lexical tone and the adjective /ɖɯ˩ₐ/ 'big'.

To venture speculative hypotheses about the origin of these variegated tone patterns, first, they may belong to different historical layers, and hence reflect different tone rules, which applied at different diachronic stages. For instance, 'deep forest', 'dog' and 'prinsepia' might be earlier than 'wild animal' and 'lean meat', as the compounds look less transparent semantically. The morpheme /na/ could be analyzed as a suffix in some cases, and as an adjective in others, on the analogy of the analysis of the morpheme /mɔ¹³/ by Lidz (2010: 182), distinguishing the adjective 'old' from its use as a suffix meaning 'dear (indicating respect)'.

---

[11] Interestingly, the association of darker fur with wildness (less disposition to domestication) is confirmed by scientific studies of animal domestication (Trut 1999). The phenomenon is apparently due (at least in part) to links between levels of stress in an individual and amount of melanine, itself reflected in darker fur (Burchill & Thody 1986): individuals in the wild experience greater stress. Wild yaks have darker hair than domestic yaks (Leslie & Schaller 2009).

Another possibility is that some of these compounds are not based on the association of a monosyllabic noun with a monosyllabic adjective, but constitute a reduced form of longer words. For instance, the syllable /si˧/ in /si˧na˧/ could result from the truncation of the disyllable /si˧ɕi˧/, meaning 'forest'.[12] Evidence for the possibility to truncate this disyllable comes from /tʰo˧ɕi˧/ 'pine forest', which combines a monosyllable for 'pine' with the *second* syllable of /si˧ɕi˧/ 'forest'. In the case of 'eldest son' and 'tadpole', such a process appears rather implausible, as these disyllables seem to have a straightforward link to the monosyllabic nouns 'son' and 'head', respectively. If one nonetheless tries to push this hypothesis, one might hypothesize that 'tadpole' was built on the basis of a disyllabic noun, which in principle could still be present in another dialect.

A third possibility is that the adjective is not the same in all of these words: in synchrony, there exists an adjective /na˧/ (not homophonous with /na˩ᵦ/ 'black, dark') which means 'important, serious (e.g. a wound)', and this adjective, or some other adjective pronounced [na], may have provided the second syllable in some adjectival compounds. This does not apply to 'eldest son' and 'tadpole', where the adjective seems recognizably identical – unless interpretation of 'tadpole' as 'big head' is not the correct etymology, but 'big head' seems fitting enough as the name of this small and amusing animal, which is an obvious candidate for frequent replacement through expressive coinages.

So far, consistency in the tone patterns of adjectival compounds seems limited to synchronically trivial patterns. For instance, it does not come as a surprise that Mid-tone /ʐɯ˧/ 'liquor/spirits' and Low-tone /na˩ᵦ/ 'black' yield a compound with M+L surface tone pattern, /ʐɯ˧na˩/: this looks like a case of simple concatenation. The same tone pattern is also found with another adjective that has the same lexical tone, /dʐɤ˩ᵦ/ 'good'. Disyllabic /kɯ˧ dʐɤ˩/ was easily extracted from the compound /kɯ˧ dʐɤ˩ hã˩ dʐɤ˩/ 'auspicious day', from /kɯ˧/ 'star' and /hã˧/ 'evening, night' (a term used to count days). (The L# tone pattern of /kɯ˧ dʐɤ˩/, literally 'good star', results in the following two syllables receiving L tone, through Rule 5.) The tone pattern of /kɯ˧ dʐɤ˩/ 'good star' is the same as that of /ʐɯ˧na˩/ 'high-quality liquor'. This could suggest that both compounds belong to the same historical layer, but more examples would be necessary to investigate this issue further.

---

[12] Creissels (1982: 50-52) reports cases of synchronic variation in Mandinka where nouns that occur more frequently in compounds than on their own tend to get extracted from compounds with the changed tone that they carry inside these compounds. The changed tone eventually replaces the original lexical tone. Such processes, which operate on a word-by-word basis, detract from the regularity of tonal correspondences across dialects, greatly complicating diachronic comparison and reconstruction.

To sum up: in view of the limited number of examples found to date, and of their heterogeneity, it does not appear illuminating to pool them all into a table summarizing the tonal output of N+ADJ compounds. Provisionally, examples are simply listed in Table 3.12, arranged by adjective, by decreasing number of examples.

As a general observation, it can be seen that the patterns in noun-plus-adjective compounds are not identical to those in noun-plus-verb combinations (described in Chapter 6). For instance, 'hot water', /dʐɯ˩tsʰi˩/, has L tone, from an input of L and M on the noun and adjective respectively; in noun-plus-verb combinations (either object plus verb or subject plus verb) with the same tonal input, the output is M.

The diachronic trend is for monosyllabic nouns to become less frequent, being replaced by disyllables. As disyllabic forms of nouns become lexicalized, the tonal correspondence between the noun-plus-adjective combination and the root ceases to be accessible to the speakers of the language, making the tone patterns of disyllables more vulnerable to replacement (through analogy or contact among dialects) than in cases where the root still exists as a monosyllable. Thus, in the current state of the language 'stone' and 'ard' are only attested as disyllables, except in compounds with the adjective 'old', where they are found in monosyllabic form. This raises the issue of whether it makes sense to extract a monosyllable from the disyllabic compounds with 'old'. The root for 'stone' could be reconstructed with a H tone, as *ly˧, on the basis of this root's tonal behaviour when it stands in an adjectival compound: the compound /ly˧mo˧/ 'old stone' carries H# tone, like the adjectival compounds created by adding 'old' to the H-tone monosyllables 'person', 'horse' and 'wood'. But closer examination shows that 'old stone' is not in common use in Yongning Na, and has no clear meaning of its own. It is a recent coinage, only found in a saying – example (14) – where it serves as a parallel to /si˧mo˧/ 'old wood'; its tone pattern also follows that of 'old wood'. (Use of the symbol 'F' for 'Focalization' in the sentence-level transcription is explained in §8.3.2.)

(14) ly˧mo˧ F | dʐɯ˩ | le˧-qv˩; | si˧mo˧ F | le˧-dze˩ kv˩! | no˧ F | ə˧tse˧ | le˧-ʂɯ˧ mɤ˧-tʰɑ˧ | di˩!

ly˧mo˧	dʐɯ˩	le˧	qv˩ₐ	si˧mo˧	le˧-
old.stones	water	ACCOMP	to_carry_away	old_wood	ACCOMP
dze˩ₐ	-kv˧	no˩	ə˧tse˧	le˧-	ʂɯ˧ₐ	mɤ˧-
to_cut	ABILITIVE	2SG	INTERROG.why	ACCOMP	to_die	NEG

          tʰɑ˧˩   di˩ₐ
          PERMISSIVE   EXIST.SPATIAL

'Old stones are carried away by the stream; and old wood gets chopped down! And you, why won't you die?' (Field notes. Context: jeering an elderly person. Na tradition assigns human beings a lifespan of sixty years; people getting past seventy are considered to be well past their expected lifespan.)

Further analysis will require gathering more examples, sorting them into sets according to their tone patterns, identifying the historical layers that they belong to, and examining their process of formation. As a first step in this direction, the following paragraph discusses items that are currently on the verge of lexicalization.

3.4.3 N+ADJ combinations in the process of lexicalization

In between adjectival constructions such as /ə˧y˧ | ɖɯ˩-hĩ˩˥/ 'mother's elder brother' (example (11a) above) on the one hand, and lexical items such as /ə˧y˧-ɖɯ˧/ (also meaning 'mother's elder brother': see Table 3.12) on the other, there are cases that offer insights into the process of lexicalization. 'Elderly person' is /hĩ˧mo˧/, from /hĩ˧/ 'person' and /mo˩ₐ/ 'old'. In a set of twenty texts, this noun appears fifteen times, always in the plural, as /hĩ˧mo˧=ɻæ˩/; the fact that it is followed by a clitic shows that it is a full-fledged noun. But there is a higher number of occurrences (twenty-three) of /hĩ˧ mo˧-hĩ˩/, which also means 'elderly person', again from /hĩ˧/ 'person' and /mo˩ₐ/ 'old', but with addition of the relativizer /-hĩ˧/. This is not quite like the adjectival construction presented in §3.4.1: in that construction, the noun constitutes a tone group on its own, e.g. /tɕʰo˧ | ʂɯ˧-hĩ#˧/ 'new ladle' (example (6) above), whereas 'elderly person' is realized as /hĩ˧ mo˧-hĩ˩/, in one tone group. At a push, it would be possible to say /hĩ˧ | mo˧-hĩ˩/ 'a person that is old', but this is judged decidedly awkward in the contexts where /hĩ˧ mo˧-hĩ˩/ is attested. The interpretation that can be proposed is that /hĩ˧mo˧/ is on its way towards lexicalization – as evidenced by the tonal interaction between its two constituting morphemes – but the perception of its second syllable as an adjective remains strong enough for the relativizer to be commonly added after it. The impossibility of adding the agent marker (‡ **hĩ˧mo˧ ɳɯ˩**) or the topic marker (‡ **hĩ˧mo˧ tsʰɯ˩**) shows that /hĩ˧mo˧/ is not fully lexicalized yet. It is compulsory to add an intervening plural or relativizer: /hĩ˧mo˧=ɻæ˩ ɳɯ˩/, /hĩ˧mo˧=ɻæ˩ tsʰɯ˩/, /hĩ˧ mo˧-hĩ˩ ɳɯ˩/, and /hĩ˧ mo˧-hĩ˩ tsʰɯ˩/.

For purposes of synchronic description, the notations adopted are /hĩ˧mo˥ =ɹæ˩/ and /hĩ˧ mo˥-hĩ˩/. In /hĩ˧mo˥=ɹæ˩/, the sequence /hĩ˧mo˥/ is transcribed as a lexical unit, with no hyphen or blank space between its two syllables. In /hĩ˧ mo˥-hĩ˩/, the first syllable is analyzed as a noun, and separated by a blank space from the adjective that follows. This notational distinction aims to draw attention to the versatility of disyllables made up of a noun and an adjective. To take another example of this phenomenon, /zo˧bæ˩/, from /zo˥/ 'son; man' and /bæ˧/ 'stupid; dumb (unable to speak)', has clearly nominal uses, meaning 'dumb man; stupid man'. More than twenty examples are found in the Lake narrative, one of whose main protagonists is a dumb person. The noun can be followed by the agent adposition: /zo˧bæ˩ ɳɯ˩/ (Lake3.29, Lake4.24); there is no need for an intervening relativizer/nominalizer for quantization purposes, witness examples (15)–(17).

(15) zo˧bæ˩ d̠ɯ˩-v˩
    zo˧bæ˩   d̠ɯ˧-v˧
    dumb_person one-CLF.individual
    'a dumb person' (Lake4.4)

(16) zo˧bæ˩ tsʰɯ˩-v˩
    zo˧bæ˩   tsʰɯ˥   v˧
    dumb_person DEM.PROX CLF.individual
    'this dumb person' (Lake4.6)

(17) zo˧bæ˩ tʰv˩-v˩
    zo˧bæ˩   tʰv˥   v˧
    dumb_person DEM.DIST CLF.individual
    'that dumb person' (Lake4.12-14)

The expression /zo˧bæ˩/ can also appear right in front of a verb, as in /zo˧bæ˩ | go˩bo˧ di˥/ 'the dumb man drove cattle' (Lake4.19). But in addition to such typically nominal uses, the word also has predicative (adjectival) uses: in a context of self-deprecation where someone accuses himself of being stupid, /zo˧bæ˩/, another person may comfort him by saying (18).

(18) mɤ˧-zo˧bæ˩!
    mɤ˧-   zo˧bæ˩
    NEG   stupid
    '[No, you are] not stupid!'

The antonym of /zo˧bæ˩/ in this adjectival sense is /zo˧tʰi˧/ 'clever; clever person', which has the same structure, from /zo˧/ 'son; man' and /tʰi˧/ 'able; capable; clever; sharp'. The two words have different tones (L# tone for /zo˧bæ˩/, vs. M tone for /zo˧tʰi˧/) despite their constituting morphemes having the same tones. This tonal difference alerts us to the possibility that the two words may have different time depths. Syntactically, the two words also differ: it is not possible to say ‡ mɤ˧-zo˧tʰi˧ 'not clever', on the analogy of /mɤ˧-zo˧bæ˩/ 'not stupid' (18). The first syllable of these two words is bleached enough for them to be used as adjectives for men and women alike, but in their nominal use they can only refer to men: /zo˧bæ˩/ means 'stupid man', and /zo˧tʰi˧/ 'clever man'; the corresponding words for women are /mv˩-bæ˧mi˩/ 'stupid woman' and /mv˩tʰi˩/ 'clever woman'.

3.4.4 A lexicalized compound of ADJ+N structure

So far, only one lexicalized compound of *adjective plus noun* structure has been found: /pɤ˧lv˧/ 'nonirrigated farmland; dry land', clearly related to /pɤ˧/ 'dry' and /lv˧/ 'field'. This word shows no phonological signs of antiquity, such as a difference in consonant, vowel or tone from its etymological components. But comparative evidence suggests that it may have some time depth: it is also found in Naxi, as /pɤ˩lɯ˧/, with the same ADJ+N structure, the same meaning, and the same transparency in terms of its components (in Naxi, 'dry' is /pɤ˩/, and 'field' is /lɯ˧/). Naxi has another ADJ+N compound containing 'dry': /pɤ˩dy˩/ 'dry land (as opposed to water)' (Pinson 2012: 55; note that there is a typographical error in the phonetic transcription, /pɤ˩dy˩/, which should be /pɤ˩dy˩/, as indicated by the orthographic transcription).

3.4.5 A lexicalized compound of V+ADJ structure

As a final observation about compounds, this paragraph discusses the only lexicalized compound of V+ADJ structure observed so far: /tsʰo˧ɖɯ˩/ 'group dance', a dance that can involve from ten to about a hundred people. Its components are /tsʰo˧b/ 'to jump' (in a nominalized reading) and /ɖɯ˩a/ 'large'. An alternative interpretation whereby /ɖɯ˩a/ would have an adverbial reading ('jumping a lot') would be implausible, because /ɖɯ˩a/ does not have attested adverbial uses.

This is not a productive construction: it is not possible to create compounds such as 'banquet' from the verb 'to eat' and the adjective 'large', for instance. Still, the existence of the word /tsʰo˧ɖɯ˩/ 'group dance' can be interpreted as evidence of an occasional permeability of word classes. Across languages, the distinction between nouns and verbs may be more or less stringent (Launey 1994, *passim*). In Naish languages, there are some borderline items. For example, Na /kɤ˧tsɯ˩/, like Naxi /kɯ˧tsɯ˩/, has both verbal and nominal uses, namely 'to speak' and 'speech; language' in Naxi and 'to tell' and 'speech' in Na.

3.5 Concluding note

The complexity of the tone combination rules in various types of compounds in the Alawa dialect of Yongning Na, and the existence of exceptions to these synchronic rules, arguably shed light on the considerable diversity of patterns from one dialect to the next, and even among different speakers from the same village (not to mention the existence of variants within a single idiolect). A few compounds happen to carry the same tone sequence as would the simple juxtaposition of their constituting elements. Most carry a tone pattern that reflects their status as compounds; among these, the nature of the compound (determinative or coordinative) can also be identified from the tone pattern in a few cases, whereas in the others it must be arrived at on the basis of semantic information.

4 Classifiers

A classifier is "a type of limited noun that occurs only after numerals (...), and whose selection is determined by a preceding (overt or implicit) noun" (Matisoff 1973: 88). The term 'classifier' is understood here in the syntactic sense of any noun that may appear directly after a numeral. This includes measure words ('inch', 'armspan', 'heap'...) and time words ('day', 'month', 'year'...), which immediately follow the numeral. In view of their great importance in the language, and of the richness of their tone patterns, classifiers are dealt with in a chapter of their own. The bulk of the chapter (§4.1) deals with the tonal behaviour of classifiers in association with numerals. But classifiers also associate with demonstratives (§4.2). In addition, numeral-plus-classifier or demonstrative-plus-classifier phrases can interact tonally with a preceding noun (§4.3).

Devoting tens of pages to the topic of nominal classifiers, after long chapters devoted to the tones of nouns (Chapter 2) and of compound nouns (Chapter 3), may cause alarm to the best-disposed of readers. Will the archipelago of tables never come to an end? Is there no better way to describe the tonal grammar of Yongning Na than by recording lump after lump of morphotonological detail?

Indeed, the tone patterns of phrases containing classifiers cause a disappointment to the linguist: they cannot be accounted for by phonological sandhi, nor do they obey a well-defined set of morphotonological rules.[1] The tonal paradigms of the various categories of classifiers need to be learnt one by one. The tables recording these patterns are admittedly the most heavy-going in the present volume. But paradoxically, this chapter, which reports on the most irregular part of the Yongning Na tone system, carries a comforting message: there *is* a limit to the seemingly endless complexity of the system, even in those areas that contain most irregularities. I think (taking full responsibility for this immodest stance) that the present chapter gets close to an exhaustive description of its object, thereby showing that a comprehensive account of tone in Yongning Na is not an unreachable goal.

---

[1] Some clarifications about the terms 'tone sandhi', 'morphotonology' and 'tonal morphology' are set out in §8.1.1.

4.1 Numeral-plus-classifier phrases

Within the group of Naish languages, tonal alternations in numeral-plus-classifier phrases are vestigial in Naxi (as spoken in the plain of Lijiang), limited in Laze, and ubiquitous in Yongning Na. In the Alawa dialect of Yongning Na, the tone of the classifier is affected by the numeral to such an extent that arriving at the classifier's underlying tone is not a straightforward task. For instance, the classifier for days carries a H tone in /ɲi˧-ɲi˥/ 'two days', a LH tone in /so˩-ɲi˥/ 'three days', and a M tone in /ʐv˧-ɲi˧/ 'four days'; and the classifier for years has a MH tone in /ɲi˧-kʰv˧˥/ 'two years', a LH tone in /so˩-kʰv˥/ 'three years', and a L tone in /ʐv˧-kʰv˩/ 'four years'. This section proposes a synchronic description and analysis.[2]

For each noun in the vocabulary list collected in the course of fieldwork, a note was made of the classifiers typically associated with the noun, and this piece of information was included in the dictionary of Yongning Na (Michaud 2015a), following the example of Eugénie Henderson's dictionary of Bwe Karen (Henderson 1997). This obviously does not capture the full range of stylistic possibilities in the choice of classifiers, which are best studied from their actual use: "a noun can be accompanied by various classifiers depending on context, so it may not be adequate to describe one of these as the primary classifier at a lexical level" (François 2000: 167).[3] But this information came in handy to put together a list of classifiers, yielding a total of over one hundred monosyllabic classifiers. (Disyllabic classifiers will be dealt with separately in §4.1.7.)

4.1.1 Elicitation procedures

The logical first step in the study of the tones of classifiers consisted of conducting systematic elicitation with numerals.[4] A first data set was elicited in 2009, covering the range of numerals from 1 to 30. Elicitation yielded less than fully consistent results, due in part to the fact that the consultant was not accustomed to lengthy counting tasks. One and the same noun-plus-classifier combination was

---

[2] An earlier version of this section was published as Michaud (2013c). Among other differences, subcategories of tones for classifiers are now distinguished through subscript letters, e.g. M_a and M_b instead of the earlier notation as M1 and M2.

[3] *Original text:* le même nom peut être accompagné de plusieurs classificateurs selon les contextes, sans qu'il soit légitime d'en privilégier un comme fondamental dès le lexique.

[4] Classifiers are bound forms, which cannot be elicited in isolation (without an accompanying numeral or demonstrative). Numerals do not usually appear on their own either, but it is possible, at a push, to elicit them in isolation. The forms from one to ten are: /ɖɯ˧/ '1', /ɲi˧/ '2', /so˧/ '3', /ʐv˧/ '4', /ŋwɤ˧/ '5', /qʰv˧/ '6', /ʂɯ˧/ '7', /hõ˧/ '8', /gv˧/ '9', and /tsʰe˧/ '10'.

realized with different tone patterns during different elicitation sessions. When such discrepancies were pointed out to the consultant, she would identify one pattern as correct and reject the others as mistaken. However, these *a posteriori* judgments also wavered: a variant that had been brushed aside as mistaken would come up again in a later session, and the consultant would then insist that it was correct. Initially, I wrongly assumed that only one tone pattern could be correct, but then it gradually became clear that there are two variants for some of the phrases. For instance, the association of '9' with the classifier for threads can be realized either as /**gɤ˧-kʰɯ˧**/ or as /**gɤ˧-kʰɯ˩**/. Taking into account these two factors – that occasional mistakes are not uncommon in systematic elicitation, and that two variants can both be correct –, a comprehensive description could finally be arrived at, dissipating earlier perplexity and frustration.

The data collected in 2009, covering the range of numerals from 1 to 30, shows that some classifiers have a tantalizingly similar but not identical behaviour: for instance, the classifier for days and the classifier for steps (of stairs) yield the same tone patterns for numerals up to thirteen, but differ for 14, 15, 16, 18, 19 and 22, as shown in Table 4.1. Thus, 'fourteen steps' is //**tsʰe˩zv˧-ɖwæ˧˥**// (tone: L+H$; surface phonological form: /**tsʰe˩zv˧-ɖwæ˧**/), whereas 'fourteen days' is //**tsʰe˩zv˧-ɲi˩**// (tone: L; surface phonological form: /**tsʰe˩zv˧-ɲi˩**/).

This finding led to the decision to include the full range of numerals from 1 to 100 in a second set of recordings. A total of 2,810 numeral-plus-classifier phrases were recorded. In the recordings that cover the range from 1 to 100, the intervals [50..59] and [80..89] were not recorded, because previous elicitation had shown that their tone patterns were identical with those of [40..49] and [60..69], respectively. Shortening the list of numerals reduced consultant fatigue.

The entire set of transcribed recordings is available online, with both a surface phonological transcription and an indication of the underlying tonal pattern.

No amount of continuous speech would be enough to obtain all the numeral-plus-classifier combinations from 1 to 100, hence the choice to resort to systematic elicitation. However, some of the combinations are also attested in the transcribed narratives.

Table 4.1: Surface phonological form of the classifiers for days and for steps, in association with numerals from 1 to 30.

NUM	CLF.days	CLF.steps	comparison
1	dɯ˧-ɲi˥	dɯ˧-kʰv̩˥	same
2	ɲi˧-ɲi˥	ɲi˧-kʰv̩˥	same
3	so˩-ɲi˩	so˩-kʰv̩˩	same
4	ʐv̩˧-ɲi˧	ʐv̩˧-kʰv̩˧	same
5	ŋwɤ˧-ɲi˧	ŋwɤ˧-kʰv̩˧	same
6	qʰv̩˧-ɲi˥	qʰv̩˧-kʰv̩˥	same
7	ʂɯ˧-ɲi˧	ʂɯ˧-kʰv̩˧	same
8	hõ˧-ɲi˥	hõ˧-kʰv̩˥	same
9	gv̩˧-ɲi˧	gv̩˧-kʰv̩˧	same
10	tsʰe˩-ɲi˩	tsʰe˩-kʰv̩˩	same
11	tsʰe˩dɯ˩-ɲi˩	tsʰe˩dɯ˩-kʰv̩˩	same
12	tsʰe˩ɲi˩-ɲi˩	tsʰe˩ɲi˩-kʰv̩˩	same
13	tsʰe˩so˩-ɲi˩	tsʰe˩so˩-kʰv̩˩	same
14	tsʰe˩ʐv̩˩-ɲi˩	tsʰe˩ʐv̩˩-kʰv̩˥	different
15	tsʰe˩ŋwɤ˩-ɲi˩	tsʰe˩ŋwɤ˩-kʰv̩˥	different
16	tsʰe˩qʰv̩˩-ɲi˩	tsʰe˩qʰv̩˩-kʰv̩˥	different
17	tsʰe˩ʂɯ˩-ɲi˩	tsʰe˩ʂɯ˩-kʰv̩˩	same
18	tsʰe˩hõ˩-ɲi˩	tsʰe˩hõ˩-kʰv̩˥	different
19	tsʰe˩gv̩˩-ɲi˩	tsʰe˩gv̩˩-kʰv̩˥	different
20	ɲi˧tsi˧-ɲi˧	ɲi˧tsi˧-kʰv̩˧	same
21	ɲi˧tsi˧dɯ˧-ɲi˥	ɲi˧tsi˧dɯ˧-kʰv̩˥	same
22	ɲi˧tsi˧ɲi˧-ɲi˧	ɲi˧tsi˧ɲi˧-kʰv̩˥	different
23	ɲi˧tsi˧so˩-ɲi˩	ɲi˧tsi˧so˩-kʰv̩˩	same
24	ɲi˧tsi˧ʐv̩˧-ɲi˧	ɲi˧tsi˧ʐv̩˧-kʰv̩˧	same
25	ɲi˧tsi˧ŋwɤ˧-ɲi˧	ɲi˧tsi˧ŋwɤ˧-kʰv̩˧	same
26	ɲi˧tsi˧qʰv̩˧-ɲi˥	ɲi˧tsi˧qʰv̩˧-kʰv̩˥	same
27	ɲi˧tsi˧ʂɯ˧-ɲi˧	ɲi˧tsi˧ʂɯ˧-kʰv̩˧	same
28	ɲi˧tsi˧hõ˧-ɲi˥	ɲi˧tsi˧hõ˧-kʰv̩˥	same
29	ɲi˧tsi˧gv̩˧-ɲi˧	ɲi˧tsi˧gv̩˧-kʰv̩˧	same
30	so˧tsʰi˧-ɲi˧	so˧tsʰi˧-kʰv̩˧	same

4.1.2 Results: Nine tonal categories for monosyllabic classifiers

The nine tonal categories were brought out by distributional analysis, distinguishing sets of monosyllabic classifiers that have the same behaviour when combined with numerals. These nine categories are shown in the nine data columns of Tables 4.3a–d and 4.4a–d.

The choice of labels for the nine categories brought out by distributional analysis was guided by structural hints. The tone patterns in association with the numerals '6' and '8' is not highly informative, since almost all tonal oppositions are neutralized in this context (the only tones that are observed are H# and H$). Likewise, in phrases involving '3' and '10', only two patterns are observed. After '4' and '5', four groups can be distinguished, but if these patterns were indicative of the classifiers' lexical tone, the system would only contain two High tones (#H and H#) and two L tones (L# and L). There would be no Mid tones, and no contours. This would be completely unlike the lexical tones of the other monosyllabic nouns found in Yongning Na, which consist of H, M, L and two types of rising contours, analyzed as MH and LM.

On the other hand, the tone patterns in association with the numerals '1' and '2' make good sense as labels for tonal categories. These four patterns are H, MH, M and L, all of which exist as lexical tones for nouns. They are therefore adopted, adding a letter to distinguish the subcategories (two for H, MH and M, and three for L), by order of decreasing frequency (e.g. there are more classifiers in category M_a than M_b). Such labels for subcategories are also used for verbs, among which it is necessary to distinguish two subcategories of L tones, L_a and L_b, and three subcategories of M tones, M_a, M_b and M_c (see Chapter 6). Note, however, that tonal subcategories are established separately for nouns and verbs, and that no arguments can be proposed to identify these subcategories across parts of speech. For instance, the label 'L_a' as used for verbs does not refer to the same category as 'L_a' for classifiers. In order to preclude misunderstandings, it would be possible to use different subscript letters, for instance using Greek letters for subcategories of classifiers, and Latin letters for subcategories of verbs. But it seemed advisable to use Latin letters in all cases to avoid an extravagant profusion of symbols.

The nine categories (H_a, H_b, MH_a, MH_b, M_a, M_b, L_a, L_b and L_c) are illustrated in Table 4.2.

Table 4.2: One example of each of the nine tonal categories of monosyllabic classifiers.

classifier	tone	description: classifier for...
ɖwæ˧	H_a	steps (of stairs)
ɲi˧	H_b	days
hɑ̃˧	MH_a	nights
kv˧	MH_b	people, persons
nɑ˧	M_a	tools
dzi˧	M_b	pairs of non-separable objects, e.g. shoes
dze˩	L_a	pairs of separable objects, e.g. pots, bottles
dzi˩	L_b	trees, bamboos
ʐɤ˩	L_c	lines, patterns (in weaving or drawing)

A summary of all the tone patterns which these nine categories of classifiers yield in association with numerals in the range from 1 to 100 is presented in Tables 4.3a–d and 4.4a–d. These tables contain, in tightly packed form, the information necessary to generate the surface phonological tone patterns of all numeral-plus-classifier phrases in the Alawa dialect of Yongning Na.

The mass of information presented in Tables 4.3a–d and 4.4a–d may seem staggering. Were it not for the clear evidence from recorded data, one could suspect that this multiplicity of tone patterns was an artefact of elicitation procedures.

Variants are separated by a slash (/). For typographical reasons, the table is divided into two halves: the H and MH tones (H_a, H_b, MH_a and MH_b) in a first table (4.3), and the M and L tones (M_a, M_b, L_a, L_b and L_c) in a second table (4.4).

Numeral-plus-classifier phrases typically constitute one single tone group[5] – although speakers can choose to split them into two groups for expressive (emphatic) purposes, as will be discussed in Chapter 7. The juncture indicated by '–' does not separate the phrase into two tone groups, but into two parts, corresponding to tens on the one hand, units and the classifier on the other. This juncture is found after the first two syllables, in phrases containing numerals above twenty. These phrases consist of two syllables referring to tens ('two-ten' for 'twenty', 'three-ten' for 'thirty', and so on) followed by the last digit followed by the classifier (except for the round figures 'twenty', 'thirty' and so on: no zero is indicated, and the classifier follows directly, as in /ʐv˧tsʰi˩-kʰv˩/ 'forty years').

---

[5] The *tone group* is the unit within which tonal processes apply in Yongning Na. It could also be referred to as *phonological phrase*. Chapter 7 is devoted to this morphotonological unit, which is fundamental to Na prosody.

Table 4.3a: The underlying tone patterns of the nine categories of numeral-plus-classifier phrases. H and MH tones. Numerals from 1 to 25.

	H$_a$	H$_b$	MH$_a$	MH$_b$
1	H$	H$	MH#	MH#
2	H$	H$	MH#	MH#
3	L	L	L	L
4	#H	#H	L#	L
5	#H	#H	L#	L
6	H$	H$	H#	H$
7	#H	#H	MH#	MH#
8	H$	H$	H#	H$
9	#H	#H	L#	L
10	L	L	L	L
11	L	L	L	L
12	L	L	L	L
13	L	L	L	L
14	L+H$	L	L+H#	L+H#
15	L+H$	L	L+H#	L+H#
16	L+H$	L	L+H#	L+H#
17	L	L	L	L
18	L+H$	L	L+H#	L+H#
19	L+H$	L	L+H#	L+H#
20	#H	#H	MH#	MH#
21	H$	H$	MH#	MH#
22	H$	#H	MH#	MH#
23	−L	−L	−L	−L
24	#H	#H	−L#	−L
25	#H	#H	−L#	−L

Table 4.3b: The underlying tone patterns of the nine categories of numeral-plus-classifier phrases. H and MH tones. Numerals from 26 to 50.

	H$_a$	H$_b$	MH$_a$	MH$_b$
26	H$	H$	H#	H$
27	#H	#H	MH#	MH#
28	H$	H$	H#	H$
29	#H	#H	−L#	−L
30	#H	#H	MH#	MH#
31	H$	H$	MH#	MH#
32	H$	#H	MH#	MH#
33	−L	−L	−L	−L
34	#H	#H	−L#	−L
35	#H	#H	−L#	−L
36	H$	H$	H#	H$
37	#H	#H	MH#	MH#
38	H$	H$	H#	H$
39	#H/−L	#H	−L#	−L
40	L#−	L#−	L#−	L#−
41	L#−H$ / L#−	L#−H$ / L#−	L#−MH# / L#−	L#−MH#
42	L#−H$ / L#−	L#−#H / L#−	L#−MH# / L#−	L#−MH#
43	L#−L	L#−L / L#−	L#−L	L#−L
44	L#−#H / L#−	L#−#H / L#−	L#−L#	L#−L
45	L#−#H / L#−	L#−#H / L#−	L#−L#	L#−L
46	L#−H$	L#−H$	L#−H#	L#−H$
47	L#−#H	L#−#H	L#−MH#	L#−MH#
48	L#−H$	L#−H$	L#−H#	L#−H$
49	L#−#H / L#−L	L#−#H / L#−	L#−L#	L#−L
50	L#−	L#−	L#−	L#−

Table 4.3c: The underlying tone patterns of the nine categories of numeral-plus-classifier phrases. H and MH tones. Numerals from 51 to 75.

	H$_a$	H$_b$	MH$_a$	MH$_b$
51	L#–H$ / L#–	L#–H$ / L#–	L#–MH / L#–	L#–MH#
52	L#–H$ / L#–	L#–#H / L#–	L#–MH / L#–	L#–MH#
53	L#–	L#–	L#–L	L#–L
54	L#–#H / L#–	L#–#H / L#–	L#–L#	L#–L
55	L#–#H / L#–	L#–#H / L#–	L#–L#	L#–L
56	L#–H$	L#–H$	L#–H#	L#–H$
57	L#–#H	L#–#H	L#–MH#	L#–MH#
58	L#–H$	L#–H$	L#–H#	L#–H$
59	L#–#H / L#–	L#–#H / L#–	L#–L#	L#–L
60	LM–H$	LM–H$	LM–H#	LM–#H
61	LM–H$	LM–H$	LM–H#	LM–#H
62	LM–H$ / LM–#H	LM–#H	LM–H#	LM–H#
63	LM–H$ / LM–L	LM–H$ / LM–L	LM–H#	LM–H#
64	LM–#H	LM–#H	LM–H#	LM–H#
65	LM–#H	LM–#H	LM–H#	LM–H#
66	LM–H$	LM–H$	LM–H#	LM–H#
67	LM–#H	LM–#H	LM–H#	LM–H#
68	LM–H$	LM–H$	LM–H#	LM–H#
69	LM–#H / LM–L	LM–L	LM–H#	LM–H#
70	L#–	L#–	L#–	L#–
71	L#–H$ / L#–	L#–H$	L#–MH# / L#–	L#–MH#
72	L#–H$ / L#–	L#–#H	L#–MH# / L#–	L#–MH#
73	L#–L	L#–L	L#–L	L#–L
74	L#–#H	L#–#H	L#–MH# / L#–	L#–L
75	L#–#H	L#–#H	L#–MH# / L#–	L#–L

Table 4.3d: The underlying tone patterns of the nine categories of numeral-plus-classifier phrases. H and MH tones. Numerals from 76 to 100.

	H$_a$	H$_b$	MH$_a$	MH$_b$
76	L#–H$	L#–H$	L#–H# / L#–	L#–H#
77	L#–#H	L#–#H	L#–MH# / L#–	L#–MH#
78	L#–H$	L#–H$	L#–H# / L#–	L#–H#
79	L#–#H / L#–L	L#–#H	L#–L#	L#–L
80	LM–H$	LM–H$	LM–H#	LM–H#
81	LM–H$	LM–H$	LM–H#	LM–H#
82	LM–H$	LM–#H	LM–H#	LM–H#
83	LM–H$	LM–H$ / LM–L	LM–H#	LM–H#
84	LM–#H	LM–H$	LM–H#	LM–H#
85	LM–#H	LM–#H	LM–H#	LM–H#
86	LM–H$	LM–H$	LM–H#	LM–H#
87	LM–#H	LM–#H	LM–H#	LM–H#
88	LM–H$	LM–H$	LM–H#	LM–H#
89	LM–#H	LM–#H	LM–H#	LM–H#
90	L#–	L#–	L#–	L#–
91	L#–H$	L#–H$	L#–MH# / L#–	L#–MH# / L#–
92	L#–H$	L#–#H	L#–MH# / L#–	L#–MH# / L#–
93	L#–L	L#–L	L#–L	L#–L
94	L#–#H	L#–#H	L#–L# / L#–	L#–L
95	L#–#H	L#–#H	L#–L# / L#–	L#–L
96	L#–H$	L#–H$	L#–H# / L#–	L#–H# / L#–
97	L#–#H	L#–#H	L#–MH# / L#–	L#–MH# / L#–
98	L#–H$	L#–H$	L#–H# / L#–	L#–H# / L#–
99	L#–L	L#–#H	L#–L# / L#–	L#–L
100	#H	#H	MH#	MH#

Table 4.4a: The underlying tone patterns of the nine categories of numeral-plus-classifier phrases. M and L tones. Numerals from 1 to 25.

	M_a	M_b	L_a	L_b	L_c
1	M	M	L#	L#	L#
2	M	M	L#	L#	L#
3	M	M	L	M	M
4	L	L	H#	H#	H#
5	L	L	H#	H#	H#
6	H#	H$	H#	H#	H#
7	M	M	L#	L#	L#
8	H#	H$	H#	H#	H#
9	L	L	H#	H# / L#	H#
10	M	M	L	M	L
11	M	M	L#	L#	L#
12	M	M	L#	L#	L#
13	M	M	L#	L#	L#
14	L+H#	L	L+H#	L+H#	L+H#
15	L+H#	L	L+H#	L+H#	L+H#
16	L+H#	L	L+H#	L+H#	L+H#
17	M	M	L#	L#	L#
18	L+H#	L	L+H#	L+H#	L+H#
19	L+H#	L	L+H#	L+H#	L+H#
20	M	M	−L	−L	−L
21	M	M	−L#	−L#	−L#
22	M	M	−L#	−L#	−L#
23	−L / M	M / −L	−L	−L	−L
24	−L	−L	H#	H#	H#
25	−L	−L	H#	H#	H#

Table 4.4b: The underlying tone patterns of the nine categories of numeral-plus-classifier phrases. M and L tones. Numerals from 26 to 50.

	M$_a$	M$_b$	L$_a$	L$_b$	L$_c$
26	H#	H$	H#	H#	H#
27	M	M	−L#	−L#	−L#
28	H#	H$	H#	H#	H#
29	−L	−L	H#	−L# / H#	H#
30	M	M	−L#	−L	−L#
31	M	M	−L#	−L#	−L#
32	M	M	−L#	−L#	−L#
33	−L	−L	−L	−L	−L
34	−L	−L	H#	H#	H#
35	−L	−L	H#	H#	H#
36	H#	H$	H#	H#	H#
37	M	L	−L#	−L#	−L#
38	H#	H$	H#	H#	H#
39	−L	−L	H# / −L#	H# / −L#	H# / −L#
40	L#−	L#−	L#−	L#−	L#−
41	L#−	L#−M / L#−	L#−L# / L#−	L#−L# / L#−	L#−L# / L#−
42	L#−	L#−M / L#−	L#−L# / L#−	L#−L# / L#−	L#−L# / L#−
43	L#−	L#−M / L#−	L#−M / L#−L	L#−M / L#−	L#−M / L#−
44	L#−H# / L#−	L#−	L#−H# / L#−	L#−H# / L#−	L#−H# / L#−
45	L#−H# / L#−	L#−	L#−H# / L#−	L#−H# / L#−	L#−H# / L#−
46	L#−H# / L#−	L#−H$ / L#−	L#−H# / L#−	L#−H# / L#−	L#−H# / L#−
47	L#−M / L#−	L#−M / L#−	L#−L# / L#−	L#−L# / L#−	L#−L# / L#−
48	L#−H# / L#−	L#−H$ / L#−	L#−H# / L#−	L#−H# / L#−	L#−H# / L#−
49	L#−H# / L#−	L#−L	L#−H# / L#−	L#−H# / L#−	L#−H# / L#−
50	L#−	L#−	L#−	L#−	L#−

Table 4.4c: The underlying tone patterns of the nine categories of numeral-plus-classifier phrases. M and L tones. Numerals from 51 to 75.

	M_a	M_b	L_a	L_b	L_c
51	L#–	L#–M / L#–	L#–L# / L#–	L#–L# / L#–	L#–L# / L#–
52	L#–	L#–M / L#–	L#–L# / L#–	L#–L# / L#–	L#–L# / L#–
53	L#–	L#–M / L#–	L#–M / L#–L	L#–M / L#–	L#–M / L#–
54	L#–H# / L#–	L#–	L#–H# / L#–	L#–H# / L#–	L#–H# / L#–
55	L#–H# / L#–	L#–	L#–H# / L#–	L#–H# / L#–	L#–H# / L#–
56	L#–H# / L#–	L#–H$ / L#–	L#–H# / L#–	L#–H# / L#–	L#–H# / L#–
57	L#–M / L#–	L#–M / L#–	L#–L# / L#–	L#–L# / L#–	L#–L# / L#–
58	L#–H# / L#–	L#–H$ / L#–	L#–H# / L#–	L#–H# / L#–	L#–H# / L#–
59	L#–H# / L#–	L#–L	L#–H# / L#–	L#–H# / L#–	L#–H# / L#–
60	LM–H#	LM–H$	LM–H#	LM–H#	LM–H#
61	LM–H# / L+MH#–M	LM–H$	LM–H#	LM–H#	LM–H#
62	LM–H# / L+MH#–M	LM–H$	LM–H#	LM–H#	LM–H#
63	LM–H# / L+MH#–M	LM–H$	LM–H#	LM–H#	LM–H#
64	LM–H# / L+MH#–L	LM–H$	LM–H#	LM–H#	LM–H#
65	LM–H# / L+MH#–L	LM–H$	LM–H#	LM–H#	LM–H#
66	LM–H#	LM–H$	LM–H#	LM–H#	LM–H#
67	LM–H# / L+MH#–M	LM–#H	LM–H#	LM–H#	LM–H#
68	LM–H#	LM–H$	LM–H#	LM–H#	LM–H#
69	LM–H# / L+MH#–L	LM–H$ / LM–L	LM–H#	LM–H#	LM–H#
70	L#–	L#–	L#–	L#–	L#–
71	L#– / L#–M	L#–M / L#–	L#–L# / L#–	L#–L# / L#–	L#–L# / L#–
72	L#– / L#–M	L#–M / L#–	L#–L# / L#–	L#–L# / L#–	L#–L# / L#–
73	L#– / L#–M	L#–M / L#–	L#–L	L#–M / L#–	L#–M / L#–
74	L#– / L#–H#	L#–L	L#–H# / L#–	L#–H# / L#–	L#–H# / L#–
75	L#– / L#–H#	L#–L	L#–H# / L#–	L#–H# / L#–	L#–H# / L#–

Table 4.4d: The underlying tone patterns of the nine categories of numeral-plus-classifier phrases. M and L tones. Numerals from 75 to 100.

	M_a	M_b	L_a	L_b	L_c
76	L#–H# / L#–	L#–H$ / L#–	L#–H# / L#–	L#–H# / L#–	L#–H# / L#–
77	L#–M / L#–	L#–M / L#–	L#–L# / L#–	L#–L# / L#–	L#–L# / L#–
78	L#–H# / L#–	L#–H$ / L#–	L#–H# / L#–	L#–H# / L#–	L#–H# / L#–
79	L#–L / L#–H#	L#–L	L#–H# / L#–	L#–H# / L#–	L#–H# / L#–
80	LM–H#	LM–H$	LM–H#	LM–H#	LM–H#
81	LM–H# / L+MH#–M	LM–H$	LM–H#	LM–H#	LM–H#
82	LM–H# / L+MH#–M	LM–H$	LM–H#	LM–H#	LM–H#
83	LM–H# / L+MH#–M	LM–H$	LM–H#	LM–H#	LM–H#
84	LM–H# / L+MH#–L	LM–H$	LM–H#	LM–H#	LM–H#
85	LM–H# / L+MH#–L	LM–H$	LM–H#	LM–H#	LM–H#
86	LM–H#	LM–H$	LM–H#	LM–H#	LM–H#
87	LM–H# / L+MH#–M	LM–#H	LM–H#	LM–H#	LM–H#
88	LM–H#	LM–H$	LM–H#	LM–H#	LM–H#
89	LM–H# / L+MH#–L	LM–H$ / LM–L	LM–H#	LM–H#	LM–H#
90	L#– / L#–	L#–	L#–	L#–	L#–
91	L#–M / L#–	L#–M / L#–	L#–L# / L#–	L#–L# / L#–	L#–L#
92	L#–M / L#–	L#–M / L#–	L#–L# / L#–	L#–L# / L#–	L#–L#
93	L#–M / L#–	L#–M / L#–	L#–M / L#–	L#–M / L#–	L#–M / L#–
94	L#–L / L#–H#	L#–	L#–H# / L#–	L#–H# / L#–	L#–H#
95	L#–L / L#–H#	L#–	L#–H# / L#–	L#–H# / L#–	L#–H#
96	L#–H# / L#–	L#–H$ / L#–	L#–H#	L#–H# / L#–	L#–H#
97	L#–M / L#–	L#–M / L#–	L#–L# / L#–	L#–L# / L#–	L#–L#
98	L#–H# / L#–	L#–H$ / L#–	L#–H#	L#–H# / L#–	L#–H#
99	L#–L / L#–H#	L#–L	L#–H#	L#–H# / L#–	L#–H# / L#
100	M	M	L#	L#	L#

For instance, /so˧tsʰi˧˗so˩-ɲi˩/ '33 days' can be represented as /so˧tsʰi˧–so˩-ɲi˩/ to show the juncture between the two parts (glosses for the four syllables: 'three - ten – three - CLF.days'). The items in Tables 4.3a–d and 4.4a–d that begin with '–' do not have any specified tone on their first part; that part receives a Mid tone by default. Using again the phrase '33 days' as an example, it has a –L tone pattern: a Low tone that associates after the juncture, yielding /…so˩-ɲi˩/. Since Low tones do not spread regressively ('right-to-left'), the first part of the phrase receives M tone by default (/so˧tsʰi˧…/), resulting in the final output /so˧tsʰi˧˗so˩-ɲi˩/.

Likewise, the items whose tone pattern ends with '–' do not have any specified tone on their second part. That part receives its tones by the application of the phonological tone rules that govern tonal groups in the Alawa dialect of Yongning Na. For instance, 'forty years' has the tone pattern L#–: L# tone (a final L tone) associates to the first half of the phrase, yielding /zɯ.tsʰi˩…/. As already mentioned, tones do not spread leftward; the first syllable receives a Mid tone by default, hence /zɯ˧tsʰi˩…/. At this point a phonological tonal rule applies (see §7.1.1): Rule 5, "All syllables following a H.L or M.L sequence receive L tone". This amounts to saying that a tone cannot be surrounded by higher tones within a tone group: there are no | MLM | sequences, nor are there | HMH |, | HLM |, | MLMH |, and so on. The only possible tone on the second part of the phrase is therefore L. The final output is /zɯ˧tsʰi˩-kʰv˩/, as shown in Figure 4.1.

4.1.3 Why little evidence about the tones of classifiers can be gleaned from the free forms in which they originate

In what precedes, the tones of classifiers were analyzed on the basis of synchronic distributional properties. Mention needs to be made of other methods, and why they have not provided decisive evidence so far on the phonological nature of the tonal categories of classifiers.

Relevant evidence could, in principle, come from those classifiers that correspond transparently to a free form: a noun or a verb. For example, the classifier for blows is /dɑ˧/, a cognate object of the verb /dɑ˧/ 'to hit, to strike', as exemplified in (1).

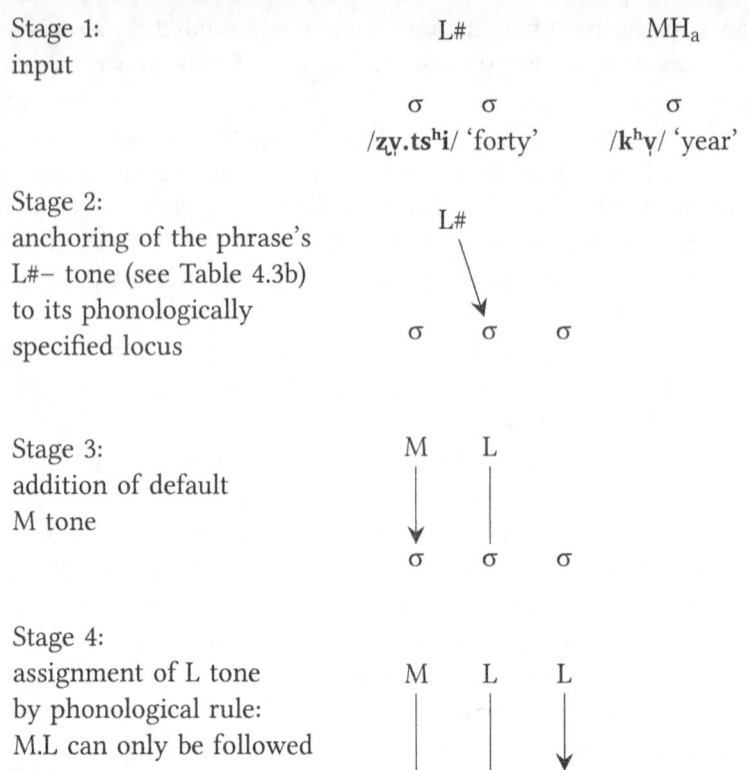

Figure 4.1: A detailed representation of tone-to-syllable association for the numeral-plus-classifier phrase /ʐʯ˧tsʰi˩-kʰɤ˩/ 'forty years'.

(1) ɖɯ˧-dɑ˧ tʰi˩-dɑ˩
    ɖɯ˧   dɑ˧   tʰi˩-   dɑ˧
    one   CLF.blows DUR to_strike
    'to strike blows' (Sister3.135)

The tonal correspondence with the verb looks transparent: both the verb and its grammaticalized form as a classifier carry MH tone. Similarly, 'mountain, hill' is /ʁwɤ˧/, and as a classifier it yields /ʁwɤ˧/ 'heap (of something)', which has the same phonological form as the free noun, including its M tone. 'Beam', /ɖʐo˧/, is also identical in form to its self-classifier /ɖʐo˧/. Taking these three examples, it seems as if the tone category of a classifier were identical to that of the corresponding free form.

Other examples, however, do not exhibit such simple correspondences. A different tonal correspondence for H-tone nouns is exemplified by /kɯ˥/ 'star', which yields /kɯ˧/ (M_b category) as a self-classifier. 'Bowl' is /qʰwɤ˧˩/ (LM tone), whereas as a classifier it yields /qʰwɤ˧˥/ 'bowlful' (MH_a category). To date, too few classifiers can be straightforwardly related to full nouns (or verbs) for the search of tonal correspondences between lexical word and classifier to be fruitful.

Classifiers borrowed from Mandarin constitute another potential source of evidence on the tones of Yongning Na classifiers. For instance, it can be assumed that the tone subcategories used to accommodate recent borrowings serve in synchrony as unmarked, default categories: H_a or H_b, MH_a or MH_b, and so on. However, only one borrowing was observed: /tɕi˥/ for 'pound (weight unit)', from Mandarin *jīn* 斤. Its tonal category is MH_a, i.e. the majority category for classifiers with a MH tone, but it would be unreasonable to draw general conclusions from this isolated example. The way forward here would consist in a more thorough study of Chinese loanwords than has been conducted so far.

4.1.4 Indirect confirmation for the H, MH, M and L categories of classifiers from frequency in surface forms

The frequency of appearance of the various tonal levels provides support (albeit weak and indirect) for the four tonal 'super-categories' of classifiers proposed here, namely H, MH, M and L. Under the (admittedly simplistic) assumption that the contribution made by the tone of the classifier will be reflected statistically in the tone patterns of numeral-plus-classifier phrases, the labels H, MH, M and L adopted here make good sense. Averaging over the entire range of tone patterns from the number 1 to the number 100, the categories that have a High tone after '1' and '2' (labelled H_a and H_b in Tables 4.3a–d and 4.4a–d) are also those with the highest proportion of H tones (either on their own: H#, #H, H$, or as part of a MH or MH# contour) and the lowest proportion of L tones. Conversely, the three tonal categories of classifiers that have a Low tone after '1' and '2' (analyzed phonologically as L_a, L_b and L_c, respectively) have the lowest proportion of H tones and the highest of L tones. The other two categories (with subgroups M_a and M_b, and MH_a and MH_b) are between these two extremes. Again as expected, M_a and M_b have a higher proportion of M tones, and a lower proportion of H tones, than MH_a and MH_b. These rule-of-thumb comparisons, which do not carry demonstrative value, are simply mentioned to convey a feel for the overall outlook of the data.

Another indirect way of approaching this data consists of examining the occasional mistakes made by the consultant.

4.1.5 The amount of mistakes in the recordings correlates with the degree of tonal complexity

As was mentioned earlier (§4.1.1), the task of realizing long series of numeral-plus-classifier phrases was challenging for the consultant. Among the 2,810 tokens, 7% have a mistaken tone pattern,[6] i.e. a tone pattern which the consultant (F4) consistently judged to be incorrect (a tonal slip of the tongue) when we returned to the data after recording sessions.

These mistakes reflect in part the phonological complexity of the tone patterns at issue. The notion that mistakes provide insights about language dates back at least to Henri Frei's *Grammar of mistakes* (1929); see also Fromkin (1973), Rossi & Peter-Defare (1998) and Nooteboom (2011). The usefulness of speech errors and word games to gain insights into tonal systems was shown by Hombert (1986: 180–181). Speakers of Mandarin, Cantonese, Minnan and Thai tend to move the tones with the syllables when changing a $C_1V_1C_2V_2$ sequence into $C_1V_2C_2V_1$ or $C_2V_2C_1V_1$, whereas speakers of Bakwiri (also known as Bakweri; Bantu branch of Niger-Congo) tend to leave tone patterns unchanged. (See also Wan & Jaeger (1998) on Mandarin.)

Figure 4.2 shows the distribution of mistakes as a factor of the range of tens: how many of the observed mistakes concern numerals between 1 and 9 (leftmost bar), 10 and 19 (second bar), etc. The ranges of numerals between 50 and 59, and between 80 and 89, are not represented: they were not included in the recordings (to reduce the consultant's fatigue), because the phonological tone patterns for 50–59 are always identical with those for 40–49, and those for 80–89 with 60–69.

Figure 4.3 shows the distribution of mistakes as a factor of the last digit (units): how many mistakes concern numbers ending in '1' (namely 1, 11, 21, 31, 41, and so on), in '2', etc.

The data is not symmetrical enough for a full-fledged statistical treatment. In particular, (i) there is more data for some tonal categories than others, (ii) some combinations have several repetitions, and (iii) there is slightly more data in the range [1..10] than for higher numerals. Some observations can nonetheless be made. The numerals ending in '6' and '8' (e.g. '6', '16', '26'; '8', '18', '28') are noticeably less subject to mistakes, and those beginning with these same numbers (e.g. '60', '61', '62', '63', '80', '81', '82', '83') are also slightly less often mispronounced than neighbouring "numeral-runs". Importantly, numerals ending in '6' and '8' are also the least complex in tonal terms, due to the neutralization

---

[6] This figure includes some items that were deleted from the sound files at an early stage of the study, before the principle of preserving the recordings unchanged was adopted.

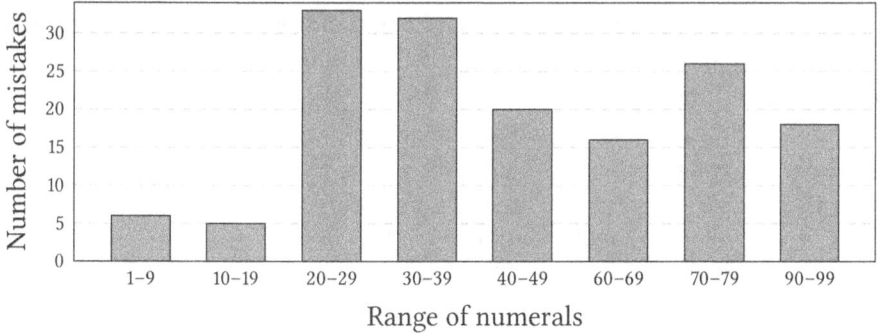

Figure 4.2: Number of mistakes in the recorded numeral-plus-classifier phrases as a factor of the range of tens.

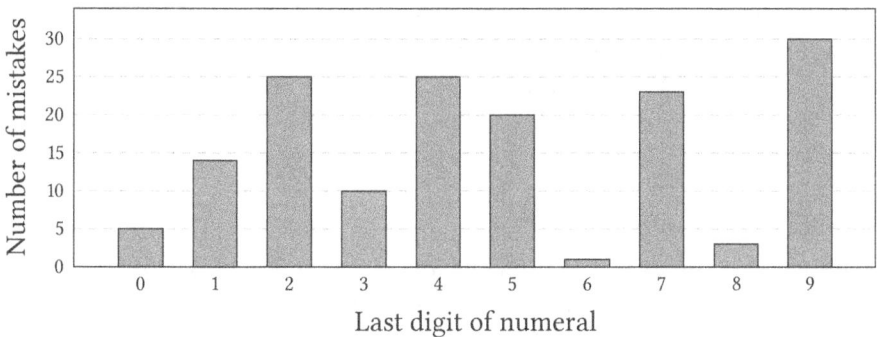

Figure 4.3: Number of mistakes in the recorded numeral-plus-classifier phrases as a function of the last digit (units).

of many tonal distinctions after these two numerals. By contrast, numeral-plus-classifier phrases containing numbers ending in '7' and '9', which display the greatest diversity in tone patterns, are among the most frequently mistaken, although '7' does not stand out within the top half of the list of mistakes, which includes {2, 4, 5, 7, 9}.

4.1.6 About variants of tone patterns

As noted at the outset of this chapter, some phrases allow for variant tone patterns. This situation is more frequent for higher numerals than for numerals below twenty. For instance, the association of '47' with the classifier for round objects can be realized either as /ʐv̩˧tsʰi˩-ʂɯ˧-ɭɯ˥/ or as /ʐv̩˧tsʰi˩-ʂɯ˩-ɭɯ˩/. No observed numeral-plus-classifier phrase has more than two acceptable variants for its tone pattern.

Many of the variants can be explained in light of the phonological rules which hold within a tone group (see §7.1.1). If the numeral-plus-classifier phrase is treated as one tone group, then these rules apply. For instance, the numeral '44' in association with the classifier for tools, /na˧a/, allows for the following two variants: /ʐv̩˧tsʰi˩–ʐv̩˧-na˥/ and /ʐv̩˧tsʰi˩–ʐv̩˧-na˩/. The first of these phrases, /ʐv̩˧tsʰi˩–ʐv̩˧-na˥/, is not a well-formed tone group, since it does not obey Rule 5: inside a tone group, all syllables following a M.L sequence receive L tone. The expression /ʐv̩˧tsʰi˩–ʐv̩˧-na˥/ is therefore to be analyzed as consisting of two tone groups: /ʐv̩˧tsʰi˩ | ʐv̩˧-na˥/ (tone pattern: L# for the first tone group, and H# for the second). If this phrase were treated as one tone group, the tones of its last two syllables would be lowered to L. This is precisely what happens in the other variant that is attested for this phrase: /ʐv̩˧tsʰi˩ʐv̩˩-na˩/ (tone pattern: L#–). The two variants can therefore be described as (i) a form consisting of two tone groups, and (ii) a simplified form, whose tonal pattern results straightforwardly from its treatment as a single tone group. (The same phenomenon is reported in the Lataddi dialect: see Dobbs & La 2016.)

The same applies to all tonal patterns in the range [40..59], [70..79] and [90..99], since the first two syllables (corresponding to '40', '50', '70' and '90' respectively) have a Mid-plus-Low pattern. This pattern precludes any tone other than L on the following syllables within the same tone group (by Rule 5). One would therefore expect all of these combinations to have two variants. This holds true as a general rule: when the consultant indicated a complex form and I tried substituting a simplified form, that form was never rejected by the consultant. On the other hand, for some combinations only the simpler form is acceptable. For instance, for '44' with a classifier of category M_b, such as /lɯ˧b/ (the classifier for round objects), one has to say /ʐv̩˧tsʰi˩ʐv̩˩-lɯ˩/ (tone pattern: L#–).

Supposing, on the analogy of category M_a, that †ʐv̩˧tsʰi˩ | ʐv̩˧-lɯ˥ was acceptable at an earlier stage of the language, it must be supposed to have fallen out of use. For category M_a, where there are currently two variants in common use, the consultant's intuition is that the complex variant, /ʐv̩˧tsʰi˩ | ʐv̩˧-na˥/, is somewhat "slow" and "clumsy": it conveys special emphasis and is only appropriate as part of an expressive strategy to draw attention to the figure at issue. To sum up, the integration of numeral-plus-classifier phrases into one tone group is the general rule.

Interestingly, when a phrase ends in two Low-tone syllables, it is possible to test whether these Low tones result from the levelling down of originally non-Low tones (as in the case of /ʐv̩˧tsʰi˩–ʐv̩˩-na˩/, mentioned above) or whether they reflect an underlying Low tone. When the phrase is divided into two tone groups, if the second group has an underlying L tone, it receives a post-lexical final H tone, by the application of Rule 7 ("If a tone group only contains L tones, a post-lexical H tone is added to its last syllable"). For example, '23 years' (category MH$_a$) can be realized either as /ɲi˧tsi˧–so˩-kʰʏ˩/ or as /ɲi˧tsi˧ | so˩-kʰʏ˥/, revealing that its underlying tone pattern is M–L, whereas with the classifier for tools it would be incorrect to say ‡ ʐʏ˧tsʰi˩ | ʐʏ˩-nɑ˥: the variant with a division into two groups is /ʐʏ˧tsʰi˩ | ʐʏ˧-nɑ˩/. This explains neatly why the contour-creating final H tone is only allowed for some of the phrases. A device for forcing the division of the phrase into two tone groups consists of inserting the syllable /lɑ˧/ 'and' before the last digit: e.g. /ʂɯ˧tsʰi˩ lɑ˩ | qʰʏ˧-ʁwɤ˥/ '79 heaps'.

4.1.7 Disyllabic classifiers, and what they reveal about the tones of numerals

Only a few disyllabic classifiers were observed. One is a reduplicated monosyllable: /tʂʰe˧~tʂʰe˧/ 'the width of a room'.[7] Others are nouns, e.g. /ji˧qʰʏ#˥/ 'bull's horn' can be used as a classifier, since bull horns were used to drink or to pour liquids, for instance to pour water into a pot. The noun 'bull's horn' is in competition, in its use as a classifier, with another classifier referring specifically to hornfuls of liquids, /qʰʏ˧tʰʏ˧/, which is more commonly used than the noun. 'Bottle', /to˩bi#˥/, can be used as a noun, /to˩bi#˥ | ɖɯ˧-ɭɯ˧/ 'a bottle', or as a classifier, /ʐɯ˧ | ɖɯ˧-to˩bi˩/ 'a bottle of liquor/spirits'. The classifier for ladlefuls is /bv̩˩dze˩/, and that for handfuls (using both hands) is /lo˩dzi˩/.

The disyllabic classifiers observed to date fall into one of four tonal categories: M, #H, L, and LM+#H. In terms of their behaviour in association with numerals, these four tonal categories fall into two sets: M and #H on the one hand, L and LM+#H on the other. Tables 4.5a and 4.5b present the data. Clearly, the relevant juncture for tone assignment in these phrases is that which precedes the classifier, even for numerals under twenty: describing the tone pattern of /ɖɯ˧-to˩bi˩/ 'one bottle' requires the recognition of a juncture preceding the classifier, i.e. /ɖɯ˧ – to˩bi˩/.

4.1.8 Two numerals plus a classifier, conveying approximation

Two numerals can accompany a classifier, conveying an approximative number. This can be likened to the coordinative construction 'NUM or NUM' in English: 'one or two', 'two or three'… This construction is less common than coordinative

---

[7] Roselle Dobbs (p.c. 2016) points out that the classifier /tʂʰe˧~tʂʰe˧/ 'the width of a room' may be reduplicated from the verb /tʂʰe˧b/ 'to stretch'.

Table 4.5a: The tonal behaviour of disyllabic classifiers with lexical M or #H tone.

numeral	example form	output tone	meaning
1	ɖɯ˧-qʰv˧tʰv˧#	#H	one hornful
2	ɲi˧-qʰv˧tʰv˧#	#H	two hornfuls
3	so˩-qʰv˩tʰv˥	L	three hornfuls
4	zv˧-qʰv˧tʰv˧#	#H	four hornfuls
5	ŋwɤ˧-qʰv˧tʰv˧#	#H	five hornfuls
6	qʰv˧-qʰv˧tʰv˧#	#H	six hornfuls
7	ʂɯ˧-qʰv˧tʰv˧#	#H	seven hornfuls
8	hõ˧-qʰv˧tʰv˧#	#H	eight hornfuls
9	gv˧-qʰv˧tʰv˧#	#H	nine hornfuls
10	tsʰe˩-qʰv˩tʰv˥	L	ten hornfuls

Table 4.5b: The tonal behaviour of disyllabic classifiers with lexical L or LM+#H tone.

numeral	example form	output tone	meaning
1	ɖɯ˧-to˩bi˩	–L	one bottle
2	ɲi˧-to˩bi˩	–L	two bottles
3	so˩-to˩bi˥	L	three bottles
4	zv˧-to˥bi˩	#H–	four bottles
5	ŋwɤ˧-to˥bi˩	#H–	five bottles
6	qʰv˧-to˥bi˩	#H–	six bottles
7	ʂɯ˧-to˩bi˩	–L	seven bottles
8	hõ˧-to˥bi˩	#H–	eight bottles
9	gv˧-to˥bi˩	#H–	nine bottles
10	tsʰe˩-to˩bi˥	L	ten bottles

compounds consisting of two numeral-plus-classifier phrases, such as /ɖɯ˧-ɲi˧ - ɲi˧-ɲi˧/ 'one day-two days' and /ɲi˧-ɲi˧ - so˧-ɲi˥/ 'two days-three days', presented in §3.3. Table 4.6 sets out the results of elicitation with the noun 'day'. A dash '–' indicates that the combination is not in use. This is not to say that there is a hard-and-fast rule against the combinations marked with a dash in Table 4.6, only that those combinations seemed less felicitous to the consultant, for various reasons that may involve considerations of homophony along with frequency of use and semantics. For instance, the expression /ɖɯ˧-ɲi˧ ɲi˧/, literally 'one-two days', actually means 'a few days', somewhat like 'a couple of days' in English. Since this expression easily covers the range from one to four, it makes the combinations '2 and 3' and '3 and 4' unnecessary. Among higher numbers, a reason why the combination '7 and 8' is deemed acceptable may be that it corresponds to 'a week or so', a span of time that has some relevance in the consultant's current conceptualization of time, in which weeks are a relevant unit because the grandchildren's schooling is punctuated by the succession of weeks. Seen in this light, the combination '6 and 7' should be about as relevant as '7 and 8', and could be acceptable at a push: ‡ qʰv˧-ʂɯ˧ ɲi˧ 'six or seven days'.

Table 4.6: Expressions conveying an approximative number: two numerals plus a classifier.

numerals	association of two numerals	meaning
1 and 2	ɖɯ˧-ɲi˧ ɲi˧	'a few days'
2 and 3	–	
3 and 4	–	
4 and 5	ʐv˧-ŋwɤ˧ ɲi˧	'four or five days'
5 and 6	ŋwɤ˧-qʰv˧ ɲi˧	'five or six days'
6 and 7	–	
7 and 8	ʂɯ˧-hõ˧ ɲi˧	'seven or eight days'
8 and 9	–	
9 and 10	gv˧-tsʰe˧ ɲi˩	'nine or ten days'

The fact that the expressions in Table 4.6 do not belong to a full, productive paradigm in the consultant's speech led to the conclusion that it would not be appropriate to attempt systematic elicitation of phrases consisting of two numerals and a classifier. There was a concern that elicitation of unusual forms (many of them new coinages) would not yield consistent results (as mentioned in §1.2.4.1). This is one of many topics that remain for future research.

4.1.9 Conclusions about numeral-plus-classifier phrases

From the mass of information set out above, it is clear that the tone patterns of numeral-plus-classifier phrases encapsulate information not derived from phonological rules. The system as presented in Tables 4.3a–d and 4.4a–d is regular and productive, in that all the classifiers of a given tone category have the same tone patterns. As this system lends itself straightforwardly to computer implementation, a simple Perl script was written.[8] It takes as its input the classifier's tone category and segmental composition and a numeral (or range of numerals) from 1 to 100. The data in Tables 4.3a–d and 4.4a–d is stored inside the script, allowing for the tone pattern to be recovered through table lookup. The surface phonological tone pattern is then assigned to the phrase on the basis of the general rules governing tone assignment in this dialect (rules which are encoded into the script), such as that simple L and M tones attach to all the syllables within their domain, tone sequences attach to syllables "left-to-right", and so on. For instance, providing as input the numeral '44' and the classifier for tools, /na˧a/ (tonal category: M_a), the script yields the following two variants for '44 tools': /zv̩˧tsʰi˩-zv̩˧-na˥/ (tone pattern: L#–H#) and /zv̩˧tsʰi˩-zv̩˩-na˩/ (tone pattern: L#–).

In the current version of the script, all of the information set out in Tables 4.3a–d and 4.4a–d is encoded in full, specifying the tone patterns of 900 combinations (9 tone categories of classifiers times 100 numerals). This allows for straightforward table-lookup, but is uneconomical from the point of view of linguistic modelling. The addition of some rules could significantly reduce the number of combinations that need to be indicated. In particular, the tone patterns of [40..49] are identical with those of [50..59]; likewise for [60..69] and [80..89]. Numerals ending in '1' also have identical patterns with those ending in '2', with a few exceptions in category H_b. The information provided for each subcategory (H_a and H_b, M_a and M_b, and so on) could also be simplified by considering one of the subcategories as the norm, and only supplying the forms for the other subcategories where they differ from that norm. However, it is clear that even after this simplification task had been conducted, large numbers of tonal patterns would still need to be specified individually. For instance, neither H_a nor H_b can be considered as a simplified version of the other. The systematic presence of a L tone in all the phrases from '10' to '19' could suggest that the patterns for H_b constitute a simplified version of those for H_a, but there also exists a complication for H_b and not for H_a, namely the presence of different tones after numerals ending in '1' and '2'. This observation is a striking counterexample to the pan-Naish generalization that the numerals '1' and '2' always have the same tone patterns – a generalization which holds for Naxi and Laze, and for all the rest of the Na data. Finally, an idiosyncratic tone pattern is observed for /to˥/ 'armful': this classifier belongs to the H_a category, but the combination '11 armfuls' is realized as /tsʰe˧ɖɯ˧-to˥/ instead of the expected /†tsʰe˩ɖɯ˩-to˥/.

---

[8] I plan to make computer tools available from an institutional repository in future. Until this plan comes to fruition, interested readers are invited to get in touch with me.

4.2 Demonstrative-plus-classifier phrases

A demonstrative and a following classifier are always integrated into one tone group, as in (2), where the proximal demonstrative //tsʰɯ˧// and the classifier for pairs or sets //dzi˧ᵦ// combine as /tsʰɯ˧-dzi˧/ 'this set'.

(2) no˩by˧ | tsʰɯ˧-dzi˧ | le˧-ʑi˩, | tʰi˧-my˧-kʰɯ˧.
    no˩by˧   tsʰɯ˧   dzi˧ᵦ   le˧-   ʑi˩ᵦ
    given_name   DEM.PROX   CLF.sets/pairs   ACCOMP   to_bring_along
    tʰi˧-   my˧ₐ   -kʰɯ˧
    DUR   to_put_on   CAUS

'Nobbu brought that set [of clothes], and made [her] wear [the clothes].' (BuriedAlive3.73)

The elicitation procedure for demonstrative-plus-classifier phrases was similar to that used for numeral-plus-classifier phrases, and similar puzzles were encountered.

As explained in the previous section, the tonal categories of classifiers were established on the basis of their behaviour when combined with numerals. The nine tonal categories of monosyllabic classifiers are: H_a and H_b; MH_a and MH_b; M_a and M_b; and L_a, L_b and L_c. As for the proximal demonstrative, /tsʰɯ#˧/, and the distal demonstrative, /tʰy#˧/, they both carry lexical #H tone. The expectations were that, in demonstrative-plus-classifier phrases, (i) there would be no difference between proximal and distal demonstratives, since they have the same lexical tone, and (ii) all classifiers within each of the nine tonal categories would have the same tonal behaviour.

The first prediction was verified: phrases containing /tsʰɯ#˧/ 'this' and /tʰy#˧/ 'that' always have the same tonal behaviour. The second prediction, on the other hand, was incorrect: some of the tonal categories for classifiers proved to be less than fully homogeneous. The account provided below starts out from the simplest cases, and progresses towards the category for which the greatest degree of divergence was found.

When combined with demonstratives, H_a and H_b behave in the same way, as do MH_a and MH_b. This is the simplest part of the picture: the distinction between H_a and H_b is neutralized in this context, and the distinction between MH_a and MH_b is likewise neutralized. Categories M_a and M_b behave differently from each other, but in a consistent and simple way, with only one possible pattern: demonstrative plus M_a-tone classifier yields L#, e.g. /tʰy˧-nɑ˩/ (classifier for tools); demonstrative plus M$_b$-tone classifier yields #H, e.g. /tʰɣ˧-l̥ɯ#˦/ (generic classifier).

Among Low tone categories of classifiers, L$_a$ and L$_c$ are relatively straightforward. All L$_a$-tone classifiers have the same behaviour, allowing two variants: H# and H$. Both variants are firmly attested. The speaker expresses a preference for the former, but this slight imbalance appears to be the same for all examples, suggesting that there does not exist any clear (lexicalized) preference for the one or the other in association with a specific classifier. L$_c$-tone classifiers allow no less than three variants: MH#, H# and H$.

Category L$_b$ is the most problematic. In the production data, there are three variants, H#, H$ and MH#. But for some classifiers of this category (e.g. /**mi**↓$_b$/, the classifier for animals, and /kʰɯ↓$_b$/, the classifier for long objects), MH# is by far the most frequent pattern, with H$ as an occasional variant, and H# rarely attested. For other classifiers, H# and H$ appear with comparable frequency, whereas MH# is seldom found.

When several variants were proposed by the investigator and the consultant was asked which ones were correct, a similar picture emerged: MH# is strongly preferred for some classifiers, with H$ as an acceptable variant, whereas H# is dispreferred (either refused as incorrect, or judged as marginally acceptable only). For other classifiers, the preferred form is with H# tone, H$ tone is an acceptable variant, and MH# tone is not. Table 4.7 presents these two sets, provisionally labelled as 'type I' and 'type II'.

The consultant's acceptance of variants fluctuated from session to session, but the distinction between types I and II was confirmed in the course of a long series of elicitation sessions. Examples from the recorded texts provide evidence to the same effect.

The tone patterns for all categories of classifiers are set out in Table 4.8, using the distal demonstrative, /tʰɣ#˦/, as an example. (As mentioned above, the tone patterns for the proximal demonstrative, /tʂʰɯ#˦/, are the same.) The corresponding online recordings are DemClf, DemClf2 and DemClf3.

The 'type I' and 'type II' distinction among L$_b$-tone classifiers constitutes an impressive extra intricacy within the classifiers' system of nine tonal categories. Category L$_b$ is a subdivision within the L category of tones; its further division into types I and II constitutes a subdivision within a subdivision. From the point of view of phonological output, type I within the L$_b$ category yields an output (MH# / H$) which does not coincide with any other within the system.

Table 4.7: The two subcategories of L_b-tone classifiers, based on their behaviour in association with demonstratives.

type	tone pattern in association with demonstrative	form	classifier for
L_b, type I	MH# most common; H$ attested; H# dispreferred or refused	bo˩ᵦ dʁ˩ᵦ dzi˩ᵦ jo˩ᵦ kʰɯ˩ᵦ lo˩ᵦ ɬi˩ᵦ mi˩ᵦ pʰʁ˩ᵦ tʰʁ˩ᵦ tɕʰi˩ᵦ wʁ˩ᵦ wo˩ᵦ	headdresses small groups trees ounces long objects valleys armspans animals fields sets of ten meals loads teams of oxen
L_b, type II	H# most common; H$ attested; MH# dispreferred or refused	pʁ˩ᵦ po˩ᵦ ʁo˩ᵦ ʂɯ˩ᵦ tsʰe˩ᵦ tʋ˩ᵦ	ladders, doors packs types, sorts times leaves large chunks

4.3 Tonal interactions with a preceding noun

Occasionally, there is tonal interaction between a numeral-plus-classifier or demonstrative-plus-classifier phrase and the preceding noun, as in (3).

(3) ə˧mi˧! | pæ˧kʰwʁ˧ so˧-ɭɯ˧ ki˩ mæ˩!
 ə˧mi˧ pæ˧kʰwʁ#˧ so˩ ɭɯ˧ ki˧ₐ mæ˧
 INTJ silver_coin three CLF to_give DISC.PTCL
 'Wow! [(S)he] is giving you three silver coins!'

189

Table 4.8: The tone patterns of demonstrative-plus-classifier phrases.

tone pattern		example	
tone of CLF	tone of DEM+CLF phrase	classifier for	DEM+CLF phrase
H_a, H_b	H$ / #H	chunks	tʰy˧-kʰwɤ˥$ / tʰy˧-kʰwɤ#˥
MH_a, MH_b	L#	cattle	tʰy˧-pʰo˩
M_a	L#	tools	tʰy˧-nɑ˩
M_b	#H	generic	tʰy˧-ɬɯ#˥
L_a	H# / H$	quantities	tʰy˧-mɤ˥ / tʰy˧-mɤ˥$
L_b, type I	MH# / H$	animals	tʰy˧-mi˧˥ / tʰy˧-mi˥$
L_b, type II	H# / H$	doors	tʰy˧-pɤ˥ / tʰy˧-pɤ˥$
L_c	MH# / H# / H$	plains	tʰy˧-di˧˥ / tʰy˧-di˥ / tʰy˧-di˥$

According to the main consultant's memories, (3) is the type of comment that uncles and aunts would make when a child received significant amounts of money on the occasion of their coming-of-age ceremony. To offer only one coin would be inappropriate, as gifts should come in pairs. Two coins is a beautiful gift. Three coins is beyond expectations (the equivalent at the time of about half a month's salary).

The tonal derivation for the phrase 'three silver coins' is as follows:

(i) the input tones are: #H for 'silver coin', //pæ˧kʰwɤ#˥//; L for 'three'; and M for the classifier, //ɬɯ˧//

(ii) the numeral-plus-classifier phrase 'three-CLF' carries M tone: //so˧-ɬɯ˧//

(iii) the phrase that results from the combination of (i) and (ii) carries a H# tone: //pʰæ˧kʰwɤ˧ so˧-ɬɯ˥#//

Other examples of such tonal interaction include (4) and (5).

(4) my˩zo˩ tʰy˩-ɬɯ˧
    my˩zo˩   tʰy˥   ɬɯ˧$_b$
    girl   DEM.DIST   CLF.generic
    'that girl' (ComingOfAge2.60; Tiger2.139, 141, 147)

(5) ə˧ɣ˧ tʰy˩-ɣ˧
     ə˧ɣ˧   tʰy˩   ɣ˧
     uncle   DEM.DIST   CLF.individual
     'that uncle' (Tiger2.109)

The underlying tonal category of such expressions can be established in the same way as that of nouns, by tests such as adding the copula. The expression 'three silver coins' /pʰæ˧kʰwɤ˧ so˧-ɭɯ˩/ in (3) yields /pʰæ˧kʰwɤ˧ so˧-ɭɯ˩ ɲi˩/, revealing that its tone is H#: //pʰæ˧kʰwɤ˧ so˧-ɭɯ˩#//. By contrast, 'that uncle', /ə˧ɣ˧ tʰy˩-ɣ˧/ (5), yields /ə˧ɣ˧ tʰy˩-ɣ˧ ɲi˩/, revealing that its tone is #H: //ə˧ɣ˧ tʰy˩-ɣ#˩//. (As for (4), its surface form suffices to determine its underlying tone: it can only be //L//.)

Why is tonal change only occasional? Here are some speculations.

First, if tone change were systematic, it would entail the neutralization of some of the tonal distinctions among classifiers. This is because the number of possible tone patterns in tone groups of three syllables or more is not as high as the combinatorial diversity in sequences of short tone groups. For instance, after disyllabic nouns carrying a L# tone, determiners would have their tones lowered to L (by application of Rule 5: "All syllables following a H.L or M.L sequence receive L tone"), which would entirely neutralize tonal oppositions among classifiers. Even if the majority of contrasts among different categories of classifiers were retained, tonal change would increase opacity, as there would be more cases where surface phonological tone on determiners differed from underlying tone. Given the richness of the tone system of classifiers, an increase in opacity would be likely to create a pressure towards the simplification of the system. The fact that tonal interaction between a noun and a following determiner is only occasional may thus favour the preservation of the current system. Functionally, having a choice between two options widens the range of stylistic possibilities.

While discourse factors are paramount in determining whether there is interaction between the noun and the phrase that determines it, the tonal category may also play a role. All other things being equal, some tones appear to resist interaction because the tonal output would be non-trivial, requiring the speaker to remember the morphologically conditioned tone combination rule that applies for this combination. Other tones are more prone to interaction because adjusting the noun with the following determiner phrase is simply a matter of applying phonological rules. For instance, if the noun's tone is L#, it feels easiest to integrate this noun with the following phrase, because the phonological consequence is a simple levelling down of the tones of the following syllables within the tone group: the noun's two syllables get M and L tone, respectively, and all syllables following this M.L sequence receive L tone by Rule 5. In this case, division into two tone groups would require the extra effort of preserving the tones of the determiner phrase from lowering. This is possible, but it requires a stylistic motivation to emphasize the two constituents.

The implication for the analysis of the tone system would be that some tones are more combination-prone than others, because the tone combination rules in which they are involved follow from phonological rules, and hence tend to be exceptionless and simple to implement. The spreading of L# onto following syllables, mentioned in the previous paragraph, appears as the best example. Other tones are less combination-prone because tone changes in which they are involved are less straightforward, and tend to allow several variants. The H$ tone category is a case in point.

Such asymmetries inside the tone system, with some tones more change-prone than others, would be reflected in the frequency of tonal interactions between a noun and a following determiner (N+DEM+CLF, N+NUM+CLF). Systematic verification of these hypotheses must be deferred until later.

4.4 Concluding note

While the tone patterns of classifiers may appear staggeringly complex, phrases containing classifiers are frequent in discourse, a factor which is known to favour the preservation of irregular morphology. As to the system's diachronic origin, some reflections are set out in §9.3.2.

If anyone read this whole chapter with uninterrupted excitement and engagement, they are invited to imagine how much more elaborate the picture would have been if Yongning Na had had the fortune to be used as a medium for the expression of concepts of number theory such as ordinals and fractions. Tibetan, for instance, has ordinals, and means to express fractions and other mathematical concepts (Liu et al. 2010), which tend to seep into other languages in the area of cultural Tibetan influence (e.g. Nar-Phu, spoken in the Manang district of Nepal: Noonan 2003: 342). Dzongkha (a Bodic language spoken in Bhutan) has fascinating complexities such as the use of fractions in its counting system (Mazaudon 1985). But in Yongning Na there are no ordinal numbers or fractions. Examples that contain ordinal numbers in other languages (such as English and Chinese) correspond to turns of phrase with cardinal numbers in Yongning Na. For instance, in (6), 'on the eighth day' is expressed as 'one day [after] seven days', i.e. 'the day after seven days had elapsed'.⁹ In (7), the equivalent of 'the first person who will come' is 'whoever comes', understood by inference from context as 'the *first* person who comes'.¹⁰ Other examples are found in Renaming. 29, 38 and Funeral.2.

(6) ʂɯ˧-hɑ̃˧ gv˧ | dɯ˧-ɲi˩, | ə˧mi˧ lɑ˧ | mv˩ | tʰi˧-to˧~to˧, | ŋv˩ɲi˩ tsɯ˩ | mv˩!

ʂɯ˧-hɑ̃˧	gv˧c	dɯ˧-ɲi$˩	ə˧mi˧	lɑ˧	mv˩
seven-CLF.nights	to_elapse	one-CLF.days	mother	and	daughter

tʰi˧-	to˧~to˧	ŋv˩a	-ɲi˩	tsɯ˩	mv˧
DUR	to_hug	to_cry	CERTITUDE	REP	AFFIRM

'On the eighth day (*literally:* the day after seven days had gone by), mother and daughter fell into each other's arms and wept!' (BuriedAlive3.129)

(7) hĩ˩ | ɲi˩ le˧-tsʰɯ˩-i̯˩-dʐo˩ ...

hĩ˩	ɲi˩	le˧-	tsʰɯ˩a	i̯˩	-dʐo˩
person	INTERROG.who	ACCOMP	to_come	to_turn_toward	TOP

'The first person who comes along... (*literally:* whoever comes along...)' (Renaming.14)

Contact with Chinese, including training in mathematics at school, currently creates a pressure towards the use of ordinals and fractions, but the result is the wholesale adoption of Chinese forms.

---

⁹ The context to example (6) is as follows. A young woman choked because she gulped down boiled eggs that got stuck in her throat; family members assumed that she was dead, and buried her. She came to herself when robbers looting her grave put her body upright to rip off the valuable garments in which she had been interred. She returned to see her mother; the mother was terrified, thinking that her daughter was become a ghost. Ghost lore has it that the dangerous period within which ghosts can return is limited to seven days, so the mother asked the daughter to stay in hiding until seven days had elapsed, and only return home after that time.

¹⁰ This example requires an explanation about context. The parents of a sick infant are advised to build a bridge, and to request the first person who crosses this bridge to give a new name to their child. This is a form of symbolic adoption, intended to give the child a new start in life. The stranger gives the infant a new name, and a small token, such as a button from their dress. Example (7) is part of the instructions that the parents receive about what they should do for their child.

5 Combinations of nouns with grammatical elements

This chapter brings together data on a wide range of constructions containing nouns, from morphological derivation – mostly nouns containing gender suffixes – and reduplication, to combinations of nouns with particles in discourse.

5.1 Derivational affixes: Gender suffixes and kinship prefix

5.1.1 Introduction to gender suffixes

The most common derivational affixes in Na are gender suffixes: /-mi/, /-zo/ and /-pʰv/,[1] carrying the meaning 'female, mother', 'son, young', and 'male', for instance in /ɬi˧mi˧/ 'female roebuck', /ɬi˧zo˩/ (variant: /ɬi˧zo#˩/) 'young roebuck', and /ɬi˩pʰv˩/ (variant: /ɬi˧pʰv#˩/) 'male roebuck' (Lidz 2010: 177-179).[2]

The suffixes /-mi/ and /-zo/ also serve as augmentative and diminutive suffixes, respectively. 'Mother' stands for 'large', and 'son' for 'small', as in numerous languages of the area (see Mazaudon 2003 on Tamang, and a cross-language discussion by Matisoff 1992). For instance, /kʰɤ˧/ 'basket (carried on back)' yields /kʰɤ˧mi˩$/ 'large basket' and /kʰɤ˧zo#˩/ 'small basket'. The augmentative or diminutive meaning has faded away from many suffixed forms, which have thereby become lexicalized. For instance, monosyllabic /ljɤ˧/ and suffixed /ljɤ˩mi˩/ are both used to refer to the same object, namely main (supporting) beams. The augmentative and diminutive suffixes are not highly productive: there is no diminutive counterpart (†ljɤ˩-zo#˩) to /ljɤ˩mi˩/ 'main beam', for instance. The slanting beams upholding the roofing (planks or tiles), which rest on the supporting beams, are called /ʐv˩lɯ˩/. When referring to a large-sized

---

[1] At this stage, no tone is indicated for these three suffixes: establishing their tone category is a key objective of §5.1.

[2] Liberty Lidz's notations are /-mi33/, /-zɔ33/ and /-pʰu33/. Consultant F4's word for 'grandmother's brother', /ə˧pʰɣ˧/, is glossed by L. Lidz as 'grandfather (father of mother or father)' in the Luoshui dialect, and transcribed as /a33-pʰɣ33/ (p. 766), but it also appears as /a33-pʰu33/ at places, e.g. pp. 269, 503 and 763.

slanting beam, it is not possible to use an augmentative †/zv˧lɯ˧-mi˩/, with the intended meaning of 'a large-sized /zv˧lɯ˧/'. Instead, constructions with the adjectives /tɕi˩a/ 'small' or /ɖɯ˩a/ 'large' are used. (About the association of adjectives to nouns in Yongning Na, see §3.4.1.)

Etymologically, the second syllable of the words /ɲi˧mi#˥/ 'sun' and /ɬi˧mi˧/ 'moon', which currently lack monosyllabic counterparts, probably originates in the same morpheme /mi/. Since these two words also have the same structure in Naxi (/ɲi˧me˧/ and /he˧me˧/) and Laze (/ɲie˧mie˧/ and /ɬie˧mie˧/), two languages closely related to Na, their disyllabic status is likely to have some historical depth. The suffix /zo/ appearing in /ɲi˧zo#˥/ 'fish', another disyllable without a monosyllabic counterpart, is also found in Laze (/ze˧/ 'son', /ɲi˩ze˧/ 'fish'), whereas Naxi has a monosyllable: /ɲi˧/.

The discussion below covers names of animals and peoples with gender suffixes, as well as the augmentative and diminutive suffixes. Needless to say, words that contain a /mi/ syllable of other origin were excluded, e.g. the name of the Yongning monastery, /dæ˩mi˧/, which is a loanword from Tibetan *dgra med*.

The suffixes for *female*, *young* and *male* are related to the free morphemes /mi˩/, /zo˧/ and /pʰv˧/, which appear in contexts such as (1)-(3). In this case, there is no mystery in the evolution from the nouns to the derivational affixes.

(1) tsʰɯ˧ | mi˩ ɲi˩.
tsʰɯ˧   mi˩   ɲi˩
DEM.PROX   female   COP
'This is a female.'

(2) tsʰɯ˧ | zo˧ ɲi˩.
tsʰɯ˧   zo˧   ɲi˩
DEM.PROX   son/young/male   COP
'This is a young/male.'

(3) tsʰɯ˧ | pʰv˧ ɲi˩.
tsʰɯ˧   pʰv˧   ɲi˩
DEM.PROX   male   COP
'This is a male.'

The free forms /zo˧/ 'young/male' and /pʰv˧/ 'male' have different tones (H and M, respectively), whereas the suffixes /-zo/ and /-pʰv/ always have the same tonal patterns, even sharing the same tonal variants, as in the example of 'roebuck'. However, neutralization of tonal oppositions on nouns in the process of grammaticalization as gender suffixes is not thoroughgoing: the tonal behaviour of /-zo/ and /-pʰv/ differs from that of the female suffix /-mi/.

From a tonal point of view, there is thus evidence that these three derivational elements have become distinct from the free nouns in which they originate. This is reminiscent of classifiers: the study of classifiers provided in Chapter 4 reveals that the tone system of classifiers is not identical to that of free nouns, and that the tone of a classifier is not necessarily the closest equivalent of that of the noun from which it derives. To repeat an example from §4.1.2, there are two tonal correspondences among classifiers for H-tone nouns, the one illustrated by 'beam', /dʐo˦/, which has /dʐo˦ₐ/ (category Hₐ) as its self-classifier, and the other illustrated by /kɯ˦/ 'star', which yields /kɯ˦ᵦ/ (Mᵦ tone category) as a self-classifier. Seen in this light, differences in tone between a noun as a full form and as a derivational suffix are not a particularly out-of-the-way finding in the context of Yongning Na morphotonology.

The difference in tone patterns between /-mi/ and the other two suffixes suffices to establish that suffixes are not toneless. But ascertaining the tones of these suffixes is not an easy matter. A simple test consists in combining them with a M-tone noun: the M tone has properties that make it suitable for use in tonal tests. M can be followed by any tone (unlike H, which can only be followed by L), and it does not spread (unlike L), so it would seem to offer the best possible context for the lexical tone of the following morpheme to manifest itself in. This works out well for verbs: a useful tonal test consists in observing a verb's tone after a M-tone morpheme such as the negation prefix, /mɤ˧-/. In this context, H-tone verbs surface with H tone, MH-tone verbs with MH tone, and so on (see §6.1.1). But the three gender suffixes all yield the same result after a M-tone monosyllable: for instance, /la˧/ 'tiger' yields /la˧mi#˥/ 'female tiger', /la˧zo#˥/ 'baby tiger' and /la˧pʰv#˥/ 'male tiger'. After disyllabic M-tone nouns, on the other hand, the results are different: thus, /si˧gɯ˧/ 'lion' yields /si˧gɯ˧-mi˩/ 'female lion', with L tone on the suffix, and /si˧gɯ˧-zo#˥/ 'baby lion', with a floating H tone. On this slender basis, the two sets of suffixes are provisionally transcribed as carrying lexical L and H tone, respectively. They are transcribed hereafter as //-mi˩//, //-zo˥// and //-pʰv˥//. It must be cautioned that this tentative identification does by no means encapsulate all the information about the tonal behaviour of these two types of suffixes, which is set out in tabular form below.

5.1.2 The facts

Tables 5.1a–g and Tables 5.2a–b present the data concerning the suffixes //-mi˩//, //-zo˥// and //-pʰv˥//. The examples are arranged by tone of the suffixed form.

Tables 5.1a–g present disyllables, and Tables 5.2a–b trisyllables. Nouns in which the suffixes are augmentative or diminutive and not gender suffixes are italicized (i.e. nouns that do not refer to animals or ethnic groups). As elsewhere, a slash separates variants. A dash '–' in a cell indicates that the form does not exist: for instance, it is not possible to use a word suffixed with /-zo/ for 'piglet' (the attested form is /bæ˩bv̩˥/). A double dagger ‡ preceding a noun indicates that it is a form that was proposed by the investigator and rejected by the consultant. For instance, "ʐæ˩mi#˥ (‡ ʐæ˩mi˩)" for 'female leopard' indicates that the tonal variant ‡ ʐæ˩mi˩, tested by the investigator on the analogy of the existence of a L-tone variant /ʑi˩mi˩/ for 'female ape', whose root belongs in the same category as 'leopard', was rejected by the consultant.

Table 5.1a includes two roots, 'thumb' and 'bee', which are not synchronically attested as monosyllables, but whose internal reconstruction yields a LM-tone root.

For two of the items that lack a monosyllabic counterpart, the tone of the root can be arrived at through internal reconstruction. Since there is a substantial number of examples (seven) of LM-tone disyllables corresponding to LM-tone monosyllables, and there is no other attested source for LM-tone disyllables, /dze˩mi˧/ 'bee' and /lo˩mi˧/ 'thumb' can be hypothesized to be derived from LM-tone roots: *dze˧ and *lo˧.

But for most of the items that lack a monosyllabic counterpart, internal reconstruction does not lead to a clear-cut conclusion, because several tone categories of roots feed into the same tone categories of disyllables. For instance, /ɲi˩zo#˥/ 'fish' may have originated in a monosyllabic root of any tone category except H, and M-tone words with the /-mi˧/ suffix, such as /ɖʐ˧mi˧/ 'fox', may be derived from any of the following four tone categories of monosyllables: LH, L, H or MH. The last two items in Table 5.1g, 'hwamei (a species of bird)' and '(cigarette) lighter', carry a tone that does not correspond to any of the attested correspondences.

The purpose of Tables 5.1a–g and 5.2a–b is to provide a bird's eye view of the tonal correspondences. It does not present information about etymology and frequency of use: for instance, that /ʝĩ˧mi˧/ 'treek trunk' (in Table 5.1e) etymologically means 'big bone'; that /po˧lo˧/ is a more common form for 'ram' than the /-pʰv̩˥/ suffixed form /jo˧pʰv̩#˥/ ≈ /jo˩pʰv̩˩/ (literally 'male sheep') shown in Table 5.1d; or that /-zo˥/ suffixed forms are more common than /-pʰv̩˥/ suffixed forms to refer to male mules and water buffalos (Table 5.1g). Some such facts are adduced in the discussion below; they can be looked up in the corresponding entries in the dictionary (Michaud 2015a).

Table 5.1a: Nouns with gender suffixes or augmentative/diminutive suffixes. Disyllabic words. LM-tone roots.

correspondences	root	suffixed forms			
		//-mi˧// 'female'/AUG	//-zo˧// 'child'/DIM	//-pʰv̩˩// 'male'
first type	sow	bo˩mi˧	–	bo˩pʰv̩˧
	hen	æ̃˩mi˧	–	–
	thumb	lo˩mi˧	–	–
	bee	dze˩mi˧	–	–
second type	yak	bv̩˩mi˧	bv̩˩zo#˥ / bv̩˩zo˧	bv̩˩pʰv̩#˥ / bv̩˩pʰv̩˧
	sparrow	dʑwæ˩mi˧	dʑwæ˩zo#˥ / dʑwæ˩zo˧	dʑwæ˩pʰv̩#˥ / dʑwæ˩pʰv̩˧
	hawk	kɤ˩mi˧	kɤ˩zo#˥ / kɤ˩zo˧	kɤ˩pʰv̩#˥ / kɤ˩pʰv̩˧
	steamer	bv̩˩mi˧	bv̩˩zo˧ / bv̩˩zo#˥	–
third type	weasel	dv̩˩mi#˥ / dv̩˩mi˧	dv̩˩zo#˥ / dv̩˩zo˧	dv̩˩pʰv̩#˥ / dv̩˩pʰv̩˧
	goose	ɑ˩mi#˥ / ɑ˩mi˧	ɑ˩zo#˥ / ɑ˩zo˧	ɑ˩pʰv̩#˥ / ɑ˩pʰv̩˧
	lizard	dzo˩mi#˥ / dzo˩mi˧	dzo˩zo#˥ / dzo˩zo˧	dzo˩pʰv̩#˥ / dzo˩pʰv̩˧
	ladle	tɕʰo˩mi#˥ / tɕʰo˩mi˧	tɕʰo˩zo#˥ / tɕʰo˩zo˧	–
	Na (people)	nɑ˩mi#˥ / nɑ˩mi˧	nɑ˩zo#˥ / nɑ˩zo˧	–
fourth type	jackal	pʰɤ˩mi˧	pʰɤ˩zo#˥ / pʰɤ˩zo˧	pʰɤ˩pʰv̩#˥ / pʰɤ˩pʰv̩˧
	road, path	zɤ˩mi˧	–	–

Table 5.1b: Nouns with gender suffixes or augmentative/diminutive suffixes. Disyllabic words. LH-tone roots.

correspondences	root	suffixed forms		
		//-mi˩// 'female'/AUG	//-zo˥// 'child'/DIM	//-pʰv˥// 'male'
first type	leopard	zæ˩mi#˥ (‡ zæ˩mi˩)	zæ˩zo#˥ (‡ zæ˩zo˩)	zæ˩pʰv#˥ (‡ zæ˩pʰv˩)
	monkey	ʐi˩mi#˥ / ʐi˩mi˩	ʐi˩zo#˥ / ʐi˩zo˩	ʐi˩pʰv#˥ / ʐi˩pʰv˩
	buffalo	tʰɑ˩mi#˥ (‡ tʰɑ˩mi˩)	tʰɑ˩zo#˥	tʰɑ˩pʰv#˥
	muntjac	tɕʰɯ˩mi#˥ / tɕʰɯ˩mi˩	tɕʰɯ˩zo#˥ / tɕʰɯ˩zo˩	tɕʰɯ˩pʰv#˥ / tɕʰɯ˩pʰv˩
	plane (tool)	tʰi˩mi#˥ (‡ tʰi˩mi˩)	tʰi˩zo#˥ (‡ tʰi˩zo˩)	–
second type (isolated example)	*slope*	to˩mi˩	to˩zo˩	–
third type	*plain*	di˧mi˧	–	–
	woman	mv˧mi˧	mv˩zo˩	–

Table 5.1c: Nouns with gender suffixes or augmentative/diminutive suffixes. Disyllabic words. M-tone roots. Only one type of correspondence.

root	suffixed forms		
	//-mi˩// 'female'/AUG	//-zo˥// 'child'	//-pʰv˥// 'male'
tiger	lɑ˧mi#˥	lɑ˧zo#˥	lɑ˧pʰv#˥
goral	se˧mi#˥	se˧zo#˥	se˧pʰv#˥
message	qʰwæ˧mi#˥	–	–

Table 5.1d: Nouns with gender suffixes or augmentative/diminutive suffixes. Disyllabic words. L-tone roots. Only one type of correspondence.

root	suffixed forms		
	//-mi˩// 'female'/AUG	//-zo˥// 'child'/DIM	//-pʰv̩˥// 'male'
daughter	mv̩˧mi˧	–	–
sheep	jo˧mi˧	jo˧zo#˥ / jo˩zo˩	jo˧pʰv̩#˥ / jo˩pʰv̩˩
roebuck	ɬi˧mi˧	ɬi˧zo#˥ / ɬi˩zo˩	ɬi˧pʰv̩#˥ / ɬi˩pʰv̩˩
bottle	kɤ˧mi˧	kɤ˩zo˩ (‡ kɤ˧zo#˥)	–
river	dʐɯ˧mi˧	–	–

Table 5.1e: Nouns with gender suffixes or augmentative/diminutive suffixes. Disyllabic words. H-tone roots.

correspondences	root	suffixed forms		
		//-mi˩// 'female'/AUG	//-zo˥// 'child'/DIM	//-pʰv̩˥// 'male'
first type	cow	ji˩mi˩	ji˧zo#˥	ji˧pʰv̩#˥
	horse	ʐwæ˩mi˩	ʐwæ˧zo#˥	ʐwæ˧pʰv̩#˥
	dog	kʰv̩˩mi˩	kʰv̩˧zo#˥	kʰv̩˧pʰv̩#˥
second type	Pumi (people)	bɤ˧mi#˥	bɤ˧zo#˥	–
	pheasant	ho˧mi#˥	ho˧zo#˥	ho˧pʰv̩#˥
	cooking pan	v̩˧mi#˥	v̩˧zo#˥	–
third type	door	kʰi˧mi˧	kʰi˧zo#˥	–
	canal	qʰæ˧mi˧	qʰæ˧zo#˥	–
	tree trunk	ʐ̩˧mi˧	–	–

Table 5.1f: Nouns with gender suffixes or augmentative/diminutive suffixes. Disyllabic words. MH-tone roots.

correspondences	root	suffixed forms		
		//-mi˩// 'female'/AUG	//-zo˩// 'child'/DIM	//-pʰv˩// 'male'
first type	cat	hwɤ˧mi˩$	hwɤ˧zo#˩ / hwɤ˧zo˩$	hwɤ˧pʰv#˩ / hwɤ˧pʰv˩$
	doe	tsʰæ˧mi˩$	tsʰæ˧zo#˩ / tsʰæ˧zo˩$	tsʰæ˧pʰv#˩ / tsʰæ˧pʰv˩$
	goat	tsʰɯ˧mi˩$	tsʰɯ˧zo#˩ / tsʰɯ˧zo˩$	tsʰɯ˧pʰv#˩ / tsʰɯ˧pʰv˩$
	crane	ʁv˧mi˩$	ʁv˧zo#˩ / ʁv˧zo˩$	ʁv˧pʰv#˩ / ʁv˧pʰv˩$
	wasp	tɕɯ˧mi˩$	tɕɯ˧zo#˩ / tɕɯ˧zo˩$	tɕɯ˧pʰv#˩ / tɕɯ˧pʰv˩$
	basket	kʰɤ˧mi˩$	kʰɤ˧zo˩$ (‡ kʰɤ˧zo#˩)	–
	needle	ʁo˧mi˩$	ʁo˧zo#˩ (‡ ʁo˧zo˩$)	–
	scales	tɕɯ˧mi˩$	tɕɯ˧zo˩$ (‡ tɕɯ˧zo#˩)	–
	bowl	qʰwɤ˧mi˩$	qʰwɤ˧zo˩$ (‡ qʰwɤ˧zo#˩)	–
	stomach	hu˧mi˩$	–	–
second type (isolated example)	building	ʐi˧mi˧	–	–

202

Table 5.1g: Nouns with gender suffixes or augmentative/diminutive suffixes. Disyllabic words without a corresponding monosyllable.

possible root tone	meaning	suffixed forms //-mi˩// 'female'/AUG	//-zo˥// 'child'/DIM	//-pʰv̩˥// 'male'
M or H	water buffalo	dʑi˧mi#˥	dʑi˧zo#˥ (‡ dʑi˩zo˩)	dʑi˧pʰv̩#˥
	granddaughter	zv̩˧mi#˥	–	–
	sun	ɲi˧mi#˥	–	–
L or LM	duck	bæ˧mi˧	bæ˧zo#˥	bæ˧pʰv̩#˥
	large vat	dzo˧mi˧	dzo˧zo#˥	–
	sword	ʁæ˧mi˧	ʁæ˧zo#˥	–
LH, L, H or MH	tummy, belly	bi˧mi˧	–	–
	fox	dʁ˧mi˧	–	–
	little sister	go˧mi˧	–	–
	moon	ɬi˧mi˧	–	–
	king, lord	ʁo˧mi˧	–	–
	louse	ʂe˧mi˧	–	–
	wife	tsʰv̩˧mi˧	–	–
LM or LH	frog	pʁ˩mi˩	–	pʁ˩pʰv̩˩
LM, LH or H	tongue	hi˩mi˩	–	–
	large comb	pv̩˩mi˩	–	–
	axe	bi˩mi˩	–	–
	heart	nv̩˩mi˩	–	–
	niece	ze˩mi˩	–	–
	mule	dɯ˩mi#˥	dɯ˩zo#˥	dɯ˩pʰv̩#˥
LM or H	bow	zv̩˩mi˩	zv̩˧zo#˥	–
any tone except LH	fish	–	ɲi˧zo#˥	–
unclear	hwamei (bird)	tɕɯ˩mi˥	–	–
	cigarette lighter	tse˧mi˥	–	–

Table 5.2a: Nouns with gender suffixes or augmentative/diminutive suffixes. Three-syllable words derived from M-tone disyllables.

correspondences	root	suffixed forms		
		//-mi˩// 'female'	//-zo˥// 'child'	//-pʰv̩˥// 'male'
first type	rabbit	tʰo˧li˧-mi˩	tʰo˧li˧-zo#˥	tʰo˧li˧-pʰv̩#˥
	snake	zv̩˧bæ˧-mi˩	zv̩˧bæ˧-zo#˥	zv̩˧bæ˧-pʰv̩#˥
	lion	si˧gɯ˧-mi˩	si˧gɯ˧-zo#˥	si˧gɯ˧-pʰv̩#˥
	earthworm	dʐɯ˧dv̩˧-mi˩	dʐɯ˧dv̩˧-zo#˥	dʐɯ˧dv̩˧-pʰv̩#˥
second type	demon	si˧bv̩˧-mi#˥	si˧bv̩˧-zo#˥	–
	ghost	tsʰo˧qʰwɤ˧-mi#˥	tsʰo˧qʰwɤ˧-zo#˥	–
	Bai (people)	ɬi˧bv̩˧-mi#˥	ɬi˧bv̩˧-zo#˥	–

Table 5.2b: Nouns with gender suffixes or augmentative/diminutive suffixes. Three-syllable words without a corresponding disyllable.

root tone	root	suffixed forms		
		//-mi˩// 'female'	//-zo˥// 'child'	//-pʰv̩˥// 'male'
L	bird	v̩˩dze˩-mi˩	v̩˩dze˩-zo˩	v̩˩dze˩-pʰv̩˩
L#	bat	dze˧bɤ˩-mi˩	dze˧bɤ˩-zo˩	dze˧bɤ˩-pʰv̩˩
	owl	mo˧jo˩-mi˩	mo˧jo˩mi˩-zo˩	mo˧jo˩mi˩-pʰv̩˩
LM+MH#	wolf	õ˩dv̩˧-mi˥	õ˩dv̩˧-zo#˥	õ˩dv̩˧-pʰv̩#˥
H#	camel	njɤ˧mv̩˥-mi˩	njɤ˧mv̩˥mi˩-zo˩	njɤ˧mv̩˥mi˩-pʰv̩˩
unclear	cicada	dʐɯ˧dze˧mi#˥	–	–
	vulture	se˩gwɤ˩-mi˧	–	–

5.1.3 Discussion

The tonal correspondences between monosyllabic roots and disyllables are not one-to-one. The diversity of tonal correspondences suggests that disyllables with these suffixes have different degrees of lexicalization, and different degrees of historical depth. It would thus be misleading to think of all the suffixed forms as the result of a synchronic, currently productive morphological process. Semantically, there is a continuum between disyllables with a clearly female meaning, such as 'sow', and disyllables in which the semantic content of the suffix has become bleached, e.g. /kʰʏ˩mi˩/ which simply means 'dog', not specifically 'she-dog'. After semantic bleaching, suffixes need to be added anew to specify gender. For instance, on the basis of /njʏ˧myˉmi˩/ 'camel', the words for 'camel calf' and 'male camel' come out as /njʏ˧myˉmi˩-zo˩/ and /njʏ˧myˉmi˩-pʰʏ˩/, respectively. But these two forms, while readily understandable, are considered awkward by the main consultant. Does this mean that the /-mi˩/ component in /njʏ˧myˉmi˩/ 'camel' is still perceived as carrying its female meaning? Not necessarily: the slight weirdness of /njʏ˧myˉmi˩-zo˩/ 'camel calf' and /njʏ˧myˉmi˩-pʰʏ˩/ 'male camel' seems due to the /...mi.zo/ and /...mi.pʰv/ sequences, where the suffix re-activates, as it were, the gender denotation of /-mi˩/ in 'camel'.

The study of combinations for which two tone patterns are acceptable, e.g. /hwʏ˧zo#˥/ and /hwʏ˧zoˉ$/ for 'male kitten', reveals that tonal variants are item-specific (lexicalized). Out of the set of nine words suffixed in /-zo˥/ or /-pʰʏ˥/ corresponding with a MH-tone root, only four allow both variants, #H and H$. Among the nine words, four refer to names of objects: 'basket', 'needle', 'scales', and 'bowl'. Interestingly, none of these four allows a tonal variant: they all fall into one category or the other (#H for 'needle', and H$ for the other three). By contrast, four of the five animal names allow both variants. The difference between the gender suffixes and size suffixes in this respect is not clear-cut: some nouns referring to objects allow two variants. For instance, 'ladle' conforms to the exceptionless existence of two tonal variants for LM-tone roots: /tɕʰo˩mi#˥/ ≈ /tɕʰo˩mi˧/, and /tɕʰo˩zo#˥/ ≈ /tɕʰo˩zo˧/. Still, there appears to be a statistical tendency for animal names to preserve a tonal flexibility reflecting the stronger perception of their internal structure by the speakers.

In some cases, it is possible to identify factors that have played a role in contributing to the current tonal output: 'little bottle', /kʏ˩zo˩/, does not have the expected #H-tone variant /†kʏ˧zo#˥/; to the consultant, the latter form immediately summoned up the given name /kʏ˧zo#˥/. Supposing that 'little bottle' once had two tonal variants, L and #H, the pressure to avoid homophony may have played a role in the selection of the variant /kʏ˩zo˩/ to the exclusion of the other.

The discussion below is arranged by tone of the root noun, in the same order as in Tables 5.1a–g and 5.2a–b. For each tone category of roots, forms suffixed with //-mi˩// are discussed first, followed by forms with //-zo˥// and //-pʰɣ˥//.

5.1.3.1 LM-tone roots

Table 5.1 brings out no fewer than four tone correspondences between monosyllables with LM tone and their suffixed forms: LM, as in /bo˩mi˧/ 'sow' and /æ˩mi˧/ 'hen'; M, as in /bv̩˧mi˧/ 'female yak', /dʐwæ˧mi˧/ 'female sparrow' and /kʁ˧mi˧/ 'female falcon'; LM+#H, in /dv̩˩mi#˥/ 'female weasel', /ɑ˩mi#˥/ 'goose', /dzo˧mi#˥/ 'female lizard', and /nɑ˩mi#˥/ 'Na woman'; and finally L, in /pʰʁ˩mi˩/ 'female jackal'.

Three LM-tone nouns outside the semantic sphere of animal names can carry the /-mi˩/ suffix, with three of the above four tone patterns. One has M tone: /bv̩˧mi˧/ 'big food steamer' (from /bv̩˩/ 'food steamer'). Another has LM+#H tone: /tɕʰo˩mi#˥/ 'big ladle' (from /tɕʰo˩/ 'ladle'). The third has L tone: /zʁ˩mi˩/ 'road, path', which does not specifically mean 'large road' anymore: the monosyllable /zʁ˩/, likewise meaning 'road, path', is falling into disuse.

Given the diversity of these patterns, it is hard to establish the relative chronology of the tone rules that produced the four types (LM, M, LM+#H, and L). A few hints may be detected nonetheless. While LM-tone monosyllables correspond to no fewer than four tone categories of suffixed forms, LM-tone suffixed forms only correspond to LM-tone monosyllables. In other words, LM-tone monosyllables are the only source of LM-tone disyllables. The examples, 'sow', 'hen', 'bee' and 'thumb', belong to basic vocabulary, suggesting that the LM::LM correspondence between monosyllable and disyllable reflects an older pattern.

The tone patterns for the //-zo˥// and //-pʰɣ˥// suffixes are fully consistent with those for the suffix //-mi˩//: in the second type of correspondences in Table 5.1, forms suffixed with //-zo˥// or //-pʰɣ˥// always have #H (with L as a variant) when the form suffixed with //-mi˩// has M; in the third type, words with any of these three suffixes have LM+#H, with LM as a variant.

On the other hand, these patterns differ widely from those observed in other syntactic structures, such as compound nouns and combinations of nouns with verbs or adjectives. Thus, different syntactic structures are reflected in different tone rules – with the added complexity of numerous lexicalized oddities.

5.1.3.2 LH-tone roots

Monosyllables with LH tone correspond to disyllables carrying LM+#H. But two items also have a L-tone variant, namely /ʐiˈmi#˥/ ≈ /ʐiˈmiˈ/ for 'female monkey' and /tɕʰɯˈmi#˥/ ≈ /tɕʰɯˈmiˈ/ for 'female muntjac'. However, /ʐæˈmi#˥/ 'female leopard' does not allow this variant: the form ‡ ʐæˈmiˈ is not acceptable. Outside the field of animal names, /tʰiˈmi#˥/ 'large plane' (from /tʰiʌ/ 'plane [carpentry tool]') cannot be realized as ‡ tʰiˈmiˈ; conversely, the word for 'large slope' (from /toʌ/ 'slope') is /toˈmiˈ/, and ‡ toˈmi#˥ is not acceptable. No certainty can be reached at present on whether two different tone rules applied at different times (in which case the existence of two variants would be a development due to analogy or dialect contact) or the two variants used to coexist for all items, some of which lost one of the variants.

Two other patterns are illustrated by only one example each. These words may be relatively old: M tone in /diˉmiˉ/ 'plain' (compare 'earth, land', /diʌ/), and LH tone in /ljɤˈmi˥/ 'main beam'.

5.1.3.3 M-tone roots

Monosyllables with M tone yield disyllables with #H tone: /lɑˉmi#˥/ 'female tiger' and /seˉmi#˥/ 'female goral'. This pattern is also found, outside the semantic field of animal names, in /qʰwæˉmi#˥/ 'message; letter'. That this rule is currently productive was verified by adding the augmentative suffix to the M-tone noun /qwæˉ/ 'bed mat', yielding /qwæˉmi#˥/ 'large bed mat'.

The situation is more complex for disyllables with //-miˈ// added as a suffix. There are two attested patterns: –L, in /siˉgɯˉ-miˈ/ 'lioness', /ʐʋˉbæˉ-miˈ/ 'female snake' and /tʰoˉliˉ-miˈ/ 'hare', and #H, in /ɬiˉbʋˉ-mi#˥/ 'woman of the Bai ethnic group'. The latter correspondence coincides with that found for monosyllables. To determine which of the two is currently productive, the suffix was added to a word to which it is not normally attached: 'earthworm', /dʐɯˉdʋˉ/, as the earthworm is a hermaphrodite. For elicitation, the imagined context was the following: a child wonders whether there are such things as male and female earthworms, and asks, 'Are there such things as female earthworms?/Do female earthworms exist?' The speaker had no hesitation in formulating the question as (4), with –L tone on the suffixed form /dʐɯˉdʋˉ-miˈ/ 'female earthworm'.

(4) dʐɯ˧dy˧-mi˧ | ə˧-dzo˩ʔ?
    dʐɯ˧dy˧-mi˧   ə˧-   dzo˩ᵇ
    female_earthworm   INTERROG   EXIST

'Are there such things as female earthworms?/Do female earthworms exist?' (Source: field notes.)

5.1.3.4 L-tone roots

Monosyllabic words carrying L tone yield M-tone disyllables: /jo˧mi˧/ 'ewe', /ɬi˧mi˧/ 'female roebuck', and /mv̩˧mi˧/ 'woman'. This last example is attested in a proverb: see (5).

(5) mv̩˧mi˧ tʂʰwɤ˩ mɤ˩-dɯ˩, | kʰv̩˧nɑ˩ zo˩ mɤ˩-dɯ˩.
    mv̩˧mi˧   tʂʰwɤ˩   mɤ˩-   dɯ˩ᵇ   kʰv̩˧nɑ˩   zo˩
    woman   dinner (evening meal)   NEG   to_get   black_dog   lunch
    mɤ˩-   dɯ˩ᵇ
    NEG   to_get

'No dinner for the [married] woman, no lunch for the black dog.' (Sister. 130, 131, 139, 158, 171 and Sister3.3, 113, 117) *Explanation:* 'No dinner for the married woman': if a married woman goes back to her original home for a visit during the day, she cannot stay for the evening meal, as she has obligations back at the household she has married into. 'No lunch for the black dog': 'black dog' here refers to any dog, in fact. Dogs only get two meals a day, one in the morning and one in the evening.

The word /mv̩˧mi˧/ 'woman' is no longer intelligible to younger speakers, such as M23. It is likely that the correspondence between L-tone roots and M-tone disyllabic forms reflects a tone rule that has a relatively great time depth. The same tone (M) is found in /kɤ˧mi˧/ 'large bottle' and /dʐɯ˧mi˧/ 'large river'.

The tone patterns for the /-zo˩/ and /-pʰv̩˩/ suffixes are identical for roots with tones L and LM.

5.1.3.5 H-tone roots

For words derived from H-tone monosyllables, we find three patterns: #H tone, in /ho˧mi#˥/ 'female pheasant' and /bɤ˧mi#˥/ 'Pumi woman'; L tone, in /ʐwæ˩mi˩/ 'mare', /ji˩mi˩/ 'cow' and /kʰv̩˩mi˩/ 'dog' (discussed further below); and M tone, in /kʰi˧mi˧/ 'main door', /qʰæ˧mi˧/ 'canal; large ditch', and /ʐ̃˧mi˧/ 'tree trunk' (etymologically 'large bone').

The first pattern makes good synchronic sense: the tones of the monosyllable and disyllable correspond neatly with each other. The semantic relationship is also clear: the monosyllabic term ('pheasant', 'Pumi') does not refer to gender, and the suffixed term does ('female pheasant', 'Pumi woman'). The second and third patterns are not phonologically transparent. Concordantly, the semantic relationship is less clear in some cases. The words for 'mare', 'cow' and 'dog' illustrate three stages in the gradual evolution of the suffix's meaning. The monosyllable for 'horse', /ʐwæ˥/, is in common use, and the word for 'mare', /ʐwæ˩mi˩/, simply specifies gender. On the other hand, the monosyllable /ji˥/ for 'cow' is not in frequent use; there are more than ten different disyllables pronounced /ji/, six of them with H tone, and the //-mi˩// suffix serves the purpose of disambiguation. In this role, while the suffix retains its female meaning, it can be said to function as an animal suffix just as much as a female suffix. The third example, /kʰʋ˩mi˩/, 'dog', is further down this evolutionary path: it refers to dogs both male and female, and the monosyllable /kʰʋ˥/ for 'dog' is seldom used (but firmly attested, witness Dog.1, 3, 45 and Dog2.68, 74-77, 79). These observations suggest that #H may be the tone of more recently derived words, and L a tone that used to obtain at an earlier stage, and that remains lexically preserved in some old words.

This conjecture is confirmed by examples from outside the semantic field of animal names: /sɑ˩mi˩/ 'Cannabis indica' (the psychotropic plant), which corresponds to monosyllabic /sɑ˥/ 'Cannabis sativa' (used to produce thread), has L tone. The semantic content of the suffix is 'large', referring to the size of the leaves (as an aside: in Mandarin too, 'cannabis' *dàmá* 大麻 is derived from 'hemp' *má* 麻 by addition of the augmentative *dà* 大 'large'). Again, this suggests that L was the tone that used to obtain at an earlier stage. By contrast, 'large pot', /ʋ˧mi#˥/ (compare /ʋ˥/ 'pot'), a less clearly lexicalized and probably more recent disyllable, carries #H tone, as does /sɯ˧ĩ̃˧mi#˥/ 'backbone, spine' (compare /sɯ˧ĩ̃#˥/ 'tree trunk').

The tone patterns for the /-zo˥/ and /-pʰʋ˥/ suffixes are identical for roots with tones H and M.

5.1.3.6 MH-tone roots

MH-tone monosyllables all correspond to disyllables with H$ tone. The following examples were observed: /hwɤ˧mi˥$/ 'she-cat'; /tsʰæ˧mi˥$/ 'hind'; /tsʰɯ˧mi˥$/ 'nanny goat'; /ʁʋ˧mi˥$/ 'female crane'; /tɕɯ˧mi˥$/ 'wasp'; and, from outside the semantic field of animal names, /kʰɤ˧mi˥$/ 'large basket', /ʁo˧mi˥$/ 'big needle', /tɕɯ˧mi˥$/ 'large basket', and /hu˧mi˥$/ 'stomach, bowels' (this last noun is now more common than monosyllabic /hu˧/, and has no strong connotation of 'big').

Words with the /-zo˥/ and /-pʰy˥/ suffixes can carry either #H, a pattern which is widely attested with these suffixes, or H$, the same tone found in items suffixed with /-mi˩/.

5.1.3.7 Some observations about other lexical tones

As predicted by Rule 5 ("All syllables following a H.L or M.L sequence receive L tone": see §7.1.1), L# tone spreads over the suffix, yielding M.L.L: /dze˧bʁ˩-mi˩/ 'female bat', /dze˧bʁ˩-zo˩/ 'little bat, pup', and /dze˧bʁ˩-pʰy˩/ 'male bat'. On this basis, a disyllabic *mo˧jo˩ can confidently be extracted from /mo˧jo˩-mi˩/ 'owl'. (Remember that the asterisk indicates a reconstruction, not an ungrammatical form.)

The tone patterns of 'cicada', 'vulture', 'hwamei (bird)' and '(cigarette) lighter' have no equivalent elsewhere, making it impossible (in the present stage of our knowledge) to extract the tones of their roots.

5.1.3.8 Concluding observations

The patterns in Tables 5.1a–g and 5.2a–b are summarized in Tables 5.3a–b. It must be emphasized that the classification into currently productive patterns and older patterns for the //-mi˩// suffix is speculative. As elsewhere, a slash (/) separates variants.

Table 5.3a: Tonal correspondences between monosyllabic base forms and disyllables containing the suffixes /-mi˩/, /-zo˥/ and /-pʰy˥/, with tentative indications on whether the tone pattern is currently productive.

	/-mi˩/		/-zo˥/, /-pʰy˥/
	older?	productive?	no distinctions in productiveness
LM	LM; L	M; LM+#H / LM	LM+#H / LM; #H / L
LH	M; LH; L	LM+#H / L	LM+#H / L
M		#H	#H
L		M	#H / L
H	L; M	#H	#H
MH		H$	#H / H$

Roots with the same lexical tones correspond to diverse tones on suffixed forms, with as many as four types of correspondences for LM tone. The total

Table 5.3b: Tonal correspondences between disyllabic base forms and trisyllabic nouns containing the suffixes /-miJ/, /-zo˧/ and /-pʰy˧/, with tentative indications on whether the tone pattern is currently productive.

	/-miJ/		/-zo˧/, /-pʰy˧/
	older?	productive?	no distinctions in productiveness
M	#H	−L (L#)	#H
H		#H	
L		L	L
L#		L#−	L#−
LM+MH#		LM+H#	LM+#H
H#		H#−	−

number of noun subsets in Tables 5.1a–g and 5.2a–b, excluding disyllabic roots, is 14. Since /-miJ/ on the one hand, and /-zo˧/ and /-pʰy˧/ on the other, fall into different tone categories, there are 2×14=28 potentially distinct tonal types of suffixed nouns. Given that many types have variants, the number of different tones on suffixed nouns could be considerable. Yet the set of tones observed on suffixed nouns is limited to six: {M, #H, H$, L, LM, LM+#H}, apart from two outliers: tones that are only found in one example each. Thus some tone categories contain large numbers of words produced through suffixation or compounding, whereas others are not fed by any currently productive combination processes. Such facts contribute to giving different lexical tone categories their own specific morphological flavours.

There are only five tone patterns for forms suffixed in //-zo˧// and //-pʰy˧//: {#H, H$, L, LM, LM+#H}. One additional pattern is attested for //-miJ//, namely M tone. The relatively greater simplicity of tone patterns for //-zo˧// and //-pʰy˧// may be linked to their more restricted distribution in the lexicon: words with the 'male' and 'child' suffix, being fewer in number, may have undergone more simplification of tone patterns by the analogical extension of productive patterns.

5.1.4 Other suffixes for 'male'

In addition to the currently productive suffix //-pʰy˧// for 'male', there also exist other, non-productive suffixes. These are mentioned for the sake of completeness, although the small number of examples greatly limits possibilities for analysis of their tone patterns.

5.1.4.1 The suffix /-ʂwæ˧/

The free form /ʂwæ˧/ currently has the meaning 'castrated/neutered male'.

(6) tʂʰɯ˧ | ʂwæ˧ ɲi˩.
    tʂʰɯ˥   ʂwæ˧   ɲi˩
    DEM.PROX castrated_male COP
    'This is a castrated male.'

The morpheme /ʂwæ˧/ may have had the meaning 'male' at an earlier stage, however, witness the noun /æ̃˧ʂwæ˥/, meaning 'rooster, cock' (compare /æ̃˩/ 'chicken'). This noun has no competitor with the suffix /-pʰv̩˥/ (it is not possible to say ‡æ̃˩pʰv̩#˥). Roselle Dobbs (p.c. 2016) reports that in Lataddi 喇塔地 'grandfather' and 'rooster' sound comically similar; it could be that an earlier form †æ̃˩pʰv̩#˥ 'rooster' fell into disuse in the Alawa dialect (studied here) because of phonetic closeness with 'grandfather'.

The suffix /-ʂwæ/ also appears in three other items in which it carries the meaning 'castrated male': see Table 5.4. Interestingly, the tone pattern is different for 'cock' and 'castrated yak', two words whose root has the same tone (LM) but in which the suffix takes different meanings: 'male' in one case, 'castrated male' in the other. It is a safe guess that /æ̃˧ʂwæ˥/ 'cock' has greater time depth.

Concerning the tone of the suffix, two of the words in which the suffix appears ('castrated yak' and 'castrated male goat') carry tone patterns that are among possible variants for the suffixes //-zo˥// 'baby, male' and //-pʰv̩˥// 'male', tentatively analyzed as carrying H tone. But the third word, /tsʰɯ˧ʂwæ˥/ 'wether, castrated male goat', does not have the same tone pattern as words containing the 'baby, male' and 'male' suffixes: /tsʰɯ˧zo#˥/ ≈ /tsʰɯ˧zo˥$/ and /tsʰɯ˧pʰv̩#˥/ ≈ /tsʰɯ˧pʰv̩˥$/ (see Table 5.1f). This constitutes evidence that the suffix /-ʂwæ/ does not carry the same tone as the //-zo˥// and //-pʰv̩˥// suffixes. The suffix /-ʂwæ/ is provisionally labelled here as carrying M tone, and transcribed as //-ʂwæ˧//, but it must be emphasized that this is mostly a way of distinguishing its tone from that of the 'baby, male' and 'male' suffixes, provisionally transcribed as //-zo˥// and //-pʰv̩˥//, respectively.

5.1.4.2 The suffix /-v̩/

Lidz (2010: 179) proposes that the suffix in /zɛ³¹-wu³³/ 'nephew' (F4: /ze˩v̩˩/) and /zu³¹-wu³³/ 'grandson' (F4: /zv̩˧v̩#˥/) comes from the root for 'uncle/senior male

Table 5.4: Names of animals with the suffix /ʂwæ˧/.

tone of root	meaning of root	suffixed form	meaning
LM	chicken	æ̃˧ʂwæ˥	rooster (not castrated)
LM	yak	bv̩˧ʂwæ˩	castrated yak
L	sheep	jo˩ʂwæ˩	wether, castrated male sheep
MH	goat	tsʰɯ˧ʂwæ˥	wether, castrated male goat

relative', which appears in /ə˧ʋ̩˥/ 'maternal uncle', and that this root also constitutes the origin of the classifier for individuals (F4: /ʋ̩˧/).

5.1.4.3 The suffix /-ʁo/

The word for 'castrated horse' is /ʐwæ˧ʁo˩/. Horses have been the object of great care and interest in this part of the Himalayas for at least two millenia (Wāng Níngshēng 1980), so it is no wonder that words belonging to this semantic field are numerous, some of them probably very old. This isolated example is clearly insufficient for linguistic analysis.

5.1.5 The kinship prefix /ə˧-/

Another non-productive but readily identifiable affix is the kinship prefix /ə˧-/. It is common to various languages of the area, such as Qiang (Evans & Huang 2007: 158–159), Yi, and Mandarin. Table 5.5 presents the examples that were observed in Yongning Na, where this prefix is "the only common noun prefix" (Lidz 2010: 167).

Monosyllabic forms do not exist, and no convincing method to extract the tone of the root could be found. It is tempting to hypothesize that the prefix does not make a tonal contribution, and that the tone of the disyllable reflects that of the root: disyllables with M, MH# and H$ tone would originate in roots with M, MH and H tone, respectively, and disyllables with L# tone would originate in roots with L, LM or LH tone. But this reasoning is highly speculative, and no evidence could be found to explore this issue further. The root /mi/ in /ə˧mi˧/ 'mother' is no doubt linked with the free form /mi˧/ 'female', and the root /pʰv/ in /ə˧pʰv̩˧/ 'grandmother's elder brother' with the free form /pʰv̩˧/ 'male', but unlike these

213

Table 5.5: Kinship terms with the prefix /ə˧-/.

kinship term	tone	meaning
ə˧ma˧	M	mother (term of address)
ə˧mi˧	M	mother; aunt
ə˧pʰv˧	M	grandmother's elder brother
ə˧si˧	M	great-grandmother; ancestor
ə˧do˧	M	boyfriend/girlfriend, lover
ə˧ʑi˥	MH#	grandmother mother's mother
ə˧v˥	MH#	maternal uncle
ə˧bo˧$	H$	paternal uncle
ə˧da˧$	H$	father
ə˧ɕjɤ˩	L#	boyfriend/girlfriend, lover
ə˧jɤ˩	L#	maternal aunt: mother's elder sister
ə˧tɕi˩	L#	maternal aunt: mother's younger sister
ə˧mv˩	L#	elder sibling (brother or sister)
ə˧zɯ˩ / ə˩zɯ˩	L# / L	dual: us two
ə˧-sɯ˩ky˩ / ə˩-sɯ˧ky˥	-L / LMH	1st person plural, inclusive

two free forms, the kinship terms /ə˧mi˧/ 'mother' and /ə˧pʰv˧/ 'grandmother's elder brother' have the same tone, so it would be problematic to extract the tones of the roots from those of the suffixed kinship terms.

From a static-synchronic point of view, it is also difficult to reach hard-and-fast conclusions, due to the limited amount of data: one prefix and four suffixes. With this qualification, one may observe that disyllables with M, H$ or L tone can be the result of suffixation as well as prefixation; that disyllables with #H, H#, LM, LH, or LM+#H tone can result from suffixation but not from prefixation; and that disyllables with MH# or L# tone can result from prefixation but not from suffixation. The issue of possible origins for the various tone categories of disyllables (by suffixation, prefixation, and compounding) is taken up in §9.2.2.

Concerning the tone of the kinship prefix, it seems reasonable to analyze it as M, since the prefix always appears with M tone except for two variants shown in the last two lines of Table 5.5. This is not really different from an analysis under which this prefix is underlyingly toneless, since M behaves in some respects as a default tone, as mentioned in §2.4.3.

Kinship terms in the Luoshui dialect (Lidz 2010: 167) are similar to those in Alawa (the dialect studied here). For instance, Luoshui /a³³ʐɯ³³/ for 'grandmother' is cognate with Alawa /ə˧ʑi˩/. Only three terms from L. Lidz's list are not attested in Alawa. One of these is /ɑ³³pɔ³¹/, for 'uncle: father's elder or younger brother'. This could be a borrowing from Mandarin *ābó* 阿伯 'brother-in-law; father's older brother'.³ Borrowing is facilitated by the similar structure in both languages, with a similar prefix (in Mandarin: *ā* 阿). A different term is in use in Alawa: /ə˧bo˩$/; its voiced initial suggests that it is not a recent borrowing from Mandarin, which does not retain voiced stops. Ethnological data sheds light on the fact that the terms for uncles on the father's side do not correspond neatly across dialects: the social relationship with one's father (and his household) was traditionally loose (see Appendix B, §B.3); accordingly, kinship terms on the father's side were not as specific as on the mother's side.

The peculiar structure of Na families invites linguistic speculation as to the origin and evolution of the terms currently used for relatives on the father's side. Fu Maoji (1980: 23; 1983: 38–39) hypothesizes that /ə˧bo˩$/ 'uncle on the father's side' used to refer to male relatives of the father's generation, on the father's side, i.e. the father and his brothers, and that the introduction of the term /ə˧dɑ˩$/ 'father' led to the specialization of /ə˧bo˩$/ to refer to uncles on the father's side. This would imply that people had a term to refer to their paternal uncles (pooled together with their father under the term /ə˧bo˩$/) before they had a term for 'father'. This may seem paradoxical: since children did not live in the same household as their paternal uncles, their link to these uncles was through the father, and the existence of the notion of 'father' would appear as a logical prerequisite for conceptualizing the broader notion of *male relatives on the father's side, belonging to the father's generation*. Fu Maoji's reasoning nonetheless makes good sense in a conceptual universe that is not based on nuclear families but on clans and extended families. If an individual is primarily identified in terms of belonging to a household, and to a generation inside the family, it would seem possible that fathers are not differentiated from their brothers in kinship terminology. Moreover, the lack of a terminological distinction between the father and his brothers does not seem excessively surprising in view of the fact that ties with the father's family were loose and distant both economically and socially.⁴

Synchronically, extension of terms used within the traditional household (i.e. on the mother's side) to the family of the father is occasionally observed, for

---

³ In *Pinyin* romanization, *b* stands for a voiceless bilabial stop: /p/, not /b/.

⁴ This reflection was proposed by Christine Mathieu (p.c. 2016). She quotes Lamu Gatusa 拉木·嘎吐萨 as reporting a word in the dialect of Labai 拉柏 that is cognate with /ə˧bo˩$/ and refers precisely to this concept: male relatives on the father's side, belonging to the father's generation, i.e. the father and his brothers. Distinctions can be made by adding the adjective 'small' to refer to the father's younger brothers, and 'big' to refer to his elder brothers.

instance publicly addressing one's father as /ə˧ʝi˩/ 'uncle on the mother's side' (field notes, consultant F4). The stylistic effect is to convey closeness – through inclusion in the household – and honour, as maternal uncles are characters to whom highest respect is due (as explained in Appendix B, §B.3.1). In view of the plasticity of terms of address, one could venture an alternative hypothesis about the origin of the term for 'uncle on the father's side': that the words /ə˧ʝi˩/ 'uncle on the mother's side' and /ə˧bo˧$/ 'uncle on the father's side' in the Alawa dialect come from terms that used to refer to the mother's older and younger brothers, respectively. This hypothesis would entail that the word /ə˧bo˧$/, corresponding to a socially less important and prestigious role than /ə˧ʝi˩/, was later applied to uncles on the father's side, while /ə˧ʝi˩/ was extended to all of the mother's brothers irrespective of age – preserving the hierarchy between /ə˧ʝi˩/ as the more important social figure and /ə˧bo˧$/ as the less important social figure, while transforming the age hierarchy into one between the mother's side and the father's side. There are two different terms for aunts: 'mother's elder sister', /ə˧jʌ˩/, and 'mother's younger sister', /ə˧tɕi˩/, so there is some plausibility in hypothesizing the existence of two different terms for uncles in an earlier state of the language. This hypothesis remains highly speculative, however.

The second term reported by Liberty Lidz that is not found in the present research data (Alawa dialect) is /ɑ³³mɔ¹³/ as another term for 'grandmother'. The third is /ɑ³³lɑ³¹/, referring to great-great-grandparents: in Alawa, the term /ə˧si˧/ is used for all ancestors of the great-grandmother's generation and above.

5.2 Reduplication

In languages that do not have morphophonological templates specific to reduplication, it is not always easy to distinguish between reduplication and other types of repetition or copying. For instance, Moravcsik (1978: 301) considers *very very* in the English example *He is very very bright* as a case of reduplication; this is debatable, because the intensifier can be repeated more than once (either an even number of times, 2×n, or an odd number of times: *He is very, very, very bright*), with gradual rather than categorical semantic-stylistic effects. In Yongning Na, reduplication is not too difficult to delimit on a phonological basis, as it has specific tonal templates as well as clearly identifiable syntactic and semantic values. Reduplication of verbs is most common; it will be described in 6.2. Reduplication involving nouns is nowhere as frequent: the only well-attested case is the reduplication of numeral-plus-classifier phrases.

5.2.1 Reduplication of numeral-plus-classifier phrases

Reduplication of a phrase consisting of the numeral 'one' (analyzed as carrying MH tone: //ɖɯ˧˥//) plus a classifier indicates iteration. The entire reduplicated phrase is integrated into a single tone group (about this crucial unit of Na morphotonology, see Chapter 7). The tone pattern of the first part of the phrase conditions that of the second, by application of the phonological rules set out in §7.1.1:

- after a H-tone classifier, the second half of the phrase receives L tone by application of Rules 4 and 5, e.g. //ɖɯ˧-ɲi˥// → /ɖɯ˧-ɲi˥~ɖɯ˧-ɲi˩/ 'day after day' (Reward.155, BuriedAlive2.85, Caravans.259)

- after a M-tone classifier, the second part is unaffected, as in //ɖɯ˧-ʁwɤ˧// → /ɖɯ˧-ʁwɤ˧~ɖɯ˧-ʁwɤ˧/ 'one heap after another' (Housebuilding.51)

- after L, the second part is lowered to L by application of Rule 5, e.g. //ɖɯ˧-ʑi˩// → /ɖɯ˧-ʑi˩~ɖɯ˧-ʑi˩/ 'one family after the other' (Healing.94, Caravans.237)

- after MH, the H part of the contour lands onto the first syllable of the second half: //ɖɯ˧-kɤ˧˥// → /ɖɯ˧-kɤ˧~ɖɯ˥-kɤ˩/ 'one tree after the other' (Housebuilding.28). The final L tone in this expression obtains by application of Rule 4.

5.2.2 Addition of the reduplicated suffix /-ʂo˧~ʂo˩/ to nouns, conveying abundance

Addition of the suffix /-ʂo˧~ʂo˩/ to nouns conveys abundance: examples include /mʁ˩-ʂo˧~ʂo˩/ 'smeared with grease, covered with grease' (7), /ʂe˧-ʂo˧~ʂo˩/ 'rich in meat, with lots of meat' (8), and /si˧-ʂo˧~ʂo˩/ 'packed with wood' (9).

(7) mv˩kʰv˧ | le˧-tsʰɯ˩-dʑo˩, | ɲi˧to˧ | tsʰɯ˧-qo˧ | le˧-tɑ˧, | tsʰɯ˧-qo˧ | le˧-tɑ˧, | mʁ˩-ʂo˩~ʂo˥ tsʁ˩ tsɯ˩ | mv˩!

mv˩kʰv˧	le˧-	tsʰɯ˩ₐ	-dʑo˩	ɲi˧to˧	tsʰɯ˧-qo˧	le˧-tɑ˧
evening	ACCOMP	to_come.PST	TOP	mouth	here	up_to

mʁ˩	-ʂo˧~ʂo˩	tsʁ˧	tsɯ˧	mv˧
animal_fat	ABUNDANCE	to_become	REP	AFFIRM

'The story goes that in the evening, when [the dumb man] came back, [his] mouth was smeared with grease up to here, up to here!' (Lake3.15)

(8) kʰv˩miɭ-ki˥, | ə... ʂe˩˧! | ɲi˩zo˩˧ | ɖɯ˩-kʰwɤ˥, | æɭ-ʂe˩˧ | ɖɯ˩-kʰwɤ˥, | boɭ-ʂe˩˧ | ɖɯ˩-kʰwɤ˥, | ji˩-ʂe˩˧ | ɖɯ˩-kʰwɤ˥, | kʰv˩miɭ-ki˥ | tʰv˩-hãɭ-dʐoɭ, | ʂe˩-ʂo˩˧ ʂo˥ | tʰi˩-ki˩-kv˩ tsɯ˥ | mv˩!

kʰv˩miɭ	-ki˩	ə...	ʂe˥	ɲi˩zo#˥	ɖɯ˩-kʰwɤ˥$
dog	DAT	hesitation	meat	fish	one-CLF.piece

æɭ-ʂe#˥	ɖɯ˩-kʰwɤ˥$	boɭ-ʂe#˥	ɖɯ˩-kʰwɤ˥$	ji˩-ʂe#˥
chicken_meat	one-CLF.piece	pork	one-CLF.piece	beef

ɖɯ˩-kʰwɤ˥$	kʰv˩miɭ	-ki˩	tʰv˩-hãɭ	-dʐo˥	ʂe˥	**-ʂo˩~ʂoɭ**
one-CLF.piece	dog	DAT	that_day	TOP	meat	**ABUNDANCE**

tʰi˩-	ki˩ₐ	-kv˩	tsɯ˥	mv˩
DUR	to_give	ABILITIVE	REP	AFFIRM

'To the dog, erm... [one would give] meat! A piece of fish, a piece of chicken, a piece of pork, a piece of beef... On that day [New Year's Eve], one would give the dog plenty of meat!' (Dog.35)

(9) naɭ-ʑi˩mi˩ tʂʰɯ˩ | ɖɯ˩-tʂɤ˥~tʂɤɭ-kiɭ-zeɭ-seɭ | **si˩-ʂo˩~ʂo˥-ɲiɭ**!

naʌ	ʑi˩mi˩	tʂʰɯ˩	ɖɯ˩-	tʂɤ˥ₐ	~
Na (endonym)	house	TOP	delimitative	to_count	ACTIVITY

ki˩ₐ	-ze˩	-seɭ	si˥	**-ʂo˩~ʂoɭ**	-ɲiɭ
to_give	PFV	COMPLETION	wood	**ABUNDANCE**	CERTITUDE

'The Na house, if one is going to count every part of it, [one will realize that] it is packed with wood!' (i.e. a huge deal of wood goes into its construction) (Housebuilding.281)

This suffix does not have a non-reduplicated counterpart, and is not part of a broader set of reduplicated nominal suffixes, so one may wonder whether it is not a reduplicated form but a simple suffix that happens to consist of two identical syllables. The reason for analyzing it as a reduplicated form is the structural parallel with reduplicated suffixes that get added to adjectives (presented in §6.7.1).

The reduplicated suffix /-ʂo˩~ʂoɭ/ can be added to a wide range of nouns, including count nouns, such as persons: a household with numerous young men may be described as /pʰæ˩tɕi˥-ʂo˩~ʂoɭ/, 'teeming with youngsters'. The wide range of semantic application of the suffix allows for the elicitation of an entire set, shown in Table 5.6. As elsewhere, the '+' sign in the transcription of surface tone patterns indicates the tone of the copula when placed after the expression as a test to ascertain the type of syllabic anchoring of a final H tone.

The tone of the suffix /-ʂo~ʂo/ can be hypothesized to be L# (hence the notation //ʂo˩~ʂoɭ// adopted here) on the basis of its behaviour after M-tone disyl-

Table 5.6: The tonal behaviour of the reduplicated suffix /-ʂo˦~ʂo˩/ depending on the tone of the preceding noun.

example	tone	example	surface pattern	analysis
dust	LM	ɖæ˩-ʂo˦~ʂo˩	L.M.L	LM+L#
pimple	LH	ji˩-ʂo˥~ʂo˩	L.H.L (=L.M.L)	LH−
star	M	kɯ˦-ʂo˦~ʂo˥	M.M.H+L	H#
grease	L	mʁ˩-ʂo˩~ʂo˥	L.L.H+L	L+H#
meat	H	ʂe˦-ʂo˦~ʂo˥	M.M.H+L	H#
mushroom	MH	mo˦-ʂo˦~ʂo˥	M.M.H+L	H#
dew	M	dʐv̩˦qʰɑ˦-ʂo˦~ʂo˩	M.M.M.L	L#
fly	#H	bv̩˦ɻ̍˦-ʂo˦~ʂo˥	M.M.M.H+L	H#
paste	MH#	ho˦dʐɯ˦-ʂo˦~ʂo˥	M.M.M.H+L	H#
mud	H$	dʐæ˦qʰæ˦-ʂo˦~ʂo˥	M.M.M.H+L	H#
egg	L	æ˩ʁv̩˩-ʂo˩~ʂo˥	L.L.L.H+L	L+H#
cake/bread	L#	dze˦dv̩˩-ʂo˩~ʂo˩	M.L.L.L	L#−
bean chaff	LM+MH#	nv̩˩tsɑ˦-ʂo˦~ʂo˥	L.M.M.H+L	LM+H#
potato	LM+#H	jʁ˩jo˦-ʂo˦~ʂo˥	L.M.M.H+L	LM+H#
sow	LM	nv̩˩lɯ˦-ʂo˦~ʂo˩	L.M.M.L	LM+L#
button	LH	pv̩˩lɯ˥-ʂo˩~ʂo˩	L.H.L.L	LH−
youngster	H#	pʰæ˦tɕi˥-ʂo˩~ʂo˩	M.H.L.L	H#−

lables and after LM-tone disyllables. In detail, the tone patterns in Table 5.6 are not straightforward; they differ from those of disyllabic postpositions, discussed in §5.5.

5.3 Possessive constructions containing pronouns

Possessive constructions were discussed in Chapter 2, where the behaviour of nouns in association with the possessive /=bv̩˦/ served as one of the tests for determining lexical tone categories. Possessive constructions containing pronouns do not have quite the same tonal patterns, however. This is one of several respects in which pronouns are special.

5.3.1 The 1ˢᵗ, 2ⁿᵈ and 3ʳᵈ person pronouns

A pronoun's tonal category is established by matching up its tone in isolation and its tone when a copula is added (a test which is also useful for nouns, as was explained in §2.2). On the basis of the tones in /njɤ˩ ɲi˧/ 'it's me', /no˩ ɲi˧/ 'it's you' and /tʂʰɯ˧ ɲi˥/ 'it's her/him', the 1SG, 2SG and 3SG pronouns are analyzed as //njɤ˩//, //no˩// and //tʂʰɯ˥//, respectively.

To build a possessive construction with a pronoun, the possessive /=bv˧/ is generally used, as in (10). The forms are /njɤ˧=bv˩/, /no˧=bv˩/ and /tʂʰɯ˧=bv˧/ for the 1ˢᵗ, 2ⁿᵈ and 3ʳᵈ persons.

(10) ə˩ji˧-ʂɯ˩ji˩, | njɤ˧=bv˩ | ʐwæ˧ tʂʰɯ˧, | ŋwɤ˩-kv˩ tsæ˥ | po˧ hɯ˧-ɲi˥!
ə˩ji˧-ʂɯ˩ji˩ njɤ˩ =bv˧ ʐwæ˥ tʂʰɯ˧ ŋwɤ˧ kv˥ tsæ˥
in_the_past 1SG POSS horse TOP five CLF to_rob
po˥ hɯ˧c -ɲi˩
to_take_away to_go.PST CERTITUDE

'Once, long ago, five of my family's horses were stolen!' *Literally:* 'Long ago, my horses (=my family's horses), five were stolen and taken away!' (Caravans.183)

This is unlike the pattern for nouns: L-tone nouns with the possessive yield L+M, and H-tone nouns yield M+H.

A further complication is that there are seemingly two variants for the 3ʳᵈ-person pronoun: /tʂʰɯ˧=bv˧/ and /tʂʰɯ˧=bv˩/. These are not tonal variants, however: they have different meanings. The latter, /tʂʰɯ˧=bv˩/, is a reduced form of /tʂʰɯ˧=i˩=bv˩/, where /=i˩/ is the associative plural. So /tʂʰɯ˧=bv˩/ means 'their', whereas /tʂʰɯ˧=bv˧/ simply means 'her/his'. Ellipsis of the associative plural /=i˩/ is complete: there is no segmental trace of it, only a tonal difference on the possessive particle. This example provides an insight into the expansion of morphotonology through segmental simplifications (a type of diachronic change that is especially well-attested among Bantu languages). This topic will be taken up in Chapter 9, where the Yongning Na tone system is approached from a dynamic-synchronic perspective.

A pronoun may also immediately precede the noun to build a possessive construction, as in (11).

(11) njɤ˧ my˩... | ə˧zɯ˩ | ʂɯ˧-bi˧, | ə˧mi˧ | tʰi˧-ʂɯ˧-kʰɯ˩!

njɤ˩	my˥	ə˧zɯ˩	ʂɯ˧	-bi˧	ə˧mi˧	tʰi˧-	ʂɯ˧
1SG	daughter	1PL.INCL	to_die	IMM_FUT	mother	DUR	to_die

-kʰɯ˩
CAUS

'My dear daughter... We are going to die [=we can't avoid death, now that the tiger is at our door]; let Mum die [=let me sacrifice myself, so you can survive]!' (Tiger.16)

Combinations of pronouns and nouns as in (11) were systematically elicited. The results are identical for the 1SG and 2SG pronouns, //njɤ˩// and //no˩//. They are shown in Table 5.7. The corresponding recording is: PossessPro.

Table 5.7: The tones of possessive constructions consisting of a 1SG pronoun and a noun.

tone	head	meaning	example	tone pattern
LM	bo˥	pig	njɤ˧ bo˩	L#
LH	my˥	daughter	njɤ˧ my˩	L#
M	zɯ˧	life, existence	njɤ˧ zɯ#˥	#H
L	dʑɯ˩	water	njɤ˧ dʑɯ#˥	#H
#H	hĩ˥	human being	njɤ˧ hĩ#˥	#H
MH#	tsʰɯ˥	goat	njɤ˧ tsʰɯ˥	MH#
M	po˧lo˧	ram	njɤ˧ po˧lo˧	M
#H	ʐwæ˧zo#˥	colt	njɤ˧ ʐwæ˧zo#˥	#H
MH#	hwɤ˧li˥	cat	njɤ˧ hwɤ˧li˥	MH#
H$	kv̩˧ʂe˥$	flea	njɤ˧ kv̩˧ʂe˥$	H$
L	kʰv̩˩mi˩	dog	njɤ˧ kʰv̩˩mi˩	-L
L#	dɑ˧ʝi˩	mule	njɤ˧ dɑ˧ʝi˩	L#
LM+MH#	ʝi˩tsæ˥	waist	njɤ˧ ʝi˩tsæ˩	-L
LM+#H	bi˩tsʰɤ#˥	whiskers	njɤ˧ bi˩tsʰɤ˩	-L
LM	bo˩mi˧	sow	njɤ˧ bo˩mi˩	-L
LH	bo˩ɬɑ˥	boar	njɤ˧ bo˩ɬɑ˩	-L
H#	kʰv̩˧nɑ˥	dog	njɤ˧ kʰv̩˧nɑ˥	H#

In all these phrases, the pronoun //njɤ˩// carries the same tone as in isolation: a M tone. (Neutralization of //L//, //M// and //H// to /M/ in isolation is the general rule for monosyllabic nouns and pronouns: see §2.2.1.) The patterns for monosyllabic nouns cannot be obtained through the application of a simple set of general rules. On the other hand, the patterns for disyllables are extremely simple. They consist of the succession of the pronoun, as said in isolation: /njɤ˧/, followed by the noun, which carries the same tone as when it appears on its own, except that some tone levels are deleted to comply with the phonological requirements on a well-formed tone group. This affects the tone categories in which a L tone is attached to the first syllable of the noun: L, LM+MH#, LM+#H, LM, and LH. For these categories, the sequence found on the first two syllables (M tone on the pronoun, and L tone on the initial syllable of the disyllabic noun) is incompatible with any tone other than L on following syllables, by Rule 5 ("All syllables following a H.L or M.L sequence receive L tone": see §7.1.1). For instance, ‡ **njɤ˧ bo˩mi˧** (obtained through simple concatenation) would not be a well-formed tone group; this is repaired to /**njɤ˧ bo˩mi˩**/, lowering the final M to L. The representation in Figure 5.1 assumes that the M part of the LM tone is associated, then deleted. One could also consider that this M does not associate at all. This is an area where psycholinguistic experiments would be necessary to approach more closely the processes taking place in speakers' brains.

This construction offers an example of minimal tonal integration of two elements. It can be described as concatenation of the two parts of the expression, followed by adjustments required by phonological rules.

For disyllables, the tone patterns after the 3rd person pronoun, //**tʂʰɯ˩**//, are identical with those after the 1st and 2nd persons. For monosyllables, on the other hand, the tone patterns are different in the case of L-tone nouns: //**njɤ˧ dʑɯ#˩**// 'my water' vs. //**tʂʰɯ˧ dʑɯ˧**// 'her/his water'. This asymmetry poses yet another challenge to the language learner, who must learn (i) to distinguish the tone patterns for these two tonal sets of pronouns when they associate with a monosyllabic noun, and (ii) to overlook the difference when the following noun is disyllabic. Table 5.8 shows the entire set.

Finally, there also exists a looser construction: a simple juxtaposition of the pronoun and the noun, each in its own tone groups, as in (12).

(12) njɤ˧ | ʈʂʰe˧-dɯ˩ma˩ tʂʰɯ˩-dʑo˩, | no˧sɯ˩kv˩ | tʰv˧-ɲi˧ | lo˧ ji˧ hɯ˧ tsɯ˩.

njɤ˩	ʈʂʰe˧-dɯ˩ma˩	tʂʰɯ˧	-dʑo˥	no˧sɯ˩kv˩	tʰv˧-ɲi˧	lo˧
1SG	given_name	TOP	TOP	2PL.EXCL	that.day	work

ɟi˧	hɯ˧ɬ_c	tsɯ˥
to_do	go.PST	REP

'As for my [daughter] Erchei Ddeema... that day, you (=the members of your family) had gone away to work.' (BuriedAlive2.132)

This is not a possessive construction in the proper sense: rather, the pronoun serves as a topic. The context to this example is as follows. A young woman is unhappy with a marriage arranged by her parents, and she commits a small offence, which takes on huge proportions. Her mother has now come over to the mother-in-law's house to make things right by talking the matter over. The young woman's mother first recapitulates the whole story, clarifying what has been done by the two parties, the members of the two families. In this situation, the first person pronoun in the construction /**njɤ˧** | **ʈʂʰe˧-ɖʐɯ˩ma˩**/ emphasizes

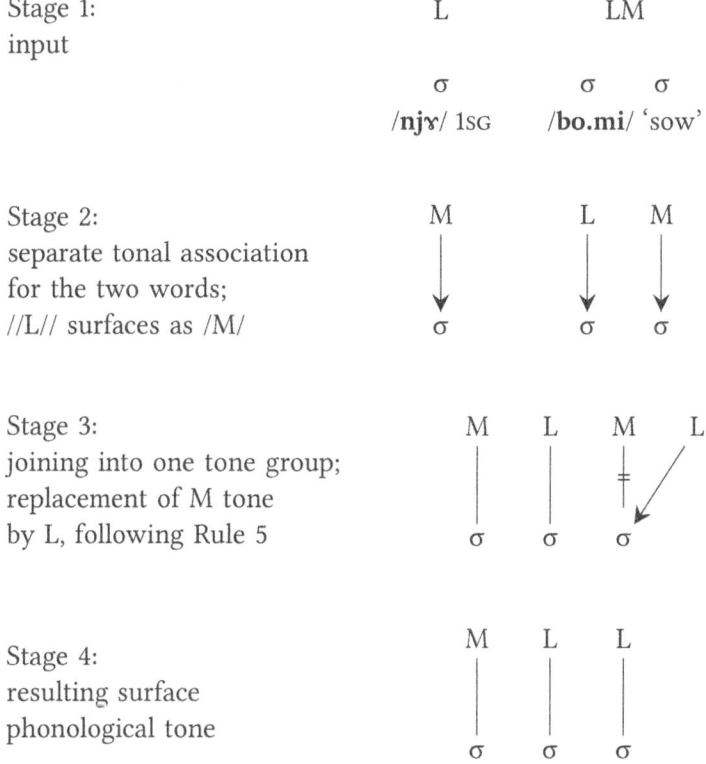

Figure 5.1: Tone-to-syllable association in /**njɤ˧ bo˩mi˩**/ 'my sow'.

Table 5.8: The tones of possessive constructions consisting of a 3SG pronoun and a noun.

tone	example	meaning	with 3SG	tone pattern
LM	bo˧˩	pig	tsʰɯ˧ bo˩	L#
LH	mv˧˩	daughter	tsʰɯ˧ mv˩	L#
M	zɯ˧	life, existence	tsʰɯ˧ zɯ#˧	#H
L	dʑɯ˩	water	tsʰɯ˧ dʑɯ˧	M
#H	hĩ˧	human being	tsʰɯ˧ hĩ#˧	#H
MH#	tsʰɯ˥	goat	tsʰɯ˧ tsʰɯ˥	MH#
M	po˧lo˧	ram	tsʰɯ˧ po˧lo˧	M
#H	ʐwæ˧zo#˧	colt	tsʰɯ˧ ʐwæ˧zo#˧	#H
MH#	hwɤ˧li˥	cat	tsʰɯ˧ hwɤ˧li˥	MH#
H$	ə˧da˥$	father	tsʰɯ˧-ə˧da#˧	#H
L	kʰv˩mi˩	dog	tsʰɯ˧ kʰv˩mi˩	-L
L#	dɑ˩ji˩	mule	tsʰɯ˧ dɑ˩ji˩	L#
LM+MH#	ji˩tsæ˥	waist	tsʰɯ˧ ji˩tsæ˩	-L
LM+#H	bi˩tsʰɤ#˧	whiskers	tsʰɯ˧ bi˩tsʰɤ˩	-L
LM	bo˩mi˧	sow	tsʰɯ˧ bo˩mi˩	-L
LH	bo˩ɬɑ˥	boar	tsʰɯ˧ bo˩ɬɑ˩	-L
H#	kʰv˧nɑ˥	dog	tsʰɯ˧ kʰv˧nɑ˥	H#

the fact that the mother is speaking on her daughter's behalf, and that, as head of the family, she assumes some responsibility for her daughter's actions.

5.3.2 The pronoun 'oneself'

The pronoun 'oneself', /õ˧/, has a different behaviour from the 1st, 2nd and 3rd person pronouns. It is not followed by the possessive, /=bv˧/, except in the frequent construction /õ˧=bv˧-õ˩/ 'one's own', 'one's proper', 'by oneself', which can in turn be followed by a noun, as in (13).

(13) õ˧=bv˧-õ˩ hɑ˩, | õ˧=bv˧-õ˩ dʑɯ˩!
õ˧ =bv˧ õ˧ hɑ˥ dʑɯ˥
oneself POSS oneself food to_eat

'One's own food, one eats it oneself! / We eat our own produce!'
(Agriculture.68; this summarizes the traditional self-sufficiency of the Na, who grew their own food crops)

After /õ˦=bʏ˥-õ˩/, all tonal oppositions are neutralized, because the following noun can only carry L tones, due to a constraint formulated in the present description as Rule 5: "All syllables following a H.L or M.L sequence receive L tone".

The pronoun /õ˦/ usually combines with a following noun, without an intervening morpheme, as in (14) and (15).

(14) õ˦ ə˦mʏ˥ ɲi˩-ze˦!
     õ˦   ə˦mʏ˩   ɲi˩   -ze˦
     self   elder_sibling COP PFV

'This is my own brother!' (Sister.57; Sister3.58. Context: a young woman recognizes a ragged stranger attending her wedding as being her long-lost brother.)

(15) õ˦-ʂe˥, õ˩ tʰæ˩!
     õ˦   ʂe˥   õ˦   tʰæ˦
     self meat self to_bite

'Each person eats her/his own slab of meat!' (Field notes. Context: describing table manners. Each family member used to receive one slice of meat and eat it up. This is unlike Chinese (Han) custom, in which each guest picks food mouthful by mouthful, with chopsticks, from dishes placed on the table.)

The construction /õ˦/ plus N, '[my/one's] own N', has a tonal behaviour of its own. On the analogy of (15), new maxims can be coined, such as (16), (17) and (18).

(16) õ˦-dʑɯ˥, õ˩ tʰɯ˩!
     õ˦   dʑɯ˩   õ˦   tʰɯ˩ᵦ
     self water self to_drink

'Each drinks from her own bottle!' (Field notes. Context: a toddler has grabbed another's bottle; parents prevent her from drinking from it.)

(17) õ˦-ɖæ˥, õ˩ bæ˩!
     õ˦   ɖæ˧   õ˦   bæ˩ₐ
     self dust self to_sweep

'one must sweep one's own garbage' (elicited example)

(18) õ˦-ly˥, õ˩ li˩!
      õ˦   ly˧   õ˦   li˧ₐ
      self field self to_look_after
   'one must look after one's own fields' (elicited)

Combinations were systematically elicited. The full set of tonal combinations is shown in Table 5.9.

Table 5.9: The tones of possessive constructions consisting of /õ˦/+N.

tone	example	meaning	with /õ˦/	tone pattern
LM	ɖæ˧	dirt, dust	õ˦-ɖæ˥	H#
LH	my˧	daughter	õ˦-my˥$	H$
M	ly˧	field	õ˦-ly˥$	H$
L	dʐɯ˩	water	õ˦-dʐɯ˥$	H$
#H	zo˥	son	õ˦-zo#˥	H#
MH#	tsʰɯ˥	goat	õ˦-tsʰɯ˥$	H$
M	go˧mi˧	younger sister	õ˦-go˧mi˥	H#
#H	ʐwæ˧zo#˥	colt	õ˦-ʐwæ˧zo#˥	#H
MH#	ə˧my˥	elder sibling	õ˦-ə˧my˥ / õ˦-ə˥my˩	MH# / MH#–
H$	ə˧da˥$	father	õ˦-ə˧da˥ / õ˦-ə˧da#˥	H# / #H
L	kʰy˩mi˩	dog	õ˦-kʰy˩mi˩	MH#–
L#	da˧ji˩	mule	õ˦-da˧ji˥	H#
LM+MH#	ji˩tsæ˥	waist	õ˦-ji˥tsæ˩	MH#–
LM+#H	bi˩tsʰʁ#˥	whiskers	õ˦-bi˥tsʰʁ˩	MH#–
LM	a˩ʁo˧	home	õ˦-a˥ʁo˩	MH#–
LH	bo˩ɬa˥	boar	õ˦-bo˥ɬa˩	MH#–
H#	kʰy˧na˥	dog	õ˦-kʰy˧na˥	H#

The behaviour of /õ˦/ in association with disyllables coincides with that of determinative compounds containing a MH-tone determiner. With monosyllables, however, the tone patterns only coincide with those of determinative compounds for nouns with LM or MH# tone.

226

5.4 Monosyllabic morphemes appearing after nouns: Enclitics, suffixes, and postpositions

Analysis of morphemes as affixes, clitics, postpositions, serial verbs, "particles" and other parts of speech raises interesting issues that differ widely from one language to another, as illustrated by the diversity of proposals and viewpoints found in a collective book about the notion of "word" (Dixon & Aikhenvald 2002). Aikhenvald (2002: 43) proposed that there is "a multidimensional continuum, from a fully bound to a fully independent morpheme". Rather than proceeding from morphosyntactic categories, the method used here is to start out from tone patterns, progressing towards an analysis in light of the morphemes' tonal behaviour. This approach yields independent evidence for syntactic analysis and part-of-speech labelling. For instance, dative /-ki˧/ and possessive /=bv˧/ turn out to have exactly the same tonal behaviour, which is distinct from that of agentive /ɳɯ˧/ (see §5.4.2), suggesting that the former two belong to the same morphosyntactic class, distinct from the latter. This can be taken as confirmation for the observation (based on syntactic behaviour) that the dative and possessive are "almost suffixal" (Lidz 2010: 155), whereas the agentive is analyzed as a case adposition.

Enclitics, suffixes, and postpositions are divided into four subsets on the basis of their behaviour after M-tone nouns. Those that surface with L tone in that context are considered to carry lexical L tone; likewise, those that surface with M, MH and H tones are considered to carry M, MH and H tones respectively. The paragraphs that follow reveal that these four broad tonal categories are not fully homogeneous; they serve as convenient headings for setting out the data.

5.4.1 L-tone morphemes

This subsection discusses three morphemes: the postposition 'on; at', and the plural and associative clitics.

The postposition //bi˩// 'on; at' surfaces with L tone after a M-tone noun, e.g. in /gv˧mi˧ bi˩/ 'on the body'. Other examples from texts and field notes include disyllabic nouns with L tone, as in /ʐæ˩sɯ˩ bi˩/ 'on the felt cape', and with LM tone, as in /lo˩qʰwɤ˧ bi˩/ 'on the hand'. In order to obtain a full set, systematic elicitation was conducted, yielding the data shown in Table 5.10.

The tone patterns indicated in Table 5.10 are those observed at the surface phonological level, not the underlying tones. In the case of /bo˩ bi˥/ 'on (a/the) pig' and /ʐæ˩ bi˥/ 'on (a/the) leopard', it is unclear whether the pattern is to be an-

Table 5.10: The behaviour of the L-tone postposition //biL// 'on; at' with monosyllabic and disyllabic nouns. There is an additional 'L PRO' row because L-tone pronouns have exceptional behaviour.

example	tone	with /biL/	surface tone pattern
pig	LM	boL biˉ	L.H
leopard	LH	ʐæL biˉ	L.H
tiger	M	laˍ biL	M.L
sheep	L	joL biˍ	L.LH
2SG	L PRO	noˍ biL	M.L
horse	H	zwæˍ biˉ	M.H
deer	MH	tsʰæˍ biˉ	M.H
fox	M	dʐˍmiˍ biL	M.M.L
colt	#H	zwæˍzoˍ biˉ	M.M.H
cat	MH#	hwɤˍliˍ biˉ	M.M.H
she-cat	H$	hwɤˍmiˍ biˉ	M.M.H
dog	L	kʰyLmiL biˉ	L.L.H
mule	L#	daˍjiL biL	M.L.L
wolf	LM+MH#	õLdyˍ biˉ	L.M.H
Naxi	LM+#H	naLhĩˍ biˉ	L.M.H
sow	LM	boLmiˍ biL	L.M.L
boar	LH	boLɬaˉ biL	L.H.L
rat	H#	hwæˍtsɯˉ biL	M.H.L

alyzed as //L.M// or //L.H//, since both are neutralized at the surface-phonological level, by Rule 6 (see §7.1.1). The data in Table 5.10 does not reveal whether the tone patterns of 'on (a/the) pig' and 'on (a/the) leopard' are underlyingly identical or not.

Additional evidence comes from plural /=ɻæL/ and associative plural /=ɨL/. As in Japhug, where the plural clitic /=ra/ can express plurality or collective meaning, these enclitics are not obligatory for non-singular arguments, even in the case of human referents (Jacques submitted). Like the postposition /biL/ 'on; at', these two enclitics are analyzed as having L tone on the basis of their tonal behaviour after M-tone nouns. Their tone patterns are identical to those of the postposition /biL/ 'on; at'. Moreover, in the case of the plural and associative plural morphemes, it is possible to add the possessive /=byˍ/ to the *N+plural* expression as a test of its underlying tone category, following the procedure used in the study of the tones of nouns (Chapter 2). This test distinguishes //L.M//, which does not depress a following possessive, from //L.H//, which does. Table 5.11 presents the facts for N+plural+possessive.

As elsewhere, not all the expressions containing pronouns are tonally identical to those containing nouns. The proximal demonstrative //tʂʰɯ˥// and the distal demonstrative //tʰv˥// yield /tʂʰɯ˧=ɹæ˧˥$/ and /tʰv=ɹæ˧˥$/, i.e. the same pattern as for monosyllabic nouns carrying H tone. But the first and second persons, //njɤ˩// and //no˩//, yield /njɤ˧=ɹæ˩/ and /no˧=ɹæ˩/ with the plural; this is different from the pattern that obtains for L-tone nouns, e.g. /jo˩=ɹæ˧/ 'sheep'.

The data in Table 5.11 brings out tonal differences between nouns and expressions made up of a noun plus a clitic. For instance, the noun /ə˧v˧/ 'uncle' yields /ə˧v˧=ɹæ˩/ 'the uncles' and /ə˧v˧=ɹæ˧=bv˩/ 'of the uncles', i.e. a tonal alternation that has no counterpart among nouns: there is no tonal category of disyllables that has a final H tone in isolation and that yields a final H tone on a following possessive. The H$ tone category of disyllables followed by the possessive yields M.M.M, not M.M.H: e.g. /kv˧ʂe˥/ 'flea' and /kv˧ʂe˧=bv˧/ 'of (a/the) flea' (see Table 2.7b). Thus, the tone carried by the expression /ə˧v˧=ɹæ˥/ 'the uncles' is not strictly identical to any of the tonal categories of disyllables. Likewise, the behaviour of the expression /hĩ˧=ɹæ˥/ 'the people', which yields /hĩ˧=ɹæ˧=bv˥/ 'of the people', has no counterpart among nouns. Stated in impressionistic terms, it is as if the behaviour of H$, the *gliding* H tone, were simplified when the expression that carries it contains a clitic: the H level then tends to attach to a following syllable, even if this syllable is a suffix. This is unlike H$-tone nouns, whose combinations with suffixes of different tone categories yield different results.

The plural marker /=ɹæ˩/ is frequently used. By contrast, the associative plural /=i̯/ has a highly specific meaning: it refers to the clan (the extended family). It is therefore mostly restricted to pronouns and family (clan) names, which are few in number. It cannot be used with kinship terms. However, it is not implausible that the morpheme /=i̯˩/ that partakes in nominalization processes is in fact the associative plural. An example is shown in (19), where /pʰæ˧~pʰæ˧/ 'to attach', in association with /=i̯˩/, comes to mean 'a couple; a pair; a set (of things, persons...) tied together'.

(19) pʰæ˧~pʰæ˧=i̯˩ ɲi˩-kv˩ tsɯ˩ | mv˩.
 pʰæ˧b   ~   =i̯˩   ɲi˩   -kv˧   tsɯ˧   mv˧
 to_tie/fasten RED ASSOCIATIVE COP ABILITIVE REP AFFIRM
 '[The mountains kv˧mv˧ and æ˧ʂæ˧] make up a couple/a pair!'
 (Mountains.99)

229

Table 5.11: The tonal behaviour of nouns followed by the plural clitic /=ɻæ˩/ plus the possessive suffix /=bv̩˩/.

example	tone	+PLURAL	+PLURAL+POSSESSIVE	tonal analysis
Na (ethnic group)	LM	nɑ˩=ɻæ˥	nɑ˩=ɻæ˥=bv̩˩	LH
daughter	LH	mv̩˩=ɻæ˥	mv̩˩=ɻæ˥=bv̩˩	LH
Han (ethnic group)	M	hæ˩=ɻæ˥	hæ˩=ɻæ˥=bv̩˩	L#
sheep	L	jo˩=ɻæ˩	jo˩=ɻæ˩=bv̩˥	L
person, human being	H	hĩ˩=ɻæ˥	hĩ˩=ɻæ˥=bv̩˩ / hĩ˩=ɻæ˩=bv̩˥	H# / H$
deer	MH	tsʰæ˩=ɻæ˥	tsʰæ˩=ɻæ˥=bv̩˩	H#
aunt	M	ə˩mi˩=ɻæ˩	ə˩mi˩=ɻæ˩=bv̩˥	-L
younger brother	#H	gi˩zɯ˩=ɻæ˥	gi˩zɯ˩=ɻæ˥=bv̩˩ / gi˩zɯ˩=ɻæ˩=bv̩˥	H$ / H#
maternal uncle	MH#	ə˩ɣɯ˩=ɻæ˥	ə˩ɣɯ˩=ɻæ˥=bv̩˩ / ə˩ɣɯ˩=ɻæ˩=bv̩˥	H$ / H#
she-cat	H$	hwɤ˩mi˩=ɻæ˥	hwɤ˩mi˩=ɻæ˥=bv̩˩ / hwɤ˩mi˩=ɻæ˩=bv̩˥	H$ / H#
woman	L	mi˩zɯ˩=ɻæ˥	mi˩zɯ˩=ɻæ˥=bv̩˩	L+H#
elder sibling	L#	ə˩mv̩˩=ɻæ˥	ə˩mv̩˩=ɻæ˥=bv̩˩	L#-
wolf	LM+MH#	õ˩ldv̩˩=ɻæ˥	õ˩ldv̩˩=ɻæ˥=bv̩˩ / õ˩ldv̩˩=ɻæ˩=bv̩˥	LM+H# / LM+H$
Naxi (ethnic group)	LM+#H	nɑ˩hĩ˩=ɻæ˥	nɑ˩hĩ˩=ɻæ˥=bv̩˩ / nɑ˩hĩ˩=ɻæ˩=bv̩˥	LM+H# / LM+H$
sow	LM	bo˩mi˩=ɻæ˩	bo˩mi˩=ɻæ˩=bv̩˥	LM-L
boar	LH	bo˩ɬɑ˩=ɻæ˩	bo˩ɬɑ˩=ɻæ˩=bv̩˥	LH-
young man	H#	pʰæ˩tɕi˩=ɻæ˩	pʰæ˩tɕi˩=ɻæ˩=bv̩˥	H#-

230

Not unexpectedly, pronouns followed by the associative plural have a tonal behaviour of their own. For the two L-tone pronouns (1SG and 2SG), the tone patterns with the associative plural are the same as with the plural: /njɤ˧=ɻ̍˩/ and /no˧=ɻ̍˩/. As for the proximal demonstrative (also serving as 3ʳᵈ person) /tʂʰɯ˩/ and the distal demonstrative /tʰv˩/, they yield /tʂʰɯ˧=ɻ̍˩/ and /tʰv˧=ɻ̍˩/, whereas the forms with the plural are /tʂʰɯ˧=ɻæ˩$/ and /tʰv=ɻæ˩$/. This difference is enough to establish that the plural and associative do not always share the same tone patterns, despite their identical behaviour in almost all cases. It must be kept in mind that, as pointed out at the outset of this section (§5.4), the four broad tonal categories set up here (morphemes with L tone, M tone, MH tone and H tone) are based on one test only: their behaviour after M-tone nouns. These four categories are not homogeneous, and only serve as convenient headings for setting out the data.

The associative /=ɻ̍˩/ is therefore presented separately in Table 5.12. Its low frequency explains the great number of gaps in the table.

The Alawa dialect of Yongning Na also has a dual morpheme /=zɯ˩/ appearing in four pronouns: first person dual exclusive /njæ˧=zɯ˩/, first person dual inclusive /ə˧=zɯ˩/, second person dual /no˧=zɯ˩/, and third person dual /tʂʰɯ˧=zɯ˩/. On the basis of these forms, the tone of the dual can be classified as belonging to the same broad tonal category as the plural and associative, namely that of L-tone morphemes – keeping in mind that this tonal category serves as a first-pass label.

The surface phonological patterns for the postposition /bi˩/ 'on; at', shown in Table 5.10, are identical in every case to those for the plural clitic /=ɻæ˩/. The underlying forms for the postposition are more difficult to arrive at, for want of a handy test such as addition of the possessive /=bv̩˧/, which works for noun phrases containing the plural clitic /=ɻæ˩/ but not for locative phrases containing the postposition /bi˩/ 'on; at'. In view of the full identity of surface phonological patterns for the clitic and the postposition, it is tempting to propose an extrapolation from the surface phonological forms in Table 5.10 to the (hypothetical) underlying forms proposed in Table 5.13. These underlying forms are based on those obtained for the plural clitic /=ɻæ˩/ (Table 5.11).

5.4.2 M-tone morphemes: Agentive, dative and topic

This section presents three morphemes that carry M tone when following a M-tone noun and are therefore analyzed as having a M lexical tone.

Tables 5.14a–b present the tonal behaviour of agentive /ŋɯ˧/, dative /-ki˧/ (whose tonal behaviour is identical with that of the possessive, /=bv̩˧/) and topic

Table 5.12: The tonal behaviour of associative plural /=ɨ̣/.

example	meaning	tone	with /=ɨ̣/	output
–	–	LM	–	–
–	–	LH	–	–
–	–	M	–	–
njɤ˩, no˩	1SG, 2SG	L	njɤ˩=ɨ̣˩, no=ɨ̣˩	L#
tʂʰɯ˥, tʰv˥	DEM.PROX, DIST	H	tʂʰɯ˧=ɨ̣˩, tʰv˧=ɨ̣˩	L#
–	–	MH	–	–
dze˧bo˧	family name	M	dze˧bo˧=ɨ̣˩	L#
–	–	#H	–	–
–	–	MH#	–	–
kv˧tsʰa˥$	family name	H$	kv˧tsʰa˧=ɨ̣˥$	H$
la˩ma˩	family name	L	la˩ma˩-ɨ̣˥$	L+H$
ə˧ɕjo˩	family name	L#	ə˧ɕjo˩=ɨ̣˩	L#–
–	–	LM+MH#	–	–
–	–	LM+#H	–	–
–	–	LM	–	–
–	–	LH	–	–
–	–	H#	–	–
dʐɤ˩kɤ˥$	family name	LM+H$	dʐɤ˩kɤ˧-ɨ̣˥$	LM+H$

marker /tʂʰɯ˧/. This last morpheme can be hypothesized to be an extension of the 3rd person singular pronoun /tʂʰɯ˥/, which also serves as a proximal demonstrative, but in view of its tonal behaviour, the topic marker is considered to have M tone, as against H tone for the 3rd person singular pronoun /tʂʰɯ˥/. Table 5.14a presents examples, and Table 5.14b the underlying tone patterns. Note that the tones of /bo˩ ɳɯ˧/ and /zæ˩ ɳɯ˥/ are neutralized at the surface phonological level due to Rule 6 ("In tone-group-final position, H and M are neutralized to H if they follow a L tone": see §7.1.1). As elsewhere, variants are separated by a slash. The difference in tone patterns between these morphemes when associated to 'horse' was carefully verified: the tones are M.L in /ʐwæ˧ ɳɯ˩/, as opposed to M.M in /ʐwæ˧-ki˧/ and /ʐwæ˧ tʂʰɯ˧/.

An exceptional pattern is observed for /di˧/ 'earth': in addition to the expected /di˩ ɳɯ˥/, attested in (20), the form /di˧ ɳɯ˧/ is also acceptable: see (21). This variant is not acceptable for other LH-tone nouns, e.g. it is not possible to say ‡ zæ˧ ɳɯ˧ for 'by (a/the) leopard'.

Table 5.13: The behaviour of the L-tone postposition //bi˩// 'on; at' as interpreted on the analogy of the plural clitic. There is an additional 'L pro' row because L-tone pronouns have exceptional behaviour.

example	tone	with /bi˩/	underlying tone
pig	LM	bo˩ bi˧	LM
leopard	LH	ʐæ˩ bi˥	LH
tiger	M	lɑ˧ bi˩	L#
sheep	L	jo˩ bi˧	L
2sg	L pro	no˧ bi˩	L#
horse	H	ʐwæ˧ bi˥	H$ / #H
deer	MH	tsʰæ˧ bi˥	H#
fox	M	dʐɤ˧mi˧ bi˩	–L
colt	#H	ʐwæ˧zo˧ bi˥	H$
cat	MH#	hwɤ˧li˧ bi˥	H$
she-cat	H$	hwɤ˧mi˧ bi˥	H$
dog	L	kʰv̩˩mi˩ bi˥	L+H$
mule	L#	dɑ˧ʑi˩ bi˩	L#–
wolf	LM+MH#	õ˩dy˧ bi˥	LM+H$
Naxi	LM+#H	nɑ˩hĩ˧ bi˥	LM+H$
sow	LM	bo˩mi˧ bi˩	LM–L
boar	LH	bo˩ɬɑ˥ bi˩	LH–
rat	H#	hwæ˧tsɯ˥ bi˩	H#–

(20) di˩-ɳɯ˥ | ə˧-sɯ˩kv̩˩ li˩-dʑo˩-ɲi˩!
di˩   ɳɯ˧   ə˧-sɯ˩kv̩˩   li˧ₐ   -dʑo˧   -ɲi˩
earth A   1PL.INCL   to_watch   PROG   CERTITUDE
'The Earth is watching us!' (Reward.145)

(21) "mv̩˧-ɳɯ˩ | ki˧! | di˧ ɳɯ˧ | ki˧!" | pi˧-ɲi˥ tsɯ˩ | mv̩˩.
mv̩˥   ɳɯ˧   ki˧ₐ   di˩   ɳɯ˧   ki˧ₐ   pi˥   -ɲi˩   tsɯ˧   mv̩˧
sky   A   to_give   earth   A   to_give   to_say   REP   PROG   AFFIRM
'"It is a gift of the Heavens! It is a gift of the Earth!" he said.' (Reward.121)

Where two variants are possible, stylistic nuances can occasionally be pinpointed. For instance, 'to the father' allows the two variants /ə˧dɑ˧-ki˧/ and

Table 5.14a: Tone patterns of agentive /ŋɯ˧/, dative /-ki˧/, and topic marker /tsʰɯ˧/ with monosyllabic and disyllabic nouns: examples in full.

example	tone	/ŋɯ˧/	/-ki˧/	/tsʰɯ˧/
pig	LM	bo˩ ŋɯ˧	bo˩-ki˧	bo˩ tsʰɯ˧
leopard	LH	ʐæ˩ ŋɯ˥	ʐæ˩-ki˥	ʐæ˩ tsʰɯ˥
tiger	M	lɑ˧ ŋɯ˧	lɑ˧-ki˧	lɑ˧ tsʰɯ˧
sheep	L	jo˧ ŋɯ˧ / jo˩ ŋɯ˥	jo˧-ki˧ / jo˩-ki˥	jo˧ tsʰɯ˧ / jo˩ tsʰɯ˥
horse	H	ʐwæ˧ ŋɯ˩	ʐwæ˧-ki˧	ʐwæ˧ tsʰɯ˧
deer	MH	tsʰæ˧ ŋɯ˥	tsʰæ˧-ki˥	tsʰæ˧ tsʰɯ˧ / tsʰæ˧ tsʰɯ˥
fox	M	ɖɯ˧mi˧ ŋɯ˧	ɖɯ˧mi˧-ki˧	ɖɯ˧mi˧ tsʰɯ˧
colt	#H	ʐwæ˧zo˧ ŋɯ˩	ʐwæ˧zo˧-ki˩	ʐwæ˧zo˧ tsʰɯ˩
cat	MH#	hwɤ˧li˧ ŋɯ˥	hwɤ˧li˧-ki˥	hwɤ˧li˧ tsʰɯ˥
she-cat	H$	hwɤ˧mi˥ ŋɯ˩ / hwɤ˧mi˥ ŋɯ˥	hwɤ˧mi˥-ki˩	hwɤ˧mi˥ tsʰɯ˧ / hwɤ˧mi˥ tsʰɯ˥
dog	L	kʰv̩˩mi˩ ŋɯ˥	kʰv̩˩mi˩-ki˥	kʰv̩˩mi˩ tsʰɯ˥
mule	L#	dɑ˧ji˩ ŋɯ˩	dɑ˧ji˩-ki˩	dɑ˧ji˩ tsʰɯ˩
wolf	LM+MH#	õ˩dv̩˧ ŋɯ˥	õ˩dv̩˧-ki˥	õ˩dv̩˧ tsʰɯ˧ / õ˩dv̩˧ tsʰɯ˥
Naxi	LM+#H	nɑ˩hĩ˧ ŋɯ˩	nɑ˩hĩ˧-ki˩	nɑ˩hĩ˧ tsʰɯ˩
sow	LM	bo˩mi˧ ŋɯ˧	bo˩mi˧-ki˧	bo˩mi˧ tsʰɯ˧
boar	LH	bo˩ɬɑ˥ ŋɯ˩	bo˩ɬɑ˥-ki˩	bo˩ɬɑ˥ tsʰɯ˩
rat	H#	hwæ˧tsɯ˥ ŋɯ˩	hwæ˧tsɯ˥-ki˩	hwæ˧tsɯ˥ tsʰɯ˩

/ə˧dɑ˥-ki˩/. The former is considered better than the latter.[5] The form /ə˧dɑ˥-ki˩/ appears in ComingOfAge2.18, in a context where emphasis is laid on the word 'father'. In this context, /ə˧dɑ˧-ki˧/ would not be syntactically wrong, but it would be less appropriate from a stylistic point of view. There appear to be (at least) two reasons for the emphatic, expressive value of /ə˧dɑ˥-ki˩/. First, the form /ə˧dɑ˥-ki˩/, as compared with /ə˧dɑ˧-ki˧/, involves a higher pitch on the

---

[5] To test the consultant's preference, the investigator says one of the two alternatives while raising his right hand, then the second while raising his left hand. The consultant indicates whether both are acceptable, and expresses a preference, often as an understatement: /tsʰɯ˧ bæ˧, | ɖɯ˧-pi˥ | ho˥/, "This one is *pretty correct*", meaning "This one is better".

Table 5.14b: Tone patterns of agentive /ɳɯ˧/, dative /-ki˧/, and topic marker /tsʰɯ˧/ with monosyllabic and disyllabic nouns.

tone of noun	/ɳɯ/	/-ki/	/tsʰɯ/
LM	L.M	L.M	L.M
LH	L.H	L.H	L.H
M	M.M	M.M	M.M
L	M.M / L.H	M.M / L.H	M.M / L.H
H	M.L	M.M	M.M
MH	M.H	M.H	M.H
M	M.M.M	M.M.M	M.M.M
#H	M.M.L	M.M.M	M.M.M
MH#	M.M.H	M.M.H	M.M.H
H$	M.H.L / M.M.H	M.M.M	M.M.M
L	L.L.H	L.L.H	L.L.H
L#	M.L.L	M.L.L	M.L.L
LM+MH#	L.M.H	L.M.H	L.M.M / L.M.H
LM+#H	L.M.L	L.M.M	L.M.M
LM	L.M.M	L.M.M	L.M.M
LH	L.H.L	L.H.L	L.H.L
H#	M.H.L	M.H.L	M.H.L

syllable that means 'father' (H tone, as against M tone). This has iconic value: there is a cross-linguistic tendency for raised pitch to be associated with emphasis, in tonal and nontonal languages alike (see §8.3). A second reason is that, in /ə˧da˦-ki˦/, the word 'father' surfaces with the same tone that it would have if said in isolation: /ə˧da˦/ (lexical form: //ə˧da˦$//). This makes the word stand out, as if extracting it from the flow of speech. By contrast, in /ə˧da˧-ki˦/ the word 'father' is tonally amalgamated with its suffix, and the constituent made up of the noun and its suffix is, in turn, woven into the mesh of its wider environment, as a neatly packaged unit whose tone pattern testifies to its syntactic elaboration. This greater degree of morphosyntactic integration befits carefully planned and constructed speech. It accounts for the perception of /ə˧da˧-ki˦/ as a "better" form outside context.

In association with agentive /ŋɯ˧/, dative /-ki˧/ and topic marker /tʂʰɯ˧/, the 1ˢᵗ and 2ⁿᵈ person pronouns behave like other L-tone items: /njɤ˩ ŋɯ˧/, /no˩ ŋɯ˧/. On the other hand, the demonstratives /tʂʰɯ˥/ (proximal, also 3ʳᵈ person singular) and /tʰy˥/ (distal) have a different behaviour from other H-tone items: they yield M.M in association with /ŋɯ˧/: /tʂʰɯ˧ ŋɯ˧/, /tʰy˧ ŋɯ˧/ (also /tʂʰɯ˧ la˧/, /tʰy˧ la˧/ 'this/that one too').

5.4.3 The MH-tone morphemes /-qɑ˧˥/ (dative/comitative) and /gi˧˥/ 'behind'

The morpheme /-qɑ˧˥/ has dative and comitative functions. It is analyzed as carrying MH tone on the basis of its behaviour after M-tone words both monosyllabic and disyllabic, and after LM-tone disyllables. Table 5.15 sets out the data. The data for the postposition /gi˧˥/ 'behind' is identical.[6]

Note that, as in all other morphosyntactic contexts, the //L.H.L// pattern is neutralized with //L.M.L// at the surface phonological level. The tone pattern for 'boar' could therefore be transcribed as /L.M.L/ in surface phonological representation. Notation as //L.H.L// reflects the analysis proposed here: that the tone of the enclitic is lowered to L because of the presence of a preceding H tone – the H part of the LH tone pattern lexically attached to the noun 'boar'. The choice of a notation as /L.M.L/ could seem advisable in order to stay closer to surface phonological form, limiting the degree of abstraction of the notation; on the other hand, this could clash with the notation of the lexical categories, wrongly suggesting that the //LH// lexical category became //LM// when this enclitic is added. This is why notation as L.H.L was chosen in Table 5.15.

5.4.4 The H-tone topic marker /-dʑo˥/, with observations about tonal contours in non-final position

The topic marker /-dʑo˥/ can appear after nouns and verbs. The tone patterns that obtain when it is associated to a noun are shown in Table 5.16. Interestingly, a MH-tone noun or verb preceding the topic marker is realized with a MH contour, e.g. /tʂʰæ˧˥-dʑo˩/ 'as for the deer' (from /tʂʰæ˧˥/ 'deer') and /mɤ˧-lɑ˧˥-dʑo˩/ 'as [he/she] did not strike' (from /lɑ˧˥/ 'to strike'). This suggests that there is a tone group boundary after the noun or verb, since contours are only realized tone-group-finally. Such a behaviour would not be unparalleled. For instance, the contrastive topic marker /-no˧˥/ and the word /tʰi˩/ 'then' always mark the beginning of a new tone group. But the tonal behaviour of the topic marker after

---

[6] Remember that, as a convention, clitics are preceded by an *equal* sign, and a hyphen is placed before suffixes and after prefixes, whereas postpositions are shown as free morphemes.

Table 5.15: The tonal behaviour of the dative/comitative marker /-qɑ˧/ following nouns.

example	tone	example	tone pattern
pig	LM	bo˩-qa˧	L.M
leopard	LH	ʐæ˩-qa˥	L.H (on surface: same as LM)
tiger	M	lɑ˧-qa˧	M.MH
sheep	L	jo˩-qɑ˧	L.LH
horse	H	ʐwæ˧-qa˩	M.L
deer	MH	tsʰæ˧-qa˥	M.H
fox	M	ɖʐɯ˧mi˧-qa˧	M.M.MH
colt	#H	ʐwæ˧zo˧-qa˩	M.M.L
cat	MH#	hwɤ˧li˧-qa˥	M.M.H
she-cat	H$	hwɤ˧mi˥-qa˩	M.H.L
dog	L	kʰv̩˩mi˩-qa˥	L.L.H
mule	L#	dɑ˥ji˩-qa˩	M.L.L
wolf	LM+MH#	õ˩dv̩˧-qa˥	L.M.H
Naxi	LM+#H	na˩hĩ˧-qa˩	L.M.L
sow	LM	bo˩mi˧-qa˧	L.M.MH
boar	LH	bo˥ɭɑ˥-qa˩	L.H.L
rat	H#	hwæ˧tsɯ˥-qa˩	M.H.L

nouns or verbs bearing a tone other than MH suggests that it is integrated within the same tone group. For instance, after a M-tone noun or verb, the pattern is M.M.H, e.g. /lɑ˧-dʑo˥/ 'as for the tiger' and /mɤ˧-hwæ˧-dʑo˥/ 'as [she/he] does not buy': these expressions clearly constitute a single tone group. The full data set is presented in Table 5.16.[7] These observations are taken up in §7.3, as part of the discussion of cases of breach of tonal grouping: how non-final syllables can come to carry a contour, and following syllables become extrametrical.

---

[7] The data was verified by using additional nouns illustrating the tonal categories: /zo˥/ 'son' for H tone, /õ˥/ 'oneself' for MH tone, /pʰɤ˧bɤ˧/ 'gift' for M tone, and /ə˧dɑ˥$/ 'father' and /mv̩˧ʁo˥$/ 'heavens' for H$ tone. The results were the same, including variant patterns: for 'gift', there are two variants, /pʰɤ˧bɤ˧-dʑo˧/ and /pʰɤ˧bɤ˧-dʑo˥/, in the same way as for the example used in Table 5.16 ('fox'). The only unexpected result was with 'plain', //di˧qo˧//. One would expect /˧di˧qo˧-dʑo˥/, on the analogy of /ɖʐɯ˧mi˧-dʑo˧/, but the observed pattern is M.M.M : /di˧qo˧-dʑo˧/. This unexpected result, confirmed across elicitation sessions, may have to do with the internal structure of this disyllable, literally meaning 'on earth'.

Table 5.16: The tonal behaviour of the topic marker /-dzo˩/ following nouns.

example	tone	example	tone pattern
pig	LM	bo˧-dzo˩	LM.L
leopard	LH	ʐæ˧-dzo˩	LH.L
tiger	M	lɑ˧-dzo˥	M.H
daughter	L	mv˩-dzo˧	LH.L
horse	H	ʐwæ˧-dzo˩	M.L
deer	MH	tsʰæ˧-dzo˩	MH.L
fox	M	dʑɯ˧mi˧-dzo˥ / dʑɯ˧mi˧-dzo˧	M.M.H / M.M.M
colt	#H	ʐwæ˧zo˧-dzo˩	M.M.L
cat	MH#	hwɯ˧li˥-dzo˩	M.MH.L
she-cat	H$	hwɯ˧mi˥-dzo˩	M.H.L
dog	L	kʰv˩mi˧-dzo˩	L.LH.L
mule	L#	dɑ˧ji˩-dzo˩	M.L.L
wolf	LM+MH#	õ˩dv˥-dzo˩	L.MH.L
Naxi	LM+#H	nɑ˩hĩ˧-dzo˩	L.M.L
sow	LM	bo˩mi˧-dzo˥	L.M.H
boar	LH	bo˩ɬɑ˧-dzo˩	L.M.L
rat	H#	hwæ˧tsɯ˥-dzo˩	M.H.L

On the basis of its behaviour after M-tone nouns (and after M-tone verbs, which will be presented in the next chapter), the topic marker is provisionally analyzed as carrying a lexical H tone. If this tonal identification is confirmed, the morpheme constitutes an extreme case of distance between underlying form and surface form: in texts, realizations with a L tone outnumber those with a H tone by a ratio of about 10 to 1. The particles indicating reported speech, /tsɯ˥/, and affirmation, /mv˧/, constitute even more spectacular cases: their underlying form hardly ever surfaces as such (see 7.1.4).

5.5 Disyllabic postpositions

Disyllabic locative postpositions include /ʁo˧tʰo˩/ 'behind', /ʁo˧dɑ˧/ 'in front of', /ɬo˧tɑ˧/ 'beside, to the side of', /ʁwæ˧gi#˥/ 'to the left', /jo˩gi˩/ 'to the right', and /-qo˧lo˩/ 'inside'. (The monosyllabic form /-qo˧/ is also attested, with the same meaning.) Table 5.17 shows the data for nouns followed by the locative

Table 5.17: The tonal behaviour of the locative postpositions /ɬo˧ta˥/ 'beside' and /ʁo˧tʰo˩/ 'behind'. There is an additional 'L PRO' row because L-tone pronouns have exceptional behaviour.

tone	example	meaning	beside	behind
LM	bo˩˥	pig	bo˩ ɬo˧ta˥	bo˩ ʁo˧tʰo˩
LH	zæ˩˥	leopard	zæ˩ ɬo˧ta˥	zæ˩ ʁo˧tʰo˩
M	lɑ˧	tiger	lɑ˧ ɬo˧ta˥	lɑ˧ ʁo˧tʰo˩
L	jo˩	sheep	jo˩ ɬo˩ta˩	jo˩ ʁo˩tʰo˩
L PRO	no˩	2SG	no˧ ɬo˧ta˥	no˧ ʁo˧tʰo˩
H	ʐwæ˥	horse	ʐwæ˧ ɬo˧ta˥	ʐwæ˧ ʁo˧tʰo˥
MH	tsʰæ˧˥	deer	tsʰæ˧ ɬo˧ta˥	tsʰæ˧ ʁo˧tʰo˥
M	ɖʐ̩˧mi˧	fox	ɖʐ̩˧mi˧ ɬo˧ta˥	ɖʐ̩˧mi˧ ʁo˧tʰo˩
#H	ʐwæ˧zo˧#˥	colt	ʐwæ˧zo˧ ɬo˧ta˥	ʐwæ˧zo˧ ʁo˧tʰo˥
MH#	hwɤ˧li˧˥	cat	hwɤ˧li˧ ɬo˧ta˥	hwɤ˧li˧ ʁo˧tʰo˥
H$	hwɤ˧mi˥$	she-cat	hwɤ˧mi˧ ɬo˧ta˥	hwɤ˧mi˧ ʁo˧tʰo˥
L	kʰv̩˩mi˩	dog	kʰv̩˩mi˩ ɬo˩ta˩	kʰv̩˩mi˩ ʁo˩tʰo˩
L#	dɑ˩ʥi˩	mule	dɑ˩ʥi˩ ɬo˩ta˩	dɑ˩ʥi˩ ʁo˩tʰo˩
LM+MH#	õ˩dv̩˥	wolf	õ˩dv̩˧ ɬo˧ta˥	õ˩dv̩˧ ʁo˧tʰo˥
LM+#H	nɑ˩hĩ#˥	Naxi	nɑ˩hĩ˧ ɬo˧ta˥	nɑ˩hĩ˧ ʁo˧tʰo˩
LM	bo˩mi˧	sow	bo˩mi˧ ɬo˧ta˥	bo˩mi˧ ʁo˧tʰo˩
LH	bo˩ɬɑ˥	boar	bo˩ɬɑ˥ ɬo˩ta˩	bo˩ɬɑ˥ ʁo˩tʰo˩
H#	hwæ˧tsɯ˥	rat	hwæ˧tsɯ˥ ɬo˩ta˩	hwæ˧tsɯ˥ ʁo˩tʰo˩

postpositions /ɬo˧ta˥/ 'beside, to the side of' and /ʁo˧tʰo˩/ 'behind, to the back of'. The data for /ʁo˧dɑ˥/ 'in front of' is identical with that for /ɬo˧ta˥/ 'beside, to the side of', and is therefore not shown in the table. Likewise, the behaviour of /tʰæ˧qo˩/ 'under' is identical with that of /ʁo˧tʰo˩/ 'behind'. Table 5.18 shows the data for the locative postpositions /ʁwæ˧gi#˥/ 'to the left' and /jo˩gi˩/ 'to the right'. The corresponding recording is: LocativePostp.

There are two rows for the L tone in Table 5.17 and Table 5.18 because L-tone pronouns, 1SG /njɤ˩/ and 2SG /no˩/, have exceptional behaviour. The difference in tonal output between pronouns and nouns is clear. For instance, with the M-tone postposition 'beside', a L-tone pronoun yields a M-tone pattern: /no˧ ɬo˧tu˧/, and it is not possible to say ‡ no˩ ɬo˩ta˩. Conversely, a L-tone noun yields a L-tone pattern: /jo˩ ɬo˩ta˩/, and it is not possible to say ‡ jo˧ ɬo˧ta˥.

The system would look nice and economical if the tone patterns in these ta-

Table 5.18: The tonal behaviour of the locative postpositions /ʁwæ˧gi#˥/ 'to the left' and /jo˩gi˩/ 'to the right'. There is an additional 'L PRO' row because L-tone pronouns have exceptional behaviour.

tone	example	meaning	to the left of	to the right of
LM	bo˩˧	pig	bo˩ ʁwæ˧gi#˥	bo˩ jo˧gi#˥
LH	z̩æ˩˥	leopard	z̩æ˩ ʁwæ˧gi#˥	z̩æ˩ jo˧gi#˥
M	lɑ˧	tiger	lɑ˧ ʁwæ˧gi#˥	lɑ˧ jo˩gi˩
L	jo˩	sheep	jo˩ ʁwæ˩gi˩	jo˧ jo˩gi˩
L PRO	no˩	2SG	no˧ ʁwæ˧gi#˥	no˧ jo˩gi˩
H	ʐwæ˥	horse	ʐwæ˧ ʁwæ˧gi#˥	ʐwæ˧ jo˥gi˩
MH	tsʰæ˩˥	deer	tsʰæ˧ ʁwæ˧gi#˥	tsʰæ˧ jo˥gi˩
M	ɖʐ̩˧mi˧	fox	ɖʐ̩˧mi˧ ʁwæ˧gi#˥	ɖʐ̩˧mi˧ jo˩gi˩
#H	ʐwæ˧zo˧#˥	colt	ʐwæ˧zo˧ ʁwæ˧gi#˥	ʐwæ˧zo˧ jo˥gi˩
MH#	hwɤ˧li˥	cat	hwɤ˧li˧ ʁwæ˧gi#˥	hwɤ˧li˧ jo˥gi˩
H$	hwɤ˧mi˥$	she-cat	hwɤ˧mi˧ ʁwæ˧gi#˥	hwɤ˧mi˧ jo˥gi˩
L	kʰv̩˩mi˩	dog	kʰv̩˩mi˩ ʁwæ˩gi˩	kʰv̩˩mi˩ jo˥gi˩
L#	dɑ˧ʝi˩	mule	dɑ˧ʝi˩ ʁwæ˩gi˩	dɑ˧ʝi˩ jo˩gi˩
LM+MH#	õ˩dv̩˥	wolf	õ˩dv̩˧ ʁwæ˧gi#˥	õ˩dv̩˧ jo˥gi˩
LM+#H	nɑ˩hĩ#˥	Naxi	nɑ˩hĩ˧ ʁwæ˧gi#˥	nɑ˩hĩ˧ jo˩gi˩
LM	bo˩mi˧	sow	bo˩mi˧ ʁwæ˧gi#˥	bo˩mi˧ jo˩gi˩
LH	bo˩ɬɑ˥	boar	bo˩ɬɑ˧ ʁwæ˩gi˩	bo˩ɬɑ˧ jo˩gi˩
H#	hwæ˧tsɯ˥	rat	hwæ˧tsɯ˥ ʁwæ˩gi˩	hwæ˧tsɯ˥ jo˩gi˩

bles were identical with those for other constructions, such as determinative compounds. Such is the case for /ʁo˧tʰo˩/ 'at the back', which behaves tonally like a L#-tone head noun in determinative compounds, and for /ɬo˧tɑ˧/ 'beside, to the side of', which behaves like a M-tone noun in determinative compounds. Not all locative postpositions share this behaviour, however: compare /hwɤ˧li˧-hi˧kʰɯ˥/ 'cat's gums (body part)' (input tones: MH# and #H; output tone: MH#) and /hwɤ˧li˧ ʁwæ˧gi#˥/ 'to the left of the cat' (same input; output tone: #H).

5.6 Adverbs

Contrary to what their name suggests, *adverbs* (a loosely defined class of words) can appear not only with verbs, but also with nouns and some other linguistic units.

5.6.1 The homophonous adverbs /lɑ˧/ 'only' and 'too, and'

The data for the two homophonous adverbs /lɑ˧/ 'only' and 'too, and' is shown in Table 5.19. Systematic elicitation of expressions made up of a noun plus these adverbs was up against some slight initial difficulties, as these expressions do not constitute complete utterances. An illustration of the pitfalls of this type of elicitation is that the combination 'only (a/the) she-cat' was first recorded with a M.M.L pattern, as /**hwɤ˧mi˧ lɑ˩**/, then with a M.M.M pattern, as /**hwɤ˧mi˧ lɑ˧**/. Later the consultant pointed out that these were both wrong, and that the correct pattern was M.H.L: /**hwɤ˧mi˥ lɑ˩**/. Homophony between this expression and 'to beat (a/the) she-cat' (likewise /**hwɤ˧mi˥ lɑ˩**/) may have contributed to the difficulty encountered at elicitation.

Table 5.19: The behaviour of /lɑ˧/ 'only; also' with monosyllabic and disyllabic nouns.

example	tone	example	abstract tone pattern
pig	LM	bo˩ lɑ˧	L.M
leopard	LH	zæ˩ lɑ˥	L.H
tiger	M	lɑ˧ lɑ˧	M.M
sheep	L	jo˩ lɑ˥	L.H
horse	H	ʐwæ˧ lɑ˩	M.L
deer	MH	tsʰæ˧ lɑ˥	M.H
fox	M	dʑɤ˧mi˧ lɑ˧	M.M.M
colt	#H	ʐwæ˧zo˧ lɑ˩	M.M.L
cat	MH#	hwɤ˧li˧ lɑ˥	M.M.H
she-cat	H$	hwɤ˧mi˥ lɑ˩	M.H.L
dog	L	kʰv̩˩mi˩ lɑ˥	L.L.H
mule	L#	dɑ˧ji˩ lɑ˩	M.L.L
wolf	LM+MH#	õ˩dv̩˧ lɑ˥	L.M.H
Naxi	LM+#H	nɑ˩hĩ˧ lɑ˩	L.M.L
sow	LM	bo˩mi˧ lɑ˧	L.M.M
boar	LH	bo˩ɬɑ˥ lɑ˩	L.H.L
rat	H#	hwæ˧tsɯ˥ lɑ˩	M.H.L

Comparison with the data for the three M-tone morphemes in Tables 5.14a–b shows that the tonal behaviour of the four morphemes /lɑ˧/, /ɳɯ˧/, /-ki˧/, and /tsʰɯ˧/ is tantalizingly similar: their tone patterns are identical for eleven of the

241

seventeen categories of nouns. The only difference between /lɑ˧/ and /ɳɯ˧/ is in combination with the L category of monosyllables, where the pattern is L.H for /lɑ˧/, as in (22), and M.M for /ɳɯ˧/, as in (23). Needless to say, the data was carefully verified across work sessions. (A recording is available: OnlyAnd.)

(22) jo˩ lɑ˩ | tsʰɯ˥
      jo˩   lɑ˧   tsʰɯ˥
      sheep   and   goat
      'sheep and goats'

(23) jo˧ ɳɯ˧
      jo˩   ɳɯ˧
      sheep   A
      'by the sheep'

To venture a hypothesis concerning these incomplete similarities, it seems plausible that grammaticalization is accompanied by a tonal evolution away from the tone of the free root. As mentioned in §5.4, it may not be coincidental that dative /-ki˧/ and possessive /=bv̩˧/, which have exactly the same tonal behaviour, also share the morphosyntactic property of being "almost suffixal" (Lidz 2010: 155), and thereby distinct from agentive /ɳɯ˧/, analyzed as a case adposition. Seen in this light, the difference in tone patterns would match that of parts of speech: one of the tone patterns is for suffixes, one for adpositions, one for adverbs/conjunctions, and one for discourse particles (in this case the topic marker).

5.6.2 The adverb /pɤ˧to˩/ 'even'

The behaviour of the adverb /pɤ˧to˩/ 'even' is presented in Table 5.20; the corresponding recording is NounsEven. This data differs from that of L#-tone locative postpositions such as /ʁo˧tʰo˩/ 'behind' and /tʰæ˧qo˩/ 'under', studied above (5.5). The tonal behaviour of /pɤ˧to˩/ also differs from that of L#-tone heads in compound nouns.

5.7 Concluding note

The facts approached in this chapter are more diverse than in the three previous ones. There is a great variety of tonal categories of grammatical elements in Yongning Na: the dative suffix /-ki˧/ and the possessive clitic /-bv̩˧/ have a different behaviour from the agentive adposition /ɳɯ˧/; a third pattern is observed for the conjunction /lɑ˧/ 'too, and'; and a fourth for the topic marker /tʂʰɯ˧/. The

Table 5.20: The tonal behaviour of /pʏ˧to˩/ 'even'. There is an additional 'L pro' row because L-tone pronouns have exceptional behaviour.

tone	example	meaning	N+/pʏ˧to˩/ 'even'
LM	bo˧˥	pig	bo˧ pʏ˩to˩
LH	zæ˧˥	leopard	zæ˩ pʏ˩to˩
M	lɑ˧	tiger	lɑ˧ pʏ˧to˩
L	jo˩	sheep	jo˩ pʏ˩to˥
L PRO	no˩	2SG	no˧ pʏ˧to˩
#H	ʐwæ˥	horse	ʐwæ˧ pʏ˧to˩
MH#	tsʰæ˥	deer	tsʰæ˧ pʏ˥to˩
M	dʏ˧mi˧	fox	dʏ˧mi˧ pʏ˥to˩
#H	ʐwæ˧zo#˥	colt	ʐwæ˧zo˧ pʏ˧to˩
MH#	hwʏ˧li˥	cat	hwʏ˧li˥ pʏ˥to˩
H$	hwʏ˧mi˥$	she-cat	hwʏ˧mi˧ pʏ˧to˩
L	kʰv˩mi˩	dog	kʰv˩mi˩ pʏ˥to˩
L#	dɑ˧ji˩	mule	dɑ˧ji˩ pʏ˩to˩
LM+MH#	õ˩dv˥	wolf	õ˩dv˧ pʏ˥to˩
LM+#H	nɑ˩hĩ#˥	Naxi	nɑ˩hĩ˧ pʏ˧to˩
LM	bo˩mi˧	sow	bo˩mi˧ pʏ˧to˩
LH	bo˩ɬɑ˥	boar	bo˩ɬɑ˧ pʏ˧to˩
H#	hwæ˧tsɯ˥	rat	hwæ˧tsɯ˥ pʏ˩to˩

complexity of Yongning Na morphotonology results from the great number of tonal paradigms. There remains much room for progress in the description and analysis of this morphotonological archipelago. In particular, systematic study of the lexicon holds potential for opening new windows onto processes of morphological derivation, revealing traces of former processes of derivation such as an animal suffix /-li/ plausibly found in /hwʏ˧li˥/ 'cat' and /pʰi˧li˩/ 'butterfly' (Naxi cognates: /hwɑ˥le˧/ and /pʰe˧le˩/).

6 Verbs and their combinatory properties

This chapter discusses the tones of verbs and adjectives, and their combinatory properties.

6.1 The lexical tones of verbs

6.1.1 Overview

For monosyllabic verbs, which are an overwhelming majority, seven tonal categories have come to light, as shown in Table 6.1.

Table 6.1: The seven tonal categories of monosyllabic verbs: behaviour in four different contexts.

example	in isolation	NEG	ACCOMP	V+'a bit'
dzɯ 'to eat'	M	M.H	M.H	M.M.M
hwæ 'to buy'		M.M	M.M	M.H.L
tɕʰi 'to sell'				M.M.M
bi 'to go'			M.L	n.a.
dze 'to cut'	LH	M.L		M.M.H
tʰɯ 'to drink'				M.M.MH
lɑ 'to strike'	MH	M.MH	M.MH	M.H.L

The four contexts shown in Table 6.1 are: (i) in isolation, (ii) with the negation prefix, (iii) with the accomplished prefix, and (iv) with /ɖɯ˧-kʰwɤ˥/ 'a piece' or /ɖɯ˧-tʰɤ˥/ 'a drop' as an object (meaning 'to V a bit').[1] These four contexts

---

[1] The two numeral-plus-classifier phrases 'a piece' and 'a drop' have the same tone: H$. The tones of numeral-plus-classifier phrases are analyzed in Chapter 4, and the H$ tone in §2.3.2.

were chosen because their combination reveals all seven categories, even though each context taken individually only distinguishes three or four. Neutralizations are reflected in cells that share the same tone pattern in a given column; they are indicated by a dashed box if the cells are adjacent, and by shading if they are nonadjacent.

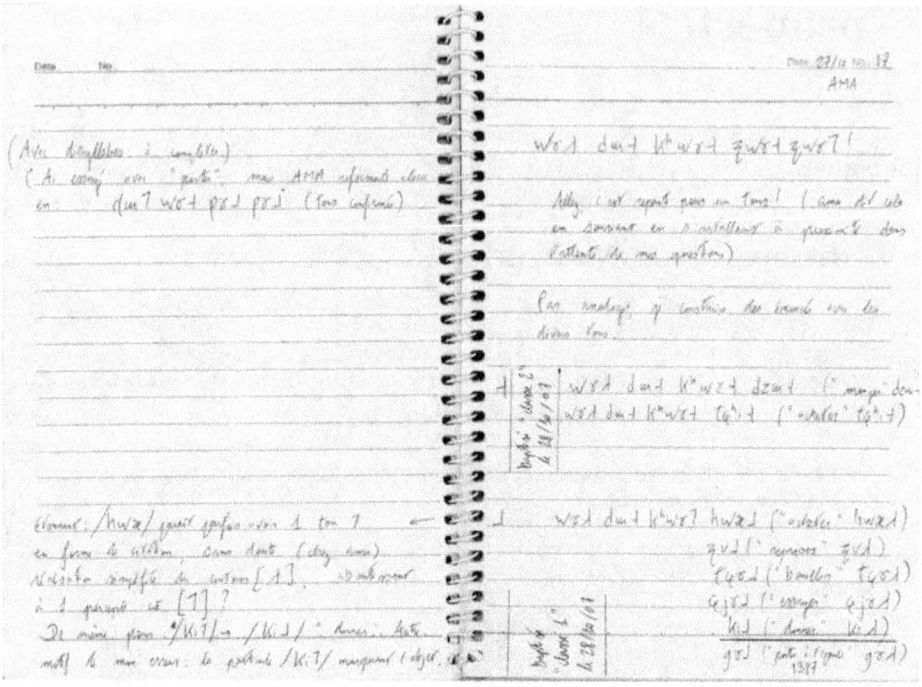

Figure 6.1: Field notes (2007). At the beginning of a work session, the consultant cheerfully said /wɤ˧ | dɯ˧-kʰwɤ˧ ʐwɤ˧~ʐwɤ˩/ 'Let's have another chat!' This construction, 'to V a bit', was written down, and elicited with various verbs. It turned out to be a useful test for the tones of verbs.

While the data in Table 6.1 demonstrates the existence of seven distinct categories, it leaves several analytic possibilities open. Observations made in the analysis of the tonal categories of nouns (in Chapter 2) clarify that the diversity of tonal patterns is highest after an initial M tone, since in that position there is no phonological prohibition against H, M, L or MH (only LM and LH are ruled out, by Rule 5, about which see §7.1.1). The behaviour of the seven classes of verbs after a M-tone prefix thus appeared as a promising guide to their underlying tone. But a complication here is that not all M-tone prefixes yield the same tonal results in association with verbs. Specifically, 'to go' yields /mɤ˧-bi˧/ with the negation prefix (tone pattern: M.M), and /le˧-bi˩/ with the accomplished prefix (tone pattern: M.L). After examining a set of M-tone prefixes, such as the prohibitive /tʰɑ˧-/ and the durative /tʰi˧-/, it appeared that the accomplished prefix is an outlier in this respect. The negation was chosen as a reference prefix to test the phonological nature of the tones of verbs.

It was observed that, following the negation prefix, a verb carries one of four tones: H, M, L, and MH. These are interpreted as four main categories. Within these, some subcategories are identified based on their different behaviour in other contexts. There are three subcategories among M-tone verbs: M_a, M_b and M_c, and two subcategories among L-tone verbs: L_a and L_b. The seven categories distinguished in Table 6.1 are therefore labelled as H, M_a, M_b, M_c, L_a, L_b and MH, as shown in Table 6.2, which has the same contents as Table 6.1 plus an indication of the underlying tones.

Table 6.2: The seven tonal categories of monosyllabic verbs: analysis into H, M, L and LH tones.

tone	example	in isolation	NEG	ACCOMP	V+'a bit'
H	dzɯ˧ 'to eat'	M	M.H	M.H	M.M.M
M_a	hwæ˧$_a$ 'to buy'		M.M	M.M	M.H.L
M_b	tɕʰi˧$_b$ 'to sell'				M.M.M
M_c	bi˧$_c$ 'to go'			M.L	n.a.
L_a	dze˩$_a$ 'to cut'	LH	M.L		M.M.H
L_b	tʰɯ˩$_b$ 'to drink'				M.M.MH
MH	lɑ˧˥ 'to strike'	MH	M.MH	M.MH	M.H.L

Realizations in isolation, which only distinguish three subsets, make sense in light of this analysis. H tone is realized as M due to the neutralization of H and M in tone-group-initial position (Rule 3; see the list of phonological tone rules in §7.1.1). M tones (M_a, M_b and M_c) are straightforwardly realized as M. Tones L_a and L_b are both realized as LH due to the post-lexical addition of a H tone to all-L tone groups (by Rule 7); L-tone verbs thus behave unlike L-tone nouns, which surface with M tone in isolation, as explained in Chapter 2. This is one of many pieces of evidence showing that the tone system of Yongning Na is not based only on a set of phonological rules that apply across-the-board in all contexts, but also has morphotonological rules: tone rules that are specific to a given morphological context.

Tones M_a and M_b yield the same tone pattern in association with the negation prefix, as do L_a and L_b, but they are distinguished in the fourth context. Conversely, the tone pairs {M_a, MH} and {M_b, H} yield the same tonal pattern when associated with the object 'a piece'/'a drop' but are distinguished after the negation prefix. Finally, tone category M_c has a different behaviour from M_a and M_b after the accomplished prefix.

Examples of predicates of the seven categories are presented in Table 6.3.

Table 6.3: Examples of the seven categories of verbs.

tone	examples
H	dzɯ˦ 'to eat', bv̩˦ 'to divide', ji˦ 'to do', se˦ 'to walk', tʂʰæ˦ 'to wash'
M_a	hwæ˧₋ₐ 'to buy', hõ˧₋ₐ 'to go away.IMP', ki˧₋ₐ 'to give', li˧₋ₐ 'to watch', mæ˧₋ₐ 'to catch hold of'
M_b	tɕʰi˧₋ᵦ 'to sell', ɖɯ˧₋ᵦ 'to obtain', dʐæ˧₋ᵦ 'to ride', pʰæ˧₋ᵦ 'to fasten', ɲi˧₋ᵦ 'to need'
M_c	bi˧₋ᵪ 'to go', hɯ˧₋ᵪ 'to go.PST', gv̩˧₋ᵪ 'to go by (of time)', ɟi˧₋ᵪ 'to come', pv̩˧₋ᵪ 'to chant'
L_a	dze˩ₐ 'to cut', bæ˩ₐ 'to sweep', ti˩ₐ 'to hit (gently)', tɕi˩ₐ 'to write', dzi˩ₐ 'to sit'
L_b	tʰɯ˩ᵦ 'to drink', dɑ˩ᵦ 'to weave', do˩ᵦ 'to see', mʁ˩ᵦ 'to eat food in powder form, typically tsamba (roasted flour)', zwʁ˩ᵦ 'to speak'
MH	ɕjʁ˧˦ 'to try; to taste', gʁ˧˦ 'to carry on one's shoulder', lɑ˧˦ 'to strike', tɕʁ˧˦ 'to boil', zv̩˧˦ 'to sew (clothes)'

The labels used for the sets of categories {L_a, L_b} and {M_a, M_b, M_c} are deliberately abstract, for want of decisive evidence about the phonological nature of the categories at issue. The letters are assigned on the basis of relative frequency in the lexicon. Among L tones, the 'to cut' type is about five times as frequent as the 'to drink' type. Among M tones, the 'to buy' type is twice as frequent as the 'to sell' type, and the 'to go' type is infrequent.

The 'to cut' and 'to drink' types, labelled here as L_a and L_b, are both analyzed as containing a L tone level, since they are realized with L tone after the negation prefix. There is limited evidence on the phonological nature of the difference between the L_a and L_b categories. One of the two could be analyzed as a simple L tone, and the other as a contour (LM or LH), on the analogy of nouns, but this would be arbitrary, since there is no compelling evidence that either of these categories consists of a contour. The apparent economy gained from using labels similar to those of nouns would come together with high costs in terms of descriptive adequacy. On nouns, the //LM// and //LH// contour tones surface as such in isolation (where they are neutralized to /LH/), unlike the //L// tone, which surfaces as /M/ in isolation. There is no such difference between the L_a and L_b categories of verbs, which both surface with a /LH/ contour in isolation.

6.1.2 About subsets of M-tone verbs

M-tone verbs, defined as those that are realized with M tone after the negation prefix, fall into three subsets: M_a, M_b and M_c. It would be satisfactory from the point of view of economy of description to reserve the label M for one of the three, and to assign to the others labels selected from the inventory of tone categories of nouns, such as #H. No evidence has been found to support such identifications, however, hence the choice to adopt noncommittal abstract labels with subscript letters.

Tone category M_c hosts five verbs that behave like M-tone verbs of the M_a category except in a few contexts, such as when preceded by the accomplished prefix, /le˧-/. These are /bi˧$_c$/ 'to go', and its past form /hɯ˧$_c$/; /gɣ˧$_c$/ 'to go by, to flow, to fly (of time)'; /ji˧$_c$/ 'to come'; and /pɣ˧$_c$/ 'to chant, to perform (a sacrifice, a ritual, a festival)'. With the accomplished prefix and the perfective suffix, the pattern is M.L.L, as shown in (1)-(2); likewise for the other three verbs: /le˧-hɯ˩-ze˩/, /le˧-gɣ˩-ze˩/, and /le˧-ji˩-ze˩/. This contrasts with the other verbs of the M tone category (i.e. the M_a and M_b subtypes), which carry M tone after the accomplished prefix.

(1) le˧-bi˩-ze˩
    le˧-   bi˧$_c$ -ze˧
    ACCOMP   to_go   PFV
    '[she/he/they...] went'

(2) le˧-pɣ˩-ze˩
    le˧-   pɣ˧$_c$ -ze˧
    ACCOMP   to_chant   PFV
    '[she/he/they...] chanted'

The difference between M_a and M_c is not related to verb valency: all M_c-tone verbs have intransitive uses, but one of the five ('to chant') can also be used transitively; conversely, not all intransitive verbs belong in this tonal category, witness 'to die', /ʂɯ˦a/, which yields /le˦-ʂɯ˦/ (Sister3.11, 95).

Since these five verbs have the same behaviour as M_a-tone verbs in most contexts, they could be described as a subset of the M_a category; a further diacritic could be added to their tone label, yielding something such as M_a' (M_a prime). However, it appeared less awkward typographically to label them as M_c, a third subcategory within M tones.

The tonal behaviour of verbs in category M_c calls for analysis. An observation that may be relevant is that the accomplished prefix /le˦-/ in association with these verbs can carry special semantic connotations. With these verbs, /le˦-/ can carry the meaning 'back/to return', as in (3) and (4):

(3) le˦-bi˩-dʐo˩, | tsʰʋ˦ | dɯ˦ mʁ˦-kv˦ tsɯ˩ | mv˩!
le˦-   bi˦ᴄ   -dʐo˩ tsʰʋ˩ dɯ˦   mʁ˦-   -kv˦   tsɯ˦
ACCOMP to_go TOP   dinner to_get NEG   ABILITIVE   REP
mv˦
AFFIRM

'If [the daughter] goes back [to her mother's home after marriage, she] cannot have dinner there.' [She must not stay there for the night, she has to go back to her new home before evening.] (Sister3.116)

(4) lv˦mi˦ so˩-tv˩ pʁ˩~pʁ˩! | le˦-bi˩-ze˩!
lv˦mi˦ so˩-tv˩   pʁ˦   ~   le˦-   bi˦ᴄ   -ze˦
stone   a_few   to_carry ACTIVITY ACCOMP to_go   PFV

'Tonight, I'll bring (back) a couple of stones! I'm going back!' (Reward.77. Context: a man is compelled by his spouse to go and steal in order to support the family; as he is about to steal sweetcorn, he decides to refrain from stealing; instead, he fills his basket with stones and goes back.)

This meaning is not always present, however, and the tone pattern is the same when the meaning is 'to go, to set off', as in (5), where the movement is clearly away from a familiar place and towards an unfamiliar one.

(5) "æ.hi.hi!" pi˦, | le˦-bi˩-zo˩-kv˩ | tsɯ˦ | mv˩!
æ.hi.hi   pi˩   le˦-   bi˦ᴄ   -zo˦   -kv˦   tsɯ˦
INTJ   to_say   ACCOMP to_go OBLIGATIVE ABILITIVE   REP
mv˦
AFFIRM

'[The mother, uncles, aunts and other relatives of the deceased wife's family shout out a cry of defiance:] "A-hi-hi!" and they set off [towards the husband's house]!' (Sister1.81)

To sum up: for want of a principled explanation for the tonal behaviour of these five verbs, it appeared best to set up a distinct synchronic tone category for them: M_c.

6.1.3 Adjectives as distinct from verbs

The issue whether adjectives constitute a distinct part of speech has been raised for various languages of Southeast Asia: for a review and discussion, with special focus on Tai, see Post (2008). "Some Tibeto-Burman languages have a definable adjective category, usually only marginally distinguishable from nouns or from verbs" (DeLancey 2015: 41). Yongning Na is one of these languages: in Na, adjectives behave in most respects like verbs, i.e. as stative verbs, but they have some tonal specificities which require that they be recognized as a formally distinct class of words.

Four main tonal categories for monosyllabic adjectives were found: L, M, H, and MH. The L tone category must further be split into two subcategories. The L_b category only contains two examples: /dʐɤ˩/ 'good' and /nɑ˩/ 'black, dark'. Details on their behaviour in context are provided in the course of this chapter.

Importantly, the MH category of adjectives and the MH category of verbs do not always have the same tonal behaviour: examples are provided in §6.4.3 below. Likewise, the L_a and L_b categories of adjectives are not fully parallel to the L_a and L_b categories of verbs in terms of their tonal behaviour. As for the M category of adjectives, no evidence was found for a division into subcategories corresponding to the M_a, M_b and M_c categories set up for verbs. These differences between the tone system of adjectives and that of verbs exemplify the morphosyntactic ramifications of tone in Yongning Na.

There also exist disyllabic adjectives. Examples include /pʰɤ˧ɖʶɯ˧/ 'expensive', from /pʰɤ˧/ 'price' and /ɖʶɯ˩/ 'large', and /lo˩ɖʶɯ˧/ 'generous', from /lo˧/ 'hand' and, again, /ɖʶɯ˩/ 'large'.

In view of the range of tone categories found on nouns, verbs and adjectives in Yongning Na, it is no wonder that they yield a wealth of diverse patterns when combined among themselves, and combined with grammatical morphemes. The structure of the Na verb phrase as schematized by Lidz (2010: 350–351) comprises: Manner adverb – Verb complex – Causative – Intensifier – Tense/aspect and modal particles, and auxiliary verbs – Quotative evidential. Additionally, the verb can be preceded by spatial indications such as 'forward'/'backward' and 'upward'/'downward'. The verb complex may be a lexical verb, an existential verb, a copula, or a serial verb construction, which may take a verbal prefix (or two prefixes, in the case of the durative prefix followed by the negation prefix).

The following sections explore the verb phrase's morphotonology. The topic of adverbials is not addressed in this chapter, because adverbials seldom interact with verbs; for a discussion, see §7.2.1.

6.2 Reduplication

Reduplication of verbs is a highly productive process in Yongning Na. From a semantic point of view, reduplication can convey various types of divergence from the prototype of the action or activity referred to by the verb. If the verb refers to an action, the reduplicated form can warp it towards representation as an activity, as in (6).

(6) jo˧-lo˧dʐo˩ tʰi˩-kʰɯ˩~kʰɯ˩. | hæ˩-lo˩pɣ˩ tʰi˩-kʰɯ˩~kʰɯ˩.
jo˧ lo˩dʐo˩ tʰi˧- kʰɯ˧ ~ hæ˩ lo˩pɣ˧ tʰi˧- kʰɯ˧
jade bracelet DUR to_put ACTIVITY gold ring DUR to_put

~

ACTIVITY

'They adorned her with jade bracelets. They adorned her with gold rings.'
(BuriedAlive2.29. Context: a bride is being prepared for a wedding.[2])

The *simplex* form /jo˧-lo˧dʐo˩ tʰi˩-kʰɯ˩/ means 'to put a jade bracelet (on someone's wrist)'. It depicts a well-delimited, unique event: in the absence of

---

[2] In view of the ethnological reports about Na family structure reviewed in Appendix B (§B. 3), it may come as a surprise that there should be folk stories about weddings in Yongning. Arranged marriages and difficult relationships between brides and mothers-in-law are typical of Confucian cultures (see e.g. Riley 1994; Chan et al. 2008), not of pre-1950s Yongning. But the argument of a story's fit to a particular culture runs both ways: a tale can be appealing because it resonates with one's cultural background, or on the contrary, it can gain appeal from exoticism. The 1990s soap opera Ke Wang 渴望 ('Yearnings'), which was a roaring success throughout China (a phenomenon studied by Wang & Singhal 1992), was also popular in Yongning, where the Na gathered at the homes of television owners to watch the story of Liu Huifang, the ideal daughter-in-law (this is narrated by F4 in the document entitled Evenings). Part of the soap opera's appeal to a Na audience may have been due to the novelty of the social relationships that it stages. A young Naxi woman from the Lijiang plain explained to me in 2010 that she loved watching Chinese soap operas "to see how Han people live", i.e. out of curiosity for cultural habits which she sees as different from Naxi custom. A study in comparative mythology and folklore in this area of the Himalayas would be necessary to trace the origin and development of stories such as that of the unhappy daughter-in-law who gets buried alive, a story also known to Laze consultant F7 (the Laze version is also available online). The thrills and spills of this story make it a good candidate for adoption by anyone who likes a good yarn.

a distinction between singular and plural, the interpretation of the noun phrase tends to be as singular, unless a numeral-plus-classifier phrase is added, as in (7).

(7) joɤ-loˈdʐoˌ | ɲiɤ-ɭɯɤ tʰiɤ-kʰɯ˦
    jo˦   loˌdʐo˦   ɲi˦   ɭɯ˦ᵦ   tʰi˦-   kʰɯ˦
    jade   bracelet   two   CLF   DUR   to_put
    'to put two jade bracelets'

By contrast, (6) means that the bride is adorned with jade bracelets and gold rings by family members. The reduplicated form leads to a plural interpretation of the nouns, presumably because successive acts of adorning are not performed with the same object: if you adorn someone more that once you would be doing this with yet another ornament, not taking one off to put it on again.

The use of reduplication illustrated by (6) is glossed as ACTIVITY. It represents the process denoted by the verb as an activity, rather than a neatly delimited event. In the text from which (6) is extracted, verb reduplication emphasizes the generosity of the family members as a unified social entity. They collectively go through the prescribed steps for the marriage ritual, giving generous measure of the prescribed offerings; each family member's individual gesture partakes in a collective activity. This builds a contrast with later events, when the young woman, feeling estranged at her in-laws' home, becomes oblivious of good manners and lapses into anti-social behaviour (solitary gluttony).

The surface semantic effect of ACTIVITY is close to that of the progressive suffix /**-dʐo˦**/. For instance, the reduplicated form of /**ʑi˦**/ 'to sleep' in (8) could be replaced by a *simplex* form followed by the progressive suffix /**-dʐo˦**/, as in (9).

(8) hĩ˦ | ɖɯ˦-tɑ˦ | le˦-ʑiˌ~ʑiˌ.
    hĩ˦   ɖɯ˦-tɑ˦   le˦-   ʑi˦   ~
    person   all   ACCOMP   to_sleep   ACTIVITY
    'Everyone was asleep.' (BuriedAlive2.94)

(9) hĩ˦ | ɖɯ˦-tɑ˦ | le˦-ʑi˦-dʐo˦.
    hĩ˦   ɖɯ˦-tɑ˦   le˦-   ʑi˦   -dʐo˦
    person   all   ACCOMP   to_sleep   PROG
    'Everyone was asleep.'

"When stative verbs reduplicate, one gets a reading of added intensity, while reduplicating non-stative verbs gives a reading of reciprocity of action, or a semantics of back-and-forth" (Lidz 2010: 373). An example is shown in (10), where the reduplicated adjective 'pleased' serves as an understatement for 'in love' ('they were in love with each other').

(10) ʁo˧dɑ˧, │ no˩bv̩˩-tsʰɯ˩ɻ̍˩ lɑ˩ │ tʂʰɯ˧=zɯ˩ │ fv̩˧~fv̩˩-ɲi˩!
ʁo˧dɑ˧ no˩bv̩˩-tsʰɯ˩ɻ̍˩ lɑ˧ tʂʰɯ˧=zɯ˩ fv̩˧ ~ -ɲi˩
before proper_name and 3DU pleased RECP CERTITUDE

'Before [my daughter married your son]... Nobbu Ci'er and [my daughter]... they used to like each other!' (BuriedAlive2.136. Context: the unhappy wife's mother explains to the husband's mother what the matter is with her daughter.)

The online texts contain more than a thousand examples of reduplication. This volume about morphotonology is not the right place to exploit these rich materials to delve any further into the study of the semantic values of reduplication in Yongning Na, to study the "paradoxes of fragmentation" (François 2004) that arise through divergence from *simplex* values, or to look for semantic and stylistic common denominators to reduplication as it applies to different parts of speech.[3] Instead, the focus here is on the morphotonological patterns of reduplication.

Table 6.4 presents the tone patterns of reduplicated verbs in Yongning Na. Two of these verbs are not the same as those in Tables 6.1-6.2: 'to go' does not easily lend itself to reduplication, and 'to chant' was therefore substituted; likewise, 'to drink' is much less commonly used in reduplicated form than 'to speak'. For each table in the present chapter, a choice of example verbs is made (mostly from the list in Table 6.3) with a view to avoiding examples that grate and jar on native ears for semantic-syntactic or pragmatic reasons. Crucially, the seven tonal categories of verbs are homogeneous: the tone patterns of all the verbs in each class are consistent. In other words, the examples 'to chant' and 'to speak' in Table 6.4 would behave in the same way as 'to go' and 'to drink' if they were in Table 6.2, and vice versa.

The patterns in Table 6.4 are valid for all the verbs for which a reduplicated form could be elicited. The only apparent exception is the disyllabic verb //wʁ˩~wʁ˩// (surface form: /wʁ˩~wʁ˧/) 'to detour past, to bypass', which looks like an unmistakeable case of reduplication, but whose L tone does not correspond to any of the patterns found for the other verbs. At a push, this verb can be used in monosyllabic form, as in (11).

---

[3] Some insights into these topics are found in Lidz (2010: 372-373, 385, 438, 440). Additionally, see Michaud & Vaissière (2007a) about reduplication in Naxi.

(11) le˧-wɤ˩-ze˩
    le˧-   ??wɤ˩   -ze˧
    ACCOMP to_bypass PFV

  '[She/he/they] bypassed' (elicited example; the question marks '??' are intended as an indication of the problematic status of the monosyllabic verb form)

In view of the M.L.L tone pattern of example (11), the monosyllable must be analyzed as carrying lexical L tone: //wɤ˩//. But this monosyllable seems to obtain by truncation of the disyllable, rather than the other way round. Thus, there are strong reasons to consider that the disyllabic form //wɤ˩~wɤ˩// 'to bypass' is not synchronically derived from a monosyllabic form, but belongs to the small and heterogeneous set of disyllabic verbs found in Yongning Na. Consequently, this verb does not constitute a counterexample to the generalizations shown in Table 6.4.

Table 6.4: The tone patterns of reduplicated verbs.

tone	example	meaning	reduplication	surface tone	underlying tone
H	dzɯ˧	to eat	dzɯ˧~dzɯ#˧	M.M	#H
M_a	hwæ˧$_a$	to buy	hwæ˧~hwæ˩	M.L	H−
M_b	tɕʰi˧$_b$	to sell	tɕʰi˧~tɕʰi˧	M.M	M
M_c	pv˧$_c$	to chant	pv˧~pv˩	M.L	M
L_a	dze˩$_a$	to cut	dze˧~dze˧	M.H	H#
L_b	ʐwɤ˩$_b$	to speak	ʐwɤ˧~ʐwɤ˩	M.L	H−
MH	lɑ˧	to strike	lɑ˩~lɑ˧	L.MH	LM+MH#

The tonal string that obtains in isolation is indicated in the "surface tone" column in Table 6.4. The underlying tone (indicated in the last column, and also used for transcribing the reduplicated expressions in the fourth column) was arrived at by examining the behaviour of reduplicated expressions in different contexts. (The corresponding recordings are VerbReduplObj and VerbReduplObj2.) Table 6.5 sets out the tone patterns that obtain in frames (12) and (13). Frame (13) is one of the few contexts where M_a and M_c yield different results.

Table 6.5: Surface phonological representation of reduplicated verbs in two different carrier phrases.

tone	example	meaning	ACCOMP+REDUPL	'to V a little'
H	dzɯ˦	to eat	le˦-dzɯ˦~dzɯ˦	dɯ˦-dzɯ˦~dzɯ˦-i˦
M$_a$	hwæ˦$_a$	to buy	le˦-hwæ˦~hwæ˧	dɯ˦-hwæ˦~hwæ˧-i˧
M$_b$	tɕʰi˦$_b$	to sell	le˦-tɕʰi˦~tɕʰi˦	dɯ˦-tɕʰi˦~tɕʰi˦-i˧
M$_c$	pɣ˦$_c$	to chant	le˦-pɣ˦~pɣ˧	dɯ˦-pɣ˦~pɣ˦-i˧
L$_a$	bæ˧$_a$	to sweep	le˦-bæ˦~bæ˦	dɯ˦-bæ˦~bæ˦-i˧
L$_b$	ʐwɣ˧$_b$	to speak	le˦-ʐwɣ˦~ʐwɣ˧	dɯ˦-ʐwɣ˦~ʐwɣ˧-i˧
MH	la˦	to strike	le˦-la˧~la˧	dɯ˦-la˧~la˧-i˧

(12) le˦-V~V
    le˦-   V   ~
    ACCOMP   *target verb*   RED
    'to V'

(13) dɯ˦-V~V-i˧
    dɯ˦-   V   ~   -i˧
    DELIMITATIVE   *target verb*   RED   INCHOATIVE
    'to V a little'

Finally, Table 6.6 shows the result of associating the object /tso˦~tso˦/ 'thing' to a reduplicated verb.

Interpretation of the tone pattern for H-tone verbs is guided by the data in Table 6.5. The presence of a H tone on the last syllable of the expression /dɯ˦-dzɯ˦~dzɯ˦-i˦/ 'to eat a little', from /dzɯ˦/ 'to eat', suggests that the reduplicated expression contains a H tone. Since this H tone does not surface when the expression is said in isolation (where the reduplicated verb surfaces as /dzɯ˦~dzɯ˦/), the tonal category cannot be //H-// (an initial H tone), nor //H#// (a final H tone), nor //H$// (a *gliding* H tone: see §2.3.2). On the other hand, its behaviour is consistent with interpretation as //#H// (a *floating* H tone), and this hypothesis is therefore adopted in Table 6.4.

Table 6.6: Reduplicated verbs with the #H-tone object 'things'.

tone	example	meaning	reduplication	'things'+reduplicated V
H	dzɯ˥	to eat	dzɯ˧~dzɯ#˥	tso˧~tso˧ dzɯ˧~dzɯ˥
M$_a$	hwæ˧$_a$	to buy	hwæ˥~hwæ˩	tso˧~tso˧ hwæ˥~hwæ˥
M$_b$	tɕʰi˧$_b$	to sell	tɕʰi˧~tɕʰi˧	tso˧~tso˧ tɕʰi˧~tɕʰi˧
L$_a$	bæ˩$_a$	to sweep	bæ˧~bæ˥	tso˧~tso˧ bæ˧~bæ˥
L$_b$	ʐwɤ˩$_b$	to speak	ʐwɤ˥~ʐwɤ˩	tso˧~tso˧ ʐwɤ˧~ʐwɤ˥
MH	lɑ˩˥	to strike	lɑ˩~lɑ˩˥	tso˧~tso˧ lɑ˥~lɑ˩

The /M.L/ surface pattern in the reduplication of M$_a$-tone verbs (e.g. /hwæ˧$_a$/ 'to buy' → /hwæ˥~hwæ˩/) could be the realization of various underlying tones, such as //L#// (a final L tone) or //H-// (a H tone associated to the first part of the reduplicated expression, i.e. its first syllable). Relevant evidence comes from the contexts shown in Table 6.5, where the first syllable of the reduplicated expression carries H tone, guiding towards an interpretation of the underlying pattern as //H-// and not //L#//.[4]

Reduplication of M$_b$-tone verbs is simplest: the reduplicated expression carries M tone in isolation (e.g. /tɕʰi˧$_b$/ 'to sell' → /tɕʰi˧~tɕʰi˧/), and it is not modified in the frames shown in Table 6.5 and Table 6.6. This strongly suggests an analysis of the reduplicated verb as carrying M tone.

Analysis for the remaining three tones is also straightforward. L$_a$ tone reduplicates to a pattern with a H tone attached to its last syllable (see Table 6.4), hence analysis as //H#//. The analysis for L$_b$ tone is identical to that for H set out above. Finally, the underlying tone //LM+MH#// postulated for the expression reduplicated from a MH-tone verb corresponds to its surface form, without any added complexities.

The relationship between the tones of monosyllabic verbs and that of reduplicated expressions is another matter. Why is it that a final H tone is found in reduplicated L$_a$-tone verbs, for instance? Why is it that MH-tone verbs get an initial L at reduplication? Phonology does not provide answers to these questions: the tone patterns found in reduplicated forms cannot be derived from those of the simple forms by phonological rules. The correspondences between simple

---

[4] An initial H tone can never surface as such, due to the neutralization of //H// and //M// in tone-group-initial position: this is referred to as Rule 3 (see §7.1.1).

and reduplicated tones need to be learnt; they constitute a component of the tonal grammar of Yongning Na.[5]

It was mentioned above that disyllabic verbs are rare and constitute a heterogeneous set. Only one case of reduplication of a disyllabic verb was observed: /sɣ˧~sɣ˧dv˧~dv˥/ 'pensively; with a heavy heart' (Reward.49), from /sɣ˧dv˧/ 'to think; to miss'. This is the only example of a correspondence between a M tone on the *simplex* form and a MH# tone on the reduplicated expression. It looks like a unique creation, rather than the result of a productive pattern.

6.3 Prefixes

6.3.1 M-tone prefixes

The prefixes described in this section can be interpreted either as M-tone prefixes, or as toneless prefixes that receive M by default; no evidence was found that they are specified for tone. They are referred to as M-tone prefixes for convenience.

The most common verbal prefixes carrying M tone are negative /mɤ˧-/, prohibitive /tʰɑ˧-/, durative /tʰi˧-/ and accomplished /le˧-/.

> The ACCOMPLISHED prefix lə³³- is used to give a reading of accomplishment to a verb with lexical aspect of ongoing state, process, or liminality. (…) The DURATIVE prefix tʰɯ³³- [in the Alawa dialect, studied in this volume: /tʰi˧/] is used to give a reading of ongoing action to verbs with lexical aspect of process or liminality. (Lidz 2010: 345)

These prefixes all have the same behaviour (apart from the exceptional case of M_c-tone verbs in association with /le˧-/, as reported in §6.1.2). A less common prefix, /mɤ˧-/, conveying imminence, has a behaviour of its own, described further below.

Table 6.7 presents the tonal behaviour of the most common prefixes. With a view to ease of reference, redundant data is provided for three prefixes: durative, prohibitive, and negation, all with identical tone patterns. Some of the combinations are found in the following online recordings: VerbProhib, VerbProhib2, VerbDurative and AccompPfv.

---

[5] In Naxi, reduplication likewise lacks a clear phonological pattern: H reduplicates to H.M, M to M.M, and L to M.L (Hé Zhìwǔ 1987: 10-11). These patterns can be analyzed as originating diachronically in total reduplication: H → H.H, M → M.M, L → L.L (Michaud & Vaissière 2007b). In Yongning Na, on the other hand, no such simple historical scenario can be proposed at present. This is an area where data from neighbouring dialects seems necessary for progress in the diachronic analysis.

Table 6.7: The tones of verbs in association with a M-tone prefix.

tone	example	meaning	DURATIVE	PROHIBITIVE	NEGATION
H	dzɯ˥	to eat	tʰi˧-dzɯ˥	tʰɑ˧-dzɯ˥	mɤ˧-dzɯ˥
M_a	hwæ˧$_a$	to buy	tʰi˧-hwæ˧	tʰɑ˧-hwæ˧	mɤ˧-hwæ˧
M_b	tɕʰi˧$_b$	to sell	tʰi˧-tɕʰi˧	tʰɑ˧-tɕʰi˧	mɤ˧-tɕʰi˧
M_c	pʏ˧$_c$	to chant	tʰi˧-pʏ˧	tʰɑ˧-pʏ˧	mɤ˧-pʏ˧
L_a	bæ˩$_a$	to sweep	tʰi˧-bæ˩	tʰɑ˧-bæ˩	mɤ˧-bæ˩
L_b	ʐwɤ˩$_b$	to speak	tʰi˧-ʐwɤ˩	tʰɑ˧-ʐwɤ˩	mɤ˧-ʐwɤ˩
MH	lɑ˧˥	to strike	tʰi˧-lɑ˧˥	tʰɑ˧-lɑ˧˥	mɤ˧-lɑ˧˥

After a M-tone prefix, the lexical tones M, H, L and MH have a straightforward realization. The subcategories M_a and M_b are neutralized in this context; likewise for L_a and L_b.

Table 6.8 sets out the facts for the accomplished prefix /le˧-/ in association with the perfective, /-ze˧/, and the morpheme indicating completion: /-se˩/. Table 6.9 lists the patterns that obtain when the verb is followed by the causative /-tsæ˧/ and certitude morpheme /-ɲi˩/.

Table 6.8: Tone patterns in constructions consisting of verbs with the accomplished M-tone prefix and a perfective or completion morpheme.

tone	example	meaning	ACCOMP	ACCOMP+V+PFV	ACCOMP+V+COMPLETION
H	dzɯ˥	to eat	le˧-dzɯ˥	le˧-dzɯ˥-ze˩	le˧-dzɯ˧-se˥
M_a	hwæ˧$_a$	to buy	le˧-hwæ˧	le˧-hwæ˧-ze˧	le˧-hwæ˧-se˩
M_b	tɕʰi˧$_b$	to sell	le˧-tɕʰi˧	le˧-tɕʰi˧-ze˧	le˧-tɕʰi˧-se˩
M_c	bi˧$_c$	to go	le˧-bi˩	le˧-bi˩-ze˩	le˧-bi˩-se˩
L_a	bæ˩$_a$	to sweep	le˧-bæ˩	le˧-bæ˩-ze˩	le˧-bæ˩-se˩
L_b	ʐwɤ˩$_b$	to speak	le˧-ʐwɤ˩	le˧-ʐwɤ˩-ze˩	le˧-ʐwɤ˩-se˩
MH	lɑ˧˥	to strike	le˧-lɑ˧˥	le˧-lɑ˧-ze˥	le˧-lɑ˧-se˥

The certitude morpheme is invariantly low in Table 6.9, in keeping with its lexical L tone; this reveals that there is no floating H tone in any of the expressions that precede it. This is important information for arriving at the underlying tone of the expressions with surface M tones, exemplified by /le˧-hwæ˧/ and /le˧-

Table 6.9: Tone patterns in constructions consisting of verbs with the accomplished M-tone prefix and causative+certitude morphemes.

tone	example	meaning	ACCOMP	ACCOMP+V+CAUS+CERTITUDE
H	dzɯ˥	to eat	le˧-dzɯ˥	le˧-dzɯ˧-tsæ˥-ɲi˩
M$_a$	hwæ˧$_a$	to buy	le˧-hwæ˧	le˧-hwæ˧-tsæ˧-ɲi˩
M$_b$	tɕʰi˧$_b$	to sell	le˧-tɕʰi˧	le˧-tɕʰi˧-tsæ˧-ɲi˩
M$_c$	pv̩˧$_c$	to chant	le˧-pv̩˧	le˧-pv̩˧-tsæ˧-ɲi˩
L$_a$	bæ˩$_a$	to sweep	le˧-bæ˩	le˧-bæ˩-tsæ˩-ɲi˩
L$_b$	ʐwɤ˩$_b$	to speak	le˧-ʐwɤ˩	le˧-ʐwɤ˩-tsæ˩-ɲi˩
MH	lɑ˧˥	to strike	le˧-lɑ˧˥	le˧-lɑ˧-tsæ˥-ɲi˩

tɕʰi˧/: if they carried a floating H tone, the following morpheme, /-ɲi˩/, would surface with H tone. The data in Table 6.9 also offers a new illustration of the behaviour that is characteristic of the MH and H tones, respectively illustrated by /le˧-lɑ˧˥/ and /le˧-dzɯ˥/. For MH-tone verbs in this construction, the M tone remains on the syllable to which it is lexically associated, and its H part is projected to the next syllable (the causative). (This is obligatorily followed by L tone on the certitude suffix, due to Rule 4: "The syllable following a H-tone syllable receives L tone".) In the case of H-tone verbs, the H tone no longer appears on the syllable to which it is lexically associated. Instead it associates to the causative, resulting in a surface phonological output that is identical to that for MH tone.

A related set of facts is presented in Table 6.10: the construction V-NEG-V, as in example (14).[6]

(14) ɲi˩ mɤ˧-ɲi˩, | mɤ˧-ŋv̩˥!
     ɲi˩   mɤ˧-   ɲi˩   mɤ˧-   ŋv̩˥
     COP NEG   COP NEG   to_know/to_get_to_know

'Whether it is actually the case… we don't know!' (Context: two persons discuss what a third person has said.)

---

[6] Two variants are possible, the one integrated into one single tone group, as in (14), the other divided into two groups: /ɲi˧ | mɤ˧-ɲi˩, | mɤ˧-ŋv̩˥!/ (same meaning and morphemic composition as (14)). In the latter case, the first syllable has the same tone as in isolation, and the negated form has the tone indicated in Table 6.7 above. These V-NEG-V constructions are typically followed by /mɤ˧-ŋv̩˥/ '[I/we] don't know' or /mɤ˧-do˩/ '[we] don't know/can't see for ourselves', sometimes with focalization of the V NEG-V portion, e.g. /hwæ˧ mɤ˧-hwæ˧ F | mɤ˧-do˩/ '[I/we] don't know whether [they] bought [it/some] or not'. (For a discussion of intonational focalization, transcribed as 'F', see §8.3.2.) In addition to the elicited data in Table 6.10, there are some examples in texts, e.g. in BuriedAlive3.133, Seeds2.85 and Dog.59.

Table 6.10: Tone patterns of the V-NEG-V construction.

tone	example	meaning	V NEG V	V | NEG V
H	dzɯ˥	to eat	dzɯ˧ mɤ˧-dzɯ˧	dzɯ˧ | mɤ˧-dzɯ˥
M$_a$	hwæ˧$_a$	to buy	hwæ˧ mɤ˧-hwæ˧	hwæ˧ | mɤ˧-hwæ˧
M$_b$	tɕʰi˧$_b$	to sell	tɕʰi˧ mɤ˧-tɕʰi˧	tɕʰi˧ | mɤ˧-tɕʰi˧
M$_c$	pv˧$_c$	to chant	pv˧ mɤ˧-pv˧	pv˧ | mɤ˧-pv˧
L$_a$	gɯ˩$_a$	to be true	gɯ˩ mɤ˩-gɯ˥	gɯ˧˩ | mɤ˧-gɯ˩
L$_b$	ʐwɤ˩$_b$	to speak	ʐwɤ˩ mɤ˥-ʐwɤ˩	ʐwɤ˧˩ | mɤ˧-ʐwɤ˩
MH	lɑ˧˥	to strike	lɑ˧ mɤ˥-lɑ˩	lɑ˧˥ | mɤ˧-lɑ˧˥

As mentioned at the outset of this section, the prefix /mɤ˧-/, conveying imminence, is infrequent: only one example is found in the first twenty-five transcribed narratives. The consultant was not comfortable pairing this prefix with verbs into a disyllabic expression, and proposed instead the three constructions (15), (16) and (17). The results are shown in Table 6.11.

(15) mɤ˧-V-bi˧
mɤ˧- V -bi˧
IMMINENCE *target verb* IMM_FUT
'will V right away'

(16) tʰi˧-mɤ˧-V
tʰi˧- mɤ˧- V
DUR IMMINENCE *target verb*
'is going to V up'

(17) le˧-mɤ˧-V
le˧- mɤ˧- V
ACCOMP NEG *target verb*
'does not V / not to V'

The results for H- and MH-tone verbs are far from trivial. As with other systematically elicited combinations, it appears safer to wait until further confirmation can be obtained (ideally from texts) before attempting an interpretation.

6.3.2 L-tone prefixes

The yes/no interrogative (polar interrogative) /ə˩-/ illustrates the case of L-tone prefixes. This interrogative is segmentally bleached, consisting of a neutral vowel

Table 6.11: Tone patterns of verbs with the prefix /my˧-/, and an antonymic construction.

tone	example	meaning	my˧-V-bi˧	tʰi˧-my˧-V	le˧-my˧-V
H	dzɯ˥	to eat	my˧-dzɯ˧-bi˧	tʰi˧-my˧-dzɯ˧	le˧-my˧-dzɯ˧
M_a	hwæ˧_a	to buy	my˧-hwæ˧-bi˧	tʰi˧-my˧-hwæ˧	le˧-my˧-hwæ˧
M_b	tɕʰi˧_b	to sell	my˧-tɕʰi˧-bi˧	tʰi˧-my˧-tɕʰi˧	le˧-my˧-tɕʰi˧
M_c	pv˧_c	to chant	my˧-pv˧-bi˧	tʰi˧-my˧-pv˧	le˧-my˧-pv˧
L_a	bæ˩_a	to sweep	my˧-bæ˧-bi˩	tʰi˧-my˧-bæ˩	le˧-my˧-bæ˩
L_b	ʐwɤ˩_b	to speak	my˧-ʐwɤ˧-bi˩	tʰi˧-my˧-ʐwɤ˩	le˧-my˧-ʐwɤ˩
MH	lɑ˩˥	to strike	my˧-lɑ˩-bi˩	tʰi˧-my˧-lɑ˩˥	le˧-my˧-lɑ˩˥

undergoing strong regressive vowel harmony. From a tonal point of view, on the other hand, it has a specification of its own. Table 6.12 sets out the facts.

Table 6.12: The tones of verbs in association with a L-tone prefix.

tone	example	meaning	interrogative
H	dzɯ˥	to eat	ə˧-dzɯ˥
M_a	hwæ˧_a	to buy	ə˩-hwæ˧
M_b	tɕʰi˧_b	to sell	ə˩-tɕʰi˧
M_c	pv˧_c	to chant	ə˩-pv˧
L_a	bæ˩_a	to sweep	ə˩-bæ˩
L_b	ʐwɤ˩_b	to speak	ə˩-ʐwɤ˩
MH	lɑ˩˥	to strike	ə˧-lɑ˥

The realizations of tones M and L after a L-tone prefix reflect the lexical tones in a straightforward way. That of tones H and MH, on the other hand, is nontrivial: both have the same pattern, in which the tone of the prefix is raised to M, and the verb carries H. The sequence /L.MH/ would not contravene Yongning Na phonotactics, so there is no phonological reason why the interrogative followed by a //MH//-tone verb should not yield /L.MH/: for instance †ə˩-lɑ˩˥ (intended meaning: 'does (s)he strike'). The sequence /L.H/ is also fine from a phonological point of view.

The origin of the raising of the interrogative morpheme's L tone in front of H-tone and MH-tone verbs constitutes a diachronic puzzle in view of the scarcity of cases of modification of a tone by that of a following morpheme in the Alawa dialect of Yongning Na. In this language variety, tone modification tends to be progressive (unlike vowel harmony, a phonetic tendency which works in the other direction: see Appendix A, §A.2.7). On the other hand, if any morpheme is likely to be modified by the tone of a following word, a schwa prefix is surely the most likely, given its phonetic and phonological lightness. The realization of schwa prefixes would warrant an experimental phonetic study in future, to investigate their duration, fundamental frequency, formant frequencies and other parameters. Synchronic patterns of phonetic variation may help formulate hypotheses about how these prefixes' current morphotonological patterns came about.

6.3.3 The marking of spatial orientation on verbs

Extensive marking of orientation on verbs is found among Na-Qiangic languages. In particular, Rgyalrongic languages "have a whole array of verbal orientation prefixes, which are obligatorily present on all perfective and imperative verb forms" (Sun 2000: 180; see also Lin 2002, and Jacques 2011b on Tangut). The three distinct pairs of directions described by J. Sun for Rgyalrongic are: eastward (i.e. in the direction of the rising sun) vs. westward; upstream vs. downstream; and uphill (upward) vs. downhill (downward). The system found in Shixing (Xumi) comprises two productive pairs of (non-obligatory) orientation prefixes, only one of which corresponds semantically with the Rgyalrongic system: upward vs. downward, the other being inward vs. outward. Shixing also displays traces of a third pair: hither and thither, found in a set construction meaning 'to V back and forth' (Chirkova 2009).

This conspicuous characteristic is sometimes awarded the status of criterion for phylogenetic classification, e.g. in proposals by Matisoff (2004: 105). But cross-dialect and cross-language differences reveal that orientation systems are no less prone to change than other areas of a language's structure. Under the hypothesis that directional prefixes have great historical depth in Sino-Tibetan, Naish must be hypothesized to have lost them. In Naish, topographically-based spatial deixis is not marked through an obligatory prefix on verbs. Indications of orientation, such as /mɤ˩tɕo˧/ 'downward' in (18), may more properly be called orientation adverbials.

(18) myˍtɕo˧ mɤ˧-hɯ˧
 myˍtɕo˧   mɤ˧-   hɯ˧c
 downward   NEG   to_go.PST

'[The dog, who had come to sit on the wooden platform close to the fire pit, where dogs are not allowed] did not/would not get down!' (Example from a discussion about Sister3.22.)

The only monosyllabic indications of orientation in common use, for which one could claim the status of prefixes, are /gɤˍ-/ 'upward' and /myˍ-/ 'downward'. For instance, /ʂo˩/ 'to reap, to gather in' can be used in association with /gɤˍ-/ 'upward' to mean 'to reap in, to bring back to the house and into the granary': /gɤˍ-ʂo˩/. These monosyllabic prefixes also appear as part of set constructions, such as /gɤˍ-V | myˍ-V/ 'to V in all directions', as in (19):

(19) tsʰɯ˧ne˧-ji˩ | gɤˍ-dɑ˧, | myˍ-dɑ˧, | gɤˍ-dɑ˧, | myˍ-dɑ˧, | (…) ɖɯ˧-ʂoˍ
 ʂɯˍ ji˩ tsɯˍ | myˍ! |
 tsʰɯ˧ne˧-ji˩ gɤˍ-   dɑ˧   myˍ-   dɑ˧   ɖɯ˧-ʂoˍ
 thus   upward   to_strike downward   to_strike several
 ʂɯˍ   ji˩   tsɯ˧   myˍ
 times   to_do   REP   AFFIRM

'He would give blows high and low (= hither and thither), again and again! / He would strike blows in all directions, again and again!' (Healing.38. Context: an exorcist is performing a ritual.)

In this context, the prefixes retain to some extent their literal meaning of 'upward' and 'downward': the exorcist's blows with his sword are aimed high up, then down (close to the ground), then up again, and so on. But in this construction, the spatial indications take up a broader meaning, summoning up the swift, dance-like movements of the exorcist fighting with an invisible cohort of demons surrounding him. Repetition of the prefixed verb (/gɤˍ-dɑ˧, | myˍ-dɑ˧, | gɤˍ-dɑ˧, | myˍ-dɑ˧/) participates to loosening the exact indication of spatial orientation, yielding a meaning of 'in all directions' rather than 'up and down'.

When an orientation prefix is separated from the verb by other prefixes, it can constitute a tone group on its own, as in (20). In this example, the prefix's //L// tone surfaces as /LH/ due to the prohibition of all-L tone groups: a phonological rule referred to as Rule 7 (see §7.1) repairs all-L tone groups by addition of a post-lexical H tone to their last syllable, which, in the case of the first tone group of example (20), also happens to be the *first* syllable.

(20) ... gʴ˦ | le˦-tsʰo˦-se˥-dzo˩ | tʰi˦ ...
     gʴ˩-   le˦-   tsʰo˥   -se˩   -dzo˥ tʰi˦
     upward ACCOMP to_pray COMPLETION TOP then
    'after one has prayed [*literally*: prayed up (to the ancestors)]' (Dog2.54)

Judging from available texts, monosyllabic /gʴ˩-/ 'upward' is more frequent than /mv˩-/ 'downward'. The two prefixes /gʴ˩-/ 'upward' and /mv˩-/ 'downward' have the same tonal behaviour. The disyllabic expressions /gʴ˩tɕo˦/ 'upward' and /mv˩tɕo˦/ 'downward' are generally preferred. Monosyllabic forms are tentatively labelled here as prefixes (and transcribed accordingly: with a following hyphen) and disyllabic forms as adverbials, but in the absence of language-internal criteria to distinguish the two, the divide is not as clear as this choice of terms suggests. From a tonal point of view, aside from uncommon cases such as (20), orientation prefixes belong in the same tone group as the following verb. On the other hand, orientation adverbials often constitute a tone group on their own, as discussed in §7.2.1. The data in Table 6.13 concerns cases when the orientation prefix or adverbial is integrated into the same tone group as the verb. The perfective suffix /-ze˦/ serves to reveal whether the verb carries H tone (which results in lowering of the suffix to L), M tone (which leaves the suffix unaffected), or MH tone (which results in the association of the H part of the contour to the suffix). For the sake of clarity, the surface forms are provided in full, even though in many cases the tonal behaviour of the perfective suffix /-ze˦/ derives straightforwardly from the tone pattern of the non-suffixed expression through the application of the seven phonological tone rules recapitulated in §7.1.1. For instance, L.H can only be followed by L, by virtue of Rule 4 ("A syllable following a H-tone syllable receives L tone"), so the L.H expression /**gʴ˩-se˥**/ 'to walk up(ward)' predictably yields L.H+L in (21).

(21) gʴ˩-se˥-ze˩
     gʴ˩-   se˥   -ze˦
     UPWARD to_walk PFV
    'walked up(ward)'

The original data is found in the online document SpatialOrientation. The verb /**bi˦**c/ 'to go' was accidentally omitted in the recording. This verb can combine with the disyllabic orientation adverbials, but not with monosyllabic /gʴ˩-/ 'upward' and /mv˩-/ 'downward'. The data is shown in (22)-(26). Note that the variant ‡ jo˩lo˩ bi˥ for (24) is not acceptable.

(22)   ʁo˧dɑ˧ bi˧(-ze˧)
       ʁo˧dɑ˧   bi˧c   -ze˧
       forward   to_go   PFV
       'to go forward'

(23)   ʁwæ˧gi˧ bi˧(-ze˧)
       ʁwæ˧gi˧   bi˧c   -ze˧
       leftward   to_go   PFV
       'to go to the left'

(24)   jo˩lo˩ bi˩
       jo˩lo˩   bi˧c
       rightward   to_go
       'to go to the right'

(25)   ʁo˧tʰo˩ bi˩
       ʁo˧tʰo˩   bi˧c
       backward   to_go
       'to go backward'

(26)   gʌ˩tɕo˧ bi˧(-ze˧)
       gʌ˩tɕo˧   bi˧c   -ze˧
       upward   to_go   PFV
       'to go upward'

Table 6.13a: The tonal behaviour of verbs after indications of spatial orientation: monosyllabic prefixes.

tone	example	meaning	'upward' prefix	'downward' prefix
H	se˧	to walk	gʌ˩-se˧, gʌ˩-se˧-ze˩	mv˩-se˧, mv˩-se˧-ze˩
M_a	li˧a	to look	gʌ˩-li˧, gʌ˩-li˧-ze˧	mv˩-li˧, mv˩-li˧-ze˧
M_b	tsi˧b	to set	gʌ˩-tsi˧, gʌ˩-tsi˧-ze˧	mv˩-tsi˧, mv˩-tsi˧-ze˧
L_a	kwʌ˩a	to throw	gʌ˩-kwʌ˧, gʌ˩-kwʌ˧-ze˩	mv˩-kwʌ˧, mv˩-kwʌ˧-ze˩
L_b	i̩˩b	to turn	gʌ˩-i̩˧, gʌ˩-i̩˧-ze˩	mv˩-i̩˧, mv˩-i̩˧-ze˩
MH	mi˩	to push	gʌ˩-mi˩, gʌ˩-mi˧-ze˧	mv˩-mi˩, mv˩-mi˧-ze˧

Table 6.13b: The tonal behaviour of verbs after indications of spatial orientation: adverbial //ɬo˧ta˧// 'to the side'.

tone	example	meaning	with adverbial 'to the side'
H	se˥	to walk	ɬo˧ta˧ se˧, ɬo˧ta˧ se˧-ze˧
M$_a$	li˧$_a$	to look	ɬo˧ta˧ li˧, ɬo˧ta˧ li˧-ze˧
M$_b$	tsi˧$_b$	to set	ɬo˧ta˧ tsi˧, ɬo˧ta˧ tsi˧-ze˧
L$_a$	kwɤ˩$_a$	to throw	ɬo˧ta˧ kwɤ˩, ɬo˧ta˧ kwɤ˩-ze˩
L$_b$	ɖʐ˩$_b$	to turn	ɬo˧ta˧ ɖʐ˩, ɬo˧ta˧ ɖʐ˩-ze˩
MH	mi˧˥	to push	ɬo˧ta˧ mi˧˥, ɬo˧ta˧ mi˧-ze˥

Table 6.13c: The tonal behaviour of verbs after indications of spatial orientation: adverbials //ʁo˧da˧// 'forward' and //ʁo˧tʰo˩// 'backward'.

tone	example	meaning	'forward'	'backward'
H	se˥	to walk	ʁo˧da˧ se˧, ʁo˧da˧ se˧-ze˩	ʁo˧tʰo˩ se˩, ʁo˧tʰo˩ se˩-ze˩
M$_a$	li˧$_a$	to look	ʁo˧da˧ li˧, ʁo˧da˧ li˧-ze˧	ʁo˧tʰo˩ li˩, ʁo˧tʰo˩ li˩-ze˩
M$_b$	tsi˧$_b$	to set	ʁo˧da˧ tsi˧, ʁo˧da˧ tsi˧-ze˩	ʁo˧tʰo˩ tsi˩, ʁo˧tʰo˩ tsi˩-ze˩
L$_a$	kwɤ˩$_a$	to throw	ʁo˧da˧ kwɤ˩, ʁo˧da˧ kwɤ˩-ze˩	ʁo˧tʰo˩ kwɤ˩, ʁo˧tʰo˩ kwɤ˩-ze˩
L$_b$	ɖʐ˩$_b$	to turn	ʁo˧da˧ ɖʐ˩, ʁo˧da˧ ɖʐ˩-ze˩	ʁo˧tʰo˩ ɖʐ˩, ʁo˧tʰo˩ ɖʐ˩-ze˩
MH	mi˧˥	to push	ʁo˧da˧ mi˧˥, ʁo˧da˧ mi˧-ze˥	ʁo˧tʰo˩ mi˩, ʁo˧tʰo˩ mi˩-ze˩

Table 6.13d: The tonal behaviour of verbs after indications of spatial orientation: //ʁwæ˧lo˥// 'leftward' and //ʁwæ˧-gi#˥// 'to the left side'.

tone	example	meaning	'leftward'	'to the left side'
H	se˥	to walk	ʁwæ˧lo˥ se˩, ʁwæ˧lo˥ se˩-ze˩	ʁwæ˧-gi˧ se˧, ʁwæ˧-gi˧ se˧-ze˩
M$_a$	li˧$_a$	to look	ʁwæ˧lo˥ li˩, ʁwæ˧lo˥ li˩-ze˩	ʁwæ˧-gi˧ li˩, ʁwæ˧-gi˧ li˩-ze˩
M$_b$	tsi˧$_b$	to set	ʁwæ˧lo˥ tsi˩, ʁwæ˧lo˥ tsi˩-ze˩	ʁwæ˧-gi˧ tsi˧, ʁwæ˧-gi˧ tsi˧-ze˩
L$_a$	kwɤ˩$_a$	to throw	ʁwæ˧lo˥ kwɤ˩, ʁwæ˧lo˥ kwɤ˩-ze˩	ʁwæ˧-gi˧ kwɤ˥, ʁwæ˧-gi˧ kwɤ˥-ze˩
L$_b$	ɖʐ˩$_b$	to turn	ʁwæ˧lo˥ ɖʐ˩, ʁwæ˧lo˥ ɖʐ˩-ze˩	ʁwæ˧-gi˧ ɖʐ˥, ʁwæ˧-gi˧ ɖʐ˥-ze˩
MH	mi˧˥	to push	ʁwæ˧lo˥ mi˩, ʁwæ˧lo˥ mi˩-ze˩	ʁwæ˧-gi˧ mi˩, ʁwæ˧-gi˧ mi˩-ze˩

Table 6.13e: The tonal behaviour of verbs after indications of spatial orientation: //jo˩lo˩// 'rightward' and //jo˩-gi˩// 'to the right side'.

tone	example	meaning	'rightward'	'to the right side'
H	se˥	to walk	jo˩lo˩ se˧, jo˩lo˩ se˩-ze˥	jo˩-gi˩ se˧, jo˩-gi˩ se˩-ze˥
M$_a$	li˧$_a$	to look	jo˩lo˩ li˥, jo˩lo˩ li˥-ze˩	jo˩-gi˩ li˥, jo˩-gi˩ li˥-ze˩
M$_b$	tsi˧$_b$	to set	jo˩lo˩ tsi˧, jo˩lo˩ tsi˩-ze˥ ≈ jo˩lo˩ tsi˥, jo˩lo˩ tsi˥-ze˩	jo˩-gi˩ tsi˥, jo˩-gi˩ tsi˩-ze˩ ≈ jo˩-gi˩ tsi˧, jo˩-gi˩ tsi˩-ze˥
L$_a$	kwɤ˩$_a$	to throw	jo˩lo˩ kwɤ˥, jo˩lo˩ kwɤ˥-ze˩	jo˩-gi˩ kwɤ˥, jo˩-gi˩ kwɤ˥-ze˩
L$_b$	ɖʐ˩$_b$	to turn	jo˩lo˩ ɖʐ˥, jo˩lo˩ ɖʐ˥-ze˩	jo˩-gi˩ ɖʐ˥, jo˩-gi˩ ɖʐ˥-ze˩
MH	mi˧˥	to push	jo˩lo˩ mi˥, jo˩lo˩ mi˥-ze˩	jo˩-gi˩ mi˥, jo˩-gi˩ mi˥-ze˩

Table 6.13f: The tonal behaviour of verbs after indications of spatial orientation: orientation adverbials //gɤ˩tɕo˧// 'upward' and //mɤ˩tɕo˧// 'downward'.

tone	example	meaning	'upward'	'downward'
H	se˥	to walk	gɤ˩tɕo˧ se˧,	mɤ˩tɕo˧ se˧,
			gɤ˩tɕo˧ se˧-ze˥	mɤ˩tɕo˧ se˧-ze˩
M$_a$	li˧$_a$	to look	gɤ˩tɕo˧ li˧,	mɤ˩tɕo˧ li˧,
			gɤ˩tɕo˧ li˧-ze˧	mɤ˩tɕo˧ li˧-ze˧
M$_b$	tsi˧$_b$	to set	gɤ˩tɕo˧ tsi˧,	mɤ˩tɕo˧ tsi˧,
			gɤ˩tɕo˧ tsi˧-ze˧	mɤ˩tɕo˧ tsi˧-ze˧
L$_a$	kwɤ˩$_a$	to throw	gɤ˩tɕo˧ kwɤ˩ ,	mɤ˩tɕo˧ kwɤ˩,
			gɤ˩tɕo˧ kwɤ˩-ze˩	mɤ˩tɕo˧ kwɤ˩-ze˩
L$_b$	ʈʂ˩$_b$	to turn	gɤ˩tɕo˧ ʈʂ˩,	mɤ˩tɕo˧ ʈʂ˩,
			gɤ˩tɕo˧ ʈʂ˩-ze˩	mɤ˩tɕo˧ ʈʂ˩-ze˩
MH	mi˧˥	to push	gɤ˩tɕo˧ mi˧˥,	mɤ˩tɕo˧ mi˧˥,
			gɤ˩tɕo˧ mi˧-ze˥	mɤ˩tɕo˧ mi˧-ze˥

All the data shown in Table 6.13 boils down to the underlying tone patterns summarized in Table 6.14. The tone indicated after a '+' sign is that carried by the perfective /-ze˧/ as it appears after the directional-plus-verb combination at issue. For example, the notation L.M+H for the combination of /gɤ˩-/ 'upward' and a verb with M$_b$ tone indicates that the pattern is /gɤ˩-tɕi˧/, /gɤ˩-tɕi˧-ze˥/ 'to set in an upward direction'.

An especially interesting aspect of this data is the lowering of the perfective suffix (which carries a lexical M tone: //-ze˧//) after expressions such as /mɤ˩tɕo˧ se˧/ 'to go downward', yielding /mɤ˩tɕo˧ se˧-ze˩/ '(s)he went downward'. This contrasts with expressions such as /mɤ˩tɕo˧ li˧/ 'to look downward', after which the perfective surfaces with its lexical M tone: /mɤ˩tɕo˧ li˧-ze˧/ '(s)he looked downward'. The lowering influence of an overt H tone on following tones within a tone group is a hard-and-fast phonological rule; but the expression /mɤ˩tɕo˧ se˧/ 'to go downward' does not contain a H tone at the surface phonological level. At a deeper level, referred to in this volume as the *underlying* phonological level, the expressions /mɤ˩tɕo˧ se˧/ 'to go downward' and /mɤ˩tɕo˧ li˧/ 'to look downward' must be analyzed as carrying different tones, since they behave differently with the same suffix. Since tone lowering is characteristic of H tones, it seems reasonable to posit a floating H in the underlying representation of /mɤ˩tɕo˧ se˧/ 'to go downward', thus: //mɤ˩tɕo˧ se#˥//. If the suffix //-ze˧// surfaced with H tone in any of the combinations in Table 6.14, that H tone would need to be recognized as the manifestation of a floating H tone from the directional-plus-verb expression; this would contradict headlong the interpretation proposed here: that floating H tones on such expressions only manifest themselves through *lowering* of a following tone. Importantly, the suffix //-ze˧// does *not* surface with H tone in any of the combinations in Table 6.14. This is taken as confirmation of the present analysis, in light of which the data in Table 6.14 is rewritten in Table 6.15, indicating the underlying tone patterns.

In Table 6.15, reference needs to be made to the juncture between the directional morpheme and the verb (similar to junctures internal to numeral-plus-classifier phrases and compound nouns, studied in previous chapters). This morpheme break is indicated by the symbol '–'. Thus, the indication 'L#–' refers to a final L tone (L#) attaching before the morpheme break. For instance, association of L#– to the syllable sequence /ʁo.tʰo.li/ 'to look back(ward)' requires identification of the morpheme break that follows the directional /ʁo.tʰo/ 'backward': /ʁo.tʰo – li/. The L tone associates to the last syllable of the first part of the expression, yielding /ʁo.tʰo˩/, and spreads (by Rule 1) to the following syllable, hence /ʁo.tʰo˩ li˩/. Finally, the expression's first syllable receives tone M (by Rule 2), hence /ʁo˧tʰo˩ li˩/. This is shown in Figure 6.2.

Table 6.14a: The surface tone patterns of verbs after indications of spatial orientation: monosyllabic prefixes.

tone of prefix	tone of verb					
	H	M$_a$	M$_b$	L$_a$	L$_b$	MH
L	L.H	L.M+M	L.M+M	L.H	L.H	L.MH

A further intricacy is that the behaviour of /a˩pʰo˩/ 'outside' is not fully identical with that of /jo˩gi˩/ and /jo˩lo˩/ 'to the right', even though these three spatial indications have the same lexical tone. In association with /tʰy˧a/ 'come out', /a˩pʰo˩/ 'outside' yields /a˩pʰo˩ tʰy˩/ 'to go outside, to get outside', instead of the expected /†a˩pʰo˩ tʰy˩/. The latter form is not acceptable as a variant.

Closer examination of this issue reveals yet another oddity: different verbs that belong in the same tonal category, M$_a$, have different tone patterns when associated with /a˩pʰo˩/ 'outside'. 'To look outside' (from /li˧a/ 'to look') is /a˩pʰo˩ li˩/, and ‡ a˩pʰo˩ li˩ is not an acceptable variant. The verb /tʰy˧a/ 'come out' is an outlier: it is the only M$_a$-tone verb yielding a L.L.L tone pattern in association with /a˩pʰo˩/ 'outside'.

Table 6.14b: The surface tone patterns of verbs after indications of spatial orientation: disyllabic orientation adverbials.

tone of prefix	tone of verb						
	H	M_a	M_b	M_c	L_a	L_b	MH
M	M.M.M+L	M.M.M+M	M.M.M+L	M.M.M+M	M.M.L	M.M.L	M.M.MH
#H	M.M.M+L	M.M.L	M.M.M+L	M.M.M+L	M.M.H	M.M.H	M.M.L
L	L.L.L	L.L.H	L.L.H / L.L.L	L.L.L	L.L.H	L.L.H	L.L.H
L#	M.L.L	M.L.L	M.L.L	M.L.L	M.L.L	M.L.L	M.L.L
LM	L.M.M+L	L.M.M+M	L.M.M+M	L.M.M+M	L.M.L	L.M.L	L.M.MH
H#	M.H.L	M.H.L	M.H.L	M.H.L	M.H.L	M.H.L	M.H.L

Stage 1:
association of L tone
to its specified locus:
before the juncture
between the two parts
of the expression

Stage 2:
assignment of L tone
by phonological rule:
L-tone spreading

Stage 3:
addition of M tone
to the remaining
toneless syllable

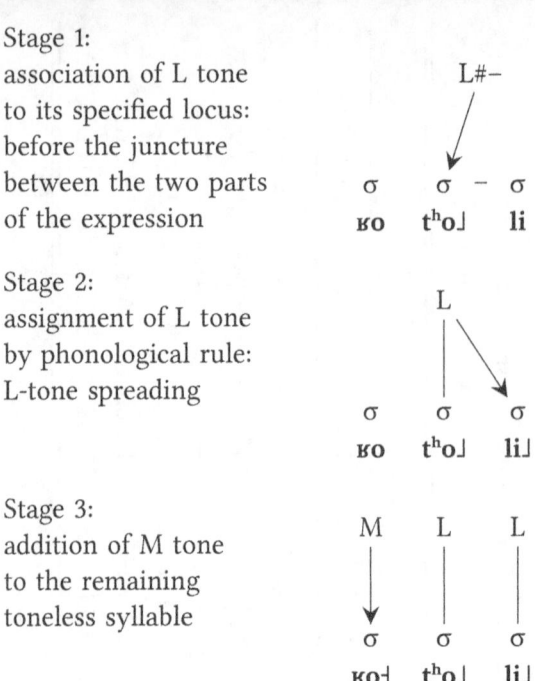

Figure 6.2: Illustration of the anchoring of tones relative to an internal juncture (notation: '–'): representation of association of L#– tone to the expression /ʁo.tʰo – li/ to yield /ʁo˦tʰo˩ li˩/ 'to look back'.

Table 6.15a: The underlying tone patterns of verbs after indications of spatial orientation: monosyllabic prefixes.

tone of prefix	tone of verb					
	H	M_a	M_b	L_a	L_b	MH
L	L.H	L.M	L.M	L.H	L.H	L.MH

In view of the fact that L.L.L and L.L.H are both acceptable variants for /jo˩gi˩/ and /jo˩lo˩/ 'to the right' followed by a M_a-tone verb, one can venture the speculation that the same pattern of variation once existed for /a˩pʰo˩/ 'outside'. Under this hypothesis, the L.L.L variant must have become dominant for 'to go outside, to get outside', to the extent that the form /a˩pʰo˩ tʰɣ˩/ came to be regarded as the only correct one.

272

Table 6.15b: The underlying tone patterns of verbs after indications of spatial orientation: disyllabic orientation adverbials.

tone of prefix	tone of verb						
	H	M$_a$	M$_b$	M$_c$	L$_a$	L$_b$	MH
M	#H	M	#H	M	L#		MH#
#H		L#		#H	H#		#H
L	L	L+H#	L+H# / L	L	L+H#		
L#	L#–						
LM	LM+#H	LM			LM+L#		LM+MH#
H#	H#–						

But even if one chooses to treat the combination /a˩pʰo˩ tʰɣ˩/ 'to go outside, to get outside' as a lexicalized oddity, the behaviour of /a˩pʰo˩/ 'outside' is still different from that of /jo˩gi˩/ and /jo˩lo˩/ 'to the right': see Table 6.16. Here again, knowledge of the input tones is not sufficient to generate the tone patterns.

Table 6.16: The tonal behaviour of verbs in association with /a˩pʰo˩/ 'outside'.

tone of verb	example	meaning of verb	tone pattern
H	a˩pʰo˩ se˩	to walk	L.L.L
M_a	a˩pʰo˩ li˥	to look	L.L.H
M_a (exceptional)	a˩pʰo˩ tʰɣ˩	to get/go	L.L.L
M_b	a˩pʰo˩ hõ˩	to go.IMPERATIVE	L.L.L
M_c	a˩pʰo˩ bi˩	to go	L.L.H
L_a	a˩pʰo˩ kwɤ˥	to throw	L.L.H
L_b	a˩pʰo˩ pʰɣ˥	to move around	L.L.H
MH	a˩pʰo˩ ʐi˥	to sleep	L.L.H

The interrogative /zo˩qo˧/ 'where' has the same behaviour as /gɤ˩tɕo˧/ 'upward' and /mʏ˩tɕo˧/ 'downward', as shown in Table 6.17. In association with /zo˩qo˧/ 'where', the verb /tʰɣ˧/, whose association with /a˩pʰo˩/ 'outside' yields an unexpected pattern (see Table 6.16), is not any different from the other M_a-tone verbs, yielding /zo˩qo˧ tʰɣ˧(-ze˧)/.

Table 6.17: The tonal behaviour of verbs in association with /zo˩qo˧/ 'where', with added information about a following perfective morpheme.

tone of verb	example	meaning of verb	tone pattern
H	zo˩qo˧ se˧(-ze˩)	to walk	L.M.M+L
M_a	zo˩qo˧ ʂe˧(-ze˧)	to look for	L.M.M+M
M_b	zo˩qo˧ pʰæ˧(-ze˧)	to attach, to fasten	L.M.M+M
M_c	zo˩qo˧ hɯ˧(-ze˧)	to go.PST	L.M.M+M
L_a	zo˩qo˧ dzi˩	to sit; to live	L.M.L
L_b	zo˩qo˧ ʝ˩	to turn toward	L.M.L
MH	zo˩qo˧ la˥	to strike, to hit	L.M.MH

274

In principle, the tonal behaviour of locative constituents in Yongning Na could shed light on their morphosyntactic treatment. Various configurations are attested cross-linguistically. For instance, in Central Bantu agreement with the verb reveals a typologically uncommon pattern: "a locative noun phrase in pre-verbal position can be analyzed as the grammatical subject" (Creissels 2011: 34), whereas in Northern Sotho, in the absence of such evidence, the construction is better analyzed as "an impersonal construction with a preposed locative constituent" (Zerbian 2006b). But the Yongning Na tone patterns presented above are not fully identical with those of any other construction. In particular, they differ from subject-plus-verb as well as from object-plus-verb constructions.

Let us now turn from pre-verbal elements to post-verbal elements.

6.4 Monosyllabic postverbal morphemes

Verbs appear after their objects. They can be followed by various morphemes, such as suffixes,[7] serialized verbs, postpositions, and discourse particles, which will be referred to here by the cover term 'postverbal morphemes'.

From the point of view of tone patterns, a key fact is that not all morphemes following verbs have the same tonal behaviour, suggesting that they have lexical tones of their own. Distributional analysis constitutes a first step in approaching these tones: finding out how many tonal categories there are for a given part of speech. After morphemes have been sorted into tonal sets, the next step consists in analyzing the underlying tones, as for nouns and verbs. On the one hand, in Yongning Na all syllables at the surface phonological level carry level tones (H, M, L, and combinations into low-rising and mid-rising contours), so it makes sense to hypothesize that the lexical tone categories all have these level tones as their building-blocks, and to attempt to pinpoint the phonological nature of the tonal categories of function words, as was done above for nouns and verbs. On the other hand, one should keep in mind the structural fact that the tone systems for different word classes are not identical. Beyond differences in the number

---

[7] Lidz (2010: 349) proposed, on the basis of data from the Luoshui dialect, that "[s]uffixation is not attested on verbs in Na"; but for the dialect under description here, it appears easiest to recognize a few postverbal morphemes as suffixes, e.g. the perfective /-ze˧/ (analyzed by Lidz (2010: 424) as a postverbal particle). In transcriptions, a hyphen is also used in cases where a verb's grammaticalized use appears distinct enough from the verb's original meaning to warrant separate recognition, for instance the immediate future, /-bi˧/, grammaticalized from the non-imperative form of 'to go', /bi˧ₑ/. The decision to treat a morpheme as a serialized verb or a suffix can be difficult. My use of hyphens fluctuated in the years of preparation of this volume, and there remain some inconsistencies in the transcriptions of texts.

of tones (among monosyllables: seven categories for verbs, five for adjectives, six for free nouns, nine for classifiers...), the behaviour of these tones in context varies across word classes, even for highly similar classes such as verbs and adjectives (as pointed out in §6.1.3). As a consequence, it is not possible to carry over the tonal analysis of a verb to its grammaticalized counterpart. For instance, the morpheme indicating completion, /-se˩/, is clearly a grammaticalized use of the verb /se˩/ 'to finish, to complete'. But this fact does not by itself warrant the conclusion that the grammaticalized morpheme carries the same lexical tone as the verb. The process of grammaticalization can be accompanied by a change of lexical tone: this is evidenced by the example of classifiers, studied in Chapter 4. Returning to postverbal morphemes, cases where they can straightforwardly be identified as originating in a lexical verb only offer indirect hints on tonal identity. The evidence on the tone categories of the grammatical morphemes studied in this chapter is therefore assembled piece by piece, and there remains room for further progress in the analysis. The reader will be reminded now and then that a given label (say, L tone) given to two different parts of speech (such as a verb and a suffix) cannot be said to refer to the same phonological entity: instead, those are two distinct morphophonological entities, which appear similar enough (at the present stage in the analysis) to warrant the use of the same label from among the set of phonologically distinctive tonal levels.

Monosyllabic elements will be discussed first, before getting on to disyllabic postpositions and combinations of affixes.

6.4.1 L-tone postverbal morphemes

6.4.1.1 Main facts

As mentioned a few lines above, the morpheme indicating completion, /-se˩/, is a grammaticalized use of the verb /se˩/ 'to finish, to complete'. This does not by itself constitute sufficient evidence that its lexical tone is L, but its tonal behaviour after M-tone verbs (where it surfaces with L tone) points in the same direction, and the tonal category in which it belongs is therefore labelled as L. Since the tonal behaviour of the desiderative morpheme is the same as that of the morpheme indicating completion, the same tonal label is applied, interpreting the desiderative as /-ho˩/. Data is shown in Table 6.18, also including data for the morpheme /-sɯ˩/ 'yet' (in the negative construction 'not yet'). Other items belonging to the same class (L tone) include the inchoative, /-i̥˩/, and the morpheme

/-dze˩/ 'to remain; to be left over'. The latter is only observed in /dzɯ˧-dze˥/ 'left over after eating' and /tʰɯ˩-dze˩/ 'left over after drinking (or smoking)'.[8]

Table 6.18: The patterns of L-tone tense-aspect-modality morphemes.

tone	example	meaning	COMPLETION	DESIDERATIVE	not yet
H	dzɯ˥	to eat	dzɯ˧-se˥	dzɯ˧-ho˥	mɤ˧-dzɯ˧-sɯ˥
M_a	hwæ˧$_a$	to buy	hwæ˧-se˩	hwæ˧-ho˩	mɤ˧-hwæ˧-sɯ˩
M_b	tɕʰi˧$_b$	to sell	tɕʰi˧-se˩	tɕʰi˧-ho˩	mɤ˧-tɕʰi˧-sɯ˩
M_c	pʏ˧$_c$	to chant	pʏ˧-se˩	pʏ˧-ho˩	mɤ˧-pʏ˧-sɯ˩
L_a	bæ˩$_a$	to sweep	bæ˩-se˩	bæ˩-ho˩	mɤ˧-bæ˩-sɯ˩
L_b	ʐwɤ˩$_b$	to speak	ʐwɤ˩-se˩	ʐwɤ˩-ho˩	mɤ˧-ʐwɤ˩-sɯ˩
MH	lɑ˩	to strike	lɑ˧-se˥	lɑ˧-ho˥	mɤ˧-lɑ˧-sɯ˥

6.4.1.2 A nominalizing suffix

It has been observed in a study of the Luoshui dialect of Yongning Na that "**di**³³ 'earth; place' grammaticalized into a locative nominalizer, and then further grammaticalized into a purposive nominalizer" (Lidz 2010: 184). For the Alawa dialect, the nominalizing morpheme is assigned L tone (hence /-di˩/) on the basis of its behaviour after M-tone verbs. It behaves differently from the L-tone morphemes discussed in the previous paragraph: /dzɯ˧-di˥/ 'food, things for eating' vs. /dzɯ˧-ho˥/ 'will eat'; /tʰæ˧-di˥/ 'thing to bite (e.g. toy given to teething babies)' vs. /tʰæ˧-ho˥/ 'will bite'. This observation is taken as confirmation that the nominalizing morpheme is to be analyzed as a suffix, belonging in a morphotonological class that is distinct from that of serialized verbs. The data is set out in Table 6.19.

As an aside, consultant M21 has different tone patterns for the L tone: L.H (e.g. /dze˩-di˥/ and /tʰɯ˩-di˥/), and not L.L. This could result from analogy with the L-tone morphemes described in §6.4.1.1, such as the morpheme indicating completion, /-se˩/, which takes H tone after a L-tone verb.

---

[8] I have not been able to come up with better English translations for these *noncompletion resultatives*, which refer to the state of affairs that results from an action that stopped short of completion (incomplete consumption of an object). Mandarin Chinese has handy equivalents: *chī shèng de* 吃剩的 for 'left over after eating' and *hē shèng de* 喝剩的 for 'left over after drinking'.

Table 6.19: The tonal behaviour of the nominalizing suffix /-di˩/.

tone	example	meaning	nominalizer	meaning
H	dzɯ˦	to eat	dzɯ˧-di˦	thing to eat, food
M$_a$	hwæ˧$_a$	to buy	hwæ˧-di˩	thing to buy, product
M$_b$	tɕʰi˧$_b$	to sell	tɕʰi˧-di˩	thing to sell, commodity
M$_c$	pv˧$_c$	to chant	pv˧-di˩	thing to chant, ritual
L$_a$	dze˩$_a$	to cut	dze˩-di˩	thing to cut, e.g. knife
L$_b$	tʰɯ˩$_b$	to drink	tʰɯ˩-di˩	thing to drink, beverage
MH	tʰæ˦	to bite	tʰæ˧-di˦	thing to bite (for infant, dog…)

6.4.2 M-tone postverbal morphemes

The imperative, /-hõ˧/, is grammaticalized from the imperative form of the verb 'to go', /hõ˩$_a$/; and the immediate future, /-bi˧/, from the non-imperative form of 'to go', /bi˧$_c$/. This constitutes a first hint that the tonal category of these two morphemes could be labelled as M. A stronger argument comes from their behaviour in association with the seven tonal categories of verbs, shown in Table 6.20. The table also shows data for the experiential /-dʐɯ˧/, which has the same tonal behaviour in all cases. The tone patterns after a verb with M, L or MH tone seem characteristic of a neutral tone: the postverbal morpheme allows the verb's MH tone to unfold over it, and the verb's L tone to spread over it; after a M-tone verb, the surface result is M, which is consistent with the phonologically inert nature of M tone, already mentioned in §2.4.3. To preview observations set out in §6.6.1, another test confirms the appropriateness of M tone as a label for the tonal category to which these morphemes belong: after the negation prefix, they surface with a M tone.

Other morphemes with the same tonal behaviour include /-ɖo˧/ 'must, have to', the volitive /-tso˧/, the obligative /-zo˧/, and the causative /-tsæ˧/.

In addition to the surface phonological forms, Table 6.20 proposes an analysis of the underlying tone, in the last column. This analysis is based on the tone patterns when the causative /-tsæ˧/ is added after the immediate future /-bi˧/, as shown in Table 6.21. The copula, in its use to convey certainty, was also added, as a further test to reveal the underlying tonal categories. In every case, the copula carries L, i.e. its lexical tone. This shows that there is no floating H tone in any of the verb phrases. The first three expressions are therefore interpreted as having

Table 6.20: The tonal behaviour of M-tone morphemes.

tone	example	meaning	IMM_FUT	experiential	imperative	analysis
H	dzɯ˦	to eat	dzɯ˦-bi˦	dzɯ˦-dzɯ˦	dzɯ˦-hõ˦	M
M$_a$	hwæ˧$_a$	to buy	hwæ˧-bi˦	hwæ˧-dzɯ˦	hwæ˧-hõ˦	M
M$_b$	tɕʰi˧$_b$	to sell	tɕʰi˧-bi˦	tɕʰi˧-dzɯ˦	tɕʰi˧-hõ˦	M
M$_c$	pv˧$_c$	to chant	pv˧-bi˦	pv˧-dzɯ˦	pv˧-hõ˦	M
L$_a$	bæ˩$_a$	to sweep	bæ˩-bi˩	bæ˩-dzɯ˩	bæ˩-hõ˩	L
L$_b$	ʐwɤ˩$_b$	to speak	ʐwɤ˩-bi˩	ʐwɤ˩-dzɯ˩	ʐwɤ˩-hõ˩	L
MH	lɑ˦	to strike	lɑ˧-bi˦	lɑ˧-dzɯ˦	lɑ˧-hõ˦	H#

Table 6.21: Tone patterns of V +IMMEDIATE FUTURE+ CAUSATIVE+COPULA.

tone	example	meaning	-bi˦-tsæ˦-ɲi˩
H	dzɯ˦	to eat	dzɯ˦-bi˦-tsæ˦-ɲi˩
M$_a$	hwæ˧$_a$	to buy	hwæ˧-bi˦-tsæ˦-ɲi˩
M$_b$	tɕʰi˧$_b$	to sell	tɕʰi˧-bi˦-tsæ˦-ɲi˩
M$_c$	pv˧$_c$	to chant	pv˧-bi˦-tsæ˦-ɲi˩
L$_a$	bæ˩$_a$	to sweep	bæ˩-bi˩-tsæ˦-ɲi˩ (‡ bæ˩-bi˩-tsæ˩-ɲi˩)
L$_b$	ʐwɤ˩$_b$	to speak	ʐwɤ˩-bi˩-tsæ˦-ɲi˩ (‡ ʐwɤ˩-bi˩-tsæ˩-ɲi˩)
MH	lɑ˦	to strike	lɑ˧-bi˦-tsæ˦-ɲi˩ (‡ lɑ˧-bi˦-tsæ˦-ɲi˩)

M tone. The underlying tone category leading to the realizations /lɑ˧-bi˦/ 'will strike' and /lɑ˧-bi˦-tsæ˦/ (not ‡ lɑ˧-bi˦-tsæ˩) 'cause to strike' is interpreted as H#.

It is reassuring to be able to report that these M-tone morphemes have the same behaviour when preceded by the negation prefix, /mɤ˦-/, e.g. in /V mɤ˦-bi˦/ 'is not going to V', /V mɤ˦-do˦/ 'ought not to V', and /V mɤ˦-zo˦/ 'must not V'. Table 6.22 shows examples with /V mɤ˦-bi˦/, and also with an added perfective, /-ze˦/. M-tone morphemes are not without complexities, however. The verb /mæ˦/ 'to achieve' carries M tone; but when it appears in serial verb constructions, where it indicates that an action achieved its goal, its behaviour is not fully identical to that of the M-tone morphemes in Table 6.20. The perfective, /-ze˦/, has the same tonal behaviour as /-mæ˦/. The behaviour of these two morphemes is recapitulated in Table 6.23. The tone patterns are in most respects like

Table 6.22: Tone patterns of V+NEGATION prefix+IMMEDIATE FUTURE.

tone	example	meaning	V NEG-IMM_FUT	V NEG-IMM_FUT-PFV
H	dzɯ˧˥	to eat	dzɯ˧˥ mɤ˧-bi˧	dzɯ˧˥ mɤ˧-bi˧-ze˩
M_a	hwæ˧$_a$	to buy	hwæ˧ mɤ˧-bi˧	hwæ˧ mɤ˧-bi˧-ze˧
M_b	tɕʰi˧$_b$	to sell	tɕʰi˧ mɤ˧-bi˧	tɕʰi˧ mɤ˧-bi˧-ze˧
M_c	pγ˧$_c$	to chant	pγ˧ mɤ˧-bi˧	pγ˧ mɤ˧-bi˧-ze˧
L_a	bæ˩$_a$	to sweep	bæ˩ mɤ˩-bi˩	bæ˩ mɤ˩-bi˩-ze˩
L_b	ʐwɤ˩$_b$	to speak	ʐwɤ˩ mɤ˩-bi˩	ʐwɤ˩ mɤ˩-bi˩-ze˩
MH	lɑ˧˥	to strike	lɑ˧ mɤ˧-bi˧	lɑ˧ mɤ˧-bi˧-ze˩

the M-tone morphemes in Table 6.20, but the pattern after a H-tone verb is M.L and not M.M. This justifies setting up a distinct tone category, distinguishing between M_a tone and M_b tone for postverbal morphemes. In the case of classifiers – about which see Chapter 4 –, a total of nine tonal categories came to light. It would not be particularly surprising to have to set up a comparable number of categories for affixes. In view of the greater morphosyntactic diversity of affixes as compared with classifiers, the number could even be higher. Obviously, the added subscript letters are simply a means of classifying: they do not reflect an analysis of the categories. An analysis would be better conducted with a fuller inventory of morphemes; it should be borne in mind that the current size of the dictionary (Michaud 2015a) is on the order of 3,000 words, i.e. only a small part of the full richness of the language's lexicon. In the present chapter, the postverbal morphemes are simply arranged into broad classes (L, M, H, and MH), reporting the encountered internal diversity of these classes, and setting up provisional subclasses, such as M_a and M_b. Subclasses M_a and M_b of M-tone postverbal morphemes contain the following items:

- M_a tone: IMPERATIVE /-hõ˧$_a$/, IMMEDIATE FUTURE /-bi˧$_a$/, EXPERIENTIAL /-dʐɯ˧$_a$/, /-ɖo˧$_a$/ 'must, have to', VOLITIVE /-tso˧$_a$/, OBLIGATIVE /-zo˧$_a$/, and CAUSATIVE /-tsæ˧$_a$/

- M_b tone: PERFECTIVE /-ze˧$_b$/, and /mæ˧$_b$/ 'to achieve'

In the data shown in Table 6.22, the H component found in the lexical categories H and MH (illustrated by /dzɯ˧˥/ 'to eat' and /lɑ˧˥/ 'to strike', respectively)

Table 6.23: The behaviour of postverbal morphemes belonging to a second subcategory of M tones: M_b.

tone	example	meaning	perfective	to achieve
H	dzɯ˥	to eat	dzɯ˧-ze˩	dzɯ˧-mæ˩
M_a	hwæ˧ₐ	to buy	hwæ˧-ze˧	hwæ˧-mæ˧
M_b	tɕʰi˧_b	to sell	tɕʰi˧-ze˧	tɕʰi˧-mæ˧
M_c	pʏ˧_c	to chant	pʏ˧-ze˧	pʏ˧-mæ˧
L_a	bæ˩ₐ	to sweep	bæ˩-ze˩	bæ˩-mæ˩
L_b	ʐwɤ˩_b	to speak	ʐwɤ˩-ze˩	ʐwɤ˩-mæ˩
MH	lɑ˧˥	to strike	lɑ˧-ze˥	lɑ˧-mæ˥

does not surface as such, but it results in the lowering of the perfective morpheme /-ze˧_b/, no fewer than three syllables distant from the verb. The phrase /dzɯ˧ mɤ˧-bi˧-ze˩/ 'will not eat anymore' constitutes one tone group, and the underlying presence of a H tone in this group makes itself felt by lowering the perfective morpheme despite the intervening syllables. The same phenomenon is observed when there is no intervening negation prefix, as shown in Table 6.24.

Table 6.24: Same data as in previous table, without intervening negation prefix.

tone	example	meaning	V+IMMEDIATE FUTURE+PERFECTIVE
H	dzɯ˥	to eat	dzɯ˧ bi˧-ze˩
M_a	hwæ˧ₐ	to buy	hwæ˧ bi˧-ze˧
M_b	tɕʰi˧_b	to sell	tɕʰi˧ bi˧-ze˧
M_c	pʏ˧_c	to chant	pʏ˧ bi˧-ze˧
L_a	bæ˩ₐ	to sweep	bæ˩ bi˩-ze˥
L_b	ʐwɤ˩_b	to speak	ʐwɤ˩ bi˩-ze˥
MH	lɑ˧˥	to strike	lɑ˧ bi˥-ze˩

In these contexts, the perfective morpheme //-ze˧_b// carries different tones depending on the lexical tone of the verb – even in the case of H tone, even though this lexical tone surfaces neither on the verb itself nor on the morpheme that follows it (the immediate future). For H-tone verbs, the perfective morpheme //-ze˧_b// is lowered to L in each of (27), (28) and (29).

(27) dzɯ˧-ze˩
    dzɯ˧   -ze˩ᵦ
    to_eat PFV
    'have eaten'

(28) dzɯ˧-bi˧-ze˩
    dzɯ˧   -bi˧ₐ   -ze˩ᵦ
    to_eat IMM.FUT PFV
    'will eat'

(29) dzɯ˧ mɤ˧-bi˧-ze˩
    dzɯ˧   mɤ˧-   -bi˧ₐ   -ze˩ᵦ
    to_eat NEG   IMM.FUT PFV
    'will not eat'

Tones that are present underlyingly but only manifest themselves in a restricted set of contexts constitute a salient aspect of the Yongning Na tone system. The surface phonological notation of 'going to buy' as /hwæ˧-bi˧/ and 'going to eat' as /dzɯ˧-bi˧/, with the same tone pattern, does not reveal the underlying presence of a H tone in the former phrase. The manifestation of the H tone of the verb is not straightforward: it does not lower a M-tone postverbal morpheme (witness /dzɯ˧-bi˧/, 'going to eat'), but it lowers the last syllable in (28).

The lowering effect of overt H tones is an exceptionless phonological regularity, formulated as Rule 4: "The syllable following a H-tone syllable receives L tone" (§7.1.1). In some morphosyntactic contexts, exemplified by Table 6.22, H tones exert a similar influence even though they remain floating, i.e. not associated to a syllable. Such complexities cannot be summarized through a small set of rules. This state of affairs explains the abundance of tables in this chapter, and in this volume as a whole.

Further data on M-tone postverbal morphemes is shown in Table 6.25, illustrating the behaviour of the progressive /-dʐo˧/. The affirmative particle /mɤ˧/ has the same behaviour. An interesting peculiarity is that a MH contour on the verb does not unfold onto these morphemes. A MH-tone verb preceding these morphemes is realized with a MH contour, e.g. /mɤ˧-lɑ˥ | -dʐo˩/ for 'to strike'. Following the same guiding principle as before, this difference in tonal behaviour requires setting up a third descriptive subcategory of M tones among postverbal morphemes: M_c.

Table 6.25: Tonal behaviour of the progressive, illustrating a third sub-category of M tones among postverbal morphemes: M_c.

tone	example	meaning	DUR+V+PROG: 'is currently V-ing'
H	dzɯ˥	to eat	tʰi˧-dzɯ˥-dʑo˩
M_a	hwæ˧ₐ	to buy	tʰi˧-hwæ˧-dʑo˧
M_b	tɕʰi˧ᵦ	to sell	tʰi˧-tɕʰi˧-dʑo˧
M_c	pɣ˧c	to chant	tʰi˧-pɣ˧-dʑo˧
L_a	bæ˩ₐ	to sweep	tʰi˧-bæ˩-dʑo˩
L_b	ʐwɤ˩ᵦ	to speak	tʰi˧-ʐwɤ˩-dʑo˩
MH	lɑ˧˥	to strike	tʰi˧-lɑ˧˥-dʑo˩ (‡ tʰi˧-lɑ˥-dʑo˩)

6.4.3 H-tone postverbal morphemes

Two postverbal morphemes are tentatively placed under the heading of "H-tone postverbal morphemes": the relativizer/nominalizer //-hĩ˥// and the topic marker //-dʑo˥//. The argument is as follows.

The relativizer/nominalizer //-hĩ˥// behaves in many tonal contexts like the M-tone postverbal morphemes presented in §6.4.2, such as the immediate future /-bi˧/. But the relativizer/nominalizer cannot host the H part of a MH contour from the preceding verb: the result is M.M, as exemplified in (30), contrasting with the M.H pattern found for M-tone morphemes, illustrated in (31). The relativizer must therefore be considered to belong to a tonal category distinct from those labelled above as L and M.

(30) lɑ˧-hĩ˧

  lɑ˧˥   -hĩ˥

  to_strike RELATIVIZER/NOMINALIZER

  'who strikes'

(31) lɑ˧-bi˥

  lɑ˧˥ -bi˧

  to_strike IMM.FUT

  'is going to strike'

In the task of assigning labels to tonal categories, I make the (debatable) assumption that the tone systems of different parts of speech all rest on the same primitives (H, M, and L levels) and on combinations among these primitives (MH,

LM and LH). An argument for identifying the tonal category of postverbal morphemes exemplified by the relativizer/nominalizer as H comes from the hypothesis that this morpheme derives from the noun for 'person, human being', which has H tone: /hĩ˩/.[9] This argument is not decisive, however: as was pointed out above, in the process of grammaticalization, a morpheme enters a tonal subsystem that differs from that of its original word class, and can come to carry a tone that is widely different from that of the original word. Another argument is that, when associated with the relativizer/nominalizer //-hĩ˩//, the adjectives in tone category L_b (such as /dʐɤ˩ᵦ/ 'good' and /na˩ᵦ/ 'black, dark') yield a L.H pattern, as shown in Table 6.26. But this argument is not decisive either: the rules are morphotonological, not simply phonological, so that a H tone in the output cannot be taken as conclusive evidence of a H tone in the input. The existence of a LH tonal category for disyllabic nouns may function as an attractor, funnelling, as it were, various morphological combinations towards a LH output.

Adjectives and verbs behave quite differently in association with the relativizer/nominalizer //-hĩ˩//. The tone patterns of verbs and corresponding adjectives are the same only for one tone category out of five (namely L_a). This comes as a surprise in view of the fact that, in many other contexts, the tonal behaviour of verbs and adjectives is pretty much the same. This could have to do with semantic-syntactic differences between the uses of the morpheme //-hĩ˩// with verbs and with adjectives: the morpheme can be categorized as a nominalizer when suffixed to an adjective, and a relativizer when suffixed to a verb.

The topic marker //-dʐo˩// commonly occurs after verb phrases, as well as after noun phrases. On the basis of its behaviour after M-tone verbs (as after M-tone nouns, which were presented in the previous chapter), the topic marker is (provisionally) analyzed as carrying a lexical H tone. Data on its behaviour in context is presented in Table 6.27a. As in Table 6.25, the MH tone does not unfold over the following morpheme: it is not correct to say ‡ mɤ˧-la˧-dʐo˩.

Importantly, the tone patterns for the topic marker, shown in Tables 6.27a and 6.27b, are different from those of the relativizer, shown in Table 6.26. The tone patterns for the topic marker show stronger surface similarity to those for the progressive morpheme, shown in Table 6.25, which is analyzed as carrying lexical M tone. The only difference between topic and progressive is that, when these morphemes combine with M-tone verbs, the topic marker gets H tone, whereas the progressive gets M tone. The logical thing to do would be to recognize two subcategories of H-tone postverbal elements (H_a and H_b), one exemplified by the relativizer, and the other by the topic marker. But categories containing only

---

[9] About the grammaticalization of this noun, see Lidz (2010: 164, 183).

Table 6.26: The tonal behaviour of the relativizer/nominalizer, analyzed as having a lexical H tone.

word class	tone	example	meaning	with RELATIVIZER
verbs	H	dzɯ˦	to eat	dzɯ˦-hĩ˦
	M$_a$	hwæ˧$_a$	to buy	hwæ˧-hĩ˦
	M$_b$	tɕʰi˧$_b$	to sell	tɕʰi˧-hĩ˦
	M$_c$	bi˧$_c$	to go	bi˧-hĩ˦
	L$_a$	bæ˩$_a$	to sweep	bæ˩-hĩ˩
	L$_b$	ʐwɤ˩$_b$	to speak	ʐwɤ˩-hĩ˩
	MH	lɑ˦	to strike	lɑ˦-hĩ˦
adjectives	H	bi˦	shallow	bi˦-hĩ#˦
	M	tɕi˧	sour	tɕi˧-hĩ#˦
	L$_a$	hỹ˩$_a$	red	hỹ˩-hĩ˩
	L$_b$	dʐɤ˩$_b$	good	dʐɤ˩-hĩ˦
	MH	tʰɑ˦	sharp	tʰɑ˦-hĩ˦$

one item are not immensely useful. The categorization of morphemes as belonging to tonal category L, M, H or MH, as proposed in §6.4.1-§6.4.4 of the present chapter, is likely to require in-depth revision in future, in light of a fuller picture of the tonal behaviour of postverbal elements. It appears too early at present to harden (hypostatize) the freshly established tonal categories of grammatical morphemes into a seemingly neat and tidy system. Yongning Na is replete with morphotonological anfractuosities; the present chapter only constitutes a step towards an orderly inventory and analysis, using "L tone", "M tone", "H tone" and "MH tone" as convenient first-pass labels.

6.4.4 MH-tone postverbal morphemes

Following the same exploratory method as outlined above in the discussion of the "L", "M" and "H" sets of postverbal morphemes, a "MH" set is postulated, likewise based on fragmentary evidence. The abilitive /-kv˦/ derives from the verb /kv˦/ 'to be able to'; this link, together with similarities in tonal behaviour, leads to adoption of the label "MH" for the tone category of the abilitive, and of other morphemes that share its tonal behaviour. Examples are provided in Table 6.28: in addition to the abilitive, /-kv˦/, they are the permissive, /-tʰɑ˦/, and the causative, /kʰɯ˦/. Other MH-tone postverbal elements include the reported-

Table 6.27a: The tonal behaviour of the topic marker with verbs.

tone	example	meaning	V+TOP	NEG+V+TOP
H	dzɯ˥	to eat	dzɯ˧-dzo˩	mɤ˧-dzɯ˥-dzo˩
M_a	hwæ˧ₐ	to buy	hwæ˧-dzo˥	mɤ˧-hwæ˧-dzo˥
M_b	tɕʰi˧ᵦ	to sell	tɕʰi˧-dzo˥	mɤ˧-tɕʰi˧-dzo˥
M_c	bi˧_c	to go	bi˧-dzo˥	mɤ˧-bi˧-dzo˥
L_a	bæ˩ₐ	to sweep	bæ˩-dzo˩	mɤ˧-bæ˩-dzo˩
L_b	ʐwɤ˩ᵦ	to speak	ʐwɤ˩-dzo˩	mɤ˧-ʐwɤ˩-dzo˩
MH	la˥	to strike	la˥-dzo˩	mɤ˧-la˥-dzo˩

Table 6.27b: The tonal behaviour of the topic marker with adjectives.

tone	example	meaning	ADJ+TOP	NEG+ADJ+TOP
H	bi˥	shallow	bi˧-dzo˩	mɤ˧-bi˥-dzo˩
M	tɕi˧	sour	tɕi˧-dzo˥	mɤ˧-tɕi˧-dzo˥
L_a	hỹ˩ₐ	red	hỹ˩-dzo˩	mɤ˧-hỹ˩-dzo˩
L_b	dʐɤ˩ᵦ	good	dʐɤ˩-dzo˩	mɤ˧-dʐɤ˩-dzo˩
MH	tʰa˥	sharp	tʰa˥-dzo˩	mɤ˧-tʰa˥-dzo˩

speech particle /tsɯ˥/. The MH tone surfaces as such after M, in keeping with the general phonological tendency that the M tone does not interfere with following tones. The MH tone is lowered to L after H; the interpretation proposed is that the H tone does not surface as such due to the neutralization of M and H in tone-group-initial position (this is formulated in §7.1.1 as Rule 3: "In tone-group-initial position, H and M are neutralized to M"), but that this H tone is present underlyingly and lowers all following tones to L (through Rules 4 and 5). A L tone on the verb spreads over a MH-tone postverbal morpheme (e.g. //bæ˩ₐ// → //bæ˩-kv˩// 'is apt to sweep'), as does the H part of a MH contour (//la˥// → //la˧-kv˥// 'is apt to strike'), delinking the MH tone on the postverbal morpheme.

The phrase /dʐɤ˩ kʰɯ˥/ ('good'+CAUSATIVE) is in common use as a blessing on special occasions such as the New Year and the rite of passage into adulthood. It could be translated as 'Best wishes!' or 'Let there be good/happiness!' Its L.H tone pattern is also observed on combinations that do not constitute set phrases, showing that it is not an exception. The other phrases in Table 6.28, /bi˧ kʰɯ˩/ ('shallow'+CAUSATIVE), /ɖɯ˩ kʰɯ˩/ ('large'+CAUSATIVE), /tsʰi˧ kʰɯ˥/

Table 6.28: The tonal behaviour of MH-tone morphemes after verbs and adjectives.

word class	tone	example	meaning	ABILITIVE	PERMISSIVE	CAUSATIVE
verbs	H	dzɯ˥	to eat	dzɯ˧-kv̩˩	dzɯ˧-tʰɑ˩	dzɯ˧ kʰɯ˩
	M_a	hwæ˧	to buy	hwæ˧-kv̩˥	hwæ˧-tʰɑ˥	hwæ˧ kʰɯ˥
	M_b	tɕʰi˧	to sell	tɕʰi˧-kv̩˥	tɕʰi˧-tʰɑ˥	tɕʰi˧ kʰɯ˥
	M_c	pv̩˧	to chant	pv̩˧-kv̩˥	pv̩˧-tʰɑ˥	pv̩˧ kʰɯ˥
	L_a	bæ˩	to sweep	bæ˩-kv̩˩	bæ˩-tʰɑ˩	bæ˩ kʰɯ˩
	L_b	ʐwɤ˩	to speak	ʐwɤ˩-kv̩˩	ʐwɤ˩-tʰɑ˩	ʐwɤ˩ kʰɯ˩
	MH	lɑ˥	to strike	lɑ˧-kv̩˥	lɑ˧-tʰɑ˥	lɑ˧ kʰɯ˥
adjectives	H	bi˥	shallow	bi˧-kv̩˩	bi˧-tʰɑ˩	bi˧ kʰɯ˩
	M	tsʰi˧	hot	tsʰi˧-kv̩˥	tsʰi˧-tʰɑ˥	tsʰi˧ kʰɯ˥
	L_a	ɖɯ˩ɑ	large	ɖɯ˩-kv̩˩	ɖɯ˩-tʰɑ˩	ɖɯ˩ kʰɯ˩
	L_b	dʐɤ˩	good	dʐɤ˩-kv̩˥	dʐɤ˩-tʰɑ˥	dʐɤ˩ kʰɯ˥
	MH	tʰɑ˥	sharp	tʰɑ˧-kv̩˥	tʰɑ˧-tʰɑ˥	tʰɑ˧ kʰɯ˥

('hot'+CAUSATIVE) and /tʰɑ˧ kʰɯ˥/ ('sharp'+CAUSATIVE), all have straightforward causative meanings: 'to make shallow', e.g. to cause the level of water in a field to become shallow by decreasing the flow of water sent into it; 'to enlarge', e.g. to increase the size of a farm by adding another building; 'to heat up'; and 'to sharpen'.

Table 6.28 shows that not all postverbal elements grouped under the provisional heading "MH" have exactly the same tonal behaviour. A difference in tone pattern between the causative and abilitive constructions is found in association with L_b-tone adjectives. (This difference has been verified through elicitation, on several occasions; examples are found in Caravans.203 and ComingOfAge2.61, 72, 73, 91, 92.) The pattern is L.MH in /dʐɤ˩-kv̩˥/ ('good'+ABILITIVE), and L.H in /dʐɤ˩ kʰɯ˥/ ('good'+CAUSATIVE). This requires the recognition of at least two subcategories of MH-tone postverbal morphemes. As explained above, it appears too early at present to propose a final inventory. The labels "L tone", "M tone", "H tone" and "MH tone" are used here for a first-pass inventory.

6.5 Disyllabic postverbal morphemes

6.5.1 M.H tone

A first tonal category of disyllabic postverbal elements is illustrated by /-kwɤ˧tɕɯ˥/ 'after; as; because'. This postposition mostly appears as part of a trisyllabic expression: /-kwɤ˧tɕɯ˥-la˩/. This expression is transcribed with a hyphen before the syllable /-la˩/ because this last syllable can be detached from the other two. In texts, out of 140 examples, ten are without /-la˩/, as in (32). (The other examples are Lake3.54, 59, 67, Sister.34, Sister3.133, Caravans.80, 137, Renaming.18, and BuriedAlive2.48.)

(32) bo˩-gʏ˥, | bo˩-ha˥ ki˩-hĩ˩=bʏ˩, | tʂʰwæ˩-ne/ | ɖɯ˧-ɭɯ˧ | dʑo˧-kwɤ˧tɕɯ˥, | tʂʰɯ˧-qo˧ | tʰi˧-dzi˩-kwɤ˩tɕɯ˩, | tɕʰo/ | ɖɯ˧-na˧ | tʰi˧-po˧ tsɯ˥ | mv̩˩.

bo˩-gʏ˥	bo˩-ha#˥	ki˧ₐ	-hĩ˥	=bʏ˧	tʂʰwæ˩
pig_manger	pig_feed	to_give	NMLZ	POSS	boat (loan: Chinese 船)
-ne	ɖɯ˧-ɭɯ˧	dʑo˧ᵦ	-kwɤ˧tɕɯ˥	tʂʰɯ˧-qo˧	tʰi˧-	dzi˩ₐ	-kwɤ˧tɕɯ˥
like	one-CLF	EXIST	as	here	DUR	to_sit	as
tɕʰo/	ɖɯ˧-na˧	tʰi˧-	po/	-tsɯ˥	mv̩˧
ladle	one-CLF.tools	DUR	to_bring	REP	AFFIRM

'As there was a pig manger, [you know,] the thing for giving swill, that was like a boat (=that had the shape of a boat), as [they] sat [in this manger]… it is said that they brought a ladle [with them].' (Lake3.53-54)

Thus, while addition of /-la/ (presumably the morpheme //la˧//, meaning 'and, also') is a well-established habit, the expression can be employed without it. No special nuance of meaning was found, except that the formulation without /-la/ is felt to be more pithy and economical. Example (32) clarifies that the presence or absence of /-la˩/ is not conditioned by the semantic interpretation of the postposition as meaning either 'when; after' or 'because, since': among the two occurrences in (32), both without an accompanying /-la˩/, the postposition /-kwɤ˧tɕɯ˥/ has a causal reading ('since, because') at first occurrence, and a temporal reading ('as, when') at second occurrence.

The monosyllabic form ‡ -kwɤ˧ is not attested in this dialect, even though it is reported in another hamlet of the Yongning plain, Walabie (ʁwɤ˧la˩-bi˩; Chinese: 瓦拉片) (Roselle Dobbs, p.c. 2016).

The lexical tone of /-kwɤ˧tɕɯ˥/ is deduced from its behaviour in association with the adjective /dʐɤ˩ᵦ/ 'good'. The observed pattern is /dʐɤ/-kwɤ˧tɕɯ˥-la˩/, which does not constitute a well-formed tone group (since it contains two H

Table 6.29: The tonal behaviour of /-kwɤ˧tɕɯ˧(-la˩)/, 'after; because'.

word class	tone	example	meaning	V+'after; because'
verbs	H	**dzɯ˥**	to eat	dzɯ˧-kwɤ˩tɕɯ˩(-la˩)
	M_a	**hwæ˧**	to buy	hwæ˧-kwɤ˧tɕɯ˩(-la˩)
	M_b	**tɕʰi˧_b**	to sell	tɕʰi˧-kwɤ˧tɕɯ˥(-la˩)
	M_c	**bi˧_c**	to go	bi˧-kwɤ˧tɕɯ˥(-la˩)
	L_a	**bæ˩_a**	to sweep	bæ˩-kwɤ˩tɕɯ˥(-la˩)
	L_b	**zwɤ˩_b**	to speak	zwɤ˩-kwɤ˩tɕɯ˥(-la˩)
	MH	**la˩˥**	to strike	la˩˥-kwɤ˩tɕɯ˩-(la˩) / la˧-kwɤ˥tɕɯ˩-(la˩)
adjectives	H	**bi˥**	shallow	bi˧-kwɤ˩tɕɯ˩(-la˩)
	M	**tɕi˧**	sour	tɕi˧-kwɤ˧tɕɯ˥(-la˩)
	L_a	**hỹ˩_a**	red	hỹ˩-kwɤ˧tɕɯ˥(-la˩)
	L_b	**dʐɤ˩_b**	good	dʐɤ˥-kwɤ˧tɕɯ˥(-la˩)
	MH	**tʰa˩˥**	sharp	tʰa˩˥-kwɤ˩tɕɯ˩(-la˩)

tones) and must therefore be analyzed as a sequence of two tone groups: /dʐɤ˥ | -kwɤ˧tɕɯ˧-la˩/. In this context, the tones carried by /-kwɤ˧tɕɯ˧/, namely /M.H/, must be supposed to reflect the underlying tone of the expression: a final H tone, i.e. //H#//. As for the added morpheme, interpreted as //la˧//, meaning 'and, also', it receives L tone through Rule 4 ("A syllable following a H-tone syllable receives L tone").

The sequence /dʐɤ˥-kwɤ˧tɕɯ˧-la˩/ 'because/since [it is] good' illustrates the existence of cases in which a rising contour is realized on the verb, and does not unfold over the postverbal expression. A second case in point is with MH-tone verbs and adjectives, e.g. /la˩˥-kwɤ˩tɕɯ˩(-la˩)/ 'because/since [someone] beat [something]'. Variants in which the MH contour unfolds over the first syllable of the following morpheme ((/la˧-kwɤ˥tɕɯ˩(-la˩)/) are considered acceptable, and there is one example in a text (BuriedAlive2.48), but the majority case is with the contour sitting on the verb.

Since contours are only realized tone-group-finally, this suggests that there is a tone-group boundary before the postposition //-kwɤ˧tɕɯ˧// 'as, because'. Such behaviour is not unparalleled in this dialect. For instance, the contrastive topic marker //-no˩// and the word /tʰi˧/ 'then' always mark the beginning of a new tone group. This interpretation would be consistent with the fact that the syllable preceding //-**kwɤ˧tɕɯ˥**// 'as, because' tends to be lengthened – a cue to the presence of an intonational boundary.[10] In early transcriptions, a comma was used to reflect a perceived pause, transcribing e.g. /le˧-tsɑ˥, | -kwɤ˧tɕɯ˩/ 'because [they] rowed' (Lake3.59).

But a difficulty with this analysis is that after some of the tonal categories of verbs, the tone patterns that are observed on //-**kwɤ˧tɕɯ**˥// 'because' suggest that the verb and the postverbal element are part of the same tone group. Spreading of a L tone from the verb onto the following syllable demonstrates that the verb and its postverbal element are integrated into the same tone group.

One possible way of handling this would be to postulate that the division into tone groups is determined by the lexical tone of the words at issue: there would be one single tone group (e.g. /| **hwæ˧-kwɤ˧tɕɯ˥-lɑ˩** |/ 'when [she/he] buys') except with a verb carrying MH tone (or an adjective carrying MH or L_b): /| **lɑ˥** | -**kwɤ˩tɕɯ˩-lɑ˩** |/, 'when [she/he] strikes'. But there are more difficulties here. The first is that some lexical tones leave both solutions open. The MH tone allows two variants, the one with the two morphemes in different tone groups (no tonal interaction: /lɑ˥ | -kwɤ˧tɕɯ˥/) and the other with integration into the same group (the H part of the MH contour associates to the following syllable, and triggers a lowering of the following tone to L, hence /lɑ˧-kwɤ˥tɕɯ˩/). As for the case of verbs carrying lexical M tone, it is simply impossible to determine the underlying division of the expression into tone groups on the basis of the surface tones, because the pattern is /M.M.H/ in both cases, and could be interpreted as made up of either one or two tone groups: | M.M.H | or | M | M.H |, e.g. | **hwæ˧-kwɤ˧tɕɯ˥-lɑ˩** | or | **hwæ˧** | -**kwɤ˧tɕɯ˥-lɑ˩** | for 'because (she/he) buys'. Since the M tone does not exert an influence on the following tone, the surface phonological output is the same in both cases.

Another difficulty is that the situation of the MH tone (for verbs and adjectives) and that of the L_b tone (for adjectives) are different. The tones of the postverbal element are all lowered to L when following a MH-tone verb, whereas they surface unscathed after the rising contour on a L_b-tone adjective. Lowering to L after a preceding H tone level is a phonological rule in the Alawa dialect of Yongning Na (Rule 4: "The syllable following a H-tone syllable receives L tone"; see §7.1.1); the tone rules operate within the tone group, never across a tone-group juncture. The fact that /kwɤ.tɕɯ-lɑ/ is lowered to L after a MH-tone verb (e.g. /lɑ˧-kwɤ˩tɕɯ˩-lɑ˩/ for 'to strike') strongly suggests that the expression /kwɤ.tɕɯ-lɑ/ does not make up an independent tone group. The sequence /-kwɤ˩tɕɯ˩-lɑ˩/ in

---

[10] On articulatory, acoustic and perceptual cues to intonational boundaries, see Byrd & Saltzman (2003).

/lɑ˧-kwɤ˩tɕɯ˩-lɑ˩/ 'when (she/he) strikes' is not a well-formed tone group, since it only contains L tones.

This special situation is analyzed as the result of a stylistic process of emphasis, which became habitually associated with certain morphemes. The analysis is set out as part of the discussion of the tone group as a key phonological unit in Yongning Na (§7.2).

6.5.2 M.L tone

Two categories of disyllabic postverbal elements have a tantalizingly similar behaviour. They are illustrated by the postposition /-ʁo˧to˩/ 'on top of; during' and the adverb /-**pʰæ˧di˩**/ 'as if/it seems that', as shown in Table 6.30. Some examples from texts are shown below, illustrating cases where /-**pʰæ˧di˩**/ is preceded by a verb with H tone (33), L$_a$ tone (34) and L$_b$ tone (35), as well as by a postverbal element carrying MH tone (36).

(33) tʰi˩ | hĩ˧=ɻæ˩-dʑo˩ | wɤ˩ | ji˧kʰv˩-dʑo˩ | mv˧-pʰæ˧di˩!
tʰi˩   hĩ˧   =ɻæ˩   -dʑo˩   wɤ˩   ji˧kʰv˩   -dʑo˩   mv˧
then   people   PL   TOP   again   some   TOP   to_understand
-pʰæ˧di˩
it_seems_that

'It seems that some people understood in the end!' (FoodShortage2.72)

(34) mv˩ tsʰɯ˩-v˩ | qʰwɤ˩-pʰæ˩di˩-dʑo˩ | tʰi˩ | kʰi˧ | tʰi˧-tv˧ tsɯ˧ | mv˩.
mv˩   tsʰɯ˩   v˧   qʰwɤ˩$_a$ -pʰæ˧di˩   -dʑo˩   tʰi˩
daughter   DEM   CLF.individual   clever   it_seems_that   TOP   then
kʰi˧   tʰi˧-   tv˧   tsɯ˧   mv˧
door   DUR   to_support   REP   AFFIRM

'That girl was clever, as it turned out: she propped herself against the door. / That girl reacted smartly: she immediately propped herself against the door [so as to keep the tiger out].' (Tiger.14)

(35) le˧-ʂɯ˧ le˧-nv˩-dʑo˩ | tʰi˩ | hĩ˧ | ɬo˧tɑ˧ | wɤ˩ | dɯ˧-v˧ ɲɯ˧ |
do˩-pʰæ˩di˩ tsɯ˩ | mv˩!
le˧-   ʂɯ˧$_a$ le˧-   nv˩   -dʑo˩   tʰi˩   hĩ˧
ACCOMP to_die   ACCOMP to_bury   TOP   then   person
ɬo˧tɑ˧   wɤ˩   dɯ˧ v˧   ɲɯ˧   do˩$_b$ -pʰæ˧di˩
to_the_side   again   one   CLF.individual   A   to_see   it_seems_that

291

tsɯ˥ -mʌ˧
REP   AFFIRM

'When she died and was buried… apparently, someone close by had seen [what had really happened to her]!' (BuriedAlive2.24)

(36) kʰʌ˩mi˩ lɑ˥ | dʑʌ˧nɑ˥mi˩ tʂʰɯ˩-dʐo˩ | dɯ˩-pi˥ | tʰi˩-kʌ˩-pʰæ˥di˩ mæ˩!
kʰʌ˩mi˩   lɑ˧   dʑʌ˧nɑ˥mi˩   tʂʰɯ˩   -dʐo˩   dɯ˩-pi˥   tʰi˩   -kʌ˥
dog   also heron   TOP   TOP   a_little skilful ABILITIVE
-pʰæ˥di˩   mæ˧
it_seems_that   OBVIOUSNESS

'The Dog and the Heron were rather talented, it seems!' (Dog2.108)

Table 6.30: The behaviour of two disyllabic suffixes analyzed as carrying M.L tone.

tone	example	meaning	V+/-pʰæ˥di˩/ 'as if'	V+/-ʁo˧to˩/ 'during'
H	dzɯ˥	to eat	dzɯ˩-pʰæ˥di˥	dzɯ˩-ʁo˧to˩
M$_a$	hwæ˧$_a$	to buy	hwæ˩-pʰæ˥di˩	hwæ˩-ʁo˧to˩
M$_b$	tɕʰi˧$_b$	to sell	tɕʰi˩-pʰæ˥di˩	tɕʰi˩-ʁo˧to˩
M$_c$	pʌ˧$_c$	to chant	pʌ˩-pʰæ˥di˩	pʌ˩-ʁo˧to˩
L$_a$	bæ˩$_a$	to sweep	bæ˩-pʰæ˥di˥	bæ˩-ʁo˧to˥
L$_b$	ʐwɤ˩$_b$	to speak	ʐwɤ˩-pʰæ˥di˥	ʐwɤ˩-ʁo˧to˥
MH	lɑ˥	to strike	lɑ˩-pʰæ˥di˥ / lɑ˩-pʰæ˥di˥	lɑ˩-ʁo˥to˩

The only difference between the two expressions is found in association with H-tone verbs. This difference is enough to require recognition of the tones of the postpositions /-pʰæ˥di˩/ 'as if' and /-ʁo˧to˩/ 'during' as belonging to two different morphotonological categories. The difference may be one between postpositions and adverbs; it could reflect the internal structure of the disyllabic expressions; or, in the absence of any such synchronic conditioning, it may have to be recognized as a difference between tonal categories, like the various other distinctions transcribed in this volume by means of subscript letters added to the tone (e.g. in the M$_a$, M$_b$ and M$_c$ subcategories of M-tone verbs). This is one of many issues requiring further examination.

6.6 Combinations of postverbal morphemes

6.6.1 Postverbal morphemes preceded by the negation prefix

It is common for a verb to be separated from a following morpheme by the negation prefix, as in example (37).

(37)   … pʰʏ˧ mɤ˧-tʰɑ˩-ɲi˩ ho˩ mæ˧!

   pʰʏ˥   mɤ˧   tʰɑ˥   -ɲi˩   ho˩

   to_take_off   NEG   PERMISSIVE   CERTITUDE   DESIDERATIVE

   mæ˧

   OBVIOUSNESS

   '[I] was not able to take off [the bracelets]!' (BuriedAlive2.88)

One could expect the tonal behaviour of such expressions to be computed progressively ("left-to-right") in some simple way. But as is often the case in Yongning Na morphotonology, no simple algorithm can be proposed that would account for all the data. A telling example is that of MH-tone verbs, such as /pʰʏ˥/ 'to take off'. In example (37), the H part of the MH contour reassociates to the negation prefix, yielding /pʰʏ˧-mɤ˥.../ and resulting in the lowering of all following tones to L (through Rules 4 and 5). When the postverbal morpheme carries M tone, on the other hand, the H part of the MH contour is not present in the surface phonological form, e.g. in /pʰʏ˧ mɤ˧-bi˧/ 'will not take off'. Unfolding of the MH contour does not take place: ‡ pʰʏ˧-mɤ˥-bi˩ is not an acceptable variant. The data is therefore set out here in static tabular form, rather than as a set of rules.

6.6.1.1 M-tone postverbal morphemes preceded by the negation

Table 6.31 shows combinations of a verb, a negation prefix, and a morpheme that carries M_a or M_b tone. The example morphemes are the immediate future, /bi˧ₐ/, and /mæ˧ᵦ/ 'to succeed, to achieve'. Note that the verb used to illustrate the M_c tone category in Table 6.31 is /ji˧c/ 'to come' rather than /bi˧c/ 'to go', to avoid the form /bi˧ mɤ˧-bi˧/ 'am not going to go'. This expression is well-formed, but rather confusing because homophony of the verb and the postverbal morpheme makes the entire expression homophonous with a V NEG-V construction, meaning 'whether [she/he…] goes or not'.

Table 6.31: Combinations of verb, negation prefix and M-tone morpheme.

tone	example	meaning	'am not going to V' (tone: M_a)	'cannot manage to V' (tone: M_b)
H	dzɯ˦	to eat	dzɯ˦ mɤ˦-bi˦	dzɯ˦ mɤ˦-mæ˧
M_a	hwæ˧$_a$	to buy	hwæ˦ mɤ˦-bi˦	hwæ˦ mɤ˦-mæ˦
M_b	tɕʰi˧$_b$	to sell	tɕʰi˦ mɤ˦-bi˦	tɕʰi˦ mɤ˦-mæ˦
M_c	ji˧$_c$	to come	ji˦ mɤ˦-bi˦	ji˦ mɤ˦-mæ˦
L_a	dze˩$_a$	to cut	dze˩ mɤ˩-bi˥	dze˩ mɤ˩-mæ˥
L_b	tʰɯ˩$_b$	to drink	tʰɯ˩ mɤ˩-bi˥	tʰɯ˩ mɤ˩-mæ˥
MH	tʰæ˧˥	to bite	tʰæ˦ mɤ˦-bi˦	tʰæ˦ mɤ˥-mæ˧

6.6.1.2 MH-tone postverbal morphemes preceded by NEG or PROHIB

This paragraph presents three constructions that share the same tone patterns: /V mɤ˦-tʰɑ˥/, V-NEG-PERMISSIVE: '[one] must not V'; /V mɤ˦-kʰɯ˥/, V-NEG-CAUS: 'not to let [someone] V'; and /V tʰɑ˦-kʰɯ˥/, V-PROHIB-CAUS: 'do not cause to V', 'do not let [someone] V'. Examples from texts include (38)-(40).

(38) le˦-ʂɯ˦-dʐo˦, | dʑi˦hỹ˥ | mv˦ mɤ˦-kʰɯ˥! |
le˦- ʂɯ˦ -dʐo˦ dʑi˦hỹ˥$ mv˦ mɤ˦- -kʰɯ˥
ACCOMP to_die PROG clothes to_put_on NEG CAUS
'When someone dies, [we] do not clothe [the corpse]!' (BuriedAlive3.58)

(39) so˦ɲi˩-so˩hã˥ | qæ˥ | -dʐo˩ | tʰi˥, | le˦-qæ˥, | mv˩-mɤ˩-tʰɑ˥!
so˦ɲi˩-so˩hã˥ qæ˥ -dʐo˥ tʰi˥ le˦- qæ˥
3_days_and_nights to_burn TOP then ACCOMP to_burn
mv˩ mɤ˦- -tʰɑ˥
to_consume/to_burn_up NEG possible
'The corpse was burnt [on the pyre] for three days and three nights, but it was not possible to burn it up!' (Sister3.93)

(40) ʂæ˦dæ˦ | di˩-tʰɑ˩-kʰɯ˥!
ʂæ˦dæ˦ di˩$_a$ -tʰɑ˥ -kʰɯ˥
differences_in_length EXIST PROHIB CAUS
'[The tree trunks] must not be different lengths! / There must not be differences in length!' (Housebuilding.19. Context: selecting trees that will be felled as lumber for building a house.)

The data for all tone categories of nouns is shown in Tables 6.32 and 6.33, bringing out the full identity among the tone patterns for the three constructions.

Table 6.32: The tone patterns of /V mɤ˧-tʰɑ˥/ '[one] must not V' and /V tʰɑ˧-kʰɯ˥/ 'do not let [someone] V/do not cause to V'.

tone	example	meaning	'[one] must not V'	'do not cause to V'
H	dzɯ˥	to eat	dzɯ˧ mɤ˧-tʰɑ˩	dzɯ˧ tʰɑ˧-kʰɯ˩
Mₐ	hwæ˧ₐ	to buy	hwæ˧ mɤ˧-tʰɑ˥	hwæ˧ tʰɑ˧-kʰɯ˥
M_b	tɕʰi˧_b	to sell	tɕʰi˧ mɤ˧-tʰɑ˥	tɕʰi˧ tʰɑ˧-kʰɯ˥
M_c	bi˧_c	to go	bi˧ mɤ˧-tʰɑ˥	bi˧ tʰɑ˧-kʰɯ˥
Lₐ	dze˩ₐ	to cut	dze˩ mɤ˩-tʰɑ˥	dze˩ tʰɑ˩-kʰɯ˥
L_b	tʰɯ˩_b	to drink	tʰɯ˩ mɤ˩-tʰɑ˥	tʰɯ˩ tʰɑ˩-kʰɯ˥
MH	tʰæ˥	to bite	tʰæ˧ mɤ˥-tʰɑ˩	tʰæ˧ tʰɑ˥-kʰɯ˩

The tones for V/ADJ-NEG-ABILITIVE, /V mɤ˧-ky˥/ '[one] cannot V', are entirely identical with those for /V mɤ˧-tʰɑ˥/ '[one] must not V' and /V tʰɑ˧-kʰɯ˥/ 'do not cause to V', as shown in Table 6.33, which also includes adjectives.

Table 6.33: The tone patterns of V/ADJ+NEG-ABILITIVE.

word class	tone	example	meaning	V/ADJ+NEG-ABILITIVE
verbs	H	dzɯ˥	to eat	dzɯ˧ mɤ˧-ky˩
	Mₐ	hwæ˧ₐ	to buy	hwæ˧ mɤ˧-ky˥
	M_b	tɕʰi˧_b	to sell	tɕʰi˧ mɤ˧-ky˥
	M_c	bi˧_c	to go	bi˧ mɤ˧-ky˥
	Lₐ	bæ˩ₐ	to sweep	bæ˩ mɤ˩-ky˥
	L_b	ʐwɤ˩_b	to speak	ʐwɤ˩ mɤ˩-ky˥
	MH	lɑ˥	to strike	lɑ˧ mɤ˥-ky˩
adjectives	H	bi˥	shallow	bi˧ mɤ˧-ky˩
	M	tsʰi˧	hot	tsʰi˧ mɤ˧-ky˥
	Lₐ	ɖɯ˩ₐ	large	ɖɯ˩ mɤ˩-ky˥
	L_b	dʐɤ˩_b	good	dʐɤ˩ mɤ˧-ky˥
	MH	tʰɑ˥	sharp	tʰɑ˧ mɤ˥-ky˩

6.6.1.3 L-tone postverbal morphemes preceded by negation prefix

Table 6.34: The tone patterns of the construction /V mɤ˧-ho˩/ 'will not V'.

tone	example	meaning	'will not V'
H	dzɯ˥	to eat	dzɯ˧ mɤ˧-ho˥
M$_a$	hwæ˧$_a$	to buy	hwæ˧ mɤ˧-ho˩
M$_b$	tɕʰi˧$_b$	to sell	tɕʰi˧ mɤ˧-ho˩
M$_c$	bi˧$_c$	to go	bi˧ mɤ˧-ho˩
L$_a$	dze˩$_a$	to cut	dze˩ mɤ˥-ho˥
L$_b$	tʰɯ˩$_b$	to drink	tʰɯ˩ mɤ˩-ho˥
MH	tʰæ˩	to bite	tʰæ˧ mɤ˧-ho˥

The data concerning L-tone postverbal morphemes preceded by the negation prefix is set out in Table 6.34. In the expressions in Table 6.34, the verb is in initial position; following an exceptionless phonological rule stated in §7.1.1 as Rule 3, "in tone-group-initial position, H and M are neutralized to M", the verb can only receive one of two tones: L or M. Thus L-tone verbs appear with their lexical L tone, and all others (M, H and MH) surface with M tone.

Tone assignment on the second and third syllables cannot be summarized in terms of a set of phonological rules. Some data subsets show regularities, however. When the verb that constitutes the first syllable of the expression has M tone, the third morpheme (that following the negation prefix) surfaces with its lexical tone, i.e. the last morpheme's tone is unchanged. For instance, the MH-tone abilitive /-kv˩/ carries MH tone in /hwæ˧ mɤ˧-kv˩/ 'cannot buy', and the L-tone desiderative /-ho˩/ carries L tone in /hwæ˧ mɤ˧-ho˩/ 'will not buy'. This relates to the tendency for M to behave as a neutral tone: M tone does not place any restriction on the tonal level that follows.

When the initial morpheme has H tone, on the other hand, this H tone precludes H tone on any of the syllables that follow, even though it does not surface as such. This results in the replacement of a following MH tone by L, hence /dzɯ˧ mɤ˧-kv˩/ 'cannot eat', not ‡ dzɯ˧ mɤ˧-kv˩. It would theoretically be possible for the H part of the MH contour of the third morpheme to be deleted, yielding ‡ dzɯ˧ mɤ˧-kv˧. But the data suggests that Yongning Na treats lexical tones as unitary in this respect: either the MH tone is compatible with what precedes, and it surfaces; or it is not, and it is lowered to L.

As for the cases where the initial morpheme has L tone, it is an open question why the L tone does not spread all the way to the third syllable, yielding //†dzeɻ mʁɻ-tʰaɻ// 'one must not cut' (which would be realized on the surface as /†dzeɻ mʁɻ-tʰa˦/, through the application of Rule 7: "If a tone group only contains L tones, a post-lexical H tone is added to its last syllable"). It does not seem to be the case that the H tone observed in /dzeɻ mʁɻ-tʰa˦/ is what remains of the MH lexical tone after its initial portion (M) is removed: such a process of truncation of the first portion of a MH tone is unattested anywhere else in the language. Rather, it looks as if the MH tone of the third syllable were deleted by a morphotonological rule, leaving it toneless, at which point phonology takes over: Rule 7 results in assignment of a H tone to the toneless syllable.

6.6.2 Postverbal morphemes preceded by the interrogative particle: Tonal oppositions are neutralized

The interrogative particle is analyzed as carrying L tone. The data in Table 6.35 reveals a complete neutralization of tonal oppositions on the morphemes placed after the interrogative particle. The three morphemes shown in the table have different tones: the immediate future /-bi˧$_a$/ has M_a tone; the desiderative /-ho˧/ has L tone; and the permissive /-tʰa˦/ has MH tone. The tone patterns for /mæ˧$_b$/, 'to manage to', are entirely identical. (They are not shown in Table 6.35.)

Table 6.35: The tone patterns for V+INTERROGATIVE+postverbal morpheme.

tone	example	meaning	'going to V?'	'will V?'	'can V?'
H	dzɯ˦	to eat	dzɯ˧ ə˧-bi˧	dzɯ˧ ə˧-ho˧	dzɯ˧ ə˧-tʰa˧
M_a	hwæ˧$_a$	to buy	hwæ˧ ə˧-bi˦	hwæ˧ ə˧-ho˦	hwæ˧ ə˧-tʰa˦
M_b	tɕʰi˧$_b$	to sell	tɕʰi˧ ə˧-bi˦	tɕʰi˧ ə˧-ho˦	tɕʰi˧ ə˧-tʰa˦
M_c	bi˧$_c$	to go	bi˧ ə˧-bi˦	bi˧ ə˧-ho˦	bi˧ ə˧-tʰa˦
L_a	dze˧$_a$	to cut	dze˧ ə˧-bi˦	dze˧ ə˧-ho˦	dze˧ ə˧-tʰa˦
L_b	tʰɯ˧$_b$	to drink	tʰɯ˧ ə˧-bi˦	tʰɯ˧ ə˧-ho˦	tʰɯ˧ ə˧-tʰa˦
MH	tʰæ˦	to bite	tʰæ˧ ə˦-bi˧	tʰæ˧ ə˦-ho˧	tʰæ˧ ə˦-tʰa˧

6.7 Morphemes surrounding adjectives

6.7.1 Addition of reduplicated suffixes to adjectives

Although adjectives behave in the same way as verbs in many respects (i.e. as stative verbs), as explained in §6.1.3, they do not reduplicate in the same way. Adjectives are intensified by suffixation of a reduplicated syllable that does not carry any meaning of its own. In some cases, the monosyllabic form of the adjective has fallen into disuse: for instance, /bæ˩-lɑ˩~lɑ˥/ 'limp, flabby (e.g. of meat without bones)' and /bæ˩-ʁwæ˩~ʁwæ˥/ 'loose (of knot)' point to a monosyllabic adjective *bæ˩ 'loose, limp', but in the present state of the language this root is not attested on its own. Another lexical peculiarity is that some such expressions have shorter variants: for instance, 'short (of persons)', /to˩tʉ˩~tʉ˥/, has a variant /to˩tʉ˩/. Comparison with closely related dialects will be necessary to verify whether the disyllable is a shortened version of the trisyllable: it might also be that a disyllabic adjective /to˩tʉ˩/ underwent expressive reduplication of its second syllable. Evidence from other dialects would also be necessary to find out what was the lexical tone of the monosyllabic root from which the longer expressions are derived. All the examples of expressions made up of an adjective and reduplicated suffix observed so far carry the same tone pattern (L.L.H), but there are too few examples to tell whether this is a morphotonological hallmark of ADJ+*reduplicated suffix* expressions, or mere coincidence.

6.7.2 Demonstrative and intensive constructions

In Yongning Na, in addition to the construction with the relativizer /-hĩ˥/, adjectives are often used in demonstrative or intensive constructions such as (41).

(41)   tsʰʉ˧-_____-gʏ˧
      tsʰʉ˧   _____   gʏ˧
      DEM.PROX *target adjective* to_be/to_become
      'thus ADJ' (e.g. 'thus big', 'thus thick')

The morpheme /gʏ˧/, grammaticalized from a verb meaning 'to be; to become', indicates the degree of a quality, as exemplified in (42).

(42)   tsʰʉ˧ | no˧ | ɲi˧gʏ˧ | ʂwæ˧ mɤ˧-gʏ˧.
      tsʰʉ˧ no˩ ɲi˧gʏ#˩ ʂwæ˧ mɤ˧- gʏ˧
      3SG   2SG nose   tall   NEG to_be/to_become
      'Her nose is not as prominent as yours.' (Source: field notes.)

In the demonstrative construction 'thus ADJ', all tonal oppositions on the adjective are neutralized, as shown in Table 6.36. Examples are found in narratives, e.g. Sister.28 and BuriedAlive3.144.

Table 6.36: Demonstrative construction /tsʰɯ˧-ADJ-gv˧/ 'thus ADJ'.

tone	example	meaning	'thus ADJ'	meaning	tone pattern
H	ɖæ˥	short	tsʰɯ˧-ɖæ˧-gv˧	thus short	M.M.M
M	hwɤ˧	broad	tsʰɯ˧-hwɤ˧-gv˧	thus broad	M.M.M
L$_a$	tɕi˩$_a$	short	tsʰɯ˧-tɕi˧-gv˧	thus short	M.M.M
MH	ɬo˧˥	deep	tsʰɯ˧-ɬo˧-gv˧	thus deep	M.M.M

The same M...M tone pattern is observed in cases where the adjective is reduplicated, e.g. /tsʰɯ˧-ɖɯ˧~ɖɯ˧-gv˧/ 'thus big' (Agriculture.55), from /ɖɯ˩$_a$/ 'big' (see also FoodShortage.43, 85).[11]

Tonal oppositions are likewise neutralized in the construction 'as ADJ (as)', /tʰɑ˧-REDUPLICATED ADJ-gv˩/, shown in Table 6.37.

Table 6.37: Tone patterns in the construction 'as ADJ as'.

tone	example	meaning	'as ADJ as'	meaning	tone pattern
H	ɖæ˥	short	tʰɑ˧-ɖæ˥~ɖæ˩-gv˩	as short as	M.H.L.L
M	hwɤ˧	broad	tʰɑ˧-hwɤ˥~hwɤ˩-gv˩	as broad as	M.H.L.L
L$_a$	tɕi˩$_a$	short	tʰɑ˧-tɕi˥~tɕi˩-gv˩	as short as	M.H.L.L
MH	ɬo˧˥	deep	tʰɑ˧-ɬo˥~ɬo˩-gv˩	as deep as	M.H.L.L

In contrast to the data in Tables 6.36 and 6.37, tonal oppositions are not fully neutralized in the construction in (43), which means 'thus ADJ', much like (41).[12] As shown in Table 6.38, adjectives of MH lexical tone category stand out by their distinct tone pattern in (43): M.M.H, vs. M.M.M for all other tone categories of adjectives.

---

[11] Related constructions include: DEM+ADJ+AUGMENTATIVE /-mi˩/, e.g. /tsʰɯ˧-ʂwæ˧-mi˧-zo˥/ 'thus tall', where /-zo/ is an adverbializer (Dog.12), and the intensive construction /qʰɑ˧- ADJ -mi˧/ 'so ADJ', e.g. /qʰɑ˧-ɖɯ˧-mi˧-hĩ˧/ 'thus huge, extremely big' (Lake3.28), where /-hĩ˥/ is the relativizer/nominalizer.

[12] The analysis of the morpheme /-i̯˩/ in (43) remains uncertain: it may be the inceptive/inchoative morpheme //-i̯˧//.

(43) tsʰɯ˧-_____-i˧˥
  tsʰɯ˧   _____   i˧˥
  DEM.PROX target adjective INCEPTIVE?
 'thus ADJ' (e.g. 'thus big', 'thus thick')

Table 6.38: Tone patterns in the construction /tsʰɯ˧-ADJ-i˧˥/ 'thus ADJ'.

tone	example	meaning	'thus ADJ'	meaning	tone pattern
H	bv˥	thick	tsʰɯ˧-bv˧-i˧˥	thus thick	M.M.M
M	fv˧	happy	tsʰɯ˧-fv˧-i˧˥	thus happy	M.M.M
L$_a$	ɖɯ˩$_a$	large	tsʰɯ˧-ɖɯ˧-i˧˥	thus large	M.M.M
MH	hæ˧˥	supple	tsʰɯ˧-hæ˧-i˥	thus supple	M.M.H

6.8 Object followed by non-prefixed verb

Cross-linguistically, the object is the nominal argument that has strongest syntactic association to the verb. Their tie is so strong that it has even been used as a defining property of the notion of object (Creissels 1991: 38). From a morphotonological point of view, it is reasonable to hypothesize that there will be at least as much tonal change in the association of an object and a verb as in the association of a subject and a verb (studied below, §6.10).

The association of an object and a verb in Yongning Na could in theory be ambiguous with that of a subject and a verb. In Na, there is no indexing of the subject or object on verbs, no case marking, and no fixed position of the subject and object relative to the verb: the verb appears after all noun phrases, except in the case of constituents tacked on at the end of the utterance as an afterthought. The postposition that forces an interpretation of a noun as agent (/ɳɯ˧/) is not compulsory. Different tone rules applying in S+V and O+V could be one of the means to disambiguate, but in practice S+V (without intervening morphemes) is relatively uncommon, and disambiguation is generally effected through context.

When eliciting object-plus-verb combinations, the phrases were contextualized so as to avoid reinterpretation as subject-verb combinations. For instance, the association of 'wolf' and 'to eat' immediately suggests agent role for 'wolf'. A subject noun phrase was therefore added to lead to an interpretation that corresponds to the desired pattern, with 'wolf' as object: see (44). (The added noun phrase does not influence the tone of the object-plus-verb combination, because it is followed by a tone-group boundary.)

(44) lɑ˦ ɳɯ˦ | õ˩dy˦ dzɯ˦-ze˩.
     lɑ˦   ɳɯ˦   õ˩dy˧   dzɯ˧   -ze˧ᵦ
     tiger   A   wolf   to_eat   PFV
     'The tiger ate the wolf.'

A sample of the elicited data is shown in Table 6.39, with nouns illustrating the various tone categories as objects of the L_b-tone verb /do˩ᵦ/ 'to see'. The same results obtain when using numeral-plus-classifier phrases instead of disyllabic nouns. For instance, /ɖɯ˦-bæ˦/ 'something', made up of the numeral 'one' and a classifier for sorts of things, behaves tonally in the same way as disyllabic lexical units carrying the same tone (M), such as /po˦lo˦/ 'ram' and /qæ˦do˦/ 'timber'; and combinations with /ɖɯ˦-kʰwɤ˩$/ 'a piece' yield the same tone patterns as those with /dʑi˦hỹ˩$/ 'clothes'.

6.8.1 The facts

Table 6.40 presents the tone rules that apply in object-plus-verb phrases. Recordings available online include (i) some combinations among monosyllables: ObjectVerb, (ii) a full set, except for L_b-tone verbs: ObjectVerb2, and (iii) L_b-tone verbs: ObjectVerb3.

The notation adopted in Table 6.40 requires disambiguation for sequences ending in a M tone, namely M.M and L.M: object-plus-verb phrases realized with one of these patterns in isolation may have different underlying patterns. Consider (45) and (46):

(45) li˩ hwæ˦
     li˧   hwæ˦ₐ
     tea   to_buy
     'to buy tea'

(46) æ̃˩ hwæ˦
     æ̃˧   hwæ˦ₐ
     chicken to_buy
     'to buy chicken'

The phrases /li˩ **hwæ˦**/ 'to buy tea' and /æ̃˩ **hwæ˦**/ 'to buy chicken' both surface with a /L.M/ pattern. But they yield different results with a following perfective morpheme, /**-ze˧ᵦ**/, as shown in (47)-(48).

Table 6.39: A sample of object plus verb combinations: the verb /doJ_b/ 'to see'.

tone of N	example	meaning	resulting phrase	tone pattern
LM	boʌ	pig	boJ do˧	L.M+L
LH	z̪æʌ	leopard	z̪æJ do˥	L.H
M	la˧	tiger	la˧ doJ	M.L
L	joJ	sheep	joJ doʌ	L.L
H	z̪wæ˥	horse	z̪wæ˧ do˥	M.MH
MH	tsʰæ˥	deer	tsʰæ˧ do˥	M.MH
M	po˧lo˧	ram	po˧lo˧ doJ	M.M.L
#H	z̪wæ˧zo#˥	colt	z̪wæ˧zo˧ do˥	M.M.MH
MH#	hwɤ˧li˥	cat	hwɤ˧li˧ do˥	M.M.MH
H$	kv̩˧ʂe˥$	flea	kv̩˧ʂe˧ do˥	M.M.MH
L	kʰv̩Jmi J	dog	kʰv̩Jmi J doʌ	L.L.L
L#	da˧jiJ	mule	da˧ji J doJ	M.L.L
LM+MH#	õJdv̩˥	wolf	õJdv̩˧ do˥	L.M.MH
LM+#H	nv̩Jtɕʰi#˥	fine chaff	nv̩Jtɕʰi˧ do˥	L.M.MH
LM	boJmi˧	sow	boJmi˧ doJ	L.M.L
LH	boJɬa˥	boar	boJɬa˧ doJ	L.H.L
H#	hwæ˧tsæ˥	squirrel	hwæ˧tsæ˥ doJ	M.H.L

(47)   liJ hwæ˧-zeJ
       liʌ   hwæ˧ₐ   -ze˧_b
       tea   to_buy   PFV
       'bought tea'

(48)   ãJ hwæ˧-ze˧
       ãʌ   hwæ˧ₐ   -ze˧_b
       chicken   to_buy   PFV
       'bought chicken'

Table 6.40 therefore contains information on the tonal realization of a following perfective morpheme, /-ze˧_b/, where relevant: the tone pattern of 'to buy tea', an example of the combination of input tones //LH// (on the noun) and //M// (on the verb), is transcribed in the table as /L.M+L/, and that of 'to buy chicken' simply as /L.M/. The pattern /M.M+L/ is likewise distinguished from /M.M+M/. The tone on the accomplished prefix is preceded by a '+' sign.

In the cases where the tone of the postverbal element results straightforwardly from the phonological rules of tone association of Yongning Na (as recapitulated in Chapter 7), no information is indicated in the table. These cases are the following: when the last tone of the object-plus-verb phrase is /H/ or /L/, /-ze˧ꜜ/ always receives L tone; and when it is /MH/, /-ze˧ꜜ/ receives the /H/ part of the contour.

As in the other tables, a slash separates variants. For instance, for 'has sold leopards' (input: //LH// and //M$_b$//), two variants are acceptable, as shown in (49).

(49) /ʐæ˩ tɕʰi˧-ze˩/ ≈ /ʐæ˩ tɕʰi˩-ze˧/
    ʐæ˩   tɕʰi˧$_b$ -ze˧
    leopard to_sell   PFV
    'sold leopards'

For //L// and //M$_b$//, two patterns are also possible: L.L, and M.M+M, as shown in (50).

(50) /jo˩ tɕʰi˩-ze˧/ ≈ /jo˧ tɕʰi˧-ze˧/
    jo˩   tɕʰi˧$_b$ -ze˧$_b$
    sheep   to_sell   PFV
    'has sold sheep'

If the input is //LH// and //H//, two patterns are also possible: L.L, and L.H, as illustrated by (51) and (52).

(51) /di˩ dy˩-ze˧/ ≈ /di˩ dy˧-ze˩/
    di˩   dy˧   -ze˧$_b$
    earth to_dig PFV
    'has dug earth'

(52) /(lɑ˧ ɳɯ˧ |) tʰɑ˩ dzɯ˩-ze˧/ ≈ /(lɑ˧ ɳɯ˧ |) tʰɑ˩ dzɯ˧-ze˩/
    lɑ˧   ɳɯ˧   tʰɑ˩   dzɯ˧   -ze˧$_b$
    tiger   A   buffalo to_eat PFV
    '(the tiger) has eaten (a) buffalo'

Finally, a note concerning the L.M.L / L.M.MH output (from input //LM+#H// and //L$_b$//): examples include (53), (54) and (55). The consultant expressed a preference for the L.M.MH realization.

(53) /nv˩tɕʰi˧ do˥/ ≈ /nv˩tɕʰi˧ do˩/
　　　nv˩tɕʰi#˥　do˩$_b$
　　　fine_chaff　to_see
　　　'to see fine chaff'

(54) /pi˩ti˧ do˥/ ≈ /pi˩ti˧ do˩/
　　　pi˩ti#˥　do˩$_b$
　　　nugget　to_see
　　　'to see nuggets (of silver)'

(55) /nɑ˩hĩ˧ do˥/ ≈ /nɑ˩hĩ˧ do˩/
　　　nɑ˩hĩ#˥　do˩$_b$
　　　Naxi　to_see
　　　'to see (the) Naxi'

The following paragraphs offer observations about the tone patterns of object-plus-noun combinations, and how they relate to other parts of the morphotonological system.

6.8.2 Object-plus-verb combinations reveal the tonal opposition between //LM// and //LH// monosyllabic nouns

The opposition between the //LM// and //LH// categories of nouns (illustrated by //bo˧// 'pig' and //z̢æ˧// 'leopard') is neutralized in most contexts. Among object-plus-verb combinations, two contexts distinguish them: their association with a M-tone verb, e.g. /bo˩ hwæ˧-ze˧/ 'bought pigs' vs. /z̢æ˩ hwæ˧-ze˩/ 'bought leopards', and with a H-tone verb, e.g. /bo˩ dzɯ˧/ 'to eat pigs' vs. /ɣɯ˩ dzɯ˧/ 'to eat skin'. ('Skin' /ɣɯ˧/ appeared as a semantically more suitable noun than 'leopard' as the object of the verb 'to eat'; but /z̢æ˩ dzɯ˧/ 'to eat leopards' is syntactically well-formed nonetheless.)

6.8.3 About tonal variants

There are interesting fine details in the use of tonal variants. Any L-tone monosyllabic noun acting as object of a L$_b$-tone verb can yield a L.L pattern: for instance, /ɬi˩ z̢i˧/ 'to grab/seize a roebuck', /mv˩ z̢i˧/ 'to grab/seize (a/one's) daughter', /ɬi˩ do˧/ 'to see a roebuck', and /mv˩ do˧/ 'to see (a/one's) daughter'. On the other hand, the M.L variant is only observed for some nouns: it is possible to say /ɬi˧ z̢i˩/ 'to grab/seize a roebuck' and /ɬi˧ do˩/ 'to see a roebuck', but not ‡ mv˧ z̢i˩

Table 6.40: The tone patterns of object-plus-verb combinations.

tone of noun	tone of verb					
	H	M_a	M_b	L_a	L_b	MH
LM	L.M+L	L.M+M	L.M+M	L.M+L	L.M+L	L.MH
LH	L.L / L.H	L.H	L.L / L.H	L.H	L.H / L.L	L.MH
M	M.M+L	M.M+M	M.M+M	M.L	M.L	M.MH
L	L.L	M.M+M	M.M+M / L.L	L.L	L.L / M.L	L.L
H	M.M+L	M.L	M.M+L	M.H	M.MH	M.L
MH	M.H	M.H	M.H	M.H	M.MH	M.H
M	M.M.M+L	M.M.M+M	M.M.M+M	M.M.L	M.M.L	M.M.MH
#H	M.M.M+L	M.M.L	M.M.M+L	M.M.H	M.M.MH	M.M.L
MH#	M.M.MH	M.M.H+L	M.M.MH	M.M.H	M.M.MH	M.M.H
H$	M.M.M+L	M.H.L	M.M.M+L	M.M.H	M.M.MH	M.H.L
L	L.L.L	L.L.H	L.L.L	L.L.H	L.L.L	L.L.H
I #	M.L.L	M.L.L	M.L.L	M.L.L	M.L.L	M.L.L
LM+MH#	L.M.M+L	L.MH	L.M.M+L	L.M.H	L.M.MH	L.MH
LM+#H	L.M.M+L	L.M.L	L.M.M+L	L.M.H	L.M.L / L.M.MH	L.M.L
LM	L.M.M+L	L.M.M+M	L.M.M+M	L.M.L	L.M.L	L.M.MH
LH	L.H.L	L.H.L	L.H.L	L.H.L	L.H.L	L.H.L
H#	M.H.L	M.H.L	M.H.L	M.H.L	M.H.L	M.H.L

(intended meaning: 'to grab/seize (a/one's) daughter') or ‡ mý˧ do˩ (intended meaning: 'to see (a/one's) daughter').

In some cases, it is possible to distinguish one variant that is more common for frequently occurring combinations of words. For instance, with a L-tone object and a LM-tone verb, there are two variants (M.M+M and L.L), but the former variant is more common for the expression 'to drink water': it is customary to say /dʐɯ˧ tʰɯ˧/. The latter variant, /dʐɯ˩ tʰɯ˧˥/, is understandable, but sounds weird. Conversely, the elicited phrase 'to grab sheep' yields /jo˩ ʐi˧˥/. The analysis proposed here is that object-plus-verb combinations with this pair of input tones (L and LM) tend to acquire a M.M+M tone pattern as a result of high frequency of occurrence (this amounts to lexicalization). If this analysis is correct, the reason why the consultant did not choose the variant /jo˧ ʐi˧/ for 'to grab sheep' is because this tone pattern carries a hint that the activity at issue is common – a part of everyday routine. This is slightly weird from a semantic point of view, because grabbing sheep is not part of the consultant's activity as a farmer: there are no sheep on her farm. The M.M+M variant /jo˧ ʐi˧/ could make sense in the context of sheep shearing, for instance, where sheep-grabbing is part of the shearing routine.

6.8.4 Exceptional combinations

Two //LH// nouns, 'leopard' and 'monkey', yield a L.M+L pattern in combination with a //H//-tone verb, instead of the expected L.L pattern, as shown in (56) and (57).

(56) ʐæ˩ dzɯ˧-ze˩ (†ʐæ˩ dzɯ˩-ze˥)
     ʐæ˧˥   dzɯ˥   -ze˧ᵦ
     leopard   to_eat   PFV
     'has eaten leopards'

(57) ʐi˩ dzɯ˧-ze˩ (†ʐi˩ dzɯ˩-ze˥)
     ʐi˧˥   dzɯ˥   -ze˧ᵦ
     monkey   to_eat   PFV
     'has eaten monkeys'

The combination of 'to eat' and 'leopard' is semantically odd, as leopards are predators rather than game, but that with 'monkey' is fine, and the same result was obtained in several elicitation sessions. This is provisionally analyzed as an exceptional pattern: another of the complexities that need to be learnt individually.

In Table 6.40, two variants were indicated for the combination of a //LH// noun and a //M_b// verb: L.L and L.H. For some combinations of words, both patterns are acceptable: for 'has sold leopards', it is possible to say /zæ˩ tɕʰi˧-ze˩/, as well as /zæ˩ tɕʰi˩-ze˩/. But some other combinations have apparently lexicalized with one tone pattern or the other: 'brought in the harvest' can only be /bæ˩ ʂo˧-ze˩/, not /†bæ˩ ʂo˩-ze˩/, whereas 'to eat skin' (with the same input tones) can only be /ɣɯ˩ dzɯ˩-ze˩/, not /†ɣɯ˩ dzɯ˧-ze˩/. It may be that combinations tend to receive a L.H pattern as they lexicalize, as suggested above. Sporadic tone change accompanying lexicalization is well-attested cross-linguistically. Or it may be that L.H is an older pattern, and is therefore more common on lexicalized combinations, whereas L.L is innovative.

Two further exceptions corresponding to highly lexicalized combinations are /kʰv˧ sæ˧/ 'to hunt', literally 'to lead a dog', from //kʰv˧// 'dog' and //sæ˧// 'to lead along', and /mv˧ tsʰi˧/ 'to light a fire', from //mv˧// 'fire' and //tsʰi˧// 'to light'. The productive, regular pattern would yield a M.L tone sequence, not M.MH: /†kʰv˧ sæ˩/ and /†mv˧ tsʰi˩/. The two expressions 'to hunt' and 'to light a fire' are interpreted as remnants of a tone pattern that used to be productive at an earlier historical stage.

6.8.5 Noun plus copula behaves tonally like object plus verb

Data on the behaviour of the copula //ɲi˩_a// after each tonal category of nouns was set out in Chapter 2. It coincides exactly with the behaviour of L_a-tone verbs in object-plus-verb combinations, and not with the behaviour of L_a-tone verbs in subject-plus-verb combinations. This observation about tones provides a strong indication about the morphosyntactic status of the copula in Yongning Na.

6.8.6 Interrogative pronoun and verb

The combination of an interrogative pronoun and a verb is a special case of the combination of object and verb. The tonal patterns are not identical, however: see Table 6.41. Surprisingly, the three interrogative pronouns in Table 6.41, which are currently hypothesized to belong in the same lexical tone category, namely //LM//, show different tonal behaviours. These differences among the three pronouns were checked carefully; for instance, it has been verified that ‡ ze˩bæ˧ lɑ˧ is not an acceptable variant for 'strike which sort [of things]?', any more than ‡ ze˩gv˧ lɑ˧ for 'strike which place?'.

Table 6.41: The tonal behaviour of three interrogative pronouns preceding a verb: /zeɭbæ˧/ 'which sort', /zeɭgɤ˧/ 'which place', and /zoɭqo˧/ 'where'.

tone	example	meaning	which	which place	where
H	dzɯ˥	to eat	zeɭbæ˧ dzɯ˧	zeɭgɤ˧ dzɯ˧	zoɭqo˧ dzɯ˧
M$_a$	hwæ˧$_a$	to buy	zeɭbæ˧ hwæɭ	zeɭgɤ˧ hwæ˧	zoɭqo˧ hwæ˧
M$_b$	tɕʰi˧$_b$	to sell	zeɭbæ˧ tɕʰi˧	zeɭgɤ˧ tɕʰi˧	zoɭqo˧ tɕʰi˧
M$_c$	pv˧$_c$	to chant	zeɭbæ˧ pvɭ	zeɭgɤ˧ pv˧	zoɭqo˧ pv˧
L$_a$	bæɭ$_a$	to sweep	zeɭbæ˧ bæ˥	zeɭgɤ˧ bæɭ	zoɭqo˧ bæɭ
L$_b$	tʰɯɭ$_b$	to drink;	zeɭbæ˧ tʰɯ˥	zeɭgɤ˧ tʰɯɭ	zoɭqo˧ tʰɯɭ
	ʐwɤɭ$_b$	to speak	zeɭbæ˧ ʐwɤ˥	zeɭgɤ˧ ʐwɤɭ	zoɭqo˧ ʐwɤɭ
MH	la˧˥	to strike	zeɭbæ˧ la˥	zeɭgɤ˧ la˧˥	zoɭqo˧ la˧˥

6.9 Object and prefixed verb

When an object associates to a prefixed verb, they can form a single tone group, as in (58), or the prefixed verb may be preceded by a tone group boundary, as in (59).

(58)   baɭlaɭ tʰi˥-mv̩ɭ
       baɭlaɭ   tʰi˧-   mv̩˧$_a$
       clothes   DUR   to_put_on
       'to put on clothes' (ComingOfAge2.37)

(59)   ə˧mv̩˧ ɲɯ˥, | ʐæɭsɯ˧ | tʰi˧-mv̩˧
       ə˧mv̩˧   ɲɯ˧   ʐæɭsɯɭ   tʰi˧   mv̩˧$_a$
       elder_sibling A   coarse_felt DUR   to_put_on
       'the elder brother put on [his] coarse felt cloak' (Sister3.57)

The same stylistic choice is open for numeral-plus-classifier phrases in object position. Example (60) illustrates a case of integration of object ('a bowl') and verb ('to pour'). The length of the tone group is not the reason for separating the prefixed verb from the object as two tone groups: in (60) we have a tone group comprising six syllables, but in (59) if the second tone group were not divided it would be just four syllables. Motivations for the placement of tone-group boundaries are discussed in detail in §7.2.

(60) ʐɯ˧ | ɖɯ˧-qʰwɤ˧ tʰi˩-pʰv̩˩ tsɯ˩ | mv̩˩.
 ʐɯ˧   ɖɯ˧ qʰwɤ˧   tʰi˧-   pʰv̩˧   tsɯ˧ mv̩˧
 liquor/spirits one CLF.bowls DUR   to_pour   REP   AFFIRM
 'it is said that [she] poured a bowl of liquor [for her brother].' (Sister3.41)

When the object and prefixed verb are integrated into one tone group, it seems at first glance as if the adjustment were purely phonological, the computation of tones within the group proceeding from the beginning ("left-to-right"). In example (60), for instance, it looks as if the MH contour on the numeral-plus-classifier unfolds over the prefixed verb: /ɖɯ˧-qʰwɤ˧/ 'one bowl(ful)' plus /tʰi˧-pʰv̩˧/ 'to pour' would be analyzed as yielding /ɖɯ˧-qʰwɤ˧ tʰi˧.../ by unfolding of the MH contour, the H part of the noun phrase's MH contour reassociating to the durative prefix //tʰi˧-// (hence /tʰi˧-/). The final result /ɖɯ˧-qʰwɤ˧ tʰi˧-pʰv̩˩/ would obtain by application of Rules 4 and 5: "A syllable following a H-tone syllable receives L tone", and "All syllables following a H.L or M.L sequence receive L tone". A similar analysis can be extended to almost all cases – but not quite all of them, leading to the conclusion (now familiar to the reader) that in this part of the system too, the adjustment between tones is not purely phonological. The association of an object and a prefixed verb therefore still belongs within morphophonology, although only a small step would be required for it to become a purely phonological process: simplifying the handful of forms that do not currently obtain on the basis of phonological rules.

The facts are set out and discussed in detail below.

6.9.1 The facts

The data is arranged by tone. The behaviour of tones M_a, M_b and M_c is identical, as is that of tones L_a and L_b; the data presented is therefore limited to one M-tone verb (Table 6.42) and one L-tone verb (Table 6.44). The patterns that do not conform with the regularities discussed below (§6.9.2) are shaded in gray.

Examples in texts are abundant: the durative prefix /tʰi˧-/ appears over 700 times in twenty texts, illustrating a broad range of combinations. In example (61), this prefix appears after a LH-tone noun, a context in which it gets a H tone. Other interesting examples are found in Funeral.69, 108, 190, 238, 253, Healing.103, Housebuilding.40, 110, 121, 217, 239, Mountains.7, 88, 161, Reward.40, 73, Seeds2.51, 62 and Sister3.41, 95.

Table 6.42: Objects plus the M-tone verb **hwæ˧a** 'to buy' prefixed by the durative /tʰi˧-/.

tone	head	meaning	hwæ˧a 'to buy'	tone pattern
LM	bo˩˧	pig	bo˩ tʰi˧-hwæ˧	L.M.M
LH	mv̩˩˥	daughter	mv̩˩ tʰi˥-hwæ˩	L.H.L
M	lɑ˧	tiger	lɑ˧ tʰi˧-hwæ˧	M.M.M
L	ʝo˩	sheep	ʝo˧ tʰi˧-hwæ˧	M.M.M
#H	hĩ˥	human being	hĩ˧ tʰi˥-hwæ˩	M.L.L
MH#	tsʰɯ˧˥	goat	tsʰɯ˧ tʰi˥-hwæ˩	M.H.L
M	po˧lo˧	ram	po˧lo˧ tʰi˧-hwæ˧	M.M.M.M
#H	ʐwæ˧zo#˥	colt	ʐwæ˧zo˧ tʰi˩-hwæ˩	M.M.L.L
MH#	hwɤ˧li˧˥	cat	hwɤ˧li˧ tʰi˥-hwæ˩	M.M.H.L
H$	kv̩˧se˥$	flea	kv̩˧se˥ tʰi˩-hwæ˩	M.H.L.L
L	kʰv̩˩mi˩	dog	kʰv̩˩mi˩ tʰi˥-hwæ˩	L.L.H.L
L#	dɑ˧ji˩	mule	dɑ˧ji˩ tʰi˩-hwæ˩	M.L.L.L
LM+MH#	v̩˩tsʰɤ˧˥	vegetables	v̩˩tsʰɤ˧ tʰi˥-hwæ˩	M.M.H.L
LM+#H	ɑ˩mi#˥	goose	ɑ˩mi˧ tʰi˩-hwæ˩	L.M.L.L
LM	bo˩mi˧	sow	bo˩mi˧ tʰi˧-hwæ˧	L.M.M.M
LH	bo˩ɬɑ˥	boar	bo˩ɬɑ˥ tʰi˩-hwæ˩	L.H.L.L
H#	kʰv̩˧nɑ˥	dog	kʰv̩˧nɑ˥ tʰi˩-hwæ˩	M.H.L.L

(61) lwɤ˩ tʰi˥-kʰɯ˩ | tɕɤ˧-kv̩˥ mæ˩, | ə˧ji˧-ʂɯ˥ji˩!
lwɤ˩   tʰi˧-   kʰɯ˥   tɕɤ˥   -kv̩˥   mæ˧
ashes DUR to_put to_boil ABILITIVE OBVIOUSNESS
ə˧ji˧-ʂɯ˥ji˩
in_the_old_times

'One would add ashes and boil [linen thread], in the old times!'
(FoodShortage.71)

6.9.2 Data analysis

The most straightforward cases are presented first, followed by the more complex ones.

Table 6.43: Objects plus the H-tone verb **dzɯ˦** 'to eat' prefixed by the durative /tʰi˧-/.

tone	head	meaning	dzɯ˦ 'to eat'	tone pattern
LM	bo˩˧	pig	bo˩ tʰi˧-dzɯ˦	L.M.H
LH	mv˩˥	daughter	mv˩ tʰi˥-dzɯ˩	L.H.L
M	lɑ˧	tiger	lɑ˧ tʰi˧-dzɯ˦	M.M.H
L	jo˩	sheep	jo˩ tʰi˩-dzɯ˩˥	L.L.LH
#H	hĩ˥	human being	hĩ˧ tʰi˩-dzɯ˩	M.L.L
MH#	tsʰɯ˧˥	goat	tsʰɯ˧ tʰi˥-dzɯ˩	M.H.L
M	po˧lo˧	ram	po˧lo˧ tʰi˧-dzɯ˦	M.M.M.H
#H	ʐwæ˧zo˧#˥	colt	ʐwæ˧zo˧ tʰi˩-dzɯ˩	M.M.L.L
MH#	hwɤ˧li˧˥	cat	hwɤ˧li˧ tʰi˥-dzɯ˩	M.M.H.L
H$	kv˧se˥$	flea	kv˧se˥ tʰi˩-dzɯ˩	M.H.L.L
L	kʰv˩mi˩	dog	kʰv˩mi˩ tʰi˩-dzɯ˩	L.L.H.L
L#	dɑ˧ji˩	mule	dɑ˧ji˩ tʰi˩-dzɯ˩	M.L.L.L
LM+MH#	v˩tsʰɤ˧˥	vegetables	v˩tsʰɤ˧ tʰi˥-dzɯ˩	L.M.H.L
LM+#H	ɑ˩mi#˥	goose	ɑ˩mi˧ tʰi˥-dzɯ˩	L.M.H.L
LM	bo˩mi˧	sow	bo˩mi˧ tʰi˧-dzɯ˦	L.M.M.H
LH	bo˩ɬɑ˥	boar	bo˩ɬɑ˥ tʰi˩-dzɯ˩	L.H.L.L
H#	kʰv˧nɑ˥	dog	kʰv˧nɑ˥ tʰi˩-dzɯ˩	M.H.L.L

6.9.2.1 The tone of the verb expresses itself when the noun phrase has LM or M tone

As observed in §6.9.2 of Chapter 2, M tends to behave as an inert tone in Yongning Na: it does not spread or otherwise affect following tones. The behaviour of M-tone nouns in association with a prefixed verb is in keeping with this observation: when the noun phrase has M tone, the prefixed verb surfaces with the same tones as in isolation. The same is true of LM-tone noun phrases.

6.9.2.2 Tonal oppositions on verbs are neutralized after a disyllabic noun phrase with L#, LH or H# tone

Tones L#, LH and H# on disyllables preclude any tone other than L on syllables that follow within the tone group, by application of Rules 4 and 5: "A syllable following a H-tone syllable receives L tone", and "All syllables following a H.L

Table 6.44: Objects plus the L-tone verb diJₐ 'to have' prefixed by the durative /tʰi˧-/.

tone	head	meaning	diJₐ 'to have'	tone pattern
LM	boJ˧	pig	boJ tʰi˧-diJ	L.M.L
LH	mv˧˥	daughter	mv˧ tʰi˧-di˥	L.L.H
M	la˧	tiger	la˧ tʰi˧-diJ	M.M.L
L	joJ	sheep	jo˧ tʰi˧-diJ	M.M.L
#H	hi˥	human being	hi˧ tʰi˧-di˥	M.M.H
MH#	tsʰɯ˥	goat	tsʰɯ˧ tʰi˧-di˥	M.M.H
M	po˧lo˧	ram	po˧lo˧ tʰi˧-diJ	M.M.M.L
#H	zwæ˧zo#˥	colt	zwæ˧zo˧ tʰi˧-di˥	M.M.M.H
MH#	hwɤ˧li˥	cat	hwɤ˧li˧ tʰi˧-di˥	M.M.M.H
H$	kv˧ʂe˥$	flea	kv˧ʂe˧ tʰi˧-di˥	M.M.M.H
L	kʰv˩mi˩	dog	kʰv˩mi˩ tʰi˩-di˥	L.L.L.H
L#	da˧ji˩	mule	da˧ji˩tʰi˩-di˩	M.L.L.L
LM+MH#	v˩tsʰɤ˥	vegetables	v˩tsʰɤ˧ tʰi˧-di˥	L.M.M.H
LM+#H	a˩mi#˥	goose	a˩mi˧ tʰi˧-di˥	L.M.M.H
LM	bo˩mi˧	sow	bo˩mi˧ tʰi˧-diJ	L.M.M.L
LH	bo˩tɑ˥	boar	bo˩tɑ˥ tʰi˩-diJ	L.H.L.L
H#	kʰv˧nɑ˥	dog	kʰv˧nɑ˥ tʰi˩-diJ	M.H.L.L

or M.L sequence receive L tone". All tonal oppositions on verbs are therefore neutralized after a disyllabic noun phrase carrying one of these three tones.

6.9.2.3 Patterns that cannot be fully explained by phonological regularities

The patterns discussed in the two preceding paragraphs can be explained fully on the basis of phonological regularities that apply throughout the system. This is not true of all patterns, however. The overall proportion is that about three combinations out of four follow a set of phonological tendencies. This figure appears high enough to formulate the tentative hypothesis that these tendencies represent the default case, and that the remaining cases are likely to be learnt individually.

The phonological tendencies are as follows.

(i) Tone //LH// on a monosyllabic noun projects its H portion onto the next syllable, in this case the durative prefix /tʰi˧/.

Table 6.45: Objects plus the MH-tone verb tʰæ˦˥ 'to bite' prefixed by the durative /tʰi˦-/.

tone	head	meaning	tʰæ˦˥ 'to bite'	tone pattern
LM	bo˧˥	pig	bo˧ tʰi˦-tʰæ˦˥	L.M.MH
LH	my˥	daughter	my˧ tʰi˥-tʰæ˧	L.H.L
M	la˦	tiger	la˦ tʰi˦-tʰæ˦˥	M.M.MH
L	jo˧	sheep	jo˧ tʰi˧-tʰæ˥	L.L.LH
#H	hĩ˥	human being	hĩ˦ tʰi˧-tʰæ˧	M.L.L
MH#	tsʰɯ˦˥	goat	tsʰɯ˦ tʰi˥-tʰæ˧	M.H.L
M	po˦lo˦	ram	po˦lo˦ tʰi˦-tʰæ˦˥	M.M.M.MH
#H	z̩wæ˦zo#˥	colt	z̩wæ˦zo˦ tʰi˧-tʰæ˧	M.M.L.L
MH#	hwɤ˦li˦˥	cat	hwɤ˦li˦ tʰi˥-tʰæ˧	M.M.H.L
H$	kv˦s̩e˥$	flea	kv˦s̩e˥ tʰi˧-tʰæ˧	M.H.L.L
L	kʰv˧mi˧	dog	kʰv˧mi˧ tʰi˥-tʰæ˧	L.L.H.L
L#	da˦ji˧	mule	da˦ji˧ tʰi˧-tʰæ˧	M.L.L.L
LM+MH#	v̩˧tsʰɤ˦˥	vegetables	v̩˧tsʰɤ˦ tʰi˥-tʰæ˧	L.M.H.L
LM+#H	a˧mi#˥	goose	a˧mi˦ tʰi˧-tʰæ˧	L.M.L.L
LM	bo˧mi˦	sow	bo˧mi˦ tʰi˦-tʰæ˦˥	L.M.M.MH
LH	bo˧ɬa˥	boar	bo˧ɬa˥ tʰi˧-tʰæ˧	L.H.L.L
H#	kʰv˦na˥	dog	kʰv˦na˥ tʰi˧-tʰæ˧	M.H.L.L

(ii) Tones //#H// and //LM+#H// do not overtly express their H tone, which remains floating, but is not deleted: this floating H tone lowers the tones of the following syllables to L.

(iii) Tone //H$// gets docked on the last syllable of the noun phrase, resulting in a lowering of the tone of following syllables to L, by Rules 4 and 5: "A syllable following a H-tone syllable receives L tone", and "All syllables following a H.L or M.L sequence receive L tone".

(iv) Tones //MH#// and //LM+MH#// project their final H level onto the following syllable.

Seen in this light, the combinations that follow the general tendencies could be described as regular, and the others as irregular. The patterns for //L//-tone verbs are irregular because they contravene tendencies (i), (ii) and (iv). (The behaviour of L-tone verbs is analyzed further in the next section, §6.9.2.4.) The pattern for

313

a //LM+#H// noun and a //H//-tone verb is also irregular: in view of tendency (ii), one would expect L.M.L.L, instead of the observed L.M.M.H: see (62).

(62) a˩mi˧ tʰi˧-dzɯ˥ (†a˩mi˧ tʰi˩-dzɯ˩)
    a˩mi#˧ tʰi˧- dzɯ˥
    goose   DUR   to_eat
    'eating a goose'

The issue of regularity and irregularity in morphotonological paradigms will be taken up again in the typological discussion in Chapter 10.

6.9.2.4 The behaviour of L-tone verbs: Attempting a generalization

L-tone verbs are those that exhibit the greatest proportion of irregular patterns: patterns that do not follow the four phonological tendencies described in the paragraph that precedes. It appears possible to attempt a generalization nonetheless. One way to describe what happens in this particular morphosyntactic context is as follows: when the noun phrase contains a H tone, this H tone moves all the way to the last syllable of the resulting verb phrase, unless it is unmovably fixed to one of the syllables.

This generalization reflects the identical tonal treatment of the prefixed verb after a disyllable with //H#// or //LH// tone. When a //H#// or //LH// tone is lexically associated to a disyllabic noun, a H tone is unmovably attached to the last syllable of the noun. On the other hand, tones //#H//, //LM+#H//, //H$//, //MH#// and //LM+MH#// share the property of containing a H tone whose syllabic anchoring is context-sensitive.

An apparent counterexample to this generalization is //LH// tone: disyllabic //LH//-tone nouns yield L.H.L.L, but monosyllabic //LH//-tone nouns yield L.L.H, as in (63).

(63) mv˩ tʰi˩-do˥
    mv˧   tʰi˧- do˩ᵦ
    daughter DUR   to_see
    'to see (a/the) daughter'

At this point, one may consider that this difference of treatment demonstrates clearly that the morphotonology at play here is irregular, and that the analyst should refrain from devising clever accounts that are more systematic and neater than the facts. The above regularity would then need to be abandoned. Experience in learning and speaking the language suggests otherwise, however, and encourages the investigator to venture some more speculations about how the observed patterns relate to one another.

The different treatment of //LH// tone on monosyllabic and disyllabic nouns could be related to the fact that, although the tonal category is identical, its association to syllables is different for monosyllables and disyllables. When the noun has two syllables, the H part of the //LH// tone is unmovably attached to the second syllable, making this tone category an easy one for the language learner. In the case of monosyllables, on the other hand, for want of a sufficient number of syllables (which constitute the tone-bearing unit in Yongning Na), there is some pressure for the H part to reassociate to a later syllable. In various morphosyntactic contexts, the H part of //LH// does not surface on the noun to which it is lexically associated. To sum up, there is a hard-and-fast syllabic anchoring for //LH// tone when it associates to a disyllable, whereas on a monosyllable its anchoring is looser. Viewed in this light, it does not come as a great surprise that //LH// on a monosyllabic noun should pattern as one of the movable H tones (alongside //#H//, //LM+#H//, //H$//, //MH#// and //LM+MH#//) rather than as one of the unmovable H tones.

This generalization is *ad hoc*, in the sense that it is based on the data for this specific morphosyntactic context. But it does not appear absurd to consider that it has psychological reality, allowing learners to memorize the patterns for tones //#H//, //LM+#H//, //H$//, //MH#// and //LM+MH#// (as well as //LH//-tone monosyllables) all at one go.

Still on a speculative note, this analysis predicts high cross-dialect variation for //L//-tone verbs. Cases that do not conform to regularities (i-iv) as set out in §6.9.2.3 are especially numerous for //L//-tone verbs; the force of analogy would tend to simplify the system by eliminating these irregularities. This is an empirical question to investigate on the basis of data from other dialects.

6.10 Subject and verb

Tonal interaction between subject and verb is illustrated by (64–65). The verb 'to fall' carries different tones in (64a) and (64b), as does the verb 'to come' in (65a) and (65b).

(64)   a. bi˧ gi˧-ze˩.
            bi˩   gi˩   -ze˩ᵦ
            snow to_fall PFV
            'It has snowed.'

b. hiɭ giɭ-ze꜓.
   hiɭ   gi꜓   -ze꜓₆
   rain   to_fall   PFV
   'It has rained.'

(65) a. hĩ˧bæ˧ tsʰɯ˧-ze꜓.
   hĩ˧bæ#˧   tsʰɯɭₐ   -ze꜓₆
   guest   to_come.PST   PFV
   'The guest has come. / The guests have come.'

b. dɑ˧pɤ˧ tsʰɯɭ-zeɭ.
   dɑ˧pɤ˧   tsʰɯɭₐ   -ze꜓₆
   priest   to_come.PST   PFV
   'The priest has come. / The priests have come.'

Subject-plus-verb phrases are relatively infrequent in Yongning Na. This is due in part to the high frequency of post-nominal morphemes and verbal prefixes (which separate the subject from the verb in the linear ordering of the sentence) and, for transitive verbs, to the subject-object-verb word order. When the verb is preceded by a particle, such as the accomplished prefix /le˧-/ or the durative prefix /tʰi˧-/, the noun and the verb belong to two different tone groups, and they do not interact. Compare, for instance, the realizations of the MH-tone verb /qæ˧/ 'to burn' in /my˧ | le˧-qæ˧-ze꜓/ 'the fire burned' and /my˧ qæɭ/ 'the fire burns'.

The elicited data analyzed in this section is based on intransitive verbs, so as to avoid possible confusions between S+V and O+V constructions. Following the same procedure as for nouns, two contexts were used to arrive at underlying tone categories: S+V, and S+V+perfective. For instance, (65a) without the PFV yields /hĩ˧-bæ˧ tsʰɯ˧/ 'the guests arrive'. The tone pattern for this combination of subject and predicate can therefore be described as /M.M.MH/, and further analyzed as //MH#//: a MH contour associating to the last syllable.

6.10.1 The facts

For systematic elicitation, the following verbs were used: /se꜓/ 'to walk', /ʂɯ˧ₐ/ 'to die', /tsʰo˧₆/ 'to jump', /tsʰɯɭₐ/ 'to come.PST', /ʐwɤɭ₆/ 'to speak', and /bæ꜓/ 'to run'. The nouns used were kinship terms and animal names. Table 6.46 presents the results. The //LM// and //LH// tone categories of monosyllables always yield the same output, so they are pooled together in the table.

When the subject-plus-verb combination ends in a /H/ or /L/ tone, the perfective morpheme carries /L/ tone. When it ends in a /MH/ tone, the postverbal morpheme receives the /H/ part of the contour. When it ends on a /M/ tone, the tone of the postverbal morpheme cannot be predicted; in these cases, it is indicated in the table, preceded by a '+' sign.

The recording SubjectVerb contains all of the combinations in Table 6.46.

About one fourth of the tone patterns for subject-plus-verb phrases differ from the corresponding object-plus-verb phrases. Among identical combinations are those where the noun has a //L#// or //H#// tone, since these fixed-position tones lower the tones of all following syllables to L (by application of Rules 4 and 5: see §7.1.1).

As with other types of combinations, such as numeral-plus-classifier and object-plus-verb, the tone patterns in Table 6.46 cannot be obtained on the basis of a set of phonological tone rules. Among the more surprising patterns is //LH// plus //LM//, yielding L.M.M+H, as in /bo˩ɬɑ˧ tʰɯ˧-ze˥/ 'the boar drank'. The noun has a //LH// lexical tone, which would be expected to cause neutralization of all tonal contrasts on the following morpheme (here, on the verb). The five other combinations involving a //LH//-tone noun do indeed yield L.H.L, but that with a //L$_b$//-tone verb yields L.M.MH. This pattern is conspicuously unrelated to the phonological tendencies observed in the language.

In subject-verb combinations as elsewhere, the //L.M// and //L.H// sequences are neutralized on the surface. Notation as //L.H// is interchangeable with //L.M+L//. The former was chosen for the sake of descriptive simplicity: it only requires two tone symbols, and it corresponds to one of the tones attested on disyllabic nouns. (The argument for using //L.H// rather than //L.M.L// as a label for this category of disyllabic nouns was set out in §2.3.5.)

An especially interesting issue is how the perfective acquires its tone after a M-tone verb. The interpretation proposed here is that structural gap-filling in the tonal paradigm has taken place, with far-reaching consequences for the system. This issue will be analyzed in the chapter devoted to the analysis of Yongning Na in dynamic perspective: Chapter 9, §9.1.

6.10.2 Variants resulting from a division into two tone groups

Some deviant patterns are observed in recorded data when the association of subject and verb is, as it were, incomplete: both the subject and the verb receive the tone that they would have in isolation. For example, 'the tiger jumped' can be realized as /lɑ˧ | tsʰo˧-ze˩/ instead of the regular /lɑ˧ tsʰo˧-ze˧/. This amounts to a division into two tone groups, as transcribed by the vertical bar |. There

Table 6.46: The tone patterns of subject-plus-verb combinations, in surface phonological transcription.

tone of noun	tone of verb					
	H	Ma	Mb	La	Lb	MH
LM, LH	L.H	L.M+M	L.M+M	L.H	L.H	L.MH
M	M.M+L	M.M+M	M.M+M	M.L	M.L	M.MH
L	M.M+L	L.L	M.M+M	L.L	L.L / M.L	L.L
H	M.M+L	M.M+L	M.M+L	M.MH	M.MH	M.L
MH	M.H	M.H	M.H	M.MH	M.MH	M.H
M	M.M.M+L	M.M.M+M	M.M.M+M	M.ML	M.ML	M.M.MH
#H	M.M.M+L	M.M.M+L	M.M.M+L	M.M.MH	M.M.MH	M.M.L
MH#	M.M.MH	M.M.MH	M.M.MH	M.M.MH	M.M.MH	M.M.MH
H$	M.M.M+L	M.M.M+L	M.M.M+L / M.M.M+H	M.M.MH	M.M.MH	M.H.L
L	L.L.L	L.L.L	L.L.L	L.L.L	L.L.L	L.L.H
L#	M.L.L	M.L.L	M.L.L	M.L.L	M.L.L	M.L.L
LM+MH#	L.M.M+L	L.M.M+L	L.M.M+L	L.M.MH	L.M.MH	L.MH
LM+#H	L.M.M+L	L.M.M+M	L.M.M+M	L.M.L	L.M.MH	L.M.MH
LM	L.M.M+L	L.M.M+M	L.M.M+M	L.M.L	L.M.L	L.M.MH
LH	L.H.L	L.H.L	L.H.L	L.H.L	L.H.L	L.H.L
H#	M.H.L	M.H.L	M.H.L	M.H.L	M.H.L	M.H.L

are borderline cases, however, without a true division into two tone groups. If the two parts (the subject on the one hand, the verb plus its suffix on the other) were really treated as two tone groups, a post-lexical H tone would be added to all-L groups such as the subject /bo˩/ 'pig' in (66) and the verb phrase /tsʰɯ˩-ze˩/ 'came' in (67).

(66) bo˩ | tsʰo˧-ze˩.
 bo˩ tsʰo˩ᵦ -ze˧ᵦ
 pig to_jump PFV
 'The pig jumped.'

(67) jo˧ | tsʰɯ˩-ze˩.
 jo˩ tsʰɯ˩ₐ -ze˧ᵦ
 sheep to_come.PST PFV
 'The sheep have come.'

Such variants exist for all combinations. When subject and verb are thus separated, it is possible to make a pause before the verb. The stylistic effect is to emphasize the subject. The topic of stylistic options in the division of the utterance into tone groups, which has great importance in Yongning Na prosody, is addressed in Chapter 7.

When the demonstratives //tʂʰɯ˥// and //tʰy˥// appear in subject position, they are always separated from the verb by a tone group boundary, as illustrated by example (68).

(68) tʂʰɯ˧ | tsʰɯ˩-ze˩!
 tʂʰɯ˥ tsʰɯ˩ₐ -ze˧ᵦ
 3SG to_come.PST PFV
 '(S)he has come!'

This is unlike H-tone nouns, which tend to be integrated in the same tone group as the verb, as in /ʐwæ˧ tsʰɯ˥/ 'the horse came', from //ʐwæ˥// 'horse' plus the same verb 'to come' as in (68). The peculiar status of demonstratives was also noted when exploring other nooks and crannies of the Yongning Na morphotonological system (see §5.4.2, in particular).

6.10.3 Nouns plus the existential verb /dʐoL_b/ behave tonally like subject-verb combinations

The existential verb /dʐoL_b/ patterns like other L_b-tone verbs. The association of a noun and the existential behaves tonally like the combination of a subject and a verb (shown in Table 6.46 above). The data is shown in Table 6.47.

Table 6.47: The tone of the existential verb /dʐoL_b/ in association with a noun.

example	meaning	tone	with existential	tone pattern
boʌ	pig	LM	boJ dʐo˥(-zeJ)	L.H
zæʌ	leopard	LH	zæJ dʐo˥(-zeJ)	L.H
la˧	tiger	M	la˧ dʐoJ	L.M
joJ	sheep	L	ɬi˧ dʐoJ	M.L
zwæ˥	horse	H	zwæ˧ dʐo˦	M.MH
tsʰæ˦	deer	MH	tsʰæ˧ dʐo˦	M.MH
ɖʐ˧mi˧	fox	M	ɖʐ˧mi˧ dʐoJ	M.M.L
zwæ˧zo#˦	colt	#H	zwæ˧zo˧ dʐo˦	M.M.MH
hwɤ˧li˦	cat	MH#	hwɤ˧li˧ dʐo˦	M.M.MH
hwɤ˧mi˥$	she-cat	H$	hwɤ˧mi˧ dʐo˦	M.M.MH
kʰvJmiJ	dog	L	kʰvJmiJ dʐoʌ	L.L.L
da˧jiJ	mule	L#	da˧jiJ dʐoJ	M.L.L
õJdʏ˦	wolf	LM+MH#	õJdʏ˧ dʐo˦	L.M.MH
naJhĩ#˦	Naxi	LM+#H	naJhĩ˧ dʐo˦	L.M.MH
boJmi˧	sow	LM	boJmi˧ dʐoJ	L.M.L
boJɬa˦	boar	LH	boJɬa˦ dʐoJ	L.H.L
hwæ˧tsɯ˦	rat	H#	hwæ˧tsɯ˦ dʐoJ	M.H.L

A subtle difference between the existential verb /dʐoL_b/ and other L_b-tone verbs is that the association of other verbs with a L-tone subject noun yields L.L, with a M.L variant for some nouns only, whereas the existential verb only allows the M.L pattern (for all nouns carrying lexical L tone).

7 Tone assignment rules and the division of utterances into tone groups

The present chapter sets out and discusses (i) the rules of tone assignment, whereby surface phonological tones can be derived from the underlying tones, and (ii) the principles underlying the division of the utterance into tone groups, a key unit for tonal processes. One of the first readers of this book (Boyd Michailovsky, who went through the first draft in 2012) pointed out that, to him, the really engaging part of the study was in this chapter, where the archipelago of tables of the earlier chapters gives way to linguistic analysis in the full sense: conveying a feel for the stylistic choices open to the speakers (§7.2-7.3), and thereby shedding light on Yongning Na morphotonology in use.

The unit within which tonal processes apply in Yongning Na is referred to here as a *tone group*. Its boundaries are indicated in transcriptions by means of the International Phonetic Alphabet symbol '|'. Successive tone groups are entirely independent from the point of view of their phonological tones: tones never spread or otherwise influence one another across tone-group boundaries, i.e. tonal computation takes place independently for successive tone groups.[1]

In a model of prosodic hierarchy such as the universal model proposed by Selkirk (1986) and Nespor & Vogel (1986), made up of utterance phrase ⊃ intonational phrase ⊃ phonological phrase ⊃ phonological word ⊃ foot ⊃ syllable ⊃ mora, tone groups may be considered as constituting one *phonological phrase* each. The term "tone group" is nonetheless used here in preference to "phonological phrase", for several reasons. First and foremost, the defining characteristic of this phonological unit is that it serves as the domain of tonal processes.

---

[1] From a phonetic point of view, successive tone groups are linked to one another through a variety of phenomena, from the most local – such as tonal coarticulation – to the most global: in particular, *declination* at the level of utterances and of higher-level discourse units. But these intonational phenomena, discussed in Chapter 8, do not affect the phonological tonal string of the utterance: conceptually, intonation needs to be distinguished from the processes whereby the surface phonological string of a tone group obtains.

Na does not have segmental rules such as the lenition of word-medial consonants observed in other languages of the area, such as Qiang (LaPolla & Huang 2003: 31–32) and Shixing (Chirkova 2009: 12–13), which provide evidence for the phonological word as a prosodic domain. Another reason for favouring the label "tone group" over "phonological phrase" is that, in Yongning Na, two levels are plausible candidates for identification with the level of the "phonological phrase": the tone group, and the tonal phrase, discussed further below.

In Yongning Na, the tone group is the highest unit for tonal computation, and the syllable is the smallest unit: the tone-bearing unit at the surface phonological level. In between these two levels, I propose to distinguish the following additional levels:

- the lexical word, to which tone categories are lexically associated;

- the tonal word: a combination of lexical words, such as noun plus verb in S+V or O+V combinations, and noun plus noun in compounds;

- the tonal phrase: a tonal word plus any added clitics and affixes.

Using the lexical word //kʰv̩˩mi˩// 'dog' as an example, a tonal word is shown in (1): the object-plus-verb combination 'to hit a dog'. A tonal phrase is shown in (2): it consists of the tonal word (1) plus the perfective suffix //-ze˧˥//.

(1) kʰv̩˩mi˩ ti˥
    kʰv̩˩mi˩   ti˩ₐ
    dog   to_tap/to_hit_gently
    'to hit a dog (gently)'

(2) kʰv̩˩mi˩ ti˥-ze˩
    kʰv̩˩mi˩   ti˩ₐ   -ze˧˥ᵦ
    dog   to_tap/to_hit_gently   PFV
    'has hit a dog (gently)'

A different possibility would be to use "prosodic stem" instead of *tonal word*, and "prosodic word" instead of *tonal phrase*. This would clear the way for use of "phonological phrase" instead of *tone group*. But an issue is that the tonal word as characterized here tends to include more material than the "prosodic stem", which "usually coincides with the morphological stem" (Van de Velde 2008a: 17; see also Downing & Kadenge 2015). Therefore, the terms "prosodic stem", "prosodic word" and "phonological phrase" are not used in the present volume. It is hoped that the description proposed here in terms of *lexical words, tonal words, tonal phrases* and *tone groups* is explicit enough to be fully intelligible and translatable, as it were, into various theoretical frameworks.

This chapter starts out from the phonological part of the picture: the tone-to-syllable association rules (§7.1). The discussion then moves on to the topic of the division of the utterance into tone groups, which links up with stylistic issues (§7.2).

7.1 A summary of tone-to-syllable association rules

This section summarizes the tone-to-syllable association rules of Yongning Na. The description is based on the notion of derivation, from an underlying level to a surface phonological level.[2] For instance, the LM and LH lexical tone categories are underlyingly distinct, but when a word is spoken in isolation, the opposition of LM and LH is neutralized at the surface phonological level due to a contextual neutralization of the M and H levels: M and H do not contrast with each other in contexts where they appear in tone-group-final position and are preceded by a L tone. In places where there is potential for confusion between underlying phonological level and surface phonological level, double slashes are used for transcriptions at the //underlying phonological level//, as against simple slashes for the /surface phonological level/. This is visually unattractive, but desperate tones call for desperate measures.

7.1.1 The phonological tone rules

The tone-to-syllable association rules yield the surface phonological tones of a given tone group, on the basis of its underlying tones. Seven phonological

---

[2] The notion of derivation from underlying representations to surface phonological representations is a great help in phonological analysis, to the point that it may not seem to require special justification. But this notion has come under criticism from various quarters: in the view of some authors, instead of derivation, it is more satisfactory to reason in terms of sets of (surface) forms that stand in close relationship with one another. Hyman (2015) concludes from his review of this issue that underlying representations should be maintained as a central tool of phonological analysis. Of course this does not mean that underlying representations constitute an adequate tool for exploring all the questions that linguists may be interested in raising, or that they constitute the final word in phonological description. The ultimate aim is to approach the actual processes taking place in the speaker's brain. When formulating generalizations, such as the tone rules proposed below, efforts were made to keep in mind issues of psychological (cognitive) plausibility. Mid- and long-term perspectives for modelling with more elaborate tools are briefly mentioned in this volume's conclusion (Chapter 12).

tone rules have been found to apply in Yongning Na. For ease of reference, a list is provided first, before the analysis and discussion.

> Rule 1: L tone spreads progressively ("left-to-right") onto syllables that are unspecified for tone.
>
> Rule 2: Syllables that remain unspecified for tone after the application of Rule 1 receive M tone.
>
> Rule 3: In tone-group-initial position, H and M are neutralized to M.
>
> Rule 4: The syllable following a H-tone syllable receives L tone.
>
> Rule 5: All syllables following a H.L or M.L sequence receive L tone.
>
> Rule 6: In tone-group-final position, H and M are neutralized to H if they follow a L tone.
>
> Rule 7: If a tone group only contains L tones, a post-lexical H tone is added to its last syllable.

The following paragraphs explain the motivation for positing these seven phonological rules.

The tone association rules for each of the lexical tone categories have been set out in the course of Chapter 2, e.g. describing in §2.3.1 and §2.3.2 the association of tone to syllables for the three types of High tones: H#, #H and H$. The same rules hold for the tones of more complex entities *(tonal words)* such as compound nouns or numeral-plus-classifier phrases. Unless otherwise specified, the tone pattern associates to the tonal word syllable by syllable ("left-to-right"), one tone level after another. When there are fewer syllables than tone levels, two levels associate to the last syllable.

Thus, L tone and M tone associate to the first syllable of the tonal word. For LM tone, the first syllable receives L, and the second receives M. For LH, the first syllable likewise receives L, and the second receives H. These four tonal categories (L, M, LM and LH) are the simplest in terms of tone-to-syllable association. The other tone categories (#H, MH#, H$, L#, LM+MH#, LM+#H, and H#) all have a specific syllabic anchoring, described in §2.3, and reflected in the special symbols used in the present transcription.

In the case of the mixed tone categories LM+MH# and LM+#H, their first part (LM) attaches to syllables following the usual rules (like a simple LM tone) and their second part (MH# or #H, respectively) attaches as indicated by the added diacritic. Thus, for LM+MH# tone, the first syllable receives L, the second receives M, and the last receives a MH contour. In the special case where only two syllables are available, the MH contour associates to the second syllable, overriding its M tone. In the case of tone category LM+#H, the first syllable likewise receives a L tone and the second a M tone; the H level associates to the first syllable following the tonal phrase, if a suitable carrier is available. (These two tone categories never associate to a monosyllable.)

At this point in the tone-to-syllable mapping process, some syllables remain toneless. For instance, the lexical disyllable //dɑ.ji˩// 'mule', the compound //**po.lo-ɬi.pi˩**// 'ram's ear', the numeral-plus-classifier //gv-ʂɯ˩// 'nine times' and the object-plus-verb combination //dʐ.mi zi˩// 'to grab a fox', all of which have L# tone, are only specified for tone on their last syllable. Tonal nuclei carrying L tone constitute a mirror image of this situation: they are only specified for tone on their *first* syllable. For instance, the noun //v˩dze// 'bird', the compound //kʰv˩mi-hṽ// 'dog's hair', the numeral-plus-classifier //so˩-dze// 'three pairs', and the object-plus-verb combination //li˩ tɕʰi// 'to sell tea' all carry L tone, which attaches to their first syllable. Their other syllables receive a surface phonological tone through the phonological rules set out below.

First, L tone spreads, and toneless syllables receive M tone by default.

> Rule 1: L tone spreads progressively ("left-to-right") onto syllables that are unspecified for tone.
>
> Rule 2: Syllables that remain unspecified for tone after the application of Rule 1 receive M tone.

The phrasing of Rule 2 makes it explicit that these rules need to be ordered: if Rule 2 applied before Rule 1, there would be no tonally unspecified syllables left for L tone to spread over.

Taking up the above examples, Rule 1 yields the following results:

> //v˩dze// → /v˩dze˩/ 'bird'
> //kʰv˩mi-hṽ// → /kʰv˩mi˩-hṽ˩/ 'dog's hair'
> //so˩-dze// → /so˩-dze˩/ 'three pairs'
> //li˩ tɕʰi// → /li˩ tɕʰi˩/ 'to sell tea'

Application of Rule 2 yields:

> //dɑ.ji˩// → /dɑ˧ji˩/ 'mule'
> //po.lo-ɬi.pi˩// → /po˧lo˧-ɬi˧pi˩/ 'ram's ear'
> //gv-ʂɯ˩// → /gv˧-ʂɯ˩/ 'nine times'
> //dʐ.mi zi˩// → /dʐ˧mi˧ zi˩/ 'to grab a fox'

After application of Rules 1 and 2, there remain no toneless syllables. (In Yongning Na, it is an exceptionless observation that each syllable carries tone at the surface phonological level.) The rules that apply next refer to the boundaries of the tone group: tonal oppositions are neutralized in certain positions within the tone group (Rules 3-6), and a repair rule adds a H tone on the last syllable of the tone group if the whole group only contains L tones (Rule 7).

> Rule 3: In tone-group-initial position, H and M are neutralized to M.
>
> Rule 4: The syllable following a H-tone syllable receives L tone.
>
> Rule 5: All syllables following a H.L or M.L sequence receive L tone.
>
> Rule 6: In tone-group-final position, H and M are neutralized to H if they follow a L tone.
>
> Rule 7: If a tone group only contains L tones, a post-lexical H tone is added to its last syllable.

Rule 6 is proposed on the basis of the observation that there is no opposition between H and M on a tone-group-final syllable when the syllables that precede it carry L tone. This also applies to contours: LH and LM contours are neutralized to LH in tone-group-final position. Thus, a tone-group-final syllable following a L-tone syllable can only have one of the following tones at the surface phonological level: L, H, LH, or MH. There is no opposition between L...L.LH and L...L.LM, any more than between L...L.H and L...L.M. In transcriptions, it appeared advisable to adhere to the principle of providing a surface transcription of tone, with no more tonal oppositions than are really present at the phonological surface. This required choosing one of two alternatives: transcribing the product of neutralization of M and H as M, or as H. A phonological reason for transcribing the product of the neutralization of H and M in this context as H (rather than M) was that it appeared more appropriate to represent a two-term opposition by means of the two extreme values of the tone scale (L and H).

An annoying consequence is that, in transcriptions, the same word can appear with a L.M pattern in certain positions, and with L.H in others, even though from a phonetic point of view the realizations may be indistinguishable. The paradox is carried to an extreme in (3).

(3) mo˩ky˧ tʰy˧-ky˩-ze˩. | mo˩ky˧!
mo˩ky#˧   tʰy˧ₐ   -ky˧   -ze˧ᵦ   mo˩ky#˧
meadow_mushroom to_grow   ABILITIVE PFV   meadow_mushroom

'[Starting in the third month,] meadow mushrooms grow. Meadow mushrooms!' (Mushrooms.149)

In example (3), the second occurrence of the word //moʌkỵ#˩// is transcribed as /moʌkỵ˩/, with a H tone on the last syllable, because of its tone-group-final position, whereas the first occurrence is transcribed as /moʌkỵ˧/. Phonetically, on the other hand, the second occurrence is realized *lower* than the first, due to utterance-final lowering.[3] I can't say that I am perfectly happy with this transcription, but it is principled and structured, and the result is unequivocal. Readers are invited to think of more elegant solutions.

Rule 7 ("If a tone group only contains L tones, a post-lexical H tone is added to its last syllable") is proposed on the basis of the observation that there are no tone groups that carry no other tone than L. It is through application of Rule 7 that L-tone expressions receive a final rising contour when spoken in isolation: when the post-lexical H tone is added to a syllable that carries a L tone, this results in a LH contour on that syllable. Taking up the same examples as above, application of Rule 7 is as follows:

/ʋ˩dze˩/ → /ʋ˩dze˥/ 'bird'
/kʰʋ˩mi˩-hỹ˩/ → /kʰʋ˩mi˩-hỹ˥/ 'dog's hair'
/so˩-dze˩/ → /so˩-dze˥/ 'three pairs'
/li˩ tɕʰi˩/ → /li˩ tɕʰi˥/ 'to sell tea'[4]

7.1.2 About the ordering of rules

As mentioned above, the rules need to be ordered. If Rule 7, which adds a H tone to all-L sequences, applied before Rule 2, which assigns M tone to toneless syllables, a sequence such as 'has not come', made up of the negation prefix, /mɤ˧-/, and the verb /tsʰɯ˩ₐ/ 'to come.PST', would have only L tones (/mɤ-tsʰɯ˩/) when Rule 7 applied, and would receive a final H tone (‡ **mɤ-tsʰɯ˥**) before receiving a M

---

[3] For a discussion of intonational factors that come into play in the phonetic realization of tones, see Chapter 8.

[4] At one point, the added tone was analyzed as M (Michaud 2008b). The choice between M and H may seem to be a non-issue, since LM and LH are neutralized in this position. However, the M tone in Yongning Na is not phonologically active: it does not spread, float or otherwise reassociate. A tone rule such as that which affects all-L tone groups is therefore much more likely to involve the H tone than the M tone. In two-tone systems, addition of a final H tone in domains having only L tone is common: it is attested in Lhasa Tibetan (Sun 1997: 498-499), Japanese (Haraguchi 1999: 19), the Bantu languages Matengo and Kimatuumbi (Odden 2005: 415), and Shixing (Chirkova & Michaud 2009). In a three-tone system, describing the added tone as M could cause confusion for cross-language comparisons. For these reasons, the post-lexical tone of Yongning Na is analyzed here as a H tone.

tone on its first syllable (‡ mɤ˧-tsʰw˧). Its realization as /mɤ˧-tsʰwꜝ/ illustrates the fact that Rule 7 applies after all the other rules.

Rules 3 and 4 ("H and M are neutralized to M in tone-group-initial position", and "A syllable following a H-tone syllable receives L tone") likewise need to be ordered. If Rule 4 applied first, an underlying sequence such as //dzɯ˥-bi˧// 'will eat' would have its second syllable lowered to L, yielding /dzɯ˥-bi˩/, and finally /dzɯ˧-bi˩/, by application of Rule 3. The observed surface phonological pattern is /dzɯ˧-bi˧/, with M tone on the second syllable, not L tone.

7.1.3 A discussion of alternative formulations

The generalizations formulated here in the form of Rules 1-7 could also be captured through other formulations. For instance, it may seem simpler to collapse Rules 4 and 5 into one rule to the effect that "H tone can only be followed by L tones". By the application of that rule, all syllables following a H-tone syllable would receive L tone. But a further rule would then have to be formulated specifically for the M.L sequence: "All syllables following a M.L sequence receive L tone". The choice to adopt the present formulation for Rule 5 ("All syllables following a H.L or M.L sequence receive L tone") is based on the intuition that the same mechanism is at play in both cases: H.L and M.L are both stepping-down sequences, from a higher tone level to a lower one. The generalization is that stepping-down sequences can only be followed by L tones.

This could also be phrased as a static constraint: "There can be no trough within a tone group", or "A tone cannot be surrounded by higher tones within a tone group". This would rule out sequences such as ‡ MLH, ‡ MLM or ‡ MHLM. However, such a static constraint would not provide any information on how the offending sequences are avoided or repaired in Yongning Na, whereas Rule 5 is explicit on this point: the tones which would result in such sequences are all lowered to L.

Rule 4 precludes ...H.H... sequences, so the H tone can be said to be culminative. In this light, the H tone might also be analyzed as a HL contour. In the early stages of analysis of the tone system of Yongning Na, I attempted an account in which the underlying phonological entities were not tones, but steps up and down the three-level tonal score: up one level, from L to M or M to H; or down from H or M to L. Proposals in this vein have been made for Japanese, where the fall from H to L can be considered as one phonological entity (which can be called a tonal accent), rather than a succession of two distinct phonological entities (Kubozono 2012: 1399). Under a tonal account, the tonal accents of Japanese dialects have to be represented as a sequence of two tones, which is uneconomical. A "dynamic treatment of tone" was also attempted for Igbo (Niger-Congo family): such is the title of Mary Clark's dissertation (Clark 1976). In the case of Yongning Na, if HL were reinterpreted as a "high fall", ML could be called a "low fall"; LM would be a "low rise", and MH a "high rise". However, the existence of contours on a single syllable argues in favour of a tonal analysis of the Yongning Na system. The dynamic treatment, which was abandoned for Igbo, does not appear promising for Yongning Na either. (This is of course not to say that it may not prove useful for other languages.)

Rule 4 above also precludes ...H.M... sequences. This can be described as a neutralization (to H.L) of the contrast between H.M and H.L.

7.1.4 Implications for the tones of sentence-final particles

In Yongning Na as in numerous East Asian languages, sentence-final particles play a major role in conveying evidentiality and speaker attitude. In tonal languages, these particles can have lexical tone (e.g. in Vietnamese), but there is a cross-linguistic tendency for an evolution towards reduced tonal distinctions or tonelessness (e.g. in Mandarin). The fact that these particles are located at the end of a sentence results in strong intonational modification. In Yongning Na, sentence-final position implies tone-group-final position; this exerts a strong influence on the particles' tone patterns, because the tone of the last syllable in a tone group is often determined by the tones that precede. If the tone group contains a H tone, or a M.L sequence, all following tones are lowered to L, through Rules 4 and 5. For instance, the lexical M tone of final particle //mæ˧// (expressing obviousness) is lowered to L in (4) because all tones following the M.L sequence /le˧-ʁæ˩/ are lowered to L by a phonological rule (Rule 5).

(4) tse˧ tsʰɯ˧ | le˧-ʁæ˩-ɲi˩ mæ˩.
    tse˥   tsʰɯ˧ le˧-   ʁæ˩ₐ   -ɲi˩
    earth   TOP   ACCOMP to_melt/to_fall_apart CERTITUDE
    mæ˧
    OBVIOUSNESS

'The clods of earth fall apart / the clods of earth melt [into the water].' (Agriculture.54)

Example (4) illustrates the majority case. But the final particle can also receive a H tone projected by a contour tone lexically attached to the preceding syllable, as in (5), where the lexical M tone of the affirmative //mæ˧// is replaced by a H tone (hence /mæ˧/) through reassociation of the H part of the MH contour of the abilitive //-kɣ˥//.

(5) ʐæ˩sɯ˩ | -dʐo˩ | tʂʰɯ˧ne˧-ji˧ | tʰi˧-mv˧-kɣ˧ mæ˧.
    ʐæ˩sɯ˩   dʐo˩   tʂʰɯ˧ne˧-ji˧ tʰi˧-   mv˧ₐ   -kɣ˥   mæ˧
    felt   TOP   thus   DUR to_put_on ABILITIVE OBVIOUSNESS
    'This is how we used to wear felt.' (Sister3.74)

It is only after transcribing ten texts, containing more than 150 examples of //mæ˧//, that this particle was finally observed in a context where the preceding syllables did not impose a tone on it:

(6) hɯ˧mi˧-tʂʰæ˧yɯ˧ tʰɯ˥ | le˧-qʰwɤ˧-ze˧-mæ˧! |
    hɯ˧mi˩$ tʂʰæ˧yɯ#˥ tʰɯ˩ᵦ   le˧-   qʰwɤ˧ᵦ -ze˧ᵦ   mæ˧
    stomach   medicine   to_drink ACCOMP to_heal   PFV   OBVIOUSNESS

'[nowadays, the diseased person] drinks medicines for the stomach, and [they] are healed, aren't they!' (Healing.66)

The phrase /le˧-qʰwɤ˧-ze˧/ (ACCOMP-to_heal-PFV) does not contain any contour or floating tone that would associate to a following syllable, and it does not contain a H tone, or a M.L sequence, which would impose a L tone on following syllables. The tone carried by the sentence-final particle //mæ˧// in this context is M. This makes it clear that the particle does not carry a lexical //L//, //H// or //MH// tone, and is to be interpreted as carrying //M// tone.

Likewise, the tone of the reported-speech particle //tsɯ˥// is affected by the tones that precede it within the tone group in a vast majority of cases. In a set of ten narratives, its realization with MH tone on the surface is observed in only eight cases out of more than three hundred.

To determine the lexical tones of sentence-final particles, elicitation proved a valuable complement to observations from recorded texts. Here is an example: that of the final particle /mo˩/, conveying invitation. This particle cannot appear right after the verb, in a ‡V+mo˩ construction. Invitation is expressed as (7), exemplified with the verb 'to eat' in (8).

(7) ɖɯ˧-V-i˧ mo˩
    ɖɯ˧-   V   -i˧   mo˩
    DELIMITATIVE   *target verb*   INCHOATIVE   DISC.PTCL:INVITATION
    'Please go ahead and V a little!'

(8) ɖɯ˧-dzɯ˧-i˥ mo˩!
    ɖɯ˧-   dzɯ˥   -i˥   mo˩
    DELIMITATIVE   to_eat   INCHOATIVE   DISC.PTCL:INVITATION
    'Please have some/please eat some [of it]!'

Table 7.1 shows a set of elicited data. The particle /mo˩/ carries L tone in all six cases. With verbs with H, L and MH tones, this L tone carried by the particle derives phonologically from the tonal sequence that precedes. Within a tone group, a syllable following a H tone can only have L tone (as is the case after H and MH tones); likewise, a syllable following a M.L sequence can only carry L tone. In the case of M tones, however, the preceding tone sequence (M.M.M) does not impose such a phonological constraint: it does not rule out any of L, M, H or MH on the final syllable. The L tone observed on the surface is therefore to be attributed to the lexical specification of the particle, hence analysis as //mo˩//, with lexical L tone.

Table 7.1: The tone patterns of the /ɖɯ˧-V-i˥ mo˩/ construction.

tone	example	meaning	/ɖɯ˧-V-i˥ mo˩/
H	dzɯ˥	to eat	ɖɯ˧-dzɯ˧-i˥ mo˩
M$_a$	hwæ˧$_a$	to buy	ɖɯ˧-hwæ˧-i˧ mo˩
M$_b$	tɕʰi˧$_b$	to sell	ɖɯ˧-tɕʰi˧-i˧ mo˩
L$_a$	bæ˩$_a$	to sweep	ɖɯ˧-bæ˩-i˩ mo˩
L$_b$	ʐwɤ˩$_b$	to speak	ɖɯ˧-ʐwɤ˩-i˩ mo˩
MH	lɑ˧˥	to strike	ɖɯ˧-lɑ˧-i˥ mo˩

7.2 The division of utterances into tone groups

The division of the utterance into tone groups is a central part of Na prosody. Although there are some general tendencies in the division of utterances into tone groups, and a few hard-and-fast rules, there are often several possibilities open to the speaker; different divisions into tone groups have different implications in terms of prominence of the various components. Prominence (conveying information structure) and phrasing (reflecting syntactic structure) interact in the division of an utterance into tone groups. There is therefore no one-to-one correspondence between syntactic structure and the division into tone groups.

Tone groups can have highly different syntactic compositions. A tone group may consist of a single syllable: monosyllabic nouns and verbs spoken in isolation constitute a tone group on their own. Personal pronouns can associate with other words but often appear on their own, as in (9).

(9) njɤ˧ | tso˩-bi˩-zo˩-ji˩.
 njɤ˩ tso˩ₐ bi˧c -zo˧-ji˧
 1SG to_build to_go to_have_to
 'I shall go and build [a bridge].' (Renaming.13)

Tone groups are often longer, however: e.g. compound noun and numeral-plus-classifier phrase, as in (10); noun phrase and affixed verb, as in (11); or numeral-plus-classifier phrase and affixed verb, as in (12).

(10) ə˧mi˧-mv˩ ɲi˩-ky˩
 ə˧mi˧ mv˩ ɲi˧-kv˧
 mother daughter two-CLF.persons
 'the mother and the daughter, the two of them' (Lake4.93)

(11) dzɯ˧-di˧ mɤ˧-dʑo˧
 dzɯ˩ -di mɤ˧ dʑo˧
 to_eat NMLZ NEG EXIST
 'there was no food' (Seeds2.69)

(12) dzo˧ | ɖɯ˧-pɤ˩ tso˩ ə˩-bi˩?
 dzo˩ ɖɯ˧-pɤ˩ tso˩ₐ ə-˩ -bi˧
 bridge one-CLF to_build INTERROG IMM_FUT
 'will [you] build a bridge?' (Renaming.10)

The present description starts with the simplest case: that of morphemes which always constitute a tone group on their own.

7.2.1 Morphemes that always constitute a tone group on their own

Some morphemes always constitute a tone group on their own. They could be referred to as *tonal standalones*. These include the gap-filler /tʰi˩/ '(and) so, (and) then'; the contrastive topic marker /-no˦/; /wɤ˩/ 'again; also', which in quite a few cases does not have its full lexical meaning and is close to a simple gap-filler; and the intensifier /ɖwæ˦/ 'very'. The first three happen to appear in succession in (13): /tʰi˩ | -no˦ | wɤ˩/.

(13) tʰi˧-gv̩˩-se˩-dzo˩ | tʰi˧ | -no˧ | wɤ˧ | qwɤ˧ tʰi˧-gv̩˩.
    tʰi˧-   gv̩˩ₐ   -se˩   -dzo˧   tʰi˧   -no˧
    DUR   to_make/to_build   COMPLETION   TOP   then   CNTR.TOP
    wɤ˧   qwɤ˧   tʰi˧-   gv̩˩ₐ
    again/also   fire_pit   DUR   to_make/to_build

'After one has finished to build [the cupboard], well, one builds the fire pit!' (Housebuilding.144)

One could speculate that /tʰi˧/ '(and) so, (and) then' and /wɤ˧/ 'again' are favoured as gap-fillers because of their properties with respect to tone-group divisions. The gap-filler /tʰi˧/ appears in most sentences in the narratives told by consultant F4: more than 1,500 occurrences among twenty narratives. The gap-filler /wɤ˧/ appears more than 120 times among the same twenty narratives. These two items may owe part of their conspicuous success as gap-fillers to the phonological fact that they demarcate tone groups clearly. Since they always constitute a tone group on their own, they create a pause in the computation of tone sequences.

But one may just as well hypothesize the inverse causal link: that these words tended to be set off from the rest of the utterance due to their function as gap-fillers, eventually resulting in the present situation where they systematically constitute tone groups on their own. An argument in favour of this hypothesis is provided by items that are in the process of entering the set of *tonal standalones*. The adverb //ɖɯ˧ njɤ˧// 'continuously, ceaselessly' is a case in point. It was elicited in association with verbs exemplifying the six tone categories of verbs, yielding the results shown in Table 7.2. In narratives, however, the adverb is always followed by a tone-group boundary, as in (14), where //ɖɯ˧ njɤ˧// 'continuously, ceaselessly' and //ʐwɤ˩ᵦ// 'to say' are not integrated in the same tone group. (There are more than thirty examples in the first twenty texts recorded.)

(14) hĩ˧mo˧=ɻæ˩-ɳɯ˩ | ɖɯ˧-njɤ˧ | ʐwɤ˩-ky˧ | mæ˩ (…)
    hĩ˧mo˧=ɻæ˩-ɳɯ˩   ɖɯ˧-njɤ˧   ʐwɤ˩ₐ   -ky˧   mæ˧
    elders=PL-A   constantly   to_say   ABILITIVE   OBVIOUSNESS

'The elders would always say…' (Dog2.32)

Using the context of this narrative, it was attempted to combine the adverb with the verb, but the consultant judged this wrong, even when truncating the sentence after the main verb: ‡ ɖɯ˧ njɤ˧ ʐwɤ˧. This judgment highlights the fact that the data in Table 7.2 was elicited at a push: in the present state of the language, these expressions verge on the incorrect, and the adverb is well advanced

Table 7.2: The tone patterns of phrases made up of the adverb //ɖɯ˧ njɤ˧// 'continuously, ceaselessly' followed by a verb.

tone	example	meaning	result	tone pattern
H	dzɯ˥	to eat	ɖɯ˧-njɤ˧ dzɯ˧	M.M.M
M$_a$	hwæ˧$_a$	to buy	ɖɯ˧-njɤ˧ hwæ˧	M.M.L
M$_b$	tɕʰi˧$_b$	to sell	ɖɯ˧-njɤ˧ tɕʰi˧	M.M.M
L$_a$	dze˧$_a$	to cut	ɖɯ˧-njɤ˧ dze˥	M.M.MH
L$_b$	ʐwɤ˧$_b$	to speak	ɖɯ˧-njɤ˧ ʐwɤ˥	M.M.MH
MH	lɑ˥	to strike	ɖɯ˧-njɤ˧ lɑ˥	M.M.MH

on its way towards the status of *tonal standalone*. This example illustrates how easily different data collection methods can lead to different conclusions. The combination of different types of data, collected with suitable precautions, appears indispensable for cumulative progress in research.[5]

A discourse factor that arguably plays a leading role in the evolution of the adverb //ɖɯ˧ njɤ˧// 'continuously, ceaselessly' is the emphasis that is associated with it from a semantic-pragmatic point of view. This adverb sometimes carries emphatic stress in narratives. The scenario would thus be one of generalization (lexicalization) of intonational emphasis.

7.2.2 Topicalized constituents always end a tone group

A tone group boundary is always found after topicalized constituents. In detail, the situation is as follows:

- the topic marker /-dʐo˥/ always terminates a tone group. No exception has been found among 2,000 examples from narratives.

- the topic marker /tʂʰɯ˧/ likewise terminates a tone group, except in the many cases where it is followed by another topic marker: /-dʐo˥/.

- the contrastive topic marker /-no˥/ always constitutes a tone group on its own, as mentioned above and illustrated by (15).

---

[5] See the set of themed articles *How to Study a Tone Language* edited by Steven Bird & Larry Hyman, in volume 8 of the journal *Language Documentation and Conservation* (2014). A case of diverging notations in a level-tone language is analyzed by Roux (2003), leading to similar recommendations for precautions in the investigation method. Some views on this topic are set out in Niebuhr & Michaud (2015).

(15) hwɤ˧li˧ | -no˧, | ʐv̩˧kʰv̩˩-ŋwɤ˩kʰv̩˩. |
     hwɤ˧li˧   -no˧   ʐv̩˧kʰv̩˩   ŋwɤ˩kʰv̩˩
     cat   CNTR.TOP   four.years five.years

'As for the cat, [it has a lifespan of] four or five years.' (Dog2.84. Context: the previous discussion hinges on the dog's lifespan, and the speaker now moves on to the topic of cats.)

7.2.3 Options left to the speaker in the division into tone groups

Apart from the cases presented in §7.2.1–7.2.2, the speaker generally has several options. They may choose to integrate large chunks of speech into a single tone group; or they may divide the utterance into a number of tone groups, with the stylistic effect of emphasizing these individual components one after the other. This parallels observations about the intonation of numerous languages, e.g. observations about Russian and German by Karcevskij (1931: 204): "Within certain limits, it is possible to change the position of the rhythmic breaks that separate a sentence into parts".[6] An interesting characteristic of Yongning Na is that this division exerts a strong influence on tone, since tonal processes never apply across tone-group junctures.

For instance, /**dzɯ˧-di˧**/ 'things to eat; food', from /**dzɯ˩**/ 'to eat' and the nominalizer /**-di˩**/, can combine with /**mɤ˧-dʑo˧**/ 'there isn't' to mean 'there isn't any food, there is nothing to eat'; the noun and the negated verb can either be integrated into one tone group, as /**dzɯ˧-di˧ mɤ˧-dʑo˧**/, or separated, as /**dzɯ˧-di˧ | mɤ˧-dʑo˧**/. The latter option is illustrated by (16):

(16) dzɯ˧-di˧ | mɤ˧-dʑo˧, | tʰɯ˩-di˩ | mɤ˧-dʑo˧!
     dzɯ˩   -di˩   mɤ˧- dʑo˧$_b$ tʰɯ˩$_b$ -di˩ mɤ˧- dʑo˧$_b$
     to_eat NMLZ NEG EXIST to_drink NMLZ NEG EXIST

'[Before mankind had learnt to grow crops], there was nothing to eat and nothing to drink!' (Seeds2.67)

In (16), separating the noun phrase /**dzɯ˧-di˧**/ 'food' and the negated existential verb /**mɤ˧-dʑo˧**/ 'there isn't' into two tone groups has the effect of emphasizing the two noun phrases, /**dzɯ˧-di˧**/ 'food; things to eat' and /**tʰɯ˩-di˩**/ 'drink; beverage'. The following sentence in the story repeats the statement 'There was no food', continuing the same strategy of bringing out the noun phrase 'food',

---

[6] *Original text*: Dans certaines limites, nous pouvons déplacer les anti-cadences séparant les membres de la phrase.

this time with the topic marker /-dzo˥/ (17). The effect is to emphasize how dire the situation was getting.

(17) dzɯ˦-di˦ | -dzo˩, | mɤ˦-dzo˦-ɲi˦ tsɯ˩ | mv˩!
     dzɯ˥ -di˩ -dzo˥ mɤ˦- dzo˦ᵦ -ɲi˩ tsɯ˦ mv˦
     to_eat NMLZ TOP NEG EXIST CERTITUDE REP AFFIRM

'As for food, it's said that there was none!' (Seeds2.68)

Then the narrator recapitulates as (18):

(18) dzɯ˦-di˦ mɤ˦-dzo˦ | -dzo˩ | tʰi˩ ...
     dzɯ˥ -di˩ mɤ˦- dzo˦ᵦ -dzo˥ tʰi˩
     to_eat NMLZ NEG EXIST TOP so/then

'As there was nothing to eat, ...' (the narrative moves on to: 'there were some exceptional, smart people, who stood up and did something about it') (Seeds2.69)

At this juncture, 'there was no food' is integrated into one tone group, and followed by the topic marker /-dzo˥/. This provides an exemplary illustration of the integration of larger chunks of information into one tone group as this information changes status from new to old and backgrounded.

Long tone groups within which phonological and morphosyntactic tone rules are allowed full play, undisturbed by local intrusions of pragmatic phenomena of emphasis, yield a stylistic effect of carefully constructed, poised, stately speech. Conversely, in lively speech, tone-group boundaries are inserted here and there to highlight the word or phrase that precedes. Even function words can be emphasized in this way, as in (19).

(19) ɬo˦pv˥ ti˩-kv˩ | tsɯ˦ | mv˩!
     ɬo˦pv˥ ti˩ₐ -kv˦ tsɯ˦ mv˦
     kow-tow to_hit ABILITIVE REP AFFIRM

'It is said that [on that occasion, the whole family] will kow-tow!' (Sister3.138)

A simpler formulation would be /ɬo˦pv˥ ti˩-kv˩ tsɯ˩ | -mv˩/. The formulation in (19) emphasizes the reported-speech particle /tsɯ˦/. This evidential particle is used whenever the speaker only has indirect knowledge of the situation at issue, and therefore it appears over and over again in narratives. But in the context of (19), it takes on its full meaning, because the narrator never witnessed the ritual that she describes. The emphasis laid on the evidential particle in the context of this sentence is one of the manifestations of speaker F4's concern to adhere to truthfulness and precision.

The stylistic choices made by a speaker can be appraised against a background of general tendencies, outlined below.

7.2.4 Some general tendencies in the division into tone groups

7.2.4.1 The role of the morphological complexity of constituents

The degree of internal complexity of the successive constituents of an utterance is among the parameters that influence its division into tone groups. A verb without prefixes or suffixes is usually just one syllable long, and easily associates with a preceding adverb or noun. For instance, /kʰɯ˧tsʰɤ˧ tsʰe˧/ 'to stretch out [one's] legs', from /kʰɯ˧tsʰɤ˧/ 'leg' and /tsʰe˧ʙ/ 'to stretch out', constitutes one tonal word, whose output tone is determined by the tone rules that apply in subject-plus-verb phrases (see §6.10). When an adverb is inserted, it can be integrated into the tone group, as in (20), where there is only one tone group for the subject, the adverb //mv˩tɕo˧// 'downward', and the verb.

(20) kʰɯ˧tsʰɤ˧ mv˩tɕo˩ tsʰe˩
     kʰɯ˧tsʰɤ˧   mv˩tɕo˧   tsʰe˧ʙ
     leg   downward   to_stretch

'to stretch (one's) leg downward'

But the adverb often marks the beginning of a new tone group, as in (21), where the subject is in a different tone group from the adverb and verb.

(21) kʰɯ˧tsʰɤ˧ | mv˩tɕo˧ tsʰe˧
     kʰɯ˧tsʰɤ˧   mv˩tɕo˧   tsʰe˧ʙ
     leg   downward   to_stretch

'to stretch (one's) leg downward'

Like directional adverbs, numeral-plus-classifier phrases often mark the beginning of a new group, as in (22). But they can also be integrated into a single tone group with a preceding noun, as in (23).

(22) ʂɤ˧~ʂɤ˧ | ɖɯ˧-pʰæ˧
     ʂɤ˧~ʂɤ˧   ɖɯ˧-pʰæ˧
     paper   one-CLF.flat_objects

'a sheet of paper'

(23) əɻmiɻ-myꜜ ɲiꜜ-kyꜜ
    əɻmiɻ   myˈ   ɲiɻ-kyˈ
    mother   daughter   two-CLF.persons

    'the mother and her daughter' *Literally:* 'mother and daughter, the two'
    (Tiger.11, 51, and Lake4.93, 96-98, 125)

The expression in (23) is a special case: /əɻmiɻ-myꜜ/ is a coordinative compound that means 'mother and daughter'; addition of the expression /ɲiɻ-kyˈ/, 'two' plus the classifier for persons, is obviously not to be understood as an instance of counting mother-and-daughter pairs. The numeral-plus-classifier phrase does not serve the usual purpose of providing a figure: in this context, it serves an anaphoric function. The expression can be paraphrased as 'these two: the mother and the daughter'.

Demonstrative-plus-classifier phrases are commonly integrated with a preceding noun. For instance, in the first version of the Lake story, the same two characters, a mother and her daughter, are referred to as /əɻmiɻ tsʰɯɻ-yɻ laꜜ | myꜜ tsʰɯꜜ-yˈ/, 'that mother and that daughter': see (24).

(24) əɻmiɻ tsʰɯɻ-yɻ laꜜ | myꜜ tsʰɯꜜ-yˈ
    əɻmiɻ   tsʰɯɻ-yɻ   laɻ   myˈ   tsʰɯɻ-yɻ
    mother   DEM-CLF.individual   and   daughter   DEM-CLF

    'that mother and that daughter' (Lake.52).

7.2.4.2 The role of information structure: Considerations of prominence

Information structure also influences the division into tone groups, in a way which is often difficult to disentangle from the influence of morphological complexity. Consider (25):

(25) kʰyꜜmiꜜ-ʂeˈ, | dzɯɻ mʁɻ-ɖoɻ piɻ-zoˈ!
    kʰyꜜmiꜜ-ʂeꜜ   dzɯˈ   mʁɻ-   ɖoɻₐ   piˈ   -zo
    dog-meat   to_eat   NEG   ought_to to_say   ADVB

    'It's said that one mustn't eat dog meat! / It's said that dog meat is something one must not eat!' (Dog2.37)

In (25), the noun phrase 'dog meat' is set into relief by constituting a tone group on its own. Despite the absence of a morphemic indication that it is topicalized, such as use of a topic marker /tsʰɯɻ/ or /-dʐoˈ/, it clearly has the status of topic. In this context, tonal integration with a following verb would not be stylistically appropriate.

Likewise, in (26), the adverbial 'outside', /əɬpʰoɭ/, constitutes a tone group on its own. Another option would be to integrate it tonally with the following verb. (The tonal paradigms for *spatial adverbial+verb* combinations are set out in Chapter 6.) In this context, integration into a single tone group would be stylistically acceptable. Separation into two tone groups has the effect of providing the information gradually, giving the impression that the speaker is constructing the utterance as she is saying it, rather than delivering long, carefully preplanned chunks of speech.

(26) əˈɟi˧-ʂɯ˥ɟi˩-dʐo˩, | kʰv˧-tʂʰɯ˧-dʐo˩, | dʐʁʌ | əɬpʰoʌ | kʰɯ˧ mʁ˥-kv˩!
 əˈɟi˧-ʂɯ˥ɟi˩   dʐo˥   kʰv˥   -tʂʰɯ˥   -dʐo˥   dʐʁʌ   əɬpʰoɭ   kʰɯ˥   mʁ˥-
 in_the_past   TOP   dog   TOP   TOP   INTS   outside   to_let   NEG
 -kv˥
 ABILITIVE

 'In the old times, one wouldn't usually let dogs go outside! / In the old times, dogs weren't usually allowed to leave the house!' (Dog2.75)

It is uncommon for a verb preceded by the accomplished prefix /le˧-/ to interact tonally with a preceding noun phrase. In Caravans.191, for instance, 'the uncle comes back' is realized as /ə˧v˥ | le˧-tsʰɯ˩/, not as /ə˧v˥ le˥-tsʰɯ˩/, although the latter form is also acceptable. Cases where tonal interaction does take place are characterized by a strong degree of semantic givenness, as in (27):

(27) ɖɯ˧-v˧ le˧-tsʰɯ˩, | ɲi˧-kv˧ le˧-tsʰɯ˥, | so˩-kv˩ le˩-tsʰɯʌ.
 ɖɯ˧-v˧   le˧-   tsʰɯ˩ₐ   ɲi˧-kv˥   so˩-kv˩
 one-CLF.individual   ACCOMP   to_come.PST   two-CLF   three-CLF

 'One person came, then two, then three.' (Field notes: explanation proposed by consultant F4 during a discussion of Lake4.126)

It would not be incorrect to say /ɖɯ˧-v˧ | le˧-tsʰɯ˩, | ɲi˧-kv˥ | le˧-tsʰɯ˩, | so˩-kv˩ | le˧-tsʰɯ˩/, but this would be inappropriate in a context where the emphasis is on the count (one person, then two, then three), not on the verb. There would be no point in setting the subject apart from the verb, hence the division into three tone groups, rather than six.

When an explanation is added as an afterthought, a relatively long sequence of syllables can be integrated into one tone group, as in (28), where the last tone group contains ten syllables.

(28) jʁ˧ŋʁ˧-dʐo˧, | ə˧ɟi˧-ʂɯ˥ɟi˩, | hæ˩-bɑ˥lɑ˩! | hæ˩-bɑ˥lɑ˩-bɑ˩lɑ˩ le˩-po˩ jo˩-kv˩ mæ˩!

339

ʝɤ˧ŋɤ˧	-dʑo˩	ə˩ʝi˧-ʂɯ˩ʝi˩	hæ˩-ɓɑ˥ɭɑ˩	hæ˩-ɓɑ˥ɭɑ˩-ɓɑ˩ɭɑ˩	le˩-
Chengdu	TOP	in_the_past	silk	silk_clothes	ACCOMP
po˥	jo˩	-kv˥	mæ˩		
to_bring	to_come	ABILITIVE	OBVIOUSNESS		

'From Chengdu, in the past... Silk!! [The people who went on caravans] would bring back silk clothing [from their journeys to Chengdu]!' (Caravans.104-105)

In a context where the narrator is explaining which goods used to be transported by caravan, the essential information is already given in the word 'silk'. The portion of sentence /le˩-po˩-jo˩-kv˩-mæ˩/ '[they] would bring back' is added as an explanation; its integration in the same tone group as the preceding noun, 'silk', results in a levelling down of all of its tones to L, reflecting its status as backgrounded information.

As many as twelve syllables are bunched together in (29):

(29) ə˩ʑi˥, | ɖɯ˩mɑ˧-ɬɑ˩tsʰo˩ pi˩-hĩ˩ ɖɯ˩-v˩ dʐo˩-ɲi˩ tsɯ˩ | mv˩.

ə˩ʑi˥	ɖɯ˩mɑ˧-ɬɑ˩tsʰo˩	pi˥	-hĩ˥	ɖɯ˩
grandmother	GIVEN_NAME	to_say	REL/NMLZ	one
v˩	dʐo˧ₐ	-ɲi˩	tsɯ˥	mv˩
CLF.individual	EXIST	CERTITUDE	REP	AFFIRM

'[Among] women elders, it is said that there was one by the name of Ddeema Lhaco.' (Elders3.11)

The speaker lays considerable emphasis on the person's name, Ddeema Lhaco. All the rest of the sentence follows as a strongly backgrounded accompaniment to this name. Phonologically, the name and all that follows are integrated into one tone group, with the result that all the syllables from the third to the twelfth and last are lowered to L.

As a last example, consider (30).

(30) dzo˩ | le˩-gv˩ | tʰi˩-tɕɯ˥ | tʰi˩ | no˩ | le˩-tsʰɯ˩-ɲi˩-ze˩-mæ˩, | ə˩-gi˩! | hĩ˥ ɖɯ˩-v˩ mɤ˩-tsʰɯ˩! | no˩ le˩-tsʰɯ˩-ɲi˥-ze˩ mæ˩!

dzo˩	le˩-	gv˩ᵦ	tʰi˩-	tɕɯ˥	tʰi˩	no˩	le˩-
bridge	ACCOMP	to_build	DUR	to_put	then	2SG	ACCOMP
tsʰɯ˩ₐ	-ɲi˩	-ze˩ᵦ	mæ˩	ə˩-gi˩	hĩ˥	ɖɯ˩
to_come	CERTITUDE	PFV	AFFIRM	isn't_it	person	one
v˩	mɤ˩-	tsʰɯ˩ₐ	no˩	le˩-	tsʰɯ˩ₐ	-ɲi˩
CLF.individual	NEG	to_come	2SG	ACCOMP	to_come	CERTITUDE

-ze˧ᵦ	mæ˧
PFV	AFFIRM

'After the bridge is built, and left there [=and the person who built it waits for someone to cross], you come along! [=someone comes along: you, for instance!] [For a long time] nobody comes, [but at last] you come along!' (Renaming.17)

The same syntactic structure, 'you came along', is realized as two tone groups: /no˧ | le˧-tsʰɯ˩ ɲi˩-ze˩ mæ˩/, then repeated as a single tone group: /no˩ le˩-tsʰɯ˩ ɲi˩-ze˩ mæ˩/. This provides an exemplary illustration of how tone groups tend to be longer when the speaker assumes that the semantic content is already familiar to the listener.

7.2.5 Extreme cases of tonal integration: Set phrases and proverbs

7.2.5.1 Tonal integration in set phrases

Set phrases constitute a typical case of integration. For instance, there are formulae that recapitulate which of the animals symbolizing the twelve Terrestrial Branches have special affinities with one another. These subsets are used in fortune-telling: the year of birth serves as a basis on which one predicts whether or not an individual will be able to relate harmoniously with another. Among the animals that succeed one another in the twelve-year cycle, there are four sets of three, shown in (31)-(34).

(31) bv˧zv˧ ʝi˧ | æ̃˩ so˥-kʰv˩
bv˧zv˧   ʝi˥   æ̃˩   so˩   kʰv˥ₐ
snake   ox   chicken three CLF.years
'the three years of the Snake, the Ox, and the Rooster'

(32) mv˧gv˧ ʐi˥ | hwɤ˧ so˧-kʰv˥
mv˧gv˧   ʐi˥   hwɤ˧   so˩   kʰv˥ₐ
dragon   ape   rat   three   CLF.years
'the three years of the Dragon, the Ape, and the Rat'

(33) tʰo˧li˧ bo˩ | jo˩ so˩-kʰv˥
tʰo˧li˧   bo˥   jo˩   so˩   kʰv˥ₐ
rabbit   pig   sheep three CLF.years
'the three years of the Rabbit, the Pig, and the Sheep'

(34) lɑ˧ | ʐwæ˧ | kʰv˧ | so˧-kʰv˧˩
     lɑ˧   ʐwæ˥ kʰv˥ so˧   kʰv˥˩ₐ
     tiger horse dog   three CLF.years

'the three years of the Tiger, the Horse, and the Dog'

The tone grouping is not exactly the same in these four phrases. In (31), (32) and (33), the phrase is divided into two tone groups, instead of the four tone groups that would obtain if each animal name were said separately. This yields the expected effect of stronger integration than would be found in a list in which each item stood in a tone group of its own. The first tone group contains the names of two animals; the rest of the phrase, making up another tone group, contains the third animal name and the expression 'three years'. Each of the two tone groups has three syllables, creating an effect of rhythmic balance. The tone that obtains by association of two animal names conforms to the patterns observed in coordinative compounds (as set out in §3.3): disyllabic M-tone noun plus monosyllabic H-tone noun yields //#H// tone (//**bv˧zv˧ ɟi#˥**//), hence a surface form with M tone: /**bv˧zv˧ ɟi˧**/.

For ease of comparison, the forms that would obtain if each noun stood in a tone group of its own are shown as (35), (36) and (37).

(35) bv˧zv˧ | ɟi˧ | æ̃˩ | so˧-kʰv˧˩
     bv˧zv˧ ɟi˥   æ̃˩   so˧   kʰv˥˩ₐ
     snake   ox   chicken three CLF.years

modified from (31) by placing each noun in a separate tone group

(36) mv˧gv˧ | ʐi˩ | hwɤ˧ | so˧-kʰv˧˩
     mv˧gv˧ ʐi˩   hwɤ˧ so˧   kʰv˥˩ₐ
     dragon ape   rat   three CLF.years

modified from (32) by placing each noun in a separate tone group

(37) tʰo˧li˧ | bo˩ | ʝo˩ | so˧-kʰv˧˩
     tʰo˧li˧ bo˩ ʝo˧ so˧   kʰv˥˩ₐ
     rabbit pig sheep three CLF.years

modified from (33) by placing each noun in a separate tone group

In (34), on the other hand, there is an odd number of syllables, making it impossible to build two tone groups that have the same number of syllables, and to arrive at a symmetrical structure as in (31), (32) and (33). The solution chosen is to keep the three animal names separate, each constituting a distinct tone group, hence yielding four tone groups in total. This illustrates the role played by rhythmic factors. (For an introduction to the notoriously complex domain of linguistic rhythm, see Niebuhr 2009a; Cummins 2012; House 2012.)

7.2.5.2 Tonal integration in proverbs

Proverbs are also typical instances of tightly-knit tonal integration. An example is shown in (38).

(38) hĩ˧dza˧ | dʑe˧ | tʰɑ˧-ji˩, | ʈʂ̩̃˧ko˩ mi˩ tʰɑ˩-tʰv˩.
     hĩ˩   dzɑ˩ dʑe˧ tʰɑ˧- ji˩   ʈʂ̩̃˧ko˩   mi˧   tʰɑ˧-
     person poor money PROH to_borrow shinbone wound PROH
     tʰv˧ₐ
     to_get

'The poor must not borrow money; the shinbone must not receive wounds.'

The proverb's argument is that one must beware of hitting fragile spots. The listener is presumed to know that a blow to the shin is especially painful, and to imagine, by analogy, how hard it is for a poor person to reimburse a loan plus added interest. The sequence /ʈʂ̩̃˧ko˩ mi˩ tʰɑ˩-tʰv˩/, 'the shinbone must not receive wounds', is integrated into one tone group, with the stylistic effect of presenting it as a self-evident fact (an established truth), not a statement coined on the fly by the speaker, in which case the division into tone groups would have been /ʈʂ̩̃˧ko˩ | mi˧ tʰɑ˧-tʰv˧/ or /ʈʂ̩̃˧ko˩ | mi˧ | tʰɑ˧-tʰv˧/.

It is highly revealing that, even in the case of proverbs and set phrases, the speaker retains a latitude of choice in the division of the utterance into tone groups. The comparison of different versions of the same story by the same speaker yields a wealth of examples. For instance, the saying 'If you see a tiger, it means your father is going to die; if you see a panther, it means your mother is going to die', which is at the heart of the narrative Tiger, is divided into four tone groups in (39), three groups in (40), and two groups in (41).

(39) zæ˩ do˩ | ə˧mi˧ ʂɯ˧; | lɑ˧ do˩, | ə˧dɑ˧ ʂɯ˧.
     zæ˩   do˩ᵦ   ə˧mi˧   ʂɯ˧ₐ   lɑ˧   do˩ᵦ   ə˧dɑ1$ ʂɯ˧ₐ
     panther to_see mother to_die tiger to_see father to_die

'If you see a panther, it means your mother is going to die; if you see a tiger, it means your father is going to die.' (Tiger.10; Tiger2.5, 13)

(40) zæɹ do˥ | ə˦mi˦ ʂɯɹ, | la˦ doɹ əɹdaɹ ʂɯɹ.
      zæ˧   doɹb   ə˦mi˦   ʂɯ˦a   la˦   doɹb   ə˦da˥$ ʂɯ˦a
      panther   to_see   mother   to_die   tiger to_see   father   to_die

   'If you see a panther, it means your mother is going to die; if you see
   a tiger, it means your father is going to die.' (Tiger.50)

(41) la˦ doɹ əɹdaɹ ʂɯɹ, | zæɹ do˥ əɹmiɹ ʂɯɹ.
      la˦   doɹb   ə˦da˥$ ʂɯ˦a   zæ˧   doɹb   ə˦mi˦   ʂɯ˦a
      tiger   to_see   father   to_die   panther to_see   mother   to_die

   'If you see a tiger, it means your father is going to die; if you see
   a panther, it means your mother is going to die.' (Tiger.31; Tiger2.111)

As in examples (16)–(19) and (27)–(30), the stylistic nuance is that, the greater the number of tone groups, the more attention is drawn to the individual components of the sentence. The phrasing in (39) is found at first occurrence, towards the beginning of the story; later occurrences tend to have fewer tone groups, as in (40) and (41). Example (40) is an interesting intermediate case, in which the 'panther/mother' and 'tiger/father' pairs are not treated symmetrically. The context is a journey on the mountain, during which a mother and her daughter encounter a tiger; the father is not present. The interpretation of the asymmetry is clear: emphasis is laid on the omen concerning the mother. The other part of the proverb, mentioning the father, is less relevant; it is not entirely omitted (which could compromise recognition of the proverb), but it is backgrounded by integrating it into one tone group.[7]

As a final example, let us examine (42).

(42) hi˦ ŋɯɹ mʁɹ-doɹ, | my˦ ŋɯɹ | do˧!
      hi˦   ŋɯ˦   mʁ˦-   doɹb   my˥   ŋɯ˦   doɹb
      person/human A   NEG   to_see   sky/heavens   A   to_see

   'People may not see, but the *heavens* see!'

This saying is used as a reminder that other people's gaze is not the touchstone of good conduct, and that one's actions should be guided by the same rules whether seen or unseen. The most common realization of this saying is (42), where the first part ('What people do not see') is integrated into one tone group,

---

[7] The order of the two clauses, 'panther/mother+tiger/father' or 'tiger/father+panther/mother', does not exert a direct influence on the division into tone groups. Both orders are acceptable: the order found in (39)-(40) is not necessarily a departure from a canonical order exemplified by (41), or the other way round.

whereas the second is divided into two. This emphatically brings out the verb /do˩ᵦ/ 'to see, to observe', which being on its own in the tone group receives a final H tone and is realized with a rise, /LH/, following Rule 7: "If a tone group only contains L tones, a post-lexical H tone is added to its last syllable". (Variants are found in the narrative Reward.28, 36, 62 and 114.)

7.2.6 Two cases of resistance to tonal integration

Some expressions resist integration into one tone group. As mentioned in §3.1.1, tonal changes in compounding are only observed when the second term (the head) has fewer than three syllables. A typical example is the proper name "Lake Lugu", shown in example (1a) of Chapter 3. As for the phrase /sɑ˧ | zo˩bv̩˧˥lɯ˩/, meaning 'the universe, the whole world' (Mountains.69), it is also perceived as composed of two distinct parts, /sɑ˧/ and /zo˩bv̩˧˥lɯ˩/, even though the first syllable, /sɑ˧/, is no longer intelligible by itself, and does not appear on its own. The trisyllable /zo˩bv̩˧˥lɯ˩/ can be employed on its own, to mean 'the universe', like the four-syllable expression. The existence of this trisyllabic form may be part of the reason why the four-syllable form /sɑ˧ | zo˩bv̩˧˥lɯ˩/ 'the universe' does not get integrated into a single tone group. (If such integration took place, it would yield a M.L.L.L tone pattern, †sɑ˧-zo˩bv̩˩lɯ˩, by application of Rule 5: "All syllables following a H.L or M.L sequence receive L tone".)

On the other hand, the same argument cannot be invoked to explain the absence of tonal integration in the Na word for 'field penny-cress', a foetid plant with round flat pods (*Thlaspi arvense*). It is called /ʁv̩˧=bv̩˧ | v̩˩tsʰɤ˧/, literally 'the crane's vegetable'. One would expect this expression to be treated as one tone group, since it constitutes one lexical item. But the fact that the name can still be transparently analyzed as a possessive construction probably contributes to slowing down its phonological integration into one tone group. Importantly, this plant is not commonly used, and the word therefore has low frequency in discourse, limiting the pressure towards phonetic-phonological simplification.

7.2.7 Illustration: Sample derivations

This section recapitulates some of the mechanisms described in this section by providing sample derivations for two sentences from transcribed texts.

(43) dzɯ˧ | dɯ˧-qʰv˧tʰv˧ tʰi˩-kʰɯ˩.
    dzɯ˩   dɯ˧-qʰv˧tʰv#˩   tʰi˩-   kʰɯ˧
    water one-CLF.hornful   DUR   to_put

'[People who travel all day] put a hornful of water [in their bag, so as to have something to drink].' (Tiger2.51)

In example (43), the noun 'water' constitutes a tone group on its own, hence its realization with M tone, following the regular pattern shown in Table 2.7a. The second tone group contains five syllables: /dɯ˧-qʰv˧tʰv˧ tʰi˩-kʰɯ˩/. First, the tone of the numeral-plus-classifier phrase is determined, following the table-lookup rules set out in Chapter 4 (Table 4.5a). This yields //dɯ˧-qʰv˧tʰv#˩// 'one hornful'. Association of this object with the prefixed verb //tʰi˩-kʰɯ˧// 'to put (into)' also operates as table lookup (see Chapter 6). This yields the surface phonological string, M.M.M.L.L. Thus, knowledge of a tone group's internal morphosyntactic structure and of the tones of its constituting elements suffices to arrive at the surface tone sequence.

As a second sample derivation, let us consider a slightly more complex example: (44).

(44) ə˧my˥ | le˧-tsʰɯ˩ | tʰi˧ʌ, | go˧mi˧ ɲɯ˧ | ə˧my˥ | mɤ˧-sɯ˥ tsɯ˩ | mv˩!
    ə˧my˥   le˧-   tsʰɯ˩ₐ   tʰi˧ʌ   go˧mi˧
    elder_sibling ACCOMP   to_come.PST   gap_filler:well younger_sister
    ɲɯ˧   ə˧my˥   mɤ˧-   sɯ˥   tsɯ˥   mv˧
    A/TOP   elder_sibling NEG   to_know   REP   AFFIRM

'[When] the big brother came back, the younger sister didn't recognize him!' (Sister.49)

In (44), the group | ə˧my˥ | 'elder sibling' simply consists of a noun, so that the levels of the tonal word and tone group coincide. In the absence of suffixes or final particles, the noun's lexical tone, MH, is realized on the last syllable of the tonal word, which is also the last syllable of the tone group. The tone pattern of the group | le˧-tsʰɯ˩ | 'came back' obtains as described in Table 6.8. The word /tʰi˧ʌ/ '(and) then, (and) so' always constitutes a tone group on its own, as explained in §7.2.1. The tone pattern of the group | go˧mi˧ ɲɯ˧ | 'by the sister' obtains as described in Table 5.14a. In the group | mɤ˧-sɯ˥ tsɯ˩ |, the verb 'to know, to recognize', //sɯ˥//, is flanked by the negation prefix //mɤ˧-// and the sentence-final particle //tsɯ˥// (reported speech). The negation prefix surfaces with its lexical M tone, the verb with its H tone, and the sentence-final particle, being preceded by a H tone, receives L through Rule 4.

The final particle //mʏ˧// (affirmative) was already encountered in various examples in which it appears after a tone-group break, and carries L tone: / | mʏ˩/. It does not constitute a well-formed tone group, since a tone group cannot contain only L tones. The special case of this particle, analyzed here as *extrametrical*, brings us to the topic of breaches of tonal grouping, which introduce extrametrical syllables into the system.

7.3 Cases of breach of tonal grouping and their consequences for the system

Breach of tonal grouping occurs when non-final syllables come to carry a contour. This causes following syllables to become extrametrical. In turn, this has consequences for the tonal system: considerations of analytical consistency lead to positing extrametrical syllables even in some contexts where they are not preceded by a tonal contour, as in the case of the affirmative final particle / | mʏ˩/ in example (44).

7.3.1 The stylistic option of realizing a contour on a word in non-final position

Syllables that are not in final position within the tone group cannot carry a contour (//MH//, //LM// or //LH//). This is an important part of the definition of the tone group as a phonological unit. But this rule is at odds with a stylistic device whereby a word is emphasized by cutting short the tone group immediately after it. This device suspends tonal calculation, and allows the realization of a contour on the emphasized word, as in (45).

(45) le˧-tsɑ˧˥, | le˧-tsɑ˧˥, | le˧-tsɑ˧˥ | -kwɤ˩tɕɯ˩, | le˧-lv˧˥!
     le˧-   tsɑ˧˥   -kwɤ˩tɕɯ˩ le˧-   lv˧˥
     ACCOMP to_row   because   ACCOMP to_escape

'By rowing, rowing, rowing, they managed to escape!' (Lake3.59)

The context to this example is highly emotional: a mother and her daughter are rowing for their lives, struggling against the flood that has come over the plain where they lived, now suddenly become a lake. The verb 'to row' is repeated, and the sentence chopped into short tone groups, as if mimicking the oar chopping into the water in a rapid succession of rowing strokes. The verb is strongly articulated phonetically, each time with its lexical rising tone, and the conjunction /-kwɤ˩tɕɯ˩/ is tacked on at the end as if it were an afterthought. It would be possible to integrate the conjunction with the preceding tone group, as in (46), with the expected unfolding of the MH contour over the verb and the first syllable of the conjunction. But this deliberate, neatly structured variant would be stylistically inappropriate in this context.

(46)   le˧-tsɑ˦, | le˧-tsɑ˦, | le˧-tsɑ˧-kwɤ˦tɕɯ˨, | le˧-lv˦!
       le˧-   tsɑ˦   -kwɤ˦tɕɯ˨   le˧-   lv˦
       ACCOMP   to_row   because   ACCOMP to_escape

'By rowing, rowing, rowing, they managed to escape!' *Modified from* (45)

An example using the same conjunction as in (45), but where the expected division into tone groups is respected, and where the expected process of unfolding of a contour tone takes place, is found in (47).

(47)   lo˨dʑo˩ | tṣʰɯ˧ne˧-ji˩ | mv˨tɕo˧ pʰv˧-kwɤ˩tɕɯ˨-ŋɯ˨, | "qʰʰʰ...ə!" | pi˧ tsɯ˨ | mv˧. |
       lo˨dʑo˩   tṣʰɯ˧ne˧-ji˩   mv˨tɕo˧   pʰv˦   -kwɤ˩tɕɯ˩   -ŋɯ
       bracelet   thus   downward   to_take_off   because   TOP
       qʰʰʰ...ə!   pi˩   tsɯ˦   mv˧
       onomatopoeia:burp!   to_say   REP   AFFIRM

'When [the man] took off [the buried woman's bracelets], like this, [the corpse made a gurgling sound]: Buuurp!' (BuriedAlive2.48)

This is the only example found so far where the H part of a verb's MH contour reassociates to the conjunction //-**kwɤ˦tɕɯ˩**//, as against many examples where this contour surfaces as such on the verb prior to this conjunction (for instance in Dog.49, Tiger.46, BuriedAlive3.65, Caravans.80, Sister.50, Sister3.133, Seeds2.34, Renaming.18 and Funeral.51). Example (47) is just enough evidence to show that a realization with contour spreading is possible. Contour unfolding might once have been the norm, and the realization with a contour on the verb might have originally been a conspicuous stylistic effect, but the latter is now much more common than the former, to the point that the realization with contour unfolding is now a stylistically marked option.

Realizations of contours in non-final position are not uncommon (e.g. Housebuilding.71, 98, 100), each time with a distinct stylistic twist. For instance, in (48), avoidance of contour unfolding has an effect of emphasis, making the statement more eloquent by emphasizing the indication of certitude carried by the particle /-**ɲi˨**/. Contour unfolding (/**le˧-tʰæ˧-ɲi˩**/) would be less forceful in this context.

(48) "mɤ˧-dʑɤ˩ ɲi˩, | ə˧-su˩! | ə˧ʝi˧-ʂɯ˩ʝi˩, | ə˧mi˧-my˩ ɲi˩-ky˩, | zo˩no˥, | ɬi˧di˩-di˩mi˩ qo˩ dzi˩, | le˧-wo˩ | le˧-hɯ˩-zo˩, | ə˧ʑi˧-ə˧pʰɤ˧-ki˩ | le˧-hɯ˩-dʐo˩, | tsʰɯ˧ne˧-ʝi˩, | ʐæ˩ ŋɯ˥ | le˧-tʰæ˥ | lɑ˧ ŋɯ˧ | le˧-tʰæ˥ | -ɲi˩" | pi˧-zo˩!

mɤ˧-	dʑɤ˩ᵦ	ɲi˩	ə˧-	su˥	ə˧ʝi˧-ʂɯ˩ʝi˩	ə˧mi˧
NEG	good	COP	INTERROG	to_know	once_upon_a_time	mother

my˩	ɲi˧-ky˥		zo˩no˥	ɬi˧di˩-di˩mi˩	qo˧	dzi˩ₐ
daughter	two-CLF.persons	well	Yongning_plain	inside	to_dwell

le˧-wo˧	le˧-hɯ˩	-zo	ə˧ʑi˥	ə˧pʰɤ˧	-ki˧
went_back	ADVB		grandmother	grandmother's_brother	ALL

le˧-	hɯ˧ᴄ	-dʐo˥	tsʰɯ˧ne˧-ʝi˥	ʐæ˩	ŋɯ˧	le˧-
ACCOMP	to_go.PST	TOP	thus	panther	A	ACCOMP

tʰæ˥	lɑ˧	ŋɯ˧	le˧-	tʰæ˥	-ɲi˩	pi˥	-zo
to_bite	tiger	A	ACCOMP	to_bite	CERTITUDE	to_say	ADVB

'[Elders would tell stories about the tiger eating people,] saying: "That is very bad, you know! Once upon a time, a mother and her daughter who lived in the Yongning plain went to see the grandmother and her brothers; and they were actually attacked by the big cats!"' *Literally:* 'they were bitten by the panther, by the tiger' (Tiger.51)

A second stylistic consequence of the absence of contour unfolding in (48) is the symmetry between the clauses /ʐæ˩ ŋɯ˧ | le˧-tʰæ˥/ '(a/the) panther bit' and /lɑ˧ ŋɯ˧ | le˧-tʰæ˥/ '(a/the) tiger bit', which would be decreased if the tone pattern were different (/le˧-tʰæ˥/ in the first case, and /le˧-tʰæ˥-ɲi˥/ in the second). This symmetry is crucial to connect the story to the Na saying 'If you see a tiger, it means your father is going to die; if you see a panther, it means your mother is going to die' (example (41) above). The story is about a tiger killing a young woman's mother, so there is an apparent mismatch between the saying (which associates *panther* and *mother* on the one hand, and *tiger* and *father* on the other) and the story (*tiger kills mother*). Mention of both panther and tiger in (48) does not make literal sense, as there is no panther in the story. But this parallel mention clarifies that the seeming opposition between *panther* and *tiger* is not relevant, and guides towards the more general interpretation that is relevant to the story: that seeing a big cat is a bad omen, foreboding the death of a parent. Example (48) provides a clear hint that the panther and tiger in the saying are no more distinct from each other than *cats* and *dogs* in the English saying *it's raining cats and dogs*.

Another construction for which the set of narratives contains examples without the unfolding of a rising contour is /tsʰɯ˧ne˧ gy˩/, combining the adverb 'thus, in this way' with the verb 'to take place, to occur', as in (49).

(49) tsʰɯ˧-ʑi˩ | -dʑo˩, | tsʰɯ˧ne˧ gy˩ | -ɲi˩! | tʰv˧-ʑi˩ | -dʑo˩, | tsʰɯ˧ne˧ gy˩ | -ɲi˩!

tsʰɯ˧-ʑi˩   -dʑo˩   tsʰɯ˧ne˧   gy˧$_c$ -ɲi˩
DEM.PROX-CLF.households   TOP   thus   to_take_place   CERTITUDE

tʰv˧-ʑi˩
DEM.DIST-CLF.households

'This is what happened to this household! And this is what happened to that household!' (Elders3.44. Context: the narrator reports how her grandmother used to teach children the proper way to behave by taking real-life examples from events that had occurred within the community.)

In this example, a tone-group boundary is found after both occurrences of the phrase /tsʰɯ˧ne˧ gy˩/. The effect is to set this phrase into relief. The following morpheme also stands out by not being incorporated within the same tone group. This morpheme, /-ɲi˩/, is a grammaticalized form of the copula, used to convey "an epistemic strategy that marks a high degree of certitude" (Lidz 2010: 497). The context helps clarify what happens here: this is a passage in reported speech, in which the narrator adopts the tone of voice of her grandmother, whom she views as the highest authority on traditional lore.

> My grandmother knew about everything! In the old times, she would also tell us stories about people in the village, and what we must learn from them: "This household, this is what happened to them! That household, this is what happened to them! One must develop habits of doing good! One mustn't do wrong!" (Elders3.44-45)

The stylistic choice of adding a tone-group boundary before the morpheme indicating certitude conveys the assertiveness of the character to whom this passage in reported speech is assigned. Realization as /tsʰɯ˧ne˧ gy˩ | -ɲi˩/ rather than /tsʰɯ˧ne˧ gy˧-ɲi˩/ conveys an authoritative attitude. On the other hand, when the phrase 'This is how it happened' is told more casually, as an introduction to a narrative, it constitutes one tone group: see (50). A related phrasing, which likewise constitutes a set phrase and is therefore integrated into one tone group, is shown in (51).

(50) tsʰɯ˧ne˧ gʌ˧-ɲi˩ tsɯ˩ mv˧.
  tsʰɯ˧ne˧ gʌ˧c   -ɲi˩   tsɯ˩ mv˧
  thus   to_take_place CERTITUDE REP AFFIRM
  'This is how it happened.' (BuriedAlive.1)

(51) tsʰɯ˧ne˧ gʌ˧-kv˩.
  tsʰɯ˧ne˧ gʌ˧c   -kv˧
  thus   to_take_place ABILITIVE
  'This is how it would happen.' (Sister3.149, Tiger.2)

Example (52) shows that the stylistic device whereby a tone group is cut short after a certain word can be applied as early as the first syllable of a sentence. A more strongly integrated formulation would be /pʰo˩-hɯ˩-kwɤ˩tɕɯ˩-la˩/, without any special emphasis on the verb 'to flee/to rush'.

(52) pʰo˥ | hɯ˧-kwɤ˧tɕɯ˥-la˩ | tʰi˥, | go˧mi˧ tsʰɯ˧-v˧-dʑo˩, | le˧-ŋv˩, | le˧-ŋv˩, | le˧-ŋv˩, | le˧-ŋv˩, | le˧-ŋv˩-zo˩!
  pʰo˩a   hɯ˧c -kwɤ˧tɕɯ˥-la˩ tʰi˥ go˧mi˧
  to_flee/to_rush to_go.PST after   then younger_sister
  tsʰɯ˥ v˧ -dʑo˩ le˧- ŋv˩ -zo
  DEM.PROX CLF TOP   ACCOMP to_cry ADVB
  'After he rushed away, [his] younger daughter cried her eyes out!' (Sister3.68)

7.3.2 Consequences for the tone system: The emergence of extrametrical syllables

The phenomenon whereby a tone group is cut short after a certain word (noun or verb) has consequences for the general architecture of the tone system. In cases where the portion of tone group that is cut off from the verb can stand on its own as a tone group, the tenets of the system remain unaffected, such as in example (53).

(53) hæ˧, | kʰv˩mi˩-ʂe˥ | dzɯ˧-kv˩!
  hæ˧   kʰv˩mi˩-ʂe˩ dzɯ˥ -kv˧
  Chinese dog_meat to_eat ABILITIVE
  'The Chinese (Han) eat dog meat!' (Field notes, 2012)

Example (53) lays emphasis on 'dog meat'. In the Na world view, dogs and men are close friends: the dog agreed to exchange its sixty-year lifespan with the

351

thirteen-year lifespan that had initially been granted to man (see the narrative Dog). Eating dog meat is therefore taboo among the Na, and the fact that some other ethnic groups do eat dog meat comes to them as a shock. An unmarked phrasing of (53) would be /hæ˧ | kʰv̩˩mi˩-ʂe˩ dzɯ˩-kv̩˥/, in which a single tone group spans the object and verb, and tonal computation takes place.

On the other hand, when particles or conjunctions are left stranded, as in (45), they do not constitute a well-formed tone group on their own. The rules recapitulated in §7.1.1, such as the addition of a final H tone to all-L sequences, do not apply to them – otherwise one would expect a final rising contour in (45): †le˧-tsɑ˥ | -kwɤ˩tɕɯ˥. Nor are these stranded syllables integrated into the following tone group.

Several options for analysis are open here. One would be to consider that, at some phonological level, the division into tone groups is in fact left unchanged. This would entail that a contour can be realized in non-final position within a tone group, an implication which contradicts headlong the definition of the tone group used under the present analysis. A preferred option is to consider that the emphasis laid on a word, and the consequent realization of a contour on that word, modifies the utterance's division into tone groups, and that the syllables left stranded acquire extrametrical status. The notion of extrametricality rescues the general rule which serves as one of the key criteria for the definition of the tone group as a phonological unit, i.e. that contours only appear tone-group-finally.

Consider example (54):

(54) pv̩˩lɯ˥ | dʐɤ˥ | ki˩ tsɯ˩ | mv̩˩.
pv̩˩lɯ˥ dʐɤ˥   ki˧   tsɯ˥   mv̩˧
button to_pluck to_give   REP   AFFIRM

'It is said that [he] plucked a [button from his jacket] and gave it [to the child]. / He plucked a button and gave it [to the child].' (Renaming.23)

At least three stylistic options are open here. The most tightly-knit would involve a single tone group: /dʐɤ˧ ki˧ tsɯ˩/.[8] The most analytic would involve two full-fledged tone groups: /dʐɤ˥ | ki˧ tsɯ˥/. The third one, found in (54), is intermediate: the verb /dʐɤ˥/ 'to pluck' is realized with its lexical MH contour, as if it were tone-group-final, and the syllables that follow are all lowered to L, as if they belonged to the preceding tone group. The syllables /ki˩ tsɯ˩/ are extrametrical: they do not constitute a full-fledged tone group on their own.

---

[8] For the sake of simplicity, the affirmative final particle is left out of the analysis; it will be discussed in §7.3.3.

This range of stylistic variation is a salient characteristic of Yongning Na. Among other potential consequences for the evolution of the tone system, extrametrical syllables at the end of a tone group may tend to become affiliated to the following tone group instead, in cases where the sequence of (surface) tones allows for this reinterpretation. A case in point is the highly frequent sequence of topic marker //-dʐo˧// and discourse marker //tʰi˧// 'so, then'. The latter makes up a tone group on its own, as was mentioned in §7.2.1. However, in the narratives recorded by consultant F4, it is not preceded by any perceived pause, whereas there tends to be a pause before the topic marker, so that the two morphemes are pronounced in quick succession. There is thus a discrepancy between two levels: that of the division into tone groups, on the one hand, and that of linguistic rhythm, on the other. Now, the topic marker //-dʐo˧// most often surfaces as /-dʐo˩/, due to the presence of a H tone earlier on in the tone group, and the sequence of /-dʐo˩/ and /tʰi˧/ would constitute a well-formed tone group. The tone sequence L.LH can be the surface realization of underlying //L.LH//, or of underlying //L//. One may speculate that the high discourse frequency of the /-dʐo˩ tʰi˧/ sequence, which on the phonological surface looks like a tightly-knit tone group, paves the way for its reinterpretation as one tone group. Such reinterpretation is especially tempting in contexts such as (55).

(55)　… gɯ˩-ji˧ | -dʐo˩ | tʰi˧ …
　　　gɯ˩-ji˧　-dʐo˩　tʰi˧
　　　really　TOP　then
　　　'… in actual fact, …' (Mountains.58)

As explained in Appendix A (§A.5), the expression /gɯ˩-ji˧/ 'really, truly' (from /gɯ˩/ 'authentic, true') is well on its way towards reduction to a monosyllable: to my ears, it sounds like [gi˧] except when hyperarticulated. In (55), for instance, /gɯ˩-ji˧/ sounds very much like a monosyllable carrying a rising contour: [gi˧]. Now, a rising contour signals the end of a tone group. While the topic marker that follows, /-dʐo˩/, does not constitute a well-formed tone group, the sequence /-dʐo˩ tʰi˧/ would constitute one. To labour the point: although in data from speaker F4 the division into tone groups is clearly /…-dʐo˩ | tʰi˧ |/, this sequence could easily be interpreted by a language learner as a L-tone group: /| -dʐo˩ tʰi˧ |/.

7.3.3 Further examples of extrametrical elements

Additional language-internal evidence for resorting to the concept of extrametricality in the description of the Na tone system comes from the affirmative particle //-mɤ˧// and the expression /əɭ-giɭ/ 'isn't it!', 'right!'

The affirmative particle //-mɤ˧// cannot host a H level from a preceding reported-speech particle //tsɯ˥//: the sequence is realized as /tsɯ˥ mɤ˩/, not ‡ tsɯ˧ mɤ˥ or ‡ tsɯ˥ | mɤ˧. This is a case that seems to be best handled in terms of extrametricality.

The expression /əɭ-giɭ/ 'isn't it!', 'right!' is commonly tagged at the end of an utterance. Two observations suggest that this expression constitutes a tone group on its own. First, a preceding LH or MH contour does not unfold over it, as would be expected inside a tone group (Caravans.257, 287; Housebuilding.113; Mountains.159; Sister3.86). Secondly, the expression /əɭ-giɭ/ is often preceded by a short (perceived) pause. On the other hand, the fact that the expression /əɭ-giɭ/ only contains L tones implies that it does *not* constitute a tone group on its own, otherwise it would be realized as /əɭ-giʌ/ (following Rule 7). The latter, /əɭ-giʌ/, is well-formed and attested in the narratives, but it is a full-fledged question ('Is it true?'), whereas /əɭ-giɭ/ is more phatic, almost a gap-filler. For these reasons, the expression /əɭ-giɭ/ is here treated as extrametrical. In the transcriptions, it is preceded by a tone group boundary, to reflect the fact that it does not interact tonally with what precedes it.

To sum up: the tone group may be interrupted after the last syllable of a word (generally, but not exclusively, a verb or noun), leaving some syllables stranded. These syllables are described as having extrametrical status.

7.3.4 Deviant tone patterns and Mandarin loanwords: Does the existence of extrametrical syllables facilitate the introduction of loanwords with a non-final rising tone?

The phenomena described above in terms of *extrametricality* are clearly marginal. Yet they pave the way for increasingly significant changes to the tone system as a whole. They introduce unusual tone patterns which may become consolidated through loanwords: once a pattern exists in the language, however peripheral it may be, it is available for accommodating foreign combinations of sounds.

For instance, the gap-filler *jiùshi* 就是, 'quite right; exactly, precisely, just' is borrowed as /tɕo˦ʂɯ˩/, with a word-internal MH contour.[9] At first blush, this contravenes a basic phonotactic rule of Na: the restriction of contours to tone-group-final position. On the other hand, the process of emphasis described in §7.3.1 introduces tone-group-internal contours, which have now become habitually associated with some morphemes. The existence of these rising contours arguably facilitated the introduction of Mandarin loanwords with this tone pattern. In turn, loanwords contribute to the gradual spread of the previously deviant phonotactic pattern.

To carry the argument one step further, assuming that the emphatic value of tone-group-internal contours predates the borrowing of the gap-filler *jiùshi* 就是 'exactly' as /tɕo˦ʂɯ˩/, this expressive value may well have facilitated the retention of the rising tone at borrowing. Emphasis is well-suited to this item. A hint of emphasis or insistence is not inappropriate for a gap-filler: it can help convey to the addressee that the speaker wishes to keep their speech turn open. The word /tɕo˦ʂɯ˩/ is also used as a rejoinder ('Exactly!'), in Yongning Na as in Mandarin. In this usage too, a touch of emphasis is welcome, highlighting the intended message of convergence of viewpoints between the interlocutors. To put it differently, the item's lexical tone in Mandarin is congruent with its expressive interpretation in terms of Na prosody.

A cross-linguistic analogue to this situation is found in the success of the Vietnamese loanword *nhà quê* in French. The original Vietnamese is a derogatory term: 'yokel, hayseed, country bumpkin, backwoods person'. It was borrowed into French as *niakoué* (also spelt as *niacoué*) as a derogatory term for the Vietnamese, and later also for the Chinese. Lexical tones were lost in the process of borrowing, but the vowels and consonants match exactly: Vietnamese /ɲa.kwe/ was borrowed as /ɲa.kwe/. Initial ɲ has expressive value in French, as shown by a quick list of items that contain it: *gnan-gnan* 'mawkish, mushy', *gniaf* 'cobbler', *gn(i)ard* 'child', *gn(i)ouf* 'prison', *gnognot(t)e* 'worthless stuff', *gnolle* 'futile person', *gnôle* 'alcohol, hard stuff', *gnon* 'blow', *niaque (gnaque)* 'combativeness' are all slang words. The bad guy in Lyon's puppet theatre is revealingly named *Gnafron*. The only exception in the list is an Italian loanword, *gnocchi*, which apparently managed to gain integration despite the slangy flavour of its initial ɲ. Seen in this light, Vietnamese *nhà quê* /ɲa.kwe/ presumably owes some of its success in French to the overtones of its initial consonant.

---

[9] Note that the borrowing is from Southwestern Mandarin, where the syllable /tɕo/ 就 carries a rising tone, not a falling tone as in Standard Mandarin (on Southwestern Mandarin: Gui 2001; Pinson & Pinson 2008).

Returning to Yongning Na, word-initial contours in Chinese words used by consultant F4 are not restricted to expressively loaded words. The word for 'television' is a case in point.[10] Realizations in isolation fluctuate between /**tjɤ˥ʂɯ˧**/ (with a tone pattern unattested in Yongning Na, apart from Chinese words), /**tjɤ˧ʂɯ˧**/ (suggesting an underlying M or #H tone), and /**tjɤ˧ʂɯ˥**/ (unambiguously pointing to an underlying LM+MH# tone). The noun's tonal behaviour in context also fluctuates. The tones of /**tjɤ˧ʂɯ˧ li˩**/ 'to watch television', /**tjɤ˧ʂɯ˧ qo˩**/ 'on TV' and /**tjɤ˧ʂɯ˧ ɲi˩**/ 'is (a/the) TV' would suggest that the noun carries either LM+#H tone or LM+MH# tone (in light of the data set out in §5.4.2, §6.8, and §2.4.2, respectively), but a contour is sometimes realized on the first syllable: realizations such as /**tjɤ˥ʂɯ˧ ɲi˩**/ 'is (a/the) TV' are observed.

This is part of a general state of flux characterizing recent Chinese loanwords, also evidenced by fluctuation in the rhyme of the word for 'television', between /jɤ/ (which complies with Na phonotactics) and /je/ (which does not, and is phonetically closer to the Chinese model). These words remain perceived by consultant F4 as Chinese words, and have not acquired a stable Na form, but their presence paves the way for changes in the morphotonological system.

7.4 Concluding note

The division of an utterance into tone groups plays a central role in conveying phrasing and prominence. In this respect, the Na facts appear closely parallel to the division of sentences into intonational groups in English (or French) – extensively studied languages, for which a wealth of references is available (on French, see for instance Vaissière 1975; Di Cristo 1998; Rossi 1999; Martin 2015). A striking characteristic of Na is the constant interaction between these intonational choices and the language's tonal processes.

---

[10] Remember that the borrowings are from Southwestern Mandarin, where tone values are almost the reverse of Standard (Beijing) Mandarin, so that the syllable *diàn* 电 in *diànshì* 电视 'television' carries a rising tone, not a falling tone as in Standard Mandarin.

8 From surface phonological tone to phonetic realization

> ... a theory of tone must provide some means for describing intonational processes independently of tonal patterns, as well as a procedure for integrating the two structures.
>
> (Clements 1979: 547)

> If, as seems to be the case, the complexity of intonation is typical of human complexity, then there is still a long way to go before (...) intonation yields all of its secrets.
>
> (Vaissière 2004: 256)

8.1 Introduction

The established order of business when describing a language is to elucidate the phonological and morphophonological facts first, and to address issues of phonetic implementation later. In practice, tones and intonation are necessarily studied together, since they share an all-important phonetic correlate: voice fundamental frequency (F_0). This is especially clear in languages such as Na, where tones are specified only in terms of pitch: in Na, unlike in many other East/Southeast Asian languages, tones do not have length or phonation-type characteristics as part of their phonological definition. (This topic is taken up in the typological discussion, §10.1.1.)

This chapter contains observations about the phonetic implementation of tone, and intonation in general: everything that happens when surface phonological tone translates into a concrete phonetic realization.

As an introduction to this domain, Figure 8.1 shows spectrograms of /boɭ˧˦ɤ˦/ 'pig's brains' and /boɭ˧˦ɤ˦ ɲi˩/ 'is (a/the) pig's brains'.

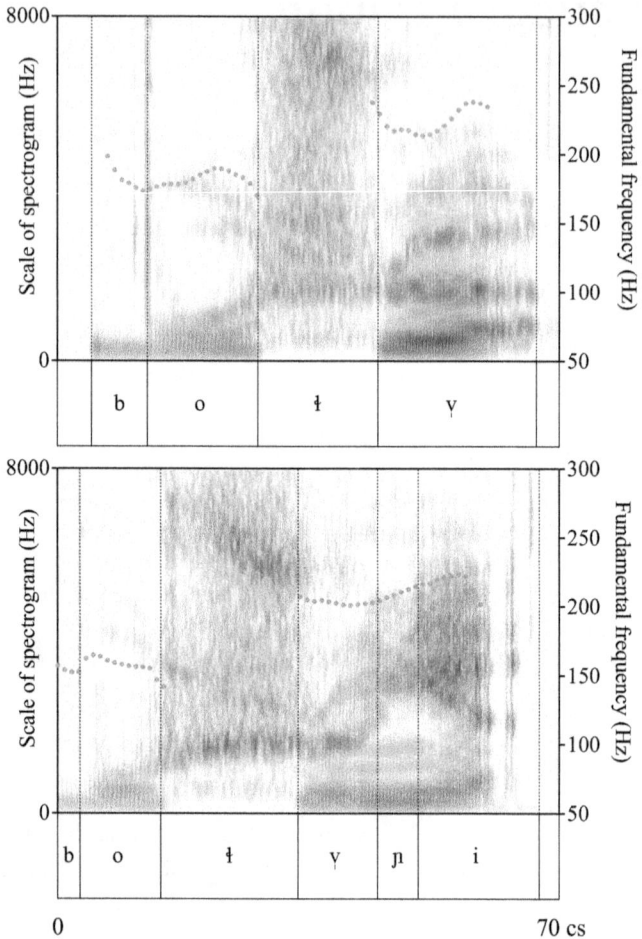

Figure 8.1: Spectrogram and F₀ tracing of 'pig's brains' and 'is (a/the) pig's brains'.

The clear rise in F_0 on the rhyme /ɤ/ in the top part of the figure is consistent with phonological description as a MH tone; and the flatter shape on the same rhyme in the bottom part of the figure, followed by higher F_0 on the copula, is consistent with phonological description as a sequence of M on one syllable and H on the next. But there is no way to read phonological tones off F_0 tracings (as emphasized e.g. by Cruz & Woodbury 2014 and Morey 2014). Figure 8.1 illustrates a phenomenon that is immediately apparent when examining any piece of experimental evidence: variability in the realization of tone. For instance, glottalization, which is common in Yongning Na in utterance-final position, is found at the end of both tokens, exerting a lowering influence on F_0 towards the offset of voicing. (In these materials, the phrases /bo˩-ɻ̍˦/ 'pig's brains' and /bo˩-ɻ̍˧ ɲi˩/ 'is (a/the) pig's brains' are both found in absolute final position, and therefore constitute entire sentences on their own.) Also, /bo˩/ 'pig' is realized with noticeably different F_0 in the top part of the figure and in the bottom part. Tone levels have some range of variation within tonal space (F_0), in the same way as vowels have some range of variation within the acoustic space (as characterized essentially by the first three formants, F1-F2-F3). In Yongning Na, rising tones are never found in initial position within a tone group, and hence the identification of an initial L tone (as on the syllable /bo˩/ 'pig') is not jeopardized by its realization with a slight rise, as in the top part of Figure 8.1. Seen in this light, the existence of slightly rising allotones (allophones of the tones) does not come as a surprise: it makes sense in view of the state of the phonological system, in the same way as, in a language that does not have contrastive aspirated consonants, plain (unaspirated) unvoiced consonants may sometimes be realized phonetically with some aspiration.

Back in the 1970s, at a time when F_0 tracings were difficult to do, necessitating expert technical skill, a specialist in Bantu tone asked a phonetician to create an F_0 tracing from a recording illustrating a specific phonological phenomenon. After receiving the desired tracing, this famous specialist of tonology said that there must be a mistake, as the F_0 tracing did not correspond to the tone pattern that his trained ear discerned clearly in the recording. In fact, there was no error in F_0 detection: the issue lay in this colleague's expectation of a neatly binary F_0 tracing, straightforwardly reflecting the phonological tone sequence (J. Vaissière, p.c. 2001). Experimental examination of spoken language reveals that, even in languages with relatively straightforward prosodic systems, such as Standard Japanese, F_0 curves are shaped by a number of factors, and do not reflect phonological tone in a crystal-clear, transparent way. Without the help of a language consultant, it is simply impossible to know for sure for a given utterance that has, for instance, a lowering of F_0 on its last syllable, whether this is due to a L tone on that syllable or to intonational final lowering of a M-tone syllable. Arriving at tonal contrasts requires factoring out intonation, and vice versa.

The following sections present salient characteristics of Na intonation. But first some concepts need to be discussed.

8.1.1 Definition of terms

Prosody as defined here consists of (i) lexically distinctive properties: stress, as in English; tone, as in Mandarin, Yorùbá or Na; tonal accent, as in Japanese[1] and Swedish; phonation-type register, as in Mon (Mon-Khmer family); (ii) intonation; and (iii) performance factors, including rhythm.

Intonation is often identified with the parameters in which it is manifested – and especially with fundamental frequency. But this identification is inappropriate, because intonation is a complex, abstract structure. It can usefully be divided into (i) two sub-systems of linguistic structure: syntactic intonation *(phrasing)*, which essentially reflects syntax in the broader sense, and pragmatic intonation *(prominence)*, which reflects information structure, and (ii) attitudinal and emotional dimensions, which convey speaker attitudes and emotions. This view of intonation is shown in Figure 8.2. It needs to be emphasized that this embedded (tree-like) graph is a highly simplified representation: its aim is to provide a visual recapitulation of the basic distinctions made here. It does not aim to reflect the delicate links among the various components of prosody, e.g. between rhythm and lexically distinctive suprasegmentals.

These definitions, taken from a publication about prosodic constituents in French (Vaissière & Michaud 2006), elaborate on proposals which (in my view) are similar in their essentials (Coustenoble & Armstrong 1937; Delattre 1965; Martin 1977; Rossi 1999). Usage still varies considerably among authors (a detailed discussion of various frameworks is proposed by Di Cristo 1998).

As defined here, tone has the function of lexical and morphological differenti-

---

[1] As mentioned in §7.1.3, several competing analyses of the prosodic systems of Japanese dialects have been proposed (for a review, see Kawahara 2015). The concept of tonal accent, also called pitch accent, has been presented by Hyman (2009) as a typical example of how *not* to do prosodic typology: the argument is that "alleged pitch-accent systems freely pick-and-choose properties from the tone and stress prototypes, producing mixed, ambiguous, and sometimes analytically indeterminate systems which appear to be intermediate". However, the description of pitch-accent systems as "intermediate" between stress and tone does not greatly clarify the issue. Hyman's questioning of pitch accent as a typological category could be extended to tone, in view of the considerable heterogeneity of prosodic systems that have been described as "tone systems" (see Brunelle & Kirby 2016 and the discussion in §10.1.1). As Hyman underlines, the goal of prosodic typology should be to classify not languages but rather the properties of their subsystems. In the present state of prosodic typology, it is not obvious to me that there is much to gain from prohibiting tonal accent as a descriptive label.

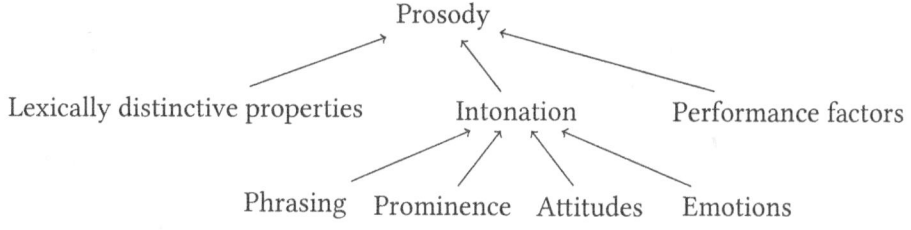

Figure 8.2: A highly schematic representation of the components of prosody.

ation, and intonation has the functions of (i) speech phrasing, (ii) coding prominence, and (iii) expressing emotions and attitudes towards the listener. Intonation is, in Bolinger's phrase, a "half-tamed savage" (Bolinger 1978: 475). *Phrasing* is on the tamer, more intellectual side; it surfaces at its clearest in deliberate oral renderings of elaborately composed texts. *Prominence* is a less tame dimension of intonation: it can still be described in terms of a linguistic system, with clear cross-linguistic differences, but the intrusion of the stronger manifestations of prominence can interfere with phrasing as determined by syntactic structure. The expression of attitudes and emotions can partly be described in terms of ethological principles, such as the Frequency Code:

> ... an innately specified 'Frequency Code' (...) associates high acoustic frequency with the primary meaning of 'small vocalizer' and thus secondary meanings as 'subordinate, submissive, non threatening, desirous of the receiver's goodwill, etc.' and associates with low acoustic frequency the primary meaning of 'large vocalizer' and such secondary meanings as 'dominant, aggressive, threatening', etc. (Ohala 1984: 1).

The phrase "syntactic intonation" may appear to be somewhat of a misnomer, insofar as intonational phrasing does not stand in a strict, one-to-one relationship with syntactic units, as was already noted in the early classics of phonetics (Grammont 1933) and confirmed by later work (Selkirk 1972; 2000: 231; Martin 1981). The phrase "syntactic intonation" is nonetheless retained in view of the fact that knowledge of a sentence's syntax offers a sufficient basis for the synthesis of an acceptable fundamental frequency contour (Vaissière 1971).

The acoustic correlates of prosody are many. They include the variations in fundamental frequency, duration and intensity and phonation type, but also the allophonic variations in the realization of the phonemes. Thus, prosody has correlates at the respiratory level (i.e. the subglottal level), at the glottis, and at the supra-glottal level (see Erickson 1998). All parameters take part in prosody simultaneously, to a greater or lesser extent.

Lastly, here are some clarifications about the concepts of 'tone sandhi', 'morphotonology' and 'tonal morphology'. *Tone sandhi* refers to phonologically specified tone change, applying automatically inside a given phonological domain. To put it differently, *tone sandhi* refers to categorical phenomena of tone change conditioned by the phonological context. The seven tonal rules of Yongning Na presented in §7.1.1 (repeated below) are tone sandhi rules, in the sense that they govern adjustments among neighbouring tones within a given phonological domain (the tone group).

Rule 1: L tone spreads progressively ("left-to-right") onto syllables that are unspecified for tone.

Rule 2: Syllables that remain unspecified for tone after the application of Rule 1 receive M tone.

Rule 3: In tone-group-initial position, H and M are neutralized to M.

Rule 4: The syllable following a H-tone syllable receives L tone.

Rule 5: All syllables following a H.L or M.L sequence receive L tone.

Rule 6: In tone-group-final position, H and M are neutralized to H if they follow a L tone.

Rule 7: If a tone group only contains L tones, a post-lexical H tone is added to its last syllable.

Morphotonology refers to categorical change in tone governed by rules that are confined to specific syntactic phrase types, e.g. the different rules that apply to object plus verb, subject plus verb, numeral plus classifier, and so on.

Finally, *tonal morphology* refers to grammatically specified tone change marking certain morphosyntactic categories. The phrase "tone cases" is used in the description of some Bantu languages, such as UMbundu (Schadeberg 1986), where a noun's tone changes according to its case. The addition of a certain tone to verbs can express a given tense/aspect/modality category.

In Yongning Na, there is no tonal morphology, in the sense that there are no tonal morphemes. The floating High tone in Yongning Na is not a morpheme (the combination of a form and a meaning): it is one of the lexical categories of nouns. As a consequence, only the first two of the three concepts characterized above – sandhi, morphotonology, and tonal morphology – are relevant to the present study.

Some authors prefer "a broad and loose usage of the term" *sandhi* covering both sandhi and morphotonology as defined here (Chen 2000: x). But while it is advisable to cast the net wide in language surveys (such as the survey of Chinese dialects by Chen 2000), the distinction between sandhi and morphotonology is crucial to the present study. The reason for writing a book-length description is that tonal changes in Yongning Na are not simply a matter of phonology: in addition to sandhi (as defined here: a phonological phenomenon), Yongning Na has a host of syntactically restricted tone rules, i.e. morphotonology.

8.1.2 About tools for intonational transcription

There does not yet exist a standardized system for transcribing intonation. This is easy to understand in view of the intricacy of this linguistic domain, described above.

> Since Bolinger first raised the question explicitly in 1951, there has been considerable argument over whether intonation is better described as pitch contours, like the kinetic tones of the British tradition, or as a sequence of pitch phonemes or significant levels (the American approach exemplified by Pike 1945, Wells 1945, Trager & Smith 1951, Hockett 1955, and now Liberman 1975 and the autosegmental school originated by Goldsmith 1976). (Ladd 1978: 531)

Under the second of these approaches, intonation is modelled by means of discrete levels, as if it were tonal. This approach is known as "autosegmental-metrical", and has dominated discussions of intonation since the 1980s. A reason for its popularity is that it seemed to hold promise for implementation in speech synthesis (Pierrehumbert 1981) and prosodic annotation (Silverman et al. 1992). The basic tenets of "autosegmental-metrical" models are concepts borrowed from autosegmental tonology, such as level tones, downstep and tone spreading. Pitch accents, organized in a linear sequence, are considered the building blocks of an intonation contour (see the textbooks by Ladd 1996 and Gussenhoven 2004, for instance).

If one stands back to take a global view of tonal models of intonation, however, they appear as hybrid and somewhat perplexing systems (as pointed out by Martin 2001 and Wightman 2002). The posited 'intonational tones' are abstract entities, but the labels are also used as a system for phonetic transcription of linguistically significant aspects of F_0 curves as they are observed. Tonal labels tend to be assigned by eye (on the basis of F_0 curves superimposed on spectrographic displays) more than by ear, whereas 'boundary tones' are meant to reflect the perceived cohesion between successive words, and are thus grounded in aural impressions as well as on the observation of F_0 curves. "To be fair to the original spirit of Janet Pierrehumbert, who intended to describe American English and carefully avoided generalization in her thesis, applying ToBI symbols to a new language requires prior re-evaluation of the underlying principles" (Vaissière 2002).

Interestingly, before he became one of the proponents of "autosegmental-metrical" models, Bob Ladd expressed the conviction that he had "clearly demonstrate[d] the inadequacy of any approach to English intonation which treats contours as sequences of significant pitch levels" (Ladd 1978: 517).

> In short, linguistic systems force users to identify certain signals as discretely different from one another; and linguists' analyses should reflect these discrete differences. But an analysis of intonation in terms of pitch levels forces us to distinguish points along a gradient as also being discretely different – even though they are not – because the theory provides no principled way of knowing when changing a certain feature in a sequence is going to produce a 'modulation', and when it is going to produce a 'very different tune'. No amount of tinkering with theoretical mechanisms can remedy this defect; the best that any pitch-level theory can do is ignore it. To continue to ignore the difference between the gradient and the all-or-none by forcing it into a pre-ordained system of distinctions is only to put off reaching an understanding of how intonation really functions in language. (Ladd 1978: 539)

This strand of thought (which makes excellent sense to me) continued to be pursued by some scholars even during the heyday of "autosegmental-metrical" models. Alternatives to tonal models of intonation include the Kiel Intonation Model and its developments (Niebuhr & Kohler 2004; Kohler 2005; Niebuhr 2007; 2010), superpositional approaches (Vaissière 2002; 2004; Grønnum 1991; 1998a,b; Lindau 1986), and various others (Delattre 1966; Fónagy 1989; Rossi 1999; Martin 1977; 2015; Hirst & Di Cristo 1998). These approaches are currently outside the mainstream of intonation studies, in the same way as non-autosegmental analyses of tone systems fall outside mainstream (generative) phonology (some reflections on this situation are set out in Zerbian 2010; Michaud & Vaissière 2015). My evaluation of the available evidence is that tonal accounts of intonation in tone languages run into considerable difficulties, and that it is better to adopt a vocabulary which suits the data, even if it is not mainstream at present, rather than force the data into inadequate models. As a consequence, the present description adopts a functional perspective that clearly distinguishes tone and intonation.

Another distinction which is essential to prosody studies is that between an abstract level of description, on the one hand, and the level of phonetic realizations, on the other. This distinction is threatened in frameworks where 'tone' is considered synonymous with F_0. For instance, Hyman & Monaka (2008) define the term 'tonal' in a phonetic sense, to mean 'realized by F_0', and 'non-tonal' to mean 'realized by parameters other than F_0' (such as phonation types). The equation between 'tone' and 'F_0' appears so self-evident that it could seem unnatural to try to define tone in any different way. But from a classical linguistic perspective, it is crucial to make a distinction between F_0, which is an acoustic parameter, and linguistic tone, which is a functional concept.

8.1.3 Intonation in level-tone languages: A review

In addition to the above remarks about the definition of terms and the frameworks for studying intonation, it may be useful, before beginning to describe intonation in Yongning Na, to review studies of intonation in other level-tone languages. This review also paves the way for the typological analyses set out in a later chapter (§10.1).

Auditory observations on phonetic realizations of tone in a two-tone language (Lingala) are proposed by Guthrie (1940):

> ... the only possible variations in the intonation of a word or sentence are these:
> (a) A widening or narrowing of the interval between the high and the normal tones.
> (b) A raising or lowering of the pitch of voice, i.e. a change of key.
> (c) A gradual rise or fall of the pitch of voice, i.e. a continuous change of key.
>
> In Lingala the only two variations that seem to exist are (a) and (b). The gradual fall of the pitch of the voice during a sentence is so slight as to be almost imperceptible. There is, however, another modification which affects the last syllable of a phrase or sentence only. This may be called the final cadence, and means that a high tone becomes a high-falling, while a tone that is normal becomes normal falling to low. (Guthrie 1940: 472–473)

Parameter (a) is considered to possess three degrees of variation. Guthrie proposes that there are four phonetic ranges, for which – somewhat surprisingly for

21st-century readers – he brings in musical definitions: minor third (considered as the "normal range"), major third, major fourth, and major fifth. Interestingly, Guthrie believes that the tonal range is set at sentence level. This arguably reflects a characteristic of the language that he was examining (Lingala): successive level tones hang together much more closely than in complex-tone systems,[2] where attention is drawn to *local* phenomena of F_0 range expansion or compression, which do not change the phonological nature of the tone of the syllables at issue.

To venture an impressionistic description of the difference between the two types of systems: level tones make sense as part of a sequence, whereas phonetically complex tones each have a stronger identity. Level tones are subject to a range of categorical processes that modify the tonal string, such as tone spreading (a H or L tone getting copied onto successive syllables), whereas complex tones are less prone to categorical change, and more prone to noncategorical, local intonational modification conveying indications about emphasis and phrasing. This does not entail that successive complex tones are independent of one another. For instance, in Mandarin, focus placed on one syllable has consequences on neighbouring – especially on following – syllables: "focus is usually related to F_0-range-expansion of focused words that are not in the final position of an utterance and F_0-range-suppression of post-focus words" (Zhang & Hirose 2004: 449). Moreover, tonal coarticulation phenomena in Sinitic, Vietnamese or Thai are strong, and they tend to harden diachronically into sandhi patterns (Abramson 1979; Gandour & Potisuk 1992; Brunelle 2003; 2009b; Zhang & Liu 2011). So it would not make sense to view the noncategorical intonational modification of complex tones as a purely local phenomenon, or conversely, to consider that level tones cannot be subject to any local, noncategorical intonational modification. Still, the following generalization seems to hold: in the field of intonation studies, Bantuists' attention seems to be regularly drawn to sentence-level phenomena, rather than to local phenomena of pragmatic emphasis. This suggests that local variations of the sort observed in complex-tone systems (as exemplified by Vietnamese, Thai and Sinitic), where they do not affect the phonological nature of the tones, are not as salient in level-tone systems as exemplified by Bantu languages. When studying Bantu prosody, attention is drawn instead to *categorical* local changes (changes that modify the string of phonological tones), and (secondarily) to sentence-level phenomena. Echoing Guthrie's study about Lingala, a study of Chichewa intonation likewise focuses on sentence mode, specifically on the differences in F_0 between questions and statements (Myers 1996).

---

[2] On the typological distinction between level-tone systems and complex-tone systems, see §10.1.1.

Guthrie describes the intonation of Lingala in terms of five different levels.

> Although there are actually five different levels used the language remains essentially two-tone, as in learning forms the only thing to be noticed is whether any syllable has a high or a normal tone. It is, moreover, interesting to notice how regular is the system of tone ranges. Emphasis shifts the intonation to the next higher range. Interrogation move the tones two ranges higher, while the use of the subjunctive reduces the pitch to the next lower range. (Guthrie 1940: 475–476)

Description of intonation in terms of a finite number of levels was a trend of the time in American structuralist approaches to intonation. Analyses of English intonation published shortly after Guthrie's study assume that there are four relevant levels of pitch: extra high, high, mid and low (Pike 1945; Trager & Smith 1951: 42). In Trager & Smith's system, the four levels combine with four relevant levels of stress (primary, secondary, tertiary, and weak), yielding a symmetrical system of no fewer than sixteen "pitch allophones". This system is rather contrived, and the sixteen units' links to linguistic functions look really tenuous. Fortunately, Trager & Smith's proposal is about English, and informed native speakers have provided articulate critical feedback:

> ... this reviewer, at least, simply does not hear the neatly symmetrical distribution of pitch allophones with phonemes of stress as Trager and Smith describe it, he often hears nothing to justify the writing of *plus* junctures where his colleagues write them, he is sometimes in serious doubt whether to write primary or secondary stress, and he is openly astonished at the apparent claim by Trager and Smith that in final position they can distinguish four allophones of each of four pitch phonemes before each of three terminal junctures. (...) Readers dislike being told that they can 'easily supply other examples' when the most patient effort leaves them utterly baffled. (Sledd 1955)

Writing about intonation in Yongning Na is a bigger scientific responsibility, as few native speakers are likely to examine the linguist's claims in such detail.

A general issue with the framework proposed by Trager & Smith to study intonation is that it suffers from the same immoderate ambition as Hall & Trager's framework for the *analysis of culture*: "a hypothesis and methodology for the analysis of culture as a whole and specific cultural systems... a general analytic scheme into which all cultural activities, at all levels of integration and complexity, can be fitted" (Hall & Trager 1953: 57). By contrast, Guthrie's proposals have much to commend them. Guthrie clearly distinguishes the two level tones from the intonational factors that influence their realization. Moreover, although the four proposed phonetic ranges are presented in an order based on form, from narrowest to widest, the analysis hinges on the linguistic functions associated with variations in tone range. This is a fruitful approach, which brings out a wealth of interesting observations.

Less positively, Guthrie's proposal that the tonal levels constitute a closed set (five in all) is hard to reconcile with the observed diversity of intonational patterns. It is understandable that linguists should wish to operate with a finite set of basic units in all fields of linguistic description, as they do at the phonemic level, and in the study of tonal phenomena. But these tools are less than fully appropriate in the field of intonation; linguistic models that treat intonation systems on the analogy of phonemic systems fail to capture their object.

> This phenomenon [=intonation] has considerable importance in oral communication, but has specificities that make it really troublesome to the linguist, since the methods that have been tried and tested in other areas do not seem truly adequate for the analysis of intonation. (Creissels 1994: 173)[3]

It now seems clear that there is no cross-linguistically fixed number of levels to be distinguished when representing phonetic realizations of tone. On the basis of expert listening, Creissels proposes stylized representations of the phonetic realizations of certain sequences of tones (in a two-tone system) which clarify that tone implementation is language-specific. For instance, Figure 8.3 illustrates an observation made in some tonal languages of Subsaharan Africa: the first in a sequence of L tones following a H tone carries pitch that is intermediate between that of the preceding H tone and that of the following L tones. "Such realizations can be seen as the inception of a phenomenon of propagation: if the raising of the first in a sequence of L tones following a H tone becomes more noticeable, it can result in misperception as a H tone" (Creissels 1994: 215–216).[4]

---

[3] *Original text*: L'importance de ce phénomène [=l'intonation] dans la communication orale est considérable, mais sa spécificité gêne beaucoup le linguiste, car les méthodes d'analyse qui ont fait leurs preuves dans d'autres domaines ne semblent pas convenir vraiment pour l'analyse de l'intonation.

[4] *Original text*: On observe par exemple dans certaines langues que, sans que son identification comme ton bas soit remise en cause, le premier d'une séquence de tons bas succédant à un ton haut est réalisé à un niveau intermédiaire entre celui du ton haut qui le précède et celui des tons bas suivants. (...) On peut voir dans de telles réalisations l'amorce d'un phénomène de propagation : en effet, si le réhaussement du premier d'une séquence de tons bas succédant à un haut s'accentue, on peut aboutir à la confusion avec un ton haut (...).

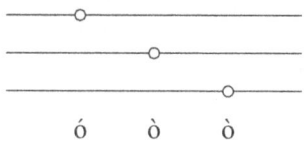

Figure 8.3: Stylized representation of the realization of a H.L.L sequence in some Subsaharan languages: as a gradual decrease in pitch from the first syllable to the third (Creissels 1994: 217).

This observation brings out the tonal coarticulation pattern's evolutionary potential. On the other hand, readers with an interest in experimental phonetics may want more detail than the schematized representation in Figure 8.3 can encapsulate. If there are three L tones in a row, are the second and third realized on the same phonetic level? Or is there gradual decrease in pitch from one syllable to the next? Is this decrease linear or asymptotic? Experimental-phonetic studies of level tones containing proposals for modelling tonal implementation are available for several two-tone systems, such as Dinka (Remijsen & Ladd 2008), Kinyarwanda (Myers 2003) and Sotho (Zerbian & Barnard 2010a,b), three-tone systems (Teo 2014: 48–65; Coupe 2003: 100–106; Laniran & Clements 2003), and four-tone systems, e.g. Mambila (Connell 2003; 2016). These studies confirm that issues of tone realization are conditioned by a host of language-specific parameters.

The present chapter aims to bring out such parameters of the Yongning Na prosodic system. No experimental phonetic tools are deployed to explore these issues: "the linguistic analysis, which may perfectly well be made on auditory basis, must come first" (Fischer-Jørgensen 1949: 4). The prospect of future experimental verification was constantly kept in mind, however, and the observations proposed below are intended as a basis for phonetic experiments.

8.2 Syntactic intonation: Phrasing and junctures

The most important unit in the prosodic organization of Na speech is the tone group, studied in Chapter 7. But from the point of view of phonetic implementation, successive tone groups are not entirely independent. Tone groups are part of higher-level prosodic units which can be defined in various ways. Two units which appear especially useful as cross-linguistic descriptive concepts, though their definition is not without problems, are the prosodic paragraph and the sentence (also referred to as 'utterance', with a view to bringing out its grounding in a communicative context, emphasized e.g. by Culioli 1995). The term 'paragraph' is open to criticism on the part of linguists who object to the transfer of concepts from the study of written texts to that of oral speech; it is a convenient term nonetheless, in view of the similarities between the division of a written text into paragraphs and that of speech into prosodic paragraphs, with a high degree of stylistic freedom in both cases. Here is a brief characterization of the prosodic paragraph and the sentence, adapted from Vaissière & Michaud (2006: 50–52).

Cross-linguistically, the peak F_0 value in a sentence tends to decrease from the first to the last sentence in a paragraph (Lehiste 1975). The end of the paragraph typically ends on an extra-low F_0 (often leading to a change in phonation type) and intensity.

At sentence level, the neutral, affirmative sentence is the basic, archetypal pattern from which other sentence modes depart (Thorsen 1980). Abstracting away from all other dimensions of prosody (such as lexically distinctive suprasegmentals, prominence, and the expression of attitudes and emotions), the F_0 curve for the sentence rises to a peak located on one of the sentence's first syllables. In the course of the sentence, a phonetic, gradual, noncategorical decrease in fundamental frequency takes place. This is known as 'declination'. Fundamental frequency therefore fluctuates within a gradually narrowed range. A final lowering marks the end of the sentence. (This corresponds to Tune 1 as described for English by Armstrong & Ward 1926.) Final lowering is a more local phenomenon, typically affecting the last syllable in declarative utterances, but this is subject to cross-language variation.

> Final lowering can be total, leading to the neutralisation of High and Low tones, as in Akan. It can be realized as a low register plateau, as in Chichewa or in Bemba (for the long stretched one), or as a gradual fall, as in Embosi, or as a sharp fall, as in Bemba (for the one syllable one). Its domain can be short (one syllable) or rather long (a stretch of tone bearing units). (Downing & Rialland 2016: 4-5)

Declination and final lowering are common across languages, as is their suspension to convey non-assertiveness (in questions, or to convey nuances of doubt and uncertainty).

From a phonetic point of view, these phenomena interact with phonological tones: the phonetic realization of a phonological H, M or L differs considerably depending on the position of the syllable inside the sentence and the prosodic paragraph. For instance, in Yongning Na the 1st, 2nd and 3rd-person pronouns

//njɤ˧//, //no˧//, and //tʂʰɯ˧// all have M tone in isolation due to the neutralization, in this position, of the lexical categories L, M and H. Their surface phonological representation in isolation is therefore /njɤ˧/, /no˧/ and /tʂʰɯ˧/, respectively. But in my first notes I transcribed them with H tone, as [njɤ˥], [no˥] and [tʂʰɯ˥]. This was due to their realization on a high pitch in isolation. In that context, their pitch is noticeably higher than that of a M tone in tone-group-initial position later on inside a prosodic paragraph.

Moreover, since the opposition between M and H is neutralized in tone-group-initial position, a phonetically high realization runs no risk of being misinterpreted by native listeners. As a consequence, M tones in this position have the entire upper part of the tonal phonetic space as their range of intonational variation. In my first field notes, I transcribed (1) as ‡ **njɤ˥ mɤ˧-dzɯ˥**; I was led to this phonologically inappropriate notation by the considerable phonetic difference in pitch between the first and second syllables, and the similarity in pitch between the first and last syllables of this short sentence.

(1) njɤ˧ | mɤ˧-dzɯ˥.
    njɤ˧   mɤ˧-   dzɯ˥
    1SG   NEG   to_eat
    'I don't eat.'

These intonational facts had to be brought to light before a correct transcription of the surface phonological form of the pronouns could be arrived at.

8.3 Pragmatic intonation

"Information structure is a vast topic of research that has been pursued within different theoretical frameworks" (Krifka 2008: 244), and with different objectives in view. A few general observations about information structure in Yongning Na will be followed by a discussion of three phenomena that belong to *pragmatic intonation*: (i) emphatic stress (§8.3.1), (ii) focalization through local intonational modification of tone (§8.3.2), and (iii) intonational backgrounding of function words (§8.5.1).[5]

The following generalization about Qiang proposed by LaPolla & Huang (2003: 221) also applies to Yongning Na (and other Sino-Tibetan languages):

> The structure of the clause is to some extent affected by pragmatic factors, but this only applies to the order of noun phrases in the clause.

---

[5] This section contains passages adapted from Michaud & Brunelle (2016).

The utterance-initial position is the unmarked topic position (though secondary topics can follow the primary topic), while the position immediately before the verb is the unmarked focus position, and so the focused element will generally appear there. The verb always appears in final position; there is no possibility for the actor of a clause to appear in postverbal position, even if it is focal. The only exception to this is the occasional afterthought clarification of a noun phrase that was omitted or expressed as a pronoun in the clause.

Information structure in Na has accordingly been described as 'topic-comment', extending an observation made by Chao Yuen-ren about Sinitic: "the grammatical meaning of subject and predicate in a Chinese sentence is topic and comment, rather than actor and action" (Chao 1968: 69; see also Shi 2000; LaPolla 2009).

> The primary information structure in Na is topic/comment rather than subject/predicate. (…) [A] topic can be a nominal argument, which the rest of the sentence will comment upon, but the topic can also be an adverbial, an independent clause, or a dependent clause. (Lidz 2010: 296)

Example (2) provides an illustration.

(2) le˧-dzɯ˥ | bi˧mi˧ go˩.
le˧-   dzɯ˥   bi˧mi˧   go˩ₐ
ACCOMP to_eat stomach/belly to_ache

'[If] [you] eat [of it], [your] stomach [will] hurt!' (Field notes. Context: on the mountain, pointing out a berry that is not edible.)

8.3.1 Emphatic stress and its toned-down avatars

An 'up' arrow ↑ is used to mark emphatic stress, as in (3), following a convention used by Mazaudon (2004). In Mazaudon's transcriptions of Tamang, tone is indicated to the left of the syllable, and the mark for intonational emphasis is added to the right; for Yongning Na, since tone is indicated to the right of the syllable, the arrow ↑ indicating emphatic stress is placed to the left of the syllable that carries it.

(3) tʰi˩, | ə˧my˧ ji˩-hĩ˩ | -dʑo˩, | ↑zo˧ ɲi˩ tsɯ˩ | mv̩˩.
tʰi˩   ə˧my˧   ji˩   -hĩ˩   dʑo˩   zo˩   ɲi˩   tsɯ˩   mv̩˧
then elder_sibling to_do REL   TOP   boy/son COP   REP   AFFIRM

'The elder [of the two siblings] was a boy.' (Sister.5)

In many contexts, emphatic stress appears on a constituent that can be predicted to receive normal focus prosody. For example, in sentence (3), one would expect the focus to be in the immediate preverbal position – the usual unmarked focus position for verb-final languages. Emphatic stress can be considered an extreme form of focus prosody. It is an extreme along a continuum: there is no hard-and-fast boundary between emphatic stress and milder realizations of focus prosody.

Emphatic stress is phonetically located on one syllable only, but from the point of view of interpretation, there is ambiguity of focus marking: either "broad focus" or "narrow focus", to use terms proposed by Lambrecht (1994). This phenomenon is extensively studied in the literature on focus projection (e.g. Selkirk 1995).

The phonetic realization of emphatic stress includes effects on the articulation of vowels and consonants. For instance, the second syllable of the verb /dʐɤ˧↑bv̩˥/ 'to play' is realized in (4) with stronger trilling of the /b/ than is found in non-emphatic contexts. This can be considered an example of 'articulatory prosodies' in the sense of Kohler & Niebuhr (2011) and Niebuhr (2013).

(4) mv̩˩zo˩=ɻæ˩ lɑ˥ | ə˧ji˧-ʂɯ˥ʝi˩ | tʰi˧/, | dʐɤ˩↑bv̩˥-ɲi˩ tsɯ˩ | mv̩˩!

mv̩˩zo˩	=ɻæ˩	lɑ˧	ə˧ji˧-ʂɯ˥ʝi˩	tʰi˧/	dʐɤ˩bv̩˥
girl	ASSOCIATIVE	with	long_ago	so/then	to_play

-ɲi˩	tsɯ˥	mv̩˧
CERTITUDE	REP	AFFIRM

'The story goes that at that time, long ago, he would have fun [i.e. flirt] with girls!' (Caravans.231)

8.3.1.1 Emphatic stress as a language universal

Emphatic stress in Na appears to be essentially the same as in English and French, hence the choice to use this label (proposed by Coustenoble & Armstrong 1937). Prototypical realizations of emphatic stress have been shown to involve supplementary activity of the expiratory muscles, resulting in a sudden increase in subglottal pressure during the articulation of a consonant (Benguerel 1973; Carton et al. 1976; Ohala 1978; Fant, Hertegård & Kruckenberg 1996), hence the term "force-accent" used by Kohler (2003). This category has been somewhat neglected in intonation studies, as tonal models of intonation have led researchers to focus their attention mostly on the acoustic parameter of fundamental frequency. But it is a good candidate for the status of universal of human language. Its linguistic functions range from the attitudinal and emotional to the pragmatic: it is the most extreme manifestation of intonational emphasis. Toned-down realizations of emphatic stress are more common than its prototypical realization: physiological effort at a subglottal level is mimicked through such strategies as F_0 excursions and consonant lengthening. Needless to say, the description of emphatic stress as a language universal by no means implies that it is uniformly present in all languages and all oral genres. Like other linguistic phenomena, it comprises important language-specific and speech-style-specific dimensions. Its frequency of use varies greatly from language to language, from speaker to speaker, and from style to style; its stylistic effect is inversely proportional to its frequency of use.

8.3.1.2 The superposition of lexical tone and intonation

The general approach adopted here is superpositional, distinguishing different levels: in particular, tone on the one hand, and intonational modifications (reflecting boundaries/junctures and information structure) on the other. Great care needs to be exercised in the analysis of these phenomena, maintaining the functional distinction between lexical tones and intonation. For instance, when picking up the phone, speakers of Mandarin say *wèi* 喂, lexically a tone-4 syllable, i.e. with sharply falling pitch; but in this context, the lexical tone can be overridden by interrogative intonation, and the pitch is often rising. One interpretation would be that the lexical tone, tone 4, is changed to another, say, tone 2, the rising tone. But rather than treating this case as an instance of tone change, it makes better sense to consider it as an example where the lexical tone has so little communicational relevance, and the expression of sentence mode and speaker attitude such importance, that their superposition leaves little trace (if any) of the lexical tone.

A compromise has to be found, in each speech act, between the competing demands of clarity, on the one hand, and expressivity, on the other. It seems clear that Na speakers are careful to avoid too great a distortion of the tonal string due to intonational emphasis. While no specific phonetic study has so far been conducted on Yongning Na data, it seems reasonable to assume that the situation is comparable to Naxi, where a study of the three basic tones (H, M and L) under emphasis reveals a proportionally milder effect of emphasis on F_0 than on intensity, as compared to English data (Michaud 2005: 107–167; Michaud, Nguyễn & Vaissière 2015).

8.3.1.3 Cases where intonation interacts with the tonal string

In some marginal cases, however, intonational modifications go so far as to affect the string of tones for the utterance. In its most vehement manifestations, emphatic stress intrudes into a sentence's prosody, wreaking havoc on tonal contrasts. Example (5) is a case in point.

(5) pʰʌ˩-tɕæ˥ɻæ˩ gʌ˩-kʌ˩-ze˩ mæ˩!
 pʰʌ˩-tɕæ˩ɻæ˥ gʌ˦ -kʌ˧ -ze˦ᵦ mæ˦
 very_white to_become ABILITIVE PFV AFFIRM
 '[after boiling, linen thread] can become really white!' (FoodShortage.73)

The usual pronunciation is /pʰʌ˩-tɕæ˩ɻæ˥/ 'very white'. In (5), the second syllable is realized phonetically with extremely high fundamental frequency on the syllable /tɕæ˩/, which is also considerably lengthened. From a phonetic point of view, its phonetic L tone is conspicuously disregarded. One way of looking at this modification would be to describe it as due to an intonational overlay: functionally, one could consider transcribing as /pʰʌ˩-↑tɕæ˩ɻæ˥-gʌ˩/, where the arrow ↑ indicates emphatic stress, and the phonological tonal string is unchanged.

This forcible intonational modification does interact with the phonological tone string of the tone group, however. If the modification of the second syllable in /pʰʌ˩-tɕæ˩ɻæ˥-gʌ˩/ only took place on an intonational level, one would expect the phonological tonal string to remain unchanged, in which case the third syllable would retain its phonological H tone. But what is observed is that the third and fourth syllables in (5) are lowered to L: /ɻæ˩-gʌ˩/. This is precisely what is expected if the second syllable carries H tone. This phenomenon is therefore analyzed as involving a categorical tone change, from a L.L.H sequence, /pʰʌ˩-tɕæ˩ɻæ˥/, to a L.H.L sequence, /pʰʌ˩-tɕæ˥ɻæ˩/.

8.3.2 Focalization through local intonational modification of tone

8.3.2.1 The main facts

In Yongning Na, there can be focalization through local intonational modification of tone on the last syllable of the word in focus. The syllable gets lengthened. A H or M level is changed to a dipping contour, and the phonetic range of a MH or LH rising contour gets expanded. As for L tone, which is canonically realized with a decrease in fundamental frequency, its phonetic falling contour becomes more noticeable under focalization. This phenomenon will be referred to, for short, as *intonational focalization*. The notation adopted is '**F**' (for 'Focalization'), written after the syllable at issue. This may seem inconsistent with the choice to place the upward arrow for emphatic stress (↑) *before* the syllable that receives emphatic stress (§8.3.1). There is a phonetic basis for this different treatment, however: emphatic stress is strongest at the *beginning* of the syllable, whereas intonational focalization is implemented through a modification that strongly affects the syllable *rhyme*.

This phenomenon was first identified in examples where the syllable receiving this intonational modification carried H tone. Modification of H tone is more conspicuous than that of M, L, MH or LH: the realization of H tone becomes a rapid dipping contour, for instance in examples (6) and (7).

(6) hĩ˦-ki˦ | ɖɯ˦-kʰwɤ˥ F | mɤ˦-pi˥!
hĩ˥   -ki˦ ɖɯ˦-kʰwɤ˥$ mɤ˦- pi˥
person DAT 1-CLF.pieces NEG to_say

'(S)he did not say anything to the people present! / (S)he did not greet anyone!' (Field notes, 2009)

(7) no˦ | njɤ˦-ki˦ | ɖɯ˦-sɑ˥ F | hwæ˦-mɤ˦-zo˦!
no˩   njɤ˩ -ki˦ ɖɯ˦-sɑ˥$ hwæ˦ₐ   mɤ˦-   -zo˦ₐ
2SG   1ST   DAT   1-CLF.things to_buy   NEG   OBLIG

'You don't need to give me anything! / There is no need to buy any presents for me!' (Trader.34)

In (6), the numeral-plus-classifier phrase /ɖɯ˦-kʰwɤ˥/ 'one piece' is given prominence through the phonetic realization of the classifier /kʰwɤ˥/ with a noticeable fall plus lengthening. Likewise for /ɖɯ˦-sɑ˥/ 'anything' (literally 'one thing') in (7). A spectrogram is shown in Figure 8.4.

This phenomenon is found in rapid speech as well as in slow repetitions.

It was later realized that the same type of prominence-lending local intonational modification could also be found for the two rising contours: high-rising (MH) and low-rising (LH). For these contours, the modification consists of lengthening and F₀ range expansion. Due to the phonetic fact that these are phonological contours, which by themselves have greater duration than simple levels, the intonational modification is less salient perceptually than for the M and H levels. Recognition of the existence of this phenomenon for the L level came last.

On the analogy of Naxi, where a reduced M- or L-tone syllable can result in the creation of contours (Michaud & He 2007) which bear some phonetic similarity to those of Yongning Na, it was first hypothesized that there must be a reduced syllable in examples such as (6): ‡ **ɖɯ˦-kʰwɤ˥-ə˩ mɤ˦-pi˥**. Likewise, example (8)

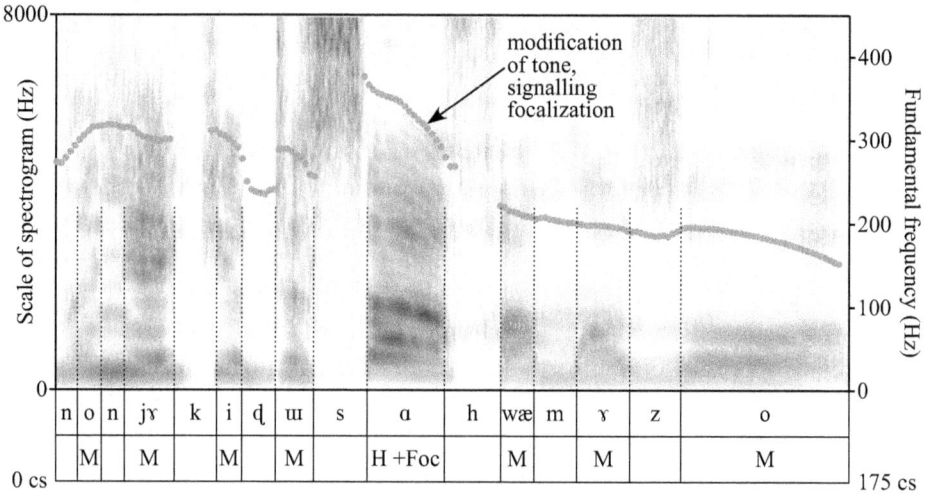

Figure 8.4: Spectrogram and F₀ curve for example (7), showing a noticeable fall plus lengthening on the syllable /sa˥/ in /ɖɯ˦-sa˥/ 'anything'. Top line of annotation: segments; bottom line: tones, with the added mention '+Foc' for the syllable receiving intonational focalization.

was initially transcribed as ‡ ə˦-dzʁ˦~dzʁ˥-ə˩ dzɯ˦. Subsequent investigation showed that these notations were inappropriate. The dip in fundamental frequency, accompanied by lengthening, is a purely intonational device: it does not involve an added syllable.

(8)   ə˦-dzʁ˦~dzʁ˥ F | dzɯ˦!
       ə˦-dzʁ˦~dzʁ˥   F   dzɯ˥
       slowly   FOCALIZATION   to_eat

'Eat slowly!/Take your time!' (Polite invitation to eat.)

The realization of focalization comprises a movement in F_0, a slight lengthening, and perhaps a slight change in the vowel, as if a final *schwa* target were added after the vowel. This is sufficiently precise and specific to preserve tonal distinctions (avoiding headlong conflict with lexical tone). To put it differently, no neutralization of lexical tonal contrasts takes place under focalization. Emphatic tone is likewise identifiable as such, from cues other than fundamental frequency. This limits the possibility of a misperception of lexical tone caused by these intonational phenomena.

8.3.2.2 Borderline cases

About two hundred instances of intonational focalization are indicated in the first twenty transcribed texts. Some cases are clearer than others. For one thing, cases where this focalization is superimposed on rising contours, and on L tones, appear less salient for phonetic reasons, as outlined above. For another, there are borderline cases, where it is not obvious whether to add a 'F' in the transcription or not. Borderline cases do not by themselves cast doubt on the categorical nature of the phenomenon. Intonational focalization can be toned down, in the same way as emphatic stress has toned-down avatars shading into non-emphatic realizations; this is a common situation in the field of intonation. On the other hand, it should be borne in mind, when consulting the texts, that the 'F' and '↑' symbols (for intonational focalization and emphatic stress, respectively) cannot be assigned with the same degree of certainty as consonants, vowels and tones. For instance, the syllable /liɬ/ 'to see' is transcribed in (9)[6] with an indication of intonational focalization, on the basis of the auditory impression that it stands out in the flow of speech. The proposed translation for /hĩ˧ liɬ F mʁɬ-ʁoɬ/ in (9) is '... could not *even* see people', to reflect the pragmatic implications of focalization on the verb 'to see'. The sequence /hĩ˧ liɬ mʁɬ-ʁoɬ/, without intonational focalization, would simply mean '... could not see people'.

(9) le˧-moɬ, | le˧-moɬ, | njʁɬɯ˧ | tsʰɯ˧ne˧ gʋ˧, | hĩ˧ liɬ F mʁɬ-ʁoɬ!

le˧-	moɬₐ	njʁɬɯ˧	tsʰɯ˧ne˧-ji˧	gʋ˧꜀	hĩ˧	li˧ₐ
ACCOMP	old	eye	thus	to_occur	person	to_look_at
F		mʁ˧-	ʁo˧			
FOCALIZATION		NEG	to_be_able_to/to_manage			

'[The dog] got older and older; and so, its eyes could not even look at people anymore / it could not even see people anymore!' (Dog2.80)

But looking at the spectrogram in Figure 8.5, it appears that the syllable /liɬ/ 'to see' is not strikingly different from its neighbours in terms of either duration or fundamental frequency. Average fundamental frequency over the vowel /i/ in /liɬ/ is two semitones lower than over the vowel /ĩ/ in the preceding syllable, /hĩ˧/ (210 Hz vs. 237 Hz), a phonetic difference that is in keeping with the phonological tones (M vs. L). The decrease in fundamental frequency between /liɬ/ and the

---

[6] In (9), the second and third syllables of /tsʰɯ˧ne˧-ji˧/ 'thus' are coalescent, and fully undistinguishable on the spectrogram (Figure 8.5). For convenience, a simplified transcription as [tsʰɯ˧ne˧ gʋ˧] is adopted in the surface phonological transcription of the sentence, and in the annotation to the spectrogram, in preference to /tsʰɯ˧ne˧-ji˧ gʋ˧/. This case of coalescence is analyzed in Appendix A, §A.3.1.

two L-tone syllables that follow can be interpreted as a straightforward case of *declination*, a phenomenon mentioned in §8.2.

The data is nonetheless compatible with the hypothesis (based on auditory impression) that the syllable /li˩/ 'to see' is highlighted by intonational means. In terms of duration, the syllable /li˩/ is 20 centiseconds long, which is slightly above the average for the passage shown in Figure 8.5 (100 centiseconds for seven syllables, i.e. about one syllable every 15 centiseconds). This difference in length cannot be dismissed as linked to the syllable's phonemes: if anything, the vowel /i/ would be expected to be intrinsically *shorter* than other vowels (Di Cristo & Hirst 1986; Whalen et al. 1998). As for fundamental frequency, the display in Figure 8.5, covering the range from 0 Hz to 450 Hz, gives the impression of a relatively smooth curve over the last four syllables, but if the scale is changed to a narrower range, as in Figure 8.6, the hump at the beginning of the vowel /i/ in /li˩/ becomes more salient visually. This hump, which results in a dip of 2.5 semitones in the brief course of this vowel, could be significant: there is no obvious contextual reason why the hump should be present, therefore it makes sense to interpret it as one of the phonetic correlates of a local intonational modification signalling some sort of emphasis, such as the phenomenon of intonational focalization transcribed here as '**F**'.

When transcribing narratives, one way to check with the speaker whether to classify a given case as having intonational focalization or not consists in playing the passage at issue, then repeating it with and without the telltale fall in pitch and lengthened rhyme, and asking the consultant to indicate which of the two realizations fits better. This entails no guarantee, however: even supposing that the investigator is successful in producing the intended distinction, the consultant may not base her decision on the realization heard on the recording. She may go for the realization which she considers (in retrospect) would have been more suitable in that context.

Pending experimental verification by perceptual tests, it seems likely that different speakers have different degrees of sensitivity to intonational detail. Toned-down versions of intonational focalization may go unnoticed by some speakers. It is a fact of life that hearers can fail to pick up intended clues. A linguist's aphorism has it that, in human communication, misunderstanding is the general case, and mutual understanding is a special case ("la compréhension est un cas particulier du malentendu": Culioli 1990: 39). The world is a cemetery of cultures, and each text is a tomb for allusions.[7]

---

[7] Lost allusions are often staged in literary works, among them Proust's *In Search of Lost Time*. The grandmother's sisters design allusions that are so carefully veiled that they are unintel-

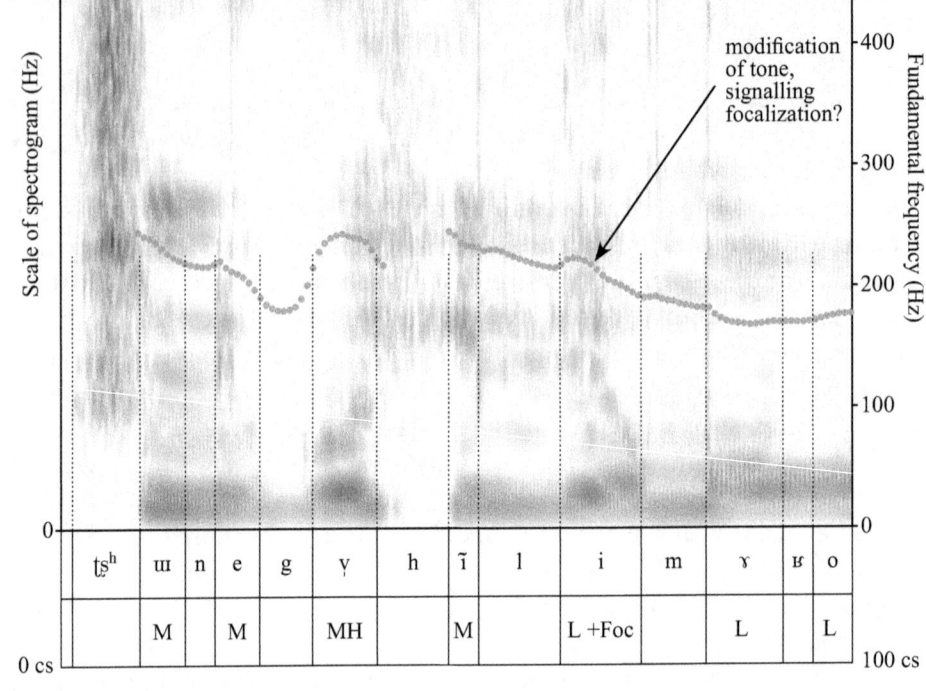

Figure 8.5: Spectrogram and F₀ curve for example (9), showing a slight fall plus hints of lengthening on the syllable /liɹ/ 'to see'. Top line of annotation: segments; bottom line: tones, with the added mention '+Foc' for the syllable presumed to receive intonational focalization.

8.3.2.3 A case in which intonational focalization has become habitual

This paragraph presents a case of habitual association of intonational focalization to a phrase. The classifier /saɹ/ 'thing' only appears in the phrase /ɖɯ˧-saɹ/ 'anything', itself restricted to negative contexts: typical examples are shown in (10) and (11).

---

ligible to the intended addressees: "... they, in their horror of vulgarity, had brought to such a fine art the concealment of a personal allusion in a wealth of ingenious circumlocution, that it would often pass unnoticed even by the person to whom it was addressed." Scott Moncrieff translation revised by Terence Kilmartin. *Original text*: "Celles-ci par horreur de la vulgarité poussaient si loin l'art de dissimuler sous des périphrases ingénieuses une allusion personnelle qu'elle passait souvent inaperçue de celui même à qui elle s'adressait."

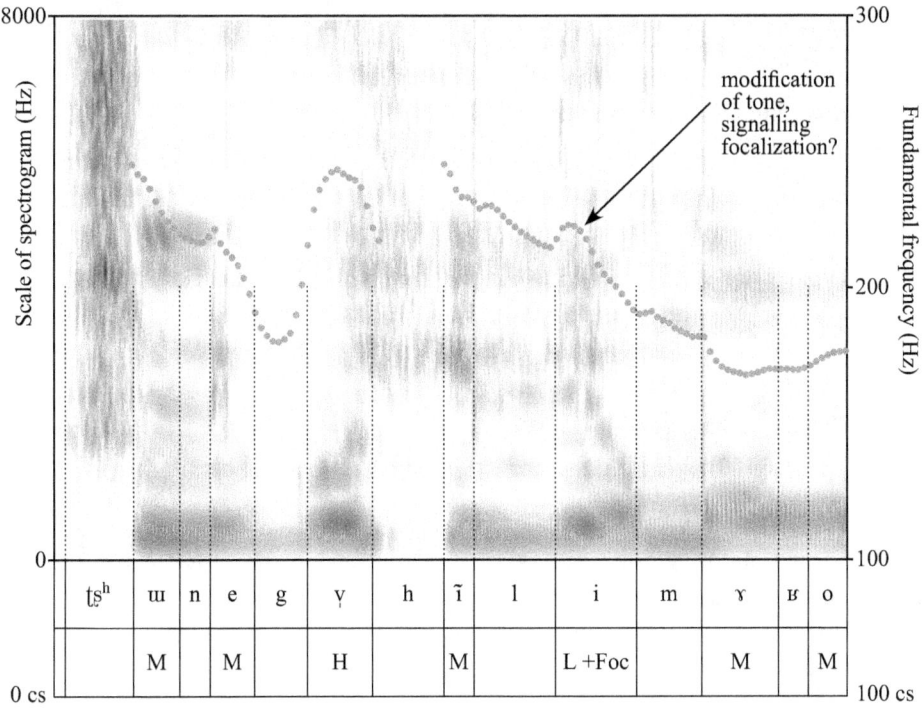

Figure 8.6: Same data as in Figure 8.5, adopting a narrower range for F₀ display.

(10) ɖɯ˧-sɑ˩ F | mɤ˧-dʑo˧.
    ɖɯ˧   sɑ˩   F   mɤ˧-   dʑo˧ᵦ
    one   CLF.things   FOCALIZATION   NEG   to_possess
    '[I/they] don't have anything at all / [I/they] have nothing at all.'

(11) ɖɯ˧-sɑ˩ F | mɤ˧-ʑi˩
    ɖɯ˧   sɑ˩   F   mɤ˧-   ʑi˩
    one   CLF.things   FOCALIZATION   NEG   to_do
    'to do nothing, to slob around the place, to do bugger all'

Out of thirty examples of /ɖɯ˧-sɑ˩/ found in twenty-five transcribed narratives, all but one are accompanied by intonational focalization. The existence of one example without intonational focalization (TraderAndHisSon.24) is enough to demonstrate that the association of this focalization with /ɖɯ˧-sɑ˩/ is habitual, and should not be considered a lexicalized characteristic of this expression in F4's speech.

8.3.2.4 Intonational focalization and the division of the utterance into tone groups

As discussed in Chapter 7, the division of the utterance into tone groups is a fundamental dimension of Yongning Na prosody. The sifting of examples reveals that intonational focalization does not necessarily entail the presence of a following tone-group boundary, as shown by (12).

(12)　ə˧ʝi˧-ʂɯ˩ʝi˩ | ɖɯ˩dzɯ˧-ɬɑ˩tsʰo˩ ɳɯ˩ | ɖɯ˧-zi˩-ki˩ F ki˩-zo˩!
　　　ə˧ʝi˧-ʂɯ˩ʝi˩　ɖɯ˩dzɯ˧-ɬɑ˩tsʰo˩　ɳɯ˧　ɖɯ˧-zi˩　　　　-ki˧
　　　long_ago　　 proper name　　　　A　　one-CLF.households DAT
　　　F　　　　　　ki˧ₐ　　-zo˧ₐ
　　　FOCALIZATION　to_give　OBLIG

'Long ago, Ddeezzhi Lhaco had to marry into someone's family!' (BuriedAlive3.143)

In the vast majority of examples, such a boundary is present, however. Moreover, there are examples where the intonational focalization is associated to the insertion of a tone-group boundary at a place where it would otherwise be highly unexpected, as in (13).

(13)　zo˧ F | ə˧mi˧ ɳɯ˧ | my˩-ki˧ʔ zwɤ˩.
　　　zo˧ʔ　　F　　　　ə˧mi˧　　ɳɯ˧　my˩　　　　　　-ki˧　zwɤ˩ᵦ
　　　son/man　FOCALIZATION　mother　A　daughter/girl　DAT　to_speak

'The young man's mother talked to the young woman.' (BuriedAlive3.161)

The emphasis placed on /zo˧/ 'son, man' causes the insertion of a tone-group boundary inside the phrase 'the young man's mother'. This results in a different sequence of tones than is found in the phrase 'the boy's mother', which, outside this context, is /zo˧-ə˧mi˩/. The division of this phrase into two tone groups results in the non-application of the tone rules which hold in determinative compounds, since tone rules never apply across tone-group boundaries.

8.4 Habitual intonational modifications as a path towards the loss of lexical tone

Expressive coinages and iconic phenomena constitute marginal elements: each of them has a lilt of its own, and only bears loose links to the rest of the linguistic system. On the other hand, these phenomena undergo continuous attraction from the more central structures that make up the language's phonological system. There is thus a tendency towards their integration into the language's phonological categories. Segmental examples are discussed in Appendix A (§A. 6); the present section is devoted to an example that concerns tone.

In Yongning Na, there are eight extra-distal locative expressions, which share a specific intonation. The argument proposed here is that this habitual intonation constitutes a path towards the loss of lexical tone on the grammatical morphemes at issue. These locative expressions are listed in Table 8.1, where their first syllable is transcribed with an exclamation mark '!' instead of a tone mark, as a provisional device to represent their telltale intonation.

Table 8.1: Extra-distal locative expressions carrying specific intonation.

locative	meaning	1ˢᵗ σ	meaning of 1ˢᵗ σ
gʁ!-qo˧	way up	gʁ˧-	upward
gʁ!-tʂʰɯ˧qo˧	way up there (PROX)	gʁ˧-	upward
gʁ!-tʰy˧qo˧	way up there (DIST)	gʁ˧-	upward
gʁ!-tʰy˧-gi#˥	way up in that direction	gʁ˧-	upward
dʁ!-qo˧	way over there	?	?
dʁ!-tʂʰɯ˧qo˧	way over there (PROX)	?	?
dʁ!-tʰy˧qo˧	way over there (DIST)	?	?
dʁ!-tʰy˧-gi#˥	way over in that direction	?	?

The two sets of extra-distal locatives shown in Table 8.1 are parallel in terms of their syntactic composition, and they share the same intonation. The realization of their first syllable is highly expressive and allows variants. Either it starts on an extra-high pitch and glides downward, at a slope left to the speaker's discretion: a sharp fall or a prolonged one. Or it is rising, the details of the rise (duration, slope and peak height) being again left to the speaker's discretion. As far as could be ascertained, the sharply falling variant emphasizes the great distance to the place at issue (paraphrase: 'in a place far, far away'), whereas the rising variant (exemplified in Figure 8.7) is used to direct the listener's attention to that place, against a background of shared knowledge (paraphrase: 'that faraway place, you know'). For instance, the context for (14) is the following: a mother thinks that her daughter has died; the young woman's lover tells the mother that her daughter is still alive, and that she is in hiding. The young man knows where the young woman is, but does not wish to disclose it to the mother. The extra-distal locative in (14) does not emphasize the great distance: paraphrase as 'Your daughter is in a faraway place' would be inappropriate. In this context, the syllable /dʐ/ in dʐ!-tʰv˧qo˧/ 'way over there' is realized as rising: see the fundamental frequency tracing in Figure 8.7.

(14) no˧ mv˩ | dʐ!-tʰv˧qo˧ dzo˩.
     no˩   mv˥   dʐ!-tʰv˧qo˧   dzo˩ᵦ
     2SG daughter DEM.EXTRA_DISTAL EXIST.animated_beings

'Your daughter is [in a place that I know,] way over there.'
(BuriedAlive3.105)

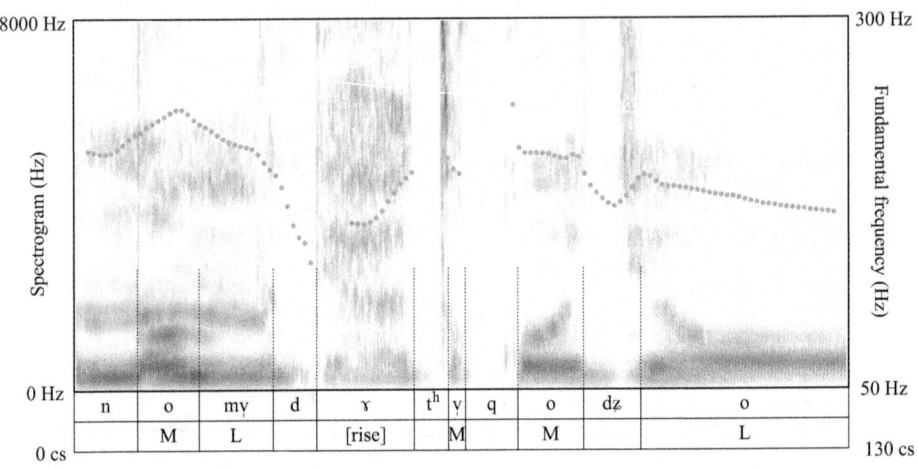

Figure 8.7: Spectrogram and F₀ curve for example (14), showing the rising realization of the syllable /dʐ/ in /dʐ!-tʰv˧qo˧/ 'way over there'.

Use of tone marks to stylize the perceived pitch of the syllable /dʐ/ in these locative expressions, such as /dʐ˥˩/ for a fall from top to bottom of the pitch range, /dʐ˦˥/ for a rise followed by a plateau, or /dʐ˧˥/ for a rise from mid-range to top of pitch range, would introduce a potential for confusion between lexical tone and intonational phenomena. Devising a set of symbols for more detailed transcription would require a full-fledged study of expressive phenomena in Yongning Na; this falls outside the scope of this exploratory chapter.

Identification of the prefix /gʐ˩-/ 'upward' in the locative expressions /gʐ˩-qo˧/, /gʐ˩-tʂʰɯ˧qo˧/, /gʐ˩-tʰv˧qo˧/ and /gʐ˩-tʰv˧-gi#˥/ of Table 8.1 is not problematic, as this prefix is attested elsewhere in the language, in a number of productive constructions, with the same meaning that it has in the extra-distal locatives (see §6.3.3). On the other hand, it is an issue how to analyze the extra-distal locatives /dʁ!-qo˧/, /dʁ!-tʂʰɯ˧qo˧/, /dʁ!-tʰy˧qo˧/ and /dʁ!-tʰy˧-gi#˥/, because the syllable /dʁ/ is synchronically orphaned. It is peculiar not only in its intonational realization, but also in its segmental composition. Apart from extra-distal locative expressions, this combination of initial and rhyme is only attested in Yongning Na in /hŷ˧dʁ˧ɻɨ#˥/ 'clumsy' and /õ˧dʁ˧ɻɨ˩/ 'fundamental(ly)'. In both of these words, the syllable /dʁ/ is followed by /ɻ/; since rhotic sounds are known (cross-linguistically) to have especially strong coarticulatory effects (see for instance West 1999), it is far from implausible that the combination /dʁ/ in these two words results from the phonologization of phonetic coarticulation.

My best guess at the time of writing is that the syllable /dʁ/ in extra-distal locatives originates in an expressive deformation of the extra-distal morpheme //dʑ˩//. This morpheme appears in /dʑ˩-tɕo˧/ 'that way, that direction', an expression now almost fallen into disuse which is structurally parallel to /tʂʰɯ˧-tɕo˧/ 'this way' and /tʰy˧-tɕo˧/ 'that way'. The expression /dʑ˩-tɕo˧/ alone is not enough to determine the tone of the extra-distal morpheme //dʑ// with certainty: it is necessary to observe a morpheme in several contexts of occurrence in order to arrive at its lexical tone, as explained step by step in the discussion of the lexical tones of nouns in Chapter 2, and verified in the discussion of grammatical words in Chapters 5–6. But the presence of a L tone on the first syllable in /dʑ˩-tɕo˧/ 'that way, that direction' suggests that the tone of the extra-distal morpheme /dʑ/ is likely to be L or LM, hence the provisional adoption of an internal reconstruction as *dʑ˩.

From a synchronic point of view, however, there is no evidence for positing an initial lexical L tone in the extra-distal locatives /dʁ!-qo˧/, /dʁ!-tʂʰɯ˧qo˧/, /dʁ!-tʰy˧qo˧/ and /dʁ!-tʰy˧-gi#˥/. This set has the same prosodic realization as the set consisting of /gʁ!-qo˧/, /gʁ!-tʂʰɯ˧qo˧/, /gʁ!-tʰy˧qo˧/, and /gʁ!-tʰy˧-gi#˥/ (shown in Table 8.1), but this realization is so distant from what one would expect on the basis of the lexical L tone of /gʁ˩-/ 'upward' that it looks like a case of neutralization of all tonal oppositions on the first syllable of these locatives.

While the synchronic data provides no evidence for one tonal notation rather than another, it also provides no evidence against adopting a notation of /dʁ-/ with L tone, as suggested by language-internal evidence. Therefore, notation as /dʁ˩-/ is provisionally adopted, rewriting Table 8.1 as Table 8.2.

The considerable intonational modification of the initial syllable in these locative expressions is transcribed in narratives through the addition of the mark for emphatic stress '↑' (see §8.3.1). This mark does not tell the full story, but has the advantage of bringing attention to the presence of a strong intonational modification resulting in a gap between the hypothesized lexical tone and the phonetic

Table 8.2: Extra-distal locative expressions carrying specific intonation.

locative	meaning	1st σ	meaning of 1st σ
gɤ˩-qo˧	way up	gɤ˩-	upward
gɤ˩-tʂʰɯ˧qo˧	way up there (PROX)	gɤ˩-	upward
gɤ˩-tʰy˧qo˧	way up there (DIST)	gɤ˩-	upward
gɤ˩-tʰy˧-gi#˧	way up in that direction	gɤ˩-	upward
dɤ˩-qo˧	way over there	*dv̩˩-	*DEM.DIST
dɤ˩-tʂʰɯ˧qo˧	way over there (PROX)	*dv̩˩-	*DEM.DIST
dɤ˩-tʰy˧qo˧	way over there (DIST)	*dv̩˩-	*DEM.DIST
dɤ˩-tʰy˧-gi#˧	way over in that direction	*dv̩˩-	*DEM.DIST

realization. Such unstable situations hold special potential for reinterpretation and change.

8.5 Key factors in the phonetic implementation of tone

This section sets out what I believe to be key factors in the phonetic implementation of tone in Yongning Na.

8.5.1 Intonational backgrounding of function words

It is a well-established cross-linguistic observation that grammatical words are less strongly articulated than lexical words: the lighter semantic weight of grammatical words relative to lexical words is reflected in a weaker phonetic realization. In languages that have distinctive stress, many grammatical words do not carry lexical stress, and those that do are sometimes destressed in discourse; in some languages that have tone, there are cases of toneless grammatical words, for instance in Mandarin (Lín Màocàn & Yán Jǐngzhù 1980; Chen & Xu 2006). Even in languages where there is no phonological difference between lexical words and grammatical words (e.g. in French, which does not have lexical stress, and in Vietnamese, which has tone on all syllables including grammatical morphemes), the phonetic difference between these two categories is noticeable. The extent of the difference in strength of articulation varies across languages: it has been found that there was less hypo-articulation of grammatical words in Vietnamese than in English or French (Brunelle, Chow & Nguyễn 2015).

Africanist colleagues report that the phonetic realization of tone sequences in some Subsaharan languages is unaffected (or almost unaffected) by the nature of the syllables that act as tone-bearing units, so that a M tone on a grammatical morpheme will be realized in the same way as if the tone-bearing syllable were a verb or a noun (Jacqueline Leroy, p.c. 2007 and Larry Hyman, p.c. 2011). In Yongning Na, on the other hand, the intonational backgrounding of grammatical words such as sentence-final particles is easily noticed.

The prohibitive prefix /tʰɑ˧-/ is a case in point. When it is followed by a reduplicated verb of tone category M_a, the tone pattern is M.H.L, e.g. /tʰɑ˧-ki˥~ki˩/ 'do not give away, do not distribute'. Phonetically, the syllable /tʰɑ˧/ is realized with rising fundamental frequency. Averaging across the eight tokens in the recording VerbProhib, there is a 6.7% rise in F_0 (standard deviation: 3.6). This rise is probably too small to be perceived as such: glissandos need a minimum slope of about 14% over a long tone-bearing unit (over 300 ms) or 18% over a short tone-bearing unit (100 ms) (Rossi 1971; Gsell 1979). The amplitude of the rise during /tʰɑ˧-/ can be compared with the 16% jump in F_0 (standard deviation: 5.0) from the prefix to the H-tone syllable that follows. To use a concept proposed as part of a model for Mandarin speech synthesis, grammatical words could be said to have a lower *strength coefficient*. In this model (called Stem-ML, for *Soft Template Mark-up Language*), the tones of syllables with a high strength coefficient are realized close to their lexical tone template, whereas the lower the coefficient, the stronger the coarticulation with following tones (Kochanski & Shih 2003). The anticipatory rise in the course of the prohibitive prefix /tʰɑ˧-/ can be interpreted as a typical example of coarticulation between a M-tone syllable with low strength coefficient and a following H-tone syllable with high strength coefficient.

For future studies of this topic, direct phonetic comparison would be possible between segmentally and tonally homophonous pairs such as the noun /bv̩˧/ 'intestine' and the possessive /=bv̩˧/, and the noun for 'person, human being', /hĩ˥/, and its grammaticalized avatar as a relativizer, /-hĩ˥/.

8.5.2 The absence of oppositions between /L.M/ and /L.H/, or between /H.M/ and /H.L/

Two of the key phonological facts about Yongning Na tone are (i) that there is no contrast between /H.M/ and /H.L/ sequences (only /H.L/ is observed), and (ii) that the contrast between //LM// and //LH//, which is postulated at the underlying phonological level, is neutralized in surface phonological forms. This leads to the following generalization: in Yongning Na surface phonological tone sequences, there is no context where a two-step shift on the tone scale (i.e. from /L/ to /H/, or from /H/ to /L/) contrasts with a one-step shift (i.e. from /L/ to /M/, or from /H/ to /M/). This is unlike the closely related language Naxi, where all combinations of tones in disyllables are attested, including /L.H/, /L.M/, /H.M/ and /H.L/.

This state of affairs has important consequences for the production and perception of tone sequences. For any pair of successive syllables within a tone group, it is enough to identify the tone of the second as being (i) higher than the preceding tone, (ii) on the same level as the preceding tone, or (iii) lower than the preceding tone.

8.5.3 Anticipatory phonetic dissimilation in M.L and M.H sequences

In some Subsaharan languages, phonetic anticipation of following tones takes place: in a L.L.H sequence, the second L tone is realized higher than the first, in a gradual progression towards the H tone (Creissels 1994: 216). Auditory impression suggests that the opposite happens in Yongning Na. If a M tone is followed by L, this M tone is realized with a higher fundamental frequency than when followed by H. This has the effect of bringing out the contrast in pitch between M and the following tone. The M tone can be said to have three allotones: that found in front of L is the highest; that found in front of M or MH is in a central phonetic range of F_0; and that found in front of H is the lowest.

Likewise, a L tone is realized lower in front of M or H than when followed by another L. Using the vertical position of letters to indicate relative pitch, an approximation of the phonetic realization of a M.M.L sequence would be [M.M.L], and a L.L.H sequence could be approximated as [L.L.H].

These coarticulatory phenomena link up with observations about the realization of like-tone sequences, L.L.L... and M.M.M... (H.H.H... sequences are never observed, since a H tone is always followed by L: this is formulated in §7.1.1 as Rule 4, "The syllable following a H-tone syllable receives L tone"). Sequences of L tones decline gradually towards a final L target that is clearly low. The first L tone in such a sequence may be realized in a relatively high range of fundamental frequency: extracted from context, it may sound like [M]. This does not threaten its correct identification within the tone sequence: a sequence such as L.L.L cannot be mistaken for M.M.L, because the latter sequence has to be realized with a significant phonetic drop from M to L (approximation: [M.M.L]). In the absence of the slight upward jump in fundamental frequency found from the first to the second M level in [M.M.L], and of any sudden drop from one syllable to the next, a sequence of syllables realized with gradually decreasing fundamental frequency is perceived as consisting of like tones. Likewise, a M.M.M like-tone sequence cannot be mistaken for M.M.L even if its last tone is depressed by intonational factors such as final lowering. Final lowering affects the last syllable, but does not raise the previous one (schematic representation: [M.M.M]), whereas a M.M.L sequence would comprise a raising of the syllable before last: [M.M.L].

These auditory impressions are summarized in Table 8.3. (Remember that the symbol σ is used to stand for syllables.) They receive some support from acoustic measurements reported in a phonetic pilot study by a speaker of Yongning Na (Ā Huì 2016); the logical next step would consist in conducting a state-of-the-art experimental study.

Table 8.3: A schematic representation of the realization of some tone sequences in Yongning Na.

phonetic outline	interpretation	cues to tonal identification
[σ.σ.σ.σ.σ]	[M.M.M.M.M]	gentle decline in F_0; overall mid range of F_0; final lowering is not considerable
[σ.σ.σ.σ.σ]	[L.L.L.L.L]	slightly steeper decline in F_0 than for all-M sequences; slightly lower starting-point and endpoint
[σ.σ.σ.σ]	M.M.M.L	raising of the syllable before last, and clear difference in pitch between the last two syllables
[σ.σ.σ.σ]	L.L.L.H	lowering of the syllable before last, and clear difference in pitch between the last two syllables

Grasping the phenomenon of anticipatory phonetic dissimilation in M.L and M.H sequences is crucial to the identification of tones in Yongning Na. The system allows for a great range of phonetic variation in sequences of L tones or M tones, since L-tone sequences may start from a relatively high pitch, as long as they descend clearly towards a phonetic low target without intervening upward jumps in pitch. M-tone sequences may be strongly affected by declination (a phonetic, gradual, noncategorical decrease in fundamental frequency in the course of the utterance: see §8.2) without putting their identification at risk. Listeners confronted with a sequence of syllables of decreasing fundamental frequency, without noticeable upward jumps, can safely interpret the sequence as carrying M.M.M... or L.L.L... tones; among these two possibilities, the overall slope of the decrease in F_0, and the range of F_0 reached at the end of the sequence, guide the listener towards interpretation as either M.M.M... or L.L.L...

Anticipatory phonetic dissimilation in M.L and M.H sequences is especially salient, but preplanning in tone production is also noticeable at the level of the entire tone group. For instance, a M.M.H sequence begins on a lower pitch than M.M.M, which itself begins lower than M.M.L. A striking example was unintentionally recorded by eliciting verbs in frame (15).

(15) no˧ ɳɯ˧ | V-zo˧-ho˩.
      no˩ ɳɯ˧ V -zo˧ₐ -ho˩
      2SG A V OBLIG FUT
      'you must now V / you will now have to V.'

The sequence 'you will now have to eat', /no˧ ɳɯ˧ | dzɯ˧-zo˧-ho˥/, was realized with high pitch on the two M-tone syllables of the utterance-initial tone group, /no˧ ɳɯ˧/ (2SG plus A), whereas the two next M-tone syllables, /dzɯ˧-zo˧/, were realized lower than average so as to maximize the contrast with the H tone that follows them. The result is a considerable drop in F_0 from /ɳɯ˧/ to /dzɯ˧/, despite their identical phonological tone. Likewise, in the elicited sentence (16), the M tones of /hu˧mi˧/ 'stomach' are realized distinctly lower than those of /ʐwæ˧zo˧=by˧/ 'of (a/the) horse'.

(16) tʂʰɯ˧ | ʐwæ˧zo˧=by˧ | hu˧mi˧ ɲi˩.
      tʂʰɯ˩ ʐwæ˧zo#˩ =by˧ hu˧mi$ ɲi˩
      DEM.PROX colt POSS stomach COP
      'This is the stomach of a colt.' (BodyPartsOfAnimals7.140)

Similar evidence comes from narratives. In (17), /ɖɯ˧-ʁæʴbæʴ/ 'one plateful' was initially transcribed as ‡ ɖɯ˧-ʁæ˧bæʴ: due to final lowering, there is a phonetic drop in F_0 from the second syllable (/ʁæʴ/) to the last syllable (/bæʴ/), even though these two syllables carry the same tone (L). This phonetic drop may be as salient (or even more salient) than that from the first syllable (/ɖɯ˧/) to the second syllable (/ʁæʴ/), which carry different tones (M and L, respectively).

(17) ʁæ˧bæ˧-qo˧ ɳɯ˧ | ʁæ˧bæ˧ | ɖɯ˧-ɭɯ˧-qo˧ ɳɯ˧, | ɖɯ˧-ʁæʴbæʴ!
      ʁæ˧bæ˧   -qo˧ ɳɯ˧ ʁæ˧bæ˧ ɖɯ˧ ɭɯ˧ᵦ -qo˧
      wooden_plate inside ABL/TOP wooden_plate one CLF inside

390

    ŋɯ˧   ɖɯ˧ ʁæ˩bæ˩
    ABL/TOP one CLF.platefuls

'[The sweets used to be presented] on a plate! [They were placed] on a plate; [one used to prepare] a plateful!' (Funeral.216)

This example brings us to the topic of the resetting of reference values for tones at junctures between tone groups.

8.5.4 Resetting of reference values for tones at junctures between tone groups

As noted in §8.2, a phonetic, gradual, noncategorical decrease in fundamental frequency takes place in the course of the sentence. This is known as 'declination'. Fundamental frequency therefore fluctuates within a gradually narrowed range. Resetting of F_0 does not take place at each boundary between two tone groups. On the other hand, there is a *resetting of reference values for tones* at each boundary between tone groups, such that a M tone in final position within a tone group and another M tone in initial position within the following tone group can have widely different fundamental frequency values. This also relates to phonological facts on possible tonal contrasts in initial, medial and final position inside a tone group: a M tone in initial position within a tone group only contrasts with L, so that it has greater freedom of phonetic variation than a M tone in final position, where contrasts are more numerous. Remember that, after a penultimate M tone, a tone group can end in any of L, M, H, MH or LH; this places precise constraints on a final M tone's position within the tonal space.

8.5.5 The realization of rising contours

It was pointed out in Chapter 2 that there only exist two types of contours on monosyllables at the surface phonological level: low-rising and mid-rising. At the surface phonological level, there is no opposition between LM and LH contours. Phonologically, the product of the neutralization is labelled LH, for the structural reason set out in §2.3.6. Phonetically, it is a low-rising contour whose endpoint is not as high as that of the MH contour. To approximate phonetic realizations in terms of three levels, they are closer to [LM] than to [LH]. This makes sense both in terms of production and in terms of perception. In production, reaching as high a phonetic target for the low-rising contour as for the mid-rising contour would require extra effort, as the rise in F_0 would have to be greater. In perception, this rise to a final target similar to that of the MH contour could make it more difficult to distinguish the (phonologically contrastive) low-rising and mid-rising contours. There are thus phonetic reasons why the product of the neutralization of LM and LH should be phonetically closer to [LM] than to [LH].

From the point of view of the tone system, this creates a tension between phonological categories and phonetic realizations. Such discrepancies hold potential for reanalysis of the system by language learners, especially in the present social context, where exposure to Na is made more limited by the pervasive presence of Mandarin, so that children do not acquire the tonal system in its full richness. This issue will be taken up in Chapter 9.

8.6 By way of recapitulation: Examples of mistaken tonal identification

In this section, the observations made above about intonation and tone implementation are recapitulated through examples of mistaken notations from early field notes: cases where tone identification was erroneous because the investigator was unaware of the language-specific factors that go to shape the final prosodic form of utterances. These examples are intended to shed light on the process of categorical interpretation of the pitch of successive syllables.

8.6.1 Anticipatory dissimilation before a L tone

The tone sequence M.M.L was often mistakenly transcribed as M.H.L, for instance in the determinative compound 'tiger's ear', shown in (18).

(18) la˧-ɬi˧pi˩
      la˧   ɬi˧pi˩
      tiger ear

'tiger's ear' (DetermCompounds6.17)

This compound was initially transcribed as ‡ la˧-ɬi˥pi˩. This was because the pitch of the second syllable, /ɬi˧/, is higher than that of the first, /la˧/, due to anticipatory dissimilation before a L tone, as described in §8.5.3: the successive pitch levels can be stylized as [M.ᴹ.L]. The difference in pitch between the first two syllables is a cue to the M.L sequence that follows: this difference is important to the identification of the tone of the third syllable as L, and not as a M tone lowered by *declination* or *final lowering*. But it must be factored out when determining the tone of the second syllable, /ɬi˧/.

8.6.2 Interplay between morphosyntax and phonology

The tone sequence M.L.L.L in (19) was mistakenly transcribed as ‡ MH.M.L.L (‡ le˧-mɤ˧pʰæ˩-ze˩) on my first field trip.

(19) le˧-mɤ˩pʰæ˩-ze˩
    le˧-   mɤ˩pʰæ˧   -ze˧$_b$
    ACCOMP to_forget   PFV
    '[I/you...] have forgotten' (Source: field notes. Also found in Dog.4)

Transcription as ‡ MH.M.L.L is relatively close to the phonetic realization, with a slight rise during the first syllable, and a gradually declining fundamental frequency during the three syllables that follow, reaching a low phonetic target on the last syllable. In order to identify the correct tone sequence, a crucial piece of information consists of the overall higher fundamental frequency on the first syllable. Details in its phonetic contour must be overlooked: whether it is flat, rising or falling is phonologically irrelevant in this context, since phonological contours are only found in tone-group-final position. Higher mean F_0 on the first syllable points to a difference in phonological level between the first syllable and those that follow. Since the first tone in a tone group can only be M or L on the surface phonological level, the first tone in (19) can safely be identified as M; since the next tone is lower, it can safely be identified as L; and from there, all the tones that follow can only be L, by application of Rule 5.

It could be that, for the listener, the identification of the sequence of syllables in (19) as one syntactic phrase (a verb phrase) helps identify it as one tone group, which in turn provides guidance in tone identification. But the issue of how morphosyntactic information and phonological information are processed in speech comprehension is, of course, to be investigated by means of psycholinguistic methods; this interesting field of research lies outside the scope of the present volume.

8.6.3 Resetting at junctures between tone groups

At a stage when I had not yet worked out clearly the existence of tone groups, sentence (20) was transcribed as ‡ njɤ˥ ɳɯ˥ hwæ˧-bi˧-ze˧: the sequence of three M tones over the last three syllables was identified correctly, but it seemed to me that the tone of the first two syllables was higher, hence the choice to transcribe them as H.

(20) njɤ˧ ŋɯ˧ | hwæ˧-bi˧-ze˧!
    njɤ˧ ŋɯ˧   hwæ˧ₐ -bi˧ₐ   -ze˧_b
    1SG   A   to_buy IMM.FUT PFV
    'I'm paying for it! / I'm the one who's buying [it]!'

Once it was recognized that there were two tone groups in (20), the considerable phonetic difference in pitch between the two groups could be interpreted as due to a difference in their overall F₀ register. There is no risk that a proficient speaker of Yongning Na would interpret the high pitch on /njɤ˧ ŋɯ˧/ as the realization of a H.H sequence, since such sequences are never found in Yongning Na (due to Rules 4 and 5: within a tone group, a H tone can only be followed by L tones). Further examples are shown in Table 8.4. In all of these cases, I based my transcription on the perceived dissimilarity in pitch between successive syllables, overlooking the fact that the overall F₀ register can differ from one tone group to the next.

Table 8.4: Some examples of mistaken tonal transcriptions due to oversight of resetting at junctures between tone groups.

meaning	phonological tone sequence	early, mistaken transcription	current transcription
you go and buy [it]	M| M.M	‡ no˥ hwæ˧hõ˧	no˧ | hwæ˧-hõ˧
one mountain	M| M.M	‡ ʁwɤ˥ dɯ˧-ɭɯ˧	ʁwɤ˧ | dɯ˧-ɭɯ˧
a drop of water	M| M.M	‡ dʑɯ˥ dɯ˧-tʰɤ˧	dʑɯ˧ | dɯ˧-tʰɤ˧
this is a mountain	M| M.L	‡ tʂʰɯ˥ ʁwɤ˧ ɲi˩	tʂʰɯ˧ | ʁwɤ˧ ɲi˩
to light a fire	M |M.MH	‡ my˥ tʰi˧-tsʰi˧˥	my˧ | tʰi˧-tsʰi˧˥
I cut a piece	M.M | M.M.H	‡ njɤ˥ ŋɯ˥ dɯ˧-kʰwɤ˧ dze˥	njɤ˧ ŋɯ˧ | dɯ˧-kʰwɤ˧ dze˥

8.6.4 The effects of pragmatic intonation

In my first field notes, example (21) was transcribed as ‡ kɯ˩ɻ̍˧ tɤ˥ due to an intonational strengthening of the verb: the phrase was provided as an answer to the question of which verb is associated with 'erhu, Chinese violin' (I began a sentence, /tʂʰɯ˧ ŋɯ˧ | kɯ˩ɻ̍˧ .../, '(S)he ... the violin', while making the gesture of playing), so that the consultant emphasized the verb in her answer. This is a form of emphatic stress as described in §8.3.1.

(21) kɯ˩ɻ̍˧ tɤ˧
    kɯ˩ɻ̍˧   tɤ˧ₐ
    Chinese_violin to_pull
    'to play erhu (Chinese violin)'

Likewise, the sentence (22) was initially transcribed as ‡ ɖɯ˧-bæ˧ | mɤ˧-tsɤ˩, with H tone on the verb. I believe that this was because the verb /tsɤ˧/ is realized phonetically with higher fundamental frequency than the preceding negation prefix, which as a grammatical morpheme is intonationally weaker, as explained in §8.5.1.

(22) ɖɯ˧-bæ˧ | mɤ˧-tsɤ˧!
     ɖɯ˧   bæ˧ₐ   mɤ˧-   tsɤ˧
     one   CLF.sorts   NEG   to_become/to_be
     'It's not the same!'

Example (23) was transcribed as ‡ mv̩˧ʁo˩ tɕɯ˩ instead of /mv̩˧ʁo˩ | tɕɯ˧/. The final syllable has a high informational load, and received some intonational emphasis. Moreover, there is no opposition between M and H in tone-group-initial position, and phonetic realizations can range into the higher part of the speaker's tonal space without risks of phonological confusions.

(23) mv̩˧ʁo˩ | tɕɯ˧.
     mv̩˧ʁo˩   tɕɯ˧
     sky/heavens   cloud
     'The sky is cloudy.'

As a final example, let us consider (24).

(24) zo˧ ɳɯ˧ | ʝi˧!
     zo˧   ɳɯ˧   ʝi˧
     man   A   to_do
     'This is a man's job! / This type of work [viz. ploughing] is men's part!'
     (Source: field notes.)

The first two syllables in (24), which constitute a tone group, carry the same surface phonological tone (M tone). In early notes, I jotted down this example as ‡ zo˧ ɳɯ˧ ʝi˧. This notation was influenced by the intonational emphasis carried by the first syllable, which resulted in a higher pitch on /zo˧/ than on the following syllable; to boot, that syllable is a grammatical element and hence prone to intonational backgrounding, a phenomenon studied in §8.5.1.

9 Yongning Na tones in dynamic-synchronic perspective

> The past century of phonetic research has illuminated our understanding of the production of sound, the properties of the acoustic signals, and to a certain extent, the perception of speech sounds. But the search for the originating causes of sound change itself remains one of the most recalcitrant problems of phonetic science.
>
> (Labov 1979: 1)

The synchronic description proposed in the present volume provides a basis for studying the historical dynamics of tone in Na: as mentioned in §1.2.2, a dynamic approach to synchrony brings out patterns of synchronic variation which, in turn, offer some glimpses into diachronic evolution. The study of variability is especially crucial to the study of tone. Variability in tone patterns tends to be high in level-tone systems with rich morphotonology, and diachronic change tends to be more rapid than in other areas of the linguistic system (such as syntax).

The argument that tonological models should be designed in such a way as to accommodate patterns of variation is found e.g. in a discussion of Bambara, a Mande language:

> Clearly, any hypothesis about the system that underlies the tonal productions of Bambara speakers should be able to account, with minimal adjustments, for observed patterns of variation. (Creissels 1992: 8)[1]

---

[1] *Original text*: il est clair que toute hypothèse sur l'organisation du système sous-jacent à un corpus de productions tonales de bambarophones doit pouvoir au prix d'un minimum d'aménagements rendre compte de possibilités éventuelles de variation.

As more data becomes available about the dialectal diversity of Na, it will be possible to investigate patterns of contact and variation with increasing precision. Four topics are discussed here: structural gap-filling, disyllabification, analogy, and the influence of bilingualism with Mandarin.

9.1 Gap-filling in tonal paradigms: The example of subject-plus-verb phrases

Structural gap-filling causes a change in the phonological system when an allophone has drifted far enough away from its original pronunciation for a new combination to nest itself in the abandoned slot. For instance, in Yongning Na it is likely that the sound [ʁ] was originally an empty-onset filler (see Appendix A, §A.3.3). The syllable /ʁo/ in /a˩ʁo˧/ 'house' is reconstructed as a simple *o at the proto-Naish stage (Jacques & Michaud 2011); it remains phonemically onsetless to this day in Laze ([a˥wu˥], phonemically /a˥u˥/) and in Naxi ([mi˧wu˩], phonemically /mi˧u˩/). After *o syllables came to be realized as [ʁo] (at the surface phonological level) in Yongning Na, there remained no [o] or [wo] syllables. But this phonetic slot was filled by syllables with other origins: the syllable /wo/ is now firmly attested, in examples such as /wo˥/ 'hard', /wo˩ᵦ/ 'classifier for teams of oxen', /wo˩kɤ#˥/ 'swing', and /wo˧/ 'turnip leaves'. The introduction of [wo] syllables precipitated the phonemicization of what was originally an empty-onset-filler: the syllable /ʁo/ in /a.ʁo/ 'house' must now be analyzed as composed of two phonemes, an initial /ʁ/ and the vowel /o/.

Gap-filling can also take place in tonal paradigms. This section is devoted to a plausible example from subject-plus-verb constructions.

Table 6.46, repeated here as Table 9.1, presents the tonal behaviour of combinations of a monosyllabic or disyllabic subject noun with a verb. Two contexts were used to arrive at underlying tone categories: S+V, and S+V+PERFECTIVE. For instance, 'the guests arrive' is /hĩ˧-bæ˧ tsʰɯ˥/, and addition of the perfective yields /hĩ˧-bæ˧ tsʰɯ˧-ze˥/ 'the guests have arrived'. The tone pattern for this combination of subject and predicate is described as /M.M.MH/, and further analyzed as //MH#//: a MH contour associating to the last syllable.

A challenge raised by the data set in Table 9.1 concerns the analysis of the surface phonological tone sequences ending in M+L, M+M and M+H. Remember that, in these notations, the tone which follows the '+' sign is that carried by the perfective /-ze˧/ when placed after the subject-plus-verb combination. The question is how the perfective acquires its /L/, /M/ or /H/ tone in these combinations. The full list of the expressions at issue is: M.M+L, M.M.M+L, M.M+M, M.M.M

Table 9.1: The tone patterns of subject-plus-verb combinations, in surface phonological transcription.

tone of noun	tone of verb						
	H	M$_a$	M$_b$	L$_a$	L$_b$	MH
LM, LH	L.H	L.M+M	L.M+M	L.H	L.H	L.MH
M	M.M+L	M.M+M	M.M+M	M.L	M.L	M.MH
L	M.M+L	L.L	M.M+M	L.L	L.L / M.L	L.L
H	M.M+L	M.M+L	M.M+L	M.MH	M.MH	M.L
MH	M.H	M.H	M.H	M.MH	M.MH	M.H
M	M.M.M+L	M.M.M+M	M.M.M+M	M.ML	M.ML	M.M.MH
#H	M.M.M+L	M.M.M+L	M.M.M+L	M.M.MH	M.M.MH	M.M.L
MH#	M.M.MH	M.M.MH	M.M.MH	M.M.MH	M.M.MH	M.M.MH
H$	M.M.M+L	M.M.M+L	M.M.M+L / M.M.M+H	M.M.MH	M.M.MH	M.H.L
L	L.L.L	L.L.L	L.L.L	L.L.L	L.L.L	L.L.H
L#	M.L.L	M.L.L	M.L.L	M.L.L	M.L.L	M.L.L
LM+MH#	L.M.M+L	L.M.M+L	L.M.M+L	L.M.MH	L.M.MH	L.MH
LM+#H	L.M.M+L	L.M.M+M	L.M.M+M	L.M.L	L.M.MH	L.M.MH
LM	L.M.M+L	L.M.M+M	L.M.M+M	L.M.L	L.M.L	L.M.MH
LH	L.H.L	L.H.L	L.H.L	L.H.L	L.H.L	L.H.L
H#	M.H.L	M.H.L	M.H.L	M.H.L	M.H.L	M.H.L

+M, M.M.M+H, L.M+M, L.M.M+M, and L.M.M+L. Among these, those ending in /M+L/, as in (1), and those ending in /M+M/, as in (2), are commonplace. On the other hand, there only exists one sequence ending in /M+H/: it results from the combination of a //H$//-tone subject and a //M_b//-tone verb, as in (3).

(1) lɑ˧ se˧-ze˩
    lɑ˧   se˩   -ze˧_b
    tiger to_walk PFV
'the tiger walked' (input tones: M on noun and H on verb)

(2) lɑ˧ ʂɯ˧-ze˧
    lɑ˧   ʂɯ˧_a   -ze˧_b
    tiger to_die PFV
'the tiger died' (input tones: M on noun and M on verb)

(3) hwɤ˧mi˧ tsʰo˧-ze˩
    hwɤ˧mi˩$ tsʰo˧_b -ze˧_b
    she_cat to_jump PFV
'the she-cat jumped' (input tones: H$ on noun and M_b on verb)

The hypothesis proposed here is that the pattern ending in /M+H/ is an innovation.

The perfective can receive one of three tones in subject-plus-verb plus perfective constructions: /M/, /H/, or /L/. Cases in which the perfective carries /M/ tone are the simplest: the morpheme does not receive any tone assignment from what precedes, and surfaces with its lexical M tone. The surface strings /M.M+M/ (for monosyllabic nouns) and /M.M.M+M/ (for disyllabic nouns) can therefore be analyzed as //M//. As for /L.M+M/ (for monosyllabic nouns) and /L.M.M+M/ (for disyllabic nouns), they can be analyzed as //LM//.

Cases where the perfective receives /H/ tone look like typical instances of the floating H tone, //#H//. This tone, which does not surface in isolation but can be manifested on a following syllable (§2.3.1), is frequently observed in Yongning Na. It is the lexical tone of a class of nouns, exemplified by 'little brother', realized in isolation as /gi˧zɯ˧/ 'little brother', and yielding /gi˧zɯ˧ ɲi˩/ when followed by the copula, as explained in §2.3.1.

It was noted in §2.3.2 that //H$// tone shows signs of variability: it is the lexical tone for which there is the greatest number of morphotonological variants, in various morphosyntactic contexts. In subject-plus-verb combinations, its association with a //M_b//-tone verb allows for two possibilities: M.M.M+L and M.M.M

+H. The latter tonal string, M.M.M+H, is not attested in any of the other subject-plus-verb combinations. A hypothesis suggested by this distribution is that this variant is an innovation which filled a slot that was empty in the surface phonological forms.

Under the hypothesis that the tone pattern M.M.M+H on subject-plus-verb plus perfective combinations represents an innovation, prior to this innovation the M.M.M+L surface pattern could have been analyzed as //#H//. The floating H tone was not manifested directly but triggered a lowering of following tones – in this instance, a lowering of the tone of the perfective morpheme.[2]

This state of affairs is reflected in the analysis in Table 9.2, which leaves out the problematic variant M.M.M+H for the combination of a subject carrying H$ tone and a verb carrying M_b tone.

Table 9.2 is a reconstruction of the set of tone rules that applied in subject-plus-verb constructions prior to the appearance of the M.M.M+H variant. If it represents a historical reality, this reconstructed stage is likely to have shallow time depth: the amount of observed idiolectal and dialectal diversity suggests that such a change can take place within a couple of generations. At the reconstructed stage represented in Table 9.2, a tone rule must be specified, to the effect that //#H// tone in subject-plus-verb combinations does not surface, but depresses following tones to L. In view of the general architecture of the Na tone system, this rule is not an *ad hoc* device to explain away an unaccountable observation: a rule to the same effect operates in other morphosyntactic contexts.

In the present state of the language, on the other hand, the M.M.M+H variant has settled in, and its simplest phonological interpretation is as the manifestation of a floating H tone – an interpretation that conflicts with the earlier system. Interpretation of the M.M.M+H pattern as underlying //#H// causes an in-depth modification in the system: as the //#H// slot in the system comes to be occupied by the new, innovative form, the M.M.M+L surface pattern, which could previously be analyzed as reflecting an underlying //#H//, requires a new interpretation, as do the other surface patterns ending in /M+L/ in Table 9.1.

A possible phonological reanalysis in view of the entire system would be as

---

[2] The floating H tone of Yongning Na, transcribed as //#H//, exists not only as a lexical category on nouns (as discussed in §2.3.1), but also as the output of some syntactically restricted tone rules (morphotonological rules), such as those that apply in compound nouns. Cases where a H tone does not surface but lowers the following tones (to L) are found in various areas of Yongning Na morphotonology. For instance, the phrase /mv˩tɕo˧ se˧/ 'to walk downward' depresses a following perfective (//-ze˧ᵦ//, which has lexical M tone) to L: /mv˩tɕo˧ se˧-ze˩/ '(s)he walked downward'; this is interpreted as evidence of the presence of a floating H tone in the expression 'to walk downward' (see §6.3.3).

Table 9.2: A phonological analysis of the tones of subject-plus-verb combinations, leaving aside the M.M.M+H variant of the combination of a H$-tone subject and a M_b-tone verb.

tone of noun	tone of verb					
	H	M_a	M_b	L_a	L_b	MH
LM, LH	LM	LM	LH	LH	LH	LM+MH#
M	M	M	#H	M.L	M.L	M.MH
L	L	M	#H	L	L	L
H	#H	#H	#H	MH#	MH#	L#
MH	H#	H#	H#	MH#	MH#	H#
M	M	M	#H	#H	#H	MH#
#H	#H	#H	#H	MH#	MH#	#H
MH#	MH#	MH#	MH#	MH#	MH#	#H
H$	#H	#H	#H	MH#	MH#	H#
L	L	L	L	L	L	L+H#
L#	L#–	L#–	L#–	L#–	L#–	L#–
LM+MH#	LM–+#H	LM–+#H	LM–+#H	LM+MH#	LM+MH#	LM+H$
LM+#H	LM–	LM–	LM–+#H	LH–	LM+MH#	LM+MH#
LM	LM–	LM–	LM–+#H	LH–	LH–	LM+MH#
LH	LH–	LH–	LH–	LH–	LM+MH#	LH–
H#	H#–	H#–	H#–	H#–	H#–	H#–

402

a floating L tone, //#L//, which would thus enter the language's tone system. The surface phonological patterns in subject-plus-verb plus perfective combinations would then be interpreted as in Table 9.3. The //#L// category is highlighted, bringing out its relatively pervasive presence in the table.

Devoting the whole of the present section to the discussion of one isolated tonal variant may seem dreadfully disproportionate. This variant deserves special attention, however, because it illustrates the constant tension between underlying forms and surface phonological forms, shedding light on types of evolution taking place in level-tone systems. From the point of view of surface phonological forms, the innovative expression discussed here can be viewed in the light of a simplification: at the (hypothetical) conservative stage presented in Table 9.2, for the combination of //H$// and //M$_b$// there is a H tone in the input, and none in the output; by contrast, in the innovative form there is an output H tone echoing the input H, creating a better fit between input and output. From the point of view of underlying forms, on the other hand, the new combination creates an analytical puzzle for linguists – and probably for language learners too. Cases like this one allow for several analytical options and hence hold potential for diachronic change.

9.2 Disyllabification

As mentioned at the outset of Chapter 3, many roots that used to be phonologically distinct have become homophonous in Na, as in other Sino-Tibetan languages that have undergone considerable phonological erosion (such as Tujia, Bai, Namuyi, or Shixing / Xumi). As a consequence, there exists a strong tendency towards disyllabification. If each tonal combination of two monosyllables created a different tonal category for the resulting disyllable, this could multiply the number of tones by squaring: six tones on monosyllables could yield 6×6=36 tones on disyllables. The observed number is much smaller: eleven tone categories for disyllabic nouns. The study of the relationship between the tones of monosyllables and those of disyllables holds promise for an understanding of the dynamics of the tone system.

9.2.1 A dynamic analysis of compound nouns

The analysis of compound nouns in Chapter 3 aimed to bring out the relationship between input nouns and the resulting compound. The notations chosen for the tones of compounds emphasized their internal makeup. For instance, the

Table 9.3: A phonological analysis of the tones of subject-plus-verb combinations positing floating L tones.

tone of noun	tone of verb					
	H	M$_a$	M$_b$	L$_a$	L$_b$	MH
LM, LH	LH	LM	LM	LH	LH	LM+MH#
M	#L	M	M	M.L	M.L	M.MH
L	#L	L	M	L	L	L
H	#L	#L	#L	MH#	MH#	L#
MH	H#	H#	H#	MH#	MH#	H#
M	#L	M	M	#L	#L	MH#
#H	#L	#L	#L	MH#	MH#	#L
MH#	MH#	MH#	MH#	MH#	MH#	#L
H$	#L	#L	#H / #L	MH#	MH#	H#
L	L	L	L	L	L	L+H#
L#	L#−	L#−	L#−	L#−	L#−	L#−
LM+MH#	LM−+#H	LM−+#H	LM−+#H	LM+MH#	LM+MH#	LM+H$
LM+#H	LM−+#H	LM−	LM−	LH−	LM+MH#	LM+MH#
LM	LM−+#H	LM−	LM−	LH−	LH−	LM+MH#
LH	LH−	LH−	LH−	LH−	LM+MH#	LH−
H#	H#−	H#−	H#−	H#−	H#−	H#−

combination of a #H-tone determiner and a LM-tone head yields a M.H surface phonological tone pattern, as in (4).

(4) ʐwæ˧-ɣɯ˩
    ʐwæ˧ ɣɯ˧˩
    horse skin
    'horse's skin' (DetermCompounds6.24, 7.67-68, 12.44)

The processes leading from the input tones to the tone of the compound can be interpreted as follows: the lexical tone of the determiner, being a floating H tone (never expressed on the lexical item itself, only on a following syllable), associates to the second syllable of the compound. The assignment of surface tones then takes place according to the general rules governing the association of tone #H in Yongning Na. Since there is a following syllable within the tone group to host it (namely, the second syllable of the compound), the H tone attaches there, and the first syllable of the compound receives M by default (through Rule 2). The notation used for this combination in Chapter 3 is #H–, using the symbol '–' to stand for the last syllable of the first part of the compound. This notation, while it is fairly complex, appears adequate insofar as it reflects a hypothesis about the way in which the tone pattern of the compound obtains. Such notations are referred to below as *source-oriented*.

In terms of end result, on the other hand, the compound in (4) belongs in tone category H#: it carries a final H tone, which does not move. Disyllabic compounds made up of the combination of a #H-tone determiner and a LM-tone head therefore feed into the lexical category of H# disyllables. Notation as H# is referred below as *result-oriented*.

Likewise, the source-oriented notation –L corresponds to the result-oriented notation L#: assigning a L tone after the juncture between the two parts of the disyllabic compound yields the same result as assigning a final L tone to the entire expression. Table 9.4 provides a summary.

The table presenting the tone patterns of disyllabic compounds (Table 3.2a of Chapter 3) is rewritten below as Table 9.5, adopting a result-oriented notation, eliminating all references to the juncture between the two parts of the compound (transcribed by means of the symbol '–' in Table 9.4). Each row corresponds to a tonal category of determiners, and each column to a tonal category of heads.[3]

---

[3] The same treatment cannot be extended to compounds of more than two syllables: it is not possible to describe the tone patterns of these compounds without referring to the juncture between the two input nouns, except by changing the entire notation, for instance specifying the tone of each syllable.

Table 9.4: Source-oriented and result-oriented notations of the tones of compounds: three examples.

		phonological analysis	
input tones	surface phonological tone	source-oriented	result-oriented
#H and LM	M.H	#H–	H#
M and LM	M.L	–L	L#
M and L	M.L	–L	L#

Table 9.5: The tones of disyllabic compounds, adopting a result-oriented notation. The four combinations transcribed differently from Table 9.4 are set in italics.

tone	LH; LM	M	L	#H	MH#
LM	LM	LM	LM	LM+#H	LM+MH#
LH	LH	L	LH		
M	*L#*	#H	*L#*	#H	MH#
L	*L*				
#H	H#	*#H*			*L#*
MH	*H#*			H$	

All of the tone categories observed on disyllabic nouns in Yongning Na are found in Table 9.5, except M. This reveals that the synchronically productive tone rules that apply in compounds feed into all of the tone categories of disyllables, apart from M.

9.2.2 Possible origins for disyllables in view of their tone

Table 9.6 flips around the morphotonological rules set out in Chapters 3 and 5 to provide an overview of possible origins of disyllabic items, in view of currently productive tone rules. The indication '–' means that no example was found. The mention *dubious* is given for H# tone as a product of suffixation because there is no firmly-attested pattern of correspondence between monosyllables and suffixed forms carrying //H#// tone, only isolated tokens whose analysis is problematic. For instance, /tse˧mi˩/ 'cigarette lighter' has //H#// tone and looks like the product of suffixation, but there is no corresponding monosyllable and hence no possibility (from this dialect alone) to establish a tone correspondence between root and suffixed form.

The bird's-eye view in Table 9.6 can provide a hint for the analysis of disyllabic words whose etymology is unclear.

Table 9.6: Possible origins of disyllabic items, in view of currently productive tone rules.

tone	compounding	suffixation	prefixation
M	–	yes	yes
#H	yes	yes	–
MH#	yes	–	yes
H$	yes	yes	yes
L	yes	yes	yes
L#	yes	–	yes
LM+MH#	yes	–	–
LM+#H	yes	yes	–
LM	yes	yes	–
LH	yes	yes	–
H#	yes	*dubious*	–

9.2.3 Recovering the tones of nouns on the basis of compounds

It is tempting to try to work backwards from the tones of compounds to those of their constituting elements. For instance, 'elder sibling (brother or sister)' is commonly realized as /ə˧my˩/ (tone: L#), but it has a variant with MH# tone: /ə˧my˥/. The tone of the coordinative compound /ə˧my˧-gi˥zɯ˩/ 'brothers' (made up of 'elder sibling' + 'younger brother') is the one expected for an input MH# tone, not an input L# tone. This could suggest that it is the MH# variant of 'elder sibling', /ə˧my˥/, that went into the creation of the compound. Seen in this light, the rarity of the MH# variant in present-day speech, where /ə˧my˩/ is far more common, suggests that the MH# variant /ə˧my˥/ is not a recent innovation but a form which is currently losing ground to /ə˧my˩/.

The greatest care must be exercised when attempting to recover tones in this way, however, since different tone rules may have applied at different stages of the language's history. As pointed out by Nathan Hill (p.c. 2016), there is at present no way to exclude the possibility that the MH# variant /ə˧my˦/ for 'elder sibling' was inferred from the compound (whatever the origin of the compound's tone may be) and constitutes an innovation.

9.3 Analogy

9.3.1 General principles

Analogy is the process whereby word forms perceived as irregular are reshaped so as to conform with more common forms: at some point, a speaker of English who was in doubt about the past tense for *dive* reasoned that *dove* is to *dive* as *drove* is to *drive*, and introduced an innovative form, *dove*, which has now become standard in North America, replacing the earlier form *dived*. From a morphological point of view, analogy can be viewed as a process of regularization. From the point of view of phonetic change, on the other hand, the piecemeal changes introduced by analogy tend to obfuscate regular correspondences.

Case studies of analogical reanalysis reveal the complexity of individual situations. For instance, in the Bantu language Eton, the stem of the possessive 'my' ends in /ɔ/ in association with nouns of classes 1 and 3: /-amɔ/, and in /a/ elsewhere: /-ama/. This irregularity is due to a mechanism of analogical morphophonological reanalysis that changed the original /a/ of the class 1/3 forms to /ɔ/. In Eton, there is a |ɔ| morphoneme whose morphologically-conditioned realizations include /wa/; commonly occurring sequences of /w/+/a/, although separated by a morpheme boundary, were reinterpreted as realizations of this morphoneme (Van de Velde 2008b). In this example, morphophonological analogy disregards morphological boundaries.

Analogy is by definition irregular and unpredictable. One may nonetheless believe that evidence from case studies gradually adds up.

> [I]t is possible to some extent to constrain the space of hypotheses involving analogy, and research on the general principles of analogy is of utmost importance for historical linguistics. (Jacques 2016: 239)

To date, studies about the principles of analogy (e.g. Kuryłowicz 1944; Lahiri 2000; Hill 2007; Blevins & Garrett 2009; Juge 2013; Hill 2014) contain little about tone, and studies about tone (e.g. Pike 1948; Fromkin 1978; Pulleyblank 1986; Gussenhoven 2004: 229-231) contain little about analogy, even though it seems intuitively clear that morphotonology can be subject to analogical levelling just like other aspects of morphophonology.

9.3.2 Analogy in Yongning Na morphotonology

Traces of analogy are also found among the tones of compounds and of affixed forms, as was pointed out in several places (in §3.3.3, 3.4.2, 5.1.3.2, 5.1.3.8 & 6.4.1.2). It appears highly plausible that the tantalizingly similar, but not identical tonal paradigms of classifiers – H_a and H_b, M_a and M_b, MH_a and MH_b, L_a, L_b and L_c (see Chapter 4) – have undergone a degree of analogical levelling, without becoming fully identical. The existence of variants for some combinations, and the consultants' occasional hesitations and confusions (errors) during elicitation sessions, all point to the presence of contradictory pressures: on the one hand the tendency towards analogical simplification, and on the other hand the tendency to maintain the distinct identity of the different classes. This is a field where the description of a single language variety reaches its limits, and a variationist approach would be called for. This study could be based on the closest language varieties: studying phenomena of accommodation between speakers within the hamlet under study, then extending the investigation to dialects spoken in the plain of Yongning and its close vicinity.

9.4 The influence of bilingualism with Mandarin

Language contact is known to be a key factor in linguistic change. An exemplary illustration of how the study of present-day contact dynamics can shed light on prosodic systems is the analysis of Kagoshima Japanese by Kubozono (2007). The Kagoshima dialect has two prosodic patterns for words: one (Tone A) with a high tone on the penultimate syllable (i.e. a fall from the penultimate to the last syllable), and the other (Tone B) with a high tone on the final syllable (i.e. no fall in pitch in the course of the word). At the time of study, this dialect was undergoing tonal change through influence from Tokyo Japanese, the national standard: words that involve an abrupt pitch fall in Tokyo tended to be reinterpreted as carrying Tone B, and vice versa. This sheds light on the issue of the tonal or accentual nature of this prosodic system: "the tonal changes in question can best be understood if an accentual analysis of Kagoshima Japanese prosody is adopted in preference to the traditional tonal analysis" (Kubozono 2007: 348; supporting evidence from a follow-up study of twenty speakers is reported by Ota, Nikaido & Utsugi 2016).

Since the present volume is synchronic in orientation, past contact between Na, Tibetan, Chinese, Pumi, Lisu, Naxi and other languages will not be investigated (apart from brief remarks in §11.2.1). Instead, this section focuses on the current landscape of language contact, in which Mandarin has, by far, the leading role. To take the example of the main consultant, Mandarin is the only language other than her mother tongue of which she has any knowledge.[4] The guiding principle in focusing on the influence of Mandarin is that "extracting as much historical information from clear contact phenomena as possible before attempting greater time depths may be the order of investigation most likely to be fruitful" (Souag 2010: 485).

Mandarin is a latecomer to this area. The feudal chieftain of Yongning spoke Na, and the Na language had a dominant situation in the plain of Yongning up until the mid-20th century. There were few (Han) Chinese migrants to Yongning, and they learnt Na, which was the locally dominant language, used in the Yongning marketplace by speakers of other languages, such as Pumi, Lisu, and Nosu (Nuosu / Yi). While there can be no doubt that the Na language received various influences in the course of its development, bilingualism was not widespread: speakers of other languages were bilingual in Yongning Na, rather than the other way round. Numerous Na speakers had very little command of other languages, or none at all. This situation is somewhat uncommon in this area, at the border between Sichuan and Yunnan. For instance, the small community of Na speakers in the neighbouring county of Muli 木里 (Shuiluo 水落 township) are bilingual in Shixing (Xumi) and have some command of Tibetan and Pumi; and the variety of Na spoken in Guabie 瓜别 has long been influenced by other languages, in particular Pumi and Nosu.

While Yongning still preserves the role of a meeting place and market place in the eyes of inhabitants of neighbouring mountain villages, for instance for the Nosu and Pumi people from small villages around Yongning (Wellens 2006: 85), language shift from Na to Mandarin is now under way in Yongning. All of the Na

---

[4] Since moving to Lijiang (2010), she has had relatively frequent contacts with Naxi speakers, however, and this has led to at least one amendment to her Na vocabulary. The Naxi are referred to by the Na as //naɭhĩ˧˥//, by a calque of the word structure of the Naxi word /naɭɕi˩/, made up of an endonym which is segmentally identical in both languages (/na/), and of the word for 'person, human being': Naxi /ɕi˩/, Na //hĩ˩//. Initially, the main consultant used this Na pronunciation when discussing with Naxi people in Lijiang. But to a Naxi listener, the realization /naɭhĩ˩/ does not sound right: the Naxi do not have nasalization in the syllable for 'person, human being'. Whether at Naxi speakers' suggestion, or through a spontaneous process of adjustment, she began to refer to the Naxi as /naɭɕi˩/, denasalizing the second syllable. This amounts to borrowing the word from Naxi, instead of calquing it with Na morphemes.

here have some command of Mandarin. While some members of the community regret the fact that their language is falling into gradual disuse, proficiency in Mandarin – one of the keys to success in society – tends to be ranked far above proficiency in Na. The blending of Na with Mandarin, rather than being stigmatized, is accepted with tolerance. This attitude facilitates language change. While a pool of variation is present at every moment and for any language, linguistic change in the strict sense requires the acceptance of innovative, deviant forms by the community of speakers.

All the level-tone systems spoken within China are currently subject to the same pressure towards reinterpretation of their tones by analogy with those of Mandarin. The Yongning Na sociolinguistic scene currently offers interesting opportunities for studying the effects of bilingualism – specifically, NON-EGALITARIAN BILINGUALISM, to take up a notion from Haudricourt (1961) – in languages with widely different tone systems. The account of Na tone presented in Chapters 2 to 7 of this volume makes it clear how much this system differs from that of the Chinese dialects to which speakers of Na are currently exposed (Southwestern Mandarin and Standard Mandarin). As discussed in Chapter 10, tones in Yongning Na are phonetically simple, consisting of three levels and combinations thereof, whereas tones in Mandarin are phonetically complex. The tone system of Yongning Na includes some oppositions that are neutralized when a word is said in isolation. When they learn Mandarin, Na speakers come to terms with a differently structured tone system: one in which (leaving aside marginal phenomena of toneless syllables and tone sandhi) each syllable has its own tone, which surfaces as such in isolation. The discrepancy between the underlying forms and the surface forms of Yongning Na tones makes them difficult to handle for bilingual speakers who have more exposure to Mandarin than to Na.[5]

9.4.1 Loss of tone categories that do not surface in isolation

Among younger speakers, especially those who went to boarding school, and who predominantly use Southwestern Mandarin, there is a tendency to overlook the differences that are neutralized in isolation, such as that between the //H#// and //H$// tones. The surface tone pattern of a word is reinterpreted as its underlying pattern, causing an upheaval in the architecture of the tonal system. For

---

[5] On the effects of bilingualism with Mandarin on the tone systems of other minority languages in rural southwest China, see the two case studies presented by Stanford & Evans (2012). These concern (i) Sui (Tai-Kadai family), which has a system of six phonetically complex tones in unchecked syllables and two in checked syllables, and (ii) Southern Qiang (Sino-Tibetan family), whose tone system is based on a binary opposition between H and L levels.

instance, the family name of the main language consultant is realized in isolation as /la˧tʰa˧mi˥/, and the associative form ('the Latami clan, the Latami family') is /la˧tʰa˧mi˧=ɳ̍˩/. This reveals that the H tone on the last syllable of /la˧tʰa˧mi˥/ is the realization of a *gliding* H tone (tone category H$), and the underlying form is //la˧tʰa˧mi˥$//. But if one ignores these alternations, and takes the M.M.H surface tone pattern in /la˧tʰa˧mi˥/ at face value, one will interpret the word as carrying a H tone on its last syllable, i.e. as belonging in phonological category //H#// (//la˧tʰa˧mi˥#//). As a consequence, when building phrases, e.g. creating an associative form ('the Latami clan') by addition of the suffix /=ɳ̍˩/, the H tone is left sitting on the last syllable of the lexical word, hence †la˧tʰa˧mi˥=ɳ̍˩. This is what happens in the speech of consultant F5, who is proficient in both Na and Mandarin. (She was aged 35 at the time of fieldwork.)

An especially difficult opposition to learn is that between the LM and LH patterns over disyllables, because it only surfaces when the word is followed by a clitic. For instance, //bo˩mi˧// 'sow, female pig' and //bo˩ɬa˧// 'boar, male pig' carry the same tones not only in isolation (/bo˩mi˥/ and /bo˩ɬa˥/) but also in most other contexts. The few contexts in which their tone patterns are disambiguated are exemplified by /bo˩mi˧=bv̩˧/ 'of (a) sow' vs. /bo˩ɬa˥=bv̩˩/ 'of (a) boar', where the H part of the lexical LH pattern results in the lowering of the following possessive particle, to L. Under such circumstances, it does not come as a surprise that the lexical opposition between LM and LH should be lost by some speakers, such as F5. In her speech, the tones of 'sow' and 'boar' are strictly identical: LM and LH have merged.

9.4.2 Simplification of morphosyntactic tone rules

Examining the tables in Chapters 3 to 6, the complexity of Na tonal morphosyntax may look mind-boggling. But the rules are productive, and the syntactic structures at issue (subject-plus-verb, object-plus-verb, compound nouns…) are so frequent that they are not particularly challenging to learn as part of the process of first language acquisition, for children steeped in a Na linguistic environment. On the other hand, for a speaker with limited practice, these combinations become problematic: they become difficult to remember and apply if one does not practise the language regularly. This holds true of the visiting linguist, as well as of Na speakers below age sixty, many of whom use more Mandarin than Na in daily life.

Evidence about ongoing language change can be gathered from deviant patterns, which to the linguist are harbingers of language change. They include a range of phenomena, from occasional slips of the tongue to ingrained habits.

Instances of hesitation and of pattern simplification can be found in the speech of M23, a bilingual language consultant. In subject-plus-verb and object-plus-verb combinations as well as in compounds, //L// tone, which surfaces as /M/ in isolation, tends to be neutralized with //M// tone: consultant M23 realizes 'the sheep came' as /jo˧ | tsʰɯ˩-ze˩/ (example (67) of Chapter 6), instead of (5). In F4's speech, the M.L.L pattern for 'the sheep came' is a variant condemned as a slip of the tongue; in M23's speech, it has become the usual form.

(5) jo˩ tsʰɯ˩-ze˩
    jo˩   tsʰɯ˩ₐ   -ze˧_b
    sheep to_come.PST PFV
    'the sheep have come'

Likewise, in M23's speech the combination 'sheep's muzzle' is //jo˧-ɲi˧gʌ˧//, i.e. a simple concatenation of the surface forms of the two nouns, unlike the conservative pattern found in F4's speech, shown in (6).

(6) jo˩-ɲi˩gʌ˧
    jo˩   ɲi˧gʌ˧
    sheep nose/muzzle
    'sheep's muzzle'

In the conservative form, (6), the tone of the compound is phonologically identical with the lexical L tone of the determiner, //jo˩// 'sheep'. This yields //jo˩-ɲi˩gʌ˩// 'sheep's muzzle', surfacing as /jo˩-ɲi˩gʌ˧/ following the post-lexical addition of a final H tone, due to Rule 7: all-L tone groups are not allowed in Yongning Na; if a tone group only contains L tones, a post-lexical H tone is added to its last syllable. A speaker needs a good command of the grammar of Na to implement the conservative tone pattern in this compound. The L tone of 'sheep', which does not even surface in isolation, has the effect of imposing itself onto no fewer than three syllables in succession in the compound, overriding the lexical tone of the head noun. The realization of 'nose, muzzle' in isolation is /ɲi˧gʌ˧/; in (6), it is changed to /ɲi˩gʌ˩/. Such tonal processes are alien to Mandarin. In light of this discrepancy, it is understandable that some less proficient speakers of Yongning Na who are exposed to Mandarin on a day-to-day basis should come to have hesitations, and should (occasionally or regularly) go for a simple succession of the tones as they surface in isolation, as is the case in their second language (Mandarin), instead of applying the rules of Yongning Na tonal grammar.

413

These examples illustrate the complexity of phenomena of language variation and change. As mentioned above, a change can constitute a simplification from one point of view and a complexification from other points of view. Saying /jo˧ | tsʰɯ˩-ze˩/ for 'the sheep arrived', with a M.L.L tone pattern instead of the conservative L.L.L pattern shown in (5), can be seen as a simplification insofar as the subject bears the same tone as in isolation. But it is a complexification insofar as it increases the frequency of occurrence of contexts in which the lexical L tone of 'sheep' does not surface, making it more difficult for language learners to arrive at the identity of this word's lexical tone.

9.4.3 Straightening out irregular tone patterns

In addition to losing some tone categories, less proficient speakers tend to regularize irregular patterns, for want of having memorized the exceptions. For instance, the word for 'powder, flour' is /tsa˧bɤ˧/, with M tone. According to the synchronic rules that govern the tone patterns of compound nouns, the combination of this word with /lv˧mi˧/, 'stone', should yield a simple M-tone output, †lv˧mi˧-tsa˧bɤ˧. (The compound means 'fine sand'.) However, in the speech of the older generation of speakers, compounds involving /tsa˧bɤ˧/, 'powder, flour', are irregular: they all carry L tone on their second half (the head noun 'powder, flour'). They belong in a set of expressions referred to as 'Tibetan compounds' in §3.2.11.3 and §3.3.3: compounds involving Tibetan loanwords, and whose second part systematically receives L tone. Examples were shown in Table 3.6 and Table 3.10. This irregularity is lost in the speech of less proficient speakers, who realize these compounds with a M.M.M.M tonal string (phonological analysis: /M/), as ‡ lv˧mi˧-tsa˧bɤ˧ 'fine sand', ‡ qʰa˧dze˧-tsa˧bɤ˧ 'sweetcorn flour', ‡ dze˧ɭɯ˧-tsa˧bɤ˧ 'wheat flour', and so on.

9.4.4 Cases where MH tone fails to unfold: Towards a syllable-tone system?

Naxi, a close relative of Yongning Na, has few phenomena of tone change. In the A-sher dialect, the reduction of a morpheme carrying H tone results in re-association of this tone to the syllable to its left (Michaud 2006b; Michaud & He 2007). Informal observations and exchanges with Naxi speakers living in the city of Lijiang suggest that even these simple instances of tone change are disappearing from Lijiang Naxi. For instance, the conditional is /se˧/ in A-sher, but this syllable is preceded by a floating H tone (its full form can be transcribed as //˦ se˧//). This is presumably the historical product of the reduction of disyllabic

*⌝ɯ˩ se˩. The phenomenon is still reported in a dictionary compiled from 1995 to 2012: "This word is fairly unique in that it triggers the mid or low tone of the preceding syllable to become a rising tone" (Pinson 2012: 337). Impressionistic observations made in Lijiang around 2010 suggest that this morpheme becomes simplified to /se˩/ in the speech of younger speakers. It is not at all unlikely that increasing familiarity with Mandarin is exerting an influence on Naxi, leading to the reinterpretation of its tones as units attached to the syllable, rather than levels that can combine among themselves.

Of the four tones of Naxi, High, Mid, Low and Rising, the last appears especially revealing in this respect. It is clearly an innovation which emerged in a system that contained three levels: High, Mid and Low. The following historical scenario can be proposed: rising contours appeared in the Naxi language through processes of syllable reduction, and became lexicalized on some words. Lexicalized instances of rising tones paved the way for the assignment of a /LH/ tone sequence to Mandarin words with rising tone. At that point, borrowings from Southwestern Mandarin consolidated this marginal lexical tone category by giving it considerable lexical development. In recent decades, bilingualism with Mandarin gradually tilted the perception of Naxi tones towards the syllable-tone type, to the point that it is now an issue whether the rising tone of Naxi is to be analyzed as a combination of levels (L+H, or M+H) or as a phonological unit (like contours in Mandarin). It is unclear to what extent Naxi speakers, most of whom are highly proficient in Southwestern Mandarin, keep the tone systems of Naxi and Mandarin cognitively distinct. To venture a hypothesis, the lexical rising tone of Naxi currently seems to behave essentially like an indecomposable contour.

In Yongning Na, there is plentiful synchronic evidence that contours are to be analyzed as sequences of levels. There are nonetheless some weak hints of a tendency for MH contours to be treated as units associated to one syllable. When saying MH-tone monosyllabic nouns in the frame 'This is …', consultant F4 occasionally produced variants with a rising contour on the target noun. Examples are shown in (7); the standard realization is provided in (8).

(7) ‡ tsʰɯ˦ | tsʰɯ˦ ɲi˩. ≈ ‡ tsʰɯ˦ | tsʰɯ˦ ɲi˩.
    tsʰɯ˩   tsʰɯ˦   ɲi˩
    DEM.PROX   goat   COP
    'This is a sheep.'

(8) tsʰɯ˦ | tsʰɯ˦ ɲi˩.
 tsʰɯ˩   tsʰɯ˦   ɲi˩
 DEM.PROX goat   COP

'This is a sheep.'

When her attention was drawn to these discrepancies, the consultant said: /ɖɯ˦-bæ˦ lɑ˦ ɲi˩/, "It's just the same". Intonationally, realization of the MH contour on the syllable to which it is lexically attached tends to happen when the word is emphasized.

This tendency surfaces here and there in the recordings. An example is the phonetic realization of /tsʰæ˦-pʀ˥to˩/ 'even a deer' as [tsʰæ˦-pʀ˥to˩] (in the recording NounsEven.7), with (i) a H tone on [pʀ˥], due to reassociation of the H part of the MH contour of /tsʰæ˦/ 'deer', as expected, and (ii) a MH contour on [tsʰæ˦], due to incomplete dissociation of the H part of its phonological MH contour.

This is only a weak tendency, however. It by no means warrants the conclusion that Yongning Na is on its way towards adopting a syllable-tone system. A detailed cross-linguistic phonetic study would be necessary to determine to what extent such tendencies are present among the world's level-tone systems. Such a study might reveal that Yongning Na is not at all exceptional in this respect. The computation of tone sequences is not a mechanical process, and slips of the tongue whereby a H tone does not fully dissociate from the syllable to which it is lexically attached may not come as a surprise to linguists with an experience of level-tone systems. This synchronic tendency appeared well worth mentioning, however, in relation to the influence currently exerted by Mandarin.

9.4.5 A topic for future research: Influence of language contact on intonation

Intonation is especially subject to carry-over from one language to another in the speech of bilinguals. A striking example involving Vietnamese speakers in a French-speaking environment is reported by Dô, Trân & Boulakia (1998: 401). In the case of Yongning Na, a full-fledged study of intonation should include a description and analysis of the intonation of Na speakers when using Mandarin, comparing it with their intonation when using Na, and examining patterns of interaction. This is not an easy topic. The main consultant only uses Mandarin reluctantly and hesitantly: she lacks confidence and feels awkward using this language. Her own evaluation is that she will never be able to speak "proper Chinese", and will make do with "pig Chinese" until her last breath. A complicating factor is that the variety of Chinese to which she was occasionally exposed until

2000 was Southwestern Mandarin, but since the year 2000 she has had regular exposure to Standard Mandarin from listening to television. The tone systems of these two dialects of Mandarin are almost identical phonologically, but the four tones' phonetic templates differ enough between the two dialects to complicate accommodation to the intonation patterns. Consultant F4 does her part in dialogues with Mandarin-speaking relatives and acquaintances, but recording these exchanges and establishing a transcription together with the participants would have run counter to our collaboration's implicit focus on her mother tongue, Yongning Na. The consultant's comfort zone was respected, and no pieces in Mandarin were recorded.

As a (lame) consolation for not being able to offer data on this topic, here is an example from another language showing that language contact can exert a strong influence on intonation. Wolof, one of the nontonal languages of the Niger-Congo family, has been described as having typological peculiarities such as the absence of any intonational marking of focus and the optional nature of the division of sentences into intonation groups (Rialland & Robert 2001). Information structure is conveyed by verbal morphology: there are three "nonfocusing conjugations" and three "focusing conjugations"; the latter "vary according to the syntactic status of the focused constituent: subject, verb, or complement (in the wide sense of any constituent that is neither subject nor main verb)" (Rialland & Robert 2001: 895). As Wolof ascends "from its origins in the heartland of Senegal to the status of urban vernacular and national *lingua franca*" (McLaughlin 2008: 142), it is acquired as a second language by speakers of many other languages. Informal discussion with a speaker of Wolof who also speaks some Bambara suggests that, in her speech, focus is clearly marked intonationally: pitch is raised on the focused constituent 'Peer' (a proper name) in (9), as compared with (10), where it is not under focus.

(9) ... Peer moo   ko   lekk
         Peer SUBJEMPH.3SG   OPR   to_eat

'It was Peer who ate it.' (SUBJEMPH stands for *subject-emphatic*, and OPR for *object pronoun*.)

(10) ... Peer lekk   na
         Peer to_eat PFT.3SG

'Peer has eaten.' (No focused constituent.)

This testifies to the fact that carry-over of intonation patterns from Bambara to Wolof can take place for bilingual speakers. Such situations can have far-reaching consequences for the evolution of the intonation system.

10 Typological perspectives

The following statement sets a possible stage for typological work:

> [L]anguages may differ at virtually all levels in their process of categorisation – not only in how they group sounds into emic categories (phonemes) but also in the way their particular constraints group these phonemes into meta-categories (classes of phonemes). These constraints, in turn, have to be defined system-internally, even when they derive from such supposedly universal parameters as sonority. Haspelmath (2007: 129) reminds us that "structural categories of language are language-particular, and we cannot take pre-established, *a priori* categories for granted". Such a stance does not rule out the possibility of universal generalisations, but entails that they can only be based on the empirical study of language-internal structures, and the acknowledgment of cross-linguistic diversity. (François 2010: 429)

In this citation, François reminds us that every language has its own emic categories, which can only be discovered through an in-depth, language-internal analysis. Universals should not be assumed aprioristically: they are to be investigated empirically, and explored through the careful comparison of languages. This view does not amount to a relativistic claim that each language calls for its own distinct concepts: rather, it opens up a programme for comparative work that emphasizes cross-language similarities in functional terms, and in terms of evolutionary potential, instead of static characteristics.

10.1 Tonal typology

In this section, clarifications are provided about the typological distinction between "level tones" and "complex tones", which constitutes the background to the classification of Yongning Na tones as "level tones" (§10.1.1). Some reflections are then set out (§10.1.2) concerning the typological profile of Na prosody as shaped by the tone rules described in the preceding chapters.

10.1.1 Level tones and phonetically complex tones

In what can be broadly termed as "Africanist" usage, "level tone" refers to *a tone that is defined simply by a discrete level of relative pitch*. Level tones (a phrase used interchangeably with "tonal levels") are monodimensional: they are defined along a single parameter, F_0. This is unlike segments, which are defined along intersecting phonetic parameters, such as voicing, nasality, place of articulation, etc. For want of free combinability of multiple properties, level tones are not further analyzed in terms of features: level tones constitute phonological primitives (Clements, Michaud & Patin 2011: 20; Hyman 2011).

Level-tone systems have two to five levels of relative pitch: L vs. H; L vs. M vs. H; L vs. M vs. H vs T(op); or B(ottom) vs. L vs. M vs. H vs. T(op). Systems with more than three levels are relatively uncommon (Bariba: Welmers 1952; Bench, also known as Gimira: Wedekind 1983; 1985). One single case of a six-level system has been reported: Chori (Dihoff 1977), for which a reanalysis is possible (Odden 1995). Bariba, Bench and Chori are spoken in Subsaharan Africa, an area where level tones are especially common. However, level-tone representations have proved useful beyond the Subsaharan area, for which they were initially developed (on languages of the Americas: Gomez-Imbert 2001; Hargus & Rice 2005; Girón Higuita & Wetzels 2007; Michael 2010; on languages of Asia: Ding 2001; Hyman & VanBik 2002; 2004; Donohue 2003; 2005; Evans 2008; Jacques 2011a). In Yongning Na, the morphotonological alternations studied in the preceding chapters provide overwhelming evidence for a level-tone analysis. In level-tone systems, a phonetic contour is *the realization of two or more level tones on a single syllable*. The contours are phonologically decomposable; the observed movement in F_0 is the result of interpolation between the successive levels.

There are some languages for which attempts at the decomposition of contours into levels have been less successful, however, to the point of casting doubt on the relevance of decomposition for these languages. In the Austroasiatic and Tai-Kadai language families, no convincing evidence is found for the decomposition of contours into simpler units (e.g. Morey 2014: 639). In the field of Sinitic languages (Chinese dialects), Chao Yuen-ren's work on Mandarin in the early 20th century (Chao 1929; 1933) brought out the complexities of its tone system. Following sustained exchanges with Chao Yuen-ren, Kenneth Pike proposed a typological divide between (i) register-tones, defined simply in terms of discrete pitch levels, and (ii) contour-tones, about which he concludes: "the glides of a contour system must be treated as unitary tonemes and cannot be broken down into end points which constitute lexically significant contrastive pitches" (Pike 1948: 10). Later studies have emphasized the importance of phonation-type characteristics.

In some prosodic systems, phonation types are simply a low-level phonetic characteristic that occasionally accompanies tone (see, for example, an investigation into the effect of creaky voice on Cantonese tonal perception: Yu & Lam 2014). In others, they are a distinctive feature orthogonal to tone, as in the Oto-Manguean languages Mazatec (Garellek & Keating 2011) and Trique (DiCanio 2012). Finally, in a third type of system, phonation-type characteristics are part and parcel of the definition of tones. Experimental studies of this third type of tone system include Rose (1982; 1989; 1990) for the Wu branch of Sinitic, Edmondson et al. (2001) for Yi and Bai, Mazaudon & Michaud (2008) for Tamang, and Andruski & Ratliff (2000), Andruski & Costello (2004), Kuang (2013) for Hmong.

> Languages such as Black Miao and Vietnamese highlight the difficulty of drawing a line in the sand separating 'tone' languages from 'register' languages. This problem is even more strikingly illustrated by Burmese (…), which has been described both as a register system (e.g. Bradley 1982; Jones 1986) and as a tone language (e.g. Watkins 2001; Gruber 2011) (…). Gruber (2011) has shown that glottalisation, creakiness and the presence of a high pitch target are all important perceptual cues, thus demonstrating that, much like Vietnamese or Black Miao, Burmese should not be analyzed in terms of pitch or phonation type alone, nor is it straightforward to decide which property is the primary acoustic cue to the contrast. (Brunelle & Kirby 2016: 194)

Pike's two-way typology of tone, while it emphasizes typologically relevant properties of those languages which he was able to take into consideration, has some limitations when it comes to characterizing tones such as those of Vietnamese. In the Vietnamese system, the tones contrast with one another through a set of characteristics that include specific phonation types in addition to the time course of F_0 (Alves 1995; Mixdorff et al. 2003; Brunelle, Nguyễn & Nguyễn 2010; Nguyen et al. 2013; Mac et al. 2015); for such tones, characterization as "contour tones" sounds underspecific. For this reason, the term "complex tones" is used here in preference to Pike's "contour tones". To recapitulate the terms used in the present discussion: *complex-tone systems* are distinguished from *level-tone systems* (based on discrete levels of relative pitch). Complex tones include Pike's category of "contour tones", with the explicit addition of tones that comprise phonation-type characteristics.[1]

---

[1] Note that this differs from the definition used in the *World Atlas of Language Structures*, where "complex" refers to the number of oppositions, not to the nature of the tones: "[t]he languages

Under this set of definitions, "contour" refers to a unitary contour: a tone defined phonologically in terms of an overall template specifying the time course of F_0 over the tone-bearing unit. Phonologically unitary contour tones are encoded as an overall shape: "there are no objective reasons to decompose Vietnamese tone contours into level tones or to reify phonetic properties like high and low pitch into phonological units such as H and L" (Brunelle 2009a: 94; see also Brunelle, Nguyễn & Nguyễn 2010; Kirby 2010). In this type of system, the term "level tone" is used to refer to *a tone that does not exhibit any salient fluctuations in F_0*. For instance, Mandarin tone 1 and Vietnamese tone 1 (orthographic *ngang*) can be referred to as "level tones" because, unlike the other tones of Mandarin and Vietnamese, their F_0 curve is relatively stable in the course of the syllable. This does not entail that they are phonologically defined by a discrete level of relative pitch (on Mandarin: see Xu & Wang 2001).

The two types of phonological contour tones – sequences of levels on the one hand, unitary contours on the other – can be phonetically indistinguishable, so that phonetic observation must be related to functional-structural levels of description. The evidence for distinguishing the two types of contours is morphotonological. A rising contour in a Bantu language will typically exhibit phonological behaviour showing that it consists of a low level tone followed by a high level tone (Clements & Goldsmith 1984; Clements & Rialland 2007). In Yongning Na, too, there is a wealth of evidence for the analysis of contour tones into sequences of level tones. From a typological point of view, instead of positing that all tones can be decomposed into levels, it is at least as reasonable to adopt the opposite standpoint, viewing contours as nondecomposable units unless there is positive evidence to the contrary (Nick Clements, p.c. 2008).

Tonal systems thus based on levels (tone heights) are relatively unusual in Sino-Tibetan, but not unheard of. Examples include Pumi (Matisoff 1997; Ding 2006; Jacques 2011a; Daudey 2014), Cone Tibetan (Sun 2003b; Jacques 2014), Mianchi Qiang (Evans 2008), Shixing / Xumi (Chirkova & Michaud 2009), Hakha Lai (Hyman & VanBik 2002), Kuki-Thaadow (Hyman 2010), and the Lataddi dialect of Na (Dobbs & La 2016).

The distinction between level tones and complex tones is proposed as a rule-of-thumb distinction; it aims to bring attention to a considerable amount of interesting Asian data that is likely to lie below the radar of some prosodic typologists and which deserves to be more widely appreciated. Needless to say, the two-way

---

with tones are divided into those with a simple tone system – essentially those with only a two-way basic contrast, usually between high and low levels – and those with a more complex set of contrasts" (Maddieson 2011).

distinction between level tones and complex tones is by no means water-tight: there are borderline situations.

The following subsection attempts to convey a feel for the organization of the Na prosodic system by pointing out some consequences of its tone rules for the outlook of this level-tone system.

10.1.2 Typological profile of Na prosody as shaped by the tone rules

One of the salient characteristics of Yongning Na is the partial neutralization of lexical oppositions when words are said in isolation. This does not appear to have far-reaching implications for the organization of the entire tonal system, however: such neutralization is observed in numerous prosodic systems which differ widely from one another, such as Japanese (Kubozono 1993), San Juan Quiahije Chatino (Oto-Manguean family) (Cruz 2011: 91), and Sotho and Tswana (Bantu) (Creissels, Chebanne & Nkhwa 1997; Zerbian & Barnard 2010b; Zerbian 2016).

On the other hand, the levelling rules of Yongning Na (Rules 4 and 5), whereby all tones following a H tone, or a M.L sequence, are lowered to L, have far-reaching consequences for surface phonological tone sequences. These two rules result in the neutralization of tonal oppositions over large portions of tone groups – a massive phenomenon of levelling that is reminiscent of stress systems in which all syllables following a major stress are de-stressed. This rule alone makes Yongning Na tone strikingly different from the extensive set of tone systems called 'terraced-level tone languages' (Armstrong 1968). 'Terracing' refers to two processes of categorical shift in register, affecting all following tones: *downstep*, a distinctive lowering; and *upstep*, a distinctive raising. An important consequence of terracing is that tones belonging to the same 'terrace' hang together more closely than the successive tones in a language which, like Na, does not have downstep or upstep. To use an image from weaving, one could say that tones belonging to the same terrace are tightly knit together; to use an image from woodwork, they could be said to be pegged together. This intuition is reflected in Nick Clements's proposed treatment of 'terracing' in terms of a "tone level frame". "Within this framework, terracing is seen to be the result of (…) processes applying to the tone level frame itself, rather than directly to individual tones" (Clements 1979: 538). 'Terracing' places constraints on the range of fundamental frequency within which the tonal levels are realized, as shifts in register are distinctive. It makes a major contribution to shaping surface phonological tone sequences and their phonetic realization. Clements points out a key factor: categorical shift in register can take place more than one time in a tone group.

> [An] important feature of tone terracing, at least in the case of downstep, is that there is no limit on the number of register lowerings that may occur within a tone group; the only limit is the external one imposed by the lexical, grammatical, or phonological factors that govern the occurrence of downstep. (Clements 1979: 540)

This leads to preplanning strategies that can get highly elaborate: brilliant speakers anticipate the amount of downsteps that will be required in a long utterance, raise the initial pitch accordingly, and manage successive lowerings all the way to the end of the utterance. Less talented orators need to reset their F_0 when successive downsteps make them hit bottom before they reach the end of a tone group (Rialland 2001).

In Yongning Na, there is no downstep, and hence no need for such long-distance preplanning. Whenever a tone group contains a H tone, this tone serves as the tone group's climax. In terms of information processing, in cases where a H tone is identified, following syllables in the tone group contain no more tonal information: there is nothing to expect but a sequence of phonological L tones. Phonetically, the pitch gradually lands towards its floor value; the realization of the F_0 curve on the portion of the tone group that follows the H tone is free from the trammels of categorical precision.

To summarize, the 'tone level frame' (Nick Clements's term to refer to the tone space at a given point in an utterance) is subject to far fewer constraints in Yongning Na than in 'terracing' tone languages. The absence of downstep or upstep in Yongning Na, and the culminative nature of its H tone, go a long way towards explaining the different feel of its prosody compared to that of 'terracing' tone languages. There are simply fewer possible tone sequences in Yongning Na than in, for instance, Yala (Ikom), which has H, M and L tones, like Na, but also has the downstepped counterparts !H, !M and !L, and allows the full range of their combinations (Armstrong 1968). In Yongning Na, there is no contrast between a fall from M to L and one from H to L. This gives a greater range of phonetic freedom than in languages where the tonal space is more crowded. (The greater phonetic freedom found in Na is exploited for intonational purposes, as explained in §8.3.)

Like downstep, *downdrift* – the gradually lower phonetic realization of phonologically identical tones separated by a lower tone – is absent in Yongning Na, for the same reason: the two sequences of a higher tone and a lower one are H.L and M.L, both of which constitute a descent to the lowest phonological level, and these sequences can only be followed by L tones (by Rule 5), thus prohibiting sequences such as ‡M.L.M, ‡H.L.H or ‡H.M.H. This is another important trait of the typological profile of Yongning Na.

10.2 Assessing the complexity of the Na tone system

In comparison with Naxi and Laze, its immediate siblings in the Naish subgroup of Sino-Tibetan (§1.1.2.2), Na presents a high degree of tonal complexity. It has more lexical tone categories, and greater morphotonological complexity.[2] A task for the future will consist in assessing this complexity by modelling regularities and irregularities in the paradigms that make up Na morphotonology. As a stepping-stone towards this mid- and long-term goal, some dimensions of this complexity are recapitulated below and compared with other languages, not on the basis of phylogenetic or areal closeness but of synchronic typological similarities.

10.2.1 Partly regular morphotonology

Partly regular morphological paradigms are cross-linguistically widespread. Examples include the inflection of transitive verbs in Dinka (Andersen 1993: 8) (while certain inflections are marked by a particular toneme for all verbs alike, other inflections are specific to particular classes of verbs) and the inflection of interrogative pronouns in the Australian language Anguthimri (Crowley 1981: 172).

Within the tone system of Na, numeral-plus-classifier phrases constitute an area where tone patterns have proliferated. The description set out in Chapter 4 brought to light no fewer than nine tonal categories for monosyllabic classifiers, as opposed to five for monosyllabic nouns. Furthermore, the tone patterns of these nine categories of classifiers in combination with numerals need to be learnt: they do not follow from synchronically regular rules. While this complexity is not as spectacular as that found in the Ahmao language (Hmong-Mien family), where classifiers have "12 basic forms, each displaying a complex cluster of meanings" (Gerner & Bisang 2009), the Na data may nonetheless have a contribution to make to typological generalizations, as it shows that the tones of classifiers can be more complex than those of nouns.

10.2.2 Nouns and verbs: A comparable degree of complexity?

Keeping in mind that some types of nouns (especially classifiers) are more complex than others in terms of their tone categories, it seems that there is no con-

---

[2] These two variables – the number of tonal contrasts, and the number of tonal rules – are proposed as the two main dimensions of tonal complexity in an article discussing methods for measuring the degree of complexity of a tone systems (Konoshenko 2014a).

spicuous imbalance between Na nouns and verbs in terms of tonal complexity. This differs from tonal systems in Bantu, and in the Niger-Congo family at large, where verbs display less diversity of tone categories than nouns. Many Bantu languages have two tonal types of verbs (irrespective of their number of syllables), versus three or more types of monosyllabic nouns and an even greater number for nouns of two syllables and more (Creissels 1994: 183). Gbeya, Kissi, Baoulé and Urhobo do not have tonal oppositions among verbs at all (Creissels 1994: 184).

10.2.3 More progressive spreading than regressive spreading: A typologically common pattern

Under the analysis proposed here, Yongning Na has a phonological tone rule (Rule 1) whereby L tone spreads progressively ('left-to-right') onto syllables that are unspecified for tone. The H tone does not spread, in the sense of associating to several syllables in a row: there can only be one H tone per tone group. Despite this, the presence of a H tone does influence the following tones in the group: they all get lowered to L. Although the morphotonological rules are context-specific, and cannot be summarized in terms of a set of phonological rules, they also reveal an overall tendency towards progressive tone spreading, rather than the other way round. For instance, averaging over the entire set of tone rules applying in determinative compounds (§3.2), the determiner (which comes first) makes a larger contribution than the head to the tone of the entire compound. Seen in this light, Na clearly has more progressive spreading than regressive spreading of tone.

This is a typologically unsurprising pattern. Regressive tone spreading is well-attested, for instance in Tswana and Odienné Dioula, and in Kikwere as analyzed by Odden (1998: 177-178), but progressive tone spreading is more common (Creissels 1994: 206-207).

A separate but not wholly unrelated observation is that H tone in Yongning Na has a tendency to be realized late within a tone group. A H tone never associates to the first syllable within a tone group. //H#// tone associates to the last syllable of the root; so does //H$//, but it typically glides from this position to a later syllable (§2.3.2); and //#H// tone never associates to the word to which it is lexically attached, only to a later syllable (§2.3.1). This overall tendency is relatively common cross-linguistically. Late realization of H targets is more common than early realization: "perseverative tone spreading phonologises the tendency of tone targets to be realized late" (Hyman 2007b: 19). The diachronic developments leading to the present diversity of final H tones in Yongning Na seem to follow tendencies that are well-attested across languages. This is a case where synchronic complexity is not particularly surprising when viewed from the perspective of the typology of language change (i.e., from a *panchronic* perspective: see §1.2.2).

10.2.4 The dual status of the M tone is not a typological rarity

Under the present description, the M tone in Yongning Na has two facets. On the one hand it is a full-fledged, phonologically specified tone: the M element in tone categories such as LM and MH cannot be omitted. LM contrasts with L, and MH# with H#. On the other hand, the M tone serves as a default tone: by Rule 2, M tone is assigned to syllables that remain toneless after Rule 1 (L-tone spreading onto toneless syllables) has applied.

Na is not an isolated case in this respect. In Yorùbá, too, the M tone has a dual status. M tone is not lexically specified: the only two lexical tones are L and H, but following its insertion through default-tone assignment rules, M behaves as a specified tone in derivations (Akinlabi 1985).

10.3 Intonational typology: Tonal vs. non-tonal intonation

This last section of the typological discussion is devoted to intonational typology. The argument is that *tonal intonation* and *non-tonal intonation* need to be carefully distinguished, and that Yongning Na does not have tonal intonation. This is not a particularly complex argument, and its conclusion seems fully clear to me, but the present state of befuddlement in the field of intonation studies requires step-by-step exposition of the typological premises.

10.3.1 Instances of intonational tones in the world's languages

There are some well-established cases where intonation is encoded by tones that are treated on a par with lexical and morphological tones: in some tonal languages, tone can serve as a marker for functions at the phrasal level. These will be referred to as *intonational tones*. This extension of the notion of tone beyond its primary meaning (lexical and morphological tone) is made in view of the structural similarities between lexical and morphological tone, on the one hand, and certain intonational phenomena, on the other hand. It does by no means amount to a broadening of the concept of tone to intonational phenomena in general, as is the case in some versions of autosegmental-metrical models of intonation.

Firstly, tone may indicate sentence mode. "The most commonly encountered cases involve a tonal means to distinguish interrogatives from declaratives. In Hausa, a L is added after the rightmost lexical H in a yes/no question, fusing with any pre-existing lexical L that may have followed the rightmost H (…). As a result, lexical tonal contrasts are neutralized. In statements, [**káí**] 'head' is tonally distinct from [**káí**] 'you [masculine]'. But at the end of a yes/no question, they are identical, consisting of an extra-H gliding down to a raised L" (Hyman & Leben 2000: 61). The Hausa example is described as a case of intonational tone, not a case of superimposition of an intonational contour onto an underlyingly unchanged tone sequence.

Secondly, tone may serve the function of phrasing. In some languages, certain junctures of the utterance are characterized by the addition of boundary tones, which, though introduced by post-lexical rules, are integrated into the tone sequence of the utterance on a par with lexical tones. L. Hyman (p.c. 2012) points out that such phenomena are "rampant in African tone systems": for instance, the phrase-final boundary tone of Luganda acts just like any other H tone, except that it is inserted into the tonal string later than the lexical tones. Any sequence of preceding toneless moras will be raised to that H level (though there has to remain at least one L before it). For example, /**omulimi**/ 'farmer' is pronounced all-L as subject of a sentence (/òmùlìmì/), but at the end of an utterance marked by this H% it is pronounced L-H-H-H: /òmúlímí/. The phrase-final boundary tone of Luganda is transcribed as H%, where the '%' sign, representing a boundary, is a functional indication of the tone's origin.

A third intonational function that may be served by tone is to convey prominence. A clear example of intonational tone (a tone of intonational origin) is encountered in Naxi: a word that carries lexical L or M tone on its last syllable can be focused by the addition of a H tone that aligns at the right edge of the word, causing the tone of the last syllable to become rising (Michaud 2006b: 72).

In order to understand how intonational tones emerge and evolve, it appears interesting to examine not only clear-cut cases such as those reviewed in this paragraph, but also doubtful cases of intonational tone.

10.3.2 Doubtful cases of intonational tone: Crossing the fine line between intonation and tone?

Scholars have long been aware of the phonetic similarities between intonation and tones. In the mid-17th century, the European authors who devised a Latin-based writing system for Vietnamese (Rhodes 1651) had to develop a notation for a six-way tonal contrast. One of the tones was left unmarked, grave and acute accents were used for two others, and the tilde for a fourth one. For the remaining two tones, symbols from sentence-level punctuation were used: the full stop was added (below the vowel) to indicate tone 4 (orthographic *nặng*) on the basis of the perceived similarity between its final glottal constriction and the intonational expression of *finality*; and the question mark (in reduced form, on top of the vowel) was used for tone 5 (orthographic *hỏi*) due to its final rise (Haudricourt 2010). To the authors of this system, the newly coined tone marks served as mnemonic cues to the pronunciation of tone, via an analogy with intonation in Romance languages.

When Chao Yuen-ren devised a system of "tone-letters" some three centuries later (Chao 1930), he proposed it as a tool to transcribe intonation, as well as tones. Examples of application to English intonation were offered, distinguishing various ways of saying *Yes* and *Where does he live*. The original article is entirely composed in International Phonetic Alphabet, as was the standard for the journal *Le Maître phonétique*. For convenience, this excerpt from Chao (1930: 26) is given in English orthography.

42	jes˦		Ordinary affirmation.
51	jes˥		Of course.
24	jes˨˦		Go on, I'm anxious to hear the rest of it.
13	jes˩˧		I'm listening.
15	jes˩˥		But, —.
11	fijes˩		I understand of course.
44	jẽ·s˦		It's all right, although you made a mess of it.
55	jẽ·s˥		I heard all about that sort of thing.
351	jes˧˥˩		I should be most delighted.
3513	jes˧˥˩˧		So far as that's concerned, only —.

ᴍɛə˥	dəz˦	i:˦	liv˦	Ordinary interrogation.
ᴍɛə˩	dəz˦	i:˦	liv˥	Where did you say he lived?
ᴍɛə˩	dəz˦	i:˦	liv˦	No matter where he eats.
ᴍɛə˥	dəz˦	i:˩	liv˥	I didn't ask…, I asked *how* he lived.
ᴍɛə˩	dəz˦	i:˥	liv˥	Don't you know where he lives?

Under Chao's proposal, there is no ambiguity as to whether tone letters are used for tones (which Chao calls "tonemes", to bring out the analogy with phonemes, with which they share a distinctive function) or for intonation (what he calls "tone values"). "Each tone-letter consists of a vertical reference line (…), to which a simplified time-pitch curve of the tone represented is attached, for tonemes to the left of the line, and for tone-values to its right" (Chao 1930: 24–25).[3] Chao's proposal to use similar tools for the transcription of intonational differences in English and tonal oppositions in Cantonese underlines their similarity in phonetic form. In Chao's examples (English, Cantonese and Tibetan), the distinction between lexical tone and intonation is clear, but there are other cases where a language's lexical tones are reported to serve intonational purposes. Phake (Tai-Kadai language family) exemplifies the diversity of situations found in Asian languages.

10.3.2.1 The expression of negation and sentence mode in Phake

Phake, a Tai-Kadai language of Assam (India), has six lexical tones, and cases of "changed tones" (Morey 2008: 234–240). Three processes are reported.

(i) If a verb has the second tone (High falling), it changes to rising when negated. This rising tone is identical in form to the language's sixth lexical tone; speakers of the language perceive such tone change to be categorical in nature (tonal replacement). This process also appears to be extending to verbs carrying other tones (S. Morey, p.c. 2013).

(ii) According to observations made in the 1960s and 1970s, changing the lexical tone of the last syllable in a sentence to the sixth tone (a rising tone) would express a question (Banchob 1987). More recent fieldwork reports the same phenomenon, but instead of identifying the "changed tone" with one of the six lexical tones, it is suggested that it is "a special questioning tone (...). This questioning tone first rises and then falls, and here is arbitrarily notated as 7" (Morey 2008: 234).

(iii) Finally, an eighth tone is reported: an *imperative tone* "that exhibited glottal constriction and creaky voice" (Morey 2008: 239).

Observation (ii) can be reinterpreted in terms of neutralization of tonal oppositions: it does not appear implausible that question intonation in Phake would override the lexical tone of the sentence's last syllable in questions. Likewise, imperative intonation has a salient influence on some tense-aspect-modality markers, which may go so far as to override their lexical tone. As observed by Martinet (1957), "the fluctuating needs of communication and expression are reflected

---

[3] The symbols to transcribe intonation, with the stylized pitch curve to the right of the reference bar, were not taken up in the International Phonetic Alphabet.

more directly and immediately in intonation than in any other section of the phonic system". The phonation type associated to imperative mode – a contraction of the laryngeal sphincter, to convey an attitude of authority – appears to have a clear iconic motivation (see Fónagy 1983: 113–126). The "imperative tone" of Phake reflects what might be a cross-linguistic *command intonation*: short, sharp, high.[4]

It is perhaps significant that "changed tones" are reported in an area where the dominant languages are non-tonal. Speakers of Phake are also fluent in Assamese, a non-tonal language, which may create a pressure towards the simplification of the Phake tone system, e.g. through neutralization of tonal contrasts in some contexts. Overall, it would seem that intonation does not easily win the day over lexical tone. Some experimental evidence on this topic comes from a study of the Austroasiatic language Kammu, one of few languages with two dialects whose only major phonological difference is the presence or absence of lexical tones. A comparison of the two dialects concludes that the intonational systems of the two Kammu dialects are basically identical, and that the main differences between the dialects are adaptations of intonation patterns to the lexical tones when the identities of the tones are jeopardized (Karlsson, House & Svantesson 2012).

10.3.2.2 Mandarin interjections: A case of spurious tonal identification

The treatment of the interjection /**a**/ (transcribed as 啊 in Chinese writing) in a learner's dictionary of Standard Mandarin offers a clear case of spurious tonal identification. This dictionary treats the interjection as if it had lexical tone, and sets up four distinct entries for it, corresponding to the four tones of Mandarin: with tone 1, the interjection would mean "speaker gets to know something pleasant"; with tone 2, it would signal a "call for repetition"; with tone 3, "surprise or disbelief"; and with tone 4, the "sudden realization of something" (Huángfǔ Qìnglián 1994, entry "a"). This categorization is based on phonetic similarities between the pitch patterns of the four tones and intonational variants of the interjection, as recapitulated in Table 10.1.

There is in fact a considerable phonetic difference between the four-way division of the Mandarin tonal space, on the one hand, and on the other hand the

---

[4] Stephen Morey (p.c. 2016) reports that a similar "imperative tone" occurs in Tai Khamti, a nearby language, which has five citation tones. When the first attempt to mark tones in Khamti was made in the 1990s, tone marks for features such as imperative were made, and these replace the citation tone mark in texts. Whether lexical distinctions are fully neutralized in these cases remains to be investigated experimentally.

Table 10.1: Phonetic basis for the four-way categorization of the nuances expressed by the interjection /a/ in Mandarin, as proposed in some dictionaries.

tone	characterization in dictionary	example	translation of example	F₀ on interjection	canonical realization of tone
1	"speaker gets to know something pleasant"	啊！我考过了！ ā! wǒ kǎo guò-le!	Wow! I passed the exam!	overall high F₀	level, in the upper part of the speaker's range
2	"call for repetition"	啊，是吗？ á, shì ma?	Oh, is that right?	rising	rising
3	"surprise or disbelief"	啊？你在这儿干吗？ ǎ? nǐ zài zhèr gànmá?	Huh? What are you doing here?	falling-rising	falling from mid-low to lowest, with final rise in isolation
4	"sudden realization of something"	啊，现在我知道了。 à, xiànzài wǒ zhīdào-le.	Aha! Now I understand.	falling	sharply falling, from high starting-point

intonational gradations in the realization of interjections. Interestingly, the authors of the dictionary gloss the "tone-4" realization of the interjection /a/ as the "*sudden* realization of something" (emphasis added). The interjection /a/ can just as well convey the realization of something, without any hint of suddenness (Lín Yǔtáng 1972, entry "啊"). The F_0 of the interjection decreases gradually, in a manner that does not resemble tone 4 (an abruptly falling tone). The mention of suddenness was probably added because the intonational signalling of this extra nuance tends to shorten the interjection, thereby creating greater surface similarity with tone 4. From the point of view of linguistic functions, there should be no confusion: the phonetic realization of interjections in Mandarin is purely intonational, "with varying, indeterminate accent, like English *Oh! ah! aha!*" (Lín Yǔtáng 1972, entry "啊"). Mandarin interjections bypass tonal coding; the interjection /a/ has a wide range of possible realizations, and of expressive effects. The four entries set up for this interjection in the dictionary single out four of these realizations, and grant them separate status merely because they happen to be phonetically close to the language's four lexical tones. This example illustrates the potential for a misinterpretation of intonational phenomena as tonal.

10.3.3 Conditioning factors for the development of intonational tones

In light of the above survey, it appears that the presence or absence of intonational tones is a typological parameter: a parameter that varies from language to language.

The issue of whether a language has tonal intonation or not may appear as a non-issue to researchers who use autosegmental-metrical models, since these models operate with the same concepts – among which tone plays a key role – for all languages, as a matter of definition. To some extent, this is an issue of choice of terms: there often exist straightforward equivalences between observations couched in tonal and non-tonal terms. For instance, in their description of phrasing in French, Fougeron & Jun (1998: 49–51) explain that they use notations as H* tone and H% tone (or L% tone) respectively as equivalents for Delattre's (1966) *minor continuation* and *major continuation*. Such equivalences allow for converting from one framework to another – but only from a language-internal point of view. When it comes to typology, use of the same labels with widely different meanings for different languages creates difficulties. Upon close examination, it appears that the labels H% and L% as used for, say, Kinande, French, Vietnamese and Bemba refer to different phenomena in each case. In Kinande, the H% which marks the end of a phrase is a *bona fide* tone, which interacts with tones of lexical origin, for instance by causing neutralization of certain lexical tone oppositions on nouns when they are said in isolation (Hyman 2014: 558). In French, in the absence of tones at the lexical level (and at the morphological level), there is no language-internal evidence to decide whether the phenomenon at issue is tonal or not, so H% can be considered to be equivalent to *major continuation*, with added information on phonetic realization. For Vietnamese, "rising final pitch movements" are labelled as H% by Hạ & Grice (2010) for theory-internal motivations, not on the basis of structural similarities between the lexical tones of Vietnamese and the intonational phenomena at issue. Finally, in Bemba, which like Kinande belongs to the vast Bantu group within Niger-Congo, the authors of a description of this language's intonation (Kula & Hamann 2016) posit boundary tones but remain noncommittal as to the extent to which these entities are really tonal. Two of these boundary tones attach to left boundaries (H- and L-) and two attach to right boundaries (H% and L%). The left-edge boundary tones H- and L- constitute a device to refer to "global effects of pitch range expansion and compression"; using the conceptual framework advocated in the present volume, they clearly seem non-tonal. The right-edge boundary tones (H% and L%) look as if they could be similar to the intonational tones reported in Kinande. The authors take a cautious stand: "[i]t remains to be investigated whether this boundary tone replaces the lexical tone" (Kula & Hamann 2016: 331). To sum up, the generalized use of boundary-tone labels such as H% and L% may appear economical from a theoretical point of view, but it tends to veil typological differences (Ladd 2008), often leaving readers hard put to figure out whether intonation in the language at issue is actually encoded by tones.

The motivation for using tonal labels for intonational phenomena is reminiscent of the use of the feature /ATR/ (Advanced Tongue Root) to describe the four-way opposition in a vowel system containing four degrees of vowel height: /**i-e-ɛ-a**/. This device obviates the need for a multi-valued /open/ feature for vowels, considered uneconomical under certain phonological analyses (Calabrese 2000). The pinch comes when typological considerations come in: should French and other Romance languages be included in cross-linguistic studies of ATR phenomena? A common-sense answer is that it would seem best to begin by identifying a core set of languages that uncontroversially possess ATR systems (a crucial phonological test being the presence of ATR vowel harmony), and to apply due caution when considering extensions of the concept beyond this core domain.

The current vogue of tonal models of intonation as applied for the most diverse languages entails an indirect benefit for specialists of intonation, as it can lead linguists engaged in intonational descriptions of tonal languages to raise explicitly the issue of the degree of similarity of intonational tones with the other tones found in the language. For instance, a study of Tanacross Athabaskan, a two-tone language, uses the tonal notations advocated in the framework of intonational phonology, proposing four intonation contours for four utterance types: H* L% for declaratives, H* H% for polar questions (yes/no interrogatives), L* L% for imperatives, and H+L* L% for open questions (wh-questions) (Holton 2005: 263). The author espouses the logic that underpins these notations: that tone and intonation are of the same nature at a certain phonological level: "[b]oth tone and intonation can be viewed as strings of binary tone values with certain associations between the tone values and the segmental tone bearing units" (Holton 2005: 267). This opens into the question of whether intonational tones partake in the language's tone rules. In Tanacross Athabaskan there is a phenomenon of tone spreading which is conditional on the stem's tone: the tone of the stem syllable affects the assignment of tone to preceding syllables. The author raises the issue of whether the final L tone found in declaratives has an influence over tone spreading: in principle, an added tone in the sequence could modify the application of tone spreading. The observation is that the pre-stem tone spread constraint is sensitive to the underlying lexical tone, and is unaffected by the hypothesized intonational 'tone' (Holton 2005: 270). The search for categorical effects of intonational 'tones' on the tonal string yields a clear conclusion in the negative. In my view, this settles the issue: Tanacross Athabaskan does not have tonal intonation. This conclusion sheds light in retrospect on the author's caveat that "[t]he notation consists of two types of 'pitch-accents', or tones (not to be confused with lexical tones discussed in the previous section)" (Holton 2005: 263). Thanks to these analyses, it is possible to arrive at a clear understanding of the facts. But clearing the confusion and uncertainty created by the use of autosegmental-metrical notations can be a tough struggle. To call two things by the same name, assert their identity at some level, and insist that they need to be kept distinct is to ask a lot of the reader.

In most East and Southeast Asian languages, the available literature suggests that intonation is not implemented by the addition of tones in the way described for Kinande, Hausa, or Luganda and Naxi (§10.3.1). The widely-studied case of Standard Mandarin provides a clear example. Mandarin has salient intonational phenomena, which have a strong influence on the phonetic realization of tones, to the extent of making the automatic recognition of tone in continuous speech a technological challenge. But these intonational phenomena do not affect the phonological identity of the lexical tones. Instead, intonation is superimposed on tone sequences. From the point of view of linguistic structure, intonation remains on an altogether different plane from tones: it does not modify the phonological sequence of tones, even in cases where it exerts a considerable influence on their phonetic realization. This has been studied since the pioneering work of Chao (1929). The informational prominence of a syllable is reflected in local phenomena of curve expansion and lengthening on the target syllable, as well as some modifications in supraglottal articulation. Conversely, a degree of phonetic reduction is found on other syllables, including post-focus compression of F_0 range (see in particular Xu 1999).

It seems intuitively clear that multilevel tone systems (e.g. Ngamambo, Wobe) cannot allow the type of intonational flexibility in the realization of tone which is pervasive in Mandarin or Vietnamese, because such flexibility would jeopardize the identification of the utterance's tonal string. The need to distinguish a wide range of categorically different sequences makes it less economical to encode information about phrasing and prominence as modulations of F_0 superimposed on the tonal string. This creates a tendency to favour other means to convey phrasing and prominence: either by integration into the tonal string (i.e., *intonational tones* as defined here), or by the use of non-intonational means, such as word order or topicalization and focalization morphemes.

Experimental verification of such hypotheses is greatly complicated by the multifarious differences among the languages to be compared. It is hoped that the availability of an increasing number of monographs such as the present one can contribute to gradual clarification of these typological perspectives.

11 Yongning Na in its areal context

This chapter presents some observations about Yongning Na in its areal context, pointing out similarities and differences with a few other Sino-Tibetan languages of the area with which Na may have been in contact in the past. The chapter is much too short to provide adequate coverage of its topic: in Wikipedia parlance, it would be called a "stub". It nonetheless appeared useful to gather areal observations (no matter how tentative) in a separate chapter, rather than blend them into the typological discussion in Chapter 10, where they do not really belong.

11.1 Naxi and Laze: Close relatives, but not part of a convergence area

It has been observed that "the same phonological processes such as tone sandhi and lengthening obviously make reference to different prosodic domains within the same language family (Bantu)" (Zerbian 2006a: 132). High diversity is also found within Naish, even though this lower-level grouping is incomparably smaller than Bantu.

Comparison of Na with Naxi and Laze is fundamental for diachronic investigation, since Naxi and Laze are the closest known relatives of Yongning Na (see §1.1.2.2). But from an areal point of view, I have not been able to find evidence of diffusional convergence between Na and the other two. It seems as if these languages had not been part of a convergence area. On the contrary, there has been strong social, political and cultural *divergence* since the 14th century: the Naxi chiefdom of Lijiang was increasingly Sinicized (and finally came under direct Chinese administration in the 18th century), whereas the feudal chieftain system was continued in Yongning and Muli until the mid-20th century due to the failure of attempts at military conquest of the Liangshan Yi area, which constitutes the gateway to these peripheral regions (see Appendix B, §B.1). As for the Laze, they are a small group of some four hundred people who migrated from Yanbian to their current location in Muli towards the end of the 19th century. They are reported to be among the speakers of Naish languages who left Yanbian as it became a dominantly Yi area, but no information is available about sociolinguistic configurations before the influx of Yi clans, so I am not in a position to tell how areal convergence may have contributed to shaping the prosody of Laze in past centuries. The present-day areal situation is not well-understood either, as the other Naish dialects spoken in the vicinity of the Laze villages remain undocumented, as far as I know.

From a prosodic point of view, Naxi and Laze currently exemplify the *nonrestricted tone* type in the sense of Voorhoeve (1973): tones are assigned to individual syllables without regard to the tone pattern of the entire word or tone phrase. In particular, in these two languages there is no limitation on the number of H tones that appear in succession, unlike in Yongning Na, where H tone is culminative (there is at most one H tone in each tone group). Interestingly, culminativity has been proposed as an areal characteristic of the languages that have long coexisted in Muli, a county that neighbours on Yongning (Chirkova 2012: 160).[1] In terms of this important property of the prosodic system, Yongning Na does not pattern together with Naxi or Laze, but with languages that have long been spoken in Muli: Pumi, Namuyi, Shixing / Xumi, Lizu,[2] and the local dialect of Tibetan. Among these, Pumi deserves particular attention, because it is also spoken in Yongning.

11.2 Comparison with Pumi

The prosodic system of Na is remarkably close to that of Pumi (also known as Prinmi), a neighbouring Sino-Tibetan language.

11.2.1 The tone group and its role in conveying information structure

In Wadu 瓦都 Pumi as in Yongning Na, there are *tone groups*, similarly defined by a tonal criterion:

---

[1] Muli was a semi-independent kingdom ruled by Pumi hereditary lama kings until the mid-20th century. A caveat about contact phenomena is in order here: the idea is not that Muli county *as a whole* constituted one convergence area, but that convergence took place in some parts of Muli that were multilingual over long stretches of time. The high mountains and deep valleys of Muli create formidable obstacles to communication, and different parts of Muli constitute strikingly different sociolinguistic environments, with different languages in contact and different relationships of prestige between ethnic groups and their languages.

[2] *Lizu* is not to be confused with *Lisu* 傈僳语. The former is an Ersuish language, spoken by approximately 7,000 people who reside along the banks of the Yalong 雅砻 River (Tibetan: Nyag chu) (Chirkova & Chen 2013); the latter is a Yi (Loloish) language spoken by about 900,000 people in a wide area that straddles boundaries between China (Yunnan and Sichuan), Thailand, Burma and India.

> Within a tone group, the underlying tone of one lexical element (usually the left-most element) spreads (usually rightwards) to the adjacent morphemes in the same tone group (…). The remaining elements in a tone group are assigned default low surface tone. Tone does not spread across tone group boundaries. (Daudey 2014: 66)

As in Yongning Na, the tone group plays a key role in conveying information structure.

> [S]ome elements always combine with others into a single tone group, some elements always form a tone group by themselves, and for some elements, speakers can decide to combine or not combine them into tone groups. The latter elements are the most interesting, in that they allow the speaker to express pragmatic differences through the choice of combining them or not. (Daudey 2014: 68)

The parallel with the observations about Na set out in Chapter 7 is striking. Such similarities raise the issue of whether language contact is involved. The variety of Pumi studied by H. Daudey (Wadu Pumi) is spoken in the plain of Yongning, where the Na and the Pumi have lived together on good terms for at least eight centuries, so the similarities could be due to language contact. The two groups "frequently intermarry and so a fair amount of Pumi speak or understand Yongning Na to some degree. The reverse is not necessarily true" (Daudey 2014: 5). But similar characteristics are also observed in another dialect of Pumi, that of Niuwozi 牛窝子, which is not in contact with Yongning Na. This dialect is spoken close to the Ninglang county seat; it is in contact with another variety of the Na language (**lo˧gʌ˩**; in Chinese: Běiqúbà 北渠坝), not mutually intelligible with that of Yongning. (As a piece of anecdotal evidence about the degree of mutual comprehension: one of the daughters of consultant F4 married a Na from that area; the differences in dialect led the couple to adopt Mandarin to communicate with each other.) While the vocabulary adopted in the linguistic description is slightly different, the observations appears to match closely those made about Wadu Pumi and Yongning Na.

> Under the influence of intonation, the underlying H tone of a phonological word is readily removable when it is situated in the final unit of the clause (…). When this happens, the phonological word is merged with the other prosodic domain (removal of the original boundary of phonological word due to a loss of H tone in a following word […]). Sometimes, a series of low

tones may appear in the ending syllables of an utterance after the boundary of phonological word is eliminated (...). (Ding 2014: 69)

Thus, the similarities in prosodic organization between Pumi and Na are not necessarily the outcome of areal convergence. As pointed out in §7.4, the division of an utterance into intonation phrases plays a central role in conveying phrasing and prominence in the most diverse languages, including thoroughly unrelated (and extensively studied) languages such as English.[3]

11.2.2 Other similarities

There are also similarities between Na and Pumi phonological rules, such as that each prosodic domain requires at least one non-L tone, and when none is present, a H tone is added to the final syllable, yielding a rising tone, LH (Ding 2014: 60). Concerning numeral-plus-classifier phrases, Ding (2014: 69) notes that their tone patterns "are not utterly predictable from the tones of the two formatives, as other factors beyond phonology are at work". This is parallel to the situation found in Na (studied in Chapter 4 of the present volume), although judging from Picus Ding's book, the degree of complexity found in that particular variety of Pumi would seem to be smaller than in the variety of Na studied here.

The high number of points of similarity suggests that further comparison of Na and Pumi could be highly revealing. The aim would be to attain the degree of depth and precision reached by Wagner & McCurdy (2010) in their comparison of English and French.

11.3 Comparison with Yi

Naish languages have striking typological similarities with languages of the Yi (Loloish) branch of Burmese-Yi (Burmese-Lolo). From a tonal point of view, there are similarities of the kind that one would expect given the similarities in syntax: tone sandhi occurs in contexts such as compounds and numeral-plus-classifier phrases. In Nosu, for instance, there exists an alternation whereby tone ^{33} changes to the sandhi tone ^{44} (transcribed in the orthography as a final *x*) when followed by another ^{33} tone. This dissimilatory process is morphosyntactically

---

[3] Within the Sino-Tibetan family, a distant echo to the Na facts is found in Zhuokeji Rgyalrong, where "clauses that are juxtaposed without any overt linkage marker that denotes coordination or consecutivization, or any morphosyntactic marking that signals dependency of one clause on the other" can be integrated into one group (called "intonation unit") to highlight "strong rhetorical links" between these clauses (Lin 2009: 208).

conditioned, witness the existence of a tonal distinction between *nga gu* 'I called (someone)' and *ngax gu* '(Someone) called me': in this case, the tonal difference reflects one between agent and patient (Gerner 2013: 28). The morphotonology has limited extent, however: in total, there are eight contexts where tone sandhi occurs. Their description takes up no more than three pages in a grammar of half a thousand pages (Gerner 2013: 28–30).

11.4 A hypothesis about contact between two-level and three-level tone systems

Contact between two-level and three-level tone systems appears as an especially interesting topic for areal studies of tone. Pumi, with which Na has been in at least occasional contact for centuries, has two levels, L and H. Among Na dialects, two-level systems are found in Wuzhiluo 五指落, on the north edge of the swamp area known as the Grass Sea which forms the eastern end of Lake Lugu (Dobbs & La 2016) and in Shuiluo 水落, in the county of Muli 木里 (source: unpublished field notes, 2009). The dialect of Luoshui 落水, geographically close to the Yongning plain, has three levels, but among these, the highest level has a relatively marginal status (Lidz 2010). Alawa (the dialect studied in this volume) has three levels, but with a strongly restricted distribution. By contrast, dialects spoken further to the West and the Northwest, such as Labai 拉柏, clearly have three levels (L, M and H). Past contact between two-level and three-level tone systems could shed light on synchronic phenomena found in Alawa, such as the exceptionless phonological rule prohibiting tone-group-initial H tone, effectively limiting the number of tonal contrasts to two in group-initial position. This synchronic rule has far-reaching consequences: at the surface phonological level, it is impossible to have H tone (as distinct from M) on a monosyllable said in isolation, or tone patterns H.M, H.MH, H.L or H.H on disyllables said in isolation, because an isolated form (often referred to as a *citation form*) constitutes a tone group on its own. As pointed out in §2.3.1.4, correspondences between overt H tones in the Labai dialect and floating H tones in Alawa suggest the possibility that word-initial H tones in Alawa were shifted from their position on the first syllable of the word as a response to the enforcement of the rule prohibiting initial H. In this scenario, the next question is why word-initial H tones ceased to be phonotactically licit. At this point, one can entertain the possibility of contact with a two-level tone system, whose speakers had special difficulty handling a three-term tonal opposition on an initial syllable. Synchronic case studies of contact between two-level and three-level tonal systems would be useful to gain insights into the types of processes to be expected, and the possible consequences for the linguistic systems in contact. The findings of such studies, combined with additional data on present-day dialectal diversity, could shed light on the historical role played by contact in shaping the tonal systems that can be observed today.

12 Conclusion

> When one aims to please others, one may fail, whereas things that we do to please ourselves always have a chance to interest someone or other.
>
> Marcel Proust[1]

The Yongning Na tone system comprises (i) a set of phonological rules governing tone-to-syllables association, set out in §7.1, and (ii) a host of rules that are specific to certain morphosyntactic contexts, set out in Chapters 3-6. Different rules apply in the association of a verb with a subject or an object, the association of two nouns into a compound, that of a numeral and classifier, or that of a word and its affixes, for instance. These tonal paradigms constitute the core of the morphotonology of Yongning Na, and represent the bulk of what language learners must acquire to master this tone system.

As a conclusion, let us return to the initial puzzle: the first example presented in the introduction. It is now possible to set out the mechanisms whereby the surface phonological tone sequences of examples (1a–1b) obtain.

---

[1] This sentence is followed by reflections that are close to linguists' concerns: "No one is unique: our individualities are made out of a universal fabric; this is what allows for sympathy and understanding, which are such great pleasures in life. If we could analyze the soul as we analyze matter, it would become apparent that below the surface diversity of minds, as under that of material objects, there are but a few simple substances and irreducible elements; and that what we think of as our personality is made up from elements which are quite common, and which are met again pretty much everywhere in the universe." *Original text:* Quand on travaille pour plaire aux autres on peut ne pas réussir, mais les choses qu'on a faites pour se contenter soi-même ont toujours chance d'intéresser quelqu'un. Il est impossible qu'il n'existe pas de gens qui prennent quelque plaisir à ce qui m'en a tant donné. Car personne n'est original et fort heureusement pour la sympathie et la compréhension qui sont de si grands plaisirs dans la vie, c'est dans une trame universelle que nos individualités sont taillées. Si l'on savait analyser l'âme comme la matière, on verrait que, sous l'apparente diversité des esprits aussi bien que sous celle des choses, il n'y a que peu de corps simples et d'éléments irréductibles et qu'il entre dans la composition de ce que nous croyons être notre personnalité, des substances fort communes et qui se retrouvent un peu partout dans l'Univers. (*Pastiches et mélanges*, Paris: Gallimard, 1919, pp. 108–109)

(1) a. njɤ˧ ʑi˩ bi˩ -zo˩ -ho˦.
   1SG to_take to_go OBLIGATIVE DESIDERATIVE
   'I have to go and take [my luggage] now.'

b. njɤ˧ bi˧ -zo˧ -ho˩.
   1SG to_go OBLIGATIVE DESIDERATIVE
   'I have to go. / I'm afraid I have to leave.'

With morpheme-level transcriptions indicating lexical tone in terms of the lexical tone categories of Yongning Na, these sentences can be represented as (2a–2b).

(2) a. njɤ˧ | ʑi˩ bi˩-zo˩-ho˦.
   njɤ˩ ʑi˩ₐ bi˧_c -zo˧ₐ -ho˩
   1SG to_take to_go OBLIGATIVE DESIDERATIVE
   'I have to go and take [my luggage] now.'

b. njɤ˧ | bi˧-zo˧-ho˩.
   njɤ˩ bi˧_c -zo˧ₐ -ho˩
   1SG to_go OBLIGATIVE DESIDERATIVE
   'I have to go. / I'm afraid I have to leave.'

A crucial piece of information is the tone-group boundary after the 1SG subject: these utterances contain two tone groups, and tonal processes apply independently for the two groups, as set out in Chapter 7.

The first tone group only contains one syllable. Its lexical tone is L. As reported in Chapter 2, the realization of this tone in isolation is as a level, non-low tone: M, hence the surface phonological form /njɤ˧/ in (2a) and (2b).

In (2a), the second tone group consists of two serialized verbs and two suffixes. Following the morphotonological rules brought out in Chapter 6, //ʑi˩ₐ// in association with //bi˧_c// 'to go' yields //ʑi˩-bi˩//. Addition of the obligative //-zo˧ₐ// yields //ʑi˩-bi˩-zo˩//. The last suffix, desiderative //ho˩//, carries L tone. The tonal behaviour of a L-tone suffix depends on the number of syllables of the expression to which it is attached: if suffixed directly to a L-tone verb, it carries L tone; if suffixed to a L-tone expression of two syllables or more, the suffix carries H tone, hence //ʑi˩-ho˩// 'will take', with a L.L pattern, but //ʑi˩-zo˩-ho˦// 'will need to take', with a L.L.H pattern. Association of this suffix to the three-syllable expression //ʑi˩-bi˩-zo˩// thus yields a final H tone, hence //ʑi˩-bi˩-zo˩-ho˦//.

Both tone groups, //njɤ˧// and //ʑi˩-bi˩-zo˩-ho˦//, contain at least one tone other than L, so that the repair rule for all-L tone groups (referred to as Rule 7 in §7.1.1) does not apply. These tone groups therefore proceed unmodified to the surface phonological level, as /njɤ˧ | ʐi˩-bi˩-zo˩-ho˥/.

In (2b), the second tone group consists of a main verb, 'to go', and the same two suffixes as in (2a). Following the morphotonological rules brought out in Chapter 6, the M tone on the main verb does not modify the tones of the suffixes. The M tone on the obligative suffix //-zo˧ₐ// likewise leaves the following morpheme unaffected, so that all three syllables in the tone group simply surface with their lexical tone.

While it is satisfying to verify that the morphotonological patterns described in the present volume shed light on these and other examples, it must be acknowledged that this book is only one step towards the goal of advanced linguistic modelling of tone in Yongning Na. A mid- to long-term perspective is the computer-aided analysis of individual utterances on the basis of a computer model of the grammar (finite-state modelling), following the methodological suggestion of Karttunen (2006). This will require (i) implementing the entire tonal grammar of Yongning Na by computer scripts, (ii) glossing Yongning Na texts at the morpheme level, providing a unique link to the lexicon, and (iii) encoding the morphosyntactic structure of each utterance. The aim will be to generate surface phonological tone patterns for an utterance, spelling out the full set of possible variants in the division of utterances into tone groups.

The model will make it possible to verify quantitatively, over the full set of available data, the generalizations which were proposed in this volume. More ambitiously, the model will allow the investigator to set the patterns observed in a textual utterance (a real sentence from a text) against the backdrop of a set of alternatives. This opens new perspectives for appraising the speaker's stylistic choices in a narrative, such as the observed division of the sentence into tone groups, and the choice of one variant rather than another in cases where two or more tone patterns are acceptable. This holds promise for uncovering factors at play in so-called nonconditioned variation. Modelling of the various components of the language's prosody and morphosyntax could allow for an exploration of the range of stylistic possibilities allowed by the linguistic system, e.g. through the choice of congruence vs. dissonance between message and form, and between syntax and prosodic phrasing (a source of inspiration here is Delattre's approach to French intonation: 1966; 1970).

A second perspective will consist in examining the phonetic implementation of surface phonological tone sequences. This study has not begun in earnest yet, because the approved order of business consists of first understanding the system (the morphotonology, and the intonation) before launching into experimental investigation into acoustic correlates and fine phonetic details (Rice 2014; Mazaudon 2014). From the beginning of fieldwork on Yongning Na, this objective has always been kept in view, however. It motivates constant efforts to collect data that will be exploitable for this purpose: high-fidelity audio, and, for some recordings, an electroglottographic signal. The first steps will consist of modelling the tonal targets and studying coarticulation patterns. Since tone-group boundaries are systematically indicated in the Yongning Na annotations, it should be possible to obtain quantified evidence on issues such as: To what extent are tone-group boundaries accompanied by pauses? Do fine phonetic details in the realization of segments cue the presence of tone-group boundaries, i.e. to what extent are tone-group boundaries signalled by "segmental intonation" in the sense of Niebuhr (2009b)?

The ultimate aim consists of assessing the contribution of various factors to the final phonetic realization of each syllable, teasing apart and spelling out the various components of the speech signal, and their linguistic interpretation. Computer implementation may be used as a tool to bring out, by contrast, intonational phenomena, as components that are not predictable on the basis of the utterance's contrastive units: the sequence of phonemes, and the tonal string parsed into tone groups.

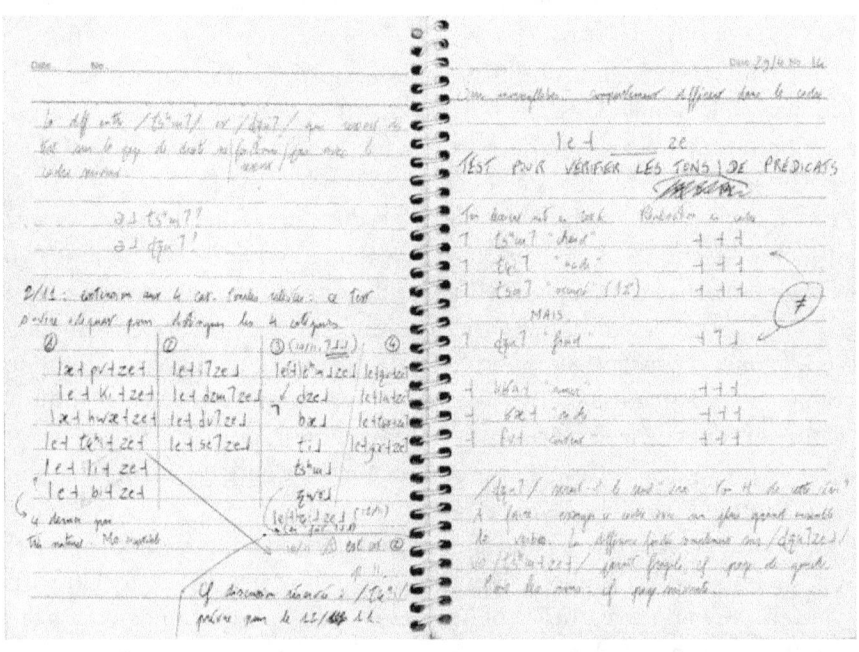

Figure 12.1: Working out tone in Yongning Na: field notes, 2007.

Appendix A: Vowels and consonants

> ... without a good sense of how languages vary, not only in terms of the symbolic units such as phonemes and allophones but also in the details of their phonetic implementation, we have little hope of understanding the possible range of language. Endangered languages in particular represent an important but often-ignored source of information about what is possible in Language.
>
> Richard Wright, University of Washington Phonetics Laboratory website

In Yongning Na, there are no restrictions on co-occurrence of tones and segments, and no special classes of segments triggering synchronic tonal processes (as is the case with depressor consonants in Bantu, e.g. in the Ikalanga language: see Hyman & Mathangwane 1998). So it did not appear appropriate to interpose a presentation of the language's segmental phonetics and phonology between the reader and the book's central topic – tone.

This Appendix offers an opportunity to smuggle into this tonal study a freestanding overview of the vowels and consonants of Yongning Na. Choices made at phonemicization are discussed in some detail, laying emphasis on those areas where phonemic analysis is cracking at the seams. Not a few of these observations could open into experimental phonetic/phonological studies, building on the availability of many hours of transcribed and annotated recordings.

The vowels and consonants of Yongning Na are phonologically inert: they are not involved in synchronic phonological rules and processes. In this respect, Yongning Na is at the opposite end of the typological continuum from a language such as Kifuliiru (Bantu), which has (i) a range of phonological rules, such as the strengthening of /h/, /l/ and /r/ to a plosive when preceded by a nasal, and

(ii) morphological rules, such as the deletion of final consonants in resultative verb forms (Van Otterloo 2011: 37–96).

When examining vowels and consonants in Yongning Na, one's attention is drawn instead to their coarticulation patterns. Due to dramatic phonological erosion since proto-Sino-Tibetan (Jacques & Michaud 2011), syllabic structure in Yongning Na has collapsed down to (C)(G)V+T, where C is a consonant, G a glide – with a severely restricted distribution –, V a syllable nucleus, and T represents tone; the brackets indicate that C and G are optional. Coarticulation constitutes a salient part of a language's sound system (Keating 1990; Kühnert & Nolan 1999). Structural approaches to phonological systems predict cross-linguistic differences in phenomena of coarticulation and articulatory reduction. To take an example, the extent to which the palatalizing influence of high, front vowels makes itself felt depends in part on the number, nature and functional yield of existing phonemic oppositions: in Na, which contrasts /ki/ and /tɕi/, the range of allophonic variation of /ki/ can safely be predicted to be narrower than in Naxi, which does not have this contrast.

Phonetic studies confirm that coarticulation is language-specific: it is sensitive to phonological inventory size and to the phonological distribution of contrasts (DiCanio 2012: 162). In the description that follows, special attention is paid to coarticulation, allophonic variation, and phenomena of articulatory reduction.

A.1 Consonant and vowel charts

Table A.1 presents consonants, and Figure A.1 presents rhymes.[1] The chart of rhymes includes syllabic /ɿ/ and /ʮ/, discussed in the following section (§A.2.1). They are respectively placed in the lower right-hand and upper right-hand areas of the chart as a rough approximation of their articulatory characteristics. The following rhymes are not shown on the chart in order to avoid overcrowding:

- rhymes that contain a glide (discussed in §A.3.1): /wæ/, /wɑ/, /wɤ/, /jæ/, /jɤ/ and /jo/
- the nasal vowels /ĩ/, /ʮ̃/, /w̃ɤ/,[2] /æ̃/ and /ɑ̃/, all appearing only after /h/

---

[1] This Appendix focuses on the Alawa dialect. Systematic comparison across dialects is not attempted here.

[2] In the rhymes /w̃ɤ/ and /w̃æ/, the diacritic for nasality is placed on the glide rather than on the final vowel because the degree of phonetic nasalization decreases throughout the course of the rhyme. About nasal rhymes in Yongning Na, see §A.2.4.

- the rhymes /ĩ/ and /w̃æ/, which always constitute syllables on their own (i.e. do not combine with any initial)
- the nasal vowel /õ/ appearing after /h/ or on its own, i.e. in the syllables /hõ/ and /õ/

Table A.1: The initials of Yongning Na.

	bilabial / labio-dental	dental	alveolo-palatal	retroflex	velar	uvular	glottal
plosive	pʰ p b	tʰ t d		tʰ ʈ ɖ	kʰ k g	qʰ q	ʔ
affricate		tsʰ ts dz	tɕʰ tɕ dʑ	tʂʰ tʂ dʐ			
nasal	m	n	ɲ	ɳ	ŋ		
fricative	f	s z	ɕ ʑ	ʂ ʐ		ʁ	h
lateral		ɬ l					
approximant				ɻ			

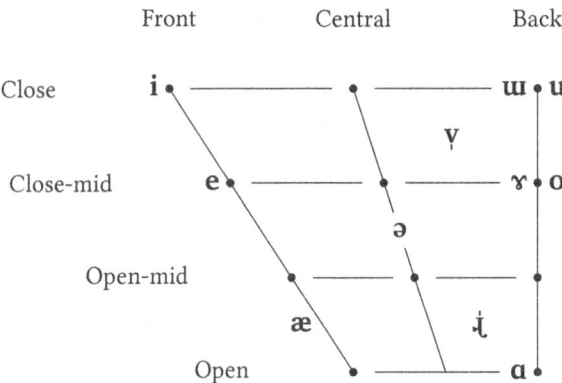

Figure A.1: The rhymes of Yongning Na.

The notation used throughout this book, and in the transcription of texts, is phonemic in orientation. However, a concern for phonetic transparency led to indicate the empty-onset fillers [ʝ], [ɣ] and [w] in transcriptions, even though they are not phonemically contrastive (as explained in §A.3.1) and hence not included in Table A.1.

All the possible vowel nuclei following each initial are listed in Tables A.2 and A.3. In the interest of space, syllables with nasal rhymes are not shown. These tables only provide a first-pass view of Na phonotactics: no indication about lexical frequency is provided, only a binary indication of presence or absence of the combination at issue. A syllable is considered as present if it is firmly attested in Na vocabulary, i.e. excluding combinations that have been introduced through lexical borrowings, vowel harmony and expressive processes, no matter how widely attested these are in the present-day state of the language. Thus, combinations of dental stops with the vowel /æ/ are indicated as nonexistent, because the only attestations are in examples such as /tʰæ˩tsɯ˧/ 'jar', borrowed from Mandarin *tánzi* 坛子, as well as /tæ˩ɻæ˩/ 'Adam's apple' and /læ˩dæ˩qæ˥/ 'armpit', where it may result from vowel harmony with the second syllable. Likewise, combinations of retroflex stops with the vowel /ɑ/ are indicated as nonexistent, because the only attestations are in the examples /tʂʰɑ˩lɑ˧/ 'to chat', /qv̩˧ɻ̍˧-tʂʰɑ˧nɑ˥#/ (the name of a mountain) and /tʂɑ˧tɑ˥/ 'written sign, tracing', three words in which the first syllable's /ɑ/ vowel may result from vowel harmony with the second syllable. Abstracting away from phenomena that can be identified as structural gap-filling highlights empty slots in the table, and cases of complementary distribution. Comments about the inventory of syllables are set out in §A.4.

Table A.2: Inventory of attested combinations of initials and rhymes, leaving aside marginal words (loanwords, expressive words…). First part.

	i	ɯ	u	v	e	ɤ	o	æ	ɑ	wæ	wɑ	wɤ	jæ	jɤ	jo
∅	✓	✓	✓	✓	✗	✗	✓	✓	✓	✗	✗	✓	✗	✓	✓
pʰ	✓	✗	✗	✓	✓	✓	✓	✓	✗	✗	✗	✗	✗	✗	✗
p	✓	✗	✗	✓	✗	✓	✓	✓	✗	✗	✗	✗	✗	✗	✗
b	✓	✗	✗	✓	✗	✓	✓	✓	✗	✗	✗	✗	✗	✗	✗
m	✓	✗	✗	✓	✗	✓	✓	✓	✗	✗	✗	✗	✗	✗	✗
tʰ	✓	✗	✗	✓	✗	✗	✓	✗	✓	✗	✗	✗	✗	✗	✗
t	✓	✗	✗	✓	✗	✓	✓	✗	✓	✗	✗	✗	✗	✗	✗
d	✓	✗	✗	✓	✗	✓	✓	✗	✓	✗	✗	✗	✗	✗	✗

Table A.3: Inventory of attested combinations of initials and rhymes, leaving aside marginal words (loanwords, expressive words...). Second part.

	i	ɯ	u	y	e	ɤ	o	æ	ɑ	wæ	wɑ	wɤ	jæ	jɤ	jo
tsʰ	✓	✓	✗	✗	✓	✓	✓	✗	✓	✗	✗	✗	✗	✗	✗
ts	✓	✓	✗	✗	✓	✓	✓	✗	✓	✗	✗	✗	✗	✗	✗
dz	✓	✓	✗	✗	✓	✓	✓	✗	✓	✗	✗	✗	✗	✗	✗
n	✓	✗	✗	✓	✓	✗	✓	✗	✓	✗	✗	✗	✗	✗	✗
s	✓	✓	✗	✗	✓	✓	✓	✗	✓	✗	✗	✗	✗	✗	✗
z	✓	✓	✗	✗	✓	✗	✓	✗	✓	✗	✗	✗	✗	✗	✗
ɬ	✓	✗	✗	✓	✗	✗	✓	✗	✓	✗	✗	✗	✗	✗	✗
l	✓	✗	✗	✓	✓	✗	✓	✗	✓	✗	✗	✗	✗	✗	✗
tɕʰ	✓	✓	✗	✗	✗	✓	✓	✗	✗	✗	✗	✗	✗	✗	✗
tɕ	✓	✓	✗	✗	✗	✓	✓	✗	✗	✗	✗	✗	✗	✗	✗
dʑ	✓	✓	✗	✗	✗	✓	✓	✗	✗	✗	✗	✗	✗	✗	✗
ɲ	✓	✗	✗	✗	✗	✗	✗	✗	✗	✗	✗	✗	✗	✗	✗
ɕ	✓	✓	✗	✗	✗	✗	✗	✗	✗	✗	✗	✗	✗	✓	✓
ʑ	✓	✗	✗	✗	✗	✗	✗	✗	✗	✗	✗	✗	✗	✗	✗
tʰ	✓	✓	✗	✗	✗	✓	✗	✓	✗	✗	✗	✗	✗	✗	✗
t	✓	✓	✗	✓	✗	✓	✗	✓	✗	✗	✗	✗	✗	✗	✗
d	✓	✓	✗	✓	✗	✓	✓	✓	✗	✗	✗	✗	✗	✗	✗
tʂʰ	✓	✓	✗	✓	✓	✓	✓	✓	✗	✗	✗	✗	✗	✗	✗
tʂ	✓	✓	✗	✓	✓	✓	✓	✓	✗	✗	✗	✗	✗	✗	✗
dʐ	✓	✓	✗	✓	✓	✓	✓	✓	✗	✗	✗	✗	✗	✗	✗
ɳ	✗	✓	✗	✓	✗	✗	✗	✓	✗	✗	✗	✗	✗	✗	✗
ʂ	✓	✓	✗	✓	✓	✓	✓	✓	✗	✓	✗	✓	✗	✗	✗
ʐ	✓	✓	✗	✓	✓	✓	✓	✓	✗	✓	✗	✓	✗	✗	✗
ɭ	✓	✗	✗	✗	✗	✗	✗	✓	✗	✓	✗	✗	✗	✗	✗
kʰ	✓	✓	✗	✓	✗	✓	✓	✗	✗	✗	✗	✓	✗	✗	✗
k	✓	✓	✗	✓	✗	✓	✓	✗	✗	✗	✗	✓	✗	✗	✗
g	✓	✓	✗	✓	✗	✓	✓	✗	✗	✗	✗	✓	✗	✗	✗
ŋ	✓	✗	✗	✓	✗	✓	✗	✗	✗	✗	✗	✓	✗	✗	✗
qʰ	✓	✗	✗	✓	✗	✗	✓	✓	✓	✓	✗	✓	✗	✗	✗
q	✓	✗	✗	✓	✗	✗	✓	✓	✓	✓	✗	✓	✗	✗	✗
ʁ	✓	✗	✗	✓	✗	✗	✓	✓	✓	✓	✗	✓	✗	✗	✗
h	✓	✓	✓	✗	✗	✓	✓	✓	✓	✓	✗	✓	✗	✗	✗
f	✗	✗	✗	✓	✗	✗	✗	✗	✗	✗	✗	✗	✗	✗	✗

A.2 Syllable nuclei: Vowels and syllabic consonants

A.2.1 Consonantal nuclei

In Na, some consonantal sounds function as syllable nuclei. In the International Phonetic Alphabet such sounds are called 'syllabic'. Fricative sounds with syllabic value are an areal characteristic. They are common in neighbouring Yi languages, which belong to the Nasoid subgroup of Loloish (also known as Ngwi; see Bradley 1979: 70), as well as in Lizu (Chirkova & Chen 2013), Ersu (Chirkova et al. 2015) and Pumi (Daudey 2014: 52). Local dialects of Mandarin also have a fricative syllable nucleus, /fɣ/: for instance 'lake', Standard Mandarin *hú* 湖, is pronounced [fɣ] (on Southwestern Mandarin: see Gui 2001; Pinson & Pinson 2008). In the absence of coda consonants in Na, 'consonantal nuclei' are also referred to in this volume as 'consonantal rhymes'. Yongning Na has the following consonantal rhymes: [ɣ], [z̩], [ʐ̩], [ɿ] and [ʅ].

A.2.1.1 The voiced fricative /ɣ/

The voiced fricative /ɣ/ can only appear as a rhyme, not as an initial. The friction for /ɣ/ is weaker than in Naxi. There is some amount of formant movement towards a central articulation: [və]. Since friction noise is slight, even at the beginning of the rhyme, this /ɣ/ could be described as close to an approximant, [ʋ]. Martinet makes a distinction between fricatives proper, which have a firm articulation and are characterized by fricative noise, and spirants, which have a relaxed articulation, tending towards a vowel-like aperture (Martinet 1956: 24; 1981). In terms of this distinction, the articulation of /ɣ/ in Yongning Na is spirant rather than fricative. After bilabial initials, /ɣ/ has a tendency towards trilling (though, again, less markedly so than in Naxi): /bɣ/ is realized close to [ʙ], /pɣ/ close to [pʙ], and /pʰɣ/ close to [pʰʙ].

In the absence of strong friction, the rhyme /ɣ/ can be difficult to distinguish from the high back vowel /o/, especially after consonants that exert similar coarticulatory effects on the rhyme. Uvular stops result in a retracted (backed) articulation of both /ɣ/ and /o/, making the opposition between syllables such as /qɣ/ and /qo/ difficult to hear at first. Minimal pairs such as /mæ˧qɣ˩/ 'tail' vs. /mæ˧qo˩/ 'end; back' constitute handy materials for learners to practise this opposition.

From a diachronic point of view, the rhyme /ɣ/ in Yongning Na (as also in Naxi) is hypothesized to originate in *u (Jacques & Michaud 2011). Seen in this light, the process of fricativization is less advanced in Yongning Na than in Lijiang Naxi.

One could find among Naish languages a continuum between [u]-like and [ɣ]-like realizations, through approximant [ʋ]. Such cases serve as reminders that the choice of symbols from the International Phonetic Alphabet does not tell the full story about phonological systems, as Martinet reminds us.

> One wonders whether the habit of constantly operating with graphic notations does not make some linguist[s] deaf to the gradual shifts which any painstaking observation can reveal. If one has been taught, not only that phonological systems are made up of discrete units, but also that these units are basically the same in all languages, (…) one can hardly avoid concluding that no change can take place except by means of jumps from one unit or allophone to another. Only those who know that linguistic identity does not imply physical sameness, can accept the notion that discreteness does not rule out infinite variety and be thus prepared to perceive the gradualness of phonological shifts. (Martinet 1988: 25)

A.2.1.2 Apicalized vowels

Apicalized vowels are found "on the tip of many tongues" across Sino-Tibetan (Baron 1974), and Na is no exception. The vowel /ɯ/ has fricative allophones after dental and retroflex fricatives and affricates; this situation is identical to that found in Naxi. For instance, /tsʰɯ˦/ 'goat' is realized [tsʰz̩˦], and /dʐɯ˩/ 'market, city' is realized [dʐʐ̩˩]. In phonetic transcription, it is customary in Asian studies to use the symbols coined by Chao Yuen-ren: [ɿ] and [ʅ], respectively. The whole set proposed by Chao Yuen-ren is shown in Table A.4; symbol descriptions are from Pullum & Ladusaw (1986: 80, 89-90).

Table A.4: Chao Yuen-ren's symbols for apicalized vowels, and closest equivalents in the International Phonetic Alphabet (IPA).

sound	symbol	symbol description	IPA
plain apical vowel	[ɿ]	long-leg turned iota	z̩
retroflex apical vowel	[ʅ]	right-tail turned iota	ʐ̩
rounded plain apical vowel	[ʮ]	curvy turned h	z̞̩
rounded retroflex apical vowel	[ʯ]	right-tail curvy turned h	ʐ̞̩

The reason that rounded apical vowels are not found in Na is that (i) there is no rounding opposition among front vowels, and hence no source for a process of apicalization such as *y > [ʮ], and (ii) among back vowels, the close vowel *u fricativized to /ɣ/, as described above (§A.2.1.1).

In addition to an opposition between plain and retroflex apical vowels, there is in Yongning Na an opposition between /i/ and another high front vowel after the alveolopalatal initials /dʑ/, /tɕ/ and /tɕʰ/. The first set – syllables /dʑi/, /tɕi/ and /tɕʰi/ – has moderate friction during the initial, and the rhyme is not strongly apicalized.

The second set consists of syllables that have an apicalized rhyme and a slightly more central vowel; these syllables can be approximated as [dʑ̩], [tɕʑ̩] and [tɕʰʑ̩], respectively. If one were to abstract from the phonetic friction found on the rhymes of these syllables, a possible phonetic notation would be as [dʑɪ], [tɕɪ] and [tɕʰɪ]. The phonemic analysis adopted here is as allophones of /ɯ/, hence /dʑɯ/, /tɕɯ/ and /tɕʰɯ/. This choice is based on structural considerations (complementary distribution), not on phonetics, and the degree of validity of this choice remains to be tested experimentally, e.g. by investigating to what extent priming[3] by canonical realizations of the vowel /ɯ/ (as in /tʰɯɹ/ 'to drink') affects reaction times in perceptual tests. Phonetically, the syllables /dʑɯ/, /tɕɯ/ and /tɕʰɯ/ are not easy to distinguish from /dzɯ/, /tsɯ/ and /tsʰɯ/, which are shown in Table A.5 with their realizations in Chao notation and in International Phonetic Alphabet.

Table A.5: Syllables with initial dental affricate and high, unrounded vowel /ɯ/, and their phonetic realizations.

phonemic analysis	Chao notation	International Phonetic Alphabet
dzɯ	[dzɿ]	[dz̩]
tsɯ	[tsɿ]	[tsz̩]
tsʰɯ	[tsʰɿ]	[tsʰz̩]

An added complexity is related to Voice Onset Time oppositions among alveolopalatal initials. Syllables with an unvoiced or aspirated initial, /tɕ/ or /tɕʰ/, have stronger affrication than those with initial /dʑ/. This has coarticulatory consequences on the following vowel, so that both /i/ and /ɯ/ are somewhat less open after /tɕ/ and /tɕʰ/ than after /dʑ/.[4]

---

[3] Priming is a memory effect in which exposure to one stimulus (the *prime*) influences the response to another stimulus.

[4] A recording (PalatalizedApicalized) was specifically conducted for words containing one of the following syllables: /dʑi/, /dʑɯ/, /tɕi/, /tɕɯ/, /tɕʰi/ and /tɕʰɯ/.

A.2.1.3 Rhotic rhymes

Further consonantal rhymes are /ɨ̣/ and its nasalized counterpart /ɨ̣̃/. From a phonetic point of view, the rhyme /ɨ̣/ does not display the considerable lowering of the third formant which is the tell-tale characteristic of rhotic vowels (Ladefoged & Maddieson 1996: 313), such as Naxi /ɚ/. The diacritic indicating syllabic status distinguishes this rhyme from the consonant phoneme /ɻ/ described in §A.3.6. As a rhyme, /ɨ̣/ can appear on its own or preceded by a retroflex fricative or affricate. Examples of syllables containing a /ɨ̣/ rhyme preceded by a retroflex affricate are presented in Table A.6, together with syllables made up of the same consonant followed by the rhyme /v/.

Table A.6: Some examples illustrating the phonemic contrast between /ɨ̣/ and /v/ after retroflex fricatives and affricates.

	v	ɨ̣
tʂʰ	/tʂʰv˧/ 'breakfast', /tʂʰv˧ɨ̣˧$/ 'ant', /bv˧tʂʰv˧/ 'cymbals'	/tʂʰɨ̣˧/ 'lungs'
tʂ	/mv˧tʂv˧/ 'wrinkles'	/tʂɨ̣˧/ 'to cough'
dʐ		no contrasts observed[a]
tʰ t ɖ tʰ t d		no contrasts observed
ʂ	/ʂv˧dv˧/ 'to think'	/ʂɨ̣˧/ 'full'
ʐ		no contrasts observed

[a] Roselle Dobbs (p.c. 2016) reports that this contrast does exist in the Lataddi dialect. Using her notations, in which /u/ corresponds to Alawa /v/, and /v/ to Alawa /ɨ̣/, the contrast is exemplified by /ʐu˥/ 'four' (homophone: 'delicious') vs. /ʐv˥/ 'horse'.

Under the present analysis, the rhyme /ɨ̣/ has a nasal counterpart, /ɨ̣̃/. Only two items have been found so far: 'bone', /ɨ̣̃˥/, which also has the meaning of 'stem'; and 'helpless, impoverished, troubled', /ɨ̣̃˥/. Notation as a nasal rhotic vowel, /ɚ̃/ or /œ̃˞/, could also be acceptable; the symbol /ɨ̣̃/ was chosen because the rhymes transcribed as /ɨ̣/ and /ɨ̣̃/ have phonetic similarities and plausibly stand in a relation of structural opposition, the one oral, the other nasal.

The word for 'bone', here transcribed as /ɨ̣̃˥/, already puzzled earlier investigators. It is transcribed phonetically as [ʔɲɹ] and analyzed phonemically as

/ŋvɹ/ by Fù Màojì (1983: 25). In this phonetic transcription, the sequence of two symbols is not to be understood as a succession of two sounds. Here, as in his other publications, Fu Maoji uses the symbol /ɹ/ to indicate a rhotic quality of the vowel. Phonemic analysis as /ŋvɹ/ does appear to be an attractive solution: nasality would be due to a nasal onset, and rhoticity to a rhotic, fricative rhyme, /vɹ/. However, in the attested syllable /ŋv/, coarticulation between the initial and rhyme does not go so far as to result in complete coalescence: the syllable retains two parts, a nasal onset [ŋ], with complete oral closure, and a rhyme [ṽ], which is partly nasalized phonetically but without oral closure. A syllable that is identical with /ŋv/ except for a feature of rhoticity would be expected to begin similarly by a nasal consonant (with complete oral closure). For this reason, this syllable is not analyzed here as a rhotic counterpart to /ŋv/ (with nasal onset and oral rhyme), but as a monophonemic syllable consisting simply of a nasal rhyme. As for its analysis as /ɨ̃/ or /ṽ/, both options are open, since there is no opposition between these on onsetless syllables. On the basis of phonetic considerations, I believe that notation as /ɨ̃/ is more adequate synchronically.

A.2.1.4 Potential for the creation of new syllabic consonants and monophonemic syllables

In syllables of simple CV (consonant+vowel) segmental structure, the consonant and vowel paired together become strongly coarticulated; their features tend to be realized over the syllable as a whole. In Naish languages, coarticulation in CV monosyllables tends to create compact units that become less and less tractable to a straightforward analysis into two distinct phonemes, until the syllable becomes monophonemic.

In addition to apicalized vowels (§A.2.1.2), syllabic nasals can also be interpreted in this light. "In various Loloish languages some or all of the nasals occur as syllabics. In most such cases the diachronic source is syllables with a nasal initial and a high vowel; sometimes one dialect has nasal syllabics where others have nasals plus a high vowel. This could be called rhyme-gobbling" (Bradley 1989: 150; see also Björverud 1998: 8). Yongning Na reveals an intermediate stage: the syllable /mv/ is phonetically realized as [m̩] except in careful (hyperarticulated) speech, but /nv/ and /ŋv/ are pronounced as [nv̩] and [ŋv̩] respectively, retaining an oral portion after the initial nasal. In the present state of the language, these are simply phonetic variants; they are mentioned to illustrate the potential for the further evolution of highly eroded syllables in Yongning Na.

A.2.2 Close vowels

Table A.7 shows that the close vowels /i/ and /e/ contrast after dental fricatives and affricates, e.g. /dzi˩/ 'to sit' vs. /dze˧˩/ 'to fly', /tsi˧˩/ 'to boil' vs. /tse˧˩/ 'to lock', /tsʰi˥/ 'classifier for animal skins' vs. /tsʰe˥/ 'salt', and /si˥/ 'wood' vs. /se˥/ 'to walk'. The syllable /zi/ has only been found in /tsʰi˧zi#˥/ 'highland barley' and /lɑ˧zi˥/ 'painter'; instances of /ze/ are more numerous.

Table A.7: Distribution of the close vowels /i/ and /e/.

initial	i	e
∅	ji˥ 'ox'	–
b p pʰ	bi˥ 'snow'	–
m	mi˧ 'wound'	–
d t tʰ	di˧˥ 'to hunt'	–
dz	dzi˧˩ 'to sit'	dze˧˩ 'to fly'
ts	tsi˧˩ 'to boil'	tse˧˩ 'to lock'
tsʰ	tsʰi˥ CLF.animal skins	tsʰe˥ 'salt'
s	si˥ 'wood'	se˥ 'to walk'
z	tsʰi˧zi#˥ 'highland barley'	ze˧˩mi˧˩ 'niece'
n	ni˥ 'amaranth'	-ne 'as, like'
l	li˧ₐ 'to look'	le˧- ACCOMPLISHED
ɬ	ɬi˥ 'to rest'	–
dʑ tɕ tɕʰ	tɕi˥ 'to shake'	–
ɕ ʑ	ɕi˧ 'rice'	–
ɲ	ɲi˥ 'to listen'	–
ɖ ʈ ʈʰ	ʈi˧˩ₐ 'to get up'	–
ɖʐ tʂ tʂʰ	–	tʂe˥ 'earth'
ʐ ʂ	–	ʐe˥ 'arrow'
ʁ ɻ	–	–
g k kʰ	gi˥ 'to owe'	–
h	hi˧˩ 'rain'	–

After the dental nasal /n/ and the dental lateral /l/, the close vowels /i/ and /e/ are marginally contrastive. The syllable /ne/ is only found in a grammatical morpheme, /-ne/ 'as, like', which appears in the interrogative /qʰɑ˧ne˧˩/ 'how', the manner demonstratives /tʂʰɯ˧ne˧-ji˥/ (proximal) and /tʰɣ˧ne˧-ji˥/ (distal), and constructions such as /tɕʰɤ˧ɲi˧-ne˧-ji˥/ 'every day; repeatedly, all the time'. The recognition of the morpheme /ne/ was delayed by the fact that the highly frequent expression /tsʰɯ˧ne˧-ji˩/ 'thus, in this way' (occurring over 500 times in 25 texts) is pronounced very close to [tsʰɯ˧ni˩], and hence was initially transcribed as ‡ tsʰɯ˧ni˩. (This adverb is analyzed further in the section devoted to on-glides, §A.3.1.) Another marginal case where it appears reasonable to posit a /e/ vowel distinct from /i/ is in combination with initial /l/. The syllable /li/ is common, appearing in about thirty words. A [le] syllable appears in the accomplished prefix /le˧-/, and in derived items, such as [njɤ˧le˧gv̩#˩] 'daytime', which is perceived by consultant F4 as meaning literally 'the day is flowing/going by', as shown in (1).[5]

(1) njɤ˧le˧gv̩#˩
    ɲi˩   le˧-   gv̩˧ᶜ
    day ACCOMP to_flow/to_go_by

'daytime', interpreted by consultant F4 as having the literal meaning 'the day is flowing/going by'

In F4's idiolect, the second syllable of 'daytime' is perceived as the accomplished prefix, and therefore does not constitute evidence for /le/ as an attested syllable in nouns. Moreover, the form /njɤ˧le˧gv̩#˩/ is only one of many avatars of the word for 'daytime' among Na dialects, some of which have /ɬi/ and not /le/ as a middle syllable (/ɲi33-ɬi31 ku33/ in Lidz 2010: 297). It appeared interesting to dwell on this example nonetheless, as it provides an insight into processes whereby marginal combinations of initials and rhymes can enter the lexicon.

To sum up, the opposition of /e/ and /i/ is restricted to syllables that have a dental initial (most examples have a fricative or affricate). This is one of the many cases where a phonemic opposition is found in highly restricted contexts; in Praguian terms, these constitute extreme cases of neutralization. This issue is taken up in the discussion of the inventory of syllables, in §A.4.

Recognition of the opposition between /i/ and /e/ after dental fricatives and affricates was delayed by the fact that, in this context, both /i/ and /e/ are apicalized, which makes their phonetic difference a very fine one. Apicalization is stronger for /ɯ/ than for /i/. Another difference is that the lips are stretched for /si/, /dzi/, /tsi/ and /tsʰi/. In the first transcriptions, the contrast between the two apicalized vowels /i/ and /ɯ/ was overlooked, and the syllables above were mistakenly transcribed as ‡ **sɯ** (for 'wood'), ‡ **zɯ** (for 'barley'), ‡ **dzɯ** (for 'to sit'), ‡ **tsɯ** (for 'to boil') and ‡ **tsʰɯ** (for the classifier for animal skins).

---

[5] Assuming that the etymological glossing in (1) is correct, the change of the first syllable from /ɲi/ to /njɤ/ remains to be accounted for.

In the many contexts where the opposition between /i/ and /e/ is neutralized, the transcription follows their phonetic realization, which is closer to [e] after retroflex fricatives and affricates, and to [i] in all other contexts (after bilabials, velars, uvulars, retroflex stops and fricatives, laterals, nasals, alveolopalatals, and glottals).

As for close back vowels, [o] and [u] are only contrastive after initial /h/. Examples of /ho/ include /tɑ˧ho˧/ 'together', /ho#˩/ 'porridge, gruel', /ho#˩/ 'partridge', /qo˩ho˩/ 'wicker box', /ho˩/ 'to sip', /ho˩ₐ/ 'correct', and /-ho˩/ DESIDERATIVE. Examples of /hu/ are fewer; they include /hu˧mi˩$/ 'stomach', /hu˩/ 'to wait', and /hu˩/ 'to miss, to long for'. Phonetically, there is stronger friction in the initial for /ho/ than for /hu/, which could be approximated phonetically as [hu] vs. [χo]. This suggests an alternative phonemic analysis, dispensing with the opposition between /u/ and /o/, positing instead an opposition between /h/ and /χ/, and rewriting /hu/ and /ho/ as /ho/ and /χo/. The phonetic difference in vowel quality appears more salient than the difference in the initial, however, hence the choice to interpret the vowel difference as phonemic.

Another way to reinterpret the syllable [hu] and eliminate the /u/ phoneme altogether would be to grant phonemic status to initial [f], analyzing the syllables [fv], [hu] and [ho] as /fv/, /hv/ and /ho/, respectively (Roselle Dobbs, p.c. 2016): see §A.3.7.

After all initials other than /h/, there is no opposition between close and close-mid rounded back vowels, [o] and [u]. Phonetic realizations are close to [o] after dentals, velars and uvulars, and more often close to [u] after the other consonants. In all the contexts where the opposition is neutralized, the notation chosen is /o/: this appeared less cumbersome than notation as an archiphoneme /O/ (or /U/).

The two sounds [o] and [u] may have stronger phonemic status in the speech of younger speakers, whose increasing proficiency in Standard Mandarin makes them familiar with a phonemic /u/ (contrasting with /oʷ/ and /ʷo/; the *Pinyin* transcription of these three vowels is: *u, ou, uo*). Southwestern Mandarin does not exert direct pressure in this direction, however, since /u/ is fricativized in this dialect of Mandarin. For instance, the word /tsʰu/ 'vinegar' is pronounced [tsʰv]. This word, which is in common use in Yongning, is accordingly pronounced as [tsʰv˩] in the speech of the older speaker F4.

A.2.3 A neutral vowel: /ə/

A clarification is necessary concerning the use of the phonetic symbol /ə/. In their 1985 book about Naxi, which includes a word list for Yongning Na, He Jiren & Jiang Zhuyi use the symbol /ə/ for two different vowels: a back unrounded vowel,

/ɤ/, realized as [ɣɤ] in an onsetless syllable; and a neutral vowel, /ə/, which always constitutes a syllable on its own, harmonizes with the following syllable's vowel, and is realized with an initial glottal stop (Michaud 2013a: 130).[6] This confusing usage was adopted for the official phonetic transcription for Naxi, which remains influential.[7]

In the present system, the symbol /ə/ is only used to transcribe the interrogative particle, and the first syllable of some lexical words, where it can plausibly be analyzed as a prefix. In particular, it is present in kinship terms referring to one's elders, such as /ə˧mi˧/ 'mother', realized as [e˧mi˧]; /ə˧mɑ˧/ 'mother (VOCATIVE)', [ɑ˧mɑ˧]; and /ə˧v˧/ 'uncle', [ɤ˧v˧]. Realizations are close to [æ] before /æ/ and apicalized allophones of /ɯ/; to [ɛ] before /i/, /ĩ/ and /e/; to [ɑ] before /ɑ/ and /wɤ/; and to [ɤ] before /ɤ/, /o/, /ɯ/, /jɤ/, /jo/ and /i̩/. Before /v/, the neutral vowel /ə/ harmonizes differently depending on whether there is an intervening consonant or not: it is realized close to [ɤ] when immediately followed by /v/, as in /ə˧v˧/ 'uncle' (phonetic approximation: [ɤ˧v˧]), and it is close to [æ] when the /v/ is preceded by a consonant, as in /ə˧pʰv˧/ 'mother's uncle; male ancestor of the second generation' and /ə˧mv˩/ 'elder sibling' (phonetic approximation: [æ˧pʰv˧] and [æ˧mv˩]).[8]

Note, however, that phonetic (incomplete) vowel harmony is not restricted to the vowel transcribed as /ə/. This topic is taken up in §A.2.7.

No phonetic difference could be found between the [ɑ] realization of /ə/ before /ɑ/, on the one hand, and the realization of the /ɑ/ vowel phoneme. For instance, the clan name [ɑ˧lɑ˧] is phonemicized as /ə˧lɑ˧/, but an interpretation as /ɑ˧lɑ˧/ cannot be ruled out.

---

[6] A likely origin for this confusion is the use of /ə/ as the official phonetic equivalent of the letter e of the *Pinyin* romanization of Standard Mandarin: /ə/ was used for a back unrounded vowel. The 'ram's horn' vowel symbol, /ɤ/, or the turned v, /ʌ/, constitute more felicitous choices than the neutral vowel /ə/, in view of phonetic realizations, which are "ɤ-like or ʌ-like" (International Phonetic Association 1949: 42). Linguists trained in mainland China in the first decades of the People's Republic of China tended to base their transcriptions on this system, reproduced in dictionaries and textbooks until the turn of the twenty-first century. Things have now changed, thanks to more accurate descriptions distinguishing a vowel /ɤ/ from a vowel /ə/, such as Lee & Zee (2003: 110).

[7] In his manuscript lexicographic notes, He Jiren used the turned v, /ʌ/, and not the neutral vowel, /ə/, but the symbol /ə/ was reintroduced when the data was edited for publication as a dictionary (Hé Jírén, Zhāo Qìnglián & Hé Jiézhēn 2011).

[8] This phonemic analysis of the kinship prefix was suggested by Roselle Dobbs.

A.2.4 Nasal rhymes

A.2.4.1 Nasal rhymes after the glottal /h/

Yongning Na has a relatively large inventory of nasal rhymes: it comprises /ĩ/, /ỹ/, /õ/, /w̃ɤ/, /æ̃/ and /ã/, and the syllables /ɨ̃/ and /w̃æ/. The first six are found after /h/, where they contrast neatly with their non-nasal counterparts: /hi/–/hĩ/, /hɣ/–/hỹ/, /ho/–/hõ/, /hwɤ/–/hw̃ɤ/, /hæ/–/hæ̃/, and /hɑ/–/hã/. Examples are provided in Table A.8.

Table A.8: Examples of /h/-initial syllables that are part of a correlation of nasality.

oral rhyme	nasal rhyme
/hi˧/ 'tooth'	/hĩ˧/ 'man'; /hĩ˧˥/ 'to stand'
/hɣ˧/ ([fɣ˧]) 'to like'	/hỹ˩/ 'red'; /hỹ˧/ 'hair'; /nv̩˧hỹ˩/ 'kidney bean'; /dʑi˧hỹ˧$/ 'clothes'; /hỹ˧~hỹ˧/ 'to stir-fry'
/ho˧˥/ 'to sip'; /ho˧/ 'to wait'	/hõ˧˥/ 'eight'; /hõ˧/ 'to go (IMPERATIVE)'
/hwɤ˩/ 'to pass over, to hand over'	/hw̃ɤ˩/ 'late'
/hæ˧/ 'Chinese'; /hæ˧˥/ 'lime'; /hæ˧pɤ˧/ 'plait'	/hæ̃˧/ 'wind'; /hæ̃˩/ 'gold'
/hɑ˧/ 'food'	/hã˧˥/ 'night'

Diachronically, these syllables illustrate a process of transfer of nasality from a syllable-initial consonant cluster to a following vowel. This process is attested in several languages of Asia. In Kam-Sui (Tai-Kadai family), Sandong Sui lost the stop part of the original cluster: the stop+nasal clusters *km-, *kn-, *tn- and *kɲ- merged with the preglottalized *ʔm-, *ʔn- and *ʔɲ- initials. The latter are preserved in Sui, e.g. /ʔma¹/ 'vegetables' and /ʔma³/ 'flexible', both corresponding to a proto-Kam-Sui *ʔm initial (Ferlus 1996: 251–252). Lakkia preserved the initial stop, while the nasal underwent lenition, nasalizing the following vowel in the process, e.g. /kũːi/ 'bear', from a stop+nasal cluster *km-. Northern Sui dialects (Pandong 潘洞 and Yang'an 阳安) illustrate a possibility for the later evolution of glottal+nasal onsets. Distinctive nasality is transferred onto the following vowel, and only the glottal remains, yielding [ʔṼ] or [ḥṼ]; the entire syllable is nasal, including the initial glottal sound (Haudricourt 1967: 176). This is exactly parallel to the facts of Yongning Na and other Naish languages, as brought out in Table A.9. (This table is taken up from a cross-linguistic (panchronic) analysis of historical transfers of nasality between consonantal onset and vowel: Michaud, Jacques & Rankin (2012).) Japhug is a conservative Sino-Tibetan language that preserves a broad range of initial clusters; after correspondences among Naish languages have been established, comparison with such conservative languages suggests hypotheses for fleshing out reconstructions (Jacques & Michaud 2011: 470-471).

Table A.9: Comparative data pointing to the development of nasality in Naish from earlier */rN-/ onsets.

	Japhug	Fengke Naxi	Yongning Na	Laze
red	**ɣɯrni**	hỹ˩	hỹ˩	–
to stand	**rma**	hỹ˧˥	hĩ˥	hĩẽ˥
person	**tɯ-rme**	hĩ˧	hĩ˥	hĩ˧
body hair	**tʁ-rme**	hỹ˥	hỹ˥	hỹ˩
to stir-fry	**rŋu**	–	hỹ˧~hỹ˧	–
two	**ʁnɯs**	ɲi˧˥	ɲi˥	ɲi˧

Table A.9 brings out a correspondence between the /ḥṼ/ syllables of Yongning Na and etyma with initial /rm-/ or /rn-/ in Japhug. This leads to the hypothesis that the /ḥṼ/ syllables found in Naish languages originate in earlier *CNV syllables. The hypothesis that the nasal vowels found in some Sino-Tibetan languages could be attributed to the influence of syllable-initial nasals was already expressed by Huáng Bùfán (1991). On the other hand, no hypotheses had been proposed until Michaud, Jacques & Rankin (2012) as to which specific sequences of phonemes were involved in the change.

The last example in Table A.9, 'two', illustrates the preservation in Naxi, Na and Laze of nasals that originate in onsets other than */rN-/. It appears reasonable to hypothesize that the *CN- onsets that led to vowel nasalization all went through a */sN-/ stage. (For general phonetic reflections on this topic see Ohala & Ohala 1993: 233: "children learning English sometimes pronounce target *sm* and *sn* clusters as voiceless nasals".)

In front of nasal rhymes, /h/ is nasalized; the lowered velum prevents the buildup of intra-oral pressure required for a strong friction noise. Since the entire syllable is nasalized, another option for phonemic analysis would be to posit a nasalized glottal fricative, /h̃/, contrasting with plain /h/. A review about "possible and impossible segments" (Walker & Pullum 1999) includes /h̃/ among the set of "possible segments" because it is firmly attested as a phoneme contrasting with /h/ in at least two languages: Kwangali (Bantu; Ladefoged & Maddieson 1996: 132-133) and Seimat (Austronesian; Blust 1998). In the case of Yongning Na, the decision to interpret nasality as a characteristic of the vowel rather than the consonant is based on the observation that nasal vowels are also found in a small set of syllables that do not have an initial glottal fricative.

A.2.4.2 Onsetless nasal syllables: /õ/, /æ̃/ and /ĩ̠/

Among onsetless nasal syllables, /õ/ contrasts with /o/, /æ̃/ with /æ/, and /ĩ̠/ with /i̠/. Examples of /o/ (realized with a glide onset, [wo]) include /wo˥/ 'hard'; examples of /õ/ include /õ˧/ '(one)self', /õ˧tʂwɤ˦/ 'mosquito' and /õ˩dv̩˧/ 'wolf'. Synchronically, initial glottalization contributes to a clear phonetic contrast between /o/, realized [wo], and /õ/, realized [ʔõ]. Examples of /ĩ̠/ and /i̠/ were presented above (§A.2.1.3). The syllable /æ̃/ has a glottalized onset: [ʔæ̃]. A non-nasalized syllable [ʔæ] is also found in the system, and is analyzed as /æ/, i.e. recognizing the phonemic status of both /æ/ and /æ̃/. Examples of /æ̃/ are relatively numerous: it is found in words such as 'chicken', 'bronze', 'plough' and 'soul'. Among disyllables, examples include /æ̃˩zɯ˩/ 'agate' vs. /æ˩gv̩˩/ 'ard';[9] /æ̃˩-mi˦/ 'hen' and /æ˩mi˦-ʁwɤ#˥/ 'the village of A-Mi' form a quasi-minimal pair.

From an evolutionary point of view, the glottal onset of [ʔõ] and [ʔæ̃] may be due to the same phenomenon of hardening of empty onsets which results in the presence of an initial [ʁ] in words such as /ʁwɤ˥/ 'village', corresponding to Naxi /wɤ˦/ (more about this phenomenon below, §A.3.1).

A.2.4.3 Phonemic analysis of the onsetless nasal syllable [w̃æ]

The syllable realized as [ʔw̃æ] appears in a single word: 'to swell, to inflate (e.g. the belly is swollen)', [ʔw̃æ˦]. It does not have a non-nasal counterpart. In the absence of an opposition with an oral syllable [wæ], nasality and initial glottalization might be considered the product of implementation rules, rather than as part of the phoneme's definition. From this perspective, phonemic analysis could be simply /wæ/. However, the Mandarin syllables *wa*, *wan* and *wang*

---
[9] The ard, also known as scratch plough, is the type of ploughing implement used in Yongning. Unlike the plough, the ard has a symmetrical share that traces a shallow furrow but does not invert the soil (Haudricourt & Jean-Brunhes Delamare 1955).

(as in *wáng* 王, a common family name) are pronounced as [ʁwæ] by consultant F4, rather than as [ʔw̃æ]. If the underlying, phonemic form of syllables such as 'to swell' were simply /wæ/, one would expect these Mandarin forms to fall into the /wæ/ category (phonetically [ʔw̃æ]), not into the /ʁwæ/ category. The transcription used here for 'to swell' is therefore /w̃æ/, granting phonological status to nasality, which plays a role in the vowel system of Yongning Na, but not to initial glottalization, which does not. To sum up the analysis: the syllable /w̃æ/, realized as [ʔw̃æ], contrasts with /wæ/, realized as [ʁwæ] (see §A.3.3).

A.2.4.4 The syllable /ĩ/

The syllable /ĩ/ appears in one single word, the interjection 'Yes!', 'Okay!', used as a response to an instruction given by a person having authority (either one's elder, or another person detaining authority): /ĩ˧/ (phonetically: [ʔĩ˧]). This item is described as having a mid tone, but could also be analyzed as a toneless interjection generally realized on a level pitch.

A.2.4.5 The nasal rhyme /õ/ appears as a variant in two Tibetan loanwords

Two Tibetan loanwords preserve a nasal rhyme /õ/ alternating with oral realizations: /o/. The examples are /tsʰo˧pæ#˥/ ≈ /tsʰõ˧pæ#˥/ 'head of caravan' (compare Written Tibetan *tshong pa* 'merchant'), and a formula of blessing: /la˧ma˧-ko˧tsʰo˧/ ≈ /la˧ma˧-ko˧tsʰõ˧/.[10] On the other hand, the word for 'monastery', /go˧bɤ˩/ (compare Written Tibetan *dgon pa*), does not have a nasalized variant ‡ gõ˧bɤ˩. Tibetan borrowings would definitely warrant in-depth study, distinguishing different layers and different degrees of integration into the Na language.

---

[10] Nathan Hill (p.c. 2016) proposes that the Na word /ko˧tsʰo˧/ ≈ /ko˧tsʰõ˧/ is a shortened form of *dkon mchog gsum*, Sanskrit *triratna*: 'the Three Jewels: Buddha, dharma (the teaching), and saṅgha (the monastic order, or community)'. Na /la˧ma˧/ is clearly from *bla ma* 'spiritual leader, great teacher (at the monastery)'; it is not obvious why this term is paired with the Three Jewels into a formula of blessing: *bla ma dkon mchog gsum*, 'the Lama and the Three Jewels' or 'the Lama's Three Jewels'. Nathan Hill's suggestion is that 'lama' may be used here to stand for the Three Roots *(tsa sum)* of the Tibetan Buddhist tradition. These Three Roots, *lama*, *yidam* and *khandroma*, are more abstract and recondite than the Three Jewels, and hence difficult to remember for people who have not received training at a monastery. Inside the set of three, the teacher, *lama*, is not only the first: it is also impersonated by a living person (a high-ranking monk), which makes the notion readily understandable. This could explain why *lama* rather than one of the other two Roots would appear in a (somewhat garbled) formula of blessing.

A.2.5 The open vowels /ɑ/ and /æ/, and the vowel /ɤ/

Na, Naxi and Laze all have an opposition between two open vowels. For Naxi, some authors transcribe them as /a/ vs. /æ/ (for instance Hé Kāixiáng et al. 1989), others as /ɑ/ vs. /æ/ (Fāng Guóyú & Hé Zhìwǔ 1995), others still as /ɑ/ vs. /a/ (Fù Màojì 1981; Hé Jírén & Jiāng Zhúyí 1985; Pinson 2012). These choices are all fine from a phonemic point of view, since the relevant structural fact is the distinction between two low vowels. But use of the symbol /a/ can cause some confusion for linguists who consult data from several sources, hence my decision to adopt a notation as /ɑ/ vs. /æ/ for all Naish languages, avoiding the symbol /a/.[11] Phonetically, the vowel transcribed as /ɑ/ is clearly a back vowel in Naxi, close to cardinal [ɑ], whereas in Na and Laze it is closer to [a]. I had not noticed any cross-language difference in the pronunciation of the vowel transcribed as /æ/ until a native speaker of Lijiang Naxi, Mu Yanjuan 木艳娟, explained to me (p.c. 2016) that in her view the front low vowel in Naxi is clearly [a] and notation as [æ] is definitely inappropriate.

In Yongning Na, the sounds [ɑ] and [ɤ] are contrastive in some contexts. Although it is clear from their present-day distribution that the opposition used to be neutralized in most contexts, this opposition has been reinforced through processes of gap-filling. (About the notion of structural gap-filling, see §A.3.3.)

After labials, only [ɤ] and not [ɑ] is found (as shown in Table A.2), except (i) in loanwords and (ii) in contexts where the vowel is likely to have been changed by vowel harmony. Thus, the combination /mɑ/ (contrasting with /mɤ/) has been introduced by Tibetan borrowings, as in the names /ɖɯ˩ma#˩/, /ɲi˩ma#˩/ and /gv̩˧mɑ˧/, and in /lɑ˧mɑ˧/ 'priest, lama', /mɑ˩ɳɯ˧-do˥bv̩˩/ 'Mani wall', and /mɑ˧pʰv̩˧/ 'butter' (the second syllable is a Na adjective meaning 'white'). Somewhat paradoxically, the first syllable of /mɑ˧pʰv̩˧/ 'butter' is perceived as semantically and phonemically different from /mɤ˩/ 'animal fat', even though 'butter tea' is /mɤ˩ɬi˩/. The combination /mɑ/ is also found in the term of address /ə˧mɑ˧/, 'Mum, mother'. Finally, there is a clan name, /lɑ˩mɑ˩/, which also contains this syllable; it may be Tibetan in origin. In the remaining two items, the syllable /mɑ/ may result from vowel harmony: /mɑ˩dzɑ˩/ 'solid ink', and /mɑ˧tsɑ˩/ 'origin, cause'. With bilabial stops, /bɑ˩/ appears in /bɑ˩lɑ˩/ 'jacket, upper outer garment', where it could result from vowel harmony, and in the final particle

---

[11] For similar reasons of consistency across descriptions of Naish languages, the vowel symbol /ɯ/ is used for Yongning Na, Naxi and Laze despite slight differences in pronunciation. In Yongning Na, this vowel is articulated less to the back than the Naxi vowel transcribed with the same symbol. From a phonetic perspective, one could argue in favour of using the symbol /ɨ/ for Yongning Na.

/ba˩/, which serves a function comparable to that of question-tags in English and belongs to the language's expressive margins. The syllable /pɑ/ is found in /pɑ˧tɕɤ˧/ 'plantain (a species of banana)', which is a loanword from Mandarin (*bājiāo* 芭蕉).

On the other hand, /ɑ/ and /ɤ/ are contrastive after affricates and fricatives, e.g. /tsɑ˧/ 'busy' vs. /tsɤ˧/ 'greedy' and /sɑ˥/ 'hemp, *Cannabis sativa*' vs. /sɤ˥/ 'blood'.

Only [ɤ] is found after velars, and only [ɑ] after uvulars, e.g. /kɤ˥/ 'to knock (on the door)' vs. /qɑ˥/ 'to help'.

After /h/, there is an opposition, witness /hɑ˩/ 'to open (one's eyes)' vs. /hɤ˩/ 'to dry beside or over a fire'.

A.2.6 A note on phonetic diphthongization

There is some diphthongization in the phonetic realization of the Na phonemes written as simple vowels, /i/, /e/, /æ/, /ɯ/, /ɤ/, /o/ and /ɑ/. There is also some formant movement during the syllabic consonants /ʅ/ and /v/. Formants in Na are not as stable as in, say, Northern (Parisian) French, whose conservative varieties provide a canonical illustration of the four-way contrast in openness among the simple vowels /i/, /e/, /ɛ/, /a/ and /u/, /o/, /ɔ/, /ɑ/.

Phonetic diphthongization in Na is at its clearest for the vowel /e/, realized phonetically close to [ej], as noted by Lidz (2010: 63, 96). This realization of /e/ is a point of similarity with Naxi, a language in which the simple vowels are otherwise stable. Phonetic diphthongization appears to date back to a century at least, as Bonin, an explorer of the turn of the twentieth century, transcribed the Naxi word /ɲi˧/ 'two' as *ngié*, and Bacot, another explorer, transcribed the Naxi name of the city of Lijiang, /ji˧gv˧dy˩/, with a *yé* for /ji˧/ (Bacot 1913: 3). Bacot indicates that "each [simple] vowel and its diphthongs [diphthongized variants] are interchangeable" (Bacot 1913: 28),[12] suggesting that diphthongization was not considerable (Michaud & Jacques 2010).

A.2.7 A note on vowel harmony

Anticipatory vowel harmony ('right-to-left' harmony) is a salient phonetic tendency in connected speech in all the Naish languages studied so far. For instance, in Laze, /ji˧dy˧/ 'family' is sometimes realized close to [jy˧dy˧]. This is not a phonological phenomenon: vowel oppositions on the first syllable of disyllables are not neutralized. But this phonetic tendency becomes lexicalized on

---

[12] *Original text*: chaque voyelle et ses diphtongues sont interchangeables.

some disyllables. For instance, in some Naxi dialects, including A-sher, 'pigswill' is /bu˩-ha˧/ (from /bu˩/ 'pig' and /ha˧/ 'food'); in other dialects, including Nda-le, it has become /ba˩-ha˧/. (This phenomenon is reported by Hé Zhìwǔ 1985: 11 but without mention of the dialects concerned.)

In detail, this phenomenon is highly language- and dialect-specific. Among the three Naish languages studied so far (Laze, Na and Naxi), Naxi is least prone to the lexicalization of such phenomena, and Laze most prone to it. The lexicalization of vowel harmony sometimes goes hand in hand with other processes such as the voicing of intervocalic voiceless consonants. A typical example in Laze is /ʂie˧-lie˧mie˧/ 'seventh month', from /ʂɯ˧/ 'seven' and /ɬie˧mie˧/ 'month': in addition to the change in the vowel of the first syllable, note the voicing of /ɬ/ to /l/.

In Na, the phonetic tendency towards regressive vowel harmony is especially strong for the vowel /æ/. For instance, /ŋwɤ˧/ 'five' plus the monetary unit /mæ˩ₐ/ is pronounced [ŋwæ˧-mæ˩] 'five yuan', although in careful (hyperarticulated) speech the pronunciation is [ŋwɤ˧-mæ˩]. Also, function words are more susceptible to vowel harmony – this is one of the manifestations of their overall weaker realization. Here are two examples.

(i) The accomplished prefix /le˧-/ is realized close to [læ] when the vowel of the following verb is /æ/ or an apical vowel.

(ii) The negation prefix /mɤ˧-/ is realized close to [mɑ] when the vowel of the following verb is an apical vowel.

Vowel harmony for these two prefixes is so strong that at one point (2008–2011) I transcribed them as /lə˧-/ and /mə˧-/, with a neutral vowel. But other morphemes such as the durative prefix /tʰi˧-/ also exhibit some vowel harmony. Pending the results of future phonetic studies of the relative degree of vowel harmony for a broad range of grammatical words, I chose to stop granting special phonemic status to the vowel in the accomplished and negation prefixes. This topic is well worth investigating further. It links up with topics of diachronic phonology: vowel harmony has the potential to introduce new phonotactic combinations into the phonological system, through sporadic lexicalization of harmonized phonetic forms. For instance, syllables containing a dental stop followed by /æ/, such as /læ/, /tæ/ and /tʰæ/, are scarce in Na, and most of them appear to originate in vowel harmony (see §A.3.5).

A.3 Initial consonants

A.3.1 On-glides

The high vowels /i/, /ɯ/ and /o/ have phonetic on-glides: they are realized as [ʝi], [ɣɯ] and [wo].

The amount of friction in the realization of /i/ led to the transcription of the on-glide as a fricative, [ʝ], rather than an approximant, [j]. The latter is used in the transcription of the complex rhymes /jo/, /jɤ/ and /jæ/, which are realized with less friction.

The phonetic realization of the syllable /ɯ/ could also be transcribed with an approximant initial: [ɰɯ]; this is the choice made in a dictionary of Naxi (Pinson 2012), a language where the phonemic analysis of this syllable is the same as in Yongning Na and the phonetic realization does not sound any different to me.

The phonetic on-glides in [ʝi], [ɣɯ] and [wo] appeared salient enough to be indicated in transcriptions, departing slightly from considerations of notational economy. However, they do not involve as much change in vowel quality (formant movement) as is found for the phonemic on-glides in the complex rhymes, /jo/, /jɤ/, /jæ/, /wɤ/, /w̃ɤ/, /wæ/, /w̃æ/, /wɑ/ and /w̃ɤ/. Onsetless syllables tend to coalesce phonetically with the preceding syllable inside polysyllabic words and tightly-knit polysyllabic expressions. For instance, I mistakenly believed for several years that the manner adverbials 'in this way, thus' and 'in that way' were /tʂʰɯ˧ni˥/ and /tʰy˧ni˥/, respectively; these are in fact /tʂʰɯ˧ne˧ ji˥/ and /tʰy˧ne˧ ji˥/, made up of a manner adverbial (/tʂʰɯ˧ne˥/, /tʰy˧ne˥/) followed by the verb 'to do', /ji˥/ (as mentioned in §A.2.2). Realization of the trisyllabic structure of these phrases did not come from phonetic evidence, but from their tonal behaviour. Consider example (2), shown here as initially transcribed:

(2) tʂʰɯ˧ni˥ | gwɤ˩-ɲi˩ mæ˩!
    tʂʰɯ˧ni˥   gwɤ˩   -ɲi˩   mæ˧
    in_this_way   to_sing   CERTITUDE   OBVIOUSNESS
    'This is how [people] used to sing!' (Caravans.51, 53, 57)

If the notation /tʂʰɯ˧ni˥/ were correct, it should be possible to link up the adverbial together with the following verb phrase into a single tone group, as ‡ tʂʰɯ˧ni˧ gwɤ˥-ɲi˩-mæ˩.[13] But this stylistic option is not open: the manner demonstrative cannot project a H tone onto a following syllable, as would be expected if it carried MH# tone. The solution to this puzzle is that the adverbial

---

[13] About the division of the utterance into tone groups, see Chapter 7.

phrase 'thus, in this way' is trisyllabic (/tsʰɯ˧ne˧-ji˥/), and remains so despite the strong phonetic coarticulation between its last two syllables. The correct notation of (2) is as in (3).

(3) tsʰɯ˧ne˧ ji˥ | gwɤ˩-ɲi˥ mæ˧!
    tsʰɯ˧ne˧   ji˥   gwɤ˩   -ɲi˩   mæ˧
    in_this_way to_do to_sing CERTITUDE OBVIOUSNESS
    'This is how [people] used to sing!' (Caravans.51, 53, 57)

Now moving on to other vowels: /æ/ and /ɑ/ may begin either with a glottal stop (hard phonetic onset) or with soft phonation: [ɦæ] ≈ [ʔæ], [ɦɑ] ≈ [ʔɑ]. Concerning the choice of one type of onset or the other, a study of glottal stops before word-initial vowels in American English concludes that "full glottal stops [ʔ] are predicted overwhelmingly by prominence and phrasing" (Garellek 2012: 20), and reviews a list of factors that would constitute a good starting-point for a future phonetic study of this topic in Yongning Na:

> ... the factors that promote the occurrence of word-initial glottalization (...) may be segmental, lexical, prosodic, or sociolinguistic. In English, segmental factors include hiatus (V#V) environments and word-initial back vowels are found to glottalize more frequently than non-back vowels. As for lexical factors, content words exhibit more frequent glottalization than function words. Sociolinguistically, women are known to use glottalization more than men. Prosodically, the presence of stress and/or a pitch accent on the word-initial vowel, as well as a larger juncture with the preceding word, are known to promote glottalization. Researchers working on other languages have found additional factors that promote the occurrence of word-initial glottalization, including presence of a preceding pause as well as speech rate and low vowel quality for German. (Garellek 2012: 1-2)[14]

Unlike in Naxi, where /ɤ/ is realized as /ɣɤ/, in Yongning Na the vowel /ɤ/ never constitutes a syllable on its own. As explained in §A.2.5, the opposition between /ɤ/ and /ɑ/ is restricted to a few contexts; synchronically, it may be considered to be neutralized in onsetless syllables.

No distinct onset portion is found for /v/, realized simply as [v]. Likewise, the rhyme /ɿ/ is not separated from the preceding rhyme by a glide or glottal stop. For instance, in /bv˧ɿ#˥/ 'fly (the insect)' the /v/ and /ɿ/ follow each other: [bvɿ].

The following paragraph discusses syllables that canonically begin with a glottal stop.

---

[14] Citations have been removed from this quotation.

A.3.2 Initial glottal stop

The rhymes /ə/ and /ĩ̩/ begin with a phonetic glottal stop when said in isolation, and also word-medially in hyperarticulated realizations: e.g. /sæ˩ĩ̩˩/ 'bone' is realized as [sæ˩ʔĩ̩˩] in careful speech, and as [sæ˩ĩ̩˩] in casual speech.

The morpheme /u˧/ is an associative first person pronoun that appears in the pronouns /u˧=ɻ̍˩/ 'my clan, my people' and /u˧=ɻæ˩/ 'us (as opposed to them)'. It is pronounced with an initial glottal stop, hence [ʔu˧=ɻ̍˩] and [ʔu˧=ɻæ˩]. The morpheme /u˧/ is the only instance of this syllable that has been observed; but one example is enough to require recognition of this syllable as distinct from the syllable realized as [wo] ≈ [wu], found in words such as //wo˥// 'hard', //wo˩kɤ#˥// 'swing' and //wo˧// 'turnip leaves'. Several solutions are open here, such as the following three (which could be combined in various ways).

(i) The syllable [ʔu] could be phonemicized as /u/, and [wo] ≈ [wu] as /wu/, granting phonemic status to the initial glide.

(ii) The syllable [ʔu] could be phonemicized as /ʔu/, and [wo] ≈ [wu] as /u/, granting phonemic status to the initial glottal stop.

(iii) The syllable [ʔu] could be phonemicized as /u/, and [wo] ≈ [wu] as /o/, ascribing the different initials to phonotactic rules of assignment of empty-onset fillers.

The most important cue to this opposition appears to lie in the initial, and would suggest granting phonemic status to the initial glottal stop or the labial-velar approximant. The provisional choice made here consists in considering the approximant as an empty-onset filler, and the glottal stop as a phonemic initial, hence its inclusion in Table A.1. Clearly, such cases of phonemic ambiguity hold potential for changes to the system; the example of initial /ʁ/, examined in the next paragraph, exemplifies the introduction of new consonants from phonemic reinterpretation of empty-onset fillers.

A.3.3 Initial /ʁ/ as a phonemicized empty-onset filler

The situation of /wɤ/, /wæ/, /o/, /ɑ/ and /æ/ is especially interesting. These rhymes can combine with an initial voiced uvular fricative, /ʁ/. (Phonetically, this /ʁ/ is weakly articulated, and can be mistaken for /w/ in some hypo-articulated tokens.) Some of the words at issue derive diachronically from onsetless syllables, such as 'village', /ʁwɤ˧/, corresponding to /wɤ˧/ in Naxi and Laze, and its homophone 'mountain', /ʁwɤ˧/, likewise corresponding to /wɤ˧/ in Naxi (where it means 'hill, hillock'); others from syllables with an initial velar or uvular cluster, such as 'sword', /ʁæ˧mi˧/, corresponding to Naxi /ŋgæ˩/.[15]

The hardening of soft onsets should in principle result in the absence of any syllable realized as [wɤ], [wæ], [o], [ɑ] or [æ], since these became [ʁwɤ], [ʁwæ], [ʁo], [ʁɑ] and [ʁæ]. This is true for /wæ/: only [ʁwæ] is attested, not [wæ] (e.g. /ʁwæ˩/ 'left, leftward', corresponding to Naxi /wæ˧/ and Laze /væ˧/). For the other syllables, however, there are oppositions between syllables with and without a /ʁ/ onset: a process of structural gap-filling has taken place. Progress in the etymological study of individual examples will be necessary to understand the various processes whereby onsetless syllables were reintroduced into the system. The hardening of empty-onset fillers must date back a relatively long way, judging from the number of onsetless syllables that currently exist: e.g., for /wɤ/, examples include the classifier for loads, /wɤ˩˥/; the noun 'serf, slave', /wɤ˧/; the adverb 'again, anew', /wɤ˥/; the verbs 'to depend on, to rely on', /wɤ˩˥/ and 'to detour past, to bypass', /wɤ˩~wɤ˩/; and the final exclamative particle /wɤ˧/, conveying obviousness.[16]

The change from proto-Naish *j to Na /ʑ/ may be part of the same process of hardening. 'To sleep', Na /ʑi˥/, corresponds to Naxi /ji˥/ (phonemically a simple /i/, to which an empty-onset-filler gets added) and Laze /zi˩/; the reconstruction proposed in Jacques & Michaud (2011) is ***jip**.

A.3.4 Velar and uvular stops

Velar and uvular stops are in complementary distribution, except in front of /ɣ/, /wɤ/, and /o/, where they are contrastive. Examples of the syllables /kɣ/, /qɣ/, /kʰɣ/, /qʰɣ/, /ko/, /qo/, /kʰo/ and /qʰo/ are provided in (4). A single instance of /qi/ (contrasting with /ki/) has also been found.

---

[15] A process of hardening of initial glides has been reported in Zeluo Ersu, where /w-/ is sometimes pronounced with frication, as [ɣʷ-] (Sūn Hóngkāi 1982). Synchronically, among the last speakers of the language, there is variation between [ʁ] and [w] sounds (Chirkova 2014).

[16] The voiced uvular fricative /ʁ/ is not uncommon in this linguistic area, but with a widely different phonemic status from one language to another. For instance, in Lizu (Chirkova & Chen 2013), it is an allophone of the voiced velar fricative /ɣ/ in front of /ɐ/ and /wɐ/, e.g. /ɣɐˬ/ [ʁɐˬ] 'needle', /ɣwɐˬ/ [ʁuɐˬ] 'to thunder'.

(4) a. /qʁ/   /kʁ/
       qʁ˧   handle   kʁ˥   garlic
       qʁ˩   to frighten   kʁ˩   to be able to
       qʁ˧tsæ˩   throat   kʁ˧tʂɯ˥$ nail
       mæ˧qʁ˩   tail   kʁ˧dʐɯ˩   tent

   b. /qʰʁ/   /kʰʁ/
       qʰʁ˩   six   mʁ˧kʰʁ˩   smoke
       qʰʁ˧   horn   kʰʁ˥   to cut (grass)
       qʰʁ˧   hole   kʰʁ˥   dog
       bʁ˧qʰʁ˩   conch shell   kʰʁ˩   year

   c. /qo/   /ko/
       qo˥   to love   ko˥   hill
       qo˧ho˩   bamboo box   ko˩   to bask
       qo˧qɑ˩   mountain pass   ko˩dʐo˩   flail
       -qo˧   inside   mæ˩ko˥   harness

   d. /qʰo/   /kʰo/
       qʰo˩   to kill   kʰo˥   to spread (e.g. a sheet)
       qʰo˧lo˧   wheel   kʰo˧lo˧   prayer wheel
       qʰo˩tʁ˩   tree stump   tse˧kʰo˩   sanctuary
       qʰo˩mʁ˩   straw hat   hæ̃˧kʰo˧   princess, young lady

   e. /qi/   /ki/
       qi˧qi˧   originally, at first ki˧   to give

This situation is unsurprising in areal context. In Lizu, velar and uvular stops only contrast before /o/, e.g. /ko˧/ 'to beg' vs. /qo\\/ 'hole, pit' (Chirkova & Chen 2013).

From a diachronic point of view, uvulars have various possible origins (Sun 2003a: 782-783); in view of cognates with uvular initials in Rgyalrong, a conservative language, the current analysis is that Na uvulars have great historical depth (Jacques & Michaud 2011: 492).

A.3.5 Retroflex stops and affricates

Yongning Na has (i) an opposition between dental and retroflex affricates, with a high functional load, and (ii) an opposition between dental and retroflex stops and nasals, but only in front of /i/, /æ/, /ʁ/ and /o/. Examples include: /tʰi˩/ 'tired' vs. /ʈʰi˩/ 'to plane (wood)'; /ti˩/ 'to get up' vs. /ʈi˩/ 'to knock, to tap (lightly)';

/tæ˧bʌ˧/ 'Buddhist priest' vs. /tæ˧pv˩/ 'thin, skinny'; /ɖo˧ɑ/ 'to allow; ought; to have to' vs. /ɖo˩/ 'to climb'. After retroflex consonants, /o/ is realized close to [u].

The consonants transcribed as retroflex are articulated much less to the back than canonical retroflex sounds such as those of Tamil or Nepali (Khatiwada 2009); a palatographic study may reveal that they are postalveolars rather than retroflexes. This is an area where there is clearly room for improvement of the International Phonetic Alphabet: separate symbols are needed for postalveolar and dental sounds, as emphasized by Ladefoged & Maddieson (1996: 21-30). This is not merely an issue of fine detail in phonetic transcription, to be handled through the addition of diacritics: the absence of distinct symbols for postalveolars can lead to the widespread adoption of retroflex symbols for non-dental sounds, creating no small amount of typological confusion and introducing a bias in cross-language studies of phonological inventories. In the absence of distinct International Phonetic Alphabet symbols for postalveolar stops, the provisional solution chosen here is to use IPA symbols for retroflex sounds.

A.3.6 Laterals /l/ and /ɬ/, and retroflexes /ɭ/ and /ɻ/

The laterals /l/ and /ɬ/ are contrastive in Yongning Na, as demonstrated by pairs such as /li˧ɑ/ 'to look' vs. /ɬi˧/ 'month' and /lo˦/ 'thick' vs. /ɬo˦/ 'deep'. Phonetically, the voiced lateral /l/ has a broad perimeter of allophonic variation. It is realized as retroflex in front of /ɯ/, e.g. in the classifier for round objects such as bowls and grains (also serving as generic classifier), /lɯ˧b/. The phonemic analysis for this syllable was only arrived at after the greatest hesitations: a broad range of options was considered, including [ɻɯ], [ɭɯ], [lv], [ly], [ly] and syllabic [l̩] or [ɻ]. The entire syllable is articulated loosely: the initial is close to an approximant, and the vowel quality is not precise, so that the syllable often resembles a monophonemic [l̩].

In front of /v/, the voiced lateral /l/ is slightly retroflex. In all contexts, /l/ is accompanied by some friction. This characteristic is at its clearest before the high front vowel /i/, but it is also observed before open vowels, including /ɑ/ and /æ/. Phonetically, it may therefore be more adequate to transcribe this allophone as [ɮ] rather than [l]. Phonologically, it would be economical to consider that the two laterals are distinguished solely by the feature of voicing; this also argues in favour of a notation as /ɮ/.

The compromise choice made here for the sake of simplicity consists in using a notation as /l/ rather than /ɮ/. On the other hand, a retroflex initial is used in the transcription of the syllable [ɭɯ] (phonemically: /lɯ/) to reflect what I perceive as a great phonetic distance between the realization of /l/ in this context and in all others; it appeared better to keep the transcriptions close to the surface forms.

These observations on the allophonic variation of /l/ shed indirect light on the distribution of the retroflex approximant /ɻ/: this phoneme may well have originated as an allophone of /l/ which drifted to such a phonetic distance that it opened a structural gap that was later filled through borrowings and processes of vowel harmony. The present-day /ɻ/ initial of Yongning Na only appears in the syllables /ɻæ/ and /ɻwæ/, which correspond to the syllables /læ/ and /lwæ/ in Laze, e.g. 'to shout, to cry': Na /ɻwæ˧/, Laze /lwæ˧/, and 'seed': Na /ɻæ˧/, Laze /læ˩/. Roselle Dobbs (p.c. 2013) indicates that in villages that belong to the area referred to in Na as /lɑ˧tʰɑ˧-di˧/, to the east of Lake Lugu, these items retain the lateral initial. Synchronically, /ɻæ/ contrasts with /læ/, but the latter only appears (i) in borrowings, such as /læ˧tsɯ˧/ 'chili peppers', from Southwestern Mandarin 辣子 [la.tsɿ], (ii) in the accomplished prefix /le˧-/, whose phonetic realizations, determined by the vowel of the following verb, include [læ], and (iii) in words where the /æ/ could have resulted from vowel harmony, e.g. /læ˧ʁæ˧/ 'raven'. (Regressive vowel harmony, which becomes sporadically lexicalized, is a salient phonetic tendency in Na: see §A.2.7.) As for the syllable /ɻwæ/, there exists no lateral counterpart /lwæ/.[17]

It can therefore be hypothesized that present-day /ɻæ/ and /ɻwæ/ originated in earlier *læ and *lwæ, which became phonetically closer to [ɻæ] and [ɻwæ], thus leaving these phonetic slots empty; the [læ] slot was then occupied by other syllables.

These diachronic reflections do not detract from the synchronic phonemic status of /ɻ/.

A.3.7 The glottal fricative /h/ and the sound [f]

Na has a glottal fricative /h/. At an earlier stage of the language, the sound [f] can be hypothesized to have been entirely absent, since early Mandarin borrowings with initial [f] in the donor language were reinterpreted as having initial /h/. For instance, 'method, solution', 办法 (Standard Mandarin: bànfǎ) was borrowed as /pæ˧hwɤ˧/.

---

[17] A tantalizingly similar synchronic situation is found in Lizu, where the /ɹ/ phoneme only occurs before /æ/, /ə/, and /wæ/, e.g. /ɹæ˥/ 'yak', /ɹə˦/ 'to laugh', and /ɹwæ˦/ 'chicken' (Chirkova & Chen 2013). The diachronic origin seems different, however, as Ersu and Duoxu evidence rather points to an earlier *r, as discussed in Yu (2012). Surface similarities in sound patterns tend to arise from areal convergence, as well as from cross-linguistic (panchronic) regularities in phonological erosion processes.

The sound [f] appears in more recent layers of borrowings, however: e.g. /fæ˧/ for 'direction', 方 (Standard Mandarin: *fāng*) and /fɑ˩ₐ/ for 'to ferment', 发 （酵） (Standard Mandarin: *fā*). A plausible scenario is that /h/ in front of oral rhymes came to be realized in Na with a friction source at a point in the vocal tract determined by the following vowel, e.g. palatal before /i/ and labial-dental before /ʋ/, hence [ɕi] and [fʋ]. Once the sound [f] had thus been introduced into Na (on a phonetic level), the way was paved for the introduction of [f]-initial loanwords. In the present state of the language, speakers of Yongning Na have no problem pronouncing a [f] sound in front of any rhyme. This can be taken as evidence that the sound [f] is no longer perceived by the speakers as an allophone of /h/. It is well-known that allophones that drift far apart acquire psychophonetic independence from one another, witness the well-documented cases of German [ç] and [x], and Standard Mandarin [ɕ] and [x]. As the psychological reality of the underlying unity among allophones wanes, the resistance against structural gap-filling decreases.

In view of this situation, and also in order to keep the transcriptions close to the surface forms, the syllable [fʋ] is transcribed as such, rather than pushing phonemicization to an extreme and analyzing it as /hʋ/. Under a flatly synchronic analysis that includes Mandarin borrowings, the sound [f] needs to be granted phonemic status, hence its inclusion in Table A.1.

This could lead to a modified treatment of the syllables [fʋ] and [hu]. The former could be phonemicized as /fʋ/, and the latter as /hʋ/; this would eliminate the /u/ phoneme altogether (Roselle Dobbs, p.c. 2016). This is one of the points of Yongning Na phonemics which are open to several analyses.

The syllable [ɕi], phonemicized as /hi/, contrasts with /ɕi/.

A.4 Comments about the inventory of syllables

The inventory of attested combinations of initials and rhymes provided at the outset of this Appendix (in Tables A.2 and A.3) reveals that numerous phonemic oppositions are found in highly restricted contexts in Yongning Na. A similar situation is found in Naxi (Michaud 2006a). The strict application of principles of Praguian synchronic description leads to an analysis of these phenomena as extreme cases of *neutralization* of phonemic contrasts. For instance, in Yongning Na the opposition between nasal and oral vowels is neutralized in all contexts except after glottal initials. It may appear counter-intuitive to speak of neutralization here: it is more usual to use this notion to describe cases where a thoroughgoing contrast disappears in a restricted environment, e.g. in Trubetzkoy's classical example: French /e/ and /ɛ/ contrast only in open syllables, the opposition being neutralized in closed syllables.

> In French (...) an opposition between **e** and **ɛ** only occurs word-finally in open syllables, e.g. *les* 'definite article.PL' vs. *lait* 'milk' and *allez* 'to go. 2PL' vs. *allait* 'to go.3SG.PST'. In all other positions the occurrence of **e** and **ɛ** is predictable: **ɛ** occurs in closed syllables, **e** in open. These two vowels must thus be considered two phonemes in open-syllable-final position, and combinatory variants of a single phoneme in all other positions. We call such oppositions *neutralizable* oppositions, the positions in which the neutralization takes place *positions of neutralization*, and those positions where the opposition is relevant *positions of relevance*. (Trubetzkoy 1969: 78)[18]

Importantly, the term *neutralization* should not be understood in a dynamic sense, whereby the opposition once existed and later has been neutralized. It has a static, flatly synchronic application (Martinet 1969: 257–259; 1970: 87–89). It is not unusual for a synchronic formulation to be the reverse image of a diachronic perspective. For instance, describing the synchronic stage during which Chinese contrasted three tones (A, B and C) on non-obstruent-final syllables, it can be said that the tonal opposition was neutralized on obstruent-final syllables (described as belonging in a fourth category: D), although this opposition never actually existed on these syllables.

In Praguian phonology, phonemes have relations of opposition with one another, and are marked for features as a consequence of these relations. If the features shared by two phonemes are not found in any other phoneme, the opposition is bilateral and neutralizable; otherwise it is multi-lateral and not neutralizable. Stated differently, only where there is opposition is a feature contrastive. An opposition is neutralized whenever one member does not occur in a specific environment. The product of neutralization is referred to as an archiphoneme.

---

[18] Some modifications to the translation were made by Roselle Dobbs. *Original text*: Im Französischen kommen aber e und ɛ nur im offenen Auslaute als Glieder einer phonologisch-distinktiven Opposition vor (*les-lait, allez-allait*); in den übrigen Stellungen ist das Vorkommen von e und ɛ mechanisch geregelt (in gedeckter Silbe ɛ, in ungedeckter e), so daß diese zwei Vokale nur im offenen Auslaut as zwei Phoneme, in den übrigen Stellungen dagegen als kombinatorische Varianten eines einzigen Phonems gewertet werden müssen. Der phonologische Gegensatz ist also im Französischen in gewissen Stellungen a u f g e h o b e n. Solche Oppositionen nennen wir a u f h e b b a r; jene Lautstellungen, in denen die Aufhebung erfolgt, A u f - h e b u n g s s t e l l u n g e n, jene, wo die Opposition relevant ist, R e l e v a n z s t e l l u n g e n. (Trubetzkoy 1939: 70)

(For a book-length treatment of neutralization from a variety of theoretical perspectives, see Silverman 2012.)

In phonological transcription, archiphonemes can be set in capitals, but this gets visually cumbersome in cases where positions of neutralization are more numerous than positions of relevance. Notations using archiphonemes are also more abstract than notations containing phonetic symbols: interpreting them requires a knowledge of the language's phonotactics. For these reasons, notations in terms of archiphonemes are not used in this volume.

From a dynamic point of view, gaps in the inventory of syllables provide structural hints about past evolutions and current tensions within the system.

A.4.1 Combinations of a dental stop and /æ/ vowel seem recent

Combinations consisting of a dental stop followed by /æ/ are scarce. The only example for /dæ/ is /læ˧dæ˧qæ˥/ 'armpit'; the two examples for /tæ/ are /tæ˧ɻæ˩/ 'Adam's apple, oesophagus' and /tæ˧pv̩˩/ 'thin, skinny'; the only example for /tʰæ/ is /tʰæ˧ɻæ˩/ 'book'. All of these except /tæ˧pv̩˩/ 'thin, skinny' can be explained as resulting from vowel harmony. Na /tʰæ˧ɻæ˩/ 'book' corresponds to Laze /tʰɑ˧ɻ˩/ and Naxi /tʰe˧ɣɯ˧/; the vowel correspondence /e:æ:ɑ/ is otherwise unattested, reinforcing the hypothesis that vowel harmony or some other exception-causing force was at play here. Na /tæ˧ɻæ˩/ 'Adam's apple, oesophagus' corresponds to Labai Na /tɑ˧i̯˧/, again an irregular correspondence, as the regular correspondences are simply æ::æ and ɑ::ɑ.

A.4.2 A marginal combination: Dental stop plus /ɤ/

Few words contain a dental stop plus /ɤ/; the only two attested combinations are /dɤ/ and /tɤ/ (no /tʰɤ/). There is an extra-distal demonstrative: 'way over there', realized as /dɤ˦-qo˧/ or /dɤ˥-qo˧/, with the locative /qo/ as its second syllable (like in /tʂʰɯ˧-qo˧/ 'here' and /tʰy˧-qo˧/ 'there'). The pitch of the first syllable reflects the intended distance: a realization with a mild rise, which could be transcribed as /dɤ˦-qo˧/, points to a less distant place than a realization with a super-high, decreasing pitch, which could be transcribed as /dɤ˥-qo˧/. The same phenomena are observed for /dɤ˦tʰy˧qo˧/ ≈ /dɤ˥tʰy˧-qo˧/ (same meaning, with added distal demonstrative) and /dɤ˦tʰy˧-gi#˥/ ≈ /dɤ˥tʰy˩-gi#˥/ 'that side, way over there' (for further details, see §8.4). The expressive load of these phrases goes a great distance towards explaining oddities in the phonemes and tone of their first syllable, where the expressivity is at its strongest.

All the other examples of syllables /dʵ/ and /tʵ/ are found with a following /ɯ̈/: /hỹ˧-dʵ˩ɯ̈#˩/ 'clumsy', /õ˧-dʵ˩ɯ̈˩/ 'fundamentally' (from /õ˩/ '(one)self'), /ʂɯ˧-tʵ˩ɯ̈˩/ 'smooth (e.g. carefully planed wood)' and /dʐɯ˩-tʵ˩ɯ̈˩/ 'humid, moist' (from /dʐɯ˩/ 'water'). These words contain a phonetic sequence which sounds like a trilled rhyme. They were initially transcribed as /dr̩/ and /tr̩/, adding another unit to the inventory of rhotic rhymes. This analysis appears correct for the phonological system of speaker F5 (F4's daughter-in-law): when repeating the phrase [hỹ˧dr̩˧~hỹ˧dr̩˧-zo˩] 'clumsily' very slowly, she still syllabifies the phonetic sequence [dr] as one syllable. In the speech of F4, though, phonetic realization is slightly less packed together, ranging between [dər] and [dəɻ] for the syllable with a voiced initial, and between [tər] and [təɻ] for the syllable with an unvoiced initial. A phonological argument demonstrating that there are two syllables, not one, comes from the noun /ho˧dʐɯ˧tʵ˩˥/ 'paste, starch', literally 'watery gruel', derived from /ho˩/ 'porridge' and /dʐɯ˩-tʵ˩ɯ̈˩/ 'humid, moist'. The noun carries H tone on its penultimate syllable and L tone on its final syllable. No HL falling tone (or any other falling tone, HM or ML) is ever observed on a single syllable in Yongning Na, so one is led to conclude that there are two syllables here: /tʵ.ɯ̈/.

Interestingly, the two tokens containing /tʵ/ have a variant with /dʵ/: /ʂɯ˧-dʵ˩ɯ̈˩/ for 'smooth', and /dʐɯ˩-dʵ˩ɯ̈˩/ for 'humid, moist'. The reverse is not true: the two tokens containing /dʵ/ do not have a variant with /tʵ/; it is not acceptable to say ‡ **hỹ˧-tʵ˩ɯ̈#˩** for 'clumsy', or ‡ **õ˧-tʵ˩ɯ̈˩** for 'fundamentally'. This suggests that /-dʵ.ɯ̈/ was, at one stage, a suffix used to derive adjectives (also used adverbially). This suffix must have ceased to be productive quite some time ago, since two of the four examples underwent a separate phonetic evolution. It may never have been highly productive.

A.4.3 After alveolopalatals, is the rhyme /o/ or /jo/?

The syllables transcribed as /tɕʰo/, /tɕo/ and /dʑo/ could also be analyzed as /tɕʰjo/, /tɕjo/ and /dʑjo/, with a /-jo/ rhyme. The correspondence between Na /dʑo/ and Naxi /gy/ (phonetically: [ɟy]) suggests that the initial became palatalized in Na by a following high front vowel or glide. From a synchronic point of view, however, it seemed more appropriate to transcribe these syllables as composed of an alveolopalatal initial followed by a back vowel.

A.4.4 Phonemic status of the retroflex nasal

There is one single instance of /nʵ/: /nʵ˩/ 'to sniff; to get to know (news)', often used in the negative: /mɤ˩-nʵ˩/ '[I] don't know'. This syllable contrasts with /nv/, e.g. /nv˩/ 'to bury'. Another possible analysis would be as [ɳɻ̩], phonemically /nɻ̩/, in which case one could dispense with positing a /ɳ/ consonant phoneme contrasting with /n/: retroflex realizations would be conditioned by a following /ɯ/ or /ɻ̩/, the combinations /nɯ/ and /nɻ̩/ being realized as [ɳɯ] and [ɳɻ̩], respectively. In the absence of a phonemic opposition, and given the phonetic proximity between these two rhymes in a retroflex context, this interpretation is not absurd. The next logical step in that perspective would be to reinterpret /ɖʵ/, /ʈʵ/ and /ʈʰʵ/ as /dɻ̩/, /tɻ̩/ and /tʰɻ̩/. This does not represent a real economy, however, since there is an opposition between dentals and retroflexes in front of other vowels (e.g. /ʈi/ vs. /ti/). The choice to transcribe as /nʵ/ is based on my auditory impression that, in the present state of the system, the rhyme is closer to [ʵ] than to [ɻ̩].

A.4.5 The palatal nasal

The palatal nasal [ɲ] only appears in the syllable [ɲi], suggesting a reanalysis as an allophone of one of the other nasal initials in the system: /m/, /n/, /ɳ/ or /ŋ/. The most plausible analysis from a language-independent perspective would be phonemicization as /ŋi/, in view of the well-documented palatalizing effects of high front vowels on velar consonants.

This analysis is possible in principle, in the absence of a syllable [ŋi] in the syllabic inventory of Yongning Na. In Naxi, analysis of palatal initials as allophones of velars is an attractive solution, because it applies throughout the system: [cʰi], [ci], [ɟi], [ɲɟi] and [ɲi] can be analyzed as /kʰi/, /ki/, /gi/, /ŋgi/ and /ŋi/ (Michailovsky & Michaud 2006: 14). However, detailed examination of the Naxi lexicon shows that this amounts to an internal reconstruction rather than a synchronic phonemic analysis, as some expressive coinages have now filled the structural gaps left empty by the palatalization of velars (Michaud & He 2015: 7). In Na, it is less tempting to phonemicize [ɲi] as /ŋi/, as there are phonemic combinations of velar initials with the vowel /i/, which are not strongly palatalized. The notation adopted therefore remains close to the surface form: /ɲi/.

A.4.6 Syllables introduced by Mandarin borrowings

Mandarin borrowings hold potential for bringing considerable changes to the phonotactics of Na syllables; in particular, they introduce many new combinations of vowels with glides. The overall situation is comparable to that of Naxi. A young Naxi from Dadong 大东, He Likun 和丽昆, did an inventory of the syllables present in his own speech, and found that recent Mandarin loanwords account for about 150 of the syllables that he uses when speaking Naxi (Michaud & He 2015). He Likun is basically bilingual in Mandarin, a situation which is common among young Naxi and Na people. On the other hand, the main consultant for Yongning Na is thirty-eight years older than He Likun, and her knowledge of Mandarin is limited. In her speech, there is a tension between a general tendency to integrate loanwords into the Na phonological system and occasional efforts at getting closer to the "correct" pronunciation in Mandarin (either Southwestern Mandarin or Standard Mandarin, depending on the addressee). This source of instability needs to be recognized when transcribing Mandarin borrowings: they typically possess both (i) an adapted form, conforming to Na phonotactics and phonetics, and (ii) forms that are closer to Mandarin, and which depart from Na phonotactics and phonetics. For instance, in the absence of a rounding opposition for front vowels, Mandarin [y] is borrowed as [i]: the Mandarin *zájūn* 杂菌 [tsa.tɕyn] 'mixed mushrooms' is pronounced /tsaJtɕiJ/. But the consultant is aware of the phonetic distance between [tɕyn] and [tɕi], and is able to make efforts towards rounding of the front vowel, getting close to [tɕɥe] ≈ [tɕɥi].

The competing pressures towards adaptation to the Na system and faithfulness to Mandarin pronunciation can sometimes be observed in the lexicon. The Chinese word for 'Westerners, foreigners', *yáng* 洋, has three forms in Yongning Na: /jɤJ/, /jeJ/ and /ʐeJ/. The most common form is /jɤJ/, as in /jɤJhoᛐ/ 'matches', from *yánghuǒ* 洋火 and /jɤJjo#˥/ 'potato', from *yángyù* 洋芋. The second, /jeJ/, appears in /jeJʐeᛐ/, from *yángrén* 洋人 'Westerner'. In turn, this word appears in a modified form in 'wild cotton flowers', /ʐeJʐeᛐ-bæJbæJ/. This is a distortion of /jeJʐeᛐ-bæJbæJ/, literally 'Westerners' flower', which is still an acceptable variant. The borrowed syllable /je/ in /jeJʐeᛐ/ 洋人 'Westerner' is Naicized by identifying it with a syllable that is well-attested in Na (/ʐe/), taking occasion of its presence in the immediate vicinity: as the second syllable of 'wild cotton flowers'. Unsurprisingly, the stylistic effect of Naicization is to sound more local, playing on a sense of closeness among speakers of Na, whereas the more faithful rendering of the Mandarin original sounds more modern and forward-looking.

A.5 Articulatory reduction: Reduced forms and their lexicalization

Phenomena of articulatory reduction pave the way for the lexicalization of new forms, sometimes resulting in the creation of new syllabic combinations. Some salient examples are presented below.

The verb /ji˩/ 'to do' is prone to reduction. Reduction is well on its way towards lexicalization for /ɡɯ˩ ji˩/ 'really, truly' (from /ɡɯ˩/ 'authentic, true'), realized as [ɡiʌ] except when hyperarticulated. Phonetic reduction is common, e.g. /no˧ | ə˧tso˧ ji˧-bi˧/ 'What are you going to do?' (2sg-interrog:what-to_do-imm.fut) is commonly realized in a hypo-articulated way that can be approximated as [no˧ ə˧tsʁ˧bi˧].

The relativizer /hĩ˩/ is articulated much more weakly than the lexical word /hĩ˩/ 'human being, person'. The initial fricative is often strongly reduced: it gets voiced throughout. Before a voiced stop, realizations as a nasal consonant (nasal stop) are observed, as in Figure A.2, which shows a spectrogram of (5).

(5) ɖwæ˩ | fv˧-hĩ˧ ɖɯ˧-ɣ˧ ɲi˩!
    ɖwæ˩ fv˧ -hĩ˩ ɖɯ˧ ɣ˧   ɲi˩
    very happy rel one clf.individual cop
    '(S)he is really happy!' (Source: field notes.)

The spectrogram shows that the sequence /hĩ˧ ɖɯ˧/ is realized phonetically close to [nɖɯ˧], as if the syllable /hĩ˩/ were realized as prenasalization of the following stop. This is not a categorical process: the claim that /hĩ˩/ becomes categorically changed to /n/ in this context would be up against insuperable phonotactic difficulties, since Na does not have a series of prenasalized stops (hence no /nɖ/ initial) and /n/ on its own is not a well-formed syllable, as it lacks a rhyme and a tone. Instead, the reduction process is phonetic; annotating the reduced realization of /hĩ˩/ in Figure A.2 as [n] is simply a convenient shorthand notation. Underlying specifications can still leave traces in the overall articulatory gesture, even though the targets normally thought of as primary are not being achieved (Nolan 1992: 272). With this reservation, it is clear that the reduction is strong; Roselle Dobbs (p.c. 2014) indicates that some younger speakers are not aware that the relativizer /hĩ˩/ is present in contexts such as the one shown in Figure A.2, and that they tend to omit it altogether.

The phrase /tʰæ˧mi˧-ɳɯ˩/ 'really, actually' is generally reduced to a monosyllable with a long rhyme, which can be approximated as [tʰææ̃˧], sometimes with a trace of the final L tone of the full expression: [tʰæ˧æ̃˩]. In the absence

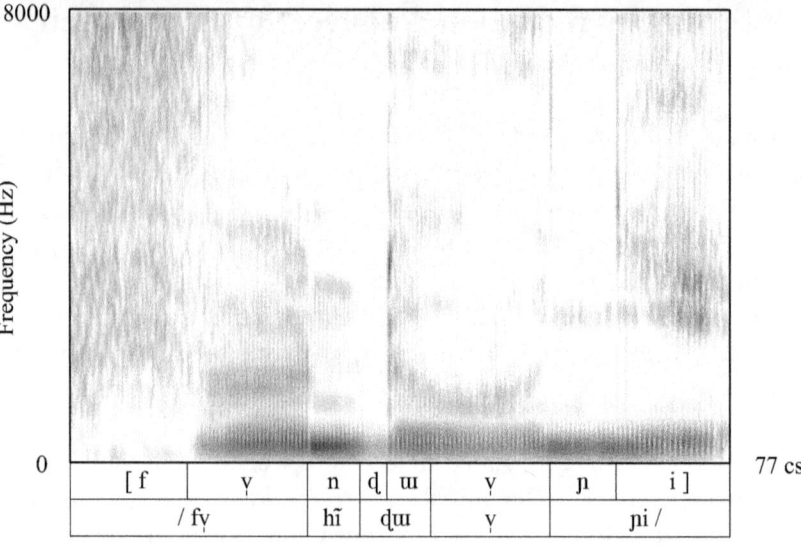

Figure A.2: An illustration of the reduction of the relativizer /hĩ/ to a nasal consonant. Top: phonetic transcription; bottom: phonemic transcription. Speaker: F5.

of a length opposition among vowels, the reduced form is unlikely to become lexicalized.

The proximal demonstrative /tṣʰɯ˩/ in association with the associative plural clitic /=ɻæ˩/ yields /tṣʰɯ˧=ɻæ˩$/ 'these things, this sort of things', and the distal demonstrative yields /tʰɤ˧=ɻæ˩$/ 'those things'. These disyllabic forms are strongly coalescent. Regressive vowel harmony is strong, yielding instances resembling [tṣʰæ˧=ɻæ˩], e.g. in Caravans.153 and Agriculture.109. Together with the weakening of the consonant /ɻ/ (which, as an approximant, is vowel-like in the first place), this leads to realizations that often resemble a monosyllable, [tṣʰæ˩] or [tʰæ˩]. Examples include Caravans.160, 165, Mountains.83, 109, Funeral.190, and BuriedAlive3.50.

The exclamative final particle, /wɤ˧/, which conveys obviousness, tends to fuse with a preceding /-ɲi˩/ (expressing certitude). In all fourteen occurrences found in F4's transcribed narratives, the combination /-ɲi˩ wɤ˧/ has its final M tone depressed to L by application of Rule 5 (see §7.1.1), and it is realized phonetically close to a monosyllable: [-ɲo˩]. This phenomenon is also highly frequent in the speech of M21.

A.6 Expressive coinages and phonostylistic observations

To conclude this chapter about Na phonemes (vowels and consonants), it appeared interesting to mention expressive coinages, and some phonostylistic observations.

A.6.1 Onomatopoeia and ideophones

Onomatopoeia constitute one aspect of expressive (phonaesthetic) coinages, which also comprise interjections, calling sounds, and ideophones. All of these present interesting morphological and phonological specificities. "Of the 446 known onsets in Japhug, forty-five clusters (including thirty-five two-consonant and eleven three-consonant clusters) are exclusively attested in ideophones or ideophonic verbs" (Jacques 2013: 264). Expressive coinages tend to have a lilt of their own, but they also undergo a continuous attraction from the language's phonological system, tending to their integration into the language's phonological categories: "ideophones fill gaps in the distribution of segments within rhymes that have been caused by sound changes" (Jacques 2013: 267). A classical case of structural gap-filling is found in Vietnamese, where the /ɔŋ/ and /oŋ/ rhymes underwent an evolution whereby lip rounding was shuffled from the vowel to the consonant, as an added final labial closure: the result can be approximated as [ʌɔŋm͡] and [ɤoŋm͡]. The slots left empty by this phonetic evolution were filled by onomatopoeic coinages, and by loanwords (Haudricourt 1952; Henderson 1985: 21; Michaud 2004b: 143).

He Likun, a native speaker of Naxi, went through each cell in a table of possible combinations of initials and rhymes in the Pianding dialect of Naxi, determining (by introspection) whether the combination was attested, and in which words. The results were supplemented by examining a word list of about 3,000 words. He identified more than fifteen syllables that are only attested in onomatopoeic words (Michaud & He 2015).

Onomatopoeia are no less abundant in Na than in Naxi. But they are scarce in the set of transcribed narratives, as could be expected of relatively formal monologues. Other data collection methods, such as recording lively conversations, will be required to explore the wealth of expressive phenomena found in Yongning Na. Here are three examples.

(i) The noise of a shock between two hard objects, for instance the sound of an axe hitting a tree trunk ('Bang!'), is rendered as [bõ]. This syllable contravenes Na phonotactics, as nasal rhymes do not normally appear after stops.

(ii) The onomatopoeia for rumbling sounds, for instance the sound of heavy loads carried over a wooden floor, or the noise of lorries, is a prolonged [ʐ]. This sound is unlike the syllable /ʐɯ/. The latter is a full-fledged syllable, which surfaces with an apicalized vowel, as [ʐʐ̩]: the beginning of the syllable is more consonant-like, and the end more vowel-like. This is the reason that Chao Yuen-ren advocated the use of special symbols for apicalized sounds (see Table A.4). In his system, the syllable would be transcribed as /ʐɿ/. In the onomatopoeic form for rumbling sound, on the other hand, friction is sustained from beginning to end, hence transcription as [ʐʐʐ].

(iii) The hissing noise of water that comes in contact with red-hot metal or incandescent wood ('Pssshhh!') is [tʂʰɻ]. The combination of initial and rhyme used to transcribe this onomatopoeia is attested in some lexical items, but its phonetic realization does not exactly match that of the syllable /tʂʰɻ/ of lexical items. To reflect this special status, a possible transcription is [tʂʰɻɻ].

A.6.2 Phonostylistic observations

Expressivity is not limited to specific areas of the lexicon, such as ideophones. The "appeal function" of speech (Bühler 1934) is constantly present. The study of this function – examining how speakers shape their utterances with a view to evoking a certain response on the part of the hearer – features prominently in the programme of phonological research set out by Trubetzkoy (1969: 14) (original text: Trubetzkoy 1939), who coined the term 'phonostylistics' (for a review: Léon 1969). The term 'psycho-phonetics' used by Fónagy (1983) is less specific and therefore perhaps less appropriate, although it has the advantage of bringing out the considerable breadth of this strand of research: studying how phonetic details convey the speaker's communicative purposes. If intonation is "a symptom of how we feel about what we say and how you feel when you say it" (Bolinger 1989: 1), phonostylistics is part and parcel of intonation studies.

But this fascinating topic is best investigated through experimental phonetic study, whereas the present volume essentially focuses on lexical tone and morphotonology; the approved order of business consists in postponing the study of expressive phenomena until the stage when the more central facts of a language's linguistic structure have been clarified. Discussion is therefore deferred to experimental phonetic studies to be conducted in future. Let us simply mention two salient cases of modification of vowels and consonants for expressive effects in Na.

The first is *lip rounding and protrusion with demonstrative (proximal) value*. Pointing with the lips is used in Na culture. (For details about this gesture, see Enfield 2001.) When the lip-pointing gesture is used during speech, lip rounding and lip protrusion get superimposed onto the speech production gestures. For instance, the vowel /ɯ/, which has neither lip rounding nor lip protrusion, acquires lip protrusion when the phrase /tʂʰɯ˧-ɭɯ˧/ 'this one' (proximal demonstrative plus generic classifier) is said while lip-pointing to an object within sight.

The second case is that of *palatalization conveying a tender emotion*. The adjective /ɳɯ˧ɕi˩/ 'lovely' can be pronounced close to /ni˧ɕi˩/. This child-speech-like variant has iconic value: palatalization, narrowing the vocal tract, is associated with smallness (Fónagy 1983: 22–23). The realization of this cross-linguistic tendency is facilitated in Na by the tendency towards regressive vowel harmony (§A.2.7).

A.6.3 Expressive uses of reduplication

Reduplication serves various grammatical functions in Yongning Na, as also in Naxi (Hé Jírén & Jiāng Zhúyí 1985: 30–33). Despite having neatly grammaticalized uses, such as lending reciprocal value to verbs, it retains an expressive dimension, especially in its sporadic application to parts of speech other than verbs and nouns. This is reflected in irregular tone patterns – and thus this Appendix finally returns to the book's central topic: tone.

The phrase /qʰɑ˧ ɲi˧/ 'how many days' reduplicates to /qʰɑ˧ ɲi˧~qʰɑ˩ ɲi˩/ 'thus and so many days' (Healing.29; the context is the following: a priest of the Na religion diagnoses the number of days of rituals it will take to cure a person's disease). The tone pattern is not the same as in numeral-plus-determiner phrases, where the expected output would be M tone throughout the phrase (see Chapter 4).

The interrogative /ə˧tso˧/ reduplicates to /ə˧tso˧~ə˧tso˩/ (Dog.48). This is also an unexpected pattern.

The word /zo˧~zo˧-mv̩˧~mv̩˩/ 'thingummy' looks a lot like it could be the product of reduplication, perhaps as a playful manipulation over /zo˧mv̩˩/ 'child'. A more common word for 'thing' is /**tso˧tso#˩**/, which may originate in a reduplication of the nominalizer /tso/. Both of the above nouns combine into /tso˧~tso˧-zo˧~zo˧-mv̩˧~mv̩˩/ 'thingummies, stuff', suggesting that they are currently perceived as having a similar internal structure.

The reduplicated form /zɯ˧~zɯ˧/ for 'life, existence' is more frequent than monosyllabic /zɯ˧/, but both are in common use.

The /lv.lv/ portion in /bi˧-lv˧~lv˥/ 'snowflake' and /dzo˧-lv˧~lv˥/ 'hailstone' looks like a reduplicated form of the classifier for kernels, /lv˧/ (Lidz 2010: xxxiv).

The phrase /tɕʏ˧~tɕʏ˧/ 'right at the moment that...' looks clearly like a reduplicated form, but the *simplex* (non-reduplicated) form could not be recovered.

Several four-syllable onomatopoeic expressions of the form ABAB were observed, all of them with a L.L.M.M tone pattern: /tsɯ˩qwæ˩~tsɯ˧qwæ˧/ 'crashing sound, for instance the sound of timber falling down' (Housebuilding.243), /zɯ˩gɯ˩~zɯ˧gɯ˧/ 'boom!' (sound of heavy shock against a door: Tiger.15), /ʐɯ˩ʐʏ˩~ʐɯ˧ʐʏ˧/ 'sound of tearing leaves to pieces' (FoodShortage2.37), and /ɕi˩hwɑ˩~ɕi˧hwɑ˧/ and /ʐɯ˩ʁæ˩~ʐɯ˧ʁæ˧/, both describing the dizziness of a character under a dazzling moonlight (Reward.17 and Reward.68). These expressions do not have an identifiable *simplex* form.

Appendix B: Historical and ethnological perspectives

This Appendix aims to shed light on the "chains of societies" (*chaînes de sociétés*: Amselle 1990; see also Tryon 1998: 329–331) that shaped Na ethnicity.

B.1 The history of Yongning in outline

B.1.1 Prehistory

The Naxi scholars Guo Dalie 郭大烈 and He Zhiwu 和志武 believe that the name *Móshā* 摩沙 appearing in a fourth-century chronicle refers, beyond any doubt, to "the Naxi", a concept which they define as including the speakers of the Yongning Na language (Guō Dàliè & Hé Zhìwǔ 1994: 102-103).[1] They thus project today's ethnic identity into a period distant by a millenium and a half. They proceed to track this people through a sequence of changes in the Chinese terms used to designate it: the term *Móshā* 摩沙 used in the Jin dynasty is followed by *Móxiē* 磨些 in the Tang dynasty, then *Móxiē* 麽些, *Móxiē* 摩些, *Mósuō* 摩娑 and *Mòxiē* 末些 in the Yuan dynasty and later. As to the earlier origin of this people, they propose that it originates in an admixture of Qiang 羌 people to an earlier aboriginal population, left unnamed.

> In the formation of the Naxi people, the main component consisted of aboriginals, who blended with Qiang 羌 people, and later assimilated some other peoples at their periphery; conversely, in peripheral areas, some Naxi were assimilated into other peoples. (Guō Dàliè & Hé Zhìwǔ 1994: 24)[2]

A further association is suggested between the Naxi and the Shiguanzang 石棺葬 culture, attested during the first millenium BC over areas that match present-day

---

[1] "This is the first certain and unequivocal mention of the Naxi in recorded history." *Original text:* 这是纳西族在历史上首次明确无误的记录。

[2] *Original text:* 纳西族的形成以土著为主，融合了北来羌人，以后又同化了周围其他一些民族，边缘地区则是纳西族被其他民族同化。

Naxi and Na settlement (Guō Dàliè & Hé Zhìwǔ 1994: 66-67). The association of incoming Sino-Tibetan peoples with a certain type of graves raised hopes similar to the association of Kurgan pit-graves with the "Indo-Europeans" (Gimbutas 1977; Anthony 2007). The Shiguanzang culture was characterized by telltale stone graves, typically located on tablelands near sites of confluence between rivers, and short bronze swords of a type also attested in China's northern steppes. The absence of clear attestation of associated settlements is suggestive of a nomadic, pastoral people using metal, contrasting with the people indigenous to the area, whose abundant settlements are clearly indicative of a Neolithic agriculturalist culture transitioning into the Bronze Age. The nomadic people are identified with the Yi 夷 tribes of Chinese chronicles, considered as ancestor to the present-day Yi 彝 ethnic group as well as to the Na and Naxi (Guō Dàliè & Hé Zhìwǔ 1994: 64-66).

This fits the overall scenario of migration of speakers of Sino-Tibetan languages from the valley of the Yellow River, hypothesizing the Yangshao 仰韶 culture as the point of origin, c. 5000 BC to 3000 BC: one of the main reconstructed lines of migration is "south-west down the river valleys along the eastern edge of the Tibetan plateau through what has been called the *ethnic corridor*" (LaPolla 2001: 236; emphasis in original).

However, Guo Dalie & He Zhiwu's proposals raise issues such as to what extent archaeological evidence lends itself to pigeon-holing into such broad cultural types, and on what evidence the naming of peoples in Chinese chronicles was based. "Most excavation reports describing and interpreting burial material from Southwest China tend to associate grave type with archaeological culture; hence their urgent desire to arrive at a clear classification of burial types; however, (...) one cultural or ethnic group can be characterized by a number of different burial rituals, while other practices might be common across such boundaries" (Hein 2013: 31).

A 1,400-page study of cultural geography and interregional contacts in prehistoric times offers a more fine-grained exploration than was possible at the time of writing of Guo & He's *History*. Systematic study of the available evidence leads to distinguish no fewer than "four subregions showing fairly distinct archaeological assemblages, burial patterns, and subsistence systems, indicating that they were probably inhabited by different cultural groups" (Hein 2013: 588).

The first is that of the Anning river 安宁河 valley. Settlements from the third millenium BC yield relatively similar finds, including "coarse sand-tempered low fired red-brown ceramics (mainly large urns with finger-tip impressed appliqué strip below the rim, *bo* and *wan* bowls, vases, and a few lids and rarely spouts), accompanied by a few polished stone woodworking tools, arrowheads, and among the surface finds also perforated stone-knives" (Hein 2013: 559). The interpretation provided is that the communities in these settlements "probably shared similar cultural tradition and thus identified themselves as part of the same larger group" (Hein 2013: 589). One of the sites, Dayangdui 大洋堆, shows evidence of outside influence c. 2000 BC followed by assimilation:

> Both in ceramic quality and execution, the early Dayangdui ceramics (...) strongly resemble ceramics from sites in Gansu 甘肅 and Qinghai 青海 attributed to the Qijia 齊傢 culture. It is therefore not unlikely that the earth-pit graves at Dayangdui were built by a group of Qijia origin. This would suggest a date between 2200 and 1800 BC (...). (Hein 2013: 562)
>
> The middle and late Dayangdui assemblages do not contain any metal objects, however, and they show a mixture of both early Dayangdui and local Neolithic trades that indicate some form of acculturation of the group of immigrants. As no similar sites of clear foreign origin have been identified in the Anning River Valley, it is likely that migration of whole groups from the North occurred rarely. (Hein 2013: 594)

In this area, there appeared megalithic graves, which were then imitated in neighbouring areas.

> Graves with stone-construction parts are common throughout Southwest China, but megalithic graves seem to be unique to the Anning River Valley. The ceramics associated with these graves indicate a local origin of this burial tradition in the Xichang area. This impression is supported by the fact that all early megalithic graves (...) are located in Xichang, while the megalithic graves in other regions such as Dechang, Mianning, Puge, and Xide all date to Phase IIa at the earliest. Why this kind of burial mode arose is uncertain, but its overall development and spread is relatively clear: it started with small constructions used for a single instance of interment of several people, possibly in a secondary mode of burial. During or after the burial, communal drinking rituals took place which seem to have become more extensive over time, as the large number of drinking vessels both in later graves and related ceramic pits shows. (...)
>
> As far as daily life and mode of subsistence are concerned, the tool assemblages from megalithic graves and related settlement sites in the Anning River Valley show an agricultural and probably settled mode of living involving the planting of rice and probably other cereals, often supplemented by hunting, and in some places fishing. Only the sites in Puge show

a continued primary reliance on hunting. Metal seems to have mainly been used for personal ornaments and only secondarily weapons or tools. (Hein 2013: 595-599)

Archaeological remains from the Neolithic to Bronze Age collected in Yongning in 1958 are considered as connected to the megalithic graves (Hein 2013: 933); it is relevant to the history of Yongning that the spread of this burial mode is hypothesized to have taken place through cultural diffusion (presumably by persons who had participated in communal rituals and later reproduced these patterns in their home settlements) rather than through military conquest. It is for future excavations to verify the existence of this connection.

The second subregion is one of remote mountains, a harsh environment where "groups of different origins conducted different kinds of burial rituals next to each other, apparently respecting each other's monuments and even adopting part of each others' burial customs and objects. In this meeting place of different groups, cultural and other forms of identity (or at least their expression in the choice of grave form, burial mode, and object assemblage) thus seem to have been extremely fluid" (Hein 2013: 602).

The third subregion is one of fertile valleys, to the Southeast. The inhabitants of the earliest settlements "practiced a hunter-gatherer lifestyle, using caves and open-air sites either as seasonal or hunting camps rather than living in permanent settlements", later "practising incipient agriculture in a particularly congenial environment, living either in permanent or semi-permanent settlements" (Hein 2013: 605-606).

The fourth and final subregion is that of the high-altitude mountains, plateaus and valleys of the Southwest, a geographical area that includes Yongning.

> The people living in Yanyuan 盐源 and Ninglang 宁蒗 (...) belonged to a clearly separate cultural group for whom armed combat – sometimes combined with horseback-riding – was a central part of their life and identity. The emphasis on horse-riding, the interment of horse heads and sheep shoulder blades in graves and the overall metal assemblage (in particular the staff heads) seen at Yanyuan are essentially foreign to the research area. Pictorial evidence for horse-riding is known from the Dian 滇 culture context, but horse skulls or long bones have never been. The interment of horse bones is instead common in the Northern Steppe and the Ordos region, and elements of horse gear similar to those seen in Yanyuan have been reported from there as well. (...) It is therefore likely that the burying

group of the "warrior graves" in Yanyuan is of a northern origin, be it the upper Minjiang 岷江 or even the steppe. (Hein 2013: 616-618)

Yanyuan 盐源, a strategic area due to its abundance in rock salt, was conquered in 225 AD by the Chinese, who refer to the population that they defeated there as the "Mosha" 摩沙. Returning to the claim of Naxi historians Guo Dalie and He Zhiwu that these "Mosha" are the ancestors of today's Naxi, the hypothesis could be rephrased as follows: military defeat led clans of this population of warriors to withdraw West, conquering new territories that included Yongning, the banks of the Yangtze, and later the plain of Lijiang – which to this day remain their area of settlement.

But there does not seem to be decisive evidence linking the Yanyuan "warrior culture" to the Naxi rather than with other Sino-Tibetan groups, who later migrated into more distant areas in present-day Yunnan and Burma. A small piece of evidence on this topic comes from the path that ritual practitioners dictate to the soul of the deceased for its journey back to the ancestral homeland. These ritual journeys, which have been studied in many parts of East and Southeast Asia, can be shown to relate to historical migrations (Blackburn 2004; Gaenszle 2012; McKhann 2012). Different clans, in different Naxi areas, have different paths, but they all pass back through Yongning, where they join with the paths of the Na, and continue northward (Guō Dàliè & Hé Zhìwǔ 1994: 50-55). The identification of place names soon becomes difficult or impossible as the distance from Yongning increases. The identification of Minya Konka 贡嘎山 as the endpoint of the journey is not unlikely to be a later addition based on the prestige of this 7,500-meter high mountain, which is a mooring point for traditions and beliefs of various peoples of this part of the Himalayas. On the other hand, it may be relevant that the path for returning souls does not go through Yanyuan: there is thus no evidence of the group's forebears ever dwelling further East than the Yongning area. Of course, this piece of ethnological evidence does not carry considerable weight, as paths could have been modified at any point in the chain of oral transmission. But it suggests that the identification of the "Mosha" 摩沙 as direct ancestors of the Na and Naxi should not be taken as proven.

> Local oral narratives and scholarly writings which discuss the origins and migrations of hill peoples of the far eastern Himalaya often share the same propositions. Firstly, both types of sources tend to plot routes of migration between an assumed original homeland area or origin place and a present-day dwelling location; direction of movement and itineraries are of shared importance here. Second, they both claim identification of contemporary

populations with their purported ancestors from past times and distant places, with implicit and explicit claims of ethnic continuity. (Huber 2012: 83)

Whatever the exact relationship of the "Mosha" to the present-day Na and Naxi, conquest of the Yanyuan area by the Chinese in 225 AD was a major landmark. Ties with the heart of the Chinese empire were established, and never entirely cut off thereafter, even during periods when the Chinese central power was weakest, such as the following four centuries.

B.1.2 Empires and indigenous chieftains

In 794 AD, the Nanzhao 南诏 kingdom, with its centre on the fertile land around lake Erhai (洱海, currently a Bai-speaking area), conquered a broad area including Yongning as well as Lijiang 丽江. After the fall of Nanzhao in 902, the kingdom of Dali (大理国, 937–1253), likewise centered around lake Erhai, exercised control over Yongning and Lijiang, which remained ruled by indigenous chieftains.

At the outset of the Yuan dynasty, a new feudal chieftain (*tǔsī* 土司) was installed in Yongning by the Mongolians, who passed through Yongning on their way to attack the kingdom of Dali. A chapter of the imperial geography *Yuan Yi Tongzhi* 《元一统志》, dated 1286, contains a transcription of the name given to Yongning as 楼头 (present-day Mandarin reading: *lóutóu*). Using the system proposed by Coblin (2007), the name 楼头 reconstructs as *ləw dəw, which is clearly cognate with the present-day name of Yongning: Naxi /ly˧dy˩/ and Na /ɬi˧di˩/, discussed in Chapter 1, §1.1. It is likely that the authors, who provide a transcription for the names 'Lijiang' (样渠头) and 'Yongning' (楼头), based themselves on the pronunciation used in Lijiang, a more important centre than Yongning (being more densely populated and more accessible); in this sense, their transcription does not constitute a direct testimony about the language spoken in Yongning. Still, this constitutes a reasonable basis on which to hypothesize that there has been linguistic continuity in Yongning since the thirteenth century.

The Yongning chieftain who surrendered to the Mongolians in 1253 reported a genealogy of thirty-one generations since his ancestors conquered Yongning. Assuming linguistic continuity, Yongning Na would have been introduced into the area at a date in the range 500-650 AD, counting twenty to twenty-five years between generations. Of course, it may also be that an earlier form of the language was already spoken in and around Yongning earlier on, and the change in the ruling class c. 500-650 AD had no great linguistic impact.

Photo B.1: The Yongning monastery. The dialect under study is spoken in Alawa, a hamlet adjacent to the monastery. Autumn 2006.

The introduction of Tibetan Buddhism dates back to about the same period as the Mongolian conquest, with the missionary efforts of monks from Muli from 1276 onward (Guō Dàliè & Hé Zhìwǔ 1994: 389). In 1356, a Kagyupa (*bka' brgyud pa*) monastery was established; in 1556, a large Gelugpa (*dge-lugs pa*) monastery was established in Yongning (Tibetan name: *dgra med dgon pa*). Earlier cults remained, with a division of labour between the Buddhist monks and Na /dɑ˧pɤ˧/ ritual practitioners; but from that time, Buddhism became a dominant religion in Yongning. (At the time of Communist takeover, there were over 700 monks at the Yongning monastery.) This led to an increasing cultural distance between Yongning and the Lijiang plain. In Lijiang, no school of Tibetan Buddhism was able to establish and maintain a central role, as sudden turns followed one another in the course of an eventful religious history; the Naxi /to˧mbɑ˩/ tradition (with Tibetan Bön religion likely as a major influence) almost acquired the status of an official cult (Jackson 1979).

During the Yuan and Ming dynasties, incessant wars took place between the feudal chieftains of Yongning, Lijiang and Yanyuan (Guō Dàliè & Hé Zhìwǔ 1994: 430–431). In 1545, Yongning united with the neighbouring areas of the five *suǒ*

493

Photo B.2: Worshippers at the Yongning monastery. Autumn 2006.

所 (Zuosuo 左所, Yousuo 右所, Qiansuo 前所, Housuo 后所, and Zhongsuo 中所). The Yangtze river constituted the border between the territories of Yongning and Lijiang.

During the Qing dynasty (1644–1912), the Naxi chiefdom of Lijiang came under direct Chinese administration, whereas the feudal chieftain system was continued in Yongning due to the failure of attempts at military conquest of the Liangshan 凉山 Yi area, which constitutes the gateway to Yongning (Guō Dàliè & Hé Zhìwǔ 1994: 460). This led to further cultural differentiation between increasingly Sinicized Lijiang, on the one hand, and on the other hand peripheral areas such as Yongning. The Yongning feudal chieftains actively resisted Chinese migration into the area, prohibiting rice cultivation and establishing alliances with Yi chieftains for military support. This accelerated the pace at which Yi families settled in the Yanyuan and Yanbian areas, eventually replacing the earlier inhabitants – speakers of closely related language varieties, referred to as "Naxi dialects" by Guo Dalie & He Zhiwu (p. 461), which in this volume will be referred to as "Naish languages", as explained further below. The Laze, a small group of some four hundred people who migrated from Yanbian to their current location in Muli towards the end of the 19th century, are apparently among the speakers of Naish languages who left Yanbian as it became a dominantly Yi area (about the Laze language, see Huáng Bùfán 2009).

During the 1920s, Yongning became a link in commercial chains between Tibet, the Yi territories centered around Ninglang, Lijiang, and inland China. "This was the first time in history that the Moso had frequent visitors from the outside on a considerable scale. (...) this period was also the onset of the syphilis epidemic" (Shih & Jenike 2002), an epidemic curbed in the 1950s.[3]

B.1.3 The People's Republic of China

After the founding of the People's Republic of China in 1949, the central government made plans for the graduated integration of frontier areas along the outer margins of the dynastic power realm: those known during the Qing dynasty as 'vassal states' (*fānshǔ* 藩屬).

> Instead of 'mobilizing the masses' like in the Yunnan interior and elsewhere in China, land reform on the volatile frontier took the form of "uniting the feudal to fight feudalism" (*lianhe fengjian fan fengjian* 联合封建反封建), a scheme designed to win over the ethnic elite. The CCP united front work saw a revival of traditions in forms of pledging allegiance, conferring official titles, and the ritual of court audiences – those who cooperated were invited to serve in the new government and local dignitaries were taken to Beijing to have an audience with the CCP leaders. (Guo 2008: 43-44)

The Liangshan 凉山 Yi area, which constitutes the gateway to Yongning, proved a hard nut to crack. Armed rebellion broke out in 1956. By 1958, the large-scale 'pacification' operations were complete (Guo 2008: 228-231), and administration of the area by the Communist state began. Since then, reforms have been applied essentially top-down. The policy is that the majority group points the way forward, and leads minority groups towards modernity and eventual assimilation. In a study about the Drung, an ethnic group located in an even less accessible area of Yunnan, Gros (2014b) argues that these policies bring about a fundamental change from the earlier relationships of vassalage between local powers and the state(s). Feudal chieftains paid tributes, and received titles in return; the balance of this exchange – how much tribute was paid, and how much recognition and autonomy was granted in return – was weighed by both parties. By contrast, top-down state policies do not partake in a logic of exchange – *don et*

---

[3] This epidemic is alluded to by Goullart, who stayed in Lijiang in the 1940s: "The Nakhi men (...) knew well enough that most of the Liukhi [/lyɨ-ɕiɨ/, the Naxi term for the Na of Yongning] tribe was infected with venereal disease" (Chapter 3 of Goullart 1955).

contre-don, as emphasized in the classic study by Marcel Mauss (1990). Post-1956 events remain a highly sensitive topic. Mazard's observation about the Nusu (Yi) also applies to the Na:

> They generally treat the years from 1958 to around 1979 as a single historical period circumscribed by the collectivisation and de-collectivisation of their land. (...) Why do many of them (...) identify this period as a whole with the Cultural Revolution, even though they know and employ the term 'Great Leap Forward' as well?
>
> One reason may be that the CCP allows overt (though limited) criticism of the Cultural Revolution; not so the Great Leap Forward (or the Anti-Rightist Campaign). The Party has never denounced the Great Leap Forward as a mistake (...). The Cultural Revolution has its villains (the Gang of Four); so do the Civil War (the Guomindang) and the Second World War (the Japanese). Discussion of the Cultural Revolution is not easy, but it is possible. When Nusu elders allude to their suffering as occuring under the 'Cultural Revolution' (even if it took place in 1959), they lay claim to a permitted register of complaints. (Mazard 2011: 172)

Recent history (since the 1980s) will only be addressed indirectly here, through a discussion of ethnic classification (§B.2) and a review of studies about the impact of tourism on Na society (§B.3.5).

B.2 Ethnic classification: Naxi, Mongolian, Mosuo, or Na

Ethnic categorization as defined by the state "crafted the prism through which the modern Chinese state, and increasingly the people of China and the world at large, have come to view and understand non-Han Chinese identity" (Mullaney 2010: 5). This categorization, which stands on each individual's identity card (*shēnfen zhèng* 身份证, literally a 'certificate of identity'), has such a strong bearing on present-day identities that it warrants separate discussion.

> ... in the China of Chiang Kai-shek, the Nationalist regime vociferously argued that the country was home to only one people, "the Chinese people" (*Zhonghua minzu* 中華民族), and that the supposedly distinct groups of the republic were merely subvarieties of a common stock. At the same time, a counterdiscourse emerged among Chinese scholars in the newly formed disciplines of ethnology and linguistics, a discourse in which China was reimagined as home to many dozens of unique ethnic groups – a newly

imported concept also translated using the term *minzu* 民族. (Mullaney 2010: 2; see also Bulag 2012)

The first census of the People's Republic of China, in 1953-1954, recorded over four hundred different ethnic identities, more than half of which concerned the province of Yunnan, which borders on multi-ethnic areas on all sides (Vietnam, Laos, Burma, Tibet, Sichuan, Guizhou and Guangxi). Until recently, little information was available on the process of ethnic identification (*mínzú shíbié* 民族识别) whereby these were subsequently grouped into some fifty officially recognized nationalities (*mínzú* 民族). Sources that have become available in the past decade reveal how small teams of researchers from diverse social science backgrounds evaluated possibilities for groupings, and gave names to these groupings, against a tight agenda (less than six months). "In the years following the end of the project, cultural and scientific works rewrote the history of China and its diversity in an effort to promote a so-called "historic" and "ancestral" model of the 56 *minzu* components" (Frangville 2011). At first, this did not exclude some fine-tuning of the ethnic categories: adjustments were made in the 1960s and 1970s, including the recognition of two ethnic minorities that were absent from the 1954 classification. In 1987, however, it was clarified that no additional nationalities would be recognized, and the figure of fifty-six was final.

> ... the idea of China as a "unified, multinational country" (*tongyi de duominzu guojia* 统一的多民族国家) is a central, load-bearing concept within a wide and heterogeneous array of discourses and practices in the contemporary People's Republic. China is a plural singularity, this orthodoxy maintains, composed of exactly fifty-six ethnonational groups (*minzu* 民族): the Han ethnic majority, which constitutes over ninety percent of the population, and a long list of fifty-five minority nationalities who account for the rest. Wherever the question of diversity is raised, this same taxonomic orthodoxy is reproduced, forming a carefully monitored orchestra of remarkable reach and consistency: anthropology museums with the requisite fifty-six displays, "nationalities doll sets" with the requisite fifty-six figurines, book series with the requisite fifty-six "brief histories" of each group, Olympic ceremonies with fifty-six delightfully costumed children, and the list goes on. Fifty-six stars, fifty-six flowers, fifty six *minzu*, one China. (Mullaney 2010: 1)

The teams who conducted surveys for the national project of ethnic identification in 1953-1954 operated separately in each province, and decisions were also made province by province. The Na living in Yunnan were considered as part of the Naxi minority. Those living in Sichuan were classified as Mongolian; this surprising choice was no doubt influenced by the powerful ring which the name 'Mongolian' retains in the area since the Mongolian army's impressive crossing of the Himalayas (passing through Yongning) and victory over the Song dynasty.

> Due to historical tensions between the Na and the Naxi, when the Sichuan Na learned that they would be classified as Naxi in the early 1950s, they protested by taking over the county government offices. As the federal government limits recognition to the fifty-six ethnicities, local officials were perplexed as to what to do, and a face-saving compromise was established such that the Sichuan Na could be classified as Mongolian, on the basis that the Mongols had invaded the area seven hundred years previously, and perhaps the Na were descendants of these Mongols. Although this designation is within historical memory, the Na in Sichuan have clearly adopted their designation as Mongolian, and colorful plastic plaques of Genghis Khan hang prominently on the walls in homes. (Lidz 2010: 9)

The claim of Mongolian descent apparently predates the systematic process of "ethnic identification" carried out by the People's Republic of China.

> Moso chiefs in both Yunnan and Sichuan Provinces claimed that they were descendants of the Mongols. According to Joseph Rock, who personally befriended key members of the Yongning chief's family (...), the general superintendent (*zongguan* 總管) of Yongning at that time "was proud of his Mongol origin, for he was a descendant of one of the Mongol officers left by Kublai Khan in Yung-ning to govern that territory" (Rock 1947: 359). Abundant historical records indicate that it was commonplace for the Mongolian conquerors to leave troops of Mongol or non-Mongol ethnic background to govern the newly subjugated territories. (...) The problem is that in all cases other than the Moso chief's, there is evidence – such as records on stelae, tombs and tombstones (some inscribed in Mongolian), records of genealogy, language or vocabulary, and legends in one form or another – to substantiate the claim. The Moso aristocrats, however, had nothing to support their claim of Mongol ancestry. (Shih 2010: 40-41)

Shih suggests that the new chieftain was "a Xifan [Pumi] officer in the Mongol troops left by Kublai Khan to rule Yongning" (Shih 2010: 51). One piece of evidence that he adduces is the identification of the Yongning chieftain's ethnicity as

"Xifan" 西番 in Ming-dynasty chronicles. The interpretation of the term "Xifan" as referring specifically to the Pumi is not self-evident, however: the label may have been used in a broad sense that included speakers of the language ancestor to Yongning Na. To this day, the Namuyi of Muli, who are speakers of a Naic language (about which see Chapter 1, §1.1.2.2), are included among the "Xifan" 西番, a cover term for various non-Tibetan groups. Another piece of evidence is ethnographic: at the succession of the Yongning chieftain, the Pumi would perform a ritual akin to /sɯ˧kʰɯ˩/, the ritual associated to the giving of a household member (typically, the giving of a bride); this is consistent with Shih's hypothesis that their ethnic group was the donor of the Yongning chieftain himself. Shih states his interpretation as follows:

> In the case of *sike* [phonetic transcription: /sɯ˧kʰɯ˩/], a household member was given to become a particular person's wife in another household. Because the status of wife necessarily ended with the life of the woman in question, *sike* was a one-time ritual between the two families concerned. In the succession ritual, however, as the historical records suggest, when a member of the Pumi was given to become the chieftain of Yongning, a territory dominated by the Moso, the status of chieftaincy was perpetual, as was the ritual of interrogation. In both cases, the rituals were performed to dramatize a reassertion of the unbreakable blood bond between the deceased and her or his natal family. (Shih 2010: 48)

Inclusion in the Mongolian minority proved a comfortable fiction: it paradoxically granted the Na of Sichuan a place of their own within the landscape of the recognized ethnic groups of Sichuan. Initially the 'Mongolian' label was taken very seriously and attempts were made to teach the Mongolian script to Naish speakers of Sichuan, with predictably poor results. The initial ethnic identification was not modified since, because of a national policy to keep the Pandora's box of ethnic labels closed. Their fictitious cousins of Mongolia do not appear to have found a subject for quarrel in the term 'Mongolian' being applied to this small group in Sichuan; and the label prevented the Na from being pooled together with closer neighbours, such as the Naxi. By contrast, the inclusion of the Na of Yunnan among the Naxi made them a minority within a minority, restricting the power and number of their representatives at various institutional levels.

In view of the historical outline summarized in §B.1, it is not difficult to understand why the Na would tend to think of themselves as distinct from the

Naxi despite the conspicuous similarities between their respective languages. Resentment about inclusion in the Naxi minority led to a search for recognition as a distinct group. From this vantage point, the endonym /na˩/ is less than ideal: /na˩/, presumed to mean 'black, dark', is also found in the endonym of the Naxi: /na˩ɕi˧/, where /ɕi˧/ means 'person, human being'. The quasi-identity of endonyms might cast doubt on the legitimacy of a sharp separation. Instead, the Na of Yunnan came to favour the exonym 'Mosuo' (*mósuō* 摩梭),[4] a name formerly used in the Chinese records, which was officially replaced after 1949 by 'Naxi' (*nàxī* 纳西).[5]

Reviving the demised term 'Mosuo' to refer to the Na of the Yongning area is a felicitous choice to substantiate claims to recognition as a group separate from the Naxi, since the words 'Mosuo' and 'Naxi' are clearly distinct from each other phonetically. Moreover, the term 'Mosuo' presents the twofold advantage of being a term of great antiquity, having been used in the Chinese chronicles since the first millenium AD, and of having fallen into disuse in the middle of the 20th century, which lends it a quaint charm and a touch of mystery. In 1990, following heated protest against the label 'Naxi', the 'Mosuo' of Yunnan were granted recognition at the provincial level as a separate subgroup within the Naxi minority. This label currently seems set to become the standard in Sichuan as well (Lǐ Dázhū 2015: 10-11). La Mingying 喇明英, a member of the Sichuan Academy of Social Sciences who identifies herself through the official label 'Mongolian' but expresses a preference for the label 'Na', reports that self-identification as 'Mosuo' is gaining ground among the younger generations on the Sichuan side of the designated 'Mosuo' tourist area.

> Disagreement among the Na about names [ethnonyms] is a cause for disputes; people sometimes even come to blows. Acknowledging one's ethnic identity, and having a sense of belonging to the community, constitute the most basic and essential factors in "ethnic identification". The multiplication of ethnic denominations for the Na of the Lake Lugu area generates great perplexity about their ethnic identity, to the point of causing preju-

---

[4] Alternative transcriptions of this name are shown in Table 1.1. As mentioned above, this exonym's origin is unclear. Chavannes (1912: 132) cites Chinese chronicles as indicating that the Mo-so tribe was formed during the Nanzhao period out of two distinct elements, the Mo and the So.

[5] Thus, the dictionary of pictograms originally published by Li Lin-ts'an 李霖灿, Chang K'un 张琨 and Ho Ts'ai 和才 as *Dictionary of Mo-So hieroglyphics* (1953) was reprinted in 2001 on the mainland under the title *Dictionary of Naxi pictograms*; all occurrences of *Móxiē* 麼些 in the book were replaced by *Nàxī* 纳西.

dice to their sense of belonging to a community and to their ethnic cohesion. (Lā Míngyīng 2015: 53)[6]

Before Communist takeover, there were three hereditary castes among the Na of Yongning: the family of the chieftain, /sɯ˩pʰi˩/, constituted the nobility, as distinct from commoners, /dze˩kʰʶ˧/, who were the majority group (about 640 families in the late 1950s); finally, a smaller group (280 families in the late 1950s) were serfs, /wʶ˧/. Historically, when outsiders joined the community – as war captives, or as immigrants from areas near and far –, they would be integrated to the serf caste, which also accommodated commoners stripped of their rank as a punishment for rebellion (Liú Lóngchū 1981). Ethnic identity as assigned by the administration (whether as 'Naxi' or 'Mongolian') lay flat earlier differences between castes; it also went along with the end of the integration of newcomers into Na society. The steady influx of settlers into Yongning, recorded in the successive editions of the county Annals (*xiànzhì* 县志; the entire collection bears the name 《中华人民共和国地方志丛书》, "Collection of local chronicles of the People's Republic of China"), results in cohabitation of persons whose official identities remain distinct, some of them "Han", others "Mosuo", "Naxi", "Pumi", "Yi" and so on, in keeping with the ideology of a multi-ethnic and unified China.

B.3 Anthropological research: The fascination of the Na's kinship system and family structure

The rich morphotonology of the Na language, which forms the central topic of this book, apparently went unnoticed until the early 21st century. On the other hand, peculiarities of the Na kinship system and family structure have long been famous well beyond the circles of specialized ethnologists. Here is an excerpt from the highly exoticized account provided by Peter Goullart, a Russian-born traveller, explorer and author who lived among the Naxi in Lijiang from 1942 to 1949, the last years of the period of intense caravan traffic (1920s to 1940s).

> The arrival of the members of a certain matriarchic tribe, living about seven days by caravan north of Likiang, always created a furore in Likiang. Whenever these men and women passed through the market or Main Street on their shopping expeditions, there was indignant whispering, giggling and

---

[6] *Original text*: 因称呼的分歧，纳人内部时有争论甚至打架的情况发生。对民族身份的承认和群体归属感是"民族认同"最基本的要素。泸沽湖地区纳人族称的多元化在很大程度上对其民族身份的认同造成很大的困惑，甚至影响了纳人的群体归属感和民族凝聚力。

squeals of outraged modesty on the part of Likiang women and girls, and salacious remarks from men. They were the inhabitants of the Yungning duchies across the Yangtze at the apex of the great bend. The Nakhi [nɑ˧-çi˧] called them Liukhi [ly˧-çi˧] and they called themselves Hlihin [ɬi˧-hĩ˧]. The structure of their society was entirely matriarchal. The property passed from mother to daughter. Each woman had several husbands and the children always cried, 'We have mama but no papa.' The mother's husbands were addressed as uncles and a husband was allowed to stay on only as long as he pleased the woman, and if he didn't, could be thrown out without much ceremony. The Yungning country was a land of free love, and all efforts of the Liukhi women were concentrated on enticing more lovers in addition to their husbands. Whenever a Tibetan caravan or other strangers were passing Yungning, these ladies went into a huddle and secretly decided where each man should stay. The lady then commanded her husbands to disappear and not to reappear until called. She and her daughters prepared a feast and danced for the guest. Afterwards the older lady bade him to make a choice between ripe experience and foolish youth. (...)

With their lips heavily rouged and eyes painted, they walked slowly, or rather undulated, through the streets, swaying their hips, smiling and casting an amorous eye on this man or that. That alone was enough to incense the less sophisticated Nakhi women. But when they walked slowly along hanging on the neck of a husband or a lover, and being held by the waist, this was too much for even the brazen Nakhi women, who spat or giggled nervously. (Goullart 1955: Chapter 3)

This sample of travellers' reports about "a land of free love" suffices to explain why the Na exert an enduring fascination on the general public. The present review does not attempt extensive coverage of the considerable anthropological, ethno-historical and sociological literature about the Na. Its aim is to convey a sense of the development of the field, of the historical evolution of approaches and viewpoints, and of the consequences in terms of local people's perception of social scientists who come to Yongning for fieldwork.

B.3.1 A major source of information: Surveys conducted in the 1960s

The in-depth research report based on sociological surveys conducted in the 1960s (Yúnnánshěng biānjízǔ 1986) constitutes a major resource for the study of Na society. The results of the survey are organized by village, and bring out subtle differences among villages and among individual households. Most later scholarship builds on the data reported in the three volumes of this report – close to one thousand pages in total.

The survey clarifies that, until the 1950s, the typical family structure in the Yongning Plain was matrilinear, with lifelong matrilocal residence. In non-technical terms, this means that brothers and sisters lived all their lives in their mother's house, together with their relatives on the mother's side: cousins, aunts and uncles, and grandmother and her brothers and sisters.

This situation bears some resemblance to that found among the Minangkabau (Indonesia) as described by Hadler (2008) and the Nayar (India) as described by Fuller (1976).

> Men marry into an extended family, but remain attached to their mothers' houses. They return to that house daily to work the fields, convalesce there in times of sickness, and are eventually buried in the maternal family graveyard. A husband and father is an evanescent figure. In the words of a Minangkabau aphorism, "The *urang sumando* is like a horsefly on the tail of a buffalo, or like ashes on a burned tree trunk. [When a little wind blows, it is gone.]" (...) Minangkabau culture has been termed matrifocal because, although men can be part of the lives of their wives and children, it is mother-centeredness that grounds the family. (Hadler 2008: 6)

Among the Nayar of India, the husband resides with his sister and visits his wife at night (Fuller 1976); in pre-1956 Na society, lovers met discreetly at the woman's home. Among the Na, as among the Minangkabau and the Nayar, the answer to the "matrilineal puzzle" (Richards 1950) – the potential conflict in authority between father and maternal uncle – was that authority rests with the uncle. Fathers did not have a prominent social role; men have commitments to their sisters' children, not to their own, who grow up in another household. "According to tradition, it is the *mamak* (maternal uncle) who provides male authority in the lives of children" (Hadler 2008: 6); likewise, among the Na, the male figure of authority was the maternal uncle, as evidenced by proverbs such as (1).

(1) mv̩˧ʁo˥ | dze˩-hĩ˩-dʑo˥, | kɤ˩-nɑ˧mi˧; | di˧qo˧ se˧-dʑo˩, | ə˧v̩˧˥.

mv̩˧ʁo˥$	dze˩$_a$	-hĩ˥	-dʑo˥	kɤ˩-nɑ˧mi˧	di˧qo˧	se˥	-dʑo˥
heavens	to_fly	NMLZ	TOP	eagle	plain	to_walk	TOP

ə˧v̩˧˥
maternal_uncle

'As the Eagle is greatest of all that fly in the sky, so the Uncle is greatest of all that walk the earth.'

A difference is that while the Minangkabau have (flimsy) marriage ties, and the Nayar practise marriage, this institution was marginal among the Na of the Yongning plain before the post-1956 social upheaval. The chieftains, being in contact with their patrilinear Chinese, Tibetan, Naxi or Pumi peers, had wives, at least as a diplomatic façade. Among commoners, on the other hand, there was no marital exchange between clans or families, and no dowry or brideprice.

The method of data collection used in the 1960s survey bears the stamp of the historical context: a time when the young People's Republic of China took stock of its new Western possessions. Clearly, unconditional obedience to instructions was expected from the surveyed human subjects. It seems that the objective was reached, and that, for the sake of the survey, the subjects provided candid, detailed statements about their family history and sentimental life story. The fact that all the data was eventually published (and reprinted in 2009), including the real names of the people who entrusted information on their private lives to the visiting ethnographers, is at variance with present-day concerns about the privacy of personal information (as set out in anthropology handbooks, e.g. Fluehr-Lobban 2014, which contains a reproduction of the Code of Ethics of the American Anthropological Association). On the other hand, the social structures described in the survey have undergone such changes since then that the survey report is simply irreplaceable.[7] To venture a comparison with the history of exploratory techniques used in experimental phonetics, the results of the 1960s survey can be likened to the X-ray data collected from the 1930s to the 1970s. This was the window of time between the technical advances that made it possible to carry out cineradiography and the realization that exposure to the high doses of radiation involved carried serious health risks for the person being filmed. This heritage data still constitutes a precious resource to study the sounds of the world's languages (Fant 1960; Leroy & Paris 1974; Bothorel et al. 1986; Bouarourou et al. 2008).

---

[7] A consultant told me in 2008 that during the Cultural Revolution, cereal rations in Yongning were made conditional to the possession of a marriage certificate. Beyond this report, indicative of a perception of a historical divide, an anthropologist would want to obtain fuller details, verifying this information with other consultants, and investigating how the policies were implemented in the various villages and how the local society responded. "The Cultural Revolution" is sometimes used as a cover term because (as mentioned at the end of §B.1) the ruling party allows some criticism of the Cultural Revolution, and not of other episodes such as the Great Leap Forward (Mazard 2011: 172).

B.3.2 Marxist interpretation: Na family structure as a confirmation of Morgan's theory

In the early 1980s, several researchers involved in the survey published books based on these materials (Zhān Chéngxù et al. 1980; Yán Rǔxián & Sòng Zhàolín 1984), before the publication of the original report. These authors adhered to an evolutionary perspective, which led them to the conclusion that Na society was a "living fossil" (huóhuà shí 活化石), a remnant of a matriarcal society that existed prior to patriarchy, constituting decisive proof of the reality of Lewis Henry Morgan's theory (1877), as embraced by Marx: that family structure evolved from the consanguine family via the matrilineal clan to the patrilineal nuclear family.

From the point of view of anthropological theory, Na family structure was taken as confirmation of an established theory (itself a "living fossil": Morgan's theory had been thoroughly discredited in the West for many decades, and only survived in China by the power of dogma), so that, in effect, the fresh data did not make a significant contribution to progress in the field. This may be likened to interpretations given of sunspots (black patches on the surface of the Sun): in the 9th century AD, they were interpreted as planetary transits obscuring part of the Sun (Wilson 1917: 93); in the 17th century, they were taken as evidence of the sun's decay, confirming the pessimistic vision of the world's gradual decadence, as expressed in the works of Walter Raleigh and Thomas Browne. "Scientific evidence can only answer the questions that scientists think fit to ask" (Hampson 1968: 21).

To preview a topic which will be taken up below, the view of Na society as a "living fossil", popularized by advertisements for the Na area as a tourist destination, created no small amount of resentment on the part of the Na (this is reported e.g. by Shih 2010: 132).

B.3.3 Bringing Na family structure to the attention of Western anthropologists: Cai Hua's *A society without fathers or husbands*

While Na society got straightforwardly pigeonholed into one of the evolutionary stages postulated by Marxist-Leninist anthropology (as the earliest stage: matriarchy), it did not conform to postwar Western models of the anthropology of kinship. Browsing through the first pages of Murdock's classic study of family structure (1949: 1–3), it is clear that the Na family does not fit within the typology. Murdock's typology considers the "first and most basic" type of family organization to be the nuclear family ("a married man and woman with their offspring"), of which the other two types of families acknowledged in his typology constitute "combinations": the polygamous family "consists of two or more nuclear families affiliated by plural marriages", and the extended family "consists of two or more nuclear families affiliated through an extension of the parent-child relationship rather than of the husband-wife relationship, i.e., by joining the nuclear family of a married adult to that of his parents" (p. 2). One can imagine the excitement with which a researcher working in Western anthropological circles would pursue the theoretical implications of the observations made in Yongning, which contradict two of Murdock's assumptions: the universality of marriage, and the universality of the nuclear family.

Such was the perspective adopted by Cai Hua 蔡华, a Yunnan-born anthropologist who wrote a Ph.D. at the *École des hautes études en sciences sociales* in Paris with Kristofer Schipper, Françoise Héritier and Olivier Herrenschmidt as advisors. Cai Hua's *Une société sans père ni mari: les Na de Chine* (A society without fathers or husbands: the Na of China) (Cai 1997) was the first book to present a study of Na family structure to a non-Chinese-reading audience. The title announces the author's vantage point: presenting the Na as a counterexample to generalizations that previously seemed firmly established. Cai Hua's book aims to draw the attention of the international community of anthropologists to a social structure that calls into question tenets of the anthropology of kinship, such as the presumed universality of marriage. Its diffusion was facilitated by an English translation (Cai 2001). As a sample of the enthusiastic response to the dizzying blend of theoretical challenges and juicy stories contained in the book, an article in the *New York Review of Books* (Geertz 2001) points out challenges to Lévi-Strauss's views on kinship (Lévi-Strauss 1949) and also provides a racy summary of the titillating part of the story:

> Sexual intercourse takes place between casual, opportunistic lovers, who develop no broader, more enduring relations to one another. The man "visits," usually furtively, the woman at her home in the middle of the night as impulse and opportunity appear, which they do with great regularity. Almost everyone of either sex has multiple partners, serially or simultaneously; simultaneously usually two or three, serially as many as a hundred

or two. There are no nuclear families, no in-laws, no stepchildren. (Geertz 2001)[8]

From the vantage point of a Western audience, an additional bonus is that the study's author is Chinese. The workings of a society "without fathers or husbands" are all the more fascinating as they are narrated by an anthropologist whose background is a patriarchal and marriage-centered culture that takes a disparaging view of Na culture as "backward". In examining Na society, Cai Hua is careful to distance himself from former colleagues such as Yan Ruxian, denouncing the evolutionary bias in their writings. This earns him the somewhat patronizing praise of colleagues who emphasize the author's scientific achievement: freeing himself from two preconceptions that could have biased his research, namely Marxist ideology and Chinese prejudice against forms of kinship and sexuality that are remote from Chinese culture (e.g. Cartier & Elisseeff 1998: 57–58).[9] The book gained international fame, and received a response from Claude Lévi-Strauss (Lévi-Strauss 2004).

The less positive side of the success story is that, in his desire to emphasize the scoop – that Na society presents radical challenges to the anthropology of kinship –, Cai Hua stretches the evidence. A reader who had access to the Chinese literature examined Cai's argument in detail and concluded that, "in setting out to

---

[8] The same two aspects – scientific significance and sexual fascination – recur in reviews of the book. Here is another example: "le propos a de quoi mettre sens dessus dessous la théorie anthropologique qui fait reposer le principe même des sociétés humaines sur l'alliance de mariage. Mais la lecture de ce livre à la fois savant et ingénu est aussi recommandée à ceux que ce problème laisse froids : le tableau des mœurs libertines des Na est digne des plus joyeux fantasmes qui circulaient en Europe dans les années 70" (Journet 1998).

[9] "Narrating the transformations imposed on Na society represents a significant achievement in itself on the part of a Han ethnologist, especially if he proves capable of standing back from Marxist ideology and from specifically Chinese prejudice about patterns of kinship and sexuality that are very distant from his own culture. Cai Hua, a young Yunnanese researcher who came over to Paris to complement his training, therefore deserves to be congratulated for achieving this difficult task, literally applying a *tabula rasa* approach to cast aside most of the prejudices that could have hampered his research." *Original text:* Relater (...) les transformations imposées à la société Na représentait en soi une contribution fort honorable de la part d'un ethnologue Han, surtout s'il se montrait capable de prendre ses distances par rapport à l'idéologie marxiste et aux préjugés proprement chinois relatifs à des formes de parenté et de sexualité très éloignées de sa culture. On saura donc tout particulièrement gré à Cai Hua, un jeune chercheur yunnanais venu à Paris compléter sa formation (...), d'avoir réussi ce difficile exercice en faisant littéralement table rase de la plupart des préjugés qui auraient pu handicaper sa recherche.

make certain points, Cai picks his unreferred cases rather selectively and ignores the cases which do not fit his argument" (Wellens 2003). The book is selective in its presentation of the data, in order to bring out forcefully the uniqueness of this society, represented as "the 'other' of the Han Chinese: a society free of the constrictions of Confucian morality" (Wellens 2003: 147).

Cai Hua became a professor in anthropology at Peking University, where he continued to focus on the anthropology of kinship. But he did not publish a Chinese version of his book. One possible reason for this choice is that he was aware that the book, tailored for a Western audience, would encounter a more critical reception on the part of scholars who have access to the ethnographic reports, and now to linguistic data as well. To call Yongning Na society "a society without fathers or husbands" is to stretch the point. The notion of 'father' is by no means absent from the language: the word /ə˧da˥/[10] unambiguously means 'father'. If one wishes to formulate the key observations by contrast with Chinese marriage customs, a more adequate description is *bù qǔ bú jià* 不娶不嫁: men do not *take* a wife into their family (*qǔ* 娶), and women do not *leave* their family to join their partner's (*jià* 嫁).

In his later foreign-languages publications, Cai Hua continued to lend Na society a prominent position in the typology of kinship structures. In a book published in French (Cai 2008), the author discusses four family structures: Chinese; Na; French; and Samo (Burkina Faso), which was studied by Cai's Ph.D. advisor Françoise Héritier. These four societies are neatly arranged into a system of binary oppositions. The first two are described as monolateral, and the latter two as bilateral; the Chinese family as masculine, and Na as feminine. French is bilateral-symmetrical, and Samo bilateral-asymmetrical. The publisher's blurb emphasizes that the author advances "new epistemological proposals which call into question a certain Western rationalism and would also be useful, it seems, to other human and social sciences".[11] The different orientations of the author's anthropological publications in Chinese and in French provide an illuminating example of the enduring divide between 'Western' and 'Chinese' scholarship, the former apparently encouraging epistemological boldness – sometimes at the expense of breadth and depth of typological surveys, and of precision in detail.

---

[10] The combination ˥ in this word's transcription refers to one of the lexical tone categories of Yongning Na: see Chapter 2, §2.3.2.

[11] *Original text*: ... de nouvelles propositions épistémologiques qui remettent en question un certain rationalisme occidental et seraient utiles, selon toute apparence, aux autres sciences humaines et sociales.

B.3.4 Beyond the initial scoop: Studies of Na society in comparative perspective

The initial scoop – encountering a society with uncommon family structure – opens into a wealth of issues for anthropologists to explore. Two important Ph.D. dissertations about the Na were completed in 1993: those of Shih Chuan-kang (1993) and Weng Naiqun (1993). These were followed in 1995 by Emily Chao's, which has a stronger focus on the Naxi. A Chinese translation of Shih's dissertation was published in 2008, and an enlarged English edition, with additional fieldwork results, in 2010. These studies provide an in-depth analysis of Na society, on the basis of new fieldwork data.

To venture a critical note about Shih Chuan-kang's publications, his conclusions on linguistic issues are sometimes hasty, as when accepting the folk etymology of the place name 'Yongning' (discussed in Chapter 1, §1.1). One may likewise entertain reasonable doubt about Shih Chuan-kang's interpretation of the exonym 'Mosuo' found in Chinese chronicles:

> In the summer of 2001, I made another field trip to Yongning under the auspices of the National Science Foundation. While being jolted around in a Mitsubishi SUV on the way from Lijiang to Yongning, I was ruminating yet again over the candidate words for which the term *Mosuo* and its variants might have been transliterated. When I was mulling over the phrase *mosi*, the legend about the English word *kangaroo* suddenly occurred to me.
>
> In the 1770s, the story goes, when Captain Cook and his explorers in Australia saw a large quadruped hopping animal they had never seen in Europe, they asked: "What is the name of this animal?" "Kangaroo," the aborigines replied. The British assumed this must be the name of the animal and introduced the word into the English vocabulary as such. It turned out, according to the legend, that the word was not the name of the animal. Rather it meant "I don't understand."
>
> Inspired by this legend, I wondered how I could have missed the point for so long. In both the Naxi and Naru [i.e. Na] languages, *mosi* means "not know," which can be used as an independent phrase to answer a question. The pronunciation of this phrase is identical in both languages. I had asked this phrase in the field countless times but never thought it was the answer to my long-standing question.
>
> Neither the historical accuracy of the kangaroo legend nor the exact meaning of the word *kangaroo* in the aboriginal language bear any direct

relevance to the origin of the word in question. Rather, the significance of this legend is that it vividly depicts a conceivable scenario in which cultural and linguistic misunderstandings could arise during the initial contact of different cultures. It is not difficult to envision another such scenario: One of the first Chinese speakers to get in touch with the group under consideration asked: "Who are you?" Responding to a language that he did not understand, the person said: "*Mosi*," meaning "I don't know (what you are talking about)." The Chinese speaker just took it as an answer to his question and recorded or repeated this "name of the people" in the closest sounds in his own language. (Shih 2010: 25–26)

"Kangaroo legend" is an apt label. 'Kangaroo' does not mean 'I don't know': it is the name of a species of kangaroo in Guugu Yimidhirr, a language of the Pama-Nyungan family. To relate the earliest Chinese names for the Na to /mɤ˧-sɯ˩/ '[I] don't know' is to build another legend in blissful ignorance of linguistic methods. Shih compares present-day Southwestern Mandarin pronunciations with present-day Na (Shih 2010: 26–27), but etymological research at such historical depth should be based on reconstructed forms. The earliest Chinese term, 摩沙, goes back to the Jin dynasty (265–420 AD). Reconstructions of Old Chinese suggest that the realization of 沙 may have been close to *sræ or *sræj (Baxter 2000). This does not match up well with reconstructions proposed to date for the proto-Naish stage: 'to know' is reconstructed as *si (Jacques & Michaud 2011).

To the linguist, these slight shortcomings in linguistic aspects of an anthropologist's publications serve as a word to the wise: great care should be exercised to avoid oversimplifications in areas other than one's own. In the same way as a lack of precision in linguistic analyses on the part of anthropologists casts the shadow of a doubt on their anthropological conclusions, linguists run a risk of missing linguistic insights by taking a simplistic view of social phenomena, and paying insufficient attention to the social nature of language.

On historical topics, a salient aspect of Shih's study is the author's relentless insistence that the Naxi and Na are distinct peoples. He proposes a distinct ancestry for the two groups, tracing the one back to the tribes referred to as *Máoniúzhǒng* 牦牛种 in Han-dynasty Chinese chronicles, and the other to the *Rǎnmáng* 冉駹 of Chinese chronicles. Identifications between present-day ethnic minorities and names given to "barbarian" tribes in early Chinese writings are the subject of sustained debate in Chinese scholarship. These identifications are highly speculative, however (Gros 2014a). Shih's statement that "patrilineal descent has been the norm for thousands of years" among the Naxi's forebears is not supported by convincing evidence. One may have an impression that the author, who expresses great sympathy for Na society throughout his study (witness the 2010 title *Quest for Harmony*), adopts his consultants' viewpoint that they are clearly distinct from the Naxi, reifies this perceived difference as a binary opposition between Na and Naxi as ethnic categories, and projects this opposition into the indefinite past.

> Shih is so preoccupied with establishing the exceptionality of the Moso that he has rather too hastily dismissed the comparative potential of similar practices found in some regions bordering Tibet. As a matter of fact, one of the merits of the book is that it presents a clear ethnography on the basis of which regional comparisons could be drawn, while fuelling the debate within anthropology of kinship in general. (Gros 2011)[12]

An unfortunate consequence of Shih Chuan-kang's entrenched belief in the great historical depth of the Na-vs.-Naxi divide is that it leads him to dismiss the studies of researchers who hypothesize that the Na and Naxi share a common ancestry, and who put forward a historical synopsis of their gradual divergence. An extreme version of this hypothesis is explored by Jackson (1979: 33–46), who points out "strong resemblances with regard to their kinship patterns in particular", and suggests that the main differences between Naxi and Na societies only have a time depth of about three centuries: in his view, they mostly result from the in-depth Sinicization of Naxi culture since the 18th century. Shih vigorously rejects Jackson's theses, and the 2010 edition of his book does not mention Christine Mathieu's (2003) study, *A history and anthropological study of the ancient kingdoms of the Sino-Tibetan borderland – Naxi and Mosuo*, which explicitly sets out to explore the historical relationship between the Na and Naxi.

Admittedly, Jackson's study calls for a thorough revision in light of more recent documentation. It must be remembered that much larger amounts of material are now available than at the time of Jackson's study; this goes a long way towards explaining occasional mistakes, such as the interpretation of the Naxi

---

[12] *Original text*: préoccupé d'établir l'exceptionnalité du cas Moso, l'auteur écarte un peu trop rapidement l'intérêt comparatif de cas assez similaires relevés dans certaines régions voisines de la bordure sino-tibétaine. C'est pourtant un des mérites de son ouvrage que de nous livrer une ethnographie claire à même de servir à une entreprise comparative régionale, comme d'alimenter le débat au sein de l'anthropologie de la parenté plus généralement.

name of the Na, /ly˩-ɕi˩/ (romanized as *Lü-khi*), as "the people of Lü, the Chinese name for the area" (p. 36), when it actually means 'the people of the Centre', and is an exact parallel (cognate) to the Na endonym /ɬi˩-hĩ˩/.[13] Also, some formulations are deliberately provocative: Jackson likes to sketch Naxi history in broad strokes, emphasizing decisive junctures such as the year "1723 A.D. when the Mu family was ignominiously dismissed and the area was 'nationalized' by the Chinese" (p. 35). During that year, Lijiang was placed under direct Chinese rule and the Mu 木 family of feudal chieftains who had ruled the area since the Yuan dynasty ceased to exercise real control. This is undoubtedly a major landmark in Naxi history. However, one may want to emphasize that the deliberate introduction of Chinese culture and Confucian ideology had begun much earlier: the Mu feudal chieftains' unswerving allegiance to China dates back to the beginning of their rule, in the 14th century. Viewed in this light, the integration of Lijiang into Chinese territory in the 18th century is not without links to decisions that were made by the ruling family several centuries earlier.

> The Mu paid tribute to the imperial court and guarded the frontier on behalf of the Chinese emperors. To develop their realm, they pacified, conscripted, and taxed the local tribes (against fierce resistance), and they also called on large numbers of Chinese migrants from the interior – peasants, artists, craftsmen, literati, Taoist and Chinese Buddhist adepts – who worked on their estates, joined their armies, populated garrisoned villages and towns in tribal territories, and assimilated into the Naxi population. The Mu kings prided themselves on their civilization, in other words: their Sinicization. They were soldiers, and they became scholars, poets and calligraphists. They built palaces in Chinese style; they also built Confucian, Taoist and Buddhist temples, and dedicated arches to the chastity of their wives in Confucian fashion. (Mathieu 2015: 359-360)

A well-documented typological parallel for the appearance of cultural differences due to Sinicization is the case of Vietnam: in-depth sinicization in the course of the first millenium AD resulted in differences of mentality between the Vietnamese (speakers of an Austroasiatic language deeply influenced by Chi-

---

[13] For the sake of simplicity, this noun is provided here in surface phonological transcription. Its underlying form is //ɬi˩-hĩ#˥//, with a floating High tone. This tonal category is analyzed in Chapter 2, §2.3.1.

nese) and their Austroasiatic neighbours.[14] Again adopting the linguist's (admittedly narrow) perspective, there appears to be evidence supporting the view of a gradual divergence between the Na and Naxi. Careful examination of kinship terms in Naxi suggests that words for relatives on the father's side are mostly borrowings or recent coinages, as they are not cognate across dialects. The same holds true of terms relating to marriage, such as 'husband', 'wife', and 'daughter-in-law'. By contrast, the terms for relatives on the mother's side are of greater antiquity, with cognates in Na and Laze. Viewed in this light, the hypothesis of a divergence in terms of family structure as the Naxi underwent growing Chinese (Confucian) influence should not be lightly dismissed. Jackson's phrasing (p. 37) is: "This is the missing key to the confusion on Nakhi kinship: legal patrilinearity yet traditional matrilinearity".

Last but not least in this review of studies of the Na's kinship system and family structure, a two-volume set of collected works in Chinese needs to be mentioned: Lātāmī (2006). This collection is organized by themes (volume I: ethnology and anthropology; volume II: language, customs, religion, culture, music, and book reviews). It covers the period from 1960 to 2005. It has some minor limitations, such as incomplete information about the original publication references of work reprinted in the collection, and typographical issues for Latin characters and transcriptions in the International Phonetic Alphabet.

---

[14] Haudricourt draws a parallel with the Germanization of the Czechs, a Western Slav group; readers unfamiliar with Haudricourt's style should be warned that allowance must be made for Haudricourt's taste for thought-provoking shortcuts. "The Vietnamese are what they are because at bottom they are culturally Chinese. This is exactly like Czechs: they speak a Slavic language, but their civilization is German. Literary German is the Prague variety of German as it was used by the imperial administration of the House of Luxembourg. This explains why there have always been insoluble national problems between Czechs and Slovaks. The Vietnamese have roughly the same history: they have assimilated enough Chinese culture to become unclassifiable in the eyes of their neighbours" (Haudricourt & Dibie 1987: 97-98). *Original text:* Les Vietnamiens sont ce qu'ils sont parce qu'en fait ils sont chinois. C'est exactement comme les Tchèques, Marcel Mauss m'avait fait remarquer avant la guerre que les Tchèques parlent une langue slave mais qu'ils ont une civilisation allemande. L'allemand littéraire c'était l'allemand de Prague utilisé par l'administration impériale de la dynastie des Luxembourg. Ce qui explique qu'il y ait toujours eu des problèmes nationaux insolubles entre les Tchèques et les Slovaques. Les Vietnamiens ont à peu près la même histoire, ils ont assimilé assez de civilisation chinoise pour se rendre inclassables aux yeux de leurs voisins.

B.3.5 Present-day sociological studies: The impact of tourism since the 1990s

Since the 1990s, tourism has developed at a staggering pace in the Yongning Na area. A number of books, both in Chinese and in Western languages, cater for the tourist industry by presenting idealized pictures of Na society against its beautiful background: Lake Lugu and the Yongning plain (e.g. Refflet 2006; Lāmù 1998). There also exists abundant scholarly literature on the effects of tourism on Na society. An especially striking contrast could be observed in the 2010s between rituals and songs as practised by villagers among themselves in the village of Lijiazui (利家嘴), far from the tourist area, and the performances staged for tourists on the shores of Lake Lugu (Milan 2013). Anthropologists report in-depth effects of tourism such as decreasing reliance on matrilineal kin as wealth increases.

> ... increased individual access to resources is associated with diminished importance of the kinship group in organising behaviour, a shift away from matrilineal inheritance and erosion of the non-conjugal visiting system. (...) Respondents in tourist-impacted areas showed more deviation from matrilineal ideology in terms of household composition and preference for marriage, trends that seem to be associated more with wealth than with cultural assimilation. (Mattison 2010: 171)

Foreign sociologists and anthropologists often take a critical stance, pointing out that "official representations of China's ethnic minorities have created an image of minority people as dangerous, feminine, and erotic", and that, in the case of the Na/Mosuo, "early state categorizations of Mosuo gender practices have led to representations of Mosuo ethnicity built around notions of women freely available for sex, to whom present lovers have no future commitments, or of a land where women rule. Matriarchy and sexual availability are central in tourists' desire to visit the Mosuo" (Walsh 2005: 449–450; see also Schein 1997; Blumenfield 2010). These authors bring to light the ironic reversal whereby "the cultural characteristics the Maoist government tried to change became celebrated as markers of Mosuo cultural uniqueness and value" (Walsh 2005: 457).

The detailed analyses proposed by Stéphane Gros (2001) in his study of the Drung (Dulong) ethnic group also apply to other groups in Yunnan and in China at large: images of "minority" identities are constructed to suit the country's projects. Assimilationist policies, which culminated during the Great Proletarian Cultural Revolution (1966–1976), translate into dual visions of pre-Liberation and post-Liberation societies. Relative toleration during the 1980s, China's "Reforms and opening up" decade (Zhu 2014), led to the recognition of acceptable cultural features that need not be eliminated along with "bad" inheritance from the past, e.g. granting cultural value to "religion" (*zōngjiào* 宗教) as (precariously) distinguished from "superstition" (*míxìn* 迷信). After 1989, the conservative backlash was accompanied by folklorization of ethnic minorities: providing timeless and monolithic representations of the officially defined ethnic minorities, marketed to cater for the tourist industry and contribute to the country's GDP. A constant is that images of the "minorities" serve as a means to assert by contrast the homogeneity and modernity of the Han "majority" (Gros 2001: 31). Another constant is the pressure towards assimilation.

> Today, on the mere surface, "leisure culture" represents market reasoning rather than a statist logic. This is, after all, what hegemony is all about: naturalization of ruling technologies. (Sigley 2013: 242)

For obvious reasons, publications by scholars with institutional or family ties to mainland China tend to refrain from such criticisms. An extensive literature focuses on proposals for striking a reasonable balance between the competing demands of economic development and "cultural preservation" (*wénhuà bǎohù* 文化保护). This perspective is in line with the national mottos of economic development, on the one hand, and preservation of social harmony, on the other. Overviews are provided by Knödel (1995) and Ho (2008). Here is an English-language sample.

> With its unique natural landscape of a plateau lake and matriarchal culture, Lugu Lake region has recently become an attractive destination for tourists and researchers. Although the present environmental conditions in Lugu Lake region are good, rapid economic and tourism development in recent years has impacted on the regional environment and the traditional Mosuo culture. (…) Unlike the attitude of other races to nature, the Mosuo's attitudes towards nature greatly benefit environmental protection. (Yan et al. 2008: 49-51)

The article leads up to a list of recommendations, the first being that "Government should play a more positive role in conservation of traditional Mosuo culture and the local environment through increased investment" (Yan et al. 2008: 54).

On a much less predictable note, the 2007 collection of articles by Mosuo scholar and poet Lamu Gatusa 拉木·嘎吐萨 preserves in (novelized) writing some interesting pieces of local history, and publications by Mosuo anthropologist Latami Dashi 拉他咪·达石 span a range of topics and locations, including the Mosuo villages of the Ninglang plain (Lātāmī 2009; 2016).

References

Ā, Huì 阿慧. 2016. *Yǒngníng Mósuōhuà "le+V+se" jiégòu de shēngdiào shíyàn fēnxi: Ālāwǎ hé Shèkuǎ de duìbǐ* 永宁摩梭话"1e+V+se"结构的声调实验分析——阿拉瓦和舍垮的对比 *(An experimental analysis of the tones in "le+V+se" verb phrases in the Yongning Mosuo language: A comparison between Alawa and Shekua dialects)*. Kunming: Yunnan University M.A. thesis.

Abramson, Arthur S. 1979. The coarticulation of tones: An acoustic study of Thai. In Therapan L. Thongkum, Vichin Panupong, Pranee Kullavanijaya & Kalaya Tingsabadh (eds.), *Studies in Tai and Mon-Khmer phonetics and phonology in honor of Eugénie J.A. Henderson*, 1–9. Bangkok: Chulalongkorn University Press.

Abramson, Arthur S., Mark K. Tiede & Theraphan Luangthongkum. 2015. Voice register in Mon: Acoustics and electroglottography. *Phonetica* 72(4). 237–256.

Adamek, Piotr. 2012. *A good son is sad if he hears the name of his father: The tabooing of names in China as a way of implementing social values.* Leiden: Leiden Institute for Area Studies, Faculty of the Humanities, Leiden University PhD thesis.

Aikhenvald, Alexandra Y. 2002. Typological parameters for the study of clitics, with special reference to Tariana. In Robert M. Dixon & Alexandra Y. Aikhenvald (eds.), *Word: A cross-linguistic typology*, 42–78. Cambridge, U.K.: Cambridge University Press.

Akinlabi, Akinbiyi. 1985. *Tonal underspecification and Yorùbá tone.* Ibadan, Nigeria: University of Ibadan PhD thesis.

Alves, Mark. 1995. Tonal features and the development of Vietnamese tones. *University of Hawai'i at Mānoa Working Papers in Linguistics* 27. 1–13.

Amselle, Jean-Loup. 1990. *Logiques métisses. Anthropologie de l'identité en Afrique et ailleurs (Hybrid logics. Anthropology of identity in Africa and elsewhere).* Paris: Payot.

Andersen, Henning. 2006. Comments on Julictte Blevins, 'A theoretical synopsis of Evolutionary Phonology'. *Theoretical Linguistics* 32(2). 167–174.

Andersen, Torben. 1993. Vowel quality alternation in Dinka verb inflection. *Phonology* 10. 1–42.

Andruski, Jean E. & James Costello. 2004. Using polynomial equations to model pitch contour shape in lexical tones: An example from Green Mong. *Journal of the International Phonetic Association* 34(2). 125–140.

Andruski, Jean E. & Martha Ratliff. 2000. Phonation types in production of phonological tone: The case of Green Mong. *Journal of the International Phonetic Association* 30. 39–62.

Anthony, David W. 2007. *The horse, the wheel, and language: How Bronze-Age riders from the Eurasian steppes shaped the modern world.* Princeton, NJ: Princeton University Press.

Arcodia, Giorgio Francesco. 2012. *Lexical derivation in Mandarin Chinese* (Taiwan Journal of Linguistics Book Series in Chinese Linguistics). Taipei: Crane Publishing Co.

Armstrong, Lilias & Ida C. Ward. 1926. *Handbook of English intonation.* Cambridge, U.K.: Heffner.

Armstrong, Robert G. 1968. Yala (Ikom): A terraced-level language with three tones. *Journal of West African Languages* 5(1). 49–58.

Audibert, Nicolas, Véronique Aubergé & Albert Rilliard. 2008. How we are not equally competent for discriminating acted from spontaneous expressive speech. In César Reis, Sandra Madureira & Plínio A. Barbosa (eds.), *Proceedings of Speech Prosody 2008*, 693–696. Campinas, Brazil: International Speech Communication Association.

Āzémíng, Cìdázhū 阿泽明·次达珠. 2013. *Mósuō Dábājīng tōngyì* 摩梭达巴经通译 *(An interpretation of Mosuo Daba scriptures).* Kunming: Yunnan Minorities Publishing House 云南民族出版社.

Bacot, Jacques. 1913. *Les Mosso, ethnographie des Mosso, leurs religions, leur langue et leur écriture, avec les documents historiques et géographiques relatifs à Likiang par Ed. Chavannes (The Mosso: An ethnography of the Mosso, their religions, their language and their writing system, with historical and geographic documents relative to Lijiang by Ed. Chavannes).* Leiden: E.J. Brill.

Baken, Ronald J. 1992. Electroglottography. *Journal of Voice* 6(2). 98–110.

Banchob, Bandhumedha. 1987. *Phake-Thai-English dictionary.* Assam, India: manuscript published by the author.

Baron, Stephen P. 1974. On the tip of many tongues: Apical vowels across Sino-Tibetan. Handout circulated at the 7th International Conference on Sino-Tibetan Language and Linguistic Studies. https://halshs.archives-ouvertes.fr/halshs-01400987.

Bauer, Laurie. 2004. Adjectives, compounds, and words. *Nordic Journal of English Studies* 3(1). 7–22.

Baxter, William H. 2000. *An etymological dictionary of common Chinese characters* [preliminary draft of 28 October 2000].

Bayer, Josef. 1984. COMP in Bavarian syntax. *Linguistic Review* 3. 209–274.

Benedict, Paul K. 1972. *Sino-Tibetan: A conspectus.* Cambridge, U.K.: Cambridge University Press.

Benguerel, André-Pierre. 1973. Corrélats physiologiques de l'accent en français (Physiological correlates of stress in French). *Phonetica* 27(1). 21–35.

Björverud, Susanna. 1998. *A grammar of Lalo.* Lund: Lund University.

Blackburn, Stuart. 2004. Memories of migration: Notes on legends and beads in Arunachal Pradesh, India. *European Bulletin of Himalayan Research* 25-26. 15–60.

Blevins, Juliette. 2004. *Evolutionary phonology: The emergence of sound patterns.* Cambridge, U.K.: Cambridge University Press.

Blevins, Juliette & Andrew Garrett. 2009. Analogical morphophonology. In Sharon Inkelas & Kristin Hanson (eds.), *The nature of the word: Essays in honor of Paul Kiparsky*, 527–546. Cambridge, MA: MIT Press.

Blumenfeld, Tami. 2010. *Scenes from Yongning: Media creation in China's Na villages.* Seattle: University of Washington PhD thesis.

Blust, Robert. 1998. Seimat vowel nasality: A typological anomaly. *Oceanic Linguistics* 37(2). 298–322.

Bolinger, Dwight Le Merton. 1951. Intonation: Levels vs. configurations. *Word* 7. 199–210.

Bolinger, Dwight Le Merton. 1978. Intonation across languages. In Joseph H. Greenberg (ed.), *Universals of human language*, vol. 2, 471–524. Stanford, CA: Stanford University Press.

Bolinger, Dwight Le Merton. 1989. *Intonation and its uses: Melody in grammar and discourse.* Stanford, CA: Stanford University Press.

Bothorel, André, Péla Simon, François Wioland & Jean-Pierre Zerling. 1986. *Cinéradiographie des voyelles et des consonnes du français.* Tech. rep. Strasbourg, France: Travaux de l'Institut de Phonétique de Strasbourg.

Bouarourou, Fayssal, Béatrice Vaxelaire, Rachid Ridouane, Fabrice Hirsch & Rudolph Sock. 2008. Gemination in Tarifit Berber: X-ray and acoustic data. In Rudolph Sock, Susanne Fuchs & Yves Laprie (eds.), *Proceedings of the 8th international seminar on speech production*, 117–120. Strasbourg, France: Institut national de recherche en informatique et en automatique.

Bradley, David. 1975a. *Lahu dialects and Proto-Loloish.* London: University of London, School of Oriental & African Studies PhD thesis.

Bradley, David. 1975b. Nahsi and Proto-Burmese-Lolo. *Linguistics of the Tibeto-Burman Area* 2(1). 93–150.

Bradley, David. 1979. *Proto-Loloish* (Scandinavian Institute of Asian Studies Monograph Series 39). London & Malmö: Curzon Press.

Bradley, David. 1982. Register in Burmese. In David Bradley (ed.), *Tonation* (Papers in Southeast Asian Linguistics 8), 117–132. Canberra: Australian National University Press.

Bradley, David. 1989. Nasals and nasality in Loloish. In David Bradley, Eugénie J.A. Henderson & Martine Mazaudon (eds.), *Prosodic analysis and Asian linguistics: To honour R.K. Sprigg* (Pacific Linguistics), 143–155. Canberra: Australian National University Press.

Brunelle, Marc. 2003. Tone coarticulation in Northern Vietnamese. In Maria-Josep Solé, Daniel Recasens & Joaquín Romero (eds.), *Proceedings of the 15th International Congress of Phonetic Sciences*, 2673–2676. Barcelona: Universitat Autònoma de Barcelona.

Brunelle, Marc. 2009a. Contact-induced change? Register in three Cham dialects. *Journal of Southeast Asian Linguistics* 2. 1–22.

Brunelle, Marc. 2009b. Northern and Southern Vietnamese tone coarticulation: A comparative case study. *Journal of Southeast Asian Linguistics* 1. 49–62.

Brunelle, Marc. 2009c. Tone perception in Northern and Southern Vietnamese. *Journal of Phonetics* 37. 79–96.

Brunelle, Marc. 2012. Dialect experience and perceptual integrality in phonological registers: Fundamental frequency, voice quality and the first formant in Cham. *Journal of the Acoustical Society of America* 131(4). 3088–3102.

Brunelle, Marc, Daryl Chow & Thụy Nhã Uyên Nguyễn. 2015. Effects of lexical frequency and lexical category on the duration of Vietnamese syllables. In The Scottish Consortium for ICPhS 2015 (ed.), *Proceedings of 18th International Congress of Phonetic Sciences*, 1–5. Glasgow: University of Glasgow.

Brunelle, Marc & James Kirby. 2016. Tone and phonation in Southeast Asian languages. *Language and Linguistics Compass* 10(4). 191–207.

Brunelle, Marc, Khắc Hùng Nguyễn & Duy Dương Nguyễn. 2010. A laryngographic and laryngoscopic study of Northern Vietnamese tones. *Phonetica* 67(3). 147–169.

Bühler, Karl. 1934. *Sprachtheorie: die Darstellungsfunktion der Sprache*. Jena: Gustav Fischer.

Bulag, Uradyn E. 2010. Can the subalterns not speak? On the regime of oral history in socialist China. *Inner Asia* 12(1). 95–111.

Bulag, Uradyn E. 2012. Good Han, bad Han: The moral parameters of ethnopolitics in China. In Thomas Mullaney, James Leibold, Stéphane Gros & Eric Vanden Bussche (eds.), *Critical Han studies: The history, representation, and identity of China's majority*, 92–109. Berkeley, CA: University of California Press.

Burchill, Susan A. & Anthony J. Thody. 1986. Dopaminergic inhibition of tyrosinase activity in hair follicular melanocytes of the mouse. *Journal of endocrinology* 111(2). 233–237.

Byrd, Dani & Elliot Saltzman. 2003. The elastic phrase: Modeling the dynamics of boundary-adjacent lengthening. *Journal of Phonetics* 31(2). 149–180.

Cai, Hua. 1997. *Une société sans père ni mari: les Na de Chine* (Ethnologies). Paris: Presses Universitaires de France.

Cai, Hua. 2001. *A society without fathers or husbands: The Na of China*. Trans. by Asti Hustvedt. New York City, NY: Zone Books.

Cai, Hua. 2008. *L'homme pensé par l'homme: du statut scientifique des sciences sociales (Man thought out by man: On the scientific status of social sciences)*. Paris: Presses Universitaires de France.

Calabrese, Andrea. 2000. The feature [Advanced Tongue Root] and vowel fronting in Romance. In Lori Repetti (ed.), *Phonological theory and the dialects of Italy*, 59–88. Amsterdam: John Benjamins.

Cartier, Michel & Danielle Elisseeff. 1998. Les Na: une structure familiale en marge [review of: Cai Hua, Une société sans père ni mari: les Na de Chine]. *Perspectives chinoises* 45. 57–59.

Carton, Fernand, Daniel Hirst, Alain Marchal & André Séguinot. 1976. *L'accent d'insistance (Emphatic stress)* (Studia Phonetica 12). Montreal: Didier.

Chan, Ko Ling, Douglas A. Brownridge, Agnes Tiwari, Daniel Y.T. Fong & Wing-Cheong Leung. 2008. Understanding violence against Chinese women in Hong Kong: An analysis of risk factors with a special emphasis on the role of in-law conflict. *Violence Against Women* 14(11). 1295–1312.

Chao, Emily Kay. 1995. *Depictions of differences: History, gender, ritual and state discourse among the Naxi of Southwest China*. Ann Arbor, MI: University of Michigan PhD thesis.

Chao, Yuen-ren. 1929. Běipíng yǔdiào de yánjiū 北平語調的研究 (Research about Beiping intonation). In *A.A. Milne: The Camberley triangle*, Appendix. Shanghai: Zhonghua Bookstore 中華書局.

Chao, Yuen-ren. 1930. A system of tone letters. *Le Maître phonétique* 45. 24–27.

Chao, Yuen-ren. 1933. Tone and intonation in Chinese. *Bulletin of the Institute of History and Philology, Academia Sinica* 4(3). 121–134.

Chao, Yuen-ren. 1968. *A grammar of spoken Chinese.* Berkeley, CA & Los Angeles, CA: University of California Press.

Chavannes, Edouard. 1912. Documents historiques et géographiques relatifs à Li Kiang. *T'oung Pao* 13(1-5). 565–653.

Chelliah, Shobhana L. & Willem J. de Reuse. 2011. *Handbook of descriptive linguistic fieldwork.* Dordrecht: Springer.

Chen, Matthew Y. 2000. *Tone sandhi: Patterns across Chinese dialects* (Cambridge Studies in Linguistics 92). Cambridge, U.K.: Cambridge University Press.

Chen, Sanping. 2016. Were "ugly slaves" in Medieval China really ugly? *Journal of the American Oriental Society* 136(1). 117–123.

Chen, Yiya & Yi Xu. 2006. Production of weak elements in speech: Evidence from f_0 patterns of neutral tone in standard Chinese. *Phonetica* 63(1). 47–75.

Chirkova, Katia. 2009. Shǐxīng, a Sino-Tibetan language of South-West China: A grammatical sketch with two appended texts. *Linguistics of the Tibeto-Burman Area* 32(1). 1–90.

Chirkova, Katia. 2012. The Qiangic subgroup from an areal perspective: A case study of languages of Muli. *Language and Linguistics* 13(1). 133–170.

Chirkova, Katia. 2014. The Duoxu language and the Ersu-Lizu-Duoxu relationship. *Linguistics of the Tibeto-Burman Area* 37(1). 104–146.

Chirkova, Katia & Yiya Chen. 2013. Illustrations of the IPA: Lizu. *Journal of the International Phonetic Association* 43(1). 75–86.

Chirkova, Katia, Yiya Chen & Tanja Kocjančič Antolík. 2013. Illustrations of the IPA: Xumi (part 2): Upper Xumi, the variety of the upper reaches of the Shuiluo river. *Journal of the International Phonetic Association* 43(3). 381–396.

Chirkova, Katia & Alexis Michaud. 2009. Approaching the prosodic system of Shixing. *Language and Linguistics* 10(3). 539–568.

Chirkova, Katia, Dehe Wang, Yiya Chen, Angélique Amelot & Tanja Kocjančič Antolík. 2015. Illustrations of the IPA: Ersu. *Journal of the International Phonetic Association* 45(2). 187–211.

Clark, Mary Morris. 1976. *A dynamic treatment of tone, with special attention to the tonal system of Igbo.* Durham, NH: University of New Hampshire PhD thesis.

Clements, Nick. 1979. The description of terraced-level tone languages. *Language* 55(3). 536–558.

Clements, Nick. 2000. Phonology. In Bernd Heine & Derek Nurse (eds.), *African languages: An introduction*, 123–160. Cambridge, U.K.: Cambridge University Press.

Clements, Nick & John Goldsmith. 1984. *Autosegmental studies in Bantu tone*. Nick Clements & Didier L. Goyvaerts (eds.) (Publications in African Languages and Linguistics 3). Dordrecht: Foris.

Clements, Nick, Alexis Michaud & Cédric Patin. 2011. Do we need tone features? In Elizabeth Hume, John Goldsmith & W. Leo Wetzels (eds.), *Tones and features*, 3–24. Berlin: De Gruyter Mouton.

Clements, Nick & Annie Rialland. 2007. Africa as a phonological area. In Bernd Heine & Derek Nurse (eds.), *A linguistic geography of Africa* (Cambridge Approaches to Language Contact), 36–85. Cambridge, U.K.: Cambridge University Press.

Coblin, South. 2007. *A handbook of 'Phags-pa Chinese*. Honolulu: University of Hawai'i Press.

Coetzee, Andries W. & Joe Pater. 2008. Weighted constraints and gradient restrictions on place co-occurrence in Muna and Arabic. *Natural Language & Linguistic Theory* 26(2). 289–337.

Connell, Bruce. 2003. Pitch realization and the four tones of Mambila. In Shigeki Kaji (ed.), *Proceedings of the symposium "Cross-linguistic studies of tonal phenomena: Historical developments, phonetics of tone"*, 181–198. Tokyo: Tokyo University of Foreign Studies, Research Institute for Languages, Cultures of Asia & Africa.

Connell, Bruce. 2016. Tone and intonation in Mambila. In Laura J. Downing & Annie Rialland (eds.), *Intonation in African tone languages* (Phonology and Phonetics 24), 131–166. Berlin: De Gruyter.

Cordier, Henri. 1908. Les Mosos (The Moso people). *T'oung Pao* series 2, vol. 9. 663–688.

Coupe, Alec. 2003. *A phonetic and phonological description of Ao: A Tibeto-Burman language of Nagaland, north-east India* (Pacific Linguistics 543). Canberra: Australian National University.

Coustenoble, Hélène & Lilias Armstrong. 1937. *Studies in French intonation*. Cambridge, U.K.: Heffer.

Creissels, Denis. 1982. A propos de défauts de mémorisation de signifiants par les locuteurs mandinka (About cases in which Mandinka speakers fail to memorize signifiers). *Mandenkan* 4. 49–56.

Creissels, Denis. 1991. *Description des langues négro-africaines et théorie syntaxique (Description of Subsaharan languages and syntactic theory)*. Grenoble: ELLUG.

Creissels, Denis. 1992. Tonologie du bambara: Bilan et perspectives (Bambara tonology: Review and prospects). *Mandenkan* 24. 1–45.

Creissels, Denis. 1994. *Aperçu sur les structures phonologiques des langues négro-africaines (Outline of the phonological structures of Subsaharan languages)*. Grenoble: ELLUG.

Creissels, Denis. 1995. *Eléments de syntaxe générale (Elements of general syntax)*. Paris: Presses Universitaires de France.

Creissels, Denis. 2011. Tswana locatives and their status in the inversion construction. *Africana Linguistica* 17. 33–52.

Creissels, Denis, Andy M. Chebanne & Heather W. Nkhwa. 1997. *Tonal morphology of the Setswana verb* (LINCOM Studies in African Linguistics 13). Munich: LINCOM Europa.

Creissels, Denis & Claire Grégoire. 1993. La notion de ton marqué dans l'analyse d'une opposition tonale binaire: le cas du mandingue (The notion of marked tone in the analysis of a binary tonal opposition: the case of Manding). *Journal of African Languages and Linguistics* 14. 107–154.

Creissels, Denis & Stéphane Robert. 1998. Morphologie verbale et organisation discursive de l'énoncé: l'exemple du tswana et du wolof (Verbal morphology and discursive organization of the utterance: The cases of Tswana and Wolof). *Faits de langues* 11-12. 161–178.

Crowley, Terry. 1981. The Mpakwithi dialect of Anguthimri. In Robert M. Dixon & Barry J. Blake (eds.), *Handbook of Australian languages*, vol. 2, 147–196. Amsterdam: John Benjamins.

Cruz, Emiliana. 2011. *Phonology, tone and the functions of tone in San Juan Quiahije Chatino*. Austin, TX: University of Texas at Austin PhD thesis.

Cruz, Emiliana & Tony Woodbury. 2014. Finding a way into a family of tone languages: The story and methods of the Chatino Language Documentation Project. *Language Documentation and Conservation* 8. 490–524.

Culioli, Antoine. 1990. *Pour une linguistique de l'énonciation I - Opérations et représentations* (L'Homme dans la langue). Paris: Ophrys.

Culioli, Antoine. 1995. *Cognition and representation in linguistic theory* (Current Issues in Linguistic Theory). Amsterdam: John Benjamins.

Cummins, Fred. 2012. Looking for rhythm in speech. *Empirical Musicology Review* 7(1-2). 28–35.

Daudey, Henriëtte. 2014. *A grammar of Wadu Pumi*. Melbourne: LaTrobe University PhD thesis.

DeLancey, Scott. 2015. Adjectival constructions in Bodo and Tibeto-Burman. In Mark W. Post, Scott DeLancey & Stephen Morey (eds.), *Language and culture in Northeast India and beyond: In honour of Robbins Burling* (Asia-Pacific Linguistics 23), 41–56. Canberra: Australian National University.

Delattre, Pierre. 1965. *Comparing the phonetic features of English, French, German and Spanish: An interim report*. Heidelberg: Julius Groos Verlag.

Delattre, Pierre. 1966. Les dix intonations de base du français (The ten basic intonation patterns of French). *The French Review* 40(1). 1–14.

Delattre, Pierre. 1970. Syntax and intonation, a study in disagreement. *The Modern Language Journal* 54(1). 3–9.

Di Cristo, Albert. 1998. Intonation in French. In Daniel Hirst & Albert Di Cristo (eds.), *Intonation systems: A survey of twenty languages*, 195–218. Cambridge, U.K.: Cambridge University Press.

Di Cristo, Albert & Daniel Hirst. 1986. Modelling French micromelody: Analysis and synthesis. *Phonetica* 43. 11–30.

DiCanio, Christian. 2012. Coarticulation between tone and glottal consonants in Itunyoso Trique. *Journal of Phonetics* 40. 162–176.

Dihoff, Ivan R. 1977. *Aspects of the tonal structure of Chori*. Madison, WI: University of Wisconsin PhD thesis.

Dimmendaal, Gerrit J. 2011. *Historical linguistics and the comparative study of African languages*. Amsterdam: John Benjamins.

Ding, Picus Sizhi. 2001. The pitch accent system of Niuwozi Prinmi. *Linguistics of the Tibeto-Burman Area* 24(2). 57–83.

Ding, Picus Sizhi. 2006. A typological study of tonal systems of Japanese and Prinmi: Towards a definition of pitch-accent languages. *Journal of Universal Language* 7. 1–35.

Ding, Picus Sizhi. 2014. *A grammar of Prinmi: Based on the Central dialect of Northwest Yunnan, China*. Leiden: Brill.

Dixon, Robert M. 2007. Field linguistics: A minor manual. *Sprachtypologie und Universalienforschung* 60(1). 12–31.

Dixon, Robert M. & Alexandra Y. Aikhenvald (eds.). 2002. *Word: A cross-linguistic typology*. Cambridge, U.K.: Cambridge University Press.

Dô, Thê Dung, Thien Huong Trân & Georges Boulakia. 1998. Intonation in Vietnamese. In Daniel Hirst & Albert Di Cristo (eds.), *Intonation systems: A survey of twenty languages*, 395–416. Cambridge, U.K.: Cambridge University Press.

Dobbs, Roselle & Mingqing La. 2016. The two-level tonal system of Lataddi Narua. *Linguistics of the Tibeto-Burman Area* 39(1). 67–104.

Donohue, Mark. 2003. The tonal system of Skou, New Guinea. In Shigeki Kaji (ed.), *Proceedings of the symposium "Cross-linguistic studies of tonal phenomena: Historical developments, phonetics of tone"*, 329–364. Tokyo: Tokyo University of Foreign Studies, Research Institute for Languages, Cultures of Asia & Africa.

Donohue, Mark. 2005. Tone and the Trans New Guinea languages. In Shigeki Kaji (ed.), *Proceedings of the symposium "Cross-linguistic studies of tonal phenomena: Tonogenesis, Japanese accentology, and other topics"*, 33–54. Tokyo: Tokyo University of Foreign Studies, Research Institute for Languages, Cultures of Asia & Africa.

Dournes, Jacques. 1990. Les traditions orales: Oralité et mémoire collective. In Gilles Quinsat (ed.), *Le grand atlas des littératures* (Les grands atlas Universalis), 86–89. Paris: Encyclopædia Universalis.

Downing, Laura J. & Maxwell Kadenge. 2015. Prosodic stems in Zezuru Shona. *Southern African Linguistics and Applied Language Studies* 33(3). 291–305.

Downing, Laura J. & Annie Rialland. 2016. Introduction. In Laura J. Downing & Annie Rialland (eds.), *Intonation in African tone languages* (Phonology and Phonetics 24), 1–16. Berlin: De Gruyter.

Dumestre, Gérard. 1987. *Le bambara du Mali: Essais de description linguistique.* Paris: Université de la Sorbonne Nouvelle & Institut National des Langues et Civilisations Orientales PhD thesis.

Duong, Khue. 2010. Rolling out Zotero across campus as a part of a science librarian's outreach efforts. *Science & Technology Libraries* 29(4). 315–324.

Edmondson, Jerold A., John Esling, Jimmy G. Harris, Li Shaoni & Lama Ziwo. 2001. The aryepiglottic folds and voice quality in the Yi and Bai languages: Laryngoscopic case studies. *Mon-Khmer Studies* 31. 83–100.

Enfield, Nicholas J. 2001. 'Lip-pointing': A discussion of form and function with reference to data from Laos. *Gesture* 1(2). 185–211.

Enfield, Nicholas J. 2006. Lao body part terms. *Parts of the body: Cross-linguistic categorisation* 28(2–3). 181–200.

Erickson, Donna. 1998. Effects of contrastive emphasis on jaw opening. *Phonetica* 55(3). 147–169.

Evans, Jonathan. 2008. 'African' tone in the Sinosphere. *Language and Linguistics* 9(3). 463–490.

Evans, Jonathan & Chenglong Huang. 2007. A bottom-up approach to vowel systems: The case of Yadu Qiang. *Cahiers de linguistique - Asie Orientale* 36(2). 147–186.

Evans, Nick. 2010. *Dying words: Endangered languages and what they have to tell us* (The Language Library). Hoboken, NJ: Wiley-Blackwell.

Fabre, Philippe. 1957. Un procédé électrique percutané d'inscription de l'accolement glottique au cours de la phonation: glottographie de haute fréquence. *Bulletin de l'Académie Nationale de Médecine* 141. 66–69.

Fāng, Guóyú 方国瑜 & Zhìwǔ Hé 和志武. 1995. *Nàxī xiàngxíng wénzì pǔ* 纳西象形文字谱 *(A dictionary of Naxi pictographic characters)*. Kunming: Yunnan People's Publishing House 云南人民出版社.

Fant, Gunnar. 1960. *Acoustic theory of speech production, with calculations based on X-ray studies of Russian articulations*. The Hague & Paris: Mouton.

Fant, Gunnar, Stellan Hertegård & Anita Kruckenberg. 1996. Focal accent and subglottal pressure. *TMH-QPSR* 2. 29–32.

Ferlus, Michel. 1979. Formation des registres et mutations consonantiques dans les langues mon-khmer (Formation of phonation-type registers and consonant shifts across Mon-Khmer languages). *Mon-Khmer Studies* 8. 1–76.

Ferlus, Michel. 1996. Remarques sur le consonantisme du proto kam-sui (Observations about the consonant system of proto Kam-Sui). *Cahiers de linguistique - Asie Orientale* 25(2). 235–278.

Ferlus, Michel. 2001. Hypercorrections in the Thổ dialect of Làng Lỡ (Nghệ An, Vietnam): An example of pitfalls for comparative linguistics. In *Quinzièmes Journées de Linguistique d'Asie Orientale*. Paris, France. https://halshs.archives-ouvertes.fr/halshs-01128106.

Ferlus, Michel. 2003. On borrowing from Middle Chinese into Proto-Tibetan: A new look at the problem of the relationship between Chinese and Tibetan. In David Bradley, Randy LaPolla, Boyd Michailovsky & Graham Thurgood (eds.), *Language variation: Papers on variation and change in the Sinosphere and the Indosphere in honour of James A. Matisoff* (Pacific Linguistics), 263–275. Canberra: Australian National University.

Fischer-Jørgensen, Eli. 1949. Kenneth L. Pike's analysis of American English intonation. *Lingua* 2. 3–13.

Fluehr-Lobban, Carolyn. 2014. Ethics. In H. Russell Bernard & Clarence C. Gravlee (eds.), *Handbook of methods in cultural anthropology*, 173–202. Lanham, MD: Rowman & Littlefield.

Fónagy, Ivan. 1983. *La vive voix: Essais de psycho-phonétique* (Langages et Sociétés 20). Paris: Payot.

Fónagy, Ivan. 1989. On status and functions of intonation. *Acta Linguistica Hungarica* 39(1-4). 53–92.

Fougeron, Cécile & Sun-Ah Jun. 1998. Rate effects on French intonation: Prosodic organization and phonetic realization. *Journal of Phonetics* 26. 45–69.

Francopoulo, Gil (ed.). 2013. *LMF: Lexical Markup Framework* (Computer Engineering and IT). Hoboken, NJ & London: Wiley & ISTE.

Frangville, Vanessa. 2011. Review of: Thomas S. Mullaney, Coming to terms with the nation: Ethnic classification in Modern China. Berkeley, University of California Press, 2011. *Perspectives chinoises* 2. 77–79.

Franich, Kathryn, Catherine O'Connor & Jonathan Barnes. 2012. Tonal merger in Medumba (Bamileke) nouns. In Michael R. Marlo, Nikki B. Adams, Christopher R. Green, Michelle Morrison & Tristan M. Purvis (eds.), *Selected proceedings of the 42nd Annual Conference on African Linguistics (ACAL): African languages in context*, 32–46. Somerville, MA: Cascadilla Proceedings Project.

François, Alexandre. 2000. L'illusion des classificateurs. *Faits de langues* 14. 165–175.

François, Alexandre. 2004. La réduplication en mwotlap: les paradoxes du fractionnement. *Faits de langues* 23-24. 177–194.

François, Alexandre. 2010. Phonotactics and the prestopped velar lateral in Hiw: Resolving the ambiguity of a complex segment. *Phonology* 27(3). 393–434.

François, Alexandre. 2014. Trees, waves and linkages: Models of language diversification. In Claire Bowern & Bethwyn Evans (eds.), *The Routledge handbook of historical linguistics*, 161–189. London: Routledge.

Frei, Henri. 1929. *La grammaire des fautes: introduction à la linguistique fonctionnelle, assimilation et différenciation, brièveté et invariabilité, expressivité (The grammar of mistakes: An introduction to functional linguistics, with a discussion of assimilation and differenciation, brevity and invariability, and expressivity)*. Bellegarde: Société anonyme des arts graphiques de France.

Fromkin, Victoria A. 1973. *Speech errors as linguistic evidence*. Berlin: De Gruyter.

Fromkin, Victoria A. (ed.). 1978. *Tone: A linguistic survey*. New York City, NY: Academic Press.

Fù, Màojì 傅懋勣. 1980. Yǒngníng Nàxīzú de mǔxì jiātíng hé qīnshǔ chēngwèi 永宁纳西族的母系家庭和亲属称谓 (The matriarchal family structure and kinship terms of Yongning Naxi people). *Ethno-National Studies* 民族研究 3.

Fù, Màojì 傅懋勣. 1981. *Nàxīyǔ túhuà wénzì "Bái biānfú qǔ jīng jì" yánjiū* 纳西语图画文字〈白蝙蝠取经记〉研究 *(A study of a Naxi pictographic manuscript "White Bat's Search for Sacred Books")* (Computational Analyses of Asian and African Languages: Monograph Series 6). 2 volumes. Tokyo: National Inter-University Research Institute of Asian, African Languages & Cultures.

Fù, Màojì 傅懋勣. 1983. La famille matriarcale et les termes de parenté chez les Naxi de Yongning (district Ninglang, Yunnan, Chine) (Matriarchal family and kinship terms among the Naxi of Yongning (Ninglang district, Yunnan, China)). *Cahiers de linguistique - Asie Orientale* 12(1). 23–42.

Fuller, Christopher J. 1976. *The Nayars today.* Cambridge, U.K.: Cambridge University Press.

Gaenszle, Martin. 2012. Where the waters dry up: The place of origin in Rai myth and ritual. In Toni Huber & Stuart Blackburn (eds.), *Origins and migrations in the extended Eastern Himalayas*, 33–47. Leiden: Brill.

Gài, Xìngzhī 盖兴之 & Zhúyí Jiāng 姜竹仪. 1990. Nàxīyǔ zài Zàng-Miǎnyǔ zhōng de dìwèi 纳西语在藏缅语中的地位 (The position of Naxi within Tibeto-Burman). *Minority Languages of China* 民族语文 1. 63–73.

Gandour, Jack & Siripong Potisuk. 1992. Tonal coarticulation in Thai disyllabic utterances: A preliminary study. *Linguistics of the Tibeto-Burman Area* 15(1). 93–110.

Garellek, Marc. 2012. Glottal stops before word-initial vowels in American English: Distribution and acoustic characteristics. *UCLA Working Papers in Phonetics* 110. 1–23.

Garellek, Marc & Patricia Keating. 2011. The acoustic consequences of phonation and tone interactions in Jalapa Mazatec. *Journal of the International Phonetic Association* 41(2). 185–205.

Geertz, Clifford. 2001. The Visit (review of: A Society Without Fathers or Husbands: The Na of China, by Cai Hua, translated from the French by Asti Hustvedt). *The New York Review of Books* 18/10/2001.

Gerner, Matthias. 2013. *A grammar of Nuosu.* Berlin: De Gruyter.

Gerner, Matthias & Walter Bisang. 2009. Inflectional classifiers in Weining Ahmao: Mirror of the history of a people. *Folia Linguistica Historica* 30(1). 183–218.

Gimbutas, Marija. 1977. The first wave of Eurasian pastoralists into Copper Age Europe. *Journal of Indo-European Studies* 5(4). 277–338.

Girón Higuita, Jesus-Mario & W. Leo Wetzels. 2007. Tone in Wãnsöhöt (Puinave). In W. Leo Wetzels (ed.), *Language endangerment and endangered languages: Linguistic and anthropological studies with special emphasis on the languages and cultures of the Andean-Amazonian border area* (Indigenous Languages of Latin America 5), 129–156. Leiden: Publications of the Research School of Asian, African & Amerindian Studies (CNWS).

Goldrick, Matthew. 2011. Using psychological realism to advance phonological theory. In John Goldsmith, Jason Riggle & Alan C.L. Yu (eds.), *Handbook of phonological theory*, second edition, 631–660. Oxford: Blackwell.

Goldsmith, John. 1976. *Autosegmental phonology.* Cambridge, MA: M.I.T. PhD thesis.

Goldsmith, John. 2002. Tone in Mituku: How a floating tone nailed down an intermediate level. In Jacques Durand & Bernard Laks (eds.), *Phonetics, phonology, and cognition*, 80–95. Oxford: Oxford University Press.

Gomez-Imbert, Elsa. 2001. More on the tone versus pitch accent typology: Evidence from Barasana and other Eastern Tukanoan languages. In Shigeki Kaji (ed.), *Proceedings of the symposium "Cross-linguistic studies of tonal phenomena: Tonogenesis, Japanese accentology, and other topics"*, 369–412. Tokyo: Tokyo University of Foreign Studies, Research Institute for Languages, Cultures of Asia & Africa.

Gordon, Raymond G. 2005. *Ethnologue: Languages of the world.* Dallas, TX: SIL International. http://www.ethnologue.com/.

Goullart, Peter. 1955. *Forgotten kingdom.* London: John Murray.

Grammont, Maurice. 1933. *Traité de phonétique.* Paris: Delagrave.

Grønnum, Nina. 1991. Prosodic parameters in a variety of regional Danish standard languages. *Phonetica* 47. 188–214.

Grønnum, Nina. 1998a. A critical remark on D. R. Ladd's Intonational Phonology. *Journal of Phonetics* 26. 109–112.

Grønnum, Nina. 1998b. Intonation in Danish. In Daniel Hirst & Albert Di Cristo (eds.), *Intonation systems: A survey of twenty languages*, 131–151. Cambridge, U.K.: Cambridge University Press.

Gros, Stéphane. 2001. Du politique au pittoresque en Chine: à propos des Dulong, nationalité minoritaire du Yunnan (From the political to the picturesque in China: About the Dulong, a minority nationality of Yunnan). *Ateliers* 24. 28–68.

Gros, Stéphane. 2011. Review of: Shih Chuan-kang, Quest for harmony. The Moso traditions of sexual union and family life. *China Perspectives* 1. 93–94.

Gros, Stéphane. 2014a. Devenirs identitaires dans les confins sino-tibétains: contextes et transformations (Changing ethnic identities in the Sino-Tibetan borderlands: Contexts and transformations). *Cahiers d'Extrême-Asie* 23. 63–102.

Gros, Stéphane. 2014b. The bittersweet taste of rice. Sloping land conversion and the shifting livelihoods of the Drung in Northwest Yunnan (China). *Himalaya* 34(2). 81–96.

Gruber, James Frederick. 2011. *An articulatory, acoustic, and auditory study of Burmese tone.* Washington: Georgetown University PhD thesis.

Gsell, René. 1979. *La prosodie du thai standard: Tons et accent.* Paris: Université Sorbonne Nouvelle – Paris 3, Institut de Phonétique PhD thesis.

Gsell, René. 1985. Hauteurs spécifiques, types consonantiques et tons statiques en thai. In Ratanakul Suriya, David Thomas & Premsrirat Suwilai (eds.), *Southeast*

Asian linguistic studies presented to André-G. Haudricourt, 389–427. Bangkok: Mahidol University.

Guérin, Maximilien. 2015. Ebauche d'une organisation des constructions verbales en wolof (A sketch of the organization of verb constructions in Wolof). In Angelina Aleksandrova, Nourdine Assani, Laurence Longo, Camille Fauth, Julien Rentz, Sarah Gemiciolglu, Adrian Görke, Inga Hennecke & Thomas Jauriberry (eds.), *Les classifications en linguistique: Problèmes, méthodologie, enjeux*, 144–159. Bochum, Germany: Westdeutscher Universitätsverlag.

Gui, Ming Chao. 2001. *Yunnanese and Kunming Chinese: A study of the language communities, the phonological systems, and the phonological developments*. Munich: LINCOM Europa.

Guō, Dàliè 郭大烈 & Zhìwǔ Hé 和志武. 1994. *Nàxīzú shǐ* 纳西族史 *(A history of the Naxi people)*. Chongqing 重庆: Sichuan Nationalities Publishing House 四川民族出版社.

Guo, Xiaolin. 2008. *State and ethnicity in China's Southwest*. Leiden: Brill.

Gussenhoven, Carlos. 2004. *The phonology of tone and intonation* (Research surveys in linguistics). Cambridge, U.K.: Cambridge University Press.

Guthrie, Malcom. 1940. Tone ranges in a two-tone language (Lingala). *Bulletin of the School of Oriental and African Studies* 10(2). 469–478.

Hạ, Kiều Phương & Martine Grice. 2010. Modelling the interaction of intonation and lexical tone in Vietnamese. In *Proceedings of Speech Prosody 2010*. Chicago, IL: International Speech Communication Association.

Hadler, Jeffrey. 2008. *Muslims and matriarchs: Cultural resilience in Indonesia through Jihad and colonialism*. Ithaca, NY: Cornell University Press.

Hagège, Claude & André-Georges Haudricourt. 1978. *La phonologie panchronique*. Paris: Presses Universitaires de France.

Hall, Edward T. & George L. Trager. 1953. *The analysis of culture*. Norman, OK: Battenberg Press.

Hampson, Norman. 1968. *The Enlightenment* (The Pelican History of European Thought IV). Baltimore, MD: Penguin Books.

Haraguchi, Shosuke. 1999. Accent. In Natsuko Tsujimura (ed.), *The handbook of Japanese linguistics*, 1–30. Malden, MA: Blackwell.

Hargus, Sharon & Keren Rice (eds.). 2005. *Athabaskan prosody* (Current issues in linguistic theory 269). Amsterdam: John Benjamins.

Harrell, Stevan. 2009. Reading threads: Clothing, ethnicity, and place in Southwest China. In *Writing with thread: Traditional textiles of southwest Chinese minorities. A special exhibition from the collection of Huang Ying Feng and the*

Evergrand Art Museum in Taoyuan, Taiwan, 99–111. Honolulu: University of Hawai'i Art Gallery.

Haspelmath, Martin. 2007. Pre-established categories don't exist: Consequences for language description and typology. *Linguistic Typology* 11(1). 119–132.

Haspelmath, Martin. 2017. Some principles for language names. *Language Documentation and Conservation* 11. 81–93.

Haudricourt, André-Georges. 1940. Méthode pour obtenir des lois concrètes en linguistique générale (Towards empirical laws in general linguistics). *Bulletin de la Société de Linguistique de Paris* 41(1). 70–74.

Haudricourt, André-Georges. 1952. Les voyelles brèves du vietnamien (The place of Vietnamese in Austroasiatic). *Bulletin de la Société de Linguistique de Paris* 48(1). 90–93.

Haudricourt, André-Georges. 1953. La place du vietnamien dans les langues austroasiatiques. *Bulletin de la Société de Linguistique de Paris* 49(1). 122–128.

Haudricourt, André-Georges. 1961. Richesse en phonèmes et richesse en locuteurs (Number of phonemes and number of speakers). *L'Homme* 1(1). 5–10.

Haudricourt, André-Georges. 1965. Les mutations consonantiques des occlusives initiales en môn-khmer (Consonant shifts in Mon-Khmer initial stops). *Bulletin de la Société de Linguistique de Paris* 60(1). 160–72.

Haudricourt, André-Georges. 1967. La langue lakkia. *Bulletin de la Société de Linguistique de Paris* 62(1). 165–182.

Haudricourt, André-Georges. 1973. La linguistique panchronique nécessaire à la linguistique comparée, science auxiliaire de la diachronie sociologique et ethnographique (On the necessity of panchronic linguistics for comparative linguistics, itself an auxiliary science of sociological-ethnographical (/anthropological) diachrony). *Ethnies* 3. 23–26.

Haudricourt, André-Georges. 2010. The origin of the peculiarities of the Vietnamese alphabet. *Mon-Khmer Studies* 39. 89–104.

Haudricourt, André-Georges & Pascal Dibie. 1987. *Les pieds sur terre*. Paris: Métailié.

Haudricourt, André-Georges & Mariel Jean-Brunhes Delamare. 1955. *L'homme et la charrue à travers le monde (Man and the plough around the world)* (Géographie humaine 25). Paris: Gallimard.

Hé, Jírén 和即仁 & Zhìwǔ Hé 和志武. 1988. Nàxīzú de shèhuì lìshǐ jí qí fāngyán diàochá 纳西族的社会历史及其方言调查 (An investigation into social history of the Naxi people and Naxi dialects). In Yunnan Ethnic Investigation Team 云南民族调查组 (ed.), *Nàxīzú shèhuì lìshǐ diàochá* 纳西族社会历史调查 *(An in-*

vestigation into the social history of the naxi people), vol. III, 119–193. Kunming: The Nationalities Publishing House of Yunnan 云南民族出版社.

Hé, Jírén 和即仁 & Zhúyí Jiāng 姜竹仪. 1985. *Nàxīyǔ jiǎnzhì* 纳西语简志 *(A brief description of the Naxi language)*. Beijing: The Ethnic Publishing House 民族出版社.

Hé, Jírén 和即仁, Qìnglián Zhào 赵庆莲 & Jiézhēn Hé 和洁珍. 2011. *Nàxīyǔ chángyòng cíhuì* 纳西语常用词汇 *(A dictionary of colloquial Naxi)*. Kunming: The Nationalities Publishing House of Yunnan 云南民族出版社.

Hé, Kāixiáng 和开祥, Lìmín Hé 和力民, Yùhuá Xí 习煜华, Yúnzhāng Hé 和云章, Shìchéng Hé 和士诚, Jíguì Hé 和即贵 & Qìngyuán Hé 和庆元. 1989. *Nàxī Dōngbā gǔjí yìzhù (sān)* 纳西东巴古籍译注（三） *(An annotated translation of Naxi Dongba classical texts, volume 3)*. Yunnan Province Minorities Ancient Books Finishing Publication Planning Office 云南省少数民族古籍整理出版规划办公室 (ed.) (Zhōngguó shǎoshù mínzú gǔjí Yúnnánshěng shǎoshù mínzú gǔjí yìcóng 中国少数民族古籍云南省少数民族古籍译丛 (The ancient books of ethnic minorities in China - Sub-collection: Ancient books of ethnic minorities in Yunnan)). Kunming: The Nationalities Publishing House of Yunnan 云南民族出版社.

Hé, Zhìwǔ 和志武. 1985. Nàxīzú de gǔwénzì hé Dōngbājīng lèibié 纳西族的古文字和东巴经类别 (The ancient script of the Naxi, and a typology of Dongba manuscripts). In Dàliè Guō 郭大烈 & Shìguāng Yáng 杨世光 (eds.), *Dōngbā wénhuà lùnjí* 东巴文化论集 *(Collected papers about Dongba culture)*, 155–172. Kunming: Yunnan Peoples's Publishing House 云南人民出版社.

Hé, Zhìwǔ 和志武. 1987. *Nàxīyǔ jīchǔ yǔfǎ* 纳西语基础语法 *(A basic grammar of Naxi)*. Kunming: The Nationalities Publishing House of Yunnan 云南民族出版社.

Hein, Anke Marion. 2013. *Cultural geography and interregional contacts in prehistoric Liangshan (Southwest China)*. Los Angeles, CA: University of California at Los Angeles PhD thesis.

Henderson, Eugénie J.A. 1952. The main features of Cambodian pronunciation. *Bulletin of the School of Oriental and African Studies* 14(1). 149–174.

Henderson, Eugénie J.A. 1985. Feature shuffling in Southeast Asian languages. In Suriya Ratanakul, David Thomas & Premsrirat Suwilai (eds.), *Southeast Asian Linguistic Studies presented to André-G. Haudricourt*, 1–22. Bangkok: Mahidol University.

Henderson, Eugénie J.A. 1997. *Bwe Karen dictionary*. London: University of London, School of Oriental & African Studies.

Henrich, Nathalie, Christophe d'Alessandro, Michèle Castellengo & Boris Doval. 2004. On the use of the derivative of electroglottographic signals for characterization of nonpathological phonation. *Journal of the Acoustical Society of America* 115(3). 1321–1332.

Hill, Eugen. 2007. Proportionale Analogie, paradigmatischer Ausgleich und Formerweiterung: ein Beitrag zur Typologie des morphologischen Wandels. *Diachronica* 24(1). 79–116.

Hill, Nathan. 2014. Grammatically conditioned sound change. *Language and Linguistics Compass* 8(6). 211–229.

Himmelmann, Nikolaus. 2006. Prosody in language documentation. In Jost Gippert, Nikolaus P. Himmelmann & Ulrike Mosel (eds.), *Essentials of language documentation*, 163–181. Berlin & New York City, NY: De Gruyter.

Hirst, Daniel & Albert Di Cristo. 1998. A survey of intonation systems. In *Intonation systems: A survey of twenty languages*, 1–43. Cambridge, U.K.: Cambridge University Press.

Ho, Sana 何撒娜. 2008. 20 shìjì 80 niándài hòu Zhōngguó xīnán shǎoshù mínzú de rénlèixué yánjiū shùpíng 20世纪80年代后中国西南少数民族的人类学研究述评 (A review of anthropological studies published since the 1980s about ethnic minorities in Southwest China). *Journal of Southwest University for Nationalities* 西南民族大学学报（人文社科版）203(7). 13–21.

Hockett, Charles F. 1955. *A manual of phonology* (Indiana University Publications in Anthropology and Linguistics 11). Baltimore, MD: Waverly Press.

Holton, Gary. 2005. Pitch, tone and intonation in Tanacross. In Sharon Hargus & Keren Rice (eds.), *Athabaskan prosody*, 249–275. Amsterdam: John Benjamins.

Hombert, Jean-Marie. 1986. Word games: Some implications for analysis of tone and other phonological constructs. In John Ohala & Jeri J. Jaeger (eds.), *Experimental phonology*, 175–186. Orlando, FL: Academic Press.

House, David. 2012. Response to Fred Cummins: Looking for rhythm in speech. *Empirical Musicology Review* 7(1-2). 45–48.

Huáng, Bùfán 黄布凡. 1991. Zàng-Miǎnyǔ shēngmǔ duì yùnmǔ yǎnbiàn de yǐngxiǎng 藏缅语声母对韵母演变的影响 (The influence of onsets over rhymes in Tibeto-Burman). *Journal of Chinese Linguistics* 中国语言学报 4. 230–244.

Huáng, Bùfán 黄布凡. 2009. Mùlǐ Shuǐtiánhuà gàikuàng 木里水田话概况 (A survey of Muli Shuitian). *Journal of Sino-Tibetan Linguistics* 汉藏语学报 3. 30–55.

Huáng, Bùfán 黄布凡 & Wàngmǔ Rénzēng 仁增旺姆. 1991. Shǐxìng yǔ 史兴语 (The Shixing language). In Qìngxià Dài 戴庆厦, Bùfán Huáng 黄布凡, Àilán Fù 傅爱兰, Wàngmǔ Rénzēng 仁增旺姆 & Júhuáng Liú 刘菊黄 (eds.), *Zàng-*

Miǎnyǔ shíwǔ zhǒng 藏缅语十五种 *(Fifteen Tibeto-Burman languages)*, 174–197. Beijing: Beijing Yanshan Press 北京燕山出版社.

Huángfǔ, Qìnglián 皇甫庆莲. 1994. *Jīngxuǎn Fǎ-Hàn - Hàn-Fǎ cídiǎn* 精选法汉-汉法词典 *(A concise French/Chinese-Chinese/French dictionary)*. Beijing: The Commercial Press & Larousse 商务印书馆与拉鲁斯出版社.

Huber, Toni. 2012. Micro-migrations of hill peoples in Northern Arunachal Pradesh: Rethinking methodologies and claims of origins in Tibet. In Toni Huber & Stuart Blackburn (eds.), *Origins and migrations in the extended Eastern Himalayas*, 83–106. Leiden: Brill.

Hyman, Larry M. 2005. Why describe African languages? In Akinbiyi Akinlabi & Oluseye Adesola (eds.), *Proceedings of the 4th World Congress of African Linguistics*, 21–42. Cologne: Rüdiger Köppe Verlag.

Hyman, Larry M. 2007a. Elicitation as experimental phonology: Thlangtlang Lai tonology. In Patrice Speeter Beddor, Maria Josep Solé & Manjari Ohala (eds.), *Experimental approaches to phonology*, 7–24. Oxford: Oxford University Press.

Hyman, Larry M. 2007b. Universals of tone rules: 30 years later. In Tomas Riad & Carlos Gussenhoven (eds.), *Tones and tunes. Volume 1: Typological studies in word and sentence prosody* (Phonology and Phonetics 12-1), 1–34. Berlin & New York City, NY: Mouton de Gruyter.

Hyman, Larry M. 2009. How (not) to do phonological typology: The case of pitch-accent. *Language Sciences* 31(2). 213–238.

Hyman, Larry M. 2010. Kuki-Thaadow: An African tone system in Southeast Asia. In Franck Floricic (ed.), *Essais de typologie et de linguistique générale. Mélanges offerts à Denis Creissels*, 31–51. Lyon: ENS Editions.

Hyman, Larry M. 2011. Do tones have features? In Elizabeth Hume, John Goldsmith & W. Leo Wetzels (eds.), *Tones and features*, 50–80. Berlin: De Gruyter Mouton.

Hyman, Larry M. 2014. How to study a tone language, with exemplification from Oku (Grassfields Bantu, Cameroon). *Language Documentation and Conservation* 8. 525–562.

Hyman, Larry M. 2015. Why underlying representations? *UC Berkeley Phonology Lab Annual Report*. 210–226.

Hyman, Larry M. & William R. Leben. 2000. Suprasegmental processes. In Geert Booij, Christian Lehmann & Joachim Mugdan (eds.), *Morphology: An international handbook on inflection and word-formation* (Handbücher zur Sprach- und Kommunikationswissenschaft 17-1), 587–594. Berlin: De Gruyter.

Hyman, Larry M. & Joyce T. Mathangwane. 1998. Tonal domains and depressor consonants in Ikalanga. In Larry M. Hyman & Charles W. Kisseberth (eds.), *The theoretical aspects of Bantu tone*, 195–230. Stanford, CA: Stanford University, Center for the Study of Language & Information Publications.

Hyman, Larry M. & Kemmonye C. Monaka. 2008. Tonal and non-tonal intonation in Shekgalagari. *UC Berkeley Phonology Lab Annual Report*. 269–288.

Hyman, Larry M. & Russell G. Shuh. 1974. Universals of tone rules: Evidence from West Africa. *Linguistic Inquiry* 5. 81–115.

Hyman, Larry M. & Kenneth VanBik. 2002. Tone and stem2 formation in Hakha Lai. *Linguistics of the Tibeto-Burman Area* 25. 113–121.

Hyman, Larry M. & Kenneth VanBik. 2004. Directional rule application and output problems in Hakha Lai tone. *Language and Linguistics* 5. 821–861.

International Phonetic Association. 1949. *The principles of the International Phonetic Association, being a description of the International Phonetic Alphabet and the manner of using it, illustrated by texts in 51 languages.* Reprinted 1963. London: International Phonetic Association.

Iverson, Gregory K. & Joseph Salmons. 2006. On the typology of final laryngeal neutralization: Evolutionary Phonology and laryngeal realism. *Theoretical Linguistics* 32(2). 205–216.

Jackson, Anthony. 1979. *Na-khi religion: An analytical appraisal of the Na-khi ritual texts* (Religion and Society 8). The Hague: Mouton.

Jacques, Guillaume. 2004. *Phonologie et morphologie du japhug (rGyalrong)*. Paris: Université Paris VII PhD thesis.

Jacques, Guillaume. 2011a. A panchronic study of aspirated fricatives, with new evidence from Pumi. *Lingua* 121(9). 1518–1538.

Jacques, Guillaume. 2011b. The structure of the Tangut verb. *Journal of Chinese Linguistics* 39(2). 419–443.

Jacques, Guillaume. 2013. Ideophones in Japhug (Rgyalrong). *Anthropological Linguistics* 55(3). 256–287.

Jacques, Guillaume. 2014. Cone. In Jackson T.-S. Sun (ed.), *Phonological profiles of little-studied Tibetic varieties* (Language and Linguistics Monograph Series 55), 269–375. Taipei: Institute of Linguistics, Academia Sinica.

Jacques, Guillaume. 2016. On the directionality of analogy in a Dhegiha paradigm. *International Journal of American Linguistics* 82(2). 239–248.

Jacques, Guillaume. Submitted. Grammaticalization in Japhug and Gyalrongic languages.

Jacques, Guillaume & Johann-Mattis List. Submitted. Save the trees: Why we need tree models in linguistic reconstruction.

Jacques, Guillaume & Alexis Michaud. 2011. Approaching the historical phonology of three highly eroded Sino-Tibetan languages: Naxi, Na and Laze. *Diachronica* 28(4). 468–498.

Jiāng, Zhúyí 姜竹仪. 1993. Nàxīyǔ dōngbù hé xībù fāngyán yǔfǎ yìtóng gàikuàng 纳西语东部和西部方言语法异同概况 (Syntactic similarities and differences between Western and Eastern dialects of Naxi). *Minority Languages of China* 民族语文 4. 43–50.

Jones, Robert B. 1986. Pitch register languages. In John McCoy & Timothy Light (eds.), *Contributions to Sino-Tibetan studies*, 135–143. Leiden: E.J. Brill.

Journet, Nicolas. 1998. Compte-rendu de: Une société sans père ni mari. Les Na de Chine. Cai Hua, Presses Universitaires de France, 1997, 372 p. *Sciences humaines* 79.

Juge, Matthew L. 2013. Analogy as a source of suppletion. In Ritsuko Kikusawa & Lawrence A. Reid (eds.), *Historical Linguistics 2011: Selected papers from the 20th International Conference on Historical Linguistics, Osaka, 25-30 July 2011* (Current Issues in Linguistic Theory 326), 175–197. Amsterdam: John Benjamins.

Karcevskij, Serge. 1931. Sur la phonologie de la phrase. *Travaux du Cercle linguistique de Prague* 4. 188–226.

Karlsson, Anastasia, David House & Jan-Olof Svantesson. 2012. Intonation adapts to lexical tone: The case of Kammu. *Phonetica* 69(1-2). 28–47.

Karttunen, Lauri. 2006. The insufficiency of paper-and-pencil linguistics: The case of Finnish prosody. In M. Butt, M. Dalrymple & T.H. King (eds.), *Intelligent linguistic architectures: Variations on themes by Ronald M. Kaplan*, 287–300. Stanford, CA: CSLI Publications.

Kawahara, Shigeto. 2015. The phonology of Japanese accent. In Haruo Kubozono (ed.), *The handbook of Japanese phonetics and phonology* (Handbooks of Japanese Language and Linguistics 2), 445–492. Berlin: De Gruyter.

Keating, Patricia. 1990. The window model of coarticulation: Articulatory evidence. In Mary Beckman & John Kingston (eds.), *Papers in Laboratory Phonology I: Between grammar and physics of speech*, 451–470. Cambridge, U.K.: Cambridge University Press.

Khatiwada, Rajesh. 2009. Illustrations of the IPA: Nepali. *Journal of the International Phonetic Association* 39(3). 373–380.

Kirby, James. 2010. Dialect experience in Vietnamese tone perception. *Journal of the Acoustical Society of America* 127(6). 3749–3757.

Kirby, James. 2011. Illustrations of the IPA: Vietnamese (Hanoi Vietnamese). *Journal of the International Phonetic Association* 41(3). 381–392.

Kirby, James. 2014. Incipient tonogenesis in Phnom Penh Khmer: Acoustic and perceptual studies. *Journal of Phonetics* 43. 69–85.

Kirby, James & Alan C.L. Yu. 2007. Lexical and phonotactic effects on wordlikeness judgments in Cantonese. In Jürgen Trouvain & William Barry (eds.), *Proceedings of the 16th International Congress of Phonetic Sciences*, 1389–1392. Saarbrücken.

Knödel, Susanne. 1995. *Die matrilinearen Mosuo von Yongning: eine quellenkritische Auswertung moderner chinesischer Ethnographien* (Kölner ethnologische Studien 22). Münster: Lit Verlag.

Kochanski, Greg P. & Chilin Shih. 2003. Prosody modelling with soft templates. *Speech Communication* 39(3-4). 311–352.

Kohler, Klaus J. 2003. Neglected categories in the modelling of prosody: Pitch timing and non-pitch accents. In Maria-Josep Solé, Daniel Recasens & Joaquín Romero (eds.), *Proceedings of the 15th International Congress of Phonetic Sciences*, 2925–2928. Barcelona: Universitat Autònoma de Barcelona.

Kohler, Klaus J. 2005. Timing and communicative functions of pitch contours. *Phonetica* 62. 88–105.

Kohler, Klaus J. & Oliver Niebuhr. 2011. On the role of articulatory prosodies in German message decoding. *Phonetica* 68. 1–31.

Konoshenko, Maria. 2008. Tonal systems in three dialects of the Kpelle language. *Mandenkan* 44. 21–42.

Konoshenko, Maria. 2014a. Studying tonal complexity, with a special reference to Mande languages. *Language Documentation and Conservation* 8. 563–586.

Konoshenko, Maria. 2014b. The syntax of tone in Guinean Kpelle. In *Proceedings of the 40th Annual Meeting of the Berkeley Linguistics Society*, vol. 40, 233–252. Berkeley, CA: Berkeley Linguistics Society.

Krifka, Manfred. 2008. Basic notions of information structure. *Acta Linguistica Hungarica* 55(3-4). 243–276.

Kuang, Jianjing. 2013. The tonal space of contrastive five level tones. *Phonetica* 70(1-2). 1–23.

Kuang, Jianjing & Patricia Keating. 2014. Glottal articulations in tense vs. lax phonation contrasts. *Journal of the Acoustical Society of America* 136(5). 2784–2797.

Kubozono, Haruo. 1993. *The organization of Japanese prosody* (Studies in Japanese Linguistics 2). Tokyo: Kurosio.

Kubozono, Haruo. 2007. Tonal change in language contact: Evidence from Kagoshima Japanese. In Tomas Riad & Carlos Gussenhoven (eds.), *Tones and tunes*.

Volume 1: Typological studies in word and sentence prosody (Phonology and Phonetics), 323–351. Berlin & New York City, NY: Mouton de Gruyter.

Kubozono, Haruo. 2012. Varieties of pitch accent systems in Japanese. *Lingua* 122(13). 1395–1414.

Kula, Nancy C. & Silke Hamann. 2016. Intonation in Bemba. In Laura J. Downing & Annie Rialland (eds.), *Intonation in African tone languages* (Phonology and Phonetics 24), 321–364. Berlin: De Gruyter.

Kuryłowicz, Jerzy. 1944. La nature des procès dits «analogiques». *Acta linguistica* 5(1). 15–37.

Kühnert, Barbara & Francis Nolan. 1999. The origin of coarticulation. In William J. Hardcastle & Nigel Hewlett (eds.), *Coarticulation: Theory, data and techniques*, 7–30. Cambridge, U.K.: Cambridge University Press.

Lā, Míngyīng 喇明英. 2015. Dāngdài yǔjìngxià Lúgūhú dìqū nà wénhuà bǎohù de sīkǎo 当代语境下泸沽湖地区纳文化保护的思考 (Reflections about the preservation of Na culture of the Lugu lake area in the contemporary linguistic context). In Xīnyú Zhào 赵心愚 & Jìquán Hé 和继全 (eds.), *Nàxīxué yánjiū (dì-yī jí)* 纳西学研究（第一辑） *(Research about the Naxi – volume 1)*, 50–64. Beijing: People's Publishing House 人民出版社.

Labov, William. 1979. *The social origins of sound change*. Vol. 47 (Series B). Trier: Linguistic Agency, University of Trier.

Labov, William. 1994. *Principles of linguistic change. Internal factors* (Language in Society 20). Oxford: Basil Blackwell.

Ladd, Robert. 1978. Stylized intonation. *Language* 54(3). 517–540.

Ladd, Robert. 1996. *Intonational phonology*. Cambridge, U.K.: Cambridge University Press.

Ladd, Robert. 2008. Review of Sun-Ah Jun (ed.) (2005) Prosodic typology: The phonology of intonation and phrasing. Oxford: Oxford University Press. *Phonology* 25. 372–376.

Ladefoged, Peter & Ian Maddieson. 1996. *The sounds of the world's languages* (Phonological Theory). Oxford, U.K. & Cambridge, MA: Blackwell.

Lahiri, Aditi (ed.). 2000. *Analogy, levelling, markedness: Principles of change in phonology and morphology* (Trends in Linguistics. Studies and Monographs [TiLSM] 127). Berlin: De Gruyter.

Lakhi, Libu, Tsering Bum & Kevin Stuart. 2010. China's Namuyi Tibetans: Life, language, and folklore. *Asian Highlands Perspectives* 2. 12–66.

Lāmǎ, Zīwò 拉玛兹偓. 1994. Nàmùyīyǔ zhīshǔ yánjiu 纳木依语支属研究 (Research on the classification of the Namuyi language). *Minority Languages of China* 民族语文 1. 50–60.

Lama, Ziwo Qiu-Fuyuan. 2012. *Subgrouping of Nisoic (Yi) languages: A study from the perspectives of shared innovation and phylogenetic estimation.* Arlington, TX: University of Texas at Arlington PhD thesis.

Lambrecht, Knud. 1994. *Information structure and sentence form: Topic, focus, and the mental representations of discourse referents.* Cambridge, U.K.: Cambridge University Press.

Lāmù, Gātǔsà 拉木·嘎吐萨. 1998. *Zǒu jìn Nǚ'érguó* 走进女儿国 *(Entering the kingdom of women).* Kunming: Yunnan Fine Arts Press 云南美术出版社.

Lāmù, Gātǔsà 拉木·嘎吐萨. 2007. *Nàxīxué lùnjí* 纳西学论集 *(A collection of articles about the Naxi).* Beijing: The Ethnic Publishing House 民族出版社.

Laniran, Yetunde O. & Nick Clements. 2003. Downstep and high raising: Interacting factors in Yorùbá tone production. *Journal of Phonetics* 31. 203–250.

LaPolla, Randy. 2001. The role of migration and language contact in the development of the Sino-Tibetan language family. In Alexandra Y. Aikhenvald & Robert M. Dixon (eds.), *Areal diffusion and genetic inheritance*, 225–254. Oxford: Oxford University Press.

LaPolla, Randy. 2009. Chinese as a Topic-Comment (not Topic-Prominent and not SVO) language. In Janet Xing (ed.), *Studies of Chinese linguistics: Functional approaches*, 9–22. Hong Kong: Hong Kong University Press.

LaPolla, Randy & Chenglong Huang. 2003. *A grammar of Qiang with annotated texts and glossary.* Berlin: Mouton de Gruyter.

Lātāmī, Dáshí 拉他咪·达石. 2006. *Mósuō shèhuì wénhuà yánjiū lùnwénjí* 摩梭社会文化研究论文集(1960-2005) *(Collected papers about Mosuo society and culture, 1960-2005).* 2 volumes. Kunming: Yunnan University Press 云南大学出版社.

Lātāmī, Wángyǒng 拉他咪·王勇. 2009. *Chéngxiāng zhī jiān de cūnluò - Nínglàng Yízú zìzhìxiàn Làngqú qūyù Mósuōrén de wénhuà shēnghuó shǐ* 城乡之间的村落—宁蒗彝族自治县蒗蕖区域摩梭人的文化生活史 *(Villages between town and countryside: A history of the cultural life of the Mosuo people in Langqu area of Ninglang Yi County).* Kunming: The Nationalities Publishing House of Yunnan 云南民族出版社.

Lātāmī, Wángyǒng 拉他咪·王勇. 2016. *Xīnsuì yǔ yōushāng: Mósuō wénhuà tiányě diàochá bàogào wénjí* 心碎与忧伤——摩梭文化田野调查报告文集 *(Grief and sorrow: A collection of fieldwork research reports about Mosuo culture).* Kunming: The Nationalities Publishing House of Yunnan 云南民族出版社.

Launey, Michel. 1994. *Une grammaire omniprédicative: Essai sur la morphosyntaxe du nahuatl classique* (Sciences du langage). Paris: CNRS Editions.

Lee, Wai-Sum & Eric Zee. 2003. Illustrations of the IPA: Standard Chinese (Beijing). *Journal of the International Phonetic Association* 33(1). 109–112.

Lehiste, Ilse. 1975. The phonetic structure of paragraphs. In Antonie Cohen & Sibout G. Noteboom (eds.), *Structure and process in speech perception*, 195–206. Berlin: Springer.

Léon, Pierre. 1969. Principes et méthodes en phonostylistique. *Langue française* 3(1). 73–84.

Leroy, Christine & Catherine Paris. 1974. Etude articulatoire de quelques sons de l'oubykh d'après film aux rayons X (An articulatory study of some of the sounds of Ubykh based on X-ray cinematography). *Bulletin de la Société de Linguistique de Paris* 49(1). 255–286.

Leslie, David & George Schaller. 2009. Bos grunniens and Bos mutus (Artiodactyla: Bovidae). *Mammalian Species*. 1–17.

Lévi-Strauss, Claude. 1949. *Les structures élémentaires de la parenté*. Paris: Presses Universitaires de France.

Lévi-Strauss, Claude. 2004. Le retour de l'oncle maternel. In Michel Izard (ed.), *Lévi-Strauss*. Paris: L'Herne.

Lewis, M. Paul, Gary F. Simons & Charles D. Fennig (eds.). 2016. *Languages of China: An Ethnologue country report*. Dallas, TX: SIL International. http://www.ethnologue.com/.

Lǐ, Dázhū 李达珠. 2015. *Dábā wénhuà: Mósuōrén de shēngmìng zhéxué* 达巴文化――摩梭人的生命哲学 *(Daba culture: The philosophy of life of the Mosuo people))* (Mósuō wénhuà cóngshū 摩梭文化丛书). Chengdu 成都: Sichuan Nationalities Publishing House 四川民族出版社.

Li, Fang-kuei. 1964. A Chipewyan ethnological text. *International Journal of American Linguistics* 30(2). 132–136.

Li, Lin-ts'an 李霖灿, K'un Chang 张琨 & Ts'ai Ho 和才. 1953. *Móxiē xiàngxíng wénzì zìdiǎn* 么些象形文字字典 *(A dictionary of Moxie (Naxi) pictographs)*. Hong Kong 香港: Shuowenshe 说文社.

Li, Lin-ts'an 李霖灿, K'un Chang 张琨 & Ts'ai Ho 和才. 2001. *Nàxī xiàngxíng biāoyīn wénzì zìdiǎn* 纳西象形标音文字字典 *(A dictionary of Naxi pictographic and phonetic characters)*. Kunming: The Nationalities Publishing House of Yunnan 云南民族出版社.

Lǐ, Zǐhè 李子鹤. 2015. Nàxī yǔyán yánjiū huígù - Jiānlùn yǔyán zài wénhuà yánjiū zhōng de jīchǔ dìwèi 纳西语言研究回顾―― 兼论语言在文化研究中的基础地位 (A review of Naxi language studies, with a discussion of the fundamental role of cultural studies for linguistic research). *Chama Gudao Yanjiu Jikan* 茶马古道研究集刊 4. 125–131.

Liberman, Mark. 1975. *The intonational system of English*. Cambridge, MA: MIT PhD thesis.

Lidz, Liberty. 2006. A synopsis of Yongning Na (Mosuo). Handout circulated at the 39th International Conference on Sino-Tibetan Languages and Linguistics, University of Washington Department of Asian Languages and Literature.

Lidz, Liberty. 2007. Evidentiality in Yongning Na (Mosuo). *Linguistics of the Tibeto-Burman Area* 30(2). 45–87.

Lidz, Liberty. 2010. *A descriptive grammar of Yongning Na (Mosuo)*. Austin, TX: University of Texas, Department of linguistics PhD thesis.

Lidz, Liberty. 2011. Agentive marking in Yongning Na (Mosuo). *Linguistics of the Tibeto-Burman Area* 34(2). 49–72.

Lidz, Liberty. 2016. Yongning Na (Mosuo). In Graham Thurgood & Randy J. LaPolla (eds.), *The Sino-Tibetan languages*, 2nd edition (Routledge Language Family Series), 840–855. London & New York City, NY: Routledge.

Lín, Màocàn 林茂灿 & Jǐngzhù Yán 颜景助. 1980. Běijīnghuà qīngshēng de shēngxué xìngzhì 北京话轻声的声学性质 (On the acoustic quality of the neutral tone in Pekinese speech). *Fangyan* 方言 (3). 166–178.

Lin, You-Jing. 2002. A dimension missed: East and West in Situ rGyalrong orientation marking. *Language and Linguistics* 3(1). 27–42.

Lin, You-Jing. 2009. *Units in Zhuokeji rGyalrong discourse: Prosody and grammar*. Santa Barbara, CA: University of California, Santa Barbara PhD thesis.

Lín, Yǔtáng 林語堂. 1972. *Dāngdài Hàn-Yīng cídiǎn* 當代漢英詞典 (*Chinese-English dictionary of modern usage*). Hong Kong 香港: Chinese University of Hong Kong Press 香港中文大學.

Lindau, M. 1986. Testing a model of intonation in a tone language. *Journal of the Acoustical Society of America* 80(3). 757–764.

Lindblom, B. 1990. Explaining phonetic variation: A sketch of the H&H theory. In William J. Hardcastle & Alain Marchal (eds.), *Speech production and speech modelling*, 403–439. Dordrecht: Kluwer.

Liu, Huidan, Weina Zhao, Minghua Nuo, Li Jiang, Jian Wu & Yeping He. 2010. Tibetan number identification based on classification of number components in Tibetan word segmentation. In *Proceedings of the 23rd International Conference on Computational Linguistics: Posters*, 719–724. Beijing: Association for Computational Linguistics.

Liú, Lóngchū 刘龙初. 1981. Lùn Yǒngníng Nàxīzú "é" děngjí de láiyuán jíqí jiējí shǔxìng 论永宁纳西族"俄"等级的来源及其阶级属性 (About the origin and social-class attributes of the "serf" caste among the Naxi of Yongning). *Ethno-National Studies* 民族研究 5. 50–58.

Luo, Chia-Ling. 2008. *The gender impact of modernization among the matrilineal Moso in China*. The Hague: Institute of Social Studies M.A. thesis.

Mac, Dang-Khoa, Thi-Lan Nguyen, Alexis Michaud & Do-Dat Tran. 2015. Influences of speaker attitudes on glottalized tones: A study of two Vietnamese sentence-final particles. In The Scottish Consortium for ICPhS 2015 (ed.), *Proceedings of 18th International Congress of Phonetic Sciences*, 1–5. Glasgow: University of Glasgow.

Maddieson, Ian. 2011. Tone. In Matthew S. Dryer & Martin Haspelmath (eds.), *The World Atlas of Language Structures online*. Leipzig: Max Planck Digital Library. http://wals.info/chapter/13.

Manessy, Gabriel. 1990. Du bon usage de la méthode comparative historique dans les langues africaines et ailleurs (On the proper use of the historical comparative method for languages of Africa and elsewhere). *Travaux du Cercle Linguistique d'Aix-en-Provence* 8. 89–107.

Martin, Philippe. 1977. Syntax and intonation: An integrated theory. *Toronto Semiotic Circle Monographs, Victoria University* 2.

Martin, Philippe. 1981. Pour une théorie de l'intonation. In Mario Rossi, Albert Di Cristo, Daniel Hirst, Philippe Martin & Yukihiro Nishinuma (eds.), *L'intonation, de l'acoustique à la sémantique*, 234–271. Paris: Klincksieck.

Martin, Philippe. 2001. ToBI: l'illusion scientifique? In *Actes du Colloque Journées Prosodie 2001*, 144–148. Grenoble: CNRS-Groupe de Recherche 34 Phonologie.

Martin, Philippe. 2015. *The structure of spoken language: intonation in Romance*. Cambridge, U.K.: Cambridge University Press.

Martinet, André. 1956. *La description phonologique avec application au parler franco-provençal d'Hauteville (Savoie)*. Genève: Droz.

Martinet, André. 1957. Phonetics and linguistic evolution. In Louise Kaiser (ed.), *Manual of phonetics*, 252–273. Amsterdam: North Holland.

Martinet, André. 1962. *A functional view of language*. Oxford: Oxford University Press.

Martinet, André. 1969. *La linguistique: Guide alphabétique*. Paris: Denoël.

Martinet, André. 1970. *La linguistique synchronique: Etudes et recherches*. Paris: Presses universitaires de France.

Martinet, André. 1981. Fricatives and spirants. In Bhakti Prasad Mallik (ed.), *Suniti Kumar Chatterji commemoration volume*, 145–151. Burdwan, West Bengal, India: Burdwan University Press.

Martinet, André. 1988. The internal conditioning of phonological changes. *La linguistique* 24(2). 17–26.

Martinet, André. 1990. La synchronie dynamique. *La linguistique* 26(2). 13–23.

Martinet, André. 1996. *The internal conditioning of phonological systems.* Thiruvananthapuram: International School of Dravidian Linguistics.

Maspero, Henri. 1912. Etude sur la phonétique historique de la langue annamite: Les initiales (Studies in Annamese historical phonetics: Initial consonants). *Bulletin de l'Ecole Française d'Extrême-Orient* 12. 1–127.

Mathieu, Christine. 2003. *A history and anthropological study of the ancient kingdoms of the Sino-Tibetan borderland - Naxi and Mosuo* (Mellen Studies in Anthropology 11). Lewiston, NY: Edwin Mellen Pr.

Mathieu, Christine. 2015. The story of Bon in the Naxi Dongba religion. In Angelo Andrea Di Castro & David Templeman (eds.), *Asian horizons: Giuseppe Tucci's Buddhist, Indian, Himalayan and Central Asian studies* (Serie Orientale Roma 106). Melbourne: Victoria Monash University Publishing.

Matisoff, James A. 1973. *The grammar of Lahu* (Linguistics 75). Berkeley, CA & Los Angeles, CA: University of California Publications.

Matisoff, James A. 1978. *Variational semantics in Tibeto-Burman: The "organic" approach to linguistic comparison.* Vol. 6. Philadelphia, PA: Institute for the Study of Human Issues.

Matisoff, James A. 1992. The mother of all morphemes: Augmentatives and diminutives in areal and universal perspective. In Martha Ratliff & Eric Schiller (eds.), *Papers from the First Annual Meeting of the Southeast Asian Linguistics Society (SEALS)*, 293–349. Tempe, AZ: Arizona State University, Program for Southeast Asian Studies.

Matisoff, James A. 1997. Dàyáng Pumi phonology and adumbrations of comparative Qiangic. *Mon-Khmer Studies* 27. 171–213.

Matisoff, James A. 2004. "Brightening" and the place of Xixia (Tangut) in the Qiangic branch of Tibeto-Burman. In Ying-chin Lin, Fang-min Hsu, Chun-chih Lee, Jackson T.-S. Sun, Hsiu-fang Yang & Dah-an Ho (eds.), *Studies on Sino-Tibetan languages: Papers in honor of Professor Hwang-cherng Gong on his seventieth birthday*, 327–352. Taipei: Language & Linguistics Monograph Series W-4.

Mattison, Siobhán M. 2010. Economic impacts of tourism and erosion of the visiting system among the Mosuo of Lugu Lake. *The Asia Pacific Journal of Anthropology* 11(2). 159–176.

Mauss, Marcel. 1990. *The gift: The form and reason for exchange in archaic societies (Essai sur le don. Forme et raison de l'échange dans les sociétés archaïques).* Trans. by William Douglas Halls. New York City, NY: W.W. Norton.

Mazard, Mireille. 2011. Powerful speech: Remembering the Long Cultural Revolution in Yunnan. *Inner Asia* 13(1). 161–182.

Mazaudon, Martine. 1985. Dzongkha number systems. In Ratanakul Suriya, David Thomas & Premsrirat Suwilai (eds.), *Southeast Asian linguistic studies presented to André-G. Haudricourt*, 124–157. Bangkok: Mahidol University.

Mazaudon, Martine. 2003. Tamang. In Graham Thurgood & Randy LaPolla (eds.), *The Sino-Tibetan languages*, 291–314. London: Routledge.

Mazaudon, Martine. 2004. *Tamang corpus of texts with synchronized recordings in the Pangloss Collection*. Paris. http://lacito.vjf.cnrs.fr/pangloss/index_en.html.

Mazaudon, Martine. 2014. Studying emergent tone-systems in Nepal: Pitch, phonation and word-tone in Tamang. *Language Documentation and Conservation* 8. 587–612.

Mazaudon, Martine & Boyd Michailovsky. 2007. La phonologie panchronique aujourd'hui: quelques repères. In Jocelyne Fernandez-Vest (ed.), *Combats pour les langues du monde: hommage à Claude Hagège*, 351–362. Paris: L'Harmattan.

Mazaudon, Martine & Alexis Michaud. 2008. Tonal contrasts and initial consonants: A case study of Tamang, a 'missing link' in tonogenesis. *Phonetica* 65(4). 231–256.

McKhann, Charles F. 1998. Naxi, Rerkua, Moso, Meng: Kinship, politics and ritual on the Yunnan-Sichuan frontier. In Michael Oppitz & Elisabeth Hsu (eds.), *Naxi and Moso ethnography*, 23–45. Zürich: Völkerkundemuseum.

McKhann, Charles F. 2012. Origin and return: Genesis and the souls of the dead in Naxi myth and ritual. In Toni Huber & Stuart Blackburn (eds.), *Origins and migrations in the extended Eastern Himalayas*, 275–298. Leiden: Brill.

McLaughlin, Fiona. 2008. The ascent of Wolof as an urban vernacular and national lingua franca in Senegal. In Cécile B. Vigouroux & Salikoko S. Mufwene (eds.), *Globalization and language vitality: Perspectives from Africa*, 142–170. London: Continuum.

Meillet, Antoine. 1936. *Linguistique historique et linguistique générale* (Collection Linguistique 40). Paris: Klincksieck.

Michael, Lev. 2010. The interaction of tone and stress in the prosodic system of Iquito (Zaparoan). *UC Berkeley Phonology Lab Annual Report*. 57–79.

Michailovsky, Boyd. 1975. Notes on the Kiranti verb (East Nepal). *Linguistics of the Tibeto-Burman Area* 2(2). 183–218.

Michailovsky, Boyd. 2011. Les langues tibéto-birmanes. In Emilio Bonvini, Joëlle Busuttil & Alain Peyraube (eds.), *Encyclopédie des sciences du langage et dictionnaire des langues*, 1037–1040. Presses Universitaires de France.

Michailovsky, Boyd & Alexis Michaud. 2006. Syllabic inventory of a Western Naxi dialect, and correspondence with Joseph F. Rock's transcriptions. *Cahiers de linguistique - Asie Orientale* 35(1). 3–21.

Michailovsky, Boyd, Martine Mazaudon, Alexis Michaud, Séverine Guillaume, Alexandre François & Evangelia Adamou. 2014. Documenting and researching endangered languages: The Pangloss Collection. *Language Documentation and Conservation* 8. 119–135.

Michaud, Alexis. 2004a. A measurement from electroglottography: DECPA, and its application in prosody. In Bernard Bel & Isabelle Marlien (eds.), *Proceedings of Speech Prosody 2004*, 633–636. Nara, Japan: International Speech Communication Association.

Michaud, Alexis. 2004b. Final consonants and glottalization: New perspectives from Hanoi Vietnamese. *Phonetica* 61(2-3). 119–146.

Michaud, Alexis. 2005. *Prosodie de langues à tons (naxi et vietnamien), prosodie de l'anglais: éclairages croisés.* Paris: Université Sorbonne Nouvelle – Paris 3 PhD thesis.

Michaud, Alexis. 2006a. Three extreme cases of neutralisation: Nasality, retroflexion and lip-rounding in Naxi. *Cahiers de linguistique - Asie Orientale* 35(1). 23–55.

Michaud, Alexis. 2006b. Tonal reassociation and rising tonal contours in Naxi. *Linguistics of the Tibeto-Burman Area* 29(1). 61–94.

Michaud, Alexis. 2008a. A first approach to the prosodic system of Laze: Fieldwork data and cross-language perspectives. In *Workshop on Tibeto-Burman Languages of Sichuan, November 21-24, 2008.* Institute of Linguistics, Academia Sinica. http://hal.archives-ouvertes.fr/halshs-01372956.

Michaud, Alexis. 2008b. Phonemic and tonal analysis of Yongning Na. *Cahiers de linguistique – Asie Orientale* 37(2). 159–196.

Michaud, Alexis. 2009. Mùlǐ Shuǐtiánhuà shēngdiào xìtǒng yánjiū 木里水田话声调系统研究 (The prosodic system of Muli Shuitian (Laze)). *Minority Languages of China* 民族语文 6. 28–33.

Michaud, Alexis. 2011. The tones of numerals and numeral-plus-classifier phrases: On structural similarities between Naxi, Na and Laze. *Linguistics of the Tibeto-Burman Area* 34(1). 1–26.

Michaud, Alexis. 2013a. Review of: Pinson, Thomas M. 2012. A Naxi-Chinese-English Dictionary (Naqxi-Habaq-Yiyu Ceeqdiail / Nàxī-Hàn-Yīng cídiǎn 纳西汉英词典). *Linguistics of the Tibeto-Burman Area* 36(2). 129–137.

Michaud, Alexis. 2013b. Studying level-tone systems in Asia: The case of the Naish languages. In *Proceedings of International Conference on Phonetics of the Languages in China (ICPLC-2013)*, 1–6. Hong Kong: City University of Hong Kong.

Michaud, Alexis. 2013c. The tone patterns of numeral-plus-classifier phrases in Yongning Na: A synchronic description and analysis. In Nathan Hill & Tom Owen-Smith (eds.), *Transhimalayan linguistics. Historical and descriptive linguistics of the Himalayan area* (Trends in Linguistics. Studies and Monographs [TiLSM] 266), 275–311. Berlin: De Gruyter Mouton.

Michaud, Alexis. 2015a. *Na-English-Chinese-French dictionary.* Paris: Huma-Num. https://halshs.archives-ouvertes.fr/halshs-01204638.

Michaud, Alexis. 2015b. Phrasing, prominence, and morphotonology: How utterances are divided into tone groups in Yongning Na. *Bulletin of Chinese Linguistics* 8. 86–116.

Michaud, Alexis & Marc Brunelle. 2016. Information structure in Asia: Yongning Na (Sino-Tibetan) and Vietnamese (Austroasiatic). In Caroline Féry & Shinichiro Ishihara (eds.), *Oxford handbook of information structure*, 774–789. Oxford: Oxford University Press.

Michaud, Alexis & Likun He. 2015. Phonemic and tonal analysis of the Pianding dialect of Naxi (Dadong County, Lijiang Municipality). *Cahiers de linguistique - Asie Orientale* 44(1). 1–35 plus online Appendices.

Michaud, Alexis & Xueguang He. 2007. Reassociated tones and coalescent syllables in Naxi (Tibeto-Burman). *Journal of the International Phonetic Association* 37(3). 237–255.

Michaud, Alexis & Guillaume Jacques. 2010. Insights into Naxi and Pumi at the end of the 19th century: Evidence on sound changes from the word lists by Charles-Eudes Bonin. *Cahiers de linguistique - Asie Orientale* 39(1). 21–40.

Michaud, Alexis & Guillaume Jacques. 2012. The phonology of Laze: Phonemic analysis, syllabic inventory, and a short word list. *Yuyanxue Luncong* 语言学论丛 45. 196–230.

Michaud, Alexis, Guillaume Jacques & Robert L. Rankin. 2012. Historical transfer of nasality between consonantal onset and vowel: From C to V or from V to C? *Diachronica* 29(2). 201–230.

Michaud, Alexis & Dashi Latami. 2011. A description of endangered phonemic oppositions in Mosuo (Yongning Na). In Tjeerd De Graaf, Xu Shixuan & Cecilia Brassett (eds.), *Issues of language endangerment*, 55–71. Beijing 北京: Intellectual Property Publishing House 知识产权出版社.

Michaud, Alexis & Dáshí Lātāmī 拉他咪·达石. 2010. Yúnnánshěng Lìjiāngshì Yǒngníng qūyù Mósuōhuà zhōng bīnlín xiāoshī de shēngdiào yǔ yīnwèi 云南省丽江市永宁区域摩梭话中濒临消失的声调与音位 (Endangered tones and phonemes in Yongning Na). *Lijiang Ethnic Studies* 丽江民族研究 4. Bō Zhāng

张波 (ed.). Lìjiāng shīfàn gāoděng zhuānkē xuéxiào mínzú wénhuà yánjiū suǒ biān 丽江师范高等专科学校民族文化研究所编, 344–355.

Michaud, Alexis, Minh Châu Nguyễn & Jacqueline Vaissière. 2015. Phonetic insights into a simple level-tone system: 'careful' vs. 'impatient' realizations of Naxi High, Mid and Low tones. In The Scottish Consortium for ICPhS 2015 (ed.), *Proceedings of 18th International Congress of Phonetic Sciences*, 1–5. Glasgow: University of Glasgow.

Michaud, Alexis & Jacqueline Vaissière. 2007a. Le devenir phonétique des formes rédupliquées: réduplication, tons lexicaux et intonation en naxi. *Faits de langues* 29. 23–35.

Michaud, Alexis & Jacqueline Vaissière. 2007b. The phonetic evolution of reduplicated expressions: Reduplication, lexical tones and prosody in Na (Naxi). In Jürgen Trouvain & William Barry (eds.), *Proceedings of the 16th International Congress of Phonetic Sciences*, 801–804. Saarbrücken.

Michaud, Alexis & Jacqueline Vaissière. 2015. Tone and intonation: Introductory notes and practical recommendations. *KALIPHO - Kieler Arbeiten zur Linguistik und Phonetik* 3. 43–80.

Milan, Pascale-Marie. 2013. Festivité, performance et agencéité chez les Na de Chine: du lien social à l'arène politique (Festivity, performance, and agency freedom among the Na of China: From social ties to political arena). *Cultures-Kairós*. No page numbers.

Milroy, James & Lesley Milroy. 1985. Linguistic change, social network and speaker innovation. *Journal of Linguistics* 21(2). 339–384.

Mixdorff, Hansjörg, Hung Nguyen Bach, Hiroya Fujisaki & Chi Mai Luong. 2003. Quantitative analysis and synthesis of syllabic tones in Vietnamese. In *Proceedings of Eurospeech*, 177–180. Geneva.

Moravcsik, Edith A. 1978. Reduplicative constructions. In Joseph H. Greenberg (ed.), *Universals of human language, volume 3: Word structure*, 297–334. Stanford, CA: Stanford University Press.

Morey, Stephen. 2008. The Tai languages of Assam. In Anthony Diller, Jerold A. Edmondson & Luo Yongxian (eds.), *The Tai-Kadai languages*, 207–253. London: Routledge.

Morey, Stephen. 2014. Studying tones in North East India: Tai, Singpho and Tangsa. *Language Documentation and Conservation* 8. 637–671.

Mullaney, Thomas. 2010. *Coming to terms with the nation: Ethnic classification in modern China*. Berkeley, CA: University of California Press.

Murdock, George P. 1949. *Social structure*. New York City, NY: McMillan.

Myers, Scott. 1996. Boundary tones and the phonetic implementation of tone in Chichewa. *Studies in African linguistics* 25(1). 29.

Myers, Scott. 2003. F_0 timing in Kinyarwanda. *Phonetica* 60. 71–97.

Nespor, Marina & Irene Vogel. 1986. *Prosodic phonology*. Dordrecht: Foris.

Nguyen, Thi-Lan, Alexis Michaud, Do-Dat Tran & Dang-Khoa Mac. 2013. The interplay of intonation and complex lexical tones: How speaker attitudes affect the realization of glottalization on Vietnamese sentence-final particles. In *Proceedings of Interspeech 2013*. Lyon: International Speech Communication Association.

Niebuhr, Oliver. 2007. The signalling of German rising-falling intonation categories: The interplay of synchronization, shape, and height. *Phonetica* 64. 174–193.

Niebuhr, Oliver. 2009a. F_0-based rhythm effects on the perception of local syllable prominence. *Phonetica* 66(1-2). 95–112.

Niebuhr, Oliver. 2009b. Intonation segments and segmental intonations. In *Proceedings of the 10th Interspeech conference*, 2435–2438. Brighton, UK: International Speech Communication Association.

Niebuhr, Oliver. 2010. On the phonetics of intensifying emphasis in German. *Phonetica* 67. 170–198.

Niebuhr, Oliver. 2013. The acoustic complexity of intonation. In Eva Liina Asu & Pärtel Lippus (eds.), *Nordic prosody XI*, 15–29. Frankfurt: Peter Lang.

Niebuhr, Oliver & Klaus J. Kohler. 2004. Perception and cognitive processing of tonal alignment in German. In *Proceedings of the international symposium on Tonal Aspects of Languages (TAL 2004)*, 155–158. Beijing.

Niebuhr, Oliver & Alexis Michaud. 2015. Speech data acquisition: The underestimated challenge. *KALIPHO - Kieler Arbeiten zur Linguistik und Phonetik* 3. 1–42.

Nishida, Tatsuo. 1985. The Hsihsia, Lolo, and Moso languages. In Graham Thurgood, James A. Matisoff & David Bradley (eds.), *Linguistics of the Sino-Tibetan area: The state of the art. Papers presented to Paul K. Benedict for his 71st birthday*. Canberra, Australia: Australian National University.

Nolan, Francis. 1992. The descriptive role of segments: Evidence from assimilation. In Gerard J. Docherty & Robert Ladd (eds.), *Papers in laboratory phonology II: Gesture, segment, prosody*, 261–280. Cambridge, U.K.: Cambridge University Press.

Nolan, Francis. 2003. Intonational equivalence: An experimental evaluation of pitch scales. In Maria-Josep Solé, Daniel Recasens & Joaquín Romero (eds.),

Proceedings of the 15th International Congress of Phonetic Sciences, 771–774. Barcelona: Universitat Autònoma de Barcelona.

Noonan, Michael. 2003. Nar-Phu. In Graham Thurgood & Randy LaPolla (eds.), *The Sino-Tibetan languages*, 336–352. London: Routledge.

Nooteboom, Sieb. 2011. Self-monitoring for speech errors in novel phrases and phrasal lexical items. *Yearbook of Phraseology* 2. 1–16.

Nurse, Derek. 2011. A brief background to writing grammars in Africa. In *The Kifuliiru language, volume 1: Phonology, tone, and morphological derivation* (author: Karen Van Otterloo), xxi–xxv. Dallas, TX: SIL International.

Odden, David. 1995. Tone: African languages. In John Goldsmith (ed.), *Handbook of phonological theory*, 444–475. Oxford: Blackwell.

Odden, David. 1998. Verbal tone melodies in Kikerewe. In Ian Maddieson & Thomas J. Hinnebusch (eds.), *Language history and linguistic description in Africa*, 177–184. Trenton: Africa World Press.

Odden, David. 2005. Comments on Nobuko Yoneda, "Tone patterns of Matengo nominals". In Shigeki Kaji (ed.), *Proceedings of the symposium "Cross-linguistic studies of tonal phenomena: Tonogenesis, Japanese accentology, and other topics"*, 411–418. Tokyo: Tokyo University of Foreign Studies, Research Institute for Languages, Cultures of Asia & Africa.

Ohala, John. 1978. The production of tone. In Victoria A. Fromkin (ed.), *Tone: A linguistic survey*, 5–39. New York City, NY & San Francisco, CA & London: Academic Press.

Ohala, John. 1984. An ethological perspective on common cross-language utilization of F_0 in voice. *Phonetica* 41. 1–16.

Ohala, John. 1989. Sound change is drawn from a pool of synchronic variation. In Leiv Egil Breivik & Ernst Håkon Jahr (eds.), *Language change: Contributions to the study of its causes*, 173–198. The Hague: Mouton de Gruyter.

Ohala, John & Manjari Ohala. 1993. The phonetics of nasal phonology: Theorems and data. In Marie Huffman & Rena Krakow (eds.), *Nasals, nasalization, and the velum*, 225–249. San Diego, CA: Academic Press.

Orlikoff, Robert F. 1998. Scrambled EGG: The uses and abuses of electroglottography. *Phonoscope* 1(1). 37–53.

Ota, Ichiro, Hitoshi Nikaido & Akira Utsugi. 2016. Tonal variation in Kagoshima Japanese and factors of language change. In Marie-Hélène Côté, Remco Knooihuizen & John Nerbonne (eds.), *The future of dialects: Selected papers from Methods in Dialectology XV* (Language Variation 1), 389–398. Berlin: Language Science Press.

Palancar, Enrique L. 2016. A typology of tone and inflection: A view from the Oto-Manguean languages of Mexico. In Enrique L. Palancar & Jean Léo Léonard (eds.), *Tone and inflection: New facts and new perspectives* (Trends in Linguistics. Studies and Monographs [TiLSM] 296), 109–139. Berlin: De Gruyter Mouton.

Pierrehumbert, Janet. 1981. Synthesizing intonation. *Journal of the Acoustical Society of America* 70(4). 985–995.

Pike, Kenneth L. 1945. *The intonation of American English* (University of Michigan Publications in Linguistics 1). Ann Arbor, MI: University of Michigan Press.

Pike, Kenneth L. 1948. *Tone languages. a technique for determining the number and type of pitch contrasts in a language, with studies in tonemic substitution and fusion.* Ann Arbor, MI: University of Michigan Press.

Pinson, Thomas M. 2012. *Nàxī-Hàn-Yīng cídiǎn* 纳西汉英词典 *(A Naxi-Chinese-English dictionary) / Naqxi-Habaq-Yiyu Ceeqdiai.* Kunming: The Nationalities Publishing House of Yunnan 云南民族出版社.

Pinson, Thomas M. & Jacqueline S. Pinson. 2008. An introduction to Kunming hua. Kunming. https://halshs.archives-ouvertes.fr/halshs-01383557.

Pittayaporn, Pittayawat & James Kirby. 2017. Laryngeal contrasts in the Tai dialect of Cao Bằng. *Journal of the International Phonetic Association* (in press).

Post, Mark. 2008. Adjectives in Thai: Implications for a functionalist typology of word classes. *Linguistic Typology* 12(3). 339–381.

Post, Mark W. 2015. Tones in Northeast Indian languages, with a focus on Tani: A fieldworker's guide. In Mark W. Post, Scott DeLancey & Stephen Morey (eds.), *Language and culture in Northeast India and beyond: In honour of Robbins Burling* (Asia-Pacific Linguistics 23), 182–210. Canberra: Australian National University.

Pulleyblank, Douglas. 1986. *Tone in lexical phonology.* Dordrecht: Reidel.

Pullum, Geoffrey K. & William A. Ladusaw. 1986. *Phonetic symbol guide.* Chicago, IL & London: The University of Chicago Press.

Refflet, Annie. 2006. *Chine inconnue: Peuples naxi du Yunnan.* Courbevoie: Editions Soline.

Remijsen, Bert & Robert Ladd. 2008. The tone system of the Luanyjang dialect of Dinka. *Journal of African Languages and Linguistics* 29(2). 173–213.

Rhodes, Alexandre de. 1651. *Dictionarium Annamiticum Lusitanum et Latinum.* Rome.

Rialland, Annie. 1997. Le parcours du "downstep", ou l'évolution d'une notion. *Bulletin de la Société de Linguistique de Paris* XCII(1). 207–243.

Rialland, Annie. 2001. Anticipatory raising in downstep realization: Evidence for preplanning in tone production. In Shigeki Kaji (ed.), *Proceedings of the sympo-*

sium *"Cross-linguistic studies of tonal phenomena: Tonogenesis, Japanese accentology, and other topics"*, 301–322. Tokyo: Tokyo University of Foreign Studies, Research Institute for Languages, Cultures of Asia & Africa.

Rialland, Annie & Stéphane Robert. 2001. The intonational system of Wolof. *Linguistics* 39(5). 839–939.

Rialland, Annie & Mamadou Badjimé Sangaré. 1989. Réanalyse des tons du bambara: des tons du nom à l'organisation générale du système (A reanalysis of the tones of Bambara: From the tones of nouns to the general organization of the system). *Studies in African Linguistics* 20(1). 1–27.

Rice, Keren. 2014. On beginning the study of the tone system of a Dene (Athabaskan) language: Looking back. *Language Documentation and Conservation* 8. 690–706.

Richards, Audrey I. 1950. Some types of family structure amongst the Central Bantu. In Alfred Reginald Radcliffe-Brown & Cyril Daryll Forde (eds.), *African systems of kinship and marriage*, 207–251. London & New York City, NY: Oxford University Press.

Riley, Nancy E. 1994. Interwoven lives: Parents, marriage, and Guanxi in China. *Journal of Marriage and the Family* 56(4). 791–803.

Rock, Joseph. 1947. *The ancient Na-khi kingdom of Southwest China* (Harvard-Yenching Institute Monograph Series 8-9). Cambridge, MA: Harvard University Press.

Rock, Joseph. 1963. *A Na-Khi – English encyclopedic dictionary* (Serie Orientale Roma 28). Roma: Instituto Italiano per il Medio ed Estremo Oriente.

Rose, Philip. 1982. Acoustic characteristics of the Shanghai-Zhenhai syllable-types. In David Bradley (ed.), *Tonation* (Papers in Southeast Asian Linguistics 8), 1–53. Canberra: Australian National University Press.

Rose, Philip. 1989. On the non-equivalence of fundamental frequency and linguistic tone. In David Bradley, Eugénie J.A. Henderson & Martine Mazaudon (eds.), *Prosodic analysis and Asian linguistics: To honour R.K. Sprigg* (Pacific Linguistics C-104), 55–82. Canberra: Australian National University.

Rose, Philip. 1990. Acoustics and phonology of complex tone sandhi: An analysis of disyllabic lexical tone sandhi in the Zhenhai variety of Wu Chinese. *Phonetica* 47. 1–35.

Rossi, Mario. 1971. Le seuil de glissando ou seuil de perception des variations tonales pour les sons de la parole (The glissando threshold: The perception threshold for tonal variations in speech sounds). *Phonetica* 23. 1–33.

Rossi, Mario. 1999. *L'intonation, le système du français: Description et modélisation*. Gap & Paris: Ophrys.

Rossi, Mario & Évelyne Peter-Defare. 1998. *Les lapsus, ou, Comment notre fourche a langué (Slips of the tongue)*. Paris: Presses universitaires de France.
Roux, Justus C. 2001. Comments on "Zulu tonology and its relationship to other Nguni languages" by Farida Cassimjee and Charles W. Kisseberth. In Shigeki Kaji (ed.), *Proceedings of the symposium "Cross-linguistic studies of tonal phenomena: Tonogenesis, Japanese accentology, and other topics"*, 361–367. Tokyo: Tokyo University of Foreign Studies, Research Institute for Languages, Cultures of Asia & Africa.
Roux, Justus C. 2003. On the perception and description of tone in the Sotho and Nguni languages. In Shigeki Kaji (ed.), *Proceedings of the symposium "Cross-linguistic studies of tonal phenomena: Historical developments, phonetics of tone"*, 155–176. Tokyo: Tokyo University of Foreign Studies, Research Institute for Languages, Cultures of Asia & Africa.
Sagot, Benoît & Géraldine Walther. 2013. Implementing a formal model of inflectional morphology. In Cerstin Mahlow & Michael Piotrowski (eds.), *Systems and frameworks for computational morphology*, 115–134. Berlin: Springer.
Schadeberg, Thilo C. 1986. Tone cases in UMbundu. *Africana Linguistica* 10(1). 423–447.
Schein, Louisa. 1997. Gender and internal orientalism in China. *Modern China* 23(1). 69–98.
Scherer, Wilhelm. 1885. *Jacob Grimm*. 2nd edition. Berlin: Weidmann.
Selkirk, Elisabeth. 1972. *The phrase phonology of English and French*. Cambridge, MA: MIT PhD thesis.
Selkirk, Elisabeth. 1986. On derived domains in sentence phonology. *Phonology Yearbook* 3. 371–405.
Selkirk, Elisabeth. 1995. Sentence prosody: Intonation, stress and phrasing. In John Goldsmith (ed.), *Handbook of phonological theory*, 550–569. Cambridge, MA: Blackwell.
Selkirk, Elisabeth. 2000. The interaction of constraints on prosodic phrasing. In Merle Horne (ed.), *Prosody: Theory and experiment. Studies presented to Gösta Bruce*, 231–261. Dordrecht: Kluwer Academic Publishers.
Shafer, Robert. 1955. Classification of the Sino-Tibetan languages. *Word* 11. 94–111.
Shi, Dingxu. 2000. Topic and topic-comment constructions in Mandarin Chinese. *Language* 76(2). 383–408.
Shih, Chuan-kang. 1993. *The Yongning Moso: Sexual union, household organization, gender and ethnicity in a matrilineal duolocal society in Southwest China*. Stanford, CA: Stanford University PhD thesis.

Shih, Chuan-kang. 2010. *Quest for harmony: The Moso traditions of sexual union and family life.* Stanford, CA: Stanford University Press.

Shih, Chuan-kang & Mark R. Jenike. 2002. A cultural-historical perspective on the depressed fertility among the matrilineal Moso in Southwest China. *Human Ecology* 30(1). 21–47.

Shih, Chuan-kang 施传刚. 2008. *Yǒngníng Mósuō* 永宁摩梭 *(Yongning Moso)* (Yúnnándàxué mínzúxué wénkù 云南大学民族学文库). Kunming: Yunnan University Press 云南大学出版社.

Sigley, Gary. 2013. The Ancient Tea Horse Road and the politics of cultural heritage in Southwest China: Regional identity in the context of a rising China. In Tami Blumenfield & Helaine Silverman (eds.), *Cultural heritage politics in China*, 235–246. Berlin: Springer.

Silverman, Daniel. 2012. *Neutralization: Rhyme and reason in phonology.* Cambridge, U.K.: Cambridge University Press.

Silverman, Daniel. 2015. Enigma variations: Response to Sampson. *Journal of Chinese Linguistics* 43(2). 697–702.

Silverman, Kim, Mary Beckman, John Pitrelli, Mari Ostendorf, Colin W. Wightman, Patti Jo Price, Janet Pierrehumbert & Julia Hirschberg. 1992. ToBI: A standard for labeling English prosody. In *Proceedings of the 1992 International Conference on Spoken Language Processing*, vol. 2, 867–870. Banff, Canada: University of Alberta.

Sledd, James. 1955. Review of: An outline of English structure by George L. Trager and Henry Lee Smith. *Language* 31(2). 312–345.

Smith, Laura Catharine & Joseph Salmons. 2008. Historical phonology and evolutionary phonology. *Diachronica* 25. 411–430.

Somé, Penou-Achille. 2000. Floating tones in Dagara: Can a low floating tone prevent a preceding high tone from spreading? *University of Alberta Papers in Experimental and Theoretical Linguistics* 5. 60–100.

Souag, Lameen. 2010. *Grammatical contact in the Sahara: Arabic, Berber, and Songhay in Tabelbala and Siwa.* London: University of London, School of Oriental & African Studies PhD thesis.

Stanford, James & Jonathan Evans. 2012. The influence of Mandarin Chinese on minority languages in rural southwest China: A sociolinguistic study of tones in contact. *International Journal of the Sociology of Language* 2012(215). 79–100.

Sūn, Hóngkāi 孙宏开. 1982. Ěrsū (Duōxù) huà jiǎnjiè 尔苏（多续）话简介 (A brief introduction to Ersu (Duoxu)). *Studies in Language and Linguistics* 语言研究 3. 241–264.

Sūn, Hóngkāi 孙宏开. 1984. Zàng-Miǎnyǔ dòngcí de hùdòng fànchóu 藏缅语动词的互动范畴 (On the category of causative verbs in Tibeto-Burman languages). *Minority Languages of China* 民族语文 4. 8–16.

Sūn, Hóngkāi 孙宏开. 2001. Nàxīyǔ zài Zàng-Miǎn yǔzú yǔyán zhōng de lìshǐ dìwèi 纳西语在藏缅语族语言中的历史地位 (The position of Naxi among Tibeto-Burman languages). *Studies in Language and Linguistics* 语言研究 42. 90–99.

Sun, Jackson T.-S. 孙天心. 1997. The typology of tone in Tibetan. In *Chinese Languages and Linguistics IV: Typological studies of languages in China*, 485–521. Taipei: Institute of History & Philology-Academia Sinica.

Sun, Jackson T.-S. 孙天心. 2000. Parallelisms in the verb morphology of Sidaba rGyalrong and Lavrung in rGyalrongic. *Language and Linguistics* 1(1). 161–190.

Sun, Jackson T.-S. 孙天心. 2003a. Phonological profile of Zhongu: A new Tibetan dialect of Northern Sichuan. *Language and Linguistics* 4(4). 796–836.

Sun, Jackson T.-S. 孙天心. 2003b. Variegated tonal developments in Tibetan. In David Bradley, Randy LaPolla, Boyd Michailovsky & Graham Thurgood (eds.), *Language variation: Papers on variation and change in the Sinosphere and the Indosphere in honour of James A. Matisoff* (Pacific Linguistics), 35–51. Canberra: Australian National University.

Teo, Amos. 2014. *A phonological and phonetic description of Sumi, a Tibeto-Burman language of Nagaland* (Asia-Pacific Linguistics Open Access Monographs). Canberra: Australian National University.

Thieberger, Nick. 2009. Steps toward a grammar embedded in data. In Patience Epps & Alexandre Arkhipov (eds.), *New challenges in typology: Transcending the borders and refining the distinctions* (Trends in Linguistics. Studies and Monographs [TiLSM] 217), 389–408. Berlin: De Gruyter.

Thieberger, Nick & Rachel Nordlinger. 2006. *Doing great things with small languages (Australian Research Council grant DP0984419)*. http : / / linguistics . unimelb.edu.au/research/projects/greatthings.html.

Thieberger, Nick, Anna Margetts, Stephen Morey & Simon Musgrave. 2016. Assessing annotated corpora as research output. *Australian Journal of Linguistics* 36(1). 1–21.

Thorsen, Nina. 1980. A study of the perception of sentence intonation: Evidence from Danish. *Journal of the Acoustical Society of America* 67. 1014–1030.

Trager, George L. & Henry Lee Smith. 1951. *An outline of English structure*. Norman, OK: Battenberg Press.

Trubetzkoy, Nikolaus S. 1939. *Grundzüge der Phonologie (Principles of phonology)*. Prague: Travaux du cercle linguistique de Prague 7.

Trubetzkoy, Nikolaus S. 1969. *Principles of phonology.* Trans. by Christiane A.M. Baltaxe. Berkeley, CA: University of California Press.

Trudgill, Peter. 2011. *Sociolinguistic typology: Social determinants of linguistic complexity.* Oxford: Oxford University Press.

Trut, Lyudmila. 1999. Early canid domestication: The farm-fox experiment. *American Scientist* 87(2). 160–169.

Tryon, Darrell. 1998. Language, space and identity in Vanuatu. In Dominique Guillaud, Maorie Seysset & Annie Walter (eds.), *Le voyage inachevé... A Joël Bonnemaison,* 329–334. Paris: ORSTOM-PRODIG.

Vaissière, Jacqueline. 1971. *Contribution à la synthèse par règles du français.* Grenoble: Université de Grenoble PhD thesis.

Vaissière, Jacqueline. 1975. Further note on French prosody. *Research Laboratory of Electronics, MIT, Quarterly Progress Report* 115. 251–262.

Vaissière, Jacqueline. 2002. Cross-linguistic prosodic transcription: French vs. English. In Nina B. Volskaya, Natalia Svetozarova & Pavel A. Skrelin (eds.), *Problems and methods of experimental phonetics. In honour of the 70th anniversary of Pr. L.V. Bondarko,* 147–164. St Petersburg: St Petersburg State University Press.

Vaissière, Jacqueline. 2004. The perception of intonation. In David B. Pisoni & Robert E. Remez (eds.), *Handbook of speech perception* (Blackwell Textbooks in Linguistics), 236–263. Oxford, U.K. & Cambridge, MA: Blackwell.

Vaissière, Jacqueline & Alexis Michaud. 2006. Prosodic constituents in French: A data-driven approach. In Ivan Fónagy, Yuji Kawaguchi & Tsunekazu Moriguchi (eds.), *Prosody and syntax: Cross-linguistic perspectives* (Usage-Based Linguistic Informatics), 47–64. Amsterdam: John Benjamins.

Van de Velde, Mark. 2008a. *A grammar of Eton.* Berlin: Mouton de Gruyter.

Van de Velde, Mark. 2008b. Un cas de changement phonologique par réanalyse morphonologique en éton. *Africana Linguistica* 14. 177–185.

Van Driem, George. 1990. An exploration of Proto-Kiranti verbal morphology. *Acta Linguistica Hafniensia: International Journal of Linguistics* 22(1). 27–48.

Van Otterloo, Karen. 2011. *The Kifuliiru language, volume 1: Phonology, tone, and morphological derivation.* Dallas, TX: SIL International.

Voorhoeve, Jan. 1967. Personal pronouns in Bamileke. *Lingua* 17(3). 421–430.

Voorhoeve, Jan. 1971. Tonology of the Bamileke noun. *Journal of African Languages* 10(2). 44–53.

Voorhoeve, Jan. 1973. Safwa as a restricted tone system. *Studies in African Linguistics* 4(1). 1–22.

Vydrin, Valentin. 2016. Tonal inflection in Mande languages: The cases of Bamana and Dan-Gwɛɛtaa. In Enrique L. Palancar & Jean Léo Léonard (eds.), *Tone and inflection: New facts and new perspectives* (Trends in Linguistics. Studies and Monographs [TiLSM] 296), 83–105. Berlin: De Gruyter Mouton.

Wagner, Michael & Katherine McCurdy. 2010. Poetic rhyme reflects cross-linguistic differences in information structure. *Cognition* 117(2). 166–175.

Walker, Rachel & Geoffrey K. Pullum. 1999. Short report: Possible and impossible segments. *Language* 75(4). 764–780.

Walsh, Eileen Rose. 2005. From Nü Guo to Nü'er Guo: Negotiating desire in the land of the Mosuo. *Modern China* 31(4). 448–486.

Wan, I-Ping & Jeri J. Jaeger. 1998. Speech errors and the representation of tone in Mandarin Chinese. *Phonology* 15. 417–461.

Wang, Min & Arvind Singhal. 1992. Ke Wang, a Chinese television soap opera with a message. *International Communication Gazette* 49(3). 177–192.

Wāng, Níngshēng 汪宁生. 1980. Gǔdài Yúnnán de yǎngmǎyè: Yúnnán shǎoshù mínzú kējìshǐ xuéxí zhájì 古代云南的养马业——云南少数民族科技史学习札记 (Horse husbandry in ancient Yunnan). *Sīxiǎng zhànxiàn* 思想战线 3(34). 38–44.

Watkins, Justin. 2001. Illustrations of the IPA: Burmese. *Journal of the International Phonetic Association* 31(2). 291–295.

Wedekind, Klaus. 1983. A six-tone language in Ethiopia: Tonal analysis of Benč non (Gimira). *Journal of Ethiopian Studies* 16. 129–156.

Wedekind, Klaus. 1985. Why Bench' (Ethiopia) has five level tones today. In Ursula Pieper & Gerhard Stickel (eds.), *Studia linguistica diachronica et synchronica*, 881–901. Berlin: Mouton.

Wellens, Koen. 2003. Revisiting the Na of Southwest China. A review of: Cai Hua, A Society Without Fathers or Husbands: The Na of China, translated from French. *Asian Ethnicity* 4(1). 147–149.

Wellens, Koen. 2006. *Consecrating the Premi house: Ritual, community and the state in the borderlands of East Tibet.* Oslo: University of Oslo, Faculty of Humanities PhD thesis.

Wells, Rulon S. 1945. The pitch phonemes of English. *Language* 21. 27–39.

Welmers, William E. 1952. Notes on the structure of Bariba. *Language* 28. 82–103.

Welmers, William E. 1969. The morphology of Kpelle nominals. *Journal of African Languages* 8(2). 73–101.

Welmers, William E. 1973. *African language structures.* Berkeley, CA: University of California Press.

Weng, Naiqun. 1993. *The Mother House: The symbolism and practice of gender among the Naze in Southwest China.* University of Rochester PhD thesis.

West, Paula. 1999. Perception of distributed coarticulatory properties of English /l/ and /r/. *Journal of Phonetics* 27(4). 405–426.

Whalen, Doug H. 2004. How the study of endangered languages will revolutionize linguistics. In Piet van Sterkernburg (ed.), *Linguistics today: Facing a greater challenge*, 321–344. Amsterdam: John Benjamins.

Whalen, Doug H., Bryan Gick, Masanobu Kumada & Kiyoshi Honda. 1998. EMG evidence for the automaticity of intrinsic F_0 of vowels. In Patricia K. Kuhl & Lawrence A. Crum (eds.), *Proceedings of the 16th International Conference on Acoustics and 135th Meeting of the Acoustical Society of America*, vol. IV, 2951–2952. New York City, NY: Acoustical Society of America.

Wightman, Colin W. 2002. ToBI or not ToBI? In Bernard Bel & Isabelle Marlien (eds.), *Proceedings of Speech Prosody 2002*. Aix-en-Provence: International Speech Communication Association.

Wilson, Edith R. 1917. A few pre-Copernican astronomers. *Popular Astronomy* 25. 88–102.

Woodbury, Tony. 2003. Defining documentary linguistics. In Peter Austin (ed.), *Language documentation and description*, vol. 1, 35–51. London: School of African & Oriental Studies.

Woodbury, Tony. 2011. Language documentation. In Peter Austin & Julia Sallabank (eds.), *The handbook of endangered languages*, 159–211. Cambridge, U.K.: Cambridge University Press.

Xu, Yi. 1997. Contextual tonal variations in Mandarin. *Journal of Phonetics* 25. 61–83.

Xu, Yi. 1998. Consistency of tone-syllable alignment across different syllable structures and speaking rates. *Phonetica* 55. 179–203.

Xu, Yi. 1999. Effects of tone and focus on the formation and alignment of f_0 contours. *Journal of Phonetics* 27(1). 55–106.

Xu, Yi & Emily Q. Wang. 2001. Pitch targets and their realization: Evidence from Mandarin Chinese. *Speech Communication* 33. 319–337.

Yán, Rǔxián 严汝娴 & Zhàolín Sòng 宋兆麟. 1984. *Yǒngníng Nàxīzú de mǔxìzhì (dì èr bǎn)* 永宁纳西族的母系制（第二版）*(The matriarchy of the Naxi people of Yongning)*. Kunming: Yunnan People's Publishing House 云南人民出版社.

Yan, Yan, Zixin He, Jing Duan, Ding Ding & Suping Zhang. 2008. Analysis of the role of the Mosuo culture in local environmental protection in Lugu Lake region. *International Journal of Sustainable Development & World Ecology* 15(1). 48–55.

Yang, Cathryn, James N. Stanford & Zhengyu Yang. 2015. A sociotonetic study of Lalo tone split in progress. *Asia-Pacific Language Variation* 1(1). 52–77.

Yáng, Fúquán 杨福泉. 2006. Nàmùyī yǔ Nà zhī zúqún guānxì kǎolüè "纳木依"与"纳"之族群关系考略 (An exploration of the ethnic relationships between Namuyi and Na). *Ethno-National Studies* 民族研究 3. 52–59.

Yáng, Lìquán 杨立权 & Qīnghuá Zhāng 张清华. 2011. *Zhōngguó shǎoshùmínzúyǔ dìmíng gàishuō* 中国少数民族语地名概说 *(A summary about toponymy in minority languages of China)*. Beijing: China Social Sciences Press 中国社会出版社.

Yáng, Xuézhèng 杨学政. 1985. Dábājiào yǔ Dōngbājiào bǐjiào yánjiū 达巴教与东巴教比较研究 (Comparative research on the Daba religion and the Dongba religion). In *Zōngjiào lùngǎo* 宗教论稿 *(Essays on religion)*, 103–196. Yunnan People's Publishing House 云南人民出版社.

Yang, Zhenhong. 2009. An overview of the Mosuo language. *Linguistics of the Tibeto-Burman Area* 32(2). 1–44.

Yáng, Zhènhóng 杨振洪. 2006. Mósuōhuà gàikuàng 摩梭话概况 (An overview of the Mosuo language). In Dáshí Lātāmī 拉他咪·达石 (ed.), *Mósuō shèhuì wénhuà yánjiū lùnwénjí (1960-2005)* 摩梭社会文化研究论文集 (1960-2005) *(Collected papers about Mosuo society and culture, 1960-2005)*, vol. 2, 28–64. Kunming: Yunnan University Press 云南大学出版社.

Yu, Dominic. 2012. *Proto-Ersuic*. Berkeley, CA: University of California at Berkeley PhD thesis.

Yu, Kristine. 2010. Representational maps from the speech signal to phonological categories: A case study with lexical tones. *UCLA Working Papers in Linguistics* 15. 1–30.

Yu, Kristine & Hiu Wai Lam. 2014. The role of creaky voice in Cantonese tonal perception. *Journal of the Acoustical Society of America* 136(3). 1320–1333.

Yúnnánshěng biānjízǔ 国家民委民族社会历史调查云南省编辑组. 1986. *Yǒngníng Nàxīzú shèhuì jí mǔxìzhì diàochá* 永宁纳西族社会及母系制调查 *(Fieldwork about the Yongning Naxi society and its matriarchal system)*. Kunming: The Ethnic Publishing House 民族出版社.

Zeitoun, Elizabeth. 2007. *A grammar of Mantauran (Rukai)*. Taipei: Institute of Linguistics, Academia Sinica.

Zerbian, Sabine. 2006a. *Expression of information structure in the Bantu language Northern Sotho*. Berlin: Humboldt-Universität zu Berlin PhD thesis.

Zerbian, Sabine. 2006b. Inversion structures in Northern Sotho. *Southern African Linguistics and Applied Language Studies* 24(3). 361–376.

Zerbian, Sabinc. 2010. Developments in the study of intonational typology. *Language and Linguistics Compass* 3(1). 1–16.

Zerbian, Sabine. 2016. Sentence intonation in Tswana (Sotho-Tswana group). In Laura J. Downing & Annie Rialland (eds.), *Intonation in African tone languages* (Phonology and Phonetics 24), 393–434. Berlin: De Gruyter.

Zerbian, Sabine & Etienne Barnard. 2010a. Realisations of a single high tone in Northern Sotho. *Southern African Linguistics and Applied Language Studies* 27(4). 357–380.

Zerbian, Sabine & Etienne Barnard. 2010b. Word-level prosody in Sotho-Tswana. In *Proceedings of Speech Prosody 2010*. Chicago, IL: International Speech Communication Association.

Zhān, Chéngxù 詹承绪, Chéngquán Wáng 王承权, Jìnchūn Lǐ 李近春 & Lóngchū Liú 刘龙初. 1980. *Yǒngníng Nàxīzú de āzhù hūnyīn hé mǔxì jiātíng* 永宁纳西族的阿注婚姻和母系家庭 *('Azhu' marriage and matriarchal family among the Naxi of Yongning)*. Shanghai: Shanghai People's Publishing House 上海人民出版社.

Zhang, Jie & Jiang Liu. 2011. Tone sandhi and tonal coarticulation in Tianjin Chinese. *Phonetica* 68(3). 161–191.

Zhang, Jinsong & Keikichi Hirose. 2004. Tone nucleus modeling for Chinese lexical tone recognition. *Speech Communication* 42(3). 447–466.

Zhang, Sihong. 2013. *A reference grammar of Ersu: A Tibeto-Burman language of China*. Townsville: James Cook University PhD thesis.

Zhíbā, Ěrchē 直巴·尔车 & Ruìjuān Xǔ 许瑞娟. 2013. *Mósuōyǔ chángyòng cíjù huìcuì* 摩梭语常用词句荟萃 *(An anthology of everyday words and expressions in the Mosuo language)*. Kunming: Yunnan People's Publishing House 云南人民出版社.

Zhu, Guobin. 2014. The right to minority language instruction in schools: Negotiating competing claims. *Human Rights Quarterly* 36(4). 691–721.

Name index

Ā, Huì 阿慧, 36, 389
Abramson, Arthur S., 26, 44, 366
Adamek, Piotr, 146
Aikhenvald, Alexandra Y., 227
Akinlabi, Akinbiyi, 427
Alves, Mark, 421
Amselle, Jean-Loup, 487
Andersen, Henning, 26
Andersen, Torben, 425
Andruski, Jean E., 421
Anthony, David W., 488
Antolík, Tanja Kocjančič, 11
Arcodia, Giorgio Francesco, 93
Armstrong, Lilias, 360, 370, 373
Armstrong, Robert G., 423, 424
Aubergé, Véronique, 27
Audibert, Nicolas, 27
Āzémíng, Cìdázhū 阿泽明·次达珠, 20

Bacot, Jacques, 466
Baken, Ronald J., 39
Banchob, Bandhumedha, 430
Barnard, Etienne, 369, 423
Barnes, Jonathan, 61
Baron, Stephen P., 453
Bauer, Laurie, 151, 152
Baxter, William H., 510
Bayer, Josef, 29
Benedict, Paul K., 13
Benguerel, André-Pierre, 373
Bisang, Walter, 425

Björverud, Susanna, 48, 456
Blackburn, Stuart, 491
Blevins, Juliette, 26, 408
Blumenfield, Tami, 514
Blust, Robert, 463
Bolinger, Dwight Le Merton, 361, 484
Bothorel, André, 504
Bouarourou, Fayssal, 504
Boulakia, Georges, 416
Bradley, David, 5, 10, 11, 421, 452, 456
Brunelle, Marc, 26, 39, 79, 360, 366, 371, 386, 421, 422
Bulag, Uradyn E., 33, 497
Bum, Tsering, 11
Burchill, Susan A., 155
Byrd, Dani, 290
Bühler, Karl, 484

Cai, Hua, 6, 506, 508
Calabrese, Andrea, 434
Cartier, Michel, 507
Carton, Fernand, 373
Chan, Ko Ling, 252
Chao, Yuen-ren 趙元任, 88, 372, 420, 429, 430, 436
Chavannes, Edouard, 500
Chebanne, Andy M., 423
Chelliah, Shobhana L., 34
Chen, Matthew Y., 363
Chen, Sanping, 142

Chen, Yiya, 11, 386, 438, 452, 471, 472, 474
Chirkova, Ekaterina, 438
Chirkova, Katia, 11, 113, 263, 322, 327, 422, 438, 452, 471, 472, 474
Chow, Daryl, 386
Clark, Mary Morris, 329
Clements, Nick, 23, 357, 369, 420, 422–424
Coblin, South, 14, 492
Coetzee, Andries W., 126
Connell, Bruce, 369
Cordier, Henri, 6
Costello, James, 421
Coupe, Alec, 369
Coustenoble, Hélène, 360, 373
Creissels, Denis, 22, 48, 50, 67, 94, 95, 156, 275, 300, 368, 369, 388, 397, 423, 426
Crowley, Terry, 425
Cruz, Emiliana, 359, 423
Culioli, Antoine, 369, 379
Cummins, Fred, 343

Daudey, Henriëtte, 5, 23, 422, 439, 452
DeLancey, Scott, 251
Delattre, Pierre, 360, 364
Di Cristo, Albert, 364
Dibie, Pascal, 513
DiCanio, Christian, 421, 448
Di Cristo, Albert, 356, 360
Di Cristo, Albert, 379
Dihoff, Ivan R., 420
Dimmendaal, Gerrit J., 12
Ding, Picus Sizhi, 19, 23, 420, 422, 440
Dixon, Robert M., 22, 35, 227
Dô, Thê Dung, 416

Dobbs, Roselle, 21, 65, 182, 422, 441
Donohue, Mark, 420
Dournes, Jacques, 33
Downing, Laura J., 322, 370
Dumestre, Gérard, 61
Duong, Khue, 45

Edmondson, Jerold A., 421
Elisseeff, Danielle, 507
Enfield, Nicholas J., 131, 485
Erickson, Donna, 362
Evans, Jonathan, 213, 411, 420, 422
Evans, Nick, 97

Fabre, Philippe, 39
Fāng, Guóyú 方国瑜, 33, 465
Fant, Gunnar, 373, 504
Fennig, Charles D., 4
Ferlus, Michel, 25, 147, 461
Fischer-Jørgensen, Eli, 369
Fluehr-Lobban, Carolyn, 504
Fónagy, Ivan, 364, 431, 484, 485
Fougeron, Cécile, 433
Francopoulo, Gil, 45
Frangville, Vanessa, 497
Franich, Kathryn, 61
François, Alexandre, 13, 164, 254, 419
Fromkin, Victoria A., 180, 408
Fù, Màojì 傅懋勣, 18, 456, 465
Fuller, Christopher J., 503

Gaenszle, Martin, 491
Gài, Xìngzhī 盖兴之, 10
Gandour, Jack, 44, 366
Garellek, Marc, 421, 469
Garrett, Andrew, 408
Geertz, Clifford, 506, 507
Gerner, Matthias, 425, 441
Gimbutas, Marija, 488

Girón Higuita, Jesus-Mario, 420
Goldrick, Matthew, 126
Goldsmith, John, 60, 363, 422
Gomez-Imbert, Elsa, 420
Gordon, Raymond G., 9
Goullart, Peter, 495, 502
Grammont, Maurice, 361
Grégoire, Claire, 67, 94
Grice, Martine, 434
Gros, Stéphane, 495, 514, 515
Gros, Stéphane, 5, 510, 511
Gruber, James Frederick, 421
Grønnum, Nina, 364
Gsell, René, 44, 387
Guérin, Maximilien, 48
Gui, Ming Chao, 355, 452
Guō, Dàliè 郭大烈, 6, 10, 487, 488, 491, 493, 494
Guo, Xiaolin, 495
Gussenhoven, Carlos, 363, 408
Guthrie, Malcom, 365, 367

Hạ, Kiều Phương, 434
Hadler, Jeffrey, 503
Hagège, Claude, 25
Hall, Edward T., 367
Hamann, Silke, 434
Hampson, Norman, 505
Haraguchi, Shosuke, 327
Hargus, Sharon, 420
Harrell, Stevan, 5
Haspelmath, Martin, 4, 419
Haudricourt, André-Georges, 12, 25, 153, 411, 429, 462, 463, 483, 513
Hé, Jiézhēn 和洁珍, 7, 460
Hé, Jírén 和即仁, 7, 9, 10, 89, 460, 465, 485
Hé, Kāixiáng 和开祥, 465

He, Likun, 479, 480, 483
He, Xueguang, 376, 414
Hé, Zhìwǔ 和志武, 6, 9, 10, 33, 258, 465, 467, 487, 488, 491, 493, 494
Hein, Anke Marion, 488–491
Henderson, Eugénie J.A., 26, 164, 483
Henrich, Nathalie, 39
Hertegård, Stellan, 373
Hill, Eugen, 408
Hill, Nathan, 408
Himmelmann, Nikolaus, 57
Hirose, Keikichi, 366
Hirst, Daniel, 364, 379
Ho, Sana 何撒娜, 515
Hockett, Charles F., 363
Holton, Gary, 435
Hombert, Jean-Marie, 180
House, David, 343, 431
Huáng, Bùfán 黄布凡, 11, 462, 494
Huang, Chenglong, 213, 322, 371
Huángfǔ, Qìnglián 皇甫庆莲, 431
Huber, Toni, 492
Hyman, Larry M., 23, 35, 53, 61, 79, 97, 323, 360, 365, 420, 422, 426, 428, 434, 447

Iverson, Gregory K., 26

Jackson, Anthony, 493, 511
Jacques, Guillaume, 13, 14, 16, 19, 25, 119, 131, 228, 263, 398, 408, 420, 422, 448, 452, 462, 466, 471, 472, 483, 510
Jaeger, Jeri J., 180
Jean-Brunhes Delamare, Mariel, 153, 463
Jenike, Mark R., 495

Jiāng, Zhúyí 姜竹仪, 9, 10, 16, 89, 465, 485
Jones, Robert B., 421
Journet, Nicolas, 507
Juge, Matthew L., 408
Jun, Sun-Ah, 433

Kadenge, Maxwell, 322
Karcevskij, Serge, 335
Karlsson, Anastasia, 431
Karttunen, Lauri, 445
Kawahara, Shigeto, 360
Keating, Patricia, 39, 421, 448
Khatiwada, Rajesh, 473
Kirby, James, 26, 79, 126, 360, 421, 422
Knödel, Susanne, 6, 515
Kochanski, Greg P., 387
Kohler, Klaus J., 364, 373
Konoshenko, Maria, 67, 113, 425
Krifka, Manfred, 371
Kruckenberg, Anita, 373
Kuang, Jianjing, 39, 421
Kubozono, Haruo, 328, 409, 423
Kula, Nancy C., 434
Kuryłowicz, Jerzy, 408
Kühnert, Barbara, 448

La, Mingqing, 21, 65, 182, 422, 441
Lā, Míngyīng 喇明英, 501
Labov, William, 26, 397
Ladd, Robert, 363, 364, 369, 434
Ladefoged, Peter, 455, 463, 473
Ladusaw, William A., 453
Lahiri, Aditi, 408
Lakhi, Libu, 11
Lam, Hiu Wai, 421
Lāmǎ, Zīwò 拉玛兹倮, 10, 11
Lambrecht, Knud, 373

Lāmù, Gātǔsà 拉木·嘎吐萨, 514
Laniran, Yetunde O., 369
LaPolla, Randy, 322, 371, 372, 488
Lātāmī, Dáshí 拉他咪·达石, 34, 513, 516
Lātāmī, Wángyǒng 拉他咪·王勇, see Lātāmī, Dáshí
Launey, Michel, xiii, 161
Leben, William R., 428
Lee, Wai-Sum, 460
Lehiste, Ilse, 370
Léon, Pierre, 484
Leroy, Christine, 504
Leslie, David, 155
Lévi-Strauss, Claude, 506, 507
Lewis, M. Paul, 4
Li, Fang-kuei, 36
Lǐ, Dázhū 李达珠, 20, 33, 500
Lǐ, Zǐhè 李子鹤, 14
Liberman, Mark, 363
Lidz, Liberty, 2, 6, 7, 21, 45, 47–49, 51, 93, 149, 155, 195, 212–214, 227, 242, 251, 253, 254, 258, 275, 277, 350, 372, 441, 458, 466, 486, 498
Lín, Yǔtáng 林語堂, 433
Lín, Màocàn 林茂灿, 386
Lin, You-Jing, 263, 440
Lindau, M., 364
Lindblom, B., 44
List, Johann-Mattis, 13
Liu, Huidan, 192
Liu, Jiang, 366
Liú, Lóngchū 刘龙初, 501
Luangthongkum, Theraphan, 26
Luo, Chia-Ling, 6

Mac, Dang-Khoa, 421
Maddieson, Ian, 422, 455, 463, 473

Manessy, Gabriel, 12
Martin, Philippe, 356, 360, 361, 363, 364
Martinet, André, 24, 25, 430, 452, 476
Martinet, André, 453
Maspero, Henri, 12
Mathangwane, Joyce T., 447
Mathieu, Christine, 20, 512
Matisoff, James A., 13, 16, 48, 163, 195, 263, 422
Mattison, Siobhán M., 514
Mauss, Marcel, 496
Mazard, Mireille, 496, 504
Mazaudon, Martine, 26, 192, 195, 372, 421, 446
McCurdy, Katherine, 440
McKhann, Charles F., 6, 491
McLaughlin, Fiona, 417
Meillet, Antoine, 147
Michael, Lev, 420
Michailovsky, Boyd, 26, 39, 94, 119, 479
Milan, Pascale-Marie, 514
Milroy, James, 29
Milroy, Lesley, 29
Mixdorff, Hansjörg, 421
Monaka, Kemmonye C., 365
Moravcsik, Edith A., 216
Morey, Stephen, 36, 359, 420, 430
Mullaney, Thomas, 496, 497
Myers, Scott, 366, 369

Nespor, Marina, 321
Nguyễn, Duy Dương, 39, 79, 421, 422
Nguyễn, Khắc Hùng, 39, 79, 421, 422
Nguyễn, Minh Châu, 374
Nguyen, Thi-Lan, 421
Nguyễn, Thụy Nhã Uyên, 386

Niebuhr, Oliver, 334, 343, 364, 373, 446
Nikaido, Hitoshi, 409
Nishida, Tatsuo, 6
Nkhwa, Heather W., 423
Nolan, Francis, 26, 448, 481
Noonan, Michael, 192
Nooteboom, Sieb, 180
Nordlinger, Rachel, 38
Nurse, Derek, xiii, 22, 23

O'Connor, Catherine, 61
Odden, David, 327, 420, 426
Ohala, John, 26, 361, 373, 462
Ohala, Manjari, 462
Orlikoff, Robert F., 39
Ota, Ichiro, 409

Palancar, Enrique L., 23
Paris, Catherine, 504
Pater, Joe, 126
Patin, Cédric, 420
Peter-Defare, Évelyne, 180
Pierrehumbert, Janet, 363
Pike, Kenneth L., 363, 367, 408, 420
Pinson, Jacqueline S., 355, 452
Pinson, Thomas M., 160, 355, 415, 452, 465, 468
Pittayaporn, Pittayawat, 26
Post, Mark W., 23, 251
Potisuk, Siripong, 44, 366
Pulleyblank, Douglas, 408
Pullum, Geoffrey K., 453, 463

Qiū, Fùyuán 邱富元, *see* Lāmǎ, Zīwò

Rankin, Robert L., 462
Ratliff, Martha, 421
Refflet, Annie, 514

Remijsen, Bert, 369
Rénzēng, Wàngmǔ 仁增旺姆, 11
Reuse, Willem J. de, 34
Rhodes, Alexandre de, 428
Rialland, Annie, 53, 60, 370, 417, 422, 424
Rice, Keren, 420, 446
Richards, Audrey I., 503
Riley, Nancy E., 252
Rilliard, Albert, 27
Robert, Stéphane, 48, 417
Rock, Joseph, 6, 498
Rose, Philip, 421
Rossi, Mario, 180, 356, 360, 364, 387
Roux, Justus C., 39, 334

Sagot, Benoît, 100
Salmons, Joseph, 26
Saltzman, Elliot, 290
Sangaré, Mamadou Badjimé, 53
Schadeberg, Thilo C., 362
Schaller, George, 155
Schein, Louisa, 514
Scherer, Wilhelm, 22
Selkirk, Elisabeth, 321, 361, 373
Shafer, Robert, 10, 13
Shi, Dingxu, 372
Shí, Gāofēng 石高峰, see Lāmù, Gātǔsà
Shih, Chilin, 387
Shih, Chuan-kang, 495
Shih, Chuan-kang 施传刚, 6, 7, 498, 499, 505, 510
Shuh, Russell G., 61
Sigley, Gary, 515
Silverman, Daniel, 67, 477
Silverman, Kim, 363
Simons, Gary F., 4
Singhal, Arvind, 252

Sledd, James, 367
Smith, Henry Lee, 363, 367
Smith, Laura Catharine, 26
Somé, Penou-Achille, 62
Sòng, Zhàolín 宋兆麟, 505
Souag, Lameen, 410
Stanford, James N., 26, 411
Stuart, Kevin, 11
Sūn, Hóngkāi 孙宏开, 11, 471
Sun, Jackson T.-S. 孙天心, 23, 119, 263, 327, 422, 472
Svantesson, Jan-Olof, 431

Teo, Amos, 369
Thieberger, Nick, 38, 41
Thody, Anthony J., 155
Thorsen, Nina, 370
Tiede, Mark K., 26
Trager, George L., 363, 367
Trubetzkoy, Nikolaus S., 476, 484
Trudgill, Peter, 29
Trân, Thien Huong, 416
Trut, Lyudmila, 155
Tryon, Darrell, 487

Utsugi, Akira, 409

Vaissière, Jacqueline, 254, 258, 356, 357, 360, 361, 364, 370, 374
VanBik, Kenneth, 79, 420, 422
Van Driem, George, 119
Van Otterloo, Karen, 448
Van de Velde, Mark, 322, 408
Vogel, Irene, 321
Voorhoeve, Jan, 61, 438
Vydrin, Valentin, 61, 113

Wagner, Michael, 440
Walker, Rachel, 463

Walsh, Eileen Rose, 514
Walther, Géraldine, 100
Wan, I-Ping, 180
Wang, Emily Q., 422
Wang, Min, 252
Wāng, Níngshēng 汪宁生, 213
Wáng, Yǒng 王勇, see Lātāmī, Dáshí
Ward, Ida C., 370
Watkins, Justin, 421
Wedekind, Klaus, 420
Wellens, Koen, 410, 508
Wells, Rulon S., 363
Welmers, William E., 113, 420
West, Paula, 385
Wetzels, W. Leo, 420
Whalen, Doug H., 38
Whalen, Dough H., 379
Wightman, Colin W., 363
Wilson, Edith R., 505
Woodbury, Tony, 38, 359

Xu, Yi, 44, 386, 422, 436
Xǔ, Ruìjuān 许瑞娟, 19

Yán, Jǐngzhù 颜景助, 386
Yán, Rǔxián 严汝娴, 505
Yan, Yan, 515
Yang, Cathryn, 26
Yáng, Fúquán 杨福泉, 6, 11
Yáng, Lìquán 杨立权, 8
Yáng, Xuézhèng 杨学政, 20
Yang, Zhengyu, 26
Yáng, Zhènhóng 杨振洪, 10, 19
Yu, Alan C. L., 126
Yu, Dominic, 13, 474
Yu, Kristine, 44, 421

Zee, Eric, 460
Zeitoun, Elizabeth, 21

Zerbian, Sabine, 275, 364, 369, 423, 437
Zhān, Chéngxù 詹承绪, 505
Zhang, Jie, 366
Zhang, Jinsong, 366
Zhāng, Qīnghuá 张清华, 8
Zhang, Sihong, 13
Zhào, Qìnglián 赵庆莲, 7, 460
Zhíbā, Ěrchē 直巴·尔车, 19
Zhu, Guobin, 515

Language index

Bai, 93
Bantu, 61, 62, 180, 275, 362, 366, 408, 422, 423, 426, 434, 447, 448, 463
Burmese, 421

Chinese, *see* Sinitic

English, 133, 151, 356, 360, 364, 367, 370, 373, 374, 386, 408, 429, 433, 462, 466, 469
Ersu, 13

French, 355, 356, 360, 373, 386, 416, 433, 434, 466, 476

Hmong, 421, 425

Japanese, 19, **328**, 328, 359, **360**, 409, 423
Japhug, 228, 462, 483
    see also Rgyalrongic

Kiranti, 119

Laze, 13, **131**, 164, 186, 196, 398, 425, **437**, 438, 462, 465–467, 470, 471, 474, 477, 494
Lisu, 410
Lizu, 438, 452, 472
Lolo, Loloish, *see* Yi

Mandarin, 44, 179, 180, 215, 329, 355, 360, 366, 374, 386, **409**, 410–413, 415, 420, 422, 431, 433, 474, 475, 480, 492
    Southwestern, 28, 33, 127, **355**, 411, 415, 417, 452, 459, 480
    Standard, 28, 355, 411, 417, 435, 459, 480
    see also Sinitic
Mande, 60, 61, 67, 94, 113, 397
Miao, *see* Hmong
Mon-Khmer, 11–13, 360

Naic, **13**
Naish, 8, **13**, 22, 28, 29, 67, 113, 161, 164, 186, 263, 398, 425, 437, 440, 453, 456, 462, 465–467, 471, 494, 499
Namuyi, 11, 13, 93, 403, 438, 499
Naxi, 5, 7, 8, **9**, 9–11, 13, 14, 16, 18, 19, 89, 133, 151, 160, 161, 164, 186, 196, 243, 374, 376, 388, 398, 410, 414, 415, 425, 428, 437, 438, 448, 452, 453, 455, 459, 460, 462, 463, 465–471, 475, 477–480, 483, 485, 487, 488, 491–494, 498–501, 509–511, 513
Nosu, 410, 440
    see also Yi

Premi, *see* Pumi

Prinmi, *see* Pumi
Pumi, 5, 19, 22, 23, 64, 201, 208, 209, 410, 422, 438–441, 498, 499, 501

Rgyalrongic, 119, 263
    see also Japhug
Romance, 13, 429, 434

Shixing, 11, 13, 93, 113, 263, 322, 403, 410, 422, 438
Shuhing, *see* Shixing
Sinitic, 11, 19, 20, 25, 193, 366, 372, 394, 411, 420, 421, 461, 476, 510
    see also Mandarin
Sino-Tibetan, 10, 13, 14, **15**, 23, 94, 263, 371, 403, 422, 425, 437, 438, 448, 453, 462, 488, 491

Tai-Kadai, 11, 12, 25, 26, 251, 420, 430, 461
Tamang, 195, 372, 421
Thai, 44, 180, 366
Tibetan, 20, 21, 23, 132, 144, 145, 147, 192, 196, 410, 414, 438, 464, 465, 488, 493, 499, 502
Tujia, 93, 403

Vietnamese, 11–13, 25, 26, 79, 329, 355, 366, 386, 416, 421, 422, 428, 433, 434, 436, 483

Xumi, *see* Shixing

Yi, 5, 10, 11, 21, 48, 213, 410, 421, 437, 440, 452, 488, 492, 494–496, 501
    see also Nosu

Subject index

adjectives, 50, 51, 148, 149, 155, 157, **251**, 251–252, 478
analogy, 124–126, 144, 157, 198, 207, 277, 315, **408**, 408, 409
anchorage, 62, 77, 82–87, 89, 115–117, 126, 178, 314, 315, 324
archiphoneme, 459, **476**
architoneme, 16

bilingualism, **409**, 410, 411
boundary (between tone groups), 236, 289, 308, 319, **331**, 333, 334, 350, 354, 382, 391, 428
boundary tone, 363, **428**, 428, 434
      see also intonational tones

citation form (i.e. form in isolation), *see* form
classifiers, **163**, 163–192, 217, 338, 409, 425, 440
clitics, 70, 73–75, 79–82, 158, 228, 229, 231, 236, 412, 482
coarticulation, 366, 369, 387, **388**, 448
comparative method (historical linguistics), 8, 10, 11, 13, 14, 25, 61, 63, 67, 74, 157, 160, 198, 210, 385, 398, 401, 452, 456, 462, 471, 472, 474, 477–479, 510
complex tones, 366, 411, **421**, 420–423

complexity, 161, 180, **425**
compounds, 93–161, 206, 242, 270, 324, 325, 332, 392, 403, 405, 407, 408, 412–414, 426
    coordinative, **93**
    determinative, **93**
conjunctions, 133, 242, 347, 348
conservative (phonological form), 403, 413
contact, *see* language contact
contour, *see* tonal contour
copula, 57–59, 69, 71–73, 75, 79, 80, 82, 91, 92, 100, 105, 191, 218, 220, 251, 278, 307, 350, 358, 400
counterexample, 124, 126, 186, 255, 314
culminative, 328

declination, **370**, 389, 391, 392
demonstratives, 50, 187, 188, 229, 231, 298, 299, 468, 477, 482, 485
derivation
    morphological, 195–216, 243, 478
    tonal, 190, **323**, 345, 346, 427
diachrony, *see* comparative method
dissimilation, 121, 389, 390, 392
disyllabification, 93, **403**, 403–408
disyllables, 54, 57, 58, 79, 93, 183, 198, 205, 238, 251, 288, 403, 406
downstep, **60**, 363, 423, 424

duration, 263, 361, 376, 378, 379, 383
dynamic synchrony, **25**, 25

emphatic stress, 334, 371, **372**, 372–376, 378, 385, 394
endonym, 2, 5, 131, 218, 500, 512
etymology, 131, 198, 407
evolutionary phonology, 26
exceptions, 63, 124, 125, 254, 286, 334, 355, 372, 453, 477
  see also irregularities
existentials, 48, 49, 251, 320, 335
exonym, 500, 509
experimental phonetics, 43, 263, **359**, 369, 447, 485
  see also phonetic realization of tones
extrametricality, **347**, 354

final lowering, 392
floating tone, **60**, 60–71, 73, 74, 77, 81, 82, 89, 93, 105, 108, 115, 119–121, 125, 126, 259, 260, 269, 270, 278, 282, 313, 330, 362, 400, 401, 403, 405, 414, 441
focalization, 371, **375**, 375–382, 436
folk etymology, 7
form
  in isolation, 16, 17, 53, 54, **57**, 57, 58, 62–64, 67, 69–74, 76, 77, 79, 80, 90, 91, 94, 99, 100, 220, 222, 229, 235, 245, 247, 249, 255–257, 301, 311, 323, 327, 332, 356, 371, 400, 411–414, 423, 432, 434, 441, 470
  surface, 54, 58, 59, 67, 87, 88, 94, 105, 118, 191, 227, 281, 321, **323**, 323, 326, 353, 358, 387, 391, 393, 398–403, 411, 414, 423
  underlying, 76, 80, 105, 164, 191, 228, 282, 321, **323**, 323, 387, 401, 403
function words, 275, 336, 371, 467, 469

gap-filling, 317, **398**, 398, 450, 465, 471, 475, 483
grammaticalization, 197, 242, 276, 284

homophony, 36, 46, 50, 64, 93, 156, 185, 205, 241, 293, 387, 403, 471

in isolation (form in isolation), *see* form
information structure, 331, 360, 371, 372, 374, 439
innovative (phonological form), 400, 401, 407, 408, 415
intensifiers, 51, 149, 332
interjections, 431–433, 464
intonation, 50, 335, 357–359, **360**, 360, 361, 363–368, 373, 374, 378, 383, 392, 416, 417, 427–431, 434, 435, 484
intonational tones, 427, 428
  see also boundary tones
irregularities, 91, 206, 270, 477
  see also exceptions

juncture (inside a tone group), 77, 80, 105–108, 123, 168, 177, 183, 270, 272, 290, 405

language contact, 12, 14, 410, 417, 439

lengthening, 50, 290, 374–377, 379, 436, 437, 481
level tones, 54, **420**, 420–423, 436, 441
lexicalization, 131, 142, 146, 148, 158, 205, 306, 307, 334, 467, 481
loanwords, 7, 132, 179, 196, 215, 355, 356, 464, 466, 480

misperception, 368, 377
mistakes, 126, 127, 165, **180**, 180, 392
monosyllables, 47, 53, 54, 57, 59, 79–81, 132, 157, 196, 198, 205, 206, 209, 222, 245, 251, 255, 257, 264, 298, 315, 325, 332, 353, 398, 400, 415, 481, 482

neutralization, 53, 58, 73, 76, 77, 80, 113–115, 119, 123–125, 180, 191, 196, 247, 286, 297, 317, 323, 326, 329, 371, 377, 385, 391, 392, 423, 430, 431, 433, 458, **475**, 476, 477
numerals, 50, 163–192, 216, 217, 252, 270, 301, 308, 309, 317, 324, 325, 332, 337, 338, 346, 376, 425, 440, 485

panchronic phonology, **25**, 25, 26, 462
phonation types, 25, 50, 361, 421, 431
phonetic realization of tones, 357–395, 422
    see also experimental phonetics
phonological erosion, 11, 46, 93, 403, 448, 456
phonostylistics, 483

phrasing, 331, 356, 360, 361, 366, 428, 433, 436, 469
possessive, 58, 59, 69, 71, 73, 75, 79–82, 94, 97, 219, 220, 223, 224, 227, 231, 242, 345, 387, 408, 412
postpositions, 133, 227, 228, 231, 236, 239, 288, 289, 291, 300
Praguian phonology, 16, 458, 475, 476
prefixes, 197, 213–215, 245–251, 258, 259, 261–266, 278, 279, 281, 293, 296, 302, 309, 312, 316, 327, 339, 346, 384, 387, 395, 407, 458, 460, 467, 474
pronouns, 48, 50, 220, 222–225, 232, 239, 307, 372, 470
prosody, 319, 331, 355, **360**, 360–362, 365, 366, 370, 373, 375, 382, 409, 419, 424

range expansion, 50, 366, 376, 434
reduplication, 46, 216, 252–255, 257, 258, 298, 485

sandhi, *see* tone sandhi
simplification, 191, 211, 345, 403, 409, 413, 414, 431
spreading, *see* tone spreading
stative verbs, 51, **251**, 253, 298
structural gap-filling, *see* gap-filling
stylistics, 144, 164, 191, 192, 216, 233, 234, 254, 291, 308, 319, 321, 323, 335–337, 343, 344, 347–353, 370, 374, 468, 480
subcategories of lexical tones, 167, 179, 186, 247, 250, 251, 259, 282, 284, 287, 292

suffixes, 47, 54, 71, 73, 74, 134, 155, 159, 196–198, 205–207, 209, 211, 212, 214, 217, 218, 229, 235, 242, 243, 249, 253, 260, 265, 269, 270, 276, 277, 298, 319, 406, 407, 412, 478

surface-phonological level, *see* derivation

tonal anchorage, *see* anchorage

tonal contour, 54–56, 58, 72, 73, 76, 77, 80–82, 88, 90, 91, 118, 123, 179, 183, 217, 236, 237, 249, 265, 282, 283, 286, 289, 290, 293, 296, 303, 309, 316, 317, 324, 325, 327–330, 347–350, 352–356, 391, 398, 416, **420**, 422

tonal intonation, **427**, 427, 433, 435

tone group, 70, 72, 78, 91, 94, 96, 105, 113, 148, 158, 168, 177, 182, 187, 191, 217, 222, 223, 236, 237, 264, 265, 269, 288–291, 297, 308, 309, 311, 319, **321**, 321–356, 362, 369, 388, 390, 391, 393–395, 405, 413, 423, 424, 426, 439, 441, 468

tone letters, 60, **88**, 88, 429

tone rules, 72, 90, 105, 114, 131, 144, 247, **323**, 327, 363, 401, 406, 412, 423

tone sandhi, **362**, 362, 363, 366, 411, 437, 440, 441

tone spreading, 87, 88, 113, 120, 126, 127, 192, 348, 363, 366, 426, 427, 435

trisyllables, 55, 56, 118, 298, 345, 468, 469

underlying form, *see* form

variants, 119, 126, 128, 129, 134, 165, 181, 182, 188, 205–207, 232, 265, 270, 272, 293, 298, 304, 306, 307, 320, 348, 383, 401, 403, 407, 408, 413, 464, 478, 480, 485

see also variation

variation, 26, 44, 129, 142, 263, 272, 315, 353, 359, 365, 370, 371, 389, 391, 397, 398, 411, 414, 448, 473, 474

dialectal, 36

see also variants

word order, **47**, 149, 316, 436

573

www.ingramcontent.com/pod-product-compliance
Lightning Source LLC
Chambersburg PA
CBHW080751300426
44114CB00020B/2693